ORGANIZING FOR
COMMUNITY
CONTROLLED
DEVELOPMENT

To Lucy —

Your community leadership & vision continue to inspire. I value your insights & actions. — Pat 3/15/03

For Lucy —

Good friend, courageous social worker, and generous teacher — guardian to Glenn B. and other thousands of Pittsburgh folk,

Jim
3/15/03

ORGANIZING FOR COMMUNITY CONTROLLED DEVELOPMENT

RENEWING CIVIL SOCIETY

Patricia Watkins Murphy
James V. Cunningham
University of Pittsburgh

SAGE Publications
International Educational and Professional Publisher
Thousand Oaks ■ London ■ New Delhi

For information:

Sage Publications, Inc.
2455 Teller Road
Thousand Oaks, California 91320
E-mail: order@sagepub.com

Sage Publications Ltd.
6 Bonhill Street
London EC2A 4PU
United Kingdom

Sage Publications India Pvt. Ltd.
B-42 Panchsheel Enclave
Post Box 4109
New Delhi 110 017 India

Printed in the United States of America

Library of Congress Cataloging-in-Publication Data

Murphy, Patricia Watkins
Organizing for community controlled development: renewing civil society /
by Patricia Watkins Murphy, James V. Cunningham.
    p. cm.
Includes bibliographical references and index.
ISBN 0-7619-0414-X-ISBN 0-7619-0415-8 (pbk.)
    1. Community development—United States. 2. Community organization—
United States. I. Cunningham, James V. II. Title.
HN90.C6 M86 2003
307.1′4′0973—dc21

                 2002152846

03   04   05   06   10   9 8 7 6 5 4 3 2 1

Acquisitions Editor:	Al Bruckner
Editorial Assistant:	MaryAnn Vail
Production Editor:	Melanie Birdsall
Copy Editor:	D. J. Peck
Typesetter:	C&M Digitals (P) Ltd.
Proofreader:	Tricia Toney
Cover Designer:	Michelle Lee
Production Artist:	Sandy Sauvajot

CONTENTS

A Personal Preface   vii
Acknowledgments   xiii

1. Introduction   1
2. The Potency of Community Power   11
3. Community Development Corporations and the Resurgence of Organizing   38
4. The Small Community   53
5. Community Organizing: Principal Tool for Change and Reform   78
6. Participation: Lifeblood of Renewal   107
7. Aliquippa: A Small Community on the Front Line   124
8. Forging an Organizational Plan   154
9. Unity in Creating a Comprehensive Community Plan   178
10. Maximizing Social Strength   200
11. Tapping Essential Resources   220
12. Capital Formation: Building Community Financial Assets   240
13. Neighborhood Preservation Through Affordable Housing   257
14. Business District Renewal: Transforming a Shopping Area   277
15. Workforce Development: Strengthening the Economic Base of the Small Community   292
16. Organizing for Community Controlled Development and the Promise of Coalition Politics   311

Index   319
About the Authors   339

A Personal Preface

We the people of the United States, since attaining sovereignty during the 18th century, have built a national network of some 60,000 small residential communities capable of sustaining individuals and providing opportunities for families. Mill towns, suburbs, urban neighborhoods, public housing communities, apartment complexes, gated villages, and rural crossroads are some of the names we give to these human settlements.

Such small communities have long been hailed as the building blocks of the nation, and many of them work well, supplying essential peace and support. Several of them distinguished themselves with their generous response to the terrorist attacks of September 11, 2001. An increasing number, however, are weakened by the growing strains of racial division, civic apathy, and economic insecurity felt since long before that fateful day. This book proposes a method for understanding and easing these strains while undertaking a renewal and rebuilding of this indispensable national network.

Renewal refers to residents of small communities gaining awareness, unifying, and educating themselves to overcome political weakness and financial anxieties so as to better meet their economic, civic, and social responsibilities. Rebuilding our small communities means reforming them to be livable, attractive, democratic, equitable, and tolerant places; more supportive of the dignity and moral integrity of people; and better able to undergird a nation facing a fractious globe that is laden with both threats and opportunities. Stephen Goldsmith, long-time energetic and creative mayor of Indianapolis, expressed it as follows: "By putting faith in our neighborhoods, we are jointly beginning a new chapter in the history of American citizenship" (Goldsmith, 2002, p. xi).

Another observer of our time who views this challenge with clarity and perspective is E. J. Dionne, Jr., a *Washington Post* columnist, a senior fellow in the Brookings Governmental Studies program, and the author-editor of *Community Works: The Revival of Civil Society in America* (Dionne, 1998). Dionne's civil society embodies the communal sector, the third sector that is independent of, but related to, the traditional two sectors of business and government. This independent third sector is people, usually acting as volunteers, undertaking collective effort through families, clans, neighborhoods, institutions, and associations of diverse kinds (p. 3).

Small place communities, when aware and unified for renewing themselves, become influential models of civic behavior. Kamikaze blows by terrorists and unconscionable acts by corporate insiders, during this new century, have shaken the government and business sectors, leaving the nation painfully in need of renewed faith and confidence. Dionne (2002) appraised it as follows: "The era of the swaggering capitalist is over. The era of the reasonable capitalist and responsible government is beginning anew. Or so we have to hope, and demand" (p. A9). The time is ripe for more leadership from the communal sector, particularly from its grassroots.

Dionne (1998) pointed to the increased attention being paid by scholars and politicians to local places and events where people relate to each other, including church-initiated associations for racial reconciliation, Parent Teacher Association (PTA) meetings, Little League games, scout meetings, block watches, living room book discussions, fantasy sports leagues, and other link-up nodes that form the foundation of a small community. Moreover, changes in the economy have brought alterations in the labor market and the structure of firms as well as in the organization of families and neighborhoods, changes that challenge third-sector associations and institutions to work hard for higher levels of fairness, understanding, inclusion, planning, action, and influence.

Even before the new century opened, Dionne (1998) predicted an era of reform and social rebuilding, which will demand serious engagement among the sectors, leading to "a rebirth and reconstruction of the communities that constitute civil society, democracy being a community of communities" (pp. 13–14). Dionne's reform argument is rooted in a conviction that "this generation has the same capacity for social inventiveness demonstrated by the Progressives Teddy Roosevelt led" early in the 20th century (p. 14).

"Social inventiveness" is what this book hopes to stimulate and facilitate. All three of the distress strains bearing down on small communities and their residents—racial division, civic apathy, and economic insecurity—are major villains draining energy and goodwill from small communities of all races and incomes and obscuring them to the potential of a new era. Fabricant and Fisher (2002), in their report on the struggle to sustain community organizations in New York City, found that "the drive to privatize every aspect of American Life conflicts with the demands associated with sustaining the polity, creating civic engagement, and building community and social cohesion" (p. 1). They maintained that this conflict is at the center of the struggle to preserve and strengthen the communal sector. Such conflict not only makes people less kind and gentle but also diverts them from public responsibility, isolating them in their private worlds and rendering them indifferent to public matters, including the humanizing and reenergizing opportunities available in their own small place communities.

Now during the 21st century, with homefront security a concern, Dionne speaks and writes urging Americans to put more faith in community, with citizens in neighborhoods taking larger roles in making and implementing local rebuilding plans while governments recognize and back up such plans with public sector power and money. Dionne is a prophet calling on ordinary people to use their common sense and goodwill to reduce fear, stress, and inequality in the nation by using small neighborhoods as their basic unit for organizing reform.

A heartening message for the post-September 11 world has come from Robert Putnam, the social scientist whose 1990s research identified widespread disconnect and isolation among Americans—a condition he labeled "bowling alone." In his coast-to-coast survey done after the September 2001 attacks, Putnam (2002) found levels of political consciousness and engagement reawakening. "In fact, they are probably higher now than they have been in the last three decades" (p. 1). Although he found that people trust one another more, from neighbors and co-workers to shop clerks and perfect strangers, he cautioned that the newly identified deep urge must be stimulated and nudged into serious community effort to produce tangible results. In short, it is a time of opportunity for reversing the decline of civic involvement, but vigorous organizing is needed to take advantage of the opportunity.

The chapters that follow suggest how residents of a small place community can unite to plan, find resources, and regenerate their local place while reconnecting themselves to public responsibilities. The authors of this book have spent their careers and volunteer time working with neighborhood people, immersed in hopeful schemes for making and remaking local places. Over time, we have learned the lesson of inclusion that social researcher Melvin Delgado confirmed with a mass of evidence. Such schemes must be "based on mutual respect and trust, with an understanding that the community (as a whole) is the best judge of what it needs and what is good for it" (Delgado, 2000, p. 12). We come to neighborhood work from different backgrounds, yet with similar sets of ideas about revitalizing small communities, including the conviction that deep participation is the rock on which sustainable revitalization rests.

The following biographical descriptions offer a glimpse into the working lives led by professional organizers who pursue community work in concert with citizen partners. These descriptions are provided in part to explain why we have written this book and partly in the hope that some readers will be drawn into the important and rewarding field of local community organizing and development.

FINDING A CAREER IN COMMUNITY BY WAY OF AFRICA

Fresh out of college and community activism, Pat Murphy spent 2 years as a Peace Corps volunteer in Niger, West Africa. While in Niger, she became immersed in the everyday lives and struggles of a small community—a sharp contrast to the issue campaigns and organizing she had been involved with in the states. With her village neighbors, she recruited people and resources for a small health clinic and helped to organize an anti-tuberculosis campaign. Having grown up in a middle-class community, she was confronted with two seemingly contradictory observations: first, the devastating effects of poverty and oppression, and second, the unshakable zest for life and drive of the people she came to know as neighbors.

Later, graduate study in community organizing and public administration at the University of Pittsburgh crystallized the economic, social, and political forces that Murphy encountered in Niger. Armed with concrete knowledge and skills as well as a deepened respect for participation and community, she became the director of a Pittsburgh neighborhood organization, the Stanton Heights Civic Association (SHCA). The group had a mixed agenda that included running a child care center and summer recreation program, coordinating a food pantry, staging neighborhood festivals, countering real estate block-busting efforts, fostering racial integration, and seeking the revitalization of a declining shopping center.

When a new community development corporation (CDC) was organized in Pittsburgh's Hill District, Murphy accepted an offer to help residents build the community's development agenda. Their mission was to spearhead efforts to rebuild the Hill, the inner-city Pittsburgh neighborhood most negatively affected by urban "renewal" during the 1960s. Her Hill experience in serious economic development honed her technical skills in housing and business district revitalization, deepened her view of the destructive role played by racism in community distress, and gave her pause over the ease with which development could disrupt or dominate an organizing agenda.

During Murphy's time in the Hill, she completed the national Development Training Institute's community development internship, gaining additional skills and a connection to the nationwide development network and dialogue. Subsequent work at Pittsburgh's city-wide Community Technical Assistance Center (CTAC) found her working with more than 50 community organizations, assisting them in building organizational strength and implementing revitalization plans for their neighborhoods.

In 1992, Murphy formed a consulting and education/training business, Cornerstones for Development, and began to work across the nation with people committed to transforming their distressed living places into resilient communities through active community organizations controlled by residents. Part-time graduate and undergraduate teaching at the University of Pittsburgh's School of Social Work provides her with additional opportunities for learning and questioning. Murphy stays grounded through board and volunteer service for local community organizations and social justice groups and by participating in and leading anti-racism discussions and workshops.

Murphy often says that she "continues to be heartened and challenged by the diversity of residents, community groups, service providers, local governments, and funders committed to the transformation of local places."

RUNNING THE CIRCLE FROM STUDENT VOLUNTEER TO RETIREE VOLUNTEER

After encountering race and housing issues as a student volunteer, Jim Cunningham found a job as a novice organizer in Chicago. He learned about the long hours, the low pay, and the frustrations and fascinations that go with the job while increasing his respect for the dedication of community volunteers. He spent 5 years organizing for an independent political organization and 3 years in the Hyde Park-Kenwood neighborhood assisting residents in their ambivalent struggles with urban renewal and racial change.

At the end of the 1950s, he transported a growing family to Pittsburgh to organize for the Allegheny Council to Improve Our Neighborhoods, better known as ACTION-Housing, a regional organization serving start-up resident groups, many of them in tight little ethnic communities. He found talented generous people in these groups and worked with them to launch planning and development initiatives. During the mid-1960s, he helped to link neighborhood groups to the "War on Poverty" with local employment centers, one-stop social service storefronts, and a variety of advocacy efforts. In time, he began teaching part-time at the University of Pittsburgh's School of Social Work and eventually joined the faculty full-time.

From the university, Cunningham was able to continue work with neighborhood people, sometimes helping young leaders to understand, through experience, that collective political influence is the key to residents getting responses from government and business. Other activities along the road included helping to form the Pittsburgh Neighborhood Alliance, which led to involvement with the National Association of Neighborhoods (NAN), and helping to prepare its organizing manual with Milton Kotler, founding director of the NAN (Cunningham & Kotler, 1983) and author of the 1960s classic *Neighborhood Government: The Local Foundations of Political Life* (Kotler, 1969). Pittsburgh organizing involved helping citizens to launch a Government Study Commission, which drafted a Home Rule Charter opening city hall to more direct participation by residents. A later referendum campaign set up the city's Civilian Police Review Board. Over the decades, University of Pittsburgh community organizing students served as interns within such advocacy efforts.

Now shifted to emeritus, Cunningham serves as a volunteer with the Race and Reconciliation group in his home parish and with Pittsburgh's "Living Wage" campaign. He continues to teach courses in economics and community organizing, including the course with Murphy that led to this book, which aims to serve learners intent on entering the world of place-based organizing.

CURRENT ACTIVITIES

Between the two of us, we have recruited, educated, and been educated by community people and their allies in a wide variety of small place communities scattered through many states and countries. As volunteers pushing diverse causes, we have served on national boards lobbying for recognition and resources for residential places and have jostled with feisty student organizers in classrooms and training workshops.

Our work has encountered conditions both harsh and hopeful. Like other long-time organizers, we have had ups and downs but gradually became confident that, through sustained effort, community people can mount sufficient collective strength to transform a distressed place while gaining in competence and mastering the art of effective negotiation, bargaining, and advocacy to extract resources of regions, states, and the nation. We have come to appreciate the reality that serious and appropriate planned change requires dogged labor by people who honor diversity, inclusiveness, and material equity. A lot is asked of those who would undertake such efforts. But we believe that this is precisely what the U.S. society must have to rescue and reinvigorate its small community inheritance and to ensure that the nation can face global challenges from a firm foundation of organized and energized grassroots.

In 1993, our academic interests converged around the knowledge gap separating community organizing and economic development at the level of the small place community. It was then that we designed and launched our university course linking the two approaches in a single model for renewal. Finding no adequate textbook, we began to gather and experiment with materials for creating one. This book is the product of many years of searching, selecting, classroom testing, integrating, and editing. Late in the process, an advanced draft and then a final draft were used and critiqued by three separate seminars of graduate students of the University of Pittsburgh, resulting in refinements and what we believe are improvements.

Pablo Eisenberg, the distinguished and outspoken long-time (now retired) director of the Center for Community Change, often has complained that too many community organizing texts have been written by academics who never practiced. He calls for joint efforts by academics and organizers, insisting that "academics can bring rigor, while practitioners bring inspiration" (personal interview, February 17, 1999). This book was written by an organizer who teaches and a teacher who organizes. We hope that we can uphold Eisenberg's faith by contributing to a practice dedicated to racial reconciliation, civic resurgence, and economic restraint that is biased toward broad-scale redistribution.

We seek to do this by proposing what we believe to be effective means for people to preserve, revitalize, and elevate their home communities, using the assets of their communities and their latent collective power, and to do this bolstered by the resources they can muster from the institutions of the wider society. Our target readers are people of all ages, races, and income levels who want to learn about the art and skills of organizing for small place renewal.

REFERENCES

Cunningham, J., & Kotler, M. (1983). *Building neighborhood organizations.* Notre Dame, IN: Notre Dame University Press.

Delgado, M. (2000). *Community social work practice in an urban context.* New York: Oxford University Press.

Dionne, E., Jr. (Ed.). (1998). *Community works: The revival of civil society in America.* Washington, DC: Brookings Institution Press.

Dionne, E., Jr. (Ed.). (2002, February 19). The capitalist evolution. *Pittsburgh Post-Gazette,* p. 9.

Fabricant. M., & Fisher, R. (2002). *Settlement houses under siege: The struggle to sustain community organizations in New York City.* New York: Columbia University Press.

Goldsmith, S. (2002). *Putting faith in neighborhoods.* Nobleville, IN: Hudson Institute Publications.

Kotler, M. (1969). *Neighborhood government: The local foundations of political life.* Indianapolis, IN: Bobbs-Merrill.

Putnam, R. (2002, February 11). Bowling together. *The American Prospect,* pp. 20–22.

ACKNOWLEDGMENTS

The inspiration for this book comes from the many people who have crossed our paths doing inspiring and challenging work on behalf of their families, neighbors and communities both here and abroad. We express our thanks and admiration, and wish them well. We dedicate this book to them and all who work for justice.

We wish to express our gratitude for encouragement and the contributions of materials, insights, ideas, opinions and experiences of colleagues in the field - both practitioner and academic. Dean Larry Davis, Dean David Epperson, Morton Coleman, Patricia Kolar, Aaron Mann, George McClomb, William Pollard, Tracy Soska, Santos (J.R.)Torres, Patricia Wright and Hide Yamatani from the University of Pittsburgh School of Social Work, and, Elizabeth Beck, Ed Blakely, Rudy Bryant, Cathy Cairns, Denys Candy, Pauline Cooper, Donal Costello, Jo Debolt, Maggie DeSantis, Pablo Eisenberg, Dave Feehan, Paul Flora, Bill Freed, Marty Johnson, Kevin Kearns, Lynette Jung Lee, Woullard Lett, Barry Maciak, Ed Marciniak, Anne McCafferty, Suzanne McDevitt, Joe McNeely, Andy Mott, Mary Ohmer, Winton Pitcoff, Douglas Rae, Carl Redwood, Rob Rogers, Alf Ronnby, Ron Schiffman, Rosa Sims, Lee Staples, Diane Sterner, Randy Stoecker, Wanda White and Wilbert Young.

We thank Brian Conway for diligent case assistance and feedback, and Anne Kearney for case research, fact checking and clerical support. Both provided fresh observations and delightful Irish wit over many cups of tea and homemade scones. Brian kept in touch with ideas from graduate school at Notre Dame. Anne was on hand to wrap up the whole last 16 months of work, an irreplaceable supporter on every aspect of the final effort. She gave a rich new meaning to the role of generalist.

Students of our class from which this book emerged offered practical feedback and friendly critiques on various draft manuscripts. We thank Melanie Bazzano, Melissa Blaszczyk, Allison Bonebreak, Rose Brooks, Megan Bursic, Yuanhzu Ding, Heather Eisiminger, David Gibson, Michael Gumpert, Thomas Hardy, Kurt Hess, Tarsha Lagrone, Heidi Latsko, Emily Lekau, Justina Kayla, Ayanna King-Lewis, Susan Klinedinst, Ayana Ledford, Jo Ella Lukon, Tracey Mannarino, Bonnie Christian Marsh, Kevin Mickens, Edwin Nwabugwu, Virginia Parker, Bertha Pitt, Constance Richardson, Samantha Roth, Kevin Russ, Yoshiko Shiga, Jill Shuey, Dorian Smith, Nicola Sysyn, Kevin Skillin, Brandi Tarr, Shannah Taylor, Don Tresor, Yvonne Van Haitsma, Tamara Wagner, Beverly Walker and Cora Young.

Special thanks to the community change agents who helped us with major case studies. They are dedicated people with tremendous responsibility who have kindly taken the time to provide us with information, facts, thoughts and helpful suggestions. From Albuquerque, NM: Mary Lou Haywood-Spells and Bob Cunningham for his research on the Barelas Neighborhood Association. From the Aliquippa Alliance for Unity and Development: David Blenk, Maryann Ilov, Bill Farra, Sylvester

Greco, Aileen Gilbert, Andrea Gillian, Jonathan Pettis, Debra Ruckert, Roseanne Stead, Jewel Whatley, and Lorenzo Williams. From the Bloomfield-Garfield Corporation: Agnes Brose, Richard Flanagan, and Richard Swartz. From the Dudley Street Neighborhood Initiative: John Barros, Jose Barros and Tom McCullough. From Greenpoint, Brooklyn, NY: Julie Lawrence and Community Board 1. From the Lyndale Neighborhood Association: Laura Johannson. From Portland, OR: Don Neureuther, Steven Rudman and Steve Young. From Rollingwood, TX: Ryan Kelley and Susan Welker. From Valmeyer, IL: Lori Brown. From Vandergrift, PA: Eugene Iagnemma and Shelia Mendicino. From the Hyde Park-Kenwood Community Conference: Jane Comiskey, George S. Cooley, Bill Gerstein, Gary B. Grant, Dorothy Horton, Margaret Matchett, Gary M. Ossewaarde, Jane Pugh, Charles G. Staples, Henry B. Stein, Joyce Teal, Stephen P. Thomas and Martin Wallace.

We are grateful to the following organizations and institutions for permission to use certain research materials: The American Prospect, The Enterprise Foundation, The Ford Foundation, The Haworth Press, Pratt Institute, The Rocky Mountain Institution. All authors are duly credited within the work.

Professional, timely and thoughtful support was provided by Dee Brown, Judy Zacharia and Debra Welkley, manuscript rewrites and production, and Bill Johnson and Blaine Walker, graphics. Donna Wolfe provided exceptional expertise as an early editor and taught us a lot about the sub-science of verbs, parallelism and readability.

Our "team" at Sage Publications has, for seven years, been patient, responsive, helpful and dedicated. Many thanks to Melanie Birdsall, Production Editor; Al Bruckner, Acquisitions Editor; Marquita Flemming, Acquisitions Assistant; Diane Foster, Senior Production Editor; Carrie Mullen, Editor; D.J. Peck, Copy Editor; Renee Piernot, Editorial Assistant; Catherine Rossbach, Acquisitions Editor; and MaryAnn Vail, Senior Editorial Assistant.

We also owe gratitude to several anonymous reviewers whose informed critiques of several versions of our manuscript provided guidance and clarity, and challenged us to persevere.

Heartfelt appreciation to our "kinship networks":

To MaryBeth, Harry and Jim Ansley, Gale McGloin, Jane Neckerman, Bonnie, Dave, Nathan and Katie Uhlenbrock, and Jim and Helen Watkins for being fine teachers and gentle boosters.

To Rita and Steve Cunningham for a ton of support that never ceased year after year.

We thank the following for permission to cite their copyrighted publications:

Aldine de Gruyter (Hawthorne, NY):
Excerpts on pp. 82–84, this volume, from R. Chaskin, P. Brown, S. Venkatesh, & A. Vidal, *Building Community Capacity.* Copyright 2001 by Walter de Gruyter, Inc. Reprinted and adapted by permission.

Allyn & Bacon (Needham, MA):
Excerpt on p. 90 from F. Rivera & J. Erlich, *Community Organizing in a Diverse Society.* Copyright 1998 by Allyn & Bacon. Reprinted and adapted by permission.
Excerpt on p. 192 from H. J. Rubin & I. S. Rubin, *Community Organizing and Development.* Copyright 1992 by Allyn & Bacon. Reprinted and adapted by permission.
Excerpts on pp. 89–90 from J. Green, *Cultural Awareness in the Human Services.* Copyright 1995 by Allyn & Bacon. Reprinted and adapted by permission.

Amherst H. Wilder Foundation (St. Paul, MN):
Excerpts on pp. 156–157 from B. Barry, *Strategic Planning Workbook for Nonprofit Organizations, Revised and Updated.* Copyright 1997. Amherst H. Wilder Foundation. Used with permission. For more information on Wilder Foundation publications, call 1–800–274–6024.

Center for Neighborhood Technology (Chicago, IL):
Excerpt on p. 42 from J. Anner & C. Vogel, (Eds.), *Dollars and Direct Action, Vol 20:2,* and *The Neighborhood Works* (a printed insert). Copyright1997. Reprinted and adapted by permission.
Use of the chart on p. 74 entitled "Spending money locally: How the multiplier works" in *Working Neighborhoods.* Copyright 1986. Updated and modernized. Reprinted and adapted by permission.

Chapin Hall Center for Children (Chicago, IL):
Excerpt on p. 69 from R. Chaskin & P. Brown, "Theories of Neighborhood Change" in *Core Issues in Comprehensive Community-Building.* Copyright 1996. Reprinted and adapted by permission.

Excerpt on p. 45 from R. Stone, "Introduction" in *Core Issues in Comprehensive Community-Building.* Copyright 1996. Reprinted and adapted by permission.

Doubleday, a division of Random House, Inc. Published as Anchor Books Doubleday (New York City):
Excerpts on pp. 179, 193, 212–213, 215 from Lisbeth Bamberger Schorr, *Common Purpose.* Copyright 1997. Reprinted and adapted by permission.

Farrar, Straus & Giroux, LLC. (New York, NY):
Excerpt on p. 32 from T. Friedman, *The Lexus and the Olive Tree: Understanding Globalization.* Copyright 1999. Reprinted and adapted by permission.

Greenwood Publishing Group, Inc. (Westport, CT):
Excerpt on p. 16 from L. Staples, *Roots to Power.* Praeger Publishers, an imprint of Greenwood Publishing Group, Inc. Copyright 1984 by Praeger Publishers. All rights reserved. Reprinted and adapted by permission.
Excerpts on pp. 53, 206–207 from R. Ahlbrandt & J. Cunningham, *A New Public Policy for Neighborhood Preservation.* Praeger Publishers, an imprint of Greenwood Publishing Group, Inc. Copyright 1979 by R. S. Ahlbrandt & J. V. Cunningham. All rights reserved. Reprinted and adapted by permission.

Harcourt, Brace & Co. Publishers (New York, NY):
Excerpt on p. 15 from J. Blum, B. Catton, E. Morgan, A. Schlesinger, K. Stampp, & C. Woodward, *The National Experience, 2nd Ed.* Copyright 1968. Reprinted and adapted by permission.

Jossey-Bass (San Francisco, CA):
Excerpts on pp. 279, 282 from B. Goldstein & R. Davis, *Neighborhoods in the Urban Economy.* Copyright 1980. Reprinted and adapted by permission.

Journal of Urban Affairs (Blackwell Publishers, UK):
Excerpt on p. 41 from R. Bratt, "CDC's Contributions Outweigh Contradictions" in *Journal of Urban Affairs 19*(1). Copyright 1997. Reprinted and adapted by permission.

Kluwer Academy/Plenum Publishers (New York, NY):
Excerpts on pp. 54–55, 207 from R. Ahlbrandt, *Neighborhoods, People, Community.* Copyright 1984. Used by permission of Kluwer Academy/Plenum Publishers.

McGraw-Hill Companies (New York, NY):
Excerpts on pp. 266, 268, 270, 274 from T. Jones, W. Pettus, & M. Pyatok, *Good Neighbors: Affordable Family Housing.* Copyright 1995. Reprinted and adapted by permission.

National Association of Social Workers, Inc.:
Excerpt on p. 142 from P. Twiss & P. Cooper, "Youth Revitalizing Main Street" in *Social Work in Education, Vol.22,* No.3. Copyright 2000. Reprinted and adapted by permission.

New Mexico Business Journal (Albuquerque, NM):
Excerpt on p. 12 from S. Shepard, *"The Buzz in Barelas."* Copyright 2001. Reprinted and adapted by permission.

New York Times (New York):
Excerpts on pp. 235–236 from P. Kilborn, *"Charity for poor lags behind."* Copyright 1999. Reprinted and adapted by permission.
Excerpt on p. 40 from N. Lemann, *"Myth of Community Development."* Copyright 1994. Reprinted and adapted by permission.
Excerpts on pp. 204–205 from S. Rimer, *"Joined at the Stoop."* Copyright 1999. Reprinted and adapted by permission.

Oxford University Press (New York, NY):
Excerpts on p. 107 (1993), p. 107 (1998), p. 107–108 (2001) from the *Human Development Report of the United Nations.* Copyright 1993, 1998 and 2001. Reprinted and adapted by permission.
Excerpts on pp. viii-ix, 6, 121 from M. Delgado, Community Social Work Practice in an Urban Context. Copyright 2000. Reprinted and adapted by permission.

F. E. Peacock Publishers, Inc. (Itasca, IL):
Excerpt on p. 100 from B. Ehrenreich, "A letter to membership of the Democratic Socialists of America, dated December 1, 1993, New York," in J. Rothman, J. Erlich, & J. Tropman, Strategies of Community Intervention, 5th Ed. Copyright 1995 Rothman et al. Reprinted and adapted by permission.
Excerpts on pp. 21–22 from C. D. Garvin & F. M. Cox, "A History of Community Organizing since the Civil War with Specific Reference to Oppressed Communities," in J. Rothman, J. Erlich, & J. Tropman, Strategies of Community Intervention, 5th Ed. Copyright 1995 Rothman et al. Reprinted and adapted by permission.
Excerpts on pp. 84, and 99–102 from J. Rothman, "Approaches to Community Intervention," in J. Rothman, J. Erlich, & J. Tropman, *Strategies of Community Intervention, 5th Ed.* Copyright 1995 Rothman et al. Reprinted and adapted by permission.

Pearson Education (Glenview, IL):
Excerpts on pp. 2, 4, 15–16, and 26 from D. Judd & T. Swanson, *City Politics.* Copyright 1994 by Harper Collins College Publishers. Used by permission of Addison-Wesley Educational Publishers, Inc.

The Pittsburgh Post-Gazette (Pittsburgh, PA):
Excerpt on p. 119 from J. McKay, "Rescued East Liberty cracker company branches out." Copyright Pittsburgh Post-Gazette, 2002. All rights reserved. Reprinted with permission.

Pratt Institute Center for Community and Environmental Development (PICCED) (New York, NY):
Excerpts on pp. 166–167 and 171–173 from R. Bryant, P. Murphy, & W. White, *Nuts and Bolts of Community Development Training Program.* Copyright March, 2000. Developed by Pratt Institute Center for Community and Environmental Development (PICCED). Reprinted and adapted by permission.
Chart on p. 71 entitled "Cash Flow Diagram," developed through PICCED. Copyright 1984. Updated and modernized. Reprinted and adapted by permission.
Excerpt on p. 20 from PICCED case study of the New Community Corporation (Newark), developed as part of PICCED's CDC Oral History Project. Reprinted and adapted by permission.

Princeton University Press (Princeton, NJ):
Excerpts on pp. 18–20 from J. Mollenkopf, *The Contested City.* Copyright 1983 by Princeton University Press. Reprinted and adapted by permission.

Random House (New York, NY):
Excerpt on p. 109 from A. Tocqueville, *Democracy in America Vol. 1.* Copyright 1954.

Sage Publications, Inc. (Thousand Oaks, CA):
Excerpts on pp. 189, 250–251, 295–296, and 301 from E. Blakely, *Planning Local Economic Development: Theory and Practice, 2nd Ed.* Copyright 1994. Reprinted and adapted by permission.
Excerpts on pp. 258–259 from J. Blair, *Local Economic Development Analysis and Practice.* Copyright 1995. Reprinted and adapted by permission.
Excerpts on pp. 294, 298, and 299 from B. Harrison & M. Weiss, *Workforce Development and Networks.* Copyright 1998. Reprinted and adapted by permission.

South End Press (Cambridge, MA):
Excerpts on pp. 24 and 67 from H. Sklar, *Chaos or Community? Seeking Solutions not Scapegoats for Bad Economics.* Copyright 1995. Reprinted and adapted by permission.

University of California Press (Berkley, CA) and Russell Sage Foundation (New York, NY):
Excerpts on pp. 8, 105, 121, 213, 231, and 315–317 from W. Wilson, *The Bridge Over the Racial Divide: Rising Inequality and Coalition Politics.* Copyright 1999. Reprinted with permission of the Regents of the University of California.

University of California (Los Angeles, CA):
Excerpts on pp. 61–62 from L. Winnick, "Place Prosperity vs. People Prosperity" in *Essays in Urban Land Economics.* Copyright 1966. Reprinted with permission of the Regents of the University of California.

The Urban Institute Press (Washington, DC):
Excerpts on pp. 9, 47–48, 49, 51, 61, 62, 102, and 232 from G. Kingsley, J. McKeely, & J. Gibson, *Community Building Coming of Age.* Copyright 1997. Reprinted and adapted by permission.
Excerpt on p. 41 from C. Walker & M. Weinheimer, *Community Development in the 1990s.* Copyright 1998. Reprinted and adapted by permission.

Viking Penguin (New York, NY):
Excerpts on pp. 213 and 314 from J. Poppendieck, *Sweet Charity?.* Copyright 1998 by Janet Poppendieck. Used by permission of Viking Penguin, a division of Penguin Putnam, Inc.

Wall Street Journal (New York, NY):
Excerpt on p. 280 from M. Porter & M. Blaxill, *Inner Cities are the Next Retailing Frontier.* Copyright November 24, 1997. Reprinted and adapted by permission of the authors.

1

INTRODUCTION

This is a book about taking care of the small place communities of America. It is about achieving a greatly strengthened grassroots foundation for national unity. It is about residents and their allies preserving and enriching what is good and useful in their local places. It is about ordinary people struggling to grow and develop themselves and their children while seeking to bring neighborhood forces of distress and decline under control. It is about creating and sustaining strong bonds among and between diverse people, demanding and getting living wages, caring for property and the environment, and maintaining a sense of place infused by a spirit of doing those things individually and collectively that need to be done.

It is also about planned efforts to increase public safety and education and to reduce drug pushing, racial exclusion, family isolation, pollution, substandard housing, and other ills that stand in the way of neighborhood well-being. And it is about people building communities that honor wide-ranging diversity and civic responsibility as well as organizations that promote and facilitate year-round participation while maintaining fruitful links to the governments, businesses, and other essential institutions that are the custodians of society's wealth.

For all of us, our place of residence has importance whether we plan to live there 6 months, 10 years, or a lifetime. It is vital to us whether we are young, old, or in the middle; single or married; with or without kids; financially struggling or comfortably making it. In this place, we get ourselves together daily to deal with an uncertain world. We find here supports for raising a family, improving our health, understanding and communicating with the outside world, and managing apprehension. The neighborhood may be the place where we escape the routine of a job, or even a place for obtaining a job as well as for coming to grips with the rich ethnic and racial differences of America. Sometimes, the small community helps us to develop in personal ways. It may be where we grow a garden, overcome an addiction, learn to shoot a basketball, launch a business, find a mate, or discover a book that changes our life.

Always, a central truth is that if a small community is to provide what is needed and expected, then it requires attention from those who live and work there and share responsibility for the community's health.

We estimate that there are at least 60,000 small communities in America if we include rural and urban neighborhoods, identifiable separate neighborhoods within large suburbs, small suburbs and towns, rural villages, and sizable housing complexes, both public and private, whether they are rental, condo, or co-op. This estimate is based on the numbers of chartered municipalities in the country, confirmed by the research and experience of others and ourselves,[1] although the proliferation of gated residential enclaves may be distorting this estimate. There is doubt as to whether all enclosed enclaves actually qualify as "communities." From our work in several states, we further estimate that at any one time probably one third of a region's small communities suffer from serious distress. The reality is that all small place communities that are not consciously and actively preserving and improving themselves are probably declining, although the decline may be slow and imperceptible for a time, like damp spots in a basement floor that suddenly become pools of water due to the sewer pipe below being blocked up by tree roots.

RACIAL ANTIPATHY

Back during the 1960s, while a minority of the population used a combination of passive and disruptive resistance to secure basic human needs for African Americans, most white Americans were Pollyannas on race. It was a decade of new beginnings. Dramatic civil rights efforts were achieving legal reforms in public accommodations, voting rights, and employment access. Concerned people generally thought that what was then called "the problem of poverty and race" was on its way to being resolved. Many went into the 1970s believing that the problem was behind them, with expectations of employment opportunities and race relations improving every year. How wrong they were. There was some progress, but there were also slips backward and failures aplenty along the route. Certain social strains did ease, but only on the surface, as urban decentralization accelerated, with affluent whites moving deep into exurbia, putting more space between themselves and people of color, the poor, and the new flows of refugees arriving in cities and their metropolitan areas.

During the 1980s, life became more painful for the minorities and the poor left behind as the economy sank into recession. Employers followed the migrating wealth to the far suburbs, and the swelling global economy imposed painful competition from low-wage foreign workforces possessed of ever rising skills. It became an exceptionally mean time for the chronic poor in cities and industrial suburbs, a condition carried into the new century while intensified by the nation's stern new welfare policies.

Poverty and race issues came back to public attention with the 1992 street rebellions in Los Angeles. As Judd and Swanstrom (1994) pointed out, these outbreaks "served as a reminder of the hazards of long neglecting the social needs of the

urban citizenry" (p. 8). By 1992, a majority of the populations in metropolitan areas resided in suburbs ironically built up with the aid of federal financing guidelines that openly promoted the merits of "protecting property values" through segregation (pp. 187–213). Segregation and exclusion hardened as dominant determinants of residential patterns. Most small town and suburban whites now have little contact with blacks. Fully 86% of suburban white people live in suburbs that have African American populations of less than 1% (pp. 12–13).

Population shifts, demographic trends, and localized increases in immigrants moving in, offer further challenges in small communities.

David Rusk, with experience as both an urban mayor (Albuquerque, New Mexico) and a "no nonsense" researcher, has dug into the consequences of population shifts within regions. His probing analysis (Rusk, 1999) of 1990 census data spotlighted disparities growing since 1950 between people who are white and people of color. Examining census data for the nation's 320 metro areas (where most Americans live), he found that only 8% of white residents were poor, while 25% of Hispanic residents and 28% of black residents were poor (p. 105). Furthermore, he found that while only one of four poor whites lived in poverty neighborhoods, one of two poor Hispanics and three of four poor blacks did. Rusk comments that to be poor and white is, in general, still to be part of the mainstream of white, middle-class society, with its expectations and access to educational and employment opportunities. "To be poor and Hispanic or poor and Black is, in general, to be isolated from mainstream society" (pp. 106–107). Although it is likely that the 2000 census data eventually will tell us more, Rusk's 1999 book was based on his own detailed observations in 58 metropolitan areas done throughout the decade and his interpretations of 1999 data from the federal school lunch program (pp. 60–61). These may hold up, but we all await his updated findings with great interest.

Equanimity of small communities has eroded under these conditions, with large numbers of affluent white families shifting further away from personal linkage with the diversity that is often celebrated as a hallmark of American society. Blakely and Snyder (1997) estimated that the United States now has more than 20,000 gated residential enclaves, with such places "increasing rapidly in number in all regions and price classes" (p. 7). At the same time, women and men of color will soon constitute a third of the nation's population and have a larger role in the nation's institutions. The stage is not set for unity and equity.

Although many speak to the need to embrace diversity and multiculturalism, the infrastructure (e.g., policies, laws, beliefs, norms, media, language) is still in place supporting personal and institutionalized prejudice, oppression, and racism. The overwhelming tendency toward white ethnocentrism and collective privilege, segregation, separation, and lack of meaningful contact, coupled with generalizations about ethnic and culturally diverse groups, fuels racial antipathy. Further compounding the climate of potential distress in which the nation's small communities find themselves is a societal decline in civic responsibility.

THE ERODING OF CIVIC INVOLVEMENT

Both authors of this book, as practitioners, have long encountered the gratification and frustrations of participation but today find the pendulum swung too close to frustration and civic paralysis. We now have a new historic symbol for civic apathy: the 2000 election. In billion-dollar campaigns carried on across the 50 states to decide the direction of the new decade, vast partisan organizations mobilized the forces of high and low technology. But they could bring out only half the vote and fell short of a clear-cut decision, which eventually took weeks to settle.

Seldom do sufficient volunteers arise to take full advantage of opportunities for building inclusive renewal organizations. Often, individual volunteers are overwhelmed by their personal survival imperatives and cannot make commitments. Others find that their networks and interests pull them beyond local connections. Some residents come onto community boards with strong community knowledge but few organizational skills and experience; therefore, they are unable to grasp opportunities to teach and motivate others without extensive on-the-job training, which is not always available. Small circles of self-appointed "leaders" hold many organizations in tight control. Volunteers are irked by the slowness of government processes, causing frustration and loss of enthusiasm. Leadership training is a hard sell to funders, but it is of enormous importance to a small community's stability and climate of responsibility. Reawakening leadership development is a theme of this book.

What is at the root of civic paralysis? Wolfe (1998) pointed to "the new realities of two-career families, suburban lifestyles, and rapid career changes" (p. 17) and even asked, "Is civil society obsolete?" Although few of the communities we work in fit Wolfe's descriptions exactly, his questions are relevant in most communities. Like Wolfe, we believe that civil society and its small communities have changed radically during the past 40 years but that small communities are neither obsolete nor irrelevant. New ways are being found to encourage involvement, and in chapters to follow we describe tactics in use as well as suggest others for accelerating civic resurgence.

Even President Bush has been pitching in with proposals for increased funding for faith-based service organizations and neighborhood charities that provide tangible aid to impoverished households. He supports tax credits for individuals who contribute money to local anti-poverty causes and has recommended allowing taxpayers who do not itemize deductions to write off their benevolent contributions in addition to taking the standard deduction. In a report issued from the White House titled *Rallying the Armies of Compassion,* Bush (2001) declared that the independent sector is on the threshold of a great renaissance, with America's nonprofit sector emerging as perhaps the most dynamic area for creative problem solving during the 21st century.

Berry, Portney, and Thomson (1993) found in their extensive studies that political officials sometimes devalue the usefulness of citizen participation, dismissing it as a force that leads to expensive delays, weakens the power of city bureaus, and makes unreasonable demands on government, which in turn bring on citizen disillusionment and alienation when demands are not met. A few local governments and other institutions have openly discouraged citizen and consumer participation. Yet these three researchers find outstanding achievements by volunteer community groups in several cities.

Moreover, Berry (1999) went forward to find that "policy decisions in Congress have moved on from questions about how to increase the economic pie to questions about how to balance economic growth with the need to enhance the environment, protect consumers, and improve personal well-being, [with] citizen groups the primary political force behind this trend" (p. 2). Berry defined citizen groups as lobbying organizations that mobilize members, donors, or activists to pursue interests other than their own vocations or professions. His conclusions flowed out of 205 rigorously studied issue battles that have gone through the congressional process since 1960.

Judd and Swanstrom (1994) pointed out that there is a declining political voice for distressed urban communities of central cities, not only because the suburbs have been growing so fast but also because low-income voters in cities have been turning out for elections at a much lower rate than have suburban voters (p. 253). But in the tumultuous 2000 election, the cities held their own with help from the old, close-in, urbanized suburbs. In general, voters concerned with distress showed that they could match those concerned with affluence vote for vote.

ECONOMIC DISPARITY AND JOBLESSNESS

As to the third strain, the stage is set for more social volatility and acrimony among, between, and within small communities as they face churning labor conditions. The economic reality of the autonomous and largely unregulated global marketplace is that sophisticated skills and learning abilities are required for getting and holding decent jobs (jobs that offer a living wage, benefits, and stability). The employment future of increasing legions of Americans, of all races, ethnicities, and classes, is now insecure and a source of worry even for many who possess what were once prized skills.

During the year ended May 31, 2002, private employers carried out layoffs and discharges encompassing 19,339,000 workers, as established by surveys of the U.S. Department of Labor (USDL, 2002). Low wages keep millions of families in poverty and wreak havoc with Welfare to Work programs, while 43 million persons (most of them in working households) lack health insurance. Of the 146.6 million persons who worked or looked for work in prosperous 1998, 14 million experienced some unemployment during the year, according to the USDL (2000, p. 2). Some did not work a day. The year 2001 opened with 1,522 mass layoff actions (50 or more people displaced in each) in January, involving a total of 200,343 workers, most of them losing better paying manufacturing jobs (USDL, 2001).

Racial disparities in employment and compensation have long been a source of hostility and bad feelings piercing small communities and their families. Historically, the USDL has reported that unemployment rates for black workers are at least double those for their white counterparts. Darity and Myers (1998), in a comprehensive analysis of data on individual and family incomes, found that even though some black workers are doing well financially, there has been a continual widening of the black-white gap since 1980: "Because blacks are found disproportionately at the bottom of the income distribution, and because public policies themselves are often hostile de facto toward racial minority groups, the overall growth in general inequality has contributed to increased racial inequality" (p. 2). They found that the black-white family income ratio "reached a low-point during the 1982 recession when black families received less than 60½ cents in income for every dollar that white families received" (pp. 7–8). Although the ratio improved after the recession, black families have never fully recovered. "They still had incomes in 1990 below their position in 1970" (p. 8). According to Darity and Myers,

> The whole debate on the widening gap between rich and poor (and the corresponding theme of the diminishing middle class) has been conducted without the proper focus on the racial dynamics of widening inequality. It has not been just a matter of rich getting richer and the poor getting poorer, but that while both affluent blacks and whites got richer, it was the black poor that got poorer. Moreover, the evidence of diminishing fortunes of the middle class derives primarily from focusing on families, and the overall deterioration in the

condition of families is magnified when the emphasis is placed on black families. (p. 2)

Each small place community is tri-dimensional, having social, political, and economic dimensions. Each of these is vulnerable to virulent forces. Racial and ethnic intolerance can poison social relationships, civic apathy can debilitate politics, and unemployment and low wages can wreak havoc on the local economy. Furthermore, the distresses become interactive and cumulative. The flight of capital cannot be slowed because the community lacks political power. Racial hostility not only savages cohesion but also enfeebles community influence with government. Apathy discourages investment and leads to neglect of public infrastructure, private property, and all other economic assets. Starting more than 50 years ago, the mass of society began to awaken to the needs and opportunities of small communities.

As authors, we have created this book from a set of nine assumptions on which we generally agree: essentiality, entropy, the survival imperative, collectivity, feasibility, resource reality, flexibility, human dignity, and local uniqueness. These grow out of our experiences and reflection and are defined as follows.

1. *Essentiality:* Most of us humans (perhaps all) require daily respite, at least brief periods during our days when we have peace and quiet and the normal pressures are suspended, giving us space for reflection and regeneration. A secure lodging in a peaceful community serves us well. For most, it is a house or an apartment owned or rented. It might be a single quiet room in a house, an apartment, or an institution of some kind. Maybe it is a trailer or a shelter under a bridge that provides some hours each day away from the struggle for survival. The need is universal, and people everywhere have met it by creating or finding a place where they are at home.

2. *Entropy:* Internal and external forces are continuously at work wearing away our small communities and all of the things that make them livable. Weather and the pounding of vehicles are putting potholes in our streets, blights are attacking our trees, and wind and rain are savaging our roofs. Big box malls and Internet retailing force the closing of local shops, while racial suspicions embitter neighborhood conversations. Layoffs discourage working people, drug pushers tempt youth, and local institutions cut their hours for lack of volunteers.

3. *The survival imperative:* A natural tendency for any living entity, including a small community, is to fight for survival. Spontaneous or planned, we find people initiating renewal. A church torched by a hate group is rebuilt by a score of volunteers. Youth reclaim a littered vacant lot as a parklet. A local plant closes, and workers and community residents go door to door collecting pledges to build a development fund. Block clubs emerge to plant community gardens and tutor children on weekends. A cadre of neighbors assemble to face the question: How can we destroy the drug underground in our community high school?

4. *Collectivity:* Most changes require power. A single person or family, in most cases, has limited power. For the difficult solutions, power must be accumulated. The wider and deeper the participation, the more influence the community will gain. In small communities, it is done by large numbers of people, representing every block and interest, pooling their individual strengths and talents.

5. *Feasibility:* People in communities will move to plan and act together so long as they have hope that success is possible within a reasonable period of time. For the United States, there is a history (discussed later) that ordinary community people can join together, amass power, and move to bring about desired changes of many kinds—social, political, and economic. Joint action, focused planning, and hopefulness, coupled with persistent extraction of resources from those with plenty, will do it.

6. *Resource reality:* Achieving desired community change is long term and expensive. Resources up to now have not been available in the required amounts. For example, extensive treatment of polluted soil or long-term recovery programs for hard-core addicts may be needed, or perhaps $100 million in demolition and new construction is necessary. Such situations occur in some small places every year. No matter how high the likely costs, if the potential gain is great

enough and the participants have arrived at an honest decision to proceed, then it can be worthwhile to make a collective effort to move ahead.

7. *Flexibility:* Community change is complex and slippery. As a collective of dedicated people work to exploit assets and reduce community distress, every legitimate strategy, tactic, and technique must be available for use. Arbitrarily putting a legal organizing strategy, tool, or tactic off-limits can greatly reduce the likelihood of success. Fear of conflict, embarrassment, and failure cannot be allowed to stand in the way.

8. *Human dignity:* Each human is sacred and important as well as worthy of honor and respect. The change process must be faithful to this truth. The collective change process is best carried on with all participants mindful of the need to maintain reverence for persons, whether friends or foes, while they labor for fairness and justice.

9. *Local uniqueness:* Each small community has its own mix of social, political, and economic conditions that arise out of the quality and character of local people, places, and things. In planning, "Local circumstances must dictate the nature of projects, and residents' backgrounds must be taken into account" (Delgado, 2000, p. 12).

The chapters that follow are guided by these assumptions as we lay out our method for invigorating America's small place communities, an approach we call Organizing for Community Controlled Development (OCCD) (see the accompanying sidebar).

Defining Organizing for Community Controlled Development

Organizing for Community Controlled Development is a comprehensive approach and direction for preserving and improving residential places that encompasses all aspects of community life—social, political, and economic. There is yet no generally used simple definition of this method and its four elements. We try to set one down here.

Organizing emphasizes that OCCD is a human activity. It is about people mobilizing and constructively deploying their human power. Organizing implies planned activity that enables community people to set and achieve useful goals and thereby control the future of their small community.

Community denotes that this method is used in a shared place and brings people together. The word community combines three notions: a common geography, common interests that unite, and interacting human participants with spiritual and material *capacities and needs.*

Controlled declares that the people mobilized have earned the right to decide the future of their place by creating a common vision and comprehensive plan through widespread participation. The people to be affected by decisions are involved in making them. They live, work, or otherwise have a legitimate interest in the community.

Development implies the blossoming of something good such as safety and security, a fair share of living wage jobs, and improved schools. It suggests making things better in a visible and purposeful way, using both consensus and confrontation as required. It implies that the future can be transformed. It suggests social change that is just, directed toward making certain that there are adequate flows of essential social, political, and economic resources coming into the community. This kind of development draws resources from the community itself and from society-at-large and uses them equitably for the community's benefit.

When we put these elements together, this definition emerges: OCCD is people coming together within their shared living place to plan and deploy resources in ways that enhance the local community, enrich society, and advance social justice.

ORGANIZING FOR COMMUNITY CONTROLLED DEVELOPMENT PRINCIPLES

Out of the thinking and work that go into healing distressed small communities and their people, there emerges the five principles set forth next. These principles underlie our comprehensive OCCD model.

Principles for Saving the Small Communities of America From Distress and Decline

1. *Inclusion:* The people of a community can best supply the ideas, decisions, and collective strength to revitalize and preserve it. "The people" include all residents and others with a legitimate interest in the community, including business people, the homeless, teachers, clergy, bankers, human service workers, and elected government representatives. Involvement needs to be at the level of the individual, family, group, and whole community. All serious matters affecting the community are potential items for the people's agenda.

2. *Comprehensiveness:* Every community has three dimensions: political, economic, and social. All three must be given attention. Each dimension is essential to community building. A healthy community is free from racial hostility, civic apathy, and economic misery, or it has a broadly based organization working seriously to make itself free.

3. *Mobilization:* Through organizing (or reorganizing), a community mobilizes its people and invigorates its *political* dimension so as to implement plans. This requires reaching out to establish fruitful relationships with relevant interests inside and outside the community. And it includes maintaining an openness to all who desire to reside in the community, with diversity viewed as a strength. Wide-scale mobilization underlies legitimacy for planning and building. Mobilization includes tapping society's institutions for the resources essential to building and rebuilding. Cooperative links to the broader society are necessary to ensure outside opportunities for residents.

4. *Adequate wealth:* Healthy communities require *resources*. This means the creation and employment of human and social capital, as well as material wealth, in ways that are fair and that lead to self-sufficiency and dignity for households and continuing vitality for the overall community. The building blocks of economic development are productive employable individuals, competent families, and concerned, fair-dealing institutions. Full employment and a living wage are essential goals.

5. *Health and spirit:* The social dimension involves both the quality of relationships among people (social fabric) and the availability of services to provide physical and spiritual well-being. The presence of opportunities for all people to learn and grow continually is a community ideal to be pursued.

OVERVIEW OF THE CONTENTS OF THIS BOOK

In the ideas to be set out within the chapters that follow, a comprehensive approach to community regeneration is taken, one that encompasses all three components of community—social, political, and economic, with some extra attention to the economic because this is the component that proves to be the most challenging to many organizers, organizations, and communities. Also addressed are key renewal issues that are encountered in community controlled development. These include the following:

1. Communities of place versus communities of identity or issue communities

2. Place-based development or people-based development

3. Local level or regional level of intervention

4. The nature, depths, and value of participation and inclusion, including happenstance as opposed to purposeful diversity

5. Indigenous, locally grown leadership in lieu of outside experts

6. The range of organizing approaches from consensus to conflict

7. The impact of funding sources on the determination of a community's agenda

8. The tension and balance of process (social) and product (economic) outcomes

9. The scale of focus, impact, and investment

The final chapter of this book looks to William Julius Wilson for a solution to the widening gap that haunts both the economic and social dimensions of community in America, a nation whose 2000 presidential election left households and small communities politically divided and frustrated.

The chapters that follow provide ideas and direction for implementing the five OCCD principles outlined earlier: inclusion, comprehensiveness, mobilization, adequate wealth, and health and spirit. Each chapter ends with a summary and continuing questions for exploration. The Preface and this introductory chapter lay out the broad themes of racial antipathy, erosion of civic involvement, and economic disparity and joblessness, our assumptions, and OCCD principles. Chapter 2 centers on community power and its history, generation, and application, presenting rich precedents for communal power challenging the traditional hegemony of business and government. Chapter 3 presents the context for understanding the recent and current models of resident-based renewal organizations, with a focus on the metamorphosis from community development corporations to a revival of comprehensive associations. Chapter 4 moves the book to a definition of small community, examining the social, political, and economic dimensions of the contemporary residential place. Chapter 4 also looks at the distress factors that beset small communities during the new century, with a focus on forces that could unravel the *social* fabric, dilute the *political* strength, and weaken the local *economic* conditions of residents, with these being the three major threats introduced in the Preface as racial division, civic apathy, and job insecurity. This opening unit introduces the major issues and provides basic definitions.

Chapters 5 to 7 center on community organizing as an effective method for mobilizing a community, built around 12 key activities. Chapter 5 concentrates on the start-up phase of a new organization (or of an old organization recharging itself), during which an early-on focus is chosen to push the organization forward in a consistent direction. Included are descriptions of several alternative "most-used" start-up directions. The nature and importance of widespread participation are described in Chapter 6, giving emphasis to a major theme of this book. Then comes a fulsome case, the effort of people in the steel town of Aliquippa, Pennsylvania, to save their community using a comprehensive direction and approach that encompasses both community organizing and economic development. This case study, in Chapter 7, illustrates the application of the 12 activities to an effort to renew the severely distressed mill town and to reduce its civic apathy and joblessness at the grassroots level. It is a case infused more with suffering than with success. It provides details on the weaknesses, needs, and opportunities identified in the chapter that precedes it.

Chapters 8 and 9 focus on planning. Chapter 8 looks at the process for making a plan for a single organization, a process using in-depth participatory decision making. Chapter 9 scrutinizes the broader planning effort involved in designing a community-wide plan that draws in all relevant groups, organizations, and institutions that are stakeholders of the community.

Chapters 10 to 15 present state-of-the-art concrete programs and ideas for community renewal amid today's turbulent technology, globalization, mobility, and racial competition. Chapter 10 points out ways in which to keep money, materials, and technical assistance coming in to ensure growth, with the case made for residents and other stakeholders to be partial providers of the resources. Chapter 11 centers on enriching social fabric, social capital, and social services within the turbulence. Chapter 12 looks at the *why* and *how* of capital formation within the community. Chapter 13 examines the role of housing in the revitalization process. Chapter 14 takes up survival and resurgence of beleaguered neighborhood business districts in the face of the Wal-Mart epidemic. Chapter 15 suggests network strategies and employer partnerships for linking good jobs to people in small communities.

Chapter 16 summarizes the definition and importance of the OCCD model, reiterating its major characteristics. Chapter 16 looks beyond today's fragmentation of communal power centers to a cohesive national alliance through which community interests would establish parity with the interests of government and business and would bargain for the scale of resources adequate to recovery and resurgence of the nation's small place communities. Envisioned is the potential of tiers of place-based organizations, reaching upward from small place communities to local, regional, and state networks and finally to a national apex interconnected and collaborating with other national communal alliances toward a workable global grid equal in influence to global business and the global alliance of sovereign nations.

In Chapter 2, we begin to understand power as related to the well-being and strengthening of America's small communities.

SUMMARY

Most Americans live a substantial part of their lives at home in small communities that offer shelter and security. An estimated one third of the nation's communities suffer from distress and disorder. This distress and disorder is seen as flowing from increasing residential segregation; growing disparities of income, wealth, and employment between white people and people of color; and the civic apathy and indifferences to poverty and segregation by people of means.

The purpose of this book is to present a method for seeking to reduce distress and disorder at the level of the small community, presented under the label Organizing for Community Controlled Development. OCCD is defined as a comprehensive approach for improving residential small communities in all three of their dimensions: social, political, and economic. The nine assumptions on which the method is based are listed, along with the five principles guiding the use of the method.

NOTE

1. According to the *Statistical Abstract of the United States* (U.S. Bureau of the Census, 2001), there are approximately 36,000 incorporated municipalities and townships in the nation, many of them small and cohesive enough to be single small communities and some of them so small as to be combined with one or more other fragments to become operating small communities. But many of them also are large and complex enough to contain two or more autonomous small communities, with perhaps as many as 100 or more neighborhoods existing in some large cities. Considering the single- and multi-neighborhood municipalities plus unincorporated villages, rural settlements, and self-contained housing complexes, both public and private, we estimate that there are at least 60,000 small communities in the nation. Kingsley, McNeely, and Gibson (1997) stated, "City planners have traditionally seen a neighborhood as a unit with around 5,000–6,000 people, roughly the size needed to support a single elementary school. . . . Community building works best at about that scale, certainly not as well in any area exceeding 10,000 population. The reason is that in larger areas you lose the frequent face-to-face interaction—the ability of people to really get to know each other that is needed to establish mutual trust and mutual obligation. . . . In areas with more people it becomes more difficult to build social capital" (p. 41). In a nation like ours, with a population running toward 300 million, and where social forces seem to cluster communities at about 5,000 people each, there would be approximately 60,000 small communities.

REFERENCES

Berry, J. (1999). *The new liberalism: The rising power of citizen groups.* Washington, DC: Brookings Institution Press.

Berry, J., Portney, K., & Thomson, K. (1993). *The rebirth of urban democracy.* Washington, DC: Brookings Institution Press.

Blakely, E., & Snyder, M. (1997). *Fortress America: Gated communities in the United States.* Washington, DC: Brookings Institution Press.

Bush, G. W. (2001). *Rallying the armies of compassion* [report]. Washington, DC: White House.

Darity, W., & Myers, S., Jr. (1998). *Persistent disparity: Race and economic inequality in the United States since 1945.* Northampton, MA: Edward Elgar.

Delgado, M. (2000). *Community social work practice in an urban context.* New York: Oxford University Press.

Judd, D., & Swanstrom, T. (1994). *City politics: Private power and public policy.* New York: HarperCollins.

Kingsley, G. T., McNeely, J. B., & Gibson, J. O. (1997). *Community building coming of age.* Baltimore, MD: Development Training Institute.

Rusk, D. (1999). *Inside game, outside game.* Washington, DC: Brookings Institution Press.

U.S. Bureau of the Census. (2001). *Statistical abstract of the United States: 2001.* Washington, DC: Author.

U.S. Department of Labor. (2000, January 31). *News.* (Washington, DC: U.S. Department of Labor, Bureau of Labor Statistics)

U.S. Department of Labor. (2001, March 2). *News.* (Washington, DC: U.S. Department of Labor, Bureau of Labor Statistics)

U.S. Department of Labor. (2002, July 30). Table 10. *News.* (Washington, DC: U.S. Department of Labor, Bureau of Labor Statistics)

Wilson, W. J. (1999). *The bridge over the racial divide: Rising inequality and coalition politics.* Berkeley: University of California Press.

Wolfe, A. (1998). Is civil society obsolete? In E. Dionne, Jr. (Ed.), *Community works: The revival of civic society in America* (pp. 17–23). Washington, DC: Brookings Institution Press.

2

THE POTENCY
OF COMMUNITY POWER

Out of the authors' experience and research has come confidence that people, working together, can muster the strength to slow, or even stop, the decline of their local living places and bring them to renewed states of stability and viability. Well-organized residents and the "natural allies" they can garner are nearly always capable of reversing social and physical decline in their home community. Natural allies include a host of people and assets such as shopkeepers, school personnel, church committees, ward politicians, Internet surfers, nonviolent gangs, idle construction workers during the winter months, retirees and elders, local banks, factory executives, high school students required to do community service projects, owners of vacant land, and money-granting foundations. The possibilities are unlimited. Every reader of this book could probably add six more potential allies who might be tapped by residents determined to seek reasurance for their small home community.

Of course, "natural enemies" also are on the prowl. Real estate speculators often lurk on the fringe of changing neighborhoods, as vultures ready to profit from racial fears or even as investor-predators who seek to ride the coattails of residents who are making heavy investments of sweat and savings to upgrade their community. Other enemies are rip-off home remodeling "contractors" who do shoddy work for inflated prices, sometimes disappearing before the job is done (after having persuaded a homeowner to "advance" the full contract price).

Residents of small communities and their allies concerned about equity and neighborhood stability have found that although they seldom hold the reins of power as do business and government, they can form organizations strong enough to provide themselves reins of countervailing community power (with power here meaning the ability to control what is going to happen in and to their own local place).

Groups of people in thousands of small communities across the nation have sought to build action and change organizations since the tumultuous 1960s, when African Americans, anti-war students, women, Native Americans, and other "left out" peoples exploded in protests that shook American society. The number of place-based, resident-led organizations bent on self-determined renewal has never been accurately and fully counted. One of the authors often heard Geno Baroni talk about 10,000 organizations, "with new ones starting up every month," before and after he was an assistant secretary at the Department of Housing and Urban Development (HUD) during the 1970s. So far as we know, there has never been a serious effort to gain a carefully calculated estimate of the number of planning and development organizations at work in small communities. We do know that the number is large, with great variations in size, structure, function, and program types. Types range from all-volunteer block clubs, to mass-based advocacy groups, to nonprofit service organizations with hundreds of employees. They also vary in attitude, but they all are aimed at maintaining and improving their local place and the spirit of its people.

To provide examples of the nature of such organizations, we briefly describe a sample of those we have worked with or studied. (We return to each of these later to illustrate an idea or to clarify a process.)

Aliquippa Alliance for Unity and Development (Aliquippa, Pennsylvania). When the 6½-mile-long integrated steel mill in Aliquippa closed during the early 1980s, thousands of families were left without means of livelihood. Response to the havoc came from workers, their families, and their supporters throughout a wide region of southwest Pennsylvania. With determined mobilization, they formed the Aliquippa Alliance for Unity and Development (AAUD) and dug in for a sustained effort. After 20 years of struggle, the AAUD has many lessons to teach us about economic development and organizing from the sheer pain and frustration of trying to revive one of America's once most prosperous industrial communities.

Barelas Neighborhood Association (Albuquerque, New Mexico). The association was founded as the Barelas Neighborhood Improvement Association in 1959 within a largely Hispanic neighborhood close-in to downtown that suffered from neglect, obsolescence, the odor of a sewage plant, lack of decent housing, and paternalistic leadership. During the 1970s, it was rejuvenated by younger, more democratic members who successfully made demands on city government and other institutions for lasting public and private investments (Cunningham & Kotler, 1983, pp. 44–50). During the new century, it has gloriously blossomed into the site of the National Hispanic Cultural Center of New Mexico, focused on living arts as well as history. The center is a $50 million anchor expected to bring 650,000 visitors a year to Albuquerque. The Hispanic Chamber of Commerce also has located there with a center that includes offices of the Small Business Administration and assistance services for start-up businesses (Shepherd, 2001).

Bloomfield-Garfield Corporation (Pittsburgh, Pennsylvania). For more than 25 years, this determined organization has negotiated new investments for its ever-threatened business street, its aged housing blocks, and its many jobless members. Now, its shopping thoroughfare is getting a $10 million facelift, it gives leadership to jobs programs for local youth and adults, and it is implementing a $30 million housing plan for six deteriorating blocks in the heart of its neighborhood. Progress has come from a persistent, broadly supported, and united effort by community people, under the firm and shrewd direction of three professional organizers, each of whom has been with the organization for more than 20 years. (The pioneering effort of this organization to deepen participation of residents is described further in Chapter 6.)

Dudley Street Neighborhood Initiative (Boston). Residents and staff of neighborhood agencies joined with the Riley Foundation to demand attention for their neighborhood devastated by garbage-strewn empty land (often caused by illegal dumping) and blighted by abandonment and arson. Militant advocacy, heavy volunteer involvement, and media support won early victories, which in time were tied down by hard-won cooperation from city government. This led to an open planning process, community control of vacant land, and a transformed and replanned neighborhood, conceived as "an urban village" (Medoff & Sklar, 1994).

Hyde Park-Kenwood Community Conference (Chicago). When Chicago's South Side was being transformed into a massive racially segregated territory after World War II, a group of black and white church and temple leaders from the Hyde Park-Kenwood neighborhood organized the conference and successfully worked together to "maintain an interracial community of high standards." The organization continues active after 50-plus years. (A case study of this organization can be found in Appendix 2.B.)

Lyndale Neighborhood Association (Minneapolis, Minnesota). A small community of 7,000 racially diverse residents used open planning to involve a wide spectrum of local people and institutions in examining the deep distress and numerous assets of their place as they built a consensus vision and a concrete plan for feasible change. Priorities set were family support, safety assurance, job development, and a livable environment, with heavy youth participation. In 2002, implementation was well along on a wide set of projects led by resident teams. One of the most innovative projects is the Lyndale Community "Hero Card," through which residents earn reward dollars when they spend at Lyndale businesses. These "dollars" can be spent in the neighborhood just like cash. More "dollars" can be earned for volunteer hours. In addition, a portion of every purchase is donated back to the association. Lyndale's community planning effort is highlighted in Chapter 9.

Rollingwood Neighborhood Association (Austin, Texas). Rollingwood is an affluent and largely white residential suburb near Austin that is known as a "sovereign neighborhood." Its population of 1,403 and their square mile of land are governed and serviced simultaneously by a chartered municipal government and the Rollingwood Neighborhood Association, with the former focused on the political and the latter focused on the social. Rollingwood's current population is diversified by a handful of families that are Hispanic or Asian. Although there are some 64,000 African Americans in Austin, none lives in Rollingwood, a fact that Rollingwood leaders attribute to homes being "too expensive here" (R. Kelley, city manager, and S. Welker, past president of the association, personal interviews, May 2002).

Together, these local place organizations, side-by-side with thousands of others like them across America, hold the potency for begetting a new nation rooted in a galaxy of energized small communities exercising peaceful and inclusive power. The experiences of these seven "key organizations" are woven through this book to illustrate and illuminate the small community struggle to vanquish distress and realize potential. Other, more briefly reported cases are also used to tie down and clarify specific points in the text.

Power is strength, the capacity for organizations like these to make and implement plans. Within the larger societal struggle for justice and fairness, collective community action is a means for mobilizing the assets and latent power of masses of people to systematically tackle hometown misery and create conditions of satisfaction. The paradigm for the societal struggle is simple, and we review it briefly here.

The main sources of power are money, public authority, and people. Money tends to be on top because it can subjugate politics, possess the media, and control real property, goods, and jobs. But people can intervene. Sometimes, people vote into elective offices able and altruistic leaders, who then use public authority to advance equity for families, communities, and society-at-large. Occasionally, there is a mayor who fulfills this role. (For the cases of two outstanding community-orientated mayors, see Appendix 2.A.)

Other times, people use mass lobbying to compel changes to laws, protect families and the environment, and carry out reforms such as the preservation and improvement of their home communities. They do this directly by their own planned projects and their collective ability to bargain with business as well as indirectly by their influence with government.

When a community organization wants to get rid of a neighborhood dump, as did Boston's Dudley Street Neighborhood Initiative at one time, there are three possible courses of action: (a) gain ownership of the land on which the dump sits and recruit resident volunteers to do the cleanup as a planned project, (b) put heavy pressure on the owners of the land and negotiate their doing the cleanup, or (c) persuade the government to force the commercial dump owners to clean up or close up. Sometimes, a combination effort is used. The tactics chosen will differ in accordance with time and place, but community power growing out of collective action can usually get the job done. Dudley Street neighbors successfully organized their own cleanup with the aid of city trucks, rakes, and shovels; pressured government to shut down illegal trash transfer stations; and eventually took ownership of much of the vacant land involved for new houses, parklets, and playgrounds (Medoff & Sklar, 1994, chap. 3). It was a 10-strike combination.

COMMUNITY POWER DURING A CENTURY OF CONTENTION

Historians agree that residential settlements in the United States primarily have economic roots. Judd and Swanstrom (1994) stated it simply: "America's cities and towns came into being as places where people could make money" (p. 1). They described the nation's 19th-century economic growth as promoted through penetration into unsettled land, with the lumber, fertile soil, and furs found there making possible "the expanding network of cities, towns, and villages." Governments in these settled places, they concluded, were "established to maximize the opportunities for individual economic advancement" (p. 2).

While the past 100 years have seen steady dominance by business forces, there have been thrusts of collective popular action. Participants in this action have included trade unionists, struggling farmers, industrial workers, intellectuals, radical churchgoers, altruistic professionals, small business owners, environmentalists, welfare rights advocates, ethnic and racial minorities, peace advocates, war veterans, women, students, social security recipients, neighborhood activists, and those alarmed by the growing and uncontrolled power of global corporations and world organizations. When able to coalesce in broad-based coalitions, these groups have achieved remarkable but inevitably temporary devolutions of regional, state, and national power. At the level of a small community, these elements are often successful when they gain influence over government and use this power to control the actions of economic organizations (e.g., a neighborhood organization pressures the county health department to enforce the housing code in the apartment buildings of an exploitive landlord). There have been more than enough triumphs to give credibility to community organizations and to elicit confidence in community power. Today, communal forces are mobilizing on a global level, as we explore later in this chapter.

POPULIST, PROGRESSIVE, AND DISRUPTIVE WORKERS

Back in 1896, a loose alliance of protesters and the aggrieved, organized in a wide assortment of local, state, and national volunteer associations and spearheaded by rural debtors, mounted a furious populist movement that made 36-year-old William Jennings Bryan the Democratic nominee for U.S. president. During the final third of the 19th century, rural and small town activists had formed 20,000 local "granges" in 32 states that provided a major component of the populist power base from which Bryan leaped to prominence.

Concern for social justice, which became widespread during the populist years, eventually did take hold in cities with an outpouring of remedial ideas, both social and political. Then, a broadened urban collective further challenged the hegemony of business and finance.

Like the rural and small town populists before them, the urban change advocates often constructed their power in part on small organizations, community by community. Betten and Austin (1990), for example, reported on the organizing of local immigrant communities by the International Institute, beginning in 1910, and on the rise and fall of the Cincinnati Experiment, which organized neighborhood-level health care improvements, starting in 1917 (p. 3).

In his story of organizing, Fisher (1994a) confirmed the neighborhood base for much early urban activism and pointed to the planned change achieved by "communitarian" organizers who came from social settlements, community centers, adult education schools, neighborhood health clinics, local labor unions, churches, ethnic societies, and political clubs dealing daily with the symptoms and suffering of urban poverty in their own neighborhoods.

At the same time, there were middle-class and wealthy persons in business, government, and the professions whose values, education, and experience gave them an understanding of the high costs and damaging effects of urban poverty, blight, and corruption as well as of the urgency for social improvements. Activists and reformers both embraced the vision of an urban environment where families were healthy and streets were peaceful. Together, "progressive" neighborhood and downtown forces, wearing both blue collars and white collars, built a movement to reduce sharply the social and economic disparities underlying disease and violence. As they made gains, their confidence increased. Eventually, they were able to successfully pressure the higher business and government forces that controlled cities. Their reforms included shifting tax burdens, so that the wealthy families and businesses paid their fair share, while initiating housing regulations, establishing recreation facilities, promoting public health, and organizing job programs for the poor (Judd & Swanstrom, 1994, p. 99). These liberal social progressive reformers are not to be confused with the conservative, efficiency-oriented, municipal reformers who sought, through legal and structural changes, to keep taxes and spending low and who believed in hiring educated experts to run municipal governments. Sometimes, of course, the two movements supported the same changes, for example, civil service for police and fire forces. But the liberal progressives relied more on the wisdom of the people than on hired experts.

Values that dominated progressive thinking, besides empathy for the poor, encompassed faith in participative democracy, hostility to large aggregations of private power, and confidence in public regulation, humanitarian temperament, and the instincts of ordinary people. Changes the movement achieved that benefited families and small communities included the strict enforcement of anti-monopoly regulations and the adoption of minimum-wage laws, employer liability, pensions for poor widows, and restrictions on hours and conditions of work, particularly for women and children, who often worked side by side in garment shops, where the hours were long and the wages were low.

Rural power coalitions, which encompassed seed and processing firms as well as farmers, won passage of the Smith-Lever Act, setting up the rural Cooperative Extension Service, through which county agents went out from land grant colleges to educate and organize. Local farmers were facilitated to initiate and carry out development plans for their farms and villages. Brunner and Yang (1949), in their history of the extension service, reported, "Participation and leadership were required. Plans had to be mutually agreed upon" (p. 14). The populist and progressive movements won many reforms but did not change the basic power arrangement. By 1915, the thrust of community power diminished as the nation turned its attention to war raging in Europe. American entrance into World War I increased the nation's dependence on industry, which stepped up production mightily and reasserted the dominance of business in national life. Working families benefited from booming wages and full employment as well as from government insistence on decent working conditions in war plants. As World War I ended in 1918, national attention became absorbed with international conflicts connected to negotiating the peace. These conflicts helped to reawaken old insecurities and biases on the home front. Progressive drives diminished during the 1920s, and the nation fell back into a period of labor strife, racial antipathy, and fears of communism.

BUSINESS RIDES HIGH

National policies were shaped by the needs and ideology of business, to the point where President Calvin Coolidge declared, "The man who builds a factory builds a temple" (Blum et al., 1968, p. 633). Throughout the decade, the principal guide for financial policy was Treasury Secretary Andrew Mellon, who believed that "the Government is just a business and can and should be run on business principles" (p. 625). Mellon used his vast influence to reduce federal expenditures, hold down taxes on profits and incomes, maintain protective tariffs, encourage employer restraint in raising wages, and minimize government control of finance and investment.

As the power pendulum froze in place on the business side during the 1920s, supporters of community interests sought to carry on through voluntary organizations such as trade unions, social agencies, independent political groups, and neighborhood associations. They were relatively weak until the tight-fisted, Mellon-guided policies began to undermine the economy. With scant incomes flowing to the mass of consumers, tariffs choking off trade, unregulated speculative investing running rampant, and masses of workers receiving low wages, the economy collapsed into the Great Depression of the 1930s, which devastated families and small communities.

OPPORTUNITY AND THE GREAT DEPRESSION

Crisis and hardship opened the way for new mobilizations of nonbusiness forces at local, state, and national levels. Industrial workers helped to elect pragmatist Franklin Roosevelt president in 1932, and then won large concessions from the Roosevelt administration, "by means of an unprecedented wave of locally organized industrial strikes" (Cloward & Piven, 1984, p. xiv) and other outbreaks of disruption. The administration was pushed to reassert government authority over economic abuses and to launch public welfare measures that would rescue families and communities from social and physical blight and would rescue employers from bankruptcy.

Pressures generated by the collective voices and militant behavior of desperate citizens in their workplaces ("sit down" strikes) and communities (rent strikes) brought daring public experiments such as the Civilian Conservation Corps, which provided jobs, training, discipline, confidence, and hope for 3 million young men between 1933 and 1942. Moving out into fields and forests, they built roads, bridges, and dams; improved the health of the forests and rural cross-roads; stopped soil erosion; enhanced flood controls; strung telephone lines; and otherwise strengthened the nation's rural and small town infrastructure while regreening its natural environment.

Programs to aid depressed, rural small town regions used the participation model of agricultural extension. Farmer committees set local production quotas and joined in decisions for implementation of the government's recovery programs. Meanwhile, the urban unemployed, pressed down by eviction enforcers who threw their furniture into the streets and by hunger that dulled the faces of their children, increasingly pursued organizing as the road to survival. Roosevelt reluctantly signed the Federal Emergency Relief Act of 1935, fearful that its cash payments would weaken the fortitude of the poor. Judd and Swanstrom (1994) explained the signing as "mandated by the want and the civic disorder that prevailed" (p. 119).

Fisher (1994b) told tales of 1930s' radicals organizing mass protests of the desperate unemployed in factories and neighborhoods throughout the nation. Tenant unions fought the unilateral control exercised by landlords. The pioneering "power" organizer Saul Alinsky began his lifelong work of mobilizing mass-based "peoples" organizations that would negotiate control of their own neighborhoods. Across the nation, 5 million elderly joined Townsend Clubs to demand poverty-ending pension checks of $200 a month.

Viewed as threats to the social order, strikers sitting down in plants and activists intimidating rent collectors and trashing government offices helped to persuade the majority of apprehensive voters to accept Roosevelt's restrained New Deal reforms, which were the alternative to the "do nothing," "let the market end the Depression" view of political conservatives. The New Deal reforms included job creation through paving mud streets and painting post offices paid for with government borrowing, while the Wagner Act baptized labor organizing and opened the way for the feisty Congress of Industrial Organizations (CIO). The CIO gave common factory workers a muscular role in society and, through their local unions, influence in their home communities. It spawned a political climate conducive to neighborhood organizing. Hanna and Robinson (1994) described unions during these years as "relating to wide segments of the community on a full menu of issues and thriving in a highly activist mode" (p. 63). The CIO organizing campaigns provided the community control-conflict model that Alinsky adapted to neighborhood organizing.

It was a dynamic decade in the history of door knocking and indigenous advocacy. Measured by the useful change achieved, the 1930s decade was fully as important to ordinary citizens as the 1960s decade was to be later. Business was no longer monopolizing public policymaking as in Mellon's day. Government listened to organizations with community roots. By 1936, the Social Security Act was on the books as a response to the Townsend Clubs, client-sensitive local welfare offices were up and running, and organizations of the still numerous jobless were recognized as legitimate negotiators for relief recipients. For the first time in the history of the United States, a national consensus emerged for a social contract to protect the poor. Programs for Unemployment Insurance and for Aid to Families with Dependent Children were put into place.

Fisher (1994b) concluded that the radical organizing of the 1930s gave neighborhood people "a sense of their own power to change the political system. It offered a community organizing experience that provided [participants] with an important theoretical and practical grassroots political education" (p. 49).

Alinsky, the brash professional who came out of the University of Chicago, was described by biographer Sanford Horwitt as an innovator who "advanced the great American radical idea that democracy is for ordinary people" (Horwitt, 1989, p. xvi). In his own book, *Reveille for Radicals,* Alinsky (1945) agitated for a fight against privilege and power, "whether it be inherited or acquired" and whether it be "political or financial or organized creed" (p. 25). Alinsky and the organizations he helped to launch were placed-based, were neighborhood oriented, and were to be significant players during the postwar years. He founded the Industrial Areas Foundation (IAF) and staffed it with able young men who he trained and nourished. Through the IAF, he deployed staff teams, by contract, to help aroused committed people in various parts of the United States master power-based organizing.

All of this occurred during an era of national reform shepherded by President Roosevelt. In his noblesse oblige mode, Roosevelt gave support and inspiration to experiments that helped the society survive until World War II ushered in a full employment economy. The war itself was won, in part, with the energy and skills of the young men who had been enrolled in the Civilian Conservation Corps and by their more mature counterparts, whose capabilities were enlarged by other Roosevelt job and infrastructure construction programs. These included the Works Progress Administration (WPA) and the Public Works Administration (PWA), whose meager paychecks were survival tickets for millions of families and whose works projects provided useful infrastructure for thousands of neighborhoods.

New Attention to Small Communities

With the war wrapped up, families and communities returned to local concerns such as the condition of their housing and neighborhoods. The modern era of community organizing had begun—nearly six decades of struggle, from the end of World War II until the present time, a time of achievements and failures, with each decade's efforts broader and more varied than those of the decades before it.

It was an era that began with business booming and the government highly regarded as an effective force for change and progress because of its having overseen the nation's survival of the Great Depression and its triumphs in World War II. People and communities during the late 1940s stood willing to sit down with public authorities to plan and cooperate. For two decades, the partnership seemed to run smoothly until aggrieved groups in the society revolted during the 1960s, with vigorous mass movements confronting the government for its failure to protect civil rights, provide economic opportunity for all, and end the futile loss of American lives in the swamps of Vietnam.

Older, well-preserved suburbs and city residential sections had long established neighborhood improvement associations and civic clubs to look after their maintenance and keep out "undesirable" households and commercial uses. During the postwar suburban housing boom, thousands of new associations and clubs came into being. Until the U.S. Supreme Court ruled them unenforceable in 1948, many groups, both old and new, used restrictive covenants for exclusion of racial minorities. However, after 1948, exclusion continued to be pursued through other means, including zoning restrictions, real estate practices, and unwritten agreements. With their twin goals of protection and enhancement, the associations were similar in character to the owner organizations that govern today's large condominium complexes and mushrooming gated communities. While increasing numbers of inner-city small communities acquired diverse racial populations, outer-edge city neighborhoods and most suburban communities remained segregated. During the immediate postwar years, affluent communities quietly preserved themselves, while the less affluent became caught up in the hope, chaos, and disappointments of the vast urban renewal program sponsored by the federal government beginning in 1949.

The Housing Act of 1949 offered financial help to old cities, towns, and neighborhoods that were willing to make "feasible plans" and roll up their sleeves to modernize themselves. More than 1,300 American communities created programs under the act during the 1950s, with local government initiatives and citizen participation becoming common and expected. The national government required at least token participation in many situations such as neighborhood renewal planning and the implementation of anti-poverty programs. Excitement and expectation abounded. A great array of revitalization organizations became active in declining and distressed residential communities, with both grassroots and business forces mobilizing. Corporate economic interests, encouraged and publicly led by "political entrepreneurs" who often were ambitious Democratic mayors, sought to renew downtowns, extend the sites of industry and large institutions, and gentrify large stocks of decrepit but fundamentally attractive and advantageously located private inner-city housing. These efforts devastated low-income families, particularly African Americans, because they destroyed poor black communities, challenged veteran neighborhood stakeholders, displaced inner-city employers, and demolished affordable housing (Mollenkopf, 1983). Low-income blacks became isolated in public housing and blighted enclaves, where many held on, maintaining their spirits through self-created networks and indigenous organizations that began to do planning and make demands on government and other sources of money and power.

Thousands of new and old neighborhood organizations of many kinds, spread through all of the states, were stimulated to intense activity by the opportunity/threat of urban renewal. One neighborhood group that sprang to life in 1949, the same year as the passage of the federal Housing Act that authorized urban renewal, was Chicago's Hyde Park-Kenwood Community Conference, mentioned earlier as a pioneering initiative of religious groups seeking to establish a stable interracial community in an inner-city area. (A case study of the conference can be found in Appendix 2.B.)

The Impact of the 1960s

The disruptive renewal activity in Hyde Park-Kenwood and hundreds of other distressed areas during the 1960s led to residential displacement and new conflict among communitarian, government, and business interests. Some groups in time were able to use the renewal process to preserve existing housing and minimize displacement. But too many programs, scattered across the nation, resulted in multi-block demolition that drove masses of people into public housing, while the cleared land was used for condominiums and corporate headquarters or, even more unsettling, was left fallow, as in Cleveland and Baltimore.

In dozens of cities, prime core land occupied by the poor was targeted by business-government partnerships for expressways, plant expansion, shopping centers, office towers, and enclaves where the displaced poor could be relocated. The powerful building trade unions, anxious to maintain high levels of job-producing economic activity, joined with business in support of this "redevelopment" effort. But over time, growing resistance from minorities and their allies slowed both planning and implementation.

By the 1950s, Alinsky's approach was spread through Chicago and other cities, showing residents of neglected urban places how to become central players, including some in Chicago who wished to slow and reshape renewal in Hyde Park-Kenwood. Alinsky's direct action model of a powerful neighborhood coalition that could force politicians, bankers, slum landlords, and corporate officials to the bargaining table was adopted by groups throughout the 1950s and was copied on a mass basis by movements during the explosive 1960s.

In a devastating attack, editor and critic Jane Jacobs charged urban renewal planners with seeking "impossibly profound changes" while employing "impossibly superficial means" (Jacobs, 1961, p. 271). She saw the process as a vicious circle "forthrightly wiping away slums and their populations, and replacing them with projects intended to produce higher tax yields." She pronounced it a failure that at best "merely shifts slums from here to there, adding its own tincture of extra hardship and disruption. At worst, it destroys neighborhoods where constructive and improving communities exist and where the situation calls for encouragement rather than destruction" (pp. 270–271).

Jacobs's criticisms were backed by social scientists such as Herbert Gans, who found that discriminatory costs, both emotional and financial, were imposed on low-income residents without fair compensation. Based on studies of renewal in Boston, Gans (1982) found that government-directed destruction of low-income homes and communities ultimately sprang from the demands of private corporate developers. He concluded that renewal policies of the early 1960s "benefit the developer most, the area residents least, and the public interest in as yet unmeasured quantity" (p. 370).

Gans (1982) traced responsibility for the destruction of viable inner-city communities and their social systems to legal procedures that grew out of years of legislative and administrative decisions starting with the Housing Act of 1949. He found these procedures embedded in the country's economic and political structure, especially in the policy of giving private developers a free hand in the most desirable cleared sites and profitable sectors of the housing market. Gans blamed this policy on realtor, builder, and banker lobbies that "insisted on [their] inclusion in all urban renewal legislation" (p. 369). He determined that the Boston redevelopment agency, "like all others the country over," had to provide sufficient incentives to attract the investments of private developers; therefore, its decisions, beginning with the selection of Boston's West End as a renewal site, were shaped "by the demands or the anticipated demands of the developer and the sources of investment capital" (p. 370). In studies of the urban ghetto disorders of the latter 1960s, he concluded that the Newark disorder of 1967 was caused in part by a plan to clear several blocks in the central-ward ghetto for a new medical school, and the Detroit riots that same year took place in a neighborhood overcrowded with those displaced from other parts of the city (p. 385).

Indictments of urban renewal continue to our day as long-term results are assessed. Halpern (1995) charged that the program during the 1950s destroyed four low-income houses for every one built; that it displaced mostly people of color; that it needlessly undermined many viable communities, each made up of thousands of "relationships, interactions, and interconnections" that had taken decades to build; and that half of the land cleared by this vast program was never developed or built on. Halpern concluded that urban renewal and public housing were complementary strategies "to buffer city centers and their ... institutions from the tide of African American migration, and to reinforce territorial segregation through zoning," largely for the benefit of private real estate developers (pp. 66–68).

Mollenkopf (1983), who studied Boston and San Francisco as well as a host of other cities of the Northeast and the Southwest, confirmed the urban renewal links between local government and local business and termed widespread local community mobilizations against urban renewal policies as a "neighborhood revolt." He found that although the business-government coalitions blunted and resisted the thrust of neighborhood activists to gain control of urban development, the coalitions eventually were forced by community resistance to ease the destruction and give up large-scale dislocation. Community groups made extensive use of militant tactics, including using outrage graffiti, picketing, and packing public hearings. Halpern (1995) reported that sit-ins, boycotts, rent strikes, marches, and street demonstrations were used to open up jobs to inner-city residents, to protest segregated and deteriorating schools, and to block urban renewal plans made without neighborhood involvement (pp. 64–74).

Just as workers and community activists earlier in the century became allied with sympathetic, reform-minded business and government professionals in building the progressive movement, the urban poor during the 1960s found themselves working side by side with idealistic young people who had been raised in the suburbs and affluent city neighborhoods. Mollenkopf (1983) described this new middle-class stratum as "urban pioneers" who lived by preference in central cities, developed "communal interests," and took up "the banner of community activism, contributing the political resources which low-income residents often lack" and helping to launch what Mollenkopf called "a powerful counter-movement" (p. 181).

Mollenkopf (1983) concluded that neighborhood activism of the 1960s and beyond, combining resistance and communal demands from alliances of poor people and middle-class activists, forced a scaling down of renewal programs, which ended massive demolition projects, created citizen review and participation procedures, and shifted policy emphasis to preservation and rehabilitation of neighborhoods as had been pioneered hesitatingly in Hyde Park-Kenwood (p. 210).

Although community forces did not win the complete control they sought, their power increased as new place-based organizations sprang up in every state. In cities, Mollenkopf (1983) noted the creation of networks of "neighborhood-based service delivery organizations that constitute a substantial political resource" (pp. 197, 210–211). With their collective strength, such networks are able to exert extensive pressure, lobbying effectively through letter writing, media campaigns, and fact-based testimony at packed public hearings; confronting and educating individual legislators in their offices; and by using a host of other techniques replete with imagination and "fire in the belly" indignation.

It seems clear that renewal displacement helped detonate the 1960s revolt of left out and victimized groups including women, anti-war protesters, radical students (both black and white), environmentalists, and the elderly as well as organizations of low-income neighborhood residents.

Ethnic and racial minorities, including Hispanics, Asian Americans, and American Indians, mobilized to lay claim to shares of "War on Poverty" monies from President Lyndon Johnson's Great Society Program. More generally, all of these aggrieved groups sought recognition and built new political organizations in the process. For instance, Nagel (1995) described how American Indians followed the civil rights model, launching activist organizations, such as the American Indian Movement and the National Indian Youth Council, and eventually protest actions. The latter involved occupation of Alcatraz Island in 1969 and the siege of Wounded Knee, South Dakota, in 1973 (pp. 956–961).

Violence in the streets, rebellions, court suits, and boycotts burgeoned. Besides restraining urban renewal, community opposition turned the society against the Vietnam war. Public policy was transformed. Institutions gave increased attention and respect to those they served.

Local community organizations grew in numbers and influence including pilot versions of the Community Development Corporation (CDC), which came into being during the mid-1960s as an anti-poverty tool for job creation in small communities that had been abandoned by business. Recognized as the first CDC, the Bedford Stuyvesant Restoration Corporation of New York City was brought into being with Senator Robert Kennedy supplying clout to make the initiative work. Another of the most productive of the original CDCs has been the New Community Corporation (NCC) of Newark. This large CDC was formed in 1968 in the city's poverty-stricken central ward through the initiatives of a local Catholic parish. Although it started small, it has never stopped growing, and as the new century began, it employed 1,200 in its service enterprises and owned and managed 2,500-plus units of housing. The Pratt Institute Center for Community and Environmental Development's (1995) *Community Development Corporations: Oral History Project* described how African American residents have directed NCC planning and development, guided by a mission statement that calls for improving "the quality of life of the people of Newark to reflect individual dignity and personal achievement" (p. 1).

Jobs and affordable housing have been this CDC's principal goals, with community residents fully engaged in their pursuit. Great sums of money have been raised through the organization's own efforts. Throughout its programs run the themes of self-sufficiency and diversification. Its network of day care centers employs hundreds and is a model of quality for the state of New Jersey. By keeping all management, maintenance, and other services in-house, the NCC provides vital jobs for residents. Its own security force has greatly reduced crime in its neighborhoods. One of its economic development projects has been a Pathmark supermarket anchoring a neighborhood shopping center.

In its study of the NCC, the Pratt Institute Center for Community and Environmental Development (1995) pointed out that the organization has refused to include any corporate or business interests on its board, while building a reputation for being responsive and accountable to residents. Today, Pratt Institute researchers rate this organizational tool created in the 1960s as "a major visible force in the economic, social, and physical revitalization of Newark's Central Ward" (p. 2).

Summing up the 1960s, Fisher (1994) viewed it as a decade when the poor and alienated did not sit passively by:

> An important and influential minority of poor people and activists joined neighborhood and national organizations, participated in demonstrations, teach-ins, and civil disobedience actions, carried signs, and demanded "Freedom Now" and "Power to the People." Like the 1930s, the 1960s was a decade of important radical ferment and social change. The decade is a critical one in a history of neighborhood organizing because of the quantity, variety, and impact of its neighborhood organizing projects. (Fisher, 1994b, p. 103)

The verve of the 1960s drew on both the progressive spirit of the early 20th century and the disruptive desperation of the 1930s. A spreading sense of outrage and injustice set loose volatile national forces that cleared the way for Presidents John F. Kennedy and Lyndon Johnson to oversee changes reaching into every small community in the nation. Jobs were expanded, wages were raised, government spending was multiplied, and housing and education were made more accessible (mostly to the advantage of white people). Medicare was invented, HUD was established, and a limited War on Poverty was launched. The federal government made emphatic its commitment to civil rights by prohibiting discrimination in the use of federal funds, establishing a commission to prevent discrimination in employment, and providing federal registration of voters in states that refused to put all eligible people on the rolls. But these changes failed to remove the stain of the unpopular war in Asia, which continued to alienate large sections of the public. The alienation was sufficient to tip the 1968 presidential election to Richard Nixon. As a conservative Republican, Nixon favored community development pursued through nongovernmental

citizen action and private business effort rather than through direct government operations, an emphasis that was to be continued throughout the rest of the century, embraced by presidents regardless of party. It was also an emphasis that gave the CDCs a dominant position in the renewal of small communities.

While shrinking resources and more conservative national administrations under Presidents Nixon and Gerald Ford reduced federally funded social programs after 1968, there remained forces at work that continued to recognize and support communal interests. A principal force was consensus among business, government, and community groups accepting the notion that residential communities were a precious asset, with CDCs a productive and acceptable conservative device for preserving and improving them.

THE 1970s

Garvin and Cox (1995) described how the quantity of community organizations continued to grow during the 1970s and beyond, with large numbers of women and ethnic groups mobilizing throughout the decade, especially in African American neighborhoods. They cited universal trends at work favorable to decentralization, resident mobilization, and local organizing, including electronic communication, multiplying volunteer support groups, the increased availability of resources from nongovernmental sources, the proliferation of personal and collaborative networks and the resurgence of the self-help spirit (pp. 93–97).

Garvin and Cox (1995) cited alternative sources of funds that partly replaced the funding streams lost when President Nixon terminated Democratic human service programs, including the War on Poverty. These encompassed urban philanthropic foundations that increased their interest in neighborhood development in most metropolitan areas, including Seattle, Portland, Denver, Chicago, and Boston. Other sources were state and local governments, United Ways, internal community self-help campaigns, labor and church organizations, neighborhood businesses, and institutions. Republicans began their own neighborhood-related programs with their

"New Federalism," which poured billions of dollars into local communities under labels such as "revenue sharing" and "Community Development Block Grant Program". Particularly the latter program has tended to favor non-profit community groups. Garvin and Cox confirmed that many of the new 1970s volunteer organizations focused on neighborhood housing, economic opportunities, health care, and consumer needs. They reported finding such groups in all ethnic communities and among all socioeconomic groups (pp. 95–97).

Landmark laws of importance to small communities, intended to provide substantial investment, were enacted during the 1970s decade. These were the Home Mortgage Disclosure Act of 1975 (HMDA) and the Community Reinvestment Act of 1977 (CRA). The CRA sprang from grassroots organizing efforts that began in Chicago under a relentless organizer named Gale Cincotta of National People's Action. This legislation requires that federally regulated lenders invest in communities from which they draw deposits. Over time, local groups have used this legislation to pull large streams of dollars into neighborhoods to finance new and rehabilitated housing (Keating & Smith, 1996, p. 54). However, the banking industry, by lobbying at the federal level with muscle and adroitness. steadily chips away at the effectiveness of these laws. Community-based forces coordinated by the National Community Reinvestment Coalition (NCRC) steadfastly push back. A drastic banking act passed at the end of 1999 by the U.S. Congress gutted the CRA. According to the NCRC, it effectively exempted more than 80% of banks and thrifts from regular service reviews by CRA examiners and community groups ("Congress Guts CRA," 1999, p. 25). (More on the CRA can be found in Chapter 12.)

During the conservative 1980s and 1990s, community organizations that focused on political and radical social agendas lost strength, while CDCs proliferated. Government and private funders pressured the CDCs to be more business-like. Some, but not all, flourished. Housing and economic development became the dominant activity for small communities seeking renewal. Fisher (1996) reported that CDCs, in responding to the pressures of funders,

became "less like community organizations and more like business and investment projects" (p. 44). He suggested that they were forced "to become so oriented to economic success that they were unable to sustain their work for community empowerment" (p. 44).

Communal forces, both old and new, struggled to maintain their influence during the 1970s as the economy slowed. Skyrocketing oil prices raised production costs at a time when obsolete equipment, rigid management policies, old-fashioned work processes, and outdated employee skills were holding back productivity gains by the nation's mature industrial corporations. At the same time, competition was rising from revived and efficient foreign producers as well as new nonunion plants in the U.S. Sunbelt. Overall return on business investments fell from 10% to less than 6%, a staggering blow to business profits and government tax revenues.

Jimmy Carter became president in 1976 as a supporter of decentralization but not of heavy government spending. He appointed activists from the ethnic and neighborhood movements to run HUD programs. In several ways, he sought to encourage volunteer activities, including promoting a national commission on neighborhoods. His administration cooperated with nationwide coalitions, including Neighborhoods USA, the National Center for Urban Ethnic Affairs, and the National Association of Neighborhoods. President Carter's principal appointee from the neighborhood sector was Geno C. Baroni, an activist Catholic priest, who had founded and led the National Center for Urban Ethnic Affairs. During the 1970s, Baroni was a leading voice calling for an alliance of urban blacks and ethnic whites to demand justice of a society that had treated both groups unfairly. He was appointed assistant secretary for neighborhood, consumer, and regulatory affairs at HUD.

In his Baroni biography, O'Rourke (1991) concluded that Baroni

turned around the federal government's policy toward neighborhoods. He deserves much credit for convincing first [HUD Secretary] Harris, then the White House domestic staff, then President Carter, that federal policies should be reshaped to preserve and improve neighborhoods where people live, shop, belong to community organizations, and attend religious institutions. (p. 142)

Baroni constantly argued for changes in government policy, urging that important attention be given to the voice of the people who live in the settled inner-city urban neighborhoods—white ethnic, black, and Hispanic. He pushed the president and Congress, with some success, to target most community development block grant money to low- and moderate-income neighborhoods. He took a lead role in the creation of the Neighborhood Self-Help Development Program, which provided a modest $15 million to 125 communities whose leaders leveraged it into a total of $198 million in private and other government funds. Baroni said the 125 programs operated by CDCs and other types of neighborhood organizations resulted in 4,500 jobs created and more than 6,000 units of affordable housing provided. But his great contribution was establishing legitimacy for neighborhoods and their organizations. His being at HUD provided an entrée that was to become permanent.

Both unemployment and inflation moved into double digits, a combination that was tagged "stagflation." Businesses began to close obsolete plants, with drastic human consequences. Firms shifted investments to exurban locations, or even to foreign shores, where the return was greater. They cut back high-wage employees, farmed out work to low-wage contractors, demanded concessions from their remaining workforces, fought unions, and left many industrial workers—black, brown, and white—isolated from the new high-performance jobs being created in the campus-like technology parks far beyond central cities.

THE 1980s AND 1990s

These conditions defeated President Carter's bid for reelection and brought Ronald Reagan to power on a platform to further reduce the role of government, and to restore the prosperity of American business, while lessening federal aid to communities by blessing them with the balm of "privatization." He aided business by drastic tax cuts and deficit spending for defense. These twin

measures stimulated the economy, increased profits, and led to the huge public debt and annual deficits that came to bedevil the government and hobble society in carrying out its responsibilities to the poor and physically/mentally challenged during the 1980s and early 1990s. Although the economic stimulation caused employment to rise, many of the new jobs were of the low-wage, part-time variety, without health benefits or stability. Incomes of the top 20% rose dramatically, while most working people found their real incomes declining. The woes of great masses of unskilled and immobile people were ignored as they fell into the ranks of the working poor or even dropped out of the workforce. More poverty for more households meant more community distress and decline.

President Reagan began the cutbacks in social programs that, during the Clinton administration, continued to become more severe, to the point where government ended the social contract that once guaranteed incomes to poor families with dependent children, the program that had been hammered out during the Great Depression of the 1930s (as described earlier). Now in the 21st century, state and local governments and their nonprofit contractors struggle to move and keep millions of supported poor in work programs, but these programs are having great difficulty because of the low wages paid by the jobs available to people who have limited skills and experience.

With government abandoning the safety net, there was further impetus for community organizations to multiply and broaden their programs, making privatization serve them as best they could. Fisher (1994a, 1994b) reported that during the 1980s and 1990s, tens of thousands of additional community-based efforts were launched around a wide range of issues and needs, an expansion that has touched most small communities. Although the decade of the 1990s remained a time of rising collective action for small communities, there was much less direct government spending on community development in spite of the federal government's ending its annual deficits and experiencing surpluses. Fisher found advocacy and service continuing to be widely used as approaches.

Fisher (1994a) saw contemporary community power as being in low gear, mired in a "politics of moderation," limited to building a capacity for governance, for forcing targets to the bargaining table, and for winning modest victories. Although the proliferation of organizations fragments community power, it also "gives voice to new constituencies and lays the groundwork for social change" (p. 19). Among the new constituencies Fisher found hopeful for moving social change beyond moderation were those that were mobilized for the World Trade Organization protests detonated in Seattle in 1999. These protests attacking "the new global corporate order" continued bursting out across the world in Davos, Switzerland; Washington, D.C.; Quebec City, Quebec; and other parts of the globe until the September 11, 2001, terrorist attacks on the United States, and then resumed afterward. (More about this global mobilization of communal forces can be found in Appendix 2.C.)

Delgado (1997) saw communities of color as a resurgent force given new vigor by the massive immigration occurring in California, Texas, and other key population areas. Linked in many situations to academic institutions, he saw "the identity politics of the dispossessed" as a powerful component for future surges of community power. Because social and economic conditions for nearly half of Americans, and for vast numbers of others throughout the world, have relatively worsened since the 1980s, with real incomes stagnant and household debts mounting, the buildup of desperate populations counterbalances the rise of wealth in the hands of the new billionaires.

On another stage, we have Berry's (1999) mountain of evidence, compiled in *The New Liberalism: The Rising Power of Citizen Groups,* demonstrating and detailing the growing power now exercised by the more sophisticated citizen organizations over policymaking in Congress. Through 205 rigorously assessed cases of issues before the Congress since 1960, Berry showed how citizen groups, such as the Environmental Defense Fund, Public Citizen, and the Community Nutrition Institute, have been the primary political force moving Congress from questions on how to increase the economic pie to questions about balancing economic growth with the need to enhance the environment, protect consumers, and improve the well-being of persons.

Sklar (1995) found that economic inequality is now so extreme that the richest 1% have as much wealth as do the entire bottom 95%, with more than 50% of all children living in poverty. "The shrinking middle class is misled into thinking that those lower on the economic ladder are pulling them down, when in reality those on the top are rising at their expense" (pp. 2–3). This widespread misery during times of unprecedented money making for some may mean a great opportunity for a resurgence of community forces if the pall of civic apathy can be dissipated. There appear to be increasing numbers of community people who are angry and ready to organize.

Earlier in this chapter we saw the monopoly of business and government broken by community people in the Dudley Street neighborhood of Boston, where for the first time a nongovernmental organization obtained the right to exercise the power of eminent domain over land. Rusk (1999) described how, in the Midwest, neighborhood churches, organized as the Northwest Indiana Federation of Interfaith Organizations, were able to challenge a similar monopoly on issues of landfills and sprawl to shift attention to child poverty, unemployment, and the growing fiscal disparities among municipalities. Former Mayor Rusk filled his book with encouraging examples of how communities have expanded their role in influencing public decisions.

If the current uncertain economy settles down and prosperity and abundance stabilize at a reasonable level, then there are going to be multiplying opportunities for community organizations to compete for resources at the scale needed. But the competition with other societal interests will be fierce and will test the mettle of the communal sector. The return of prosperity is always a somewhat shaky assumption, and perhaps more so in a global context. Moreover, President Bush's insistence on increased government spending for domestic security and military, while holding to tax cuts, could painfully squeeze community-based renewal efforts.

In Chapter 3, we look at the dominance achieved by the CDC renewal model during the 1970s and 1980s and how this dominance was challenged during the 1990s, resulting in the resurgence of models that embody advocacy and hard-nosed organizing as acceptable tools for community renewal during the new century and setting the stage for the widespread use of the flexible comprehensive model.

Fisher and Shragge (2000) labeled "social moderation" as the enemy of community progress (p. 16). They emphasized raising social policy and political demands for reform of the now dominant political economy to the top of the community sector agenda, with drastic redistribution downward as a legitimate demand for maintaining democracy and achieving economic fair play.

Given the rising levels of political consciousness discovered by Putnam (2002) in his recent polling, we are likely entering a favorable time for aggressive efforts of mobilizing, planning, and reforming our own home communities. In Chapter 3, we get up-to-date on the efforts already under way and see how they arrived at where they are.

Summary

The past 100 years provide evidence of the potency of communal power to affect public policy, as well as to change social, political, and economic conditions in local areas, when such power is organized and carefully deployed toward limited targets. Too often, power is fragmented and wasted. More prudent strategies, tougher tactics, and larger and more cohesive coalitions and alliances seem to be needed as the new century unfolds with rising tides of disparities.

The history of communal power deployment has had its bright years as well as its depressing ones. The good years reveal latent strength and intriguing possibilities. This history, in all its richness, variety, and volatility, supports the feasibility of neighbors coming together to improve their own small communities and then forming the alliances and combined networks that are able to affect the highest holders of authority in society. It is even possible, at certain times and under certain circumstances, for community power to have influence at the level of an urban region, a whole state, or even the nation and beyond. And, at special times, it is possible for this influence to prevail in wiping out discrimination, unlocking desperately needed resources, or bringing changed direction to public or corporate power, as we saw in the CRA of the 1970s. Breaking the monopoly of the traditional business-government partnerships so as to achieve equity appears more feasible after looking back at the populist movement of the 1890s, the progressive movement of the early 1900s, the desperate Depression of the 1930s, the 1960s decade of rebellion, and even the results of the popular vote in the November 2000 presidential election, where the party representing most of the poor, labor unions, people of color, and other communal types received a million more votes than the party representing most of the wealthy, business corporations, stockholders, monopolists, and authoritarian bankers.

Continuing Questions

1. Where are distressed small communities likely to find their best leadership?

2. Under what conditions can the growing numbers of community organizations be fused together in regional and national coalitions that can have a strong influence on public policy?

3. Are democratic grassroots or expert-led community organizations more effective?

4. Are communities in distress helped most by militant advocacy or cooperative partnership?

5. Are distressed communities likely to heal more fully and permanently from evolutionary or revolutionary reform?

6. Will the increased interest in global organizing diminish or increase interest in neighborhood organizing?

7. What are the compelling central issues around which a broad coalition of communal organizations might unite to gain parity and power and influence with business and government?

Appendix 2.A
Two Men of
Glory in Urban Politics

Examples of two urban mayors who used their governmental powers to advance equity for families, communities, and society-at-large were Hazen Pingree of Detroit (1890–1897) and Harold Washington of Chicago (1983–1987).

An outstanding figure was Pingree, mayor of Detroit from 1890 to his untimely death in 1897.

Pingree was the son of a poor Maine farmer who mobilized working-class ethnic voters in Detroit and used his skills and power base to end civic corruption, build a first-rate street system, cut utility costs, open up waterfronts for public use, and win reductions in street railway fares. He forced the city's business elite to carry their fair share of the city's tax burden. To lower unfair telephone rates, he organized a rival phone company. Rather than exploit ethnic hostilities, he appealed "to the unity of interests of Detroit's working-class Poles, Germans, Irish, and the middle class" (Judd & Swanstrom, 1994, pp. 71–72).

In 1983, Washington was elected mayor of Chicago. This was a "magic moment" in Chicago. He was the city's first black mayor. In his victory speech, he said, "We never stopped believing we were part of something good, something that has never happened before. We intend to revitalize this city, to open the doors and be certain that its babies are healthy and its old people are fed and well housed." His platform of inclusion, fairness, and empowerment marked a decisive shift away from the patronage politics of Chicago. He was new wine in a new bottle.

Washington put together a formidable "rainbow coalition" to bring government closer to the people with a "neighborhood agenda" that was the centerpiece of his office. Washington's populist charismatic style won him the affection of a broad-based coalition of blacks, Hispanics, and liberal whites in support of a progressive vision. He saw the "third sector" of community-based organizations as the savior for Chicago's economic, political, and social ills. It was a massive voter registration drive by these organizations that convinced Washington to run. His vision was to bring the classes and races together and to galvanize them to seek redistribution of power and opportunity. It would put emphasis on decision making by previously excluded groups and chase funds away from downtown development into neighborhood renewal (Gills, 1991).

Washington's reforms grew out of the context of massive displacement in Chicago and the widespread feeling that the social costs of urban decline could not be allowed to lie where they fall.

In appointing his staff, Washington rewarded loyalty as well as like-mindedness. This led to tension between his political followers and the leaders of neighborhood organizations as he faced the task of changing people's perceptions of what government could do and of showing that social movements could be a positive force.

Washington's handling of debates over a new central library, revised city budgets, neighborhood land use, and other key issues followed a participation mode. Washington established a Commission on Latino Affairs that widened opportunities for Hispanic people to enter politics and the workings of city hall and to begin to have a voice in the workings of local government.

Washington was more successful in implementing some parts of his program than others. He lifted the city hall veil of secrecy. He brought greater accountability to public office. Yet he might have achieved more if his relationship with his own Democratic party and the business community, to which he was ideologically opposed, had been more amicable.

If Washington had not died prematurely in 1987, his reform agenda might eventually have been implemented in full. But this is not certain given that he failed to recruit fresh cadres of community-oriented people to become leaders in the movement he inspired. According to Gills (1991), "Harold was less effective because he didn't have a strong independent movement. He was the movement!" (p. 61).

The question of Washington's legacy remains. Chicago's city government has had more respect since Washington was mayor. Some believe that it has been more open and fair. Others are not so sure.

—Brian Conway
Research Assistant

Appendix 2.B
The Hyde Park-Kenwood
Community Conference

Among the thousands of old and new neighborhood organizations that wrestled with the challenges of urban renewal after World War II was the Hyde Park-Kenwood Community Conference, formed to act for an aged but attractive lakefront location on the near South Side of Chicago that is home to the University of Chicago. The conference came into being through the initiative of black and white leaders of faith-based institutions during a time of massive southern migration. Housing was becoming overcrowded, the streets were shabby, and rumors were rife that the university was considering a move to the suburbs.

A resident who was around when it all began was Charles Staples. Still associated with the conference after 50 years, he confirms the birth event:

> Until 1948, the burgeoning black community north and south of Hyde Park-Kenwood was held back by restrictive covenants. Then the courts nullified the covenants and the newcomers moved across the old boundaries. Fears engendered in some white homeowners led to distressed sales and flight. Real estate agents warned of more losses in values and frightened increasing numbers into selling, a process referred to as "blockbusting." Houses were sold to black buyers at inflated prices. Illegal rooming houses were created. Apartments were subdivided. Racial turnover and overcrowding swept through border blocks. At a gathering of conscientious ministers, Quakers, a rabbi, and other concerned citizens, black and white, the Conference was formed in 1949, dedicated to helping build a stable integrated community of high standards, through educational and legal means as well as group methods to quell fears, and end blockbusting. University of Chicago Professor Herbert Thelan held community clinics in which he taught residents to be block leaders skilled in group dynamics. (C. G. Staples & J. Staples, personal communication, May 12, 1999)

The conference spearheaded a neighborhood movement that used block organization to ease racial tension, housing code enforcement to check illegal subdividing of apartments, political action to improve the schools and increase police patrols, and eventually neighborhood-wide planning to gain long-term stability. The planning was done, with some apprehension, in partnership with the university.

The mission of the conference officially became "building an interracial community of high standards." Early on, more than 2,000 people in a neighborhood of 70,000 became active, a membership that in time doubled to 4,000. Most who participated paid dues. Thousands more affiliated informally through a block club or attendance at public meetings. There was a conference service organized by Pierre de Vise, a young social scientist, to steer perspective renters and home buyers to specific blocks, by race, in proportions that would ensure the interracial character of the blocks. De Vise found all but one of the realtors in the neighborhood running like scared jackrabbits chased by bloodhounds. But one cooperating firm gave him solid cooperation and showed that the effort had potential.

Doubting the feasibility of the interracial mission, the University of Chicago observed from the sidelines for 3 years. Finally, when an upsurge of crime in 1952 threatened to interfere with the recruitment of quality students and faculty, the university joined in on its own terms, creating its own community arm, the South East Chicago Commission. The commission launched hard-line anti-crime activities and hired an unrelenting attorney as director and a professional city planner to design a long-range renewal plan for the entire neighborhood. The attorney was Julian Levi, the son of a rabbi, a native of Hyde Park-Kenwood who drove slumlords to the wall and showed little enthusiasm for resident participation. He became celebrated as the "bad cop" essential to the neighborhood's survival.

The twin efforts of residents and the university proceeded along what was then a new road by choosing to use planning and renewal as appropriate methods for preserving community rather than choosing to demolish it and start over. The presence of organized concerned residents was a mitigating force, restraining the university's appetite for land and radical gentrification, although the displacement of residents and small businesses ultimately was extensive. Throughout, Chicago's Mayor Richard J. Daley offered powerful support.

The conference and commission did not always travel the road cordially. Although a common interest in preserving the neighborhood drove them on, divergent views on methods and values tore them apart. Julia Abrahamson, founding conference director, recorded the differences, as did university social scientists Peter Rossi and Robert Dentler (Abrahamson, 1959; Rossi & Dentler, 1961). Issues that were fought over included the allotment of land for public housing, preservation versus demolition in certain key locations, the open sharing of information as the planning proceeded, affordable versus upscale housing standards, and democracy versus oligarchy in decision making (Cunningham, 1965).

Ostensibly, united neighborhood forces—residents, business people, the university, local politicians, churches, and other institutions—extracted large-scale government funding to implement the resulting urban renewal plan. The conference insisted on adequate relocation benefits for the displaced, as well as the inclusion of public housing, before supporting the plan. The plan was executed amid controversy during the 1960s and early 1970s. Rehabilitation and preservation, along with clearance, were used. The conference mission was largely achieved after 25 years of effort and more than $300 million of public and private investment, but at heavy costs to several thousand low-income residents, many of them people of color, who were forced out. This was far too many, in the view of some residents and outside critics. Today, Hyde Park-Kenwood is at least a biracial neighborhood of high standards. The conference still exists, but as a much scaled-down organization, now seeking to recast its vision and recapture some of the drive of the early decades.

Important to the funding of the conference during its early years were the Emil Schwarzhaupt Foundation and Carl Tjerandsen, a pioneering adult educator who served as executive secretary of the foundation. His final assessment, published after 30 years of conference effort, concluded, "The community was stabilized on a multiracial basis. Citizens were mobilized. The most blighted areas were replaced with new housing and service facilities. The Conference continued as a functioning organization" (Tjerandsen, 1980, p. 372). These achievements, he suggested, came from quality leadership, a program combining idealistic and programmatic organizational elements,

interpersonal communication standards that included the rejection of confrontation in favor of cooperation while still taking vigorous stands on issues, and encouraging the aggressive involvement of those willing to support the goal of an interracial community. Participation, his report noted, was aided by a dual structure of volunteer committees and block clubs, and operations were undergirded by an environment of strong institutions that were able to bring pressure on city government, including the police, who vigilantly sought to ensure that residents felt safe when they walked to night meetings.

As the 20th century ended, the conference celebrated 50 years of being a workhorse for small community salvation. The neighborhood population had slipped to about 40,000, the conference paid membership was less than 500, and the conference budget was minuscule. The staff members were mostly volunteers, but the organization rolled along with an office over a storefront, annual fund-raising events, and an information-packed newsletter sent out six times a year to 4,600 households and businesses, including a critical mass of households settled into cooperative and condominium apartments. The newsletter reported on important issues, but without the crisis tone of the 1950s and 1960s (Hyde Park-Kenwood Community Conference, 1999, 2000a, 2000b, 2001). Much of the information and analysis now reported in the newsletter, the *Conference Reporter*, arises out of the work and ideas of local cooperating organizations rather than out of conference initiatives. The conference serves as a kind of town crier, shouting out via post important neighborhood happenings regardless of sponsor. It provides forums and link-ups on issues and program ideas. For example, the conference has been concerned about the opening of a currency exchange charging outrageous interest on "payday loans." State legislators have been asked to find ways in which to limit interest charges. Several conference members have joined in informational leafleting aimed at awakening people to the potential of exploitation.

Crime statistics are still reported but are less frightening than during earlier decades. Newsletter readers learn that homicides and sexual assaults are down and purse snatchings are fewer but that burglaries are up. Economic integration is getting more attention than racial integration. Parking remains a pervasive irritant. Teachers, parents, and neighborhood leaders connect in local school councils, which now hire their own principals, an element of Chicago's school reform seen as key to quality education. Readers also learn that charter schools will be opening soon. The university and community are tied together on many fronts and are continuously professing their affection for one another. Public housing is being rebuilt for mixed-income tenancy. Although hackers from Poland once kidnapped the conference Web site (www.hyde-park.org), it was quickly rescued and is up and working again. Amid controversy, an ad hoc committee seeks to rejuvenate the 53rd Street collection of restaurants and shops. No Hyde Park shop left anywhere sells pillowcases or yarn. Some 50,000 spring plants will go on sale at the annual garden fair. Volunteers are monitoring $30 million in park improvements to the neighborhood piece of the Lake Michigan lakefront. Readers nominate the names of tradespersons who do quality repair work. Academic Games League annual tournament rotations are set. Some 17,000 fresh bulbs have arrived from Holland for sale at the annual Fall Conference fund-raiser. A walking tour to benefit the hunger fund will wind through the adjacent Old Bronzville, the historic South Side African American community. The university offered several $10,000 grants to local groups, which can produce beautification projects that include convincing long-term plans for maintenance. The conference reported a widespread resurgence of participative public planning for rehabilitation of Lake Shore Drive, political fund-raising reform, an evaluation of the Welfare to Work program, the restoration of lakefront parks, a new master campus construction plan for the university, and a program aimed at reducing motorcycle speeding and noise, and the Web site has developed into an "organized version of our community in cyberspace," according to the conference newsletter. (Each issue of the *Conference Reporter* adds to the neighborhood's history.)

Approaching the conference's 50th birthday, the Conference Strategic Planning Committee went to work to evaluate the past and enter the future with a "redefined and refined" mission statement and course of action. Looking toward this landmark anniversary in the history of place-based small community development organizations, one of the authors of this book polled the 23 members of the conference board to ask for their contemporary views on past achievements and failings, current objectives, and suggestions for strengthening the conference. More than half of the board members responded, providing the following findings.

Survey of Conference Board Members (1998–1999)

Three Principal Achievements

- Building a sense of community through communications and consensus while remaining faithful to pledge to preserve diversity
- Improvements in public safety
- Beautification

Three Principal Failings

- Too little Conference power and leadership built up and deployed over the years (e.g., not able to maintain early huge membership, loss of block clubs, lack of support from several interests, not doing enough to fight "Negro removal")
- Inability to sustain substantial indigenous fund-raising
- Loss of ability to attract sizable number of members from among African American population and young people

Three Current Priority Objectives

- Build the organization by recruiting a more diverse membership, targeting younger people of all races, and establishing more working alliances with other appropriate organizations both inside and outside Hyde Park-Kenwood.
- Step up information flows using state-of-the-art technology and emphasizing advocacy.
- Build financial strength on a diversified indigenous funding base (recent conference annual budgets have been less than $30,000).

Three Current Suggestions

- Dedicate more resources to organizational alliances toward gaining influence citywide and beyond.

- Intensify actions and communications to help residents and others feel more secure and confident in the neighborhood.
- Use the 50th anniversary to jump-start the conference toward enriching diversity and interaction within itself and within the buildings and blocks of the neighborhood.

Early in the anniversary year, the Strategic Planning Committee won board approval for this revised mission statement:

The Hyde Park-Kenwood Community Conference is a community organization dedicated to maintaining and enhancing an attractive, secure, diverse, and caring community. It promotes participation of its residents, businesses, institutions, and organizations in programs and activities that will advance the interests and concerns of the community.

The committee announced that it had begun to develop a strategic plan that would reflect the changing face of the community as well as the changing face of the conference. Board members were discussing an annual systematic fundraising campaign among the 4,600 households and businesses receiving the newsletter. It would require a target amount large enough to hire a staff. The staff should be able to facilitate the members in shaping an independent platform powerful enough to have influence on the direction of the community.

There was some sentiment on the board for doing recruitment of aggressive young members and for doing more militant advocacy on school improvement, neighborhood safety, the university's master planning, and other gut issues. But there was also sentiment for the organization to continue to build itself as a community clearinghouse, town forum, and interconnector, with a few special projects such as the annual garden fair. With either an advocacy or a clearinghouse direction, the basic mission of maintaining and strengthening a true, interracial urban community in Chicago could be pursued. Sustaining such a direction for more than a half century is the great achievement. The conference is also a living reminder that a resident organization can last for a long time and can serve a useful purpose in maintaining a small community so long

as there is a continuity of people willing to give of their time and talent.

Late Bulletins From the *Conference Reporter*

- The conference announced that its 50th anniversary membership drive, generously supported by the Hyde-Park Bank, had raised membership by 65%. (March–April 2000, p. 3)
- The conference has launched a brisk round of participative planning on the future of Elm Park, a run-down, underused small space that attracts troublemakers. In meetings and via the conference Web site, a lively debate has raged over three options: upgrade the park; sell land for parking to nearby plaza and relocate park; or sell to plaza, but only if replacement site is within three blocks of current park. (November–December 1999, pp. 1, 5)
- A campaign is unfolding to use tax increment financing to revitalize the shabby 53rd Street business artery. Tax increment financing allows long-range public improvements to be financed by future tax revenues expected to accrue from the improvements. (January–February 2000, p. 1)

A major project advocated for vigorously is rehabilitation of the neighborhood's four obsolete Metro rapid transit stations and extension of service on one of its bus lines. Public transit is a key asset of the neighborhood to which the conference gives attention, not only by monitoring and pushing quality service but also by advocating for attractive and safe stations. The conference does this through a permanent Transit Task Force in close partnership with the area's two city council members.

With both pride and regrets for its history, the conference has entered its second half century revived and determined to help Hyde Park-Kenwood remain a significant community in a city of great vitality. Looking toward the future, the *Conference Reporter* (July–August 2001) has carried comments from residents pointing out that many people love the fact that Hyde Park is an urban village in the sense that it features the diversity, choice, and independence of an urban neighborhood and simultaneously maintains the familiarity and intimacy of a small town. On the other hand; the neighborhood constantly faces pressure to consider finding space for a few national retail chains that might invest big money and attract more people to the community. This leaves a question to be addressed: Would this destroy the urban village?

Appendix 2.C
Global Organizing—One More Time: People Stand Up for Equity

As the year 1999 ended, a cataclysmic event, reminiscent of the 1960s, unfolded in Seattle, the global port city that is home for Boeing, Microsoft, Amazon.com, and other dragons of technology. As with all urban places mentioned in this book, Seattle has small communities where activist residents yearn for the skills and resources to organize. The 1999 event gave these residents opportunities for gaining sophisticated experience around world trade issues of grave complexity. A few weeks before the event, the *Seattle Press* reported on its front page that neighborhood-based protesting groups were springing up all over the city, particularly within Ballard, Fremont, and the northeast part of the city ("Neighborhood Groups," 1999). These excited and eager groups had the opportunity to link with exotic new potential allies from global hinterlands who shared their passions and would be acting out in Seattle on the occasion of a gathering convened by the World Trade Organization (WTO).

In late November 1999, as long planned, an optimistic Seattle welcomed trade representatives from 135 nations to a historic WTO assembly, where talks were to seek to free world business from parochial national restrictions. Before delegates could remove their jackets for serious conversation, legions of protesters representing diverse interests and languages, including the English speakers from Seattle's Ballard and Fremont, poured onto the streets around the headquarters hotel and in a few tumultuous hours redefined and expanded the struggle of the world's communal sector for recognition and justice.

Mobilized from a polyglot of nations, street crowds raged for days, bellowing against the killing of sea turtles, the exploitation of young children as laborers, the selling of genetically modified foods, the ravaging of natural environments, and the scandalous growing gap between rich and poor everywhere on the globe. Estimates of the number of protesters ran from 30,000 to 50,000. Some among the largely peaceful street multitudes resisted police commands or vandalized property, resulting in 600 arrests by week's end.

Seattle is a sometimes booming metropolis that in 1999 boasted 60,000 millionaires. For every millionaire, there was a household living on the brink whose net worth had remained stagnant or even gone negative since 1990. Some blue-collar neighborhoods had been upscaled, pushing out one population in favor of a more affluent one. Boeing faced fierce competition from Europe's Airbus, forcing Boeing to tightly control costs and making employees nervous about job security. Seattle residents in the street demonstrations included activists from the Seattle Direct Action Network, veteran environmentalists, members of an array of neighborhood groups, and unionized workers such as Boeing machinists who had overwhelmingly rejected a new contract offer shortly before the WTO conference opened its sessions.

There was no central demand on the WTO, but general targets emerged: the "excesses" of globalization, where forced currency devaluation pauperizes working people, including many in a country's middle class; multinational bodies overriding the environmental protection laws of individual nations; international corporations outsourcing manufacturing in a search for compliant workforces whose members accept sub-poverty compensation; and authoritarian governments trammeling human rights by prohibiting independent organizations from speaking out, families from bearing children, and women from freely choosing their marriage partners.

The Seattle event did not arise out of nowhere. Nongovernmental communal sector organizations have spoken out on these issues for decades. But today, we have obscure global structures that amass unprecedented resources and power and that become treaty enforcers exercising control over whole nations whose peoples and small communities have no recourse to elected bodies. These structures are created by arcane multinational agreements that are shaped and pushed by globe-circling leviathan business corporations. Human society finds itself facing forces that most people neither understand nor experience as benign. A meeting such as the WTO gathering in Seattle becomes a target—perhaps a proper and fair concrete flesh-and-blood target—for community forces that up to November 1999 had been frustrated by an inability to come nose to nose with the multinational specter they sense is oppressing them.

For a few days, Seattle was the big game, where the perceived oppressor could be confronted. There had been preliminary games. Earlier in 1999, there was a warm-up demonstration at the WTO world headquarters in Geneva, Switzerland. British periodicals reported a "carnival of capitalism" staged in London in June 1999, where Seattle-bound protest groups practiced. José Bové and his farmer insurgents in France, who have drawn world attention for years as they have acted out in support of continued state farm subsidies, came to Seattle fresh from a bulldozer attack launched against a McDonald's restaurant in a French town.

A sampling of the groups on the streets of Seattle were the International Forum on Globalization, the Sierra Club, the Council of Canadians, Public Citizen, the American Federation of Labor and Congress of Industrial Organizations (AFL-CIO), the Washington Council for Fair Trade, People for the Ethical Treatment of Animals, the Sea Turtle Restoration Project, and an array of faith-based organizations. Members of these groups and many others participating were able to persist for several days, using cell phones for efficient communication and state-of-the-art gas masks for protection against the tear gas of the police and National Guard.

In short, it was a popular demonstration against oppression and poverty, a cacophony not too different from the dissonance of the 1960s, the 1930s, and the 1900s. Moreover, the disagreements were not all in the streets. As the WTO delegates struggled to plan and negotiate, they fought each other over agricultural subsidies, investment rules, labor rights, textile tariffs, protection of intellectual property, and the WTO's own internal secrecy, an issue that became cast as "transparency versus efficiency."

By December 3, even the governmental representatives of developing countries were in rebellion, and the United States was in a deadlock with its largest trading partners. At that point, the talks collapsed and the WTO conference disintegrated. Weary delegates hustled to the airport without issuing the usual final communiqués. They flew off to their home countries exhausted and disgruntled. There were fleeting announcements of limited talks to be resumed in 2000 at the WTO headquarters in Geneva, with negotiations to be limited to some narrow aspects of agriculture and some of the services for which the WTO is responsible. A few departing delegates announced intentions to try to deal with the issues raised by protesters. On the Monday following the breakup, across the world, the media called the collapse a debacle.

At the core of the protests was the accelerated spread of globalization. Its unregulated nature places awesome volatile power in the hands of financial service corporations and billionaire "lone wolf" investors and speculators, whose decisions can devastate the economies of whole nations when their risk models miscalculate key shifts in world markets. Since 1994, risk model failure had brought widespread suffering to whole nations and their working peoples, their families, and their communities, particularly in Mexico, Thailand, Indonesia, Malaysia, South Korea, and Russia.

Friedman (1999) described globalization as the anonymous, transnational, homogenizing, standardizing market forces and technologies that make up today's economic system (p. 29). He saw these modernizing forces as clashing with "everything that roots us, anchors us, identifies us, and locates us in this world—whether it be belonging to a family, a community, a tribe, a nation, a religion, or most of all a place called home. . . . Without a sense of home and belonging, life becomes barren and rootless" (p. 27). Globalization is with us for good or for evil. The challenge is to find ways in which to meet it and tame it so that it supports and enhances lives of the poor and the homes and neighborhoods of all the globe's people. Seattle was an early shot at taming it.

Very much of such protest represents global concern for the three issue themes of this book: racial division, civic apathy, and job insecurity.

Concerns for human rights were upfront on behalf of exploited people throughout the world, including many millions in the United States. The protest was a cry for dignity for ordinary working people and especially for those paid only a fraction of a living wage.

The Seattle disruptions, in fact, were civic involvement of a high order—a transnational rolling back of apathy. If demands launched there eventually lead to open processes for making and adjudicating trade agreements, as well as for participation of nongovernmental organizations (NGOs) in the implementation of the regulations embedded in the agreements, then it would give a substantial boost to universal civic resurgence.

The cries for equity and fairness in pricing consumer products, establishing fair wages, and protecting the health and safety of working people were loud, reflecting the worldwide nervousness regarding employment and job tenure. Organizations in small place communities can find strong allies in the issue groups that were mobilized in Seattle, pointing to future communal coalition building of networks and alliances that draw in both place community and issue community forces.

Desperate and negative as the Seattle week was, it produced an unusual show of citizen energy, imaginative NGO strategies and tactics, and the power of 30,000 or 40,000 risk takers to draw the attention of the world. The WTO went back to Geneva for retooling. Worldwide, millions were inspired once more by the possibilities of communal power. The leaders of multinational economic organizations were shocked into the realization that they must give respect and attention to the third sector and its communal interests. Perhaps the event punched out a broadened social agenda that human society must face during this new century. Certainly, events following close on Seattle gave hints that a renewed era of "power in the streets" could be emerging.

At the end of January 2000, official delegates from 130 nations assembled in Montreal to work out the biosafety issue that was much yelled about in Seattle (also known as the "genetically modified products" issue).

In Montreal, the atmosphere was relatively calm. There was no detested WTO convener as there was in Seattle. Delegates from developed and developing nations alike came with expectations for reaching an agreement on a biosafety treaty. No final decision had to be made; only a tentative agreement had to be reached that participants would bring back to their home countries for ratification. Protesters were few, and demonstrations were orderly. After a week of hard bargaining, a consensus was arrived at on the right of individual nations to bar imports of genetically modified products. It was a small but significant reconciliation of environmental protection with free trade. Talks on this issue in Seattle 2 months earlier had collapsed, adding fuel to the fire in that city.

Simultaneous with the Montreal event, world corporate and political leaders gathered in Davos to discuss the growing polarization of the rich and poor, with President Clinton and others predicting a return to protectionism if the poor were not recognized and responded to. Clinton pleaded for open markets plus rules-based trade as the best combination for building shared prosperity. He also lobbied for lifting the burden of debt from developing countries. For the first time, NGOs were admitted in strength to forum sessions. Demonstrations were much smaller than those in Seattle and were tightly controlled by Swiss police, although one group broke windows in a nearby McDonald's restaurant.

The media reported from Davos that several Seattle protesters were admitted to conference sessions, where they argued that removal of barriers to trade and investment could sometimes be acceptable, but only when accompanied by regulations to prevent pollution and destruction of rainforests, to reduce economic crises that destroy jobs and savings, and to prevent depressed farm prices that undercut both small farmers and farm laborers who are without the power to bargain collectively. It became clear that such arguments held added weight because of the disruption and visibility of the Seattle protests. More such demonstrations could be useful at future world trade gatherings.

By inviting leading protesters such as Lori Wallach (of Public Citizen's Global Trade) and author Jeremy Rifkin to participate, the Davos forum took a step toward a collective solution to world trade policies and operating practices that would meet the needs of both the powerful corporate wealth creators and the poor people and poor nations of the world that have long been neglected and exploited. It can be said that a bit of inclusion was practiced at Davos.

In April, the pressure was ratcheted upward by 10,000 protesters mobilized in Washington to challenge the International Monetary Fund (IMF) and the World Bank for supporting policies and practices of "global corporatism" that subject workers to sweatshop conditions and squeeze down public expenditures for health, education, and environmental protection. The media reported that the impenetrable police force and 1,300 arrests short-circuited a shutdown of the IMF and World Bank assemblies but did not prevent protesters from winning avid attention to their issues. There was a virtual closing of the downtown area that sparked clashes between police and demonstrators and led to many arrests.

The top financial officials present announced that more attention would be paid to globalization's victims and offered a commitment to furnish unlimited money to fight AIDS in poor countries. They also promised to accelerate debt relief for the developing world, a promise that may be difficult to implement soon. Observers said that although the protesters never managed to disrupt the official meetings as they had hoped, the numerous students, environmentalists, union workers, and other activists—diverse in age, race, and nationality—impressed the sponsors with their cohesion.

Some media correspondents criticized protesters for trying to reduce a matter of incredible complexity to emotional slogans and for having affluent American students trying to speak for the poor of other nations. A few, however, saw U.S. corporate leaders softening up enough to compromise on a key issue: giving their support to inserting human standards for civil rights, conditions of labor, and care for the environment in trade agreements so as to maintain the existing partial consensus on free trade.

In June 2000, protests were planned for Detroit and Windsor, to be directed at a Windsor summit of delegates from the 34 nations of the Organization of American States. The agenda called for discussion of ways in which to bolster trade in North and South America. The Council of Canadians and other

activist organizations planned to participate. However, the proposed demonstration was largely stifled by a multinational mobilization of 4,000 security officers. The threat of disruption was heavy in the air for weeks leading up to the event and "forced" the governments to use a heavy hand.

A follow-up to the Detroit-Windsor gathering took place in April 2001 in Quebec City, with a resurgence of the Seattle chaos. Top government leaders of the entire Western Hemisphere came together to continue the effort to shape a North American Free Trade Agreement (NAFTA)-like free trade zone that would encompass 34 nations. Once again, tear gas and disruptive demonstrations drew world attention. President George W. Bush was on hand to tout free trade as the key to spreading both prosperity and freedom to U.S. "neighbors" in what would be the world's largest free trade zone. Throughout a stormy weekend, the president appealed for "a spirit of civility," while demonstrators broke through police barriers to delay the opening of conference sessions.

As an ameliorating measure, U.S. Trade Representative Robert Zoellick announced that the Bush administration would subject future trade agreements to environmental reviews. During the conference, the president sent staff members to meet with hostile labor, environmental, and human rights groups. His representatives carried the message of seeking a free trade area where there would be a commitment to "protecting the environment and improving labor standards."

Protests drew more than 20,000 participants who feared that any formal agreement among the 34 nations would protect investors but offer incentives rather than guarantees for workers and the environment. More than 150 protesters were arrested after incidents of stone throwing. But most of the demonstrators, although loud and enraged, were peaceful, with a great variety of groups participating, including Quakers. Pervasive among the groups was concern for the hemisphere's poorest and the need to hold corporations to the same rules abroad that they must observe at home. But protesting groups showed little confidence in the argument that incentives could achieve justice with the same certainty as can sanctions. Too often, they have heard business people argue with passion that labor and environmental standards do not belong in trade agreements.

Some media observers saw the protesters as obstructing economic growth that could help the world's impoverished people to move out of poverty. Others saw the protesters forcing an essential debate to settle the great world trade questions with participation and fairness. There was one certainty: What began in the streets of Seattle as communal demands for a voice in deciding global economic questions will not go away. Crucial as they are to the future of job security for ordinary people everywhere, to the core nature of freedom and democracy, and to universal recognition of dignity of individual persons and households in every small community on the globe, the insistence on collective decisions makes sense. The 34 nations have yet to achieve a final resolution.

World trade protests continued in 2001 in Genoa, Italy, with some of the same scale and fury as in Seattle, reducing the ability of delegates to hold effective discussions. In September, thousands came to Washington to demonstrate at a meeting of the international financial institutions that was canceled due to the September 11 terrorist attacks on the United States. However, many of the protesters joined anti-war marches that were opposing the violence launched against Afghanistan and calling for a firm but nonviolent response. The marchers battled with police, and 11 were arrested. Later in November in Ottawa, Ontario, a small turnout of protesters was kept in line by a massive police presence at sessions of the IMF.

The United States' largest urban police force was on hand for a February assembly of the World Economic Forum in New York City, a few months after the terrorist attacks. Subdued demonstrations occurred with some defacing of corporate symbols, but generally these actions were peaceful.

European Union leaders met in Barcelona, Spain, in March 2002 with a huge police guard to seek agreement on increased competition in energy markets and on a variety of other economic issues. A peaceful march—estimated by the press at 250,000 people—carried banners announcing "against the Europe of capital and war—another world is possible." Toward

evening, there were scuffles with the police, and 50 people arrested.

Whether the signs of a new era of protest portend a productive buildup of communal power or a short-lived period of outrage that will fade is yet to be seen, but global economic issues are not the only ones provoking protest. There have been a rash of other communal outbursts.

The number of protesters who turned up at the July-August 2000 Republican Convention in Philadelphia was reported as about 10,000. Nearly 400 were arrested in disruptive demonstrations, including 4 state police officers working undercover as protesters. A massive protective security force sought to suppress non-peaceful parades. Crowds were larger for the Democratic event that followed, but the multi-cause polyglot of groups turning up could not agree on a single target issue, and so the protests lacked the impact of the Seattle original.

The largest communal outburst of the year 2000 came May 14 when an estimated 200,000 women and their supporters took part in the Million Mom March in Washington, putting focus on demands for tougher handgun restrictions. Critics pointed out that the march lacked force because it did not carry the threat of disruption. It was disruption that had put sting and impact into Seattle. The women in the Million Mom March were not ready to picket gun stores, clog the aisles at gun shows, or sit in the offices of reluctant legislators.

In another example, in January 2000, 46,000 marchers stepped out in South Carolina to protest the Confederate flag snapping over the state capital and to launch an expanded boycott advocated by the National Association for the Advancement of Colored People (NAACP). The march came in response to a rally of 6,000 white people supporting the flag a week earlier. Later, on March 26, 2000, 3,000 New Yorkers marched at the funeral of Patrick Dorismond, a Haitian young man who was unarmed when gunned down by police. The demonstrations included horns blaring and police barriers being knocked down.

A shocking and surprising demonstration materialized in Washington on April 20, 2002, when legions of anti-global economy marchers converged on long lines of chanting Arab Americans and their supporters calling for an end to violence against people in Palestine. At some point, the streams blended into a single moving mass voicing united opposition to war and killing. The *Washington Post* (April 21, 2002) reported a police estimate of a total of 75,000 marchers, of whom 41were arrested.

Washington Post reporter Manny Fernandez describes the atmosphere as "mostly civil and occasionally comedic, with only brief flashes of arguments or hostility. . . . The emotion of the Mid-East conflict appeared to overpower issues of economic fairness, with most of the signs and chants calling for freedom for Palestinians and the end of U.S. sponsorship of Israel" (Fernandez, 2002, p. A8).

Whether the 3-year-long round of street protests that began in Seattle, challenging the benevolence and fairness of the global political economy, will persist and eventually help to win effective environmental practices, rights for working people worldwide, living wages, and limits on food modification is uncertain. However, the repeated and mounting media attention of these 3 years of periodic mass protests confirms that communal forces seeking reform are not to be denied and have in fact drawn response with their encounters. They are likely to continue to mount fresh, forceful disruptive protests that affect world opinion and global policymaking until protesters are convinced that global trade policies are tipped unequivocally toward drastic reduction of world poverty and progress toward more equal sharing of the world's income and wealth. To these forces, it is unacceptable that a billion people live on less than a dollar a day. Meanwhile, neighborhood groups participating in global protests will learn the nuances of coalition advocacy and be better prepared to exercise political influence.

Three years of renewed civic energy at the beginning of the millennium does not necessarily portend a return to the militancy of the 1960s. It is certain, however, that community organizers will be missing a useful tried-and-true tool if they do not have protest in their bag, including disruptive strains, which seem to be essential to ensure media attention.

REFERENCES

Abrahamson, J. (1959). *A neighborhood finds itself.* New York: Harper.

Alinsky, S. D. (1945). *Reveille for radicals.* Chicago: University of Chicago Press.

Berry, J. M. (1999). *The new liberalism: The rising power of citizen groups.* Washington, DC: Brookings Institution Press.

Betten, N., & Austin, M. J. (1990). *The roots of community organizing, 1917–1939.* Philadelphia: Temple University Press.

Blum, J. M., Catton, B., Morgan, E. S., Schlesinger, A. M., Jr., Stampp, K. M., & Woodward, C. V. (1968). *The national experience* (2nd ed.). New York: Harcourt, Brace.

Brunner, E., & Yang, H. (1949). *Rural America and the extension service.* New York: Columbia University Press.

Cloward, R. A., & Piven, F. F. (1984). Introduction. In L. Staples (Ed.), *Roots to power* (pp. xiii–xviii). Westport, CT: Praeger.

Congress guts CRA. (1999, September–October). *Shelterforce,* p. 25. (Orange, NJ: National Housing Institute)

Cunningham, J. (1965). *The resurgent neighborhood.* Notre Dame, IN: Fides.

Cunningham, J., & Kotler, M. (1983). *Building neighborhood organizations.* Notre Dame, IN: Notre Dame University Press.

Delgado, G. (1997). *Beyond the politics of place: New directions in community organizing* (2nd ed.). Oakland, CA: Chardon.

Fernandez, M. (2002, April 21). Demonstrations rally to Palestinian cause. *The Washington Post,* pp. A1, A8–A9.

Fisher, R. (1994a, Fall). Community organizing in the conservative '80s and beyond. *Social Policy,* pp. 11–21.

Fisher, R. (1994b). *Let the people decide: Neighborhood organizing in America* (rev. ed.). New York: Twayne.

Fisher, R. (1996). Neighborhood organizing: The importance of historical context. In W. Keating, N. Krumholz, & P. Star (Eds.), *Revitalizing urban neighborhoods.* Lawrence: University Press of Kansas.

Fisher, R., & Shragge, E. (2000). Challenging community organizing: Facing the 21st century. *Journal of Community Practice, 8*(3), 1-20.

Friedman, T. (1999). *The lexus and the olive tree: Understanding globalization.* New York: Farrar, Straus, & Giroux.

Gans, H. J. (1982). *The urban villagers* (rev. ed.). New York: Free Press.

Garvin, C. D., & Cox, F. M. (1995). A history of community organizing since the Civil War with special reference to oppressed communities. In J. Rothman, J. L. Erlich, J. E. Tropman, & F. M. Cox (Eds.), *Strategies of community intervention: Macro practice* (pp. 64–98). Itasca, IL: F. E. Peacock.

Gills, D. (1991). Chicago politics and community development: A social movement perspective. In P. Clavel & W. Wiewel (Eds.), *Harold Washington and the neighborhoods: Progressive city government in Chicago, 1983–1987* (pp. 34–63). New Brunswick, NJ: Rutgers University Press.

Halpern, R. (1995). *Rebuilding the inner city: A history of neighborhood initiatives to address poverty in the United States.* New York: Columbia University Press.

Hanna, M. G., & Robinson, B. (1994). *Strategies for community empowerment: Direct action and transformative approaches to social change practice.* Lewiston, NY: Edwin Mellen.

Horwitt, S. D. (1989). *Let them call me rebel: Saul Alinsky—His life and legacy.* New York: Knopf.

Hyde Park-Kenwood Community Conference. (1999, November–December). *The Conference Reporter,* pp. 1, 5. (Chicago)

Hyde Park-Kenwood Community Conference. (2000a, January–February). *The Conference Reporter,* p. 1. (Chicago)

Hyde Park-Kenwood Community Conference. (2000b, March–April). *The Conference Reporter,* p. 6. (Chicago)

Hyde Park-Kenwood Community Conference. (2001, July–August). *The Conference Reporter,* p. 6. (Chicago)

Jacobs, J. (1961). *The death and life of great American cities.* New York: Vintage Books.

Judd, D., & Swanstrom, T. (1994). *City politics: Private power and public policy.* New York: HarperCollins.

Keating, W., & Smith, S. (1996). Past federal policy for urban neighborhoods. In N. Krumholz & P. Star (Eds.), *Revitalizing urban neighborhoods* (pp. 50–57). Lawrence: University Press of Kansas.

Medoff, P., & Sklar, H. (1994). *Streets of hope: The fall and rise of an urban neighborhood.* Boston: South End Press.

Mollenkopf, J. H. (1983). *The contested city.* Princeton, NJ: Princeton University Press.

Nagel, J. (1995). American Indian ethnic renewal. *American Sociology Review, 60,* 956–961.

Neighborhood groups form to protest WTO. (1999, October 20). *Seattle Press,* p. A1.

O'Rourke, L. (1991). *Geno: The life and mission of Geno Baroni.* New York: Paulist Press.

Pratt Institute Center for Community and Environmental Development. (1995). New Community Corporation. In *Community development corporations: Oral history project* [loose page in a folder]. New York: Author.

Putnam, R. (2002, February 11). Bowling together. *The American Prospect, 13*(3), 20–22.

Rossi, P., & Dentler, R. (1961). *The politics of urban renewal.* Glencoe, IL: Free Press.

Rusk, D. (1999). *Inside game, outside game.* Washington, DC: Brookings Institution Press.

Shepherd, S. (2001). The buzz in Barelas. *New Mexico Business Journal, 26*(3), 36–37.

Sklar, H. (1995). *Chaos or community: Seeking solutions, not scapegoats, for bad economics.* Boston: South End Press.

Tjerandsen, C. (1980). *Education for citizenship: A foundation's experience.* Santa Cruz, CA: Emil Schwarzhaupt Foundation.

3

COMMUNITY DEVELOPMENT CORPORATIONS AND THE RESURGENCE OF ORGANIZING

Community development corporations (CDCs) emerged out of the enthusiasm and hope of the 1960s, with federal anti-poverty funds as the incentive that moved distressed communities in every state to take initiatives. These initiatives of infinite variety spawned corporations in neighborhoods large and small where they sought to use government funds for producing jobs, human services, housing, and self-determined community action that centered on health, entrepreneurship, and education. It was a vast federal-local mobilization heralding and pursuing the official ideal of the 1960s: equal economic opportunity for the poor.

As reported in Chapter 2, two of the earliest CDCs were the Bedford Stuyvesant Restoration Corporation of New York City and the New Community Corporation of Newark, both of which were launched during the late 1960s with substantial, highly visible programs that served individuals and families in large numbers. Their early achievements inspired the formation of thousands of CDC-type organizations during ensuing years. Although many were undermined by a lack of organizing skills and the failure of increasingly conservative national administrations to maintain anti-poverty funds at high levels throughout the era, there were also CDCs that tapped regional, public, and private money sources to persist and prosper.

For these decades from the 1960s to the 1990s, CDCs were the preferred instrument supported by foundations, governments, and business corporations for renewing small communities, especially where there was heavy human distress. CDCs did some money raising on their own from local sources, but most of their funds came from large institutions outside their communities. After 1975, sophisticated CDCs benefited from bank real estate investments in their communities stimulated by the Home Mortgage Act of 1975 and the Community Reinvestment Act of 1977 (described in Chapter 2). In urban areas with high civic activity, regional "intermediaries" were established with pools of funds coming from a combination of national and regional sources for redistribution to the most productive and promising CDCs in the areas.

A CDC's activities could include increasing its neighborhood's quantity and quality of affordable housing; helping existing local commercial/industrial firms to thrive, export, and create jobs; assisting the survival of neighborhood retail shops and service businesses; and midwifing small new enterprises. Most of them abandoned any vestige of mass organizing and militant advocacy. However, we will see that some CDCs never progressed beyond a narrow range of single-dimensional activities, while others were in effect transformed into businesses. In any case, CDCs became an important type of local organization working to revitalize small place communities beginning in the late 1960s, and some remain struggling to give life to distressed neighborhoods. However, today most CDCs seem to be working to remake themselves to become comprehensive models, going beyond limitations of the past.

CDCs generally have boards largely composed of community people, perhaps with a couple of experts and a status person from the outside also as members, plus small staffs whose members tend to run the organizations. CDCs primarily serve low- and moderate-income communities, although CDCs do form in neighborhoods where there are mixes of low, middle, and high incomes and even in communities where there are very few poor people. CDCs are sometimes placed under other labels such as "community-based organizations," "local development companies," and "community development organizations" and in fact can pop up in communities with all types of economic profile. Specific CDCs often have institution or place names such as St. Nicholas Neighborhood Preservation Corporation (Brooklyn, New York), Bethel New Life (Chicago), Whittier Alliance (Minneapolis), Vermont-Slausan Development Corporation (Los Angeles), Northeast Louisiana Delta (Tallulah, Louisiana), and Organizacion Progresiva de San Elizario (San Elizario, Texas).

During the 1970s, the national government transformed direct subsidies to block grants and housing vouchers. This made it possible to favor private groups, including CDCs, over public authorities when passing out housing funds (Keating & Smith, 1996, p. 53). But overall, government funding for social needs, including community development, declined during that decade, which was a time of high inflation, falling productivity, lowered profits, and rising unemployment—a condition that came to be known as "stagflation."

During the Reagan administration of the 1980s, community organizations that focused on radical political agendas lost strength, while conservative bricks-and-mortar CDCs proliferated. Government and private funders pressured the CDCs to be more cautious and disciplined. Housing and economic development became the dominant activity for small communities seeking renewal. Fisher (1996) reported that during the 1980s CDCs, in responding to the pressure of funders, became "less like community organizations and more like small business and investment projects" (p. 44). He concluded that CDCs were forced "to become so oriented to economic success that they were unable to sustain their work for community empowerment" (p. 44).

A new national program of significance created during the 1980s was the Low-Income Housing Tax Credit, introduced to offset tax benefits eliminated under the Tax Reform Act of 1986. It set up a complicated system whereby corporate investors receive tax credits for their investments in low-income projects, most of which are created by CDCs and other community-based organizations. This effort continues a practice of supplying tax incentives for private investors to encourage the production of below market-priced private housing while reducing direct public spending on government-owned and -operated housing (Keating & Smith, 1996, p. 55).

Peirce and Steinbach (1990), in a substantial study of CDCs at the end of the 1980s, hailed their enhanced capacity for producing new and repaired housing and for aiding start-up enterprises to gain stability. They credited CDCs with "creating and retaining close to 90,000 jobs" (p. 8). They praised the ability of CDCs to gain institutional support, particularly through the network of "intermediaries" that had come to include the Local Initiative Support Corporation and the Enterprise Foundation, two national resource-gathering bodies that accumulated funds from government, foundations, banks, and business corporations for regranting to promising CDCs, often through regional intermediaries. Peirce and Steinbach found that such regional and national support organizations furnished both money and technical assistance to CDCs. They also noted the CDC inventory of tools growing to include land trusts, local loan funds, community credit unions, workplace networks, limited equity cooperatives, lease purchasing, and manufactured housing. Use of these sophisticated means and mechanics increased the respect shown CDCs and gave them enhanced influence.

Difficulties arose, however. Although new private funding streams opened, there was never enough money given the scale and intensity of the tasks confronted in the most severely distressed communities. Moreover, there seemed to be too few community people willing and able to step up and take on the arduous task of board leadership. Meanwhile, support from the federal government became even weaker than it had been prior to the 1980s.

Peirce and Steinbach (1990) found a few larger, more stable community corporations allocating resources to shore up community social service needs (e.g., education, health care, addiction reduction), but they report that most CDCs were narrowly focused on the economic dimension of their communities. They advocated broader programs and added that "an objective assessment of the movement today . . . would have to conclude that the surface has only been scratched" (p. 12). Although Peirce and Steinbach attempted an objective analysis, they did not address the question of whether there are intrinsic weaknesses that prevent CDCs from successfully revitalizing small communities. Throughout the 1990s, other observers identified such weaknesses.

In a formidable critique, Shiffman with Motley (1990) acknowledged impressive "hard" production of housing and jobs but made the case that many CDCs, by eschewing organizing, social action, and advocacy, were failing to empower people and rescue neighborhoods. Fundamental change had been illusive, they argued, with problems overwhelming progress. They predicted that CDCs could not seriously affect poverty, racism, and class conflict unless they became comprehensive community development agencies in which organizing, planning, development, and evaluation confronted social and political issues as well as economic needs.

Traynor (1993) charged that CDCs that had created significant numbers of jobs, housing, and enterprises were still finding their neighborhoods "deteriorating faster than ever before," with the residents of these communities "as isolated and disenfranchised as they have ever been" (p. 4). He blamed the CDCs' limited programs, and their frequent failure to operate under the direction of community people, as preventing them from being aggressive on many key issues that affect neighborhoods. He saw the CDC as one more dependency model.

Stoecker (1996) found CDCs to be undercapitalized and generally constrained by limited resources. He surmised that CDCs have neither the scale of capital sufficient to slow community decay nor the freedom and skills needed to mobilize substantial community power, concluding that CDCs are too weak to bargain successfully with foundations, businesses, and governments. "CDCs are not adequate representatives of neighborhood interests [and] cannot take the risks necessary to produce empowering community organizing" (p. 10).

Lemann (1994) drew mass attention to the issue in an article in the *New York Times Magazine*. Acknowledging that a few CDCs had created attractive and affordable housing (Newark's New Community Corporation was cited), Lemann insisted that old urban neighborhoods were unstable and seldom sensible locations for place-based economic revitalization investments (p. 30). Moreover, he claimed that attempts at community development often took the place of other efforts that would do much more good such as improving schools and police protection. CDC efforts, he said, set up projects for failure by establishing goals that cannot be accomplished. He added that inexperienced people, who sometimes showed themselves to be incompetent or even corrupt, often led CDCs. He ridiculed the assumption of hidden "strengths" in inner-city areas and concluded that CDCs passed every test but one—the reality test. That is, they had failed to reach their goals.

Lemann's (1994) views provoked an outpouring of rebuttals, with many of them accusing him of confusing "government development" with "neighborhood development." Outrage came in spite of Lemann's hopeful views about the useful role that neighborhood organizations might take in promoting public education, safety, health, and public services—views that went largely unnoticed.

O'Donnell and Schumer (1996), whose interests centered on low-income families in Chicago, saw organizing "become more and more narrowly defined as CDCs have become enamored with bricks and mortar and technical sophistication [while] replacing residents on their boards and planning teams with bankers, developers, and realtors" (p. 12).

McDevitt (1997), who has done comparative studies of CDC-type organizations in Britain (Bristol, London, and Newcastle) and the United States (Pittsburgh and Philadelphia), concluded that "no satisfactory recipe has been developed, over 30 years of urban renewal projects, to bring back neighborhoods in decline" (p. 353).

Much came to be expected of the oft-celebrated CDCs during the post-1960s decades, too much given the stingy resources they were granted from funding sources in their own communities and from the governments, businesses, foundations, and other sources. Drained of many of their resources, old neighborhoods that were left behind were expected to save themselves through seven-figure grants for tasks that required nine-figure allotments. And no riveting cries for help went up from the civic and governmental forces involved. Only maverick voices such as that of Pablo Eisenberg, the long-time director of the Center for Community Change (Eisenberg, 2000), were setting the record straight, pointing to where the money-starved movement should go, and stating what it needed to get there.

Defenders of CDCs tried to answer the criticism. Bratt (1997) cited specific neighborhoods successfully aided by CDCs and blamed their difficulties on the financial starving of CDCs, which she attributed to disinterest in poor people and weak political mobilization to support CDCs. She suggested that CDCs could do the job if funders would raise their grants to an adequate scale and bestow them without restrictions.

Walker and Weinheimer (1998) examined the work of 300 CDCs located in 23 major cities participating in a 10-year, $250 million test of CDCs given extra funding for the period from 1991 to 2001. They focused their studies on scale and stability of funding and on quality of management. They found a rising level of funding during the test period but no indications that it could be sustained. Even with the private and federal increases in funds coming to CDCs during the test period, they judged the funding generally to be woefully inadequate given the severe community distress faced by these renewal organizations. They also noted that "several states have made it harder for urban CDCs to compete for [low-income housing] tax

credits by applying allocation formulas that favor lower-cost jurisdictions and thinly capitalized projects" (p. 9). CDCs appeared under constant pressure to provide a laundry list of new services, while city governments often stalled on handing over abandoned property so that it could be put to productive use (p. 10). Walker and Weinheimer found that most CDCs had not developed efficient management systems and reported the collapse of several CDCs.

Walker and Weinheimer (1998) expressed hope for the future of CDCs, but only with a steady infusion of increased funding and with intensified technical assistance able to develop sensitive and skilled staff, board members, and leadership, especially for communities inflicted by racial bias and other human disconnections.

David Rusk is a hopeful critic who insists on asking the tough questions. He visited Bedford-Stuyvesant in 1995 to see the CDC's plaza of shops and offices, 4,200 rebuilt homes, and an employment service that had boosted 20,000 residents into jobs. He was impressed but could not praise the effort without a look at census statistics (Rusk, 1999, pp. 21–22). Data for 1970–1990 revealed that the neighborhood had lost 27% of its population, the poverty rate had increased from 27.5% to 34.0%, and buying power had fallen by 12% (in real inflated adjusted dollars).

Not willing to make a judgment on a single case, Rusk (1999) set out to look at a national sample of 43 "exemplary" CDCs. He found that although there was economic improvement for a few of the target neighborhoods, the overall finding "in the cities across the country served by the most successful CDCs as a group still became poorer, fell farther behind the regional income level, and lost real buying power" (p. 49).

Rusk (1999) discovered patches of regeneration in the area of the largest CDCs, but they represented mostly newly moving-in middle-class residents settled in very small enclaves scattered among large areas of rising poverty and declining population. He observed, "The evidence of my experience is that, even in the midst of what is now a seven-year economic expansion, prosperity has not reached into the hearts of many of America's ghettos and barrios. The good guys are not winning" (p. 62).

Shabecoff and Brophy (1996), writing in *Shelterforce,* an important housing- and neighborhood-oriented magazine, argued that development is done not for development's sake but rather "to build community, to nourish the human spirit and social bonds among people in the neighborhood while using business skills to regenerate the neighborhood's physical and economic base and connection to mainstream institutions" (p. 8). They acknowledged that concentration on bricks and mortar is not enough "to save the 'soul' of neighborhoods. It takes paying attention to the people part of the neighborhood, setting the environment for them to care about and invest in themselves and each other" (p. 8). Shabecoff and Brophy maintained that CDCs and other community-based development organizations were already doing much to promote social development and had plans to do more. They cited examples in small communities in Detroit, Denver, and Cleveland (p. 8). This included Detroit-based Warren Conner Development Coalition's program to train residents to serve as "family coaches" providing one-to-one counseling, advice, and support to job training participants and their families. Another example was Denver's Hope Communities, which teaches mothers to care for their new infants and deal with problems in their daily lives.

Editors of two important community-oriented journals on organizing and planned change, John Anner (*Third Force*) and Carl Vogel (*The Neighborhood Works*), teamed up to assess the growing controversy (Anner & Vogel, 1997). They found specific CDC successes in Cleveland, Charlotte, Boston, Los Angeles, Chicago, and New York. But they also found that CDCs largely had forgotten their organizing roots. This resulted in homes being built in neighborhoods that continued to fall apart as CDCs worked on housing to the exclusion of other urgent needs. Likewise, such narrowness led to CDCs sheepishly following decisions made "downtown" instead of mobilizing residents to hammer out their own decisions in open sessions. These authors concluded that CDCs urgently need direction and mass support from resident grassroots forces and their allies.

An encouraging discovery by Anner and Vogel (1997) was that not only were many active people discussing the idea of reconnecting organizing and development, but some CDCs had been using both approaches all along and several groups were testing new ways in which to integrate the two processes in the same organization. For instance, they found that the Massachusetts Association of Community Development Corporations was helping 18 of its member groups expand to do both development and organizing. They cited Marc Draisen, chief executive officer of the association, as believing that such expansion would require a change of culture. Anner and Vogel predicted that it is such struggles on the ground that eventually will move CDCs generally toward becoming creative comprehensive organizations.

Combining organizing and development in a single organization, a small partnership of two or three organizations, or even a coalition of diverse organizations in the same small community obviously has become the consensus view. This approach envisions local organizations strong enough to tap into the resources of state, regional, and national foundations, governments, and corporations. In part, it is a return to the people-led efforts of the 1950s, when many neighborhood groups operated under a "whatever it takes" guiding principle, which fed the organizing movements of the 1960s. The major difference is that today's comprehensive model includes much more attention to the motivation, commitment, and capacity of participants and particularly resident participants. This is the "transformative" dimension that has become dominant in many comprehensive models.

From the experience of the authors of this book, this means undergirding the zeal and enthusiasm of residents and their allies with an understanding and acceptance of the value and worth of every person and with recognition of the failure of most economic and political institutions to yet accept and act on this principle. It also means that we admit the failure to date of community organizing and mobilization to win the wholehearted support of society's institutions. For instance, one major force disruptive of the well-being of small communities is low-wage work. The nation's social, economic, and political institutions refuse to deal with it. In fact, they seriously reject efforts by community groups to bring it to their attention. Even respected social service agencies oppose the living wage idea because they are fearful that it will put them under pressure to raise the wages of their own poorly paid employees.

Now that Ehrenreich (2001) has published her masterpiece, *Nickel and Dimed,* laying a popular base for communicating the dehumanizing impact of low-wage work, perhaps a few compassionate leaders within the institutions will begin to examine this scandal, which is far broader and deeper than the Enron collapse. It is ignoring or stepping forward on such issues that helps to define the difference between the bricks-and-mortar approach of the business-efficient CDC and the inner transformation approach of the comprehensive neighborhood initiative.

Sharply criticizing the foundations, financial intermediaries, and CDCs themselves for a "conspiracy of silence" and an "all is well image to the outside world," Eisenberg (2000) suggested that "no one has had the courage to take responsibility for the movement's failures." He has long suggested "a tough, ongoing objective analysis that looks at issues of responsibility, accountability, and integrity and deals with the challenge of organizing, advocacy, questions of leadership, and alliances with other community-based groups" (p. 25), and he still believes that it is needed.

Eisenberg (2000) stated that many current CDC leaders themselves desperately need the truth about their movement, their potential, and their options. "If community development's enormous accomplishments are to be perpetuated and strengthened, we will need a body of observers, evaluators, and critics who will put the lie to the good old public relations myth that only good news, even if incomplete, is the sure path to success" (pp. 22–25).

A counter to the censures of Rusk, Eisenberg, and the like came from Grogan and Proscio (2000), who argued that ordinary people in hundreds of small, battered, inner-city communities have rolled up their sleeves and made dramatic improvements in neighborhoods once judged to be comatose in spite of the inadequate funds available to them. Grogan and Proscio are defenders of the continued importance and potential of central cities. Their formula for revival is a strong network of thriving CDCs, a broad and

diverse support base, political leadership, and 15 or more years of patient methodical effort. From their experience and research, they found that this formula can bring "breathtaking results." They reported, "The cities that have invested the most political will and local resources in this process routinely astonish visitors who have been away from their inner-city neighborhoods for a while and are unaware of the cumulative transformations" (p. 96).

Even during the years when CDCs and their preoccupation with housing dominated neighborhood change, there were people-based organizations using a combination of organizing and development. They were not getting the attention and big money, but many were pushing their small communities forward. One example is the Aliquippa Alliance for Unity and Development (AAUD) in Pennsylvania (described and assessed in Chapters 5, 7, 8, 9, and 10, looking at both the achievements and the failures of that far-reaching small community effort).

The Emerging Comprehensive Approach

Several national support organizations beginning in the 1990s reported evidence of a growing move toward comprehensive programming by place-based local renewal efforts. The National Congress for Community Economic Development (NCCED) (the trade association for CDCs), the Community Development Research Center of the New School for Social Research, the Chapin Hall Center for Children at the University of Chicago, and the "Community Building" project created by the U.S. Department of Housing and Urban Development (HUD) in concert with the Annie E. Casey and Rockefeller foundations gave voice to affirming an emerging consensus around the comprehensive approach.

NCCED (1991) reported during the early 1990s that more than 70% of the then more than 2,000 CDCs were engaged in activities beyond development such as tenant counseling, weatherization, housing for homeless people, child care, health care, and the arts, with these programs sometimes involving organizing and advocacy (p. 7). However, these activities at the time seemed to be supplemental rather than high priority.

Later, NCCED reported steady movement toward broadening CDC agendas. Roy Priest, NCCED's chief executive, reported that during the decade the number of CDCs had risen from 2,000 to 3,600, with their total production since the 1960s being more than 550,000 housing units and 247,000 jobs created (Priest, 1999). He said that many of them were engaging in social services beyond the traditional CDC trio of housing, employment, and business-related enterprises. Priest stated that CDCs collectively had become significant "agents of economic change and instruments of public policy" (p. 2), accounting for 30% of the nation's assisted housing production, much of its revitalization of distressed neighborhoods, and an increasing amount of the employment support and training furnished to residents who are coming off welfare. For the congress and its affiliates, he concluded, "NCCED as the trade association for the community-based economic development industry is the voice for policy interests of economically distressed rural and urban communities" (p. 4). Such claims would seem to mark CDCs, with their broadening programs, as full-fledged competitors to become the comprehensive model of choice for future renewing of small place communities.

Earlier field studies by the New School of Social Research (Vidal, 1992) brought forth data from 130 of the largest and most active CDCs in 29 cities. Although Vidal's research concentrated on programs in housing, commercial real estate, and business enterprises, tucked away in her 294-page report were two relevant tables. Table III-9 told us that by the 1990s CDCs clearly had shifted away completely from a confrontational style to a more cooperative and business-like style. "The CDCs have learned how to do deals," she concluded (p. 62). But Table IV-1 confirmed that some of the CDCs studied tended to use their cooperative approach to combine hard-edged economic development with consensus organizing and social services.

O'Donnell and Schumer (1996), creators of a "Family-Focused Community Building" model, expressed what is probably the central thought of those pushing the combination approach: "It's time for organizers to take their boxing gloves off, for developers to take their hard hats off, and for funders to come out from behind their desks to begin a serious dialogue about how organizing can be integrated into—and, yes, drive—community development strategies" (pp. 14–15).

O'Donnell and Schumer (1996) also reported, significantly, that organizers "both in Chicago and nationwide were beginning to draw from the transformative 'base community' or 'popular education' tradition" (pp. 14–15). This approach builds on the notion that empowerment of people begins from within and that oppressed people need to develop a new awareness of themselves as capable of setting and achieving goals. Besides raising sights, participants in their model take action to advocate for housing and job policies that will prevent homelessness and for schemes to promote low-income homeownership. In the O'Donnell and Schumer model, parent leaders form teams to make their communities more "family friendly" (pp. 14–15). They employ means that can be economic as well as social or political—whatever it takes. (For more on the base community approach, see Appendix 3.A.)

Comprehensive is now the general term for place-based change efforts that go beyond the bricks and mortar of traditional CDCs and the charity of human services, striving to achieve a holistic model of revitalized community. It is still emerging, it is not yet a clear-cut model as the CDC was, and it probably never will be given its changing nature and many variations. The comprehensive initiatives draw in layers of goals, programs, and tactics. These are concerned with all three components of community—social, political, and economic—not limiting themselves only to the economic, as some CDCs did. In the social dimension, they seek interconnectedness by promoting wide-ranging interrelationships and friendships, toward building a sense of community and organizing networks of mutual support. In the political dimension, they facilitate interfamily discussion sessions, open to all who are willing to give it a lengthy try, where community residents gain awareness of oppression in their lives and discover techniques for broad mobilization and self-determination. They do not shrink from old-fashioned militancy where that is called for to effect needed change. In the economic dimension, they enhance the skills of workforce residents, building their capacity and earning power and reinforcing their self-confidence in linking with employers through collective arrangements based in the neighborhood.

Besides this fundamental people-transforming and people-developing activity, the comprehensive approach is dedicated to unlocking creative ideas, constructive values, and generous beliefs that can enrich and strengthen community planning as well as encourage responsible and forceful implementation of plans.

The product sought is growth in the capacity of the collective effort, not only deeper research and more feasible plans but also more powerful tactics and lasting impact derived from implementation that uses organizing and advocacy as required. In such a process, it is expected that certain values will assert themselves, including the following:

- Preference for the poor
- Recognition of the pervasive threat of race to divide
- The potency of reconciliation to heal
- The usefulness of justice as an indicator
- The importance of "owning" ideas as an incentive for invigorating collective activity
- The wisdom of a dual perspective, both short and long term
- Respect for the spiritual nature of individuals and groups
- The reality that elite people can be helpful but that elitism never is
- The joy to be found in the principle of "subsidiarity," which espouses the belief that functions that local organizations can perform effectively belong more properly to them than to a dominant central organization
- The belief that no legitimate instrument or tactic of change should ever be ruled out of the collective bag of tools for organizing and advocacy

Beyond people development and the exploitation of ideas, the comprehensive approach has its targets: the systems of society as they are found within the small community. The objectives of systems change are the vitality, livability, and fair play that make a holistic and happy community, achieved through reformed and interwoven sets of systems—social,

political, and economic—that serve it and feed it but are not allowed to dominate it.

Systems operate in every sphere of life. There are social systems revolving around basic elements of life such as security, health, and recreation/entertainment. There are political systems revolving around elections, city services, government social policies and practice, criminal justice, and taxes. There are economic systems that deal with retailing, resource management, workforce development, credit flows, and housing, among other essential activities in small communities.

As the collective initiative in a small community comes to proceed with efficiency and good feeling, improvements can be sought in the basic quality and fairness of the community's systems. This then becomes the long-term work of the emerging comprehensive effort, regardless of what model category it falls into.

Stone (1996, February) summarized the comprehensive movement by pointing out that to be comprehensive in revitalizing a small community is

> to reflect the common wisdom that people and life are complex, that no one person or place can be defined by a single attribute, and that multi-layered problems require multi-layered, often long-term solutions. . . . Revitalization represents a return to the original comprehensive intent of community development and reflects the growing recognition that housing alone cannot reshape distressed communities. (p. viii)

Some local, place-based organizations have pursued a comprehensive course for years, but most lack one or two key elements. Other long active organizations are just beginning to become comprehensive. For most, it is pursuit of a still blurry mission, now complicated by the government's concern with a global war on terrorism. But the pioneers, such as Stone, have blazed an inviting trail. And the mainstream is moving their way.

Building a change force through personal transformation, organizing, and development is a less tidy approach than the top-down, business-efficient CDC model of former decades, but it is one with more potential for *invigorating small communities*. It might not gain the quick, dramatic visible changes sometimes achieved an exclusively bricks and mortar strategy or even by a militant mass organizing thrust. However, the slow change that combination brings may be deeper, more fundamental, and longer lasting.

The comprehensive model most heavily reported on is the Comprehensive Community Initiative (CCI). Funded largely by national foundations beginning with the Ford Foundation's Neighborhood and Family Initiative (NFI) in 1990, this effort encompasses a dozen organizations following the comprehensive approach and spread across the nation, mostly in large cities. Besides Ford's multi-site NFI, there are other multi-site efforts underwritten by the Annie E. Casey Foundation, the Surdna Foundation, the Edna McConnell Clark Foundation, and the Enterprise Foundation. These sophisticated foundations, aware of the complexity and long time line of multifaceted programs, have promised grants over longer than usual periods—up to 7 years—with the possibility of grant renewal, a practice for which there are precedents. The Riley Foundation has been contributing large sums to the Dudley Street Neighborhood Initiative in Boston since 1984. The Heinz Endowments in Pittsburgh underwrote the AAUD from 1986 to 2000.

Focus in the CCI approach is not on construction of houses and shops or delivery of social services but rather on strengthening a neighborhood's capacity to effect change through indigenous leadership trained in the transformation tradition. Neighbors learn to assess assets and distresses and seek practical ways in which to use their community's existing institutions and service agencies for transforming people and community building. Residents think hard about what holds families and communities together and learn to strengthen ties not only among households but also between people and institutions as well as between and among institutions. Concerned families are nudged to join together to see, judge, and act. The burden for planning and doing lies most heavily on community residents, and therefore, visible results come only after years of training, preparation, and inclusive planning.

CCI participants find both promise and pitfalls. Frustrations as well as triumphs abound. Lessons are being mastered, however. Confidence is rising in the belief that if participants hang on for the long haul, small communities can become greatly improved living places during the 21st century, with relationships among individuals, families, organizations, and institutions that are more mutually respectful, cohesive, and productive. Collective effort built with sound planning seems able to increase a community's assets and gain long-term commitments from funders. Serious assessments of organizations seeking to use a comprehensive approach are included here. They provide objective views of the strengths and weaknesses being discovered.

Two useful assessments of comprehensive programs have been published. Pitcoff (1999) drew on the efforts of five urban neighborhoods spread across the nation, where a lead organization in each was given a 7-year, $3 million CCI grant during the 1990s by the Annie E. Casey Foundation. Their task was to bring together diverse local interests to make and test a self-determined comprehensive strategy of reform and resurgence. Each effort was to involve creation of a neighborhood governance structure rooted in resident-driven multi-group partnerships with a central goal of systems reform to humanize local service delivery, reconnect households and participants in community life, and enhance family stability.

Pitcoff (1999) found hope and motion, followed quickly by organizing pain. CCI, he discovered, was about residents taking control of established neighborhood domains but doing it armed with outside money and unannounced goals that would usurp the power of community stakeholders not previously acquiescent. Not all local leaders and groups were agreeable to being rushed into accepting a new neighborhood governance structure, adding to the volatility that could be the difference between the funder and participating residents as to which of their diverging views should dominate strategic decisions. For instance, funder staff cherished simple, logical, decisive governance structures, while residents often tended to favor complexity, with lots of nooks and closets that would provide a domain for every neighborhood warlord and his or her entourage. Progress in reducing friction came only when the community people began to insist on their rights as partners. Surprisingly to residents, funders accepted this "standing tough" as a sign of resident empowerment and maturity.

There was also hostility over the policy leadership question: Does it come most effectively from a strong staff or a broad system of board, committees, and town meetings? Pitcoff (1999) reported the tensions emerging and concluded by endorsing the overview of Cornelia Swenton from Philadelphia's Germantown neighborhood:

> There's no science to these initiatives, nor is the focus about issues like economic development, crime, or even housing. It's about how a neighborhood integrates and manages these issues, and it's about building and maintaining relationships to transform the way a community works. It's about finding sustainable solutions to problems of chronic poverty, neglect, and disenfranchisement by developing the skills and strength of those who call it home. (p. 31)

The second assessment of the comprehensive approach focuses on a strain labeled *community building*. It was compiled by veteran observers G. Thomas Kingsley of the Urban Institute, Joe McNeely of the Development Training Institute, and James O. Gibson of the D.C. Agenda Project, a private sector association addressing the fiscal and governance problems facing the District of Columbia. These three found community building primarily concerned with the blossoming of responsible residents and the life chances of their kids and only secondarily concerned with making entrepreneurs and affordable housing. Kingsley, McNeely, and Gibson (1997) identified the central theme of community building as "to obliterate feelings of dependency and to replace them with attitudes of self-reliance, self-confidence, and responsibility"—that is, change communities by changing their people (p. 3). It gives priority to establishing and reinforcing sound values that are worked out by the residents themselves. These assessors saw it working by "neighbors learning to rely on each other, working together on concrete tasks that take advantage of new self-awareness of their collective and individual assets, and in the process creating human, family, and social capital that provides a new base for a more promising future and reconnection to America's mainstream" (p. 3).

Kingsley et al. (1997) cited Indianapolis's Eastside Community Investments as starting out as a CDC with 500 resident incorporators doing large-scale housing fix-up, amassing capital by buying and selling repaired houses, and creating its own industrial park but then moving on to rejuvenating its social service system, transforming resident skills and confidence in the process. (This organization eventually ran into management and financial difficulties and heavy staff turnover before closing up [Steinbach, 1999, pp. 10–13, 15].) Washington's Kenilworth-Parkside is described as a drug-degraded public housing project transformed into a disciplined community owned by residents who send their kids to college. Baltimore's Boyd-Booth is cited for driving out drug peddling and related crime, partnering with an array of city institutions such as the police, and establishing a safe neighborhood before turning to increasing homeownership and school enhancement programs. Newark's New Community Corporation is celebrated for its new housing, institutions, and enterprises owned by the community and for providing jobs for hundreds. New York's Comprehensive Community Revitalization Program of the South Bronx is lauded for its achievement of comprehensive human services through five small-scale CDCs that organized broad resident involvement and decision making. Plans made and implemented involved youth development, new primary health care facilities, job training and employment linkages beyond the community, child care, school support, a new shopping center, crime reduction measures, and more.

Kingsley et al. (1997) saw these efforts as employing a collection of well-known and well-used techniques but as coming out of very broad resident-doing operations that transformed thinking and hopes. Besides moving to the center of community life, residents identified priority activities, reinforced values, became strategic and entrepreneurial, focused on assets of people and neighborhood, tailored efforts to local scale and conditions, built strong extractive links to the broader society, and consciously struggled to change institutional barriers and reduce racism.

Kingsley et al. (1997) saw the community building as properly directed at a total living place, taking in social fabric, confidence, and respect for collaboration. Their critique agreed with the others that neighborhood people must obtain vast new resources if they are to realize their potential for revitalizing society through building up from the bottom. Local governments must become more willing to partner. More and stronger intermediaries need to arise to facilitate rational scales of money and technical assistance, more and better training and capacity for the broad array of grassroots actors, federal and state governments that become closer partners, and all supporters being willing to hang in for the long haul and be tolerant of failures so long as there is bounce-back. They closed their report with the notion that "community building depends on rebuilding a sense of hope" (p. 13) and the traditional warning that an organization should avoid becoming dependent on a single donor.

Although Kingsley et al. (1997) saw the community-building approach as most relevant to poverty neighborhoods, they recognized that the issues dealt with can arise in any small community, especially the issues of crime, drugs, dissatisfaction with public schools, racism, job insecurity, and certainly the need for participation to overcome civic apathy. The new element, if there is one, is the transformation focus—consciously giving priority to people growth and development carried to the point where people can design, build, and govern a just neighborhood world.

One final note is in order. The jump from the standard place-based community development organizations of the 20th century to the emerging comprehensive organizations of the 21st century largely marks a shift from collective community action, which assumed that all who volunteered were competent to plan fair and effective change, to a collective community process, which assumes that participants must examine and reform themselves—their commitments, self-confidence, and capacity—before seeking to lead in making and carrying out just and equitable changes for their place community.

SUMMARY

Collective understanding by residents of processes for assessing and revitalizing their home communities has grown steadily for decades and now constitutes a widespread national effort, with several approaches emerging for achieving renewal. During the period from 1970 to 1990, a narrowly focused CDC model dominated but did not achieve the broad rebuilding capability required to restore severely deteriorated neighborhoods. Gradually during the 1990s, small communities and their allies began to transform their local renewal organizations into practical comprehensive models for change and development that encompass economic, political, and social dimensions and that seek to be open and inclusive of all who would participate. Now during the 21st century, the comprehensive approach is becoming universal, with organizing and economic development melded together. This book argues that this comprehensive approach, if applied faithfully, can bring great benefits to families and their home communities during this new century. Our version of this approach is presented in the 13 chapters that follow.

CONTINUING QUESTIONS

1. Can all CDCs make a transformation to become comprehensive? Should they?

2. What have been the contributions of CDCs to the improvement and development of small communities? Are such contributions still possible in the future?

3. Are the problems and weaknesses of CDCs something that can be cured with more organizing, participation, and money?

4. Is there any reason why a CDC cannot create in-depth participation reaching into every section and interest group in its community?

5. Are changing population, income and poverty trends in a small community a fair measure of the competence and impact of its neighborhood development organization?

6. How can a powerful neighborhood organization spearhead reform and substantial improvement of local public education? What approach is likely to be most promising?

7. Is social justice as a core value likely to gain or lose acceptance during the decade ahead?

8. Are demands for transformation of values and outlook a growing or declining trend among communal organizations regarding both their members and their communities?

9. Is a resident-led revitalization effort more effective when carried out by a single unified membership organization or when carried out by a coalition of several relevant independent groups with varied programs collaborating in the same community?

Appendix 3.A
A Transformative Model

Hanna and Robinson (1994) drew from the same base community, popular education tradition to put forth a comprehensive model designed to help community people free themselves from the manipulation of advertising, media, government bureaucracy, and similar forces that are prone to exploit individuals and families. Their model requires rigorous initiation and adherence to a long-term process, demanding carefully developed, consistent, small study groupings that "preclude an early entry into social action" (p. 153). Organizers of the study group "extract themselves first, and only then others, from various forms of systematic oppression, including many destructive aspects of mass culture" (p. 153).

In the Hanna and Robinson (1994) model, participants who have broken out of the lock of oppression proceed to learn organizing skills through action, with the goal of transforming a whole community and ultimately the society. Transformative groups are likely to use any appropriate change programs, including housing construction, power advocacy, innovative human service delivery, and enterprise development. This transformative community organizing method can be traced back to the Highlander Folk School, founded in Tennessee in 1932 by Horton (1998). The notion of transformation runs through all of the approaches currently operating under the rubrics of combination, comprehensive, and community building. Transformative groups start with organizing and leadership development but are flexible enough to move on to include economic development either through their own efforts or by a partnership with one or more other organizations.

Appendix 3.B
A Two-Tier Model

Among the more traditional combination models being offered is the two-tier model of Stoecker (1996). He proposed to clear away "the myth" that CDCs are resident controlled and to remove the barrier of small scale that inhibits CDCs. This would be done through a two-tier model: strong grassroots organizing groups at the single-neighborhood, small community level and professionally staffed CDCs at the multi-neighborhood, multi-communities level. In this model, each small grassroots group would control planning for its community, while an experienced multi-neighborhood CDC producing with economies of scale would contract to implement the plans of the small neighborhood groups. Control would lie with the grassroots groups, which would be the "principals" in the two-tier operation and have sign-off authority over funds. Stoecker cited Boston's Dudley Street Neighborhood Initiative as a strong comprehensive neighborhood group that shifted its development projects to "regular CDCs" within its part of Boston (p. 13).

Appendix 3.C
Multi-Neighborhood Efforts

The community-building study project carried out by the Development Training Institute and the Urban Institute (Kingsley, McNeely, & Gibson, 1997) for HUD recommended that complex functions, such as economic development and health care, be undertaken by "clusters of individual neighborhoods" so long as "shared objectives exist" (p. 42). Kingsley et al. saw such functions as requiring a sizable power base. At the same time, they admonished neighborhood organizations to keep the differences between the individual communities in mind as they operate and recognize that each community needs to develop its own sense of identity if social and human capital are to be built successfully.

The Pittsburgh Partnership for Neighborhood Development (PPND), an intermediary providing funding and technical assistance for Pittsburgh's CDCs, has shifted from funding individual CDCs for operations and projects to providing multi-year funding to community economic development organizations, that is, staffed multi-neighborhood collaboratives focusing on planning and resident organizing. Cross-neighborhood development projects are strongly encouraged. The PPND now places planning and organizing at the multi-neighborhood level and places implementation at the small community level. Another type of two-tier model is Pennsylvania's Mon Valley Initiative (MVI), a coalition of 17 small CDCs launched in 1987. An individual CDC or small subset of CDCs may suggest development projects and, with technical assistance from a central coalition staff, may make and implement plans. (For more about the history and programs of the PPND and the MVI, see Lubove [1996]; Ahlbrandt, Cunningham, & Trauth [1994]; Baum & Twiss [1996]; and Gittell [1992].)

The central body can supply development funds, while implementation is likely to be a joint enterprise of the local initiator and the sophisticated staff of the coalition. The MVI was originally organized by the Allegheny Conference on Community Development, the civic arm of Pittsburgh's large corporations, but it now governs itself while drawing funding from local and state governments, foundations, and the Local Initiatives Support Corporation, which is the national funding and financing intermediary founded by the Ford Foundation in 1979–1980.

linking inner-city neighborhoods to the growth nodes of the regional economy. An example would be the Ogontz Avenue Revitalization Corporation in the Northwest section of Philadelphia. A partnership between this CDC and several educational institutions and business associations involves the systematic assessment and recruitment of local workers, their training, and their linking to regional job opportunities.

Rusk (1999) titled his book *Inside Game, Outside Game.* It carries the theme that effort inside a neighborhood's boundaries without serious social, political, and economic connections to the prosperous growth areas throughout the surrounding region is doomed to failure. As the title of his book implies, Rusk's experience as a mayor and a state legislator, as well as his prodigious works of research, convinced him that seriously distressed small communities must have both an "inside game" and an "outside game" if they are to revive and recover. And he awaited final reports on the 2000 census for further evidence, fairly confident that the data would support his view.

A further variation of linking comes when a large successful CDC sells its services to a non-CDC community organization. Levavi (1996) reported that two experienced Chicago CDCs, Lakefront SRO and Century Place Development Corporation, sold their expertise to neighborhood organizations in scattered sections of Chicago, thereby making themselves "citywide CDCs" (pp. 17–19). The neighborhood group does the planning, and the citywide CDC provides the technical expertise to implement á la Stoecker (1996).

Appendix 3.D
Regional Links

The urgency for organizations to look beyond their own small community for help with development was supported by Jeremy Nowak of the Delaware Community Reinvestment Fund (Nowak, 1997). His fund's experience in bringing capital to declining neighborhoods has led to the conclusion that productive community development requires an explicit emphasis on poverty alleviation, which in turn requires

Appendix 3.E
Three CDCs in Transition to Comprehensive

The New School for Social Research, Community Development Research Center (Briggs & Mueller, 1997, pp. 1, 5), reported on "best practice" CDCs in Minneapolis, Boston, and Newark that have ventured into organizing and social programs through resident-based anti-crime programs, after-school tutoring, and resident-run social services. The center reported that each added "community-building" role did enhance sense of community as it promoted neighboring and increased resident involvement in neighborhood improvement. However, there is no evidence to show that the impacts have been sufficient to make a difference in reversing the deterioration of the communities involved. The three CDCs studied were the Whittier Alliance in Minneapolis, the Urban Edge Housing Corporation in Boston, and the New Community Corporation in Newark. The full report is contained in Briggs and Mueller (1997).

Appendix 3.F
Other Recommended Authors

Besides those already cited, other authors observing and analyzing the new emerging comprehensive models during the transition period of 1990 to 1999 include Kubisch (1996) (Aspen Institute), Stone (1996) (Chapin Hall Center for Children), Kingsley et al. (1997) (Urban Institute), Delgado (1997) (Applied Research Center), and Pitcoff (1999). All have provided original information and insight. They have added support to the central notion that new life and stability comes more readily to small communities when residents themselves become the principal initiators and "drivers" of change efforts rooted in local generosity of time and money. Participation transforms people, increases capacity, and enables ordinary people to deal with the leaders of institutions as equals. In this model, organizing gets priority, and there is the expectation that concrete and measurable change can occur in time. Implicit is the necessity for a rising tide of funding, with foundations being the obvious key source, but always with the proviso that the community itself provides a substantial "independent" share of the funding from its own pockets.

REFERENCES

Ahlbrandt, R., Cunningham, J., & Trauth, J. (1994). *Regional organizations involved in economic development in southwestern Pennsylvania* (River Communities Project). Pittsburgh, PA: University of Pittsburgh, School of Social Work.

Anner, J., & Vogel, C. (Eds.). (1997, March). Dollars and direct action [insert]. *Third Force, 20*(2).

(Oakland, CA: Center for Third World Organizing)

Baum, M., & Twiss, P. (Eds.). (1996). *Social work intervention in an economic crisis.* New York: Hayworth.

Bratt, R. (1997). CDCs: Contributions outweigh contradictions. *Journal of Urban Affairs, 19*(1), 23–28.

Briggs, X., & Mueller, E., with Sullivan, M. (1997). *From neighborhood and community: Evidence on the social effects of community development.* New York: New School for Social Research, Community Development Research Center.

Delgado, G. (1997). *Beyond the politics of place: New directions in community organizing* (2nd ed.). Oakland, CA: Chardon Press.

Ehrenreich, B. (2001). *Nickel and dimed: On (not) getting by in America.* New York: Henry Holt.

Eisenberg, P. (2000, March–April). Time to remove the rose-colored glasses. *Shelterforce,* pp. 22–25. (Orange, NJ: National Housing Institute)

Fisher, R. (1996). Neighborhood organizing: The importance of historical context. In W. D. Keating, N. Krumholz, & P. Star (Eds.), *Revitalizing urban neighborhoods* (pp. 39–49). Lawrence: University Press of Kansas.

Gittell, R. (1992) *Renewing cities.* Princeton, NJ: Princeton University Press.

Grogan, P., & Proscio, T. (2000). *Comeback cities: A blueprint for urban neighborhood revival.* Boulder, CO: Westview.

Hanna, M., & Robinson, B. (1994). *Strategies for community empowerment, direct-action, and transformative approaches to social change practice.* Lewiston, NY: Edwin Mellen.

Horton, M. (1998). *The long haul.* New York: Columbia University, Teachers College.

Keating, W. D., & Smith, J. (1996). Past federal policy for urban neighborhoods. In W. D. Keating, N. Krumholz, & P. Star (Eds.), *Revitalizing urban neighborhoods* (pp. 50–57). Lawrence: University Press of Kansas.

Kingsley, G. T., McNeely, J. B., & Gibson, J. O. (1997). *Community building coming of age.* Baltimore, MD: Development Training Institute.

Kubisch, A. C. (1996, January–February). Comprehensive community initiatives: Lessons in neighborhood transformation. *Shelterforce,* pp. 8–11, 18. (Orange, NJ: National Housing Institute)

Lemann, N. (1994, January 9). Myth of community development. *The New York Times Magazine,* pp. 27–31, 50, 54, 60.

Levavi, P. (1996, May–June). Citywide CDCs. *Shelterforce,* pp. 17–19. (Orange, NJ: National Housing Institute)

Lubove, R. (1996) *Twentieth-century Pittsburgh: The post steel era* (Vol. 2). Pittsburgh, PA: University of Pittsburgh Press.

McDevitt, S. (1997). Social work in community development: A cross-national comparison. *International Social Work, 40,* 341–357.

National Congress for Community Economic Development. (1991). Changing the odds. *NCCED Report.* (Washington, DC: Author)

Nowack, J. (1997). Neighborhood initiative and the regional economy. *Economic Development Quarterly, 11,* 3–10.

O'Donnell, S., & Schumer, E. (1996, January–February). Community building and community organizing issues in creating effective models. *Shelterforce,* pp. 12–15. (Orange, NJ: National Housing Institute)

Peirce, N. R., & Steinbach, C. F. (1990). *Enterprising communities.* Washington, DC: Council for Community-Based Development.

Pitcoff, W. (1999). *Redefining community development.* Orange, NJ: National Housing Institute.

Priest, R. O. (1999). *Community-based development: Coming of age.* [Online]. Retrieved February 2, 1999, from the World Wide Web: www.ncced. org

Rusk, D. (1999). *Inside game, outside game.* Washington, DC: Brookings Institution Press.

Shabecoff, A., & Brophy, P. (1996, May–June). The soul of the neighborhood. *Shelterforce,* pp. 8–11. (Orange, NJ: National Housing Institute)

Shiffman, R., with Motley, S. (1990). *Comprehensive and integrative planning for community development.* New York: New School for Social Research, Community Development Research Center.

Steinbach, C. (1999, March–April). After the fall. *Shelterforce,* pp. 10–13, 15. (Orange, NJ: National Housing Institute)

Stoecker, R. (1996). *The community development corporation model of urban redevelopment: A political economy critique and an alternative.* [Online]. Retrieved September 23, 1996, from the World Wide Web: http://msu.edu/~urban/comm-org/cdc/cdc.html

Stone, R. (Ed.). (1996). *Core issues in comprehensive community-building initiatives.* Chicago: University of Chicago, Chapin Hall Center for Children.

Traynor, B. (1993, March–April). Community development and community organizing. *Shelterforce,* pp. 4–7. (Orange, NJ: National Housing Institute)

Vidal, A. C. (1992). *Rebuilding communities: A national study of urban community development corporations.* New York: New School for Social Research, Community Development Research Center.

Walker, C., & Weinheimer, M. (1998). *Community development in the 1990s.* Washington, DC: Urban Institute.

4

THE SMALL COMMUNITY

Each small community in America, whether urban, suburban, or rural, is both a world of its own and a distinct piece of the global community. This chapter examines the nature and importance of the small place-based community and looks at the forces of distress that are always a threat.

Small communities have a defined territory given life by three interacting people processes: an underlying web of human relationships called a social fabric, a unique community power structure, and a set of resource flows that constitute a local economy. Like the region, state, and nation beyond, the small community has assets and liabilities and provides most of its inhabitants with shelter and a place of identity. An urban region is a mosaic of small communities punctuated by landmarks of production, power, trade, and services. Small communities are relatively simple. People comprehend them and feel at home in them, whereas the region is complex and often difficult to comprehend. The small community is where people find a useful and supportive fit as neighbors and citizens.

Small community is a level of society just above the family. It is a collection of households, businesses, and institutions. In the vision of McKnight (1995), it is "the social place used by family, friends, neighbors, neighborhood associations, clubs, civic groups, local enterprises, churches, ethnic associations, synagogues, local unions, local government, and local media" (p. 164).

Keen observation led Jacobs (1961) to affirm that the small community is formed by a "continuity of people." Jacobs was a feisty penetrating critic of urban life who revolutionized our understanding of old neighborhoods. She found that "even in seemingly irreparable milieus, if the population can be held, a slow improvement starts" (p. 277), a key notion underlying hope for the future of even severely distressed small communities. A core of stable people in a neighborhood, acting collectively, can always get it moving in a renewed direction.

Such communities are miniature worlds of delimited space where human interactions arise in part from people living and working near each other, sharing the frustrations and conveniences of locale. Mumford (1961), in his sweeping portrayal of the city in history, confirmed that neighbors, brought together not by common purposes but rather by proximity in space, can establish and preserve a sense of belonging through the interactions of mutual aid, fragile though this sense of belonging may be. Mumford cited the early Greek poet and farmer Hesiod (eighth century BC) as reporting that when households cry for help, "Neighbors hurry to your aid . . . while even your kinspeople 'dawdle' over their gear" (p. 15).

Breathing life into the small community are the repetitious human relationships that actualize attachment, pinned down and described in the massive neighborhood surveys directed by Roger Ahlbrandt (Ahlbrandt & Cunningham, 1979; Ahlbrandt, 1984). In a foreword to Ahlbrandt and Cunningham's (1979) book, Geno Baroni, who was President Jimmy Carter's in-house advocate for neighborhoods, hailed the book for identifying social fabric as "the fragile, sacred, essential, and complex ingredient that holds neighborhoods together" (Baroni, 1979, p. vii).

The "smallness" of the residential community is relative, varying according to the size of the city or region in which it is located. In a medium-sized region such as Pittsburgh, most small communities have populations of 3,000 to 15,000. A smaller region, such as Wichita, Kansas, or Tacoma, Washington, has neighborhoods with populations of 1,000 to 4,000. Rural villages such as Roscoe, Montana, and Wendell Depot, Massachusetts, and their environs may have populations of a few hundred or a few dozen. An urban housing complex, whether private or public, may also be tiny but on occasion can house several thousand families.

Leviathan cities, such as New York, Chicago, and Los Angeles, have much larger neighborhoods organized as "small communities," but usually in these we find decentralization in the form of networks of mini sub-neighborhoods. (More on the scale of residential communities can be found in Appendix 4.A.)

Across the nation, small communities of varying sizes struggle to make use of their assets to renew themselves. Although relatively minute in comparison with any city, county, or region of which they are a part, they are always potentially volatile and dynamic. Most small communities are growing and dying continuously and are improving and declining simultaneously. If a small community's maintenance and rebuilding efforts keep pace, then we say it is stable. By this, we mean that it remains livable, not that it ceases to change. But as a small community ages in a world where societal forces are often hostile, the community in time will face severe distress that must be dealt with gently and forthrightly.

The following three examples may serve as useful illustrations. Area C in Savannah, Georgia, distressed by crime, deep poverty, and houses that were falling apart, transformed an abandoned Catholic high school into a thriving family resource center that became one factor in reducing juvenile crime. The New Bedford, Massachusetts, community took hold of a dying remnant of a once great fishing port of the whaling period and turned it into a community retreat for young Boston professionals. Albuquerque's traditional Hispanic settlement, sprawled along the edge of downtown, suffered from decay, insecurity, and the inaction of its aged residents until younger spirits rebelled to form the Barelas Neighborhood Association and gradually transform it into an attractive community worthy of its prime location, as pointed out in Chapter 2.

Each small community faces a different mix of stresses and responds in its own way. Small communities have much in common, but no two are exactly alike. Most in time will have to face the scourges of race, class, and civic indifference. But each threat has a distinctive character in each location it attacks. The more we examine their complicated nature, the more evidence we find to support the need for a differential renewal strategy for each individual small community.

To better understand the nature of small community and its endless variety, we now look at its three intertwined sources of vitality: social fabric, power structure, and local economy.

Social Fabric

In the work Ahlbrandt (1984) directed, he identified seven especially powerful generators of relationships as the principal producers of social fabric. These are as follows:

1. *Kinship networks:* These are sets of two or more households linked by blood or marriage in addition to sharing the same residential area. They have fairly frequent contact face-to-face and by other means and regularly share in milestone family events. Households have a sense of needing to exchange information and news as well as to give and get advice and support.

2. *Friendship networks:* Friendship, as Keller (1968) pointed out, is a private and personal affair. When friends occupy the same neighborhood, there probably will be more occasions for exercising "close reciprocity rooted in mutual trust, affection, and respect" (p. 25), as Keller defined the state of friendship. Such relationships, when intimate and sustained, can be especially strong fibers of social fabric.

3. *Neighbors:* The links between and among neighbors arise from propinquity and may be weak or strong. Keller (1968) reminded us that the neighbor, like the relative, is "somehow an objectively given, inescapable presence in one's life space" (p. 24). The link may be temporary but can be very active and may involve exchanging tools, mutually protecting each other's property (i.e., "eyes on the street"), offering consolation during times of crisis, helping with child care, and sharing local information.

4. *Local institutions:* These are collectivities with shared purpose that have been around for a while and usually occupy high-visibility property. They can include ethnic clubs, places of worship, drugstores, senior centers, bars, family support centers, health clinics, schools, owner-operated hardware stores, and the coffee counters in corner convenience stores. These are contact points for linking people together. Other groups (including street gangs, athletic teams, and book clubs) also can be significant. Both nonprofit human service agencies and for-profit businesses over time can take on the nature of local institutions. Local institutions that persist are powerful connectors. Evidence seems to confirm churches and other centers of faith as primary among these.

5. *Internal communication mechanisms:* As people in a small place come to know more about each other, the connections attaching people to people and attaching people to place tend to strengthen. Information flows can be carried by neighborhood newspapers, newsletters of local organizations and institutions, e-mail, community bulletin boards on street corners or in supermarkets, posters on storefronts announcing spaghetti dinners and on utility poles promoting political candidates or local rock bands, neighborhood voters' guides, flyers sent home with schoolchildren, Web pages, and billboards. In addition to the print media, there can be hometown radio, cable TV, and sound trucks. Knowledge shared usually—but not always—strengthens human bonds.

6. *Common history:* Every place has a history. Shared knowledge of this history, especially when it is rich and interesting, can be a strong bond. There are now a number of useful devices for making local history visible. The short case study of Vandergrift and its volunteer organizer in Chapter 5 relates how one small community with a fascinating past is making this past a tool of recovery and revitalization. Vandergrift residents give their history visibility through a newsletter, tours, lectures, plaques on historic structures, roadside markers, a heritage society, take-home projects for schoolchildren, displays of old photos retrieved from attics, an annual dinner with a history-related speaker or video, and frequent shows and events in their carefully restored "Casino Theatre," the town's most prominent building.

7. *Shared values:* These can be a powerful force for bringing people together or scattering them apart. When groups of hopeful and committed people in small communities can explore and reach agreement on fundamental positive values, the local place gains in its ability to survive and grow.

Value questions of crucial importance to small communities today include the following. Do neighbors have responsibility to each other regarding the care and use of their own private property? Are we allowing drugs to undermine community health and well-being? Are oppression and spirituality relevant matters for attention by local community organizations? And, most sensitive and most important, when a small community is populated nearly entirely by people of the same race, what is the responsibility of the local community, its institutions, and its households to take initiatives to embrace diversity? It is a disturbing paradox that while the United States is a pluralist society with a population becoming more diverse, at the same time it has racially homogeneous settlements growing in numbers and isolation throughout the land.

Today, some writers and practitioners fittingly call these seven components "assets," and there is a growing body of literature supporting and further developing the asset concept, including work by Kretzmann and McKnight (1993) and a book-length case study of Boston's Dudley Street Neighborhood Initiative by Medoff and Sklar (1994). When these assets endure and produce benefits, neighborhood people are better able to make effectual plans and tap resources from outside their community.

The power of social fabric to hold a community together was evident in the small community of Valmeyer, Illinois, when it was devastated by two destructive floodings of the Mississippi River in 1993. The townspeople planned a new town and moved nearby to higher ground. By the year 2000, more than 250 homes had been built with the ultimate goal of 350, according to Lori Brown, the village clerk. She estimated the population at 525. Brown reported that the new institutions set up included three churches, a school, a print shop, a bank, a tavern-restaurant, a convenience store, and a post office. "We would have liked to see all this develop faster, but we are coming pretty good," she told one of the authors. "Schneider's, the old general store hangout, moved elsewhere, so we still badly need a real grocery" (phone interview, May 4, 2000).

Now, we move from social ties to power source.

COMMUNITY POWER STRUCTURE

The focus of this component is the control that arises from collective effort. Political power is continuously up for grabs. Every individual and group in a community is free to mobilize supporters and undertake collective action for change, including electing new public officials. Of course, a climate of freedom also makes it possible for others who possess money, property, legal authority, and information to seek to checkmate change that threatens their interests. Thus, a neighborhood organization may build power but still be stymied in its efforts to stop a hospital or a factory from encroachment into a residential street. But each battle the organization fights visibly, for a legitimate cause, will win it respect and transform a portion of its potential power to real influence and sometimes control.

Although many neighborhood people shy away from politics—especially the hard-knuckles attack type—Kahn (1991) reminded us,

In this country electoral politics is a traditional way through which power is exercised. It's something that is within the experience of most of the members of our organizations. They're used to participating in the political process. They see it as

a material way for individuals and organizations to try to accomplish their goals. . . . An electoral strategy that comes out of the experience of an organization's members, that focuses on issues, that is centered around not just elections but a continuing strategy to influence government, can make a real difference in all of our lives. (p. 276)

Closely linked to control also is the local economy, and we move on to that third vitality source. (Chapters 5 and 6 examine community organizing and participation as keys to fully developing a community's political infrastructure.)

THE LOCAL ECONOMY

A small residential community may be but a fragment of what we normally think of as a supply-and-demand economy, or it may be a substantial and well-developed miniature with most of the essential elements of an economy in place. Even a fragment has economic actors in the form of resident households living within the neighborhood's boundaries, receiving income, and using the income to purchase and save. These are important functions no matter how humble the place. This circular flow of receiving and spending is the heart and structure of a market economy, even down at the neighborhood level.

The wizardry of communication in tying small communities to limitless locations on the globe is understood, but not so well do we comprehend the universal connections of the world market with its limitless financial transactions. Every residential neighborhood has an economic base, usually made up largely of households providing labor that generates streams of income to maintain and sometimes strengthen the household as it purchases goods and services originating from producers spread around the world.

The key economic activity in any residential neighborhood, then, is employment. Employment of residents outside the neighborhood is basic economic activity, while employment within the neighborhood is nonbasic. For most small residential neighborhoods, the principal source of economic growth is increasing the quantity and quality of labor exports.

The Market Economy

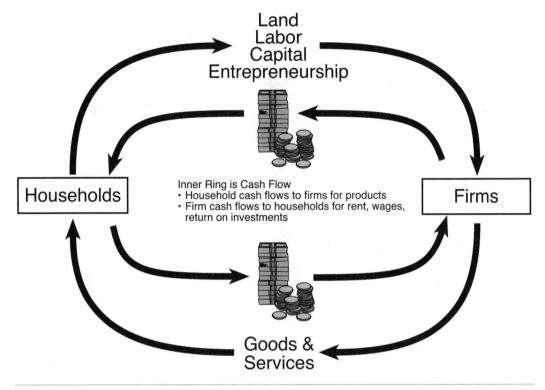

Land
Labor
Capital
Entrepreneurship

Households

Firms

Inner Ring is Cash Flow
• Household cash flows to firms for products
• Firm cash flows to households for rent, wages,
  return on investments

**Goods &
Services**

Figure 4.1 The Market Economy.   © James V. Cunningham, 2002

Like any economy, a neighborhood economy operates as a set of four resource flows (Figure 4.1). One flow involves the households spending their money to demand and purchase goods and services from firms and other suppliers. The second flow consists of the goods and services sold by suppliers to the purchasing households. Such transactions produce a third flow as the suppliers spend money to pay wages, rent, and interest on capital to demand and purchase the inputs necessary to produce the goods and services they sell. The fourth and final flow consists of the labor (including entrepreneurship talent), land and its raw materials, and capital equipment delivered to suppliers and used in the production process.

These four flows and the transactions involved are the principal activities that provide the economic base of the small community, an entity composed of all the households living within the boundaries of the neighborhood. The households continually export labor across the boundaries while importing goods and services.

This model suggests ways in which renewal organizations can stimulate increased flows. Two examples may help illustrate. In the case study of Barelas, with its growing tourist demand, the local association might enlist neighborhood musicians and actors to launch a year-round show tent and secure the development funds to make it happen. The purchase of entertainment by the visitors constitutes an export of services. In Hyde Park-Kenwood in Chicago, with its luxury condominiums, its continual concerns regarding security, and its great university with immense technical research potential, a start-up industry might be launched to develop and market worldwide advanced design production-communication security systems for households, real estate management

Basic Market Flows

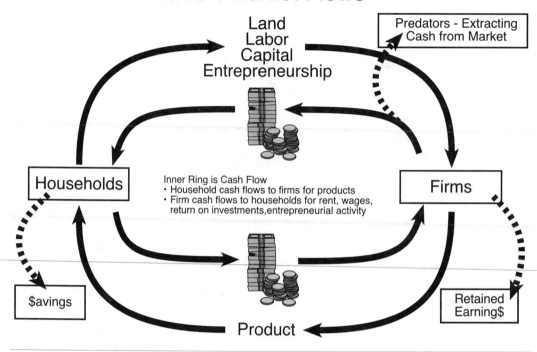

Figure 4.2   Basic Market Flows.   © James V. Cunningham, 2002

firms, and businesses, a potential export market of considerable size. Both of these projects would export products to customers outside the respective neighborhoods (with the products being entertainment and security systems). New flows of export income would come to both neighborhoods, providing jobs and capital for expansion of the young industries.

The second illustration (Figure 4.2) pictures the miniature community in a more realistic complex form, including those activities related to household savings and firms' retained earnings, two main sources of capital. The economic activity of speculators, unethical home remodelers, and other predators who prey on small communities are shown as a leakage of funds out of the area. Here, we can relate the Aliquippa Alliance for Unity and Development (see Chapter 7), which has produced a credit union and a development fund as institutions of capital formation for its community in Pennsylvania. Both institutions are supplying job-creating funds to local employers. The Lyndale Neighborhood

Association in Minneapolis has recently created a new revolving pool of capital by extracting funds from external sources and drawing on internal funds from its members and supporters to be loaned and/or granted to local firms or loaned to residential property owners. Lyndale also has a unique "Community Hero Card" that residents can use to obtain "reward dollars" by making purchases at neighborhood-area stores, restaurants, and other businesses, an incentive for residents to keep their money flowing within the community, where it can double or triple its impact.

The third illustration (Figure 4.3) is a model of the neighborhood economy set in the midst of city and region, picturing the major movements of money, goods, and services and introducing banks and their capital-supplying function as well as local community institutions as additional generators of economic activity. Broken lines indicate both import and export activity, and the arrowheads at both ends indicate dual flow simultaneously moving in both import and export directions.

The Small Economy
(Urban Neighborhood, Suburb, Industrial Town, or Rural Area)

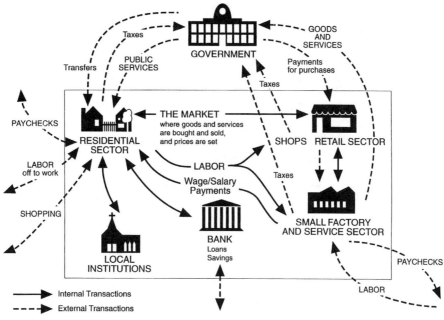

Figure 4.3   The Small Economy.   © James V. Cunningham, 2002

Government is introduced as a powerful source of economic activities and many kinds of functions that are largely located outside the community but that are always generating economic activities that affect individual small neighborhoods. Government activities that are economic in nature include collecting taxes, supplying infrastructure, making transfer payments, and even the government's hiring labor and purchasing goods and services from within the neighborhood. Also, in Figure 4.3, we begin to see more clearly the vast array of export flows that help to relate the small community to the outside economic world. Of special interest are the Aliquippa and Rollingwood (Austin) cases, where each neighborhood possesses its own local government, a situation with the advantage of local control over some economic activities such as types of investment that can be made to use vacant land, property tax rates, scale of infrastructure, and size and nature of local public workforce.

The fourth illustration (Figure 4.4) shows the relation of the miniature economy to the regional, national, and global economies. The reality today is that, with the explosion of Internet communication, this whole economic world becomes a potential market for every neighborhood everywhere but requires research and careful selection processes to find marketable goods and services. High activity, sophisticated planning, and development activities are carried out in small communities such as Bloomfield-Garfield (Pittsburgh) and Dudley Street (Boston), which possess the competence to exploit export markets with and through the firms, universities, and national funders with whom they have partnerships—or could establish such. An important product that might be first on their product lists is their own expertise and imaginative methods and models for replanning and rebuilding old but advantageously located small communities that they have created for their own areas but that they might export as valuable products. Beyond this, they might exploit the imaginative goods and services, art, and artifacts of their own households and firms for sale in the export market.

Appendix 4.C presents definitions of key socioeconomic activities under way in small communities. An understanding of the workings

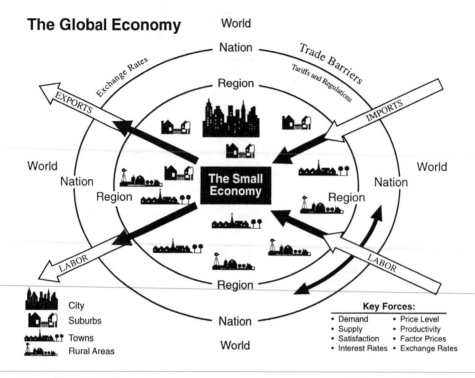

Figure 4.4   The Global Economy.   © James V. Cunningham, 2002

of the market economy can facilitate communities seeking to change and add to their export flows so as to strengthen their local economies. For small residential communities, stable export-related jobs with rising wages and salaries obviously are a most important economic component for bringing in all-important outside resources. But there are many other components in these flow charts that provide opportunities for strengthening a miniature economy. If a neighborhood group studies them carefully, with imaginations intensely applied, then ideas for a local job creation scheme can easily arise.

Like the more complex regional, national, and global economies, every miniature economy can suffer from instability and breakdown, as the following example illustrates. A Wal-Mart store rises a few miles away. Small shops fail, householders find themselves unemployed or underemployed, and homes cannot be sold or leased. But the market is not completely stagnant. Wal-Mart hires 300 persons from the county. The school principal retires, takes his savings, borrows from the bank, and opens a restaurant featuring Cajun recipes given him by

a brother in Lake Charles, Louisiana, and he soon has 30 employees and customers coming from far away. High-performance equipment is installed in the community's idle factory. Quality machine parts are produced by 22 high-wage unionized workers, most of them women. A married couple, gone from the town for 35 years, returns for retirement, bringing their flow of transfer payments with them. And so forth.

With money and product flows expanding in a small community, there is renewed stability. But next year, world wheat prices may nosedive, the surrounding farmers may suffer, and a new round of instability may begin, with job layoffs at Wal-Mart and the restaurant and a new inflow of unemployment compensation checks. This great free economy is "free" to rise or fall. But alert organized people can boost the growth and slow the decline.

We return to this local economy in Chapter 15, where we focus on workforce development, a most important economic issue and one always containing hidden strengths and ideas to be tapped for new thrusts of economic activity.

The Economists' Doubt

A serious question has long been raised by economists about the wisdom of investing time, money, and resources in revitalizing distressed communities. They ask whether salvaging old living areas is the most efficient and beneficial way in which to spend public money, especially when it comes from the national treasury. A leading critic has been the economist and author Edgar M. Hoover. He saw such investment falling victim to "the place prosperity fallacy" by ignoring the fact that a place does not correspond, for any length of time, to a fixed set of people. He wrote, "Since people have some mobility, the best way to help disadvantaged people who are living in a particular region may be to encourage them to move. Migration can, in fact, serve both the objective of efficient use of resources and the objective of interpersonal equity and distribution of opportunity" (Hoover, 1971, p. 259). Thus, the migration of rural people, such as those in the Appalachian Mountains, to Cleveland and Chicago might better be referred to as an "aided or encouraged displacement."

Hoover (1971) also saw a local economic development effort aimed at a specific small community as "wastefully nonselective in its assistance" (p. 259). In describing what he saw as the larger picture, he wrote,

> In any community or region where there are unemployed and needy people, there are also employed and prosperous people. Increased employment and income for the area as a whole may help those who need it most, but a large part of its local benefits will come to those who do not need it. Those surest to gain are generally property owners and the operators of established locally oriented business, such as utilities, banks, and commercial service firms. (p. 259)

This argument carries the rationality of scientific economics and its single-minded drive toward the maximization of the use of resources. It ignores the high costs that can be involved in the displacement of a household from a small community to which it has strong attachments. Such separation has potentially high psychological costs in loss of human relationships. Separation also can involve real economic costs

for the separating family as it is cut off from direct contact with relatives, friends, local institutions, and other sources of material support, including both in-kind and cash transfers.

Louis Winnick, an economist with the Ford Foundation during the late 1960s, was concerned about the enormous amounts of money that the federal urban renewal program was then pouring into selected city locations, mostly in central business districts (Winnick, 1966). He, too, saw this wealth going for the benefit of those who needed it least—the owners of immobile wealth such as prime-located real estate, the practice of a popular dentist, a widely circulated daily newspaper, and a prosperous hospital. But what bothered him most was massive federal investments pulling wealth from one place and giving it to another place without any compensation for the losers. He believed that this was expensive, wasteful, and inequitable.

However, Winnick (1966) did recognize social and political realities. From working with many foundation-connected development organizations, he knew that the labor force is not easily moved around and that migration of households takes a long time, requires resources, and has opportunity costs. He also saw the problem of abandonment implicit in the purely rational economic view: "It imposes a kind of a death sentence on a community" (p. 274). He concluded that, even with the unintended and unwanted inefficiencies of the place prosperity approach, mobility is not the sole answer. Winnick acknowledged that "economic opportunities also have to be brought to where the stranded poor are now living" (p. 275). In other words, some poor and impoverished families generally need additional skills and other resources before they are able to make a successful move to a new community.

For more than three decades, the controversy of people versus place has continued unresolved, with politicians remaining faithful to their local places and their voters, while theoretical economists have argued for cold efficiency.

In their assessment of community building, Kingsley, McNeely, and Gibson (1997) brought the debate up-to-date, arguing,

> Even if we had a fully effective set of people-based policies in America—e.g., an income maintenance system with the proper mix of assistance

and incentives applied equitably across the nation—it would not be enough. There are certain types of "infrastructure" needed to equip people to take advantage of the opportunities our society has to offer that are definitionally place-based, for example, decent schools and effective community-level social networks and institutions. At present, such infrastructure is not at all equitably distributed. It is particularly lacking in neighborhoods with concentrated poverty, especially those in large cities. For them, strengthening or rebuilding such place-based infrastructure may well be essential before sound people-based policies can be expected to have much effect. (p. 25)

In many old industrial areas where populations have shrunk, there are poor school districts with declining enrollment and reduced tax bases to fund education, while suburban districts in the same regions are able to finance excellent schools. If the same state or national pot financed all school districts within its jurisdiction, then more equity might be possible.

This issue stays alive as the highly competitive global economy drives us toward efficiency. Henry Cisneros, former secretary of the U.S. Department of Housing and Urban Development (HUD), pointed out that people and place policies are "not polar opposites" and in fact "can be made to blend with a reasonable sense of balance" (quoted in Kingsley et al., 1997, p. 42). He argued that moving all urban poor to the suburbs would waste vital community assets and institutions that remain in the city but, at the same time, that all people should be free to accept jobs wherever they exist.

Public policy, being short range and sensitive to the pressures of aroused voters in distressed communities, continues to tilt toward place prosperity. There is no denying that great flows of labor do follow the pulls of the market, ever moving toward growth neighborhoods in growth regions, with most of the movers being young and white. But the mature small community, with its reciprocal relationships, embedded institutions, and history relevant to long-term residents, also can claim to be a legitimate societal treasure that provides a supportive and irreplaceable environment for a still large (but probably shrinking) number of households.

Grogan and Proscio (2000), in their optimistic book on "comeback cities," reminded us that those streaming out of cities during the past 30 years have been the middle class and wealthy, ironically supported in their mobility by government funds paying for urban expressways, sewers, and other infrastructure as well as vast federal home mortgage deductions that have bolstered the net income of homeowners and particularly of suburban families with large mortgages (p. 36). This system of special refunds to homeowners has been a strong economic resource, helping households to maintain their personal properties and their local communities as well. (Chapters 11 through 15 focus on strategies to bolster local economics through place-based initiatives.)

This chapter now moves on to the reality of distress that, in some form, eventually strikes every small community. The causes of change and factors of distress are shown to be complex, interrelated, and linked. Destructive forces are numerous. The unraveling of social fabric, the weakening and disarray of political networks, and the shrinkage of the local economy are major indicators of serious distress, as is the erosion of bulwarks such as churches and extended families. However, we will see that every small community has strengths and assets for fighting back and building on, even when significant distress factors are present.

Typology of Change and Distress

Anthony Downs, in his classic analysis of the links between neighborhoods and the urban development process, classified residential areas along a continuum of five stages of neighborhood conditions, mostly using physical and financial measures (Downs, 1981).

Stage 1: Stable and Viable. These are healthy small communities that are either new and thriving or mature, well cared for, and stable. No symptoms of serious physical decline have appeared, and property values are rising. Incipient decline is dealt with swiftly as it may appear. Demands for housing remain high, with prices moving upward.

Stage 2: Minor Decline. These are generally older areas where some signs of decline are found. Younger families with few net assets are numerous. Minor deficiencies in housing are visible, and density is higher than when the neighborhood was first developed. Property values are stable or increasing slightly. Often, mortgages are federally insured because buyers do not have substantial equity. The level of public service and the social status are below those typical of Stage 1 neighborhoods. One or more resident groups may be promoting cleanup and public improvements.

Stage 3: Clear Decline. These are areas where renters may be nearly or fully dominant in the housing market. Tenant-landlord relations are poor because of high absentee ownership. Social status is below Stage 1 or 2. There are numerous low-income households. Minor physical deficiencies are visible. Many structures have been converted to higher density uses other than those for which they were designed; for example, single-family homes may be divided into multi-unit housing, with others becoming auto repair garages, plumbing shops, and the like. There may be some abandoned housing. Overall confidence in the area's future is weak unless there is a well-organized and visible community revitalization effort under way.

Stage 4: Heavily Deteriorated. These are areas where housing is shabby and even dilapidated, while most structures require major repairs and replacements. Many properties are marketable only to low-income groups through contract sales. Profitability of rental units is poor, with low or negative cash flows. Subsistence-level households are numerous and may even dominate. Unemployment is commonplace. Pessimism about the area's future is widespread as abandonment spreads.

Stage 5: Unhealthy and Nonviable. These are areas at a terminal point, marked by massive stretches of vacant land and buildings. Drug users frequent empty buildings, as do squatters. High weeds grow unrestrained. All expectations for the area's future are negative. Residents are those with the lowest incomes in the region and who therefore have limited mobility. Many consider it to be a place to move out of, not into. Demolition of buildings and land clearance may *appear* to be the most sensible alternative.

In this 1981 analysis, Downs stated that few cities contained any Stage 4 or Stage 5 areas. Of

course, there have been many changes since he wrote. In 2003, most cities have scattered patches of such distress in a few neighborhoods. In Chapter 6, we encounter the Bloomfield-Garfield Corporation and its neighborhood distressed by a six-block clump of blighted hillside housing, a telling example of a specific distressed patch. These are now neighborhoods where, due to population loss, whole blocks of housing have been abandoned, dropping these communities into the condition described by Downs as Stage 5. Population loss continues to weaken them.

In this new century, Downs (2000) sees neighborhood and housing markets working well for most households with money. What is not working is housing for the poor, who are mainly renters. He found that more than 50% of all renter households have too little income to afford decent housing, and therefore many of this 50% get confined to Stage 3, 4, or 5 neighborhoods, especially if they are people of color. "Clearly," stated Downs, "low incomes comprise by far our largest 'housing problem.' Low incomes exclude poor households, and poor minority households are deeply excluded" (p. 2). They are concentrated in adverse neighborhood environments and large-scale public housing, thereby creating increased concentration within "socially destitute environments." This does not work. "We cannot improve the quality of life for the very poor without reducing big poverty clusters" (p. 2).

Rae (2000), in his appraisal of "undercrowded cities," identified 67 shrinking cities east of the Mississippi River that have hemorrhaged population for decades (pp. 23–24). Of these, 19 are shrunken down at least 40% from their peak populations and suffer substantial numbers of vacant housing units. Cities containing one or more large clusters of afflicted neighborhoods, pocked with vacant structures, include once vibrant urban centers such as Detroit (28,000 units of vacant housing), New Orleans (50,000), Philadelphia (67,000), and St. Louis (28,700). Rae recommended that cities and their neighborhoods blighted by undercrowding face up to the reality of this condition and its consequences and start thinking and planning smaller (pp. 41–43).

To deal with life in a contracting place, local people need to achieve widespread self-mobilization and control of the resources that remain and must extract considerable public subsidies from regional, state, and national sources. Sometimes, the turnaround initiative may have to come from a multi-neighborhood coalition that encompasses the blighted patch plus nearby areas threatened by it. In cities or towns with concerned local leaders who are sophisticated about obtaining resources both inside and outside their communities, extreme deterioration and abandonment can be dealt with through a crisis partnership of government and indigenous resident and business organizations. The chapters that follow suggest the activities that would have to be undertaken.

While visible physical blight can signal severe crisis in Stage 4 or 5 communities, more stable communities can suffer psychological blight that, although not as visible, is just as severe and threatening to community cohesion and tranquility. For instance, the strain and stress of exclusion can have a devastating impact on a polished outer suburb or a gentrified center city condominium district. Distress is no stranger to seemingly stable small communities. Even an elegant enclave is not easily freed from fears of outsiders. In their intensive analysis of gated communities, Blakely and Snyder (1997) concluded,

> We must protect our neighborhood communities because they are essential and fundamental to our democratic society. Yet protecting houses and physical possessions with gates and guards is contradictory to community building. . . . It is the mutual support and shared social relationships of community that require protection and deserve our material and intellectual resources. (p. 176)

Their investigations found that high-income gated communities can fall into sharp conflict over exclusion issues.

Blakely and Snyder (1997) cited the case of Whitley Heights, a hilly enclave within Los Angeles marked by tall trees and Mediterranean-style mansions scattered along steep winding streets. It was a strong community with a sense of history and an active organization of residents that held an annual Labor Day neighborhood festival. During the 1980s, residents began getting upset by an invasion of car parkers from the commonplace streets below. As people discovered the beauty of the area, more outsiders came to use it as a shortcut, a jogging course, or a dog run and parkers jammed the once quiet streets.

Finally, the residents sought and obtained approval from the Los Angeles City Council for the installation of iron gates. At about the time that construction was to begin, downhill neighbors targeted for exclusion filed a lawsuit, calling themselves CAGE (Citizens Against Gated Enclaves). They charged that the gates were an "elitist slap in the face" (Blakely & Snyder, 1997, p. 106). After 4 years of expensive litigation, the California supreme court in 1994 held the gates to be illegal, ruling that citizens of the state could not be denied the fundamental right to access public streets.

Blakely and Snyder (1997) reported that, following the defeat, internal conflicts erupted within Whitley Heights over how to pursue the case, with its community leadership becoming exhausted. The Whitley Heights Civic Association collapsed, and its activities ceased. Recently, the community has begun to reform itself with an association composed of newcomers. But the whole affair was a long draining experience that set the community back. Blakely and Snyder summed up, "Whitley Heights may have lost its most precious resource, its sense of self as a strong community" (p. 107).

Such findings have implications through all five stages. Not only can the fear and stress that underlie exclusion undermine a Stage 1 neighborhood (gates or no gates), but increased tensions make renewal more difficult at the other stages. Resident-led renewal is a sensitive human process requiring a high degree of trust at every stage. Likewise, residents have to face, at times, the reciprocal relationships between physical and social distress that may infect any small community, as when a homeless, harmless old man begins sleeping and eating his food pantry bagged lunches on the lawns and patios of a Stage 1 manicured suburb.

Causes of Change and Factors Underlying Distress

In most cities, we have found that up to one third of neighborhoods suffer from serious distress. However, it is important to note that the categorization and measures of distress are not perfected. A dividing line between distressed areas and those not distressed is arbitrary. Although there is not universal agreement on what constitutes serious distress, there is consensus that it involves a set of reinforcing negative factors. The Committee for Economic

Development (CED, 1995) found that "the defining characteristic of distressed neighborhoods is the *simultaneous* presence of *multiple* social problems: poverty and joblessness, crime and violence, family instability and welfare dependency, and depressed property values and physical blight" (p. 10). This supports Downs's argument and reinforces the experience of this book's authors, who would add racial intolerance and growing indifference to public affairs as major depressants. It is the convergence of several negative forces that is destructive.

Each day, a variety of actors make decisions that affect the well-being and future of their community. This further complicates revitalization efforts but offers a rich vein of community residents and their allies to be recruited into improvement efforts. Such actors can include people living in, or interested in living in, the neighborhood; absentee owners of property; local employers; leaders of community organizations, associations, and institutions located in or serving the community; and a host of outside, politically influential real estate brokers, developers, salespersons and appraisers, and building property managers.

The owners and operators of businesses located in or near the neighborhood, such as the Rite-Aid drugstore, the Texaco gas station, and the Arby's restaurant, decide how much to invest and how many people to employ. The president of the savings and loan association, the bank manager, insurance companies risk assessors, the credit union loan committee, and mortgage analysts determine the access to capital and credit available to residents, businesses, and institutions. Foundations alter funding priorities and shuffle their target areas.

Local mayors, council members, and state legislators every day may make decisions and take actions that seriously affect many small communities within their jurisdictions, for example, failing to provide adequate funds for public education, creating strict and expensive regulations for in-home day care, and outlawing commercial auto repair in residential blocks. These changes may quickly dilute the incomes of some families in blue-collar neighborhoods at the same time as they raise property values for the more affluent. On the other hand, the rich variety of public decisions to be made by governmental bodies offers organized community groups a great opportunity for intervention in decision making to press for policies and goals that will meet their community goals.

Downs has found that the perceptions, expectations, and decisions of each of these actors create conditions affecting others, often reinforcing tendencies toward neighborhood change (both positive and negative) once their decisions begin to take effect.

Every community is affected by what occurs in nearby communities, making influential people and decision makers in those communities also potentially important. Beyond this, small communities always face the reality that the ultimate forces affecting them are rooted in national or even global events, for example, closing a military base, moving a sports franchise (either major or minor), and devaluing Asian currencies (which lowers import prices and brings layoffs to a local shirt-making firm). Weather-related crop failures in Latin America that force the closing of a community's fruit processing plant, resulting in 60 layoffs, is another example of the global-local connection.

Drier (1993) affirmed this reality of the outside enemies, noting that "every observer of urban neighborhood problems recognizes that the sources of urban distress and decay primarily reside outside neighborhood boundaries" (p. 8). He pointed to large-scale economic forces, including federal government actions that undermine small communities through policies that accelerate the spread of low-wage service jobs; encourage disinvestment in older communities; relax safeguards against redlining by banks and insurance companies; cut funding for housing, jobs, and social services; and favor new suburbs over older communities. These policies have subsidized the exodus of people and businesses to all-white suburban enclaves and thereby have reduced the vitality of many small, older, once diverse communities. Drier also cited government planning for expressways, urban development, stadiums, and other projects that might require large-scale clearance as sources of disruption, displacement, and destruction for small communities.

We would emphasize that scarcity of people in a settled place, whether it is an inner-city neighborhood, a restricted new suburb of four-acre estates, or a small rural community, can mean the loss of visible human presence and reduce the vibrant sense of character marking a successful small community. Isolation and unused roads may be desirable for mountain hideaways but are debilitating or even dangerous for year-round residential environments and especially for neighborhoods in stages of decline.

Empty sidewalks and anonymous cars speeding by in a neighborhood where abandoned houses and storefronts loom make for alienation and fear. Even high-income suburbs may suffer boredom and dullness from undercrowdedness when their neatly clipped hedges are left surrounded by silent sidewalks and trafficless streets during long periods of the day, with the voices of preschool children shifted to day care centers and the adults off doing their corporate and professional duties. Community vitality demands at least a small diverse mass of visible interrelated persons, as long advocated by Jane Jacobs.

Eight Forces of Distress

Eight of the most important large-scale forces with negative economic consequences for small communities are the following.

1. *Suburbanization:* New construction in suburban areas can draw stable residents away from older urban communities. Lower transportation costs resulting from a return to "cheap" gasoline (yes, this happens every few years) or new highways and bridges can generate and foster out-migration by making suburban housing less costly and more accessible. Rising real incomes in households lead some to relocate to "better" neighborhoods. Urban decay has pushed affluent middle-class families out of cities (Rusk, 1997). This exodus of higher-income residents takes away political, social, cultural, and financial support, thereby weakening community institutions left behind such as churches, schools, and recreation groups. This prompts a spiral of decline among businesses and rental properties in older communities, both urban and suburban (CED, 1995; Kasarda, 1993; Rusk, 1997). Sprawl likewise may create ugly and oppressive conditions for people and property alike, a situation of hyperdistress (see the two accompanying sidebars).

Sprawl and Distress: Inextricably Intertwined

In the 300-plus metropolitan regions of the nation, where most people live and yearn for tranquility, the dozens of menacing forces often cited as threats to community contentment have now been rolled into the one big concept: "sprawl." Definitions of sprawl seem to be still getting sorted out, with component terms and phrases spread around awkwardly as befit the illusive nature of the concept.

Investigators for cost studies, policy projects, and media feature stories have associated sprawl with greedy consumption of farmland, wetlands, and forests; travel dominance by personal fossil fuel vehicles; historic disdain for the restraints of planning; abandoned and burntout inner-city blocks; poisoning of the natural environment; and diverse exploitations of beauty and fertility. Most such actions against nature and humankind were once hailed as freedom and the good life. Today, they are accused of destroying both, and of oppressing large bodies of people to boot, in both the aged urban cores and the spreading outside rings.

Long lists of side effects are appearing: more expensive infrastructure, higher land costs, commuters spending more time in vehicles, more accidents, less efficient public transit, suspect water, social services harder to get to, weakening social fabric, the debasing of scenic and historic meadows and hillsides, shortages of workers in suburban supermarkets, a chronic surplus of discouraged job hunters in the urban cores cut off from the new job sources, rising housing costs and taxes, multiplying work absences due to illness, more (not less) segregation by race and income, and increased stress linked to travel congestion, road rage, and job dissatisfaction.

Some 40 years ago, Jacobs (1961) described the destructive process accurately: "Each day, several thousand more acres of our countryside are eaten up by the bulldozers, covered by pavement, dotted with suburbanites who have killed the thing they thought they came to find" (p. 445).

As lack of restraint and land gluttony continue to shape much of the change, and the peace and tranquility of households and their supporting institutions are threatened with creeping disaster, especially as the nearby auto junkyard is expanding beyond its shield of evergreens and coming out into the open. Meantime, the nation's grassroots renewal groups are challenged to help transform sprawl into a rational, moderated, and wisely planned process that some are calling "smart growth" or sustainability. The planning chapters that lie ahead in this book, Chapters 8 and 9, seek to frame an appropriate long-term course. Also, potentially helpful tactics and techniques are found in every chapter.

2. *Impoverishment:* Wealth is being distributed upward, and the gap between whites and people of color widens more in wealth than in income while people being displaced from the labor force become more numerous (Sklar, 1995, p. 5). In the midst of the great boom of the 1990s, Handler and Hasenfeld (1997) reported 68 million Americans to be impoverished, with "barely enough to get by . . . and little doubt that poverty is growing, both in numbers and severity" (p. 53–54). They asserted that poverty continues to spread because of the deterioration of the low-wage labor market and the changes in family structure. The destructiveness of today's low-wage work was brought up close to us by Ehrenreich (2001), as mentioned in Chapter 3.

Race Makes a Difference

As part of his analysis of urban sprawl, Rusk (1999) spelled out what it means to live in a "poor," deeply distressed neighborhood during an era of population and development shifts. "As poverty increases, the interaction between stressed families also increases, particularly as stable, middle-class families move away. Once these 'control rods' are removed and the concentration of poverty reaches a critical level, a chain reaction begins in the community, crime and delinquency rise, alcoholism and drug addiction increase, schools fall into decline, neighborhoods deteriorate, unemployment and welfare dependency increase, and social meltdown begins. Poor blacks almost invariably live in neighborhoods that have reached these critical levels; poor whites almost never do. There is a world of difference" (p. 81). Rusk observed, "We are wasting the potential talents and productive capabilities of millions of children trapped in high-poverty ghettos, barrios, and slums" (p. 323).

3. *Weaknesses in the labor market and breakdown in wages and employment:* The numbers of working poor are steadily increasing as technology replaces human labor, part-time and temporary jobs replace stable full-time jobs, and the legal minimum wage remains below the poverty level (Sklar, 1995). This deterioration of sharing in prosperity occurs within a labor market shaken by corporate mergers and restructuring and by shifts away from domestic manufacturing to service jobs and overseas manufacturing. As traditional living-wage jobs

have disappeared, long-term underemployment and unemployment have increasingly undermined household income and reduced financial support for community institutions (CED, 1995, p. 16). Most job growth currently takes place outside of cities, in areas from which many city residents are excluded due to lack of transportation, hostile racial attitudes, and low wages.

4. *Discrimination:* Race, age, and/or gender discrimination lead to lack of income, which translates into inadequate purchasing power that stunts local businesses, limits the ability of homeowners and landlords to maintain properties, and thwarts renters' efforts to accumulate assets through homeownership and saving (CED, 1995, p. 17). Downs (1981) found the decline of older urban neighborhoods to be related to "white flight" and the dual housing market it creates. He asserted that "white racial prejudice underlies the dual market system," with black buyers and renters often paying more than white ones for the same housing (p. 91). And after finding the same negatives at work nearly 20 years later, Downs (2000) pointed out, "Middle- and upper-income households of all ethnic groups do not want to live in neighborhoods containing any sizable number of poor people . . . and there is unwillingness of most whites to live in areas where more then 25[%] to 33% of the residents are African Americans no matter what their income level" (p. 20).

5. *Unfair and illegal housing practices:* Housing segregation and discrimination keep racial and ethnic minority residents out of white neighborhoods. Residential racial segregation is a powerful force of containment; locking disadvantaged people into distressed communities and economic isolation, it creates and maintains inequality. Racism underlies much white flight to the suburbs (CED, 1995, p. 17). Illegal real estate practices, such as racial steering, can cause racial clustering in some communities.

6. *Redlining and disinvestments:* Redlining is the practice of limiting or denying goods, services, or financing to an area's residents or businesses based on real or perceived risk associated with their racial, ethnic, or economic backgrounds. Appraisers, creditors, real estate agents, insurance brokers, and others associated with the housing industry continue to undervalue or avoid mortgaging property in such neighborhoods. The denial of mortgages, or the charging of extra fees and the unavailability of insurance, results in these consequences: (a) limiting the ability of some would-be homeowners to buy, (b) losing the potential stability they would bring to the neighborhood, and (c) reducing chances for some to accumulate assets for purposes such as entrepreneurship (Bates, 1993; Squires, 1992, p. 20). Redlining of emergent entrepreneurs and small businesses limits their access to the credit and working capital necessary to create and grow sources of goods, services, and local jobs. Conscious decisions by economic and political elites not to invest in, and in some cases to abandon, people and their communities accelerates physical, economic, and infrastructure decline. Such arbitrary undermining of local economies can set back a whole region.

7. *Imbalance in political clout:* Many affluent neighborhoods use zoning restrictions and political power to keep unwanted facilities (e.g., halfway houses, homeless shelters, waste disposal sites) from their areas and force them to cluster in distressed areas. In communities at the margin of distress, such facilities may accelerate the process of decline. Furthermore, the economically and politically weakened condition of the receiving neighborhoods may tempt authorities to place fewer safeguards on the facilities than they would have required in better organized and more attractive locations (CED, 1995, p. 19).

8. *Fragmentation of social service programs:* Many social service programs are available even in the most distressed communities. All have standard services but different requirements, regulations, and procedures. The lack of coordinated, comprehensive, and integrated services for the entire family means single service agencies often provide little more than marginal benefit. A major cause of this service fragmentation is categorical funding of public programs to address specific problems (Center for Integrated Services and Families and Neighborhoods, 1994, pp. 6–7; CED, 1995, p. 18). Rigid categories mean that people are likely to fall through the cracks. People or family-centered wraparound services acknowledge the interrelationship of issues maximizing impact and outcomes.

Micro Forces

In addition to these macro influences on neighborhood change, many theorists focus on micro-influences, individual behavior, and family functioning as key factors that shape the direction and pace of neighborhood decline and distress (Chaskin & Brown, 1996, p. 2). According to Chaskin and Brown (1996),

> Micro-level influences on neighborhood change often focus on individual behavior and family functioning. For example, that individuals within neighborhoods engage in delinquent or criminal behavior, [and] that they are unemployed or underemployed, are believed to have an effect on the direction and pace of neighborhood change. Similarly, individuals from outside the neighborhood, the landlord who fails to keep his properties up to code or the police officer who fails to respond to calls within the neighborhood, contribute to neighborhood decline and disinvestments. (pp. 4–5)

A household may neglect to report drug selling, a jolt-producing pothole, a burned-out pole light, or a dead animal in the street. Then, there is the pessimistic resident who vilifies political affairs to the point of discouraging his neighbors from voting, and there is the local store owner who offers high-priced, low-quality goods.

Ronnby (1994), in his report on local communities in Sweden, found that distress might be first exhibited not by physical or economic indicators but rather by residents who display bitterness, isolation, despair, hatred, disharmony and disunity, and failure to find growth and satisfaction in their lives.

Chaskin and Brown (1996) also cited attempts to link these micro and macro influences, a focus on the quantity and quality of social fabric or social capital within a community (pp. 3–4). This relationship of the social structure of a community and individual behavior within it includes variables such as the density of social ties and acquaintanceship, formal and informal mechanisms for information sharing and mutual aid, level of participation and degree of organizational density, and existence of informal mechanisms of social support and control. The role of culture—the pattern of collective norms, beliefs, structures of identity, and patterns of behavior—also shapes and informs social fabric. The general effects of urbanization, including greater specialization and division of labor and the increased size, density, and heterogeneity of settlement, are cited as factors that have weakened personal connections among residents. The increased mobility of urban populations and disjointed relationships between workplace and living place are shaking up the configuration and intensity of interpersonal networks.

Distress and decline are summarized next as they affect the three components of small community: social fabric, political structure, and local economy.

Unraveling Social Fabric

If incipient physical decline and social tension are not dealt with, human relationships and sense of community can begin to break down. Kinship and friendship networks may become fewer, and the networks remaining tend to become broken and scattered. When children grow to adulthood in shrinking declining neighborhoods, they may move away from the decay in search of more attractive housing, personal safety, full-service supermarkets, and lucrative job opportunities. Such options overcome the holding power of loving grandmothers and supportive uncles left behind. Time-pressed or aloof strangers often replace longtime neighbors. Informal helping and support systems are lost. Institutions weaken and lose influence as membership and volunteering slacken. Internal communication mechanisms are used less, and some (e.g., neighborhood newspapers) disappear.

Cooperative community spirit and pride diminish, and collective public responsibility ceases. Knowledge of the community's history and its revered traditions fade and become less binding on residents. Fewer values are shared, and there may be more clashes over beliefs. Without some kind of internal or external intervention, a community will show signs of collapse. In time, those residents remaining will tend to become focused only on personal survival and escape.

Disintegration of Political Structure

Because clout in a democratic society requires collective action, a shriveling of resident interest in public affairs, a decline in population numbers, or a loss of cohesion often means weakening and possible melting away of the internal power structure, with the attendant loss of influence beyond the community. Such disintegration may be marked by organizational leaders resigning or perhaps even moving out. Local political party committees may find minor posts once fought over now going vacant and unsought. The percentage of residents registered to vote falls. Heads of institutions who hang on may draw back into their own organizations in pursuit of survival.

Again, if new and/or longtime residents do not intervene with a burst of energy, then an essential element of community health will be lost. It may take years or even decades to restore political competency. Outside, absentee power centers may come to call the shots.

Without an operating power structure of strong indigenous institutions and local groups and associations, led by stable and competent people, the community will likely find difficulty in securing or extracting essential resources. Streets will go unrepaired and unpatrolled, mortgages will be ungranted, and milk and bread will become unavailable without a trip to another neighborhood. At worst, a criminal group may assume "shadow power" and exploit the people and place.

Weakening of the Local Economy

When flows of income into a community slow down due to unemployment, population loss, and other negative forces, there is a loss of stability, confidence, and vitality in the local market. Homeowners decline in numbers, and potential buyers of homes begin to disappear. Transience becomes common. Absentee ownership increases. Households with low incomes replace those with adequate incomes. Property values decline. Confidence in the community's future weakens. Subsistence-level households multiply and may even begin to dominate. Savings and investment disappear. This chaos of the local marketplace drives out shops, institutions, and small manufacturing plants. What goods and services are available tend to be nonlocal, of uneven quality, and overpriced, with small corporate-owned convenience stores, chain drug stores, shabby bars, and discount cigarette shops dominating what is left of the shopping street. Indigenous legitimate employment sinks, and tax revenues from the area fall. Abandonment spreads, and some business owners go bankrupt. Absentee ownership of remaining businesses is now the rule, along with imported labor.

This leakage in the community economy is illustrated by the cash flow diagram in Figure 4.5. A small community is strengthened when residents' salaries and wages are increasing along with a greater inflow of transfer payments (e.g., social security or company pension checks), rents for property owned by local people, dividends on stock owned by residents, and even funds obtained through the underground economy. But reverse forces, such as deaths of pensioners, can also be operating to reduce these needed inflows. During the 21st century, with Home Depots, CVS Drugs, 7-Eleven convenience stores, and massive green BP gasoline stations serving as gatherers of money that is sent off in flows to far-away investors, neighborhood circulation of money shrinks to a trickle, negating economic vitality.

Figure 4.5 lists tactics for trapping and recycling funds within the neighborhood, including maximizing transfers, more locally owned businesses, increased savings invested in community credit unions, or even small indigenous businesses that serve the local place, perhaps through a church. Preserving, capturing, and controlling a small community's internal flows are dealt with in Chapters 11, 12, and 14. However, there has been more thinking and writing about this opportunity than there have been actual experiments or pilot projects that could be of value to a distressed community.

If joblessness is rising among residents at the same time that social security recipients are relocating to Florida, owners of investments are moving up and out, and retail spending is shifting to malls and the Internet, then the local economy will weaken rapidly as such leakages accelerate. (For more on the weakening of the local economy, see Appendix 4.B.)

Cash Flow Diagram

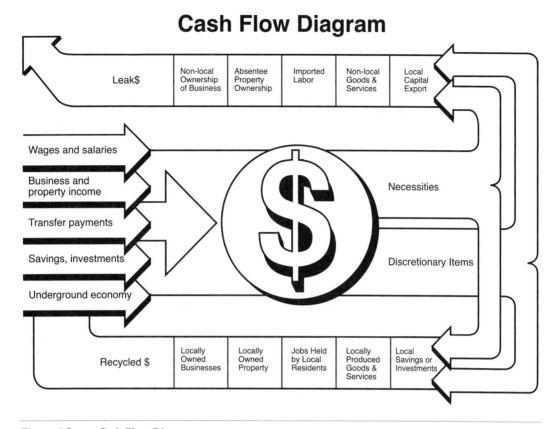

Figure 4.5   Cash Flow Diagram.
© Pratt Institute Center for Community and Environmental Development, 1984

The CED (1995) reported that local and regional problems can coexist, mutually reinforce each other, and cumulatively overwhelm the social control mechanisms of weakened communities. The committee concluded that distress is about more than poverty or individual problems; it is about the collapse of a community's ability to cope with its problems.

Research, however, continues to confirm that healthy communities foster positive outlooks among residents (CED, 1995). In such communities, residents share information through networks and institutions, work toward common goals, and acquire support. Residents connect to society outside their borders, using resources and contacts from across the metropolitan area. Through formal and informal mechanisms, healthy communities identify and address problems, reinforce social norms, and promote productive lives for individuals and their families. The authors of this book have found that such norms include respect, a spirit of inclusion, ethnic and racial tolerance, positive appreciation for population diversity, and concern for economic fairness. Understanding how to achieve and bolster such health is what this book is about.

More "clues to survival," as reported by the University of Nebraska's Heartland Center for Leadership Development, are included as Appendix 4.D. This list suggests the strengths of a small community that may be useful for stimulating and supporting the renewal initiative of residents and their allies and supporters. It is a harbinger of the practical and positive ideas set forth in later chapters.

In Chapter 5, we look at the fundamental process through which aroused communities mobilize to take charge of their own fate.

SUMMARY

For most Americans, the local settlement where they establish a home is a special and significant place. Over time, a variety of relationships can strengthen their attachment to this place and make it their community. Economic flows can give it increased importance and opportunity. Joining with their neighbors, residents can seek to defend and improve their place and renew it when it declines. Although some economists doubt the efficiency of such effort, the fact is that high opportunity costs eliminate the option of moving out for a vast number of residents of small communities. Individually and collectively, people aspire to a better world. Often, this urge becomes action driven by community initiative. Therefore, a great variety of organizations have come into being to renew local communities, to make them places of responsibility and reconciliation, and to cause investments to be made in them. Power to attract and renew resources grows as the organizations show results in their individual communities, and it grows rapidly when they coalesce in alliances and coalitions across regions and beyond.

Collective efforts for recovery and renewal confront barriers of racial division, lack of communal power, decay of social fabric, job insecurity, low wages, unemployment, and shortages of capital and credit. Understanding these barriers and determining how to face them is the essential first step toward recovery of individual communities.

The small community never remains still. It is a place of churning relationships that is constantly subject to masses of individual and group decisions while being bombarded directly and indirectly by both positive and negative forces from near and afar. These forces may be social, political, or economic or a combination of the three. The art and science of community development has made it possible for us to identify and better understand many of these forces. This knowledge makes possible productive organized efforts to reduce distress and halt the decline in small communities while beginning to move them to new stages of livability. Knowledge of the stages of decline can help to alert residents to incipient decline and give them the opportunity to organize early. Knowledge and mobilization of community assets can give residents a foundation on which to build.

CONTINUING QUESTIONS

1. Is change occurring so swiftly in contemporary society that we will soon have throwaway small communities?

2. Can a small community's consensus on values, such as "homeowners are more responsible people" and "rap music is evil," lead to the oppression of minorities within a community (e.g., women, youth, renters, racial/ethnic groups)?

3. Is it feasible to find ways in which to trap income flows within a small community?

4. What are the assets likely to be possessed even by the most distressed small community?

5. How is an authentic, collective community voice created, nurtured, and best used?

6. When assessing their small community, how much attention and weight do residents need to give to individual, institutional, and community assets?

7. Do communities need an "early warning system" to move them quickly to meet new distress? Who should set it up? Who should finance such a system?

8. What is the best measure for determining when a small community needs an organized "treatment" to relieve distress?

9. Can communities effectively battle local influences and the effects of outside societal forces without being part of regional and national alliances?

10. In a pluralistic American society that is moving toward being a nation in which people of color represent 50% of the population, can a small community be free of distress if it is all white and desirous of remaining so?

Appendix 4.A
Scale and the Small Community

Back during the 1950s, one of the authors served on the staff of Chicago's Hyde Park-Kenwood Community Conference, an early attempt at a comprehensive neighborhood renewal organization that promoted housing code enforcement and block club organizing in a community of 70,000 people (down to about 40,000 in 2002). But Hyde Park-Kenwood also had subdivisions, and each subdivision had several residential blocks, its own volunteer-led organization, and numerous volunteer block organizations. Each subdivision had relations with the conference and assumed responsibility for close-to-home issues arising in its subcommunity such as litter, street parking, petty crime, and minor housing code violations.

Marciniak (1981) helped us to understand what a small community is in a large city with his hierarchy of levels of community organization in Chicago, the city that has been his research and organizing turf since the 1940s. This city of 3 million people has about 100 traditional "communities" at the Hyde Park-Kenwood level, communities known by place names such as Rogers Park, Edgewater, Uptown, Austin, Englewood, and Beverly. Marciniak described such a community as sometimes large enough to warrant a public high school, a police district, a political ward, or a postal zone, with its economy able to support a small bank and a hospital.

Such traditional Chicago communities vary in population, with the average size being close to 30,000. Through the research and technical assistance that Marciniak (1981) has provided for local groups at Chicago's Institute of Urban Life, he long ago found that survival and renewal efforts since the 1960s have largely been carried out in small neighborhoods, which are subsections of the larger traditional communities. He estimated that there were "far more than 500" of these small neighborhoods in the city (p. 52).

As an example, within the Edgewater traditional community, Marciniak (1981) found 13 small neighborhoods that would fit this book's definition of a small community, identified by place names such as Northwest Edgewater, Grandale, Edgewater Beach, Lakewood-Balmoral, and Rosehill. It was in these small component places that he discovered the "vitality, the energy of [local] leaders, and residents' concerns for their own neighborhood's future. . . . As the neighborhoods began to define themselves, they also identified with the larger traditional community through which they could wield their individual strengths into a more effective voice" (p. 52).

Marciniak (1981) found these little social environments shaped by "face-to-face relationships and the goings on inside" school buildings, churches, and synagogues; the talk of mothers at the playground; conversations at the laundromat; shared graduation parties; and intermingling in the political precinct as well as by a wide array of other oft-repeated, place-based personal interactions (p. 50).

In 1981, Marciniak predicted that, as we would move into the 21st century, these small neighborhood communities would represent new diverse urban neighborhoods where homeowners would strain their ingenuity and pocketbooks to remain living amid the excitement of the urban place and the opportunity to establish local schools where standards of behavior and moral values would be "caught as well as taught" (Marciniak, 1981, p. 51).

Appendix 4.B
The Local Multiplier

The fewer transactions a resident's dollar triggers inside the community, the less opportunity there is for a "multiplier effect" to operate whereby the impact and stimulation of a dollar grows as it stays within the community and circulates to many people. If a householder spends at a locally owned and operated hardware store instead of at a suburban "big box" store (e.g., Lowe's, Food 4 Less), and if the hardware store spends the money to hire a local delivery boy, then the community impact is triple what it would have been if the householder had headed for the mall (Figure 4.6). As local transactions decline, distress expands.

Appendix 4.C
Definitions of Key Forces at Work in the Small Economy

Demand: Demand is created by households and firms "spending" to buy goods and services and to hire labor. As buying rises, it tends to push up prices, employment, and wages. As buying

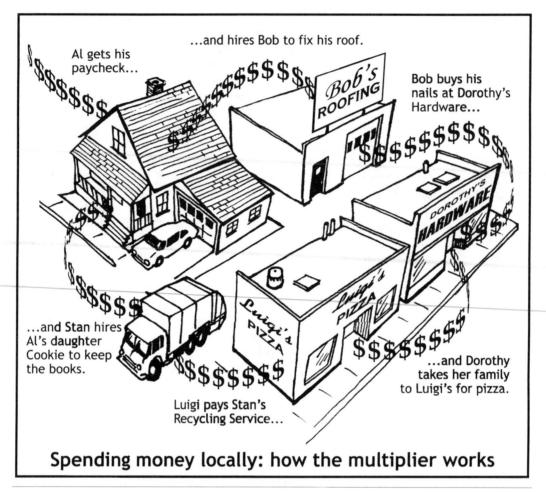

Al gets his paycheck...

...and hires Bob to fix his roof.

Bob's ROOFING

Bob buys his nails at Dorothy's Hardware...

DOROTHY'S HARDWARE

...and Stan hires Al's daughter Cookie to keep the books.

Luigi pays Stan's Recycling Service...

Luigi's PIZZA

...and Dorothy takes her family to Luigi's for pizza.

Spending money locally: how the multiplier works

Figure 4.6   Spending Money Locally: How the Multiplier Works.
© Center for Neighborhood Technology, Working Neighborhoods, 1986

declines, it tends to lower prices, lower wages, and increase unemployment.

Supply: Supply is the goods manufactured and services furnished by firms and other producers in response to demand. As supply is increased, prices tend to fall and more labor is likely to be hired. But sometimes, supply is increased by firms buying labor-saving capital equipment rather than by hiring more labor. This practice can lead to "downsizing" (layoffs). Any decline in supply will also generally result in layoffs.

Satisfaction: Satisfaction is the utility sought by consumers when they demand goods and services. The amount of satisfaction expected largely determines the price that consumers are willing to pay for a product.

Interest rates: Interest rates are the prices paid for borrowing money from a savings institution. Market rates will vary with government-set rates and the amount of risk involved in a transaction. A rise in interest rates tends to slow both demand and supply, while a decrease in rates tends to stimulate demand, with an increase in supply following.

Price level: Price level is the dollar amount at which all goods and services are being exchanged at a given point in time. If prices are rising, then the economy is tending toward inflation. If prices are falling, then it is tending toward deflation. Most economists favor stability within a narrow range of variance.

Productivity: Productivity is the value of goods and services produced by one worker in 1 hour.

The total of goods and services produced by the economy in 1 year is the principal indicator of the economy's growth or decline.

Factor prices: Factor prices are the costs to firms of land (including extracted raw materials), labor (workforce), capital (funds to run business, including the purchase of permanent equipment), and entrepreneurship (the premium paid to leaders of a firm for their coordinating skills, creativity, risk taking, and energy required to develop, produce, and market goods and services successfully). These costs, spread over a firm's products, determine a price floor below which a firm cannot sell its products for long without being forced out of business. (Total factor "costs" always include an amount for a "fair profit.")

Exchange rates: Exchange rates are the price of one nation's currency in terms of another nation's currency. Most rates now float up and down daily, depending on the demand for and supply available for any given currency. This fluctuation imposes an added risk for persons and firms buying and selling between and among nations. The risk can be reduced through hedge fund contracts, which allow future buying and selling of a currency at a fixed rate. (For example, Firm X expects a payment of 40 million yen from a Japanese customer in 6 months for a shipment of hardwoods. At the time of the hardwood sale, the exchange rate is 106 yen to 1 dollar, making the deal worth $377,400. However, in 6 months, currency fluctuation could substantially raise or lower the dollar value of the payment. To eliminate uncertainty, the firm negotiates an advance sale of the yen through a broker for a fixed price of $360,000 that still leaves Firm X with an adequate profit. The broker receives a commission from his or her buyer-client. If there is a rise in the value of the yen during the 6 months, then the buyer-client could make a windfall profit. A steep drop in the price of the yen could cause a loss.)

Savings: Personal savings are the difference between household income (after taxes) and consumption expenditures. These retained funds can be accumulated and used to improve future household income by investment in a computer, a home office, or another productive asset. Business savings are the retained earnings that a firm has after paying all costs, including dividends to stockholders or partners. Retained earnings can be used as reserve to cover future losses, for an expansion, and for investment in new processes, new capital equipment, and product research.

Appendix 4.D
Clues to Survival

The University of Nebraska's Heartland Center for Leadership Development conducted a major study in 1986 (Holladay, 1992) to answer the question: Why are some rural communities coping with fundamental restructuring, while others seem to have surrendered to crisis? The study determined that some communities were solving their economic crises, even though they appeared to have few resources. The following 20 clues point the way to potential survival:

1. Willingness to invest

2. Cooperative community spirit

3. Evidence of community pride

4. Emphasis on the quality of business and community life

5. Participatory approach to decision making

6. Realistic appraisal of future opportunities

7. Awareness of competitive positioning

8. Knowledge of the physical environment

9. Active economic development program

10. Deliberate transition of power to a younger generation of leaders

11. Acceptance of women in leadership roles

12. Strong belief in, and support for, education

13. Problem-solving approach to providing health care

14. Strong multigenerational family orientation

15. Strong presence of traditional institutions that are integral to community life

16. Attention to sound and well-maintained infrastructure

17. Careful use of fiscal resources

18. Sophisticated use of information resources

Table 4.1 Factors Underlying Decline and Revitalization

Revitalization	*Decline*
• Rising household income	• Falling household incomes
• Majority of buildings with good design or historic interest	• Majority of old buildings with poor design and no historic interest
• Population increase in a city area	• Rapid population decrease in a city or an area
• Owner occupancy increase	• Owner occupancy decrease
• Small rental units with owners living on the premises	• Large rental apartments with absentee owners
• Achieving racial unity through reconciliation and joint effort	• Spreading and intensifying racial antipathy
• Proximity to strong institutions, a lakefront, or downtown area	• Isolation away from strong institutions and amenities
• Active community organizations	• Lack of community mobilization
• Low vacancy rates in homes and rental apartments	• High vacancy rates in homes and rental apartments
• Low turnover and transience among residents	• High turnover and transience among residents
• Little vehicular traffic, especially few trucks, on residential streets	• Heavy vehicular traffic, especially trucks, on residential streets
• Low crime and vandalism	• Growing crime and vandalism
• High civic involvement and engagement	• Disappearance of civic activity and engagement
• Active efforts toward racial reconciliation	• Visible racial hostility

SOURCE: Adapted from Downs (1981, Table 5-1, p. 66).

19. Willingness to seek help from the outside

20. Conviction that, in the long run, communities have to do it themselves

These clues to potential survival and stability point to the need to focus on the economic and political, as well as on the social, aspects of the small community. They also affirm inclusiveness.

Appendix 4.E
Summary of Decline and Revitalization Factors

Downs (1981) pointed out that specific factors increase a small community's susceptibility to decline or revitalization (Table 4.1): "Any factor that reduces a neighborhood's relative desirability as a place to live or in which to invest reduces the strength of market demand for property there and increases the probability that owners will neglect their properties, thus increasing the neighborhood's susceptibility to decline. The more such factors are present simultaneously, the greater likelihood that self-reinforcing decline will begin if some triggering event occurs. In fact, a sudden change in one or more of these susceptibility factors can itself act as a detonator setting off either neighborhood revitalization or decline" (pp. 65–66). A sudden appearance of an undesirable use, such as a pornographic theater or a discount liquor store, will often galvanize community residents to come together to act. The opportunity for a community to apply for youth initiative funding or the celebration of the opening of a sizable locally owned and managed business can also serve as the spark for residents to join forces and initiate revival.

Small communities are dynamic and can easily change direction along the continuum from viable to abandoned. Within any given locale, small communities at differential stages of growth and decline can exist simultaneously. A major reality is that the revitalization of one or more small communities in any region does not mean that others will be revitalized soon (Downs, 1981, p. 69). Most communities fall within the middle range of Downs's (1981) continuum; few communities or parts of communities fall at the extreme ends. This means that many communities can benefit from attention and organizing and that most still have a "net worth" of assets over liabilities. Serious organizing during the early stages of decline can usually show positive results.

REFERENCES

Ahlbrandt, R. S. (1984). *Neighborhoods, people, community.* New York: Plenum.

Ahlbrandt, R. S., & Cunningham, J. V. (1979). *A new public policy for neighborhood preservation.* New York: Praeger.

Baroni, G. (1979). Forward. In R. S. Ahlbrandt & J. V. Cunningham, *A new public policy for neighborhood preservation* (pp. vii–ix). New York: Praeger.

Bates, T. (1993). *Banking on black enterprise: The potential of emerging firms for revitalizing urban economies.* Washington, DC: Joint Center for Political and Economic Studies.

Blakely, E., & Snyder, M. (1997). *Fortress America: Gated communities in the United States.* Washington, DC: Brookings Institution Press.

Center for Integrated Services for Families and Neighborhoods. (1994). *Strategies for distressed neighborhoods.* Sacramento, CA: Author.

Chaskin, R., & Brown, P. (1996). Theories of neighborhood change. In R. Stone (Ed.), *Core issues in comprehensive community-building initiatives* (pp. 1–15). Chicago: University of Chicago, Chapin Hall Center for Children.

Committee for Economic Development. (1995). *Rebuilding inner-city communities: A new approach to the nation's urban crisis.* New York: Author.

Downs, A. (1981). *Neighborhoods and urban development.* Washington, DC: Brookings Institution Press.

Downs, A. (2000, October). *Housing policies in the new millennium.* Speech delivered at U.S. Department of Housing and Urban Development Conference on Housing Policies for the Millennium, Washington, DC.

Drier, P. (1993, April). *Community empowerment strategies: The experience of community-based problem solving in America's urban neighborhoods—Recommendations for federal policy.* Washington, DC: U.S. Department of Housing and Urban Development, Social Science Research Council.

Ehrenreich, B. (2001). *Nickel and dimed: On (not) getting by in America.* New York: Henry Holt.

Grogan, P., & Proscio, T. (2000). *Comeback cities: A blueprint for urban neighborhood revival.* Boulder, CO: Westview.

Handler, J., & Hasenfeld, Y. (1997). *We the poor people: Work, poverty, and welfare.* New Haven, CT: Yale University Press.

Holladay, J. (1992). *Economics and community development: A southern exposure.* Dayton, OH: Kettering Foundation.

Hoover, E. M. (1971). *An introduction to regional economics.* New York: Knopf.

Jacobs, J. (1961). *The death and life of great American cities.* New York: Vintage Books.

Kahn, S. (1991). *Organizing: A guide for grassroots leaders* (rev. ed.). Washington, DC: NASW Press.

Kasarda, J. (1993). Inner city concentrated poverty and neighborhood distress: 1970. *Housing Policy Debate, 3,* 253–302.

Keller, S. (1968). *The urban neighborhood.* New York: Random House.

Kingsley, G., McNeely, J., & Gibson, J. (1997). *Community building coming of age.* Baltimore, MD: Development Training Institute.

Kretzmann, J. P., & McKnight, J. L. (1993). *Building communities from the inside out: A path toward finding and mobilizing a community's assets.* Chicago: ACTA Publications.

Marciniak, E. (1981). *Reversing urban decline.* Washington, DC: National Center for Urban Ethnic Affairs.

McKnight, J. (1995). *The careless society.* New York: Basic Books.

Medoff, P., & Sklar, H. (1994). *Streets of hope: The fall and rise of an urban neighborhood.* Boston: South End Press.

Mumford, L (1961). *The city in history: Its origins, its transformations, and its prospects.* New York: Harcourt, Brace, and World.

Rae, D. (2000, September). *Undercrowded cities.* Paper prepared for conference, "The Thinning Metropolis," Cornell University, Ithaca, NY.

Ronnby, A. (1994). *Mobilizing local communities.* London: Avery.

Rusk, D. (1997, May 26). Policies that promote poverty. *The Washington Post,* p. A21.

Rusk, D. (1999). *Inside game, outside game.* Washington, DC: Brookings Institution Press.

Sklar, H. (1995). *Chaos or community? Seeking solutions, not scapegoats for bad economics.* Boston: South End Press.

Squires, G. (Ed.). (1992). *From redlining to reinvestment: Community response to urban disinvestment.* Philadelphia: Temple University Press.

Winnick, L. (1966). Place prosperity vs. people prosperity: Welfare considerations in the geographic redistribution of economic activity. In *Essays in urban land economics: In honor of the sixty-fifth birthday of Leo Grebler* (pp. 273–283). Los Angeles: University of California, Los Angeles, Real Estate Research Program.

5

COMMUNITY ORGANIZING

Principal Tool for Change and Reform

Organizing for Community Controlled Development (OCCD) combines community organization's mobilization and advocacy power with neighborhood investment strategies to build a strengthened and revitalized community that strives to ensure that its residents can have satisfying lives as well as good jobs with living wages. Scheie (1996) investigated community-based groups from Brooklyn to San Antonio and found organizing to be the uniting process for making all of this happen. He also found that the widespread involvement of people inherent in organizing promotes accountability; folks who invest themselves as volunteers expect to see results and will demand them from both their own organization and the institutions and decision makers responsible for serving their community (p. 9). This chapter focuses on community organizing as it relates to the small place community, identifying the 12 key activities of community organizing and exploring their functions.

As described in earlier chapters, a small community might be any type of residential place, from a quiet farm village to a self-contained condominium skyscraper set in an urban center. *Strengthening* refers to residents unifying and educating themselves to overcome political weakness and financial anxieties and to meet their social, civic, and economic responsibilities. *Revitalizing* refers to making a place livable, democratic, equitable, and tolerant and

thereby able to help its residents live with dignity and moral integrity.

American society, with its focus on liberty and free competition, makes it easy for the ambitious, clever, and sometimes amoral to dominate business and politics. Such dominance often opens the way to exploitation through downsizing, speeding up, wage cutting, false financial reporting, manipulating markets, drug trafficking, stealing, cheating, abusing and neglecting property, illegal dumping, and the like. Any of these practices directly or indirectly can produce community distress, as described in Chapters 2 and 4. The result in many communities can be a loss of confidence in business and government as well as pessimism about the future.

However, we know from the American experience outlined in Chapter 2 that political freedom also makes possible successful change efforts organized out of the homes, churches, and storefront offices of community residents and their allies. Potentially oppressive forces are always with us, but increasingly they are matched by well-organized communal forces able to assert their own interests and protect and improve their small communities by helping themselves, reshaping institutions, and influencing the policies of local governments.

The systematic process for mobilizing and advocating by using communal power is called *community organizing* in this book. A substantial knowledge base for this process is available.

This chapter describes the process as applied to place communities and assesses useful activities open to those who would take the initiative to renew a distressed place community.

It is not a perfect process, even when accrued knowledge is mastered and carefully applied; there are situations without precedent, plans with flaws, and human errors and weaknesses that can impede success. Like starting a small business, building or rebuilding a community organization involves risk. It is always in part an act of faith and hope. The authors of this book have been involved in enough organizing efforts to have confidence that, over time, a small community is going to be far better off with organizing than without it.

DEFINITION OF
COMMUNITY ORGANIZING

Place-based community organizing is a process in which local people, united by concern for renewing their own small territory, plan and act together from an organizational base that they control. They are usually aided by a community organizer, either professional or volunteer, who has skill and experience and helps the body of people to plan and move toward achieving their agreed-on goals. It is a practice that involves collective human effort centered on mobilization, advocating, planning, and the negotiation of resources. Although such efforts in small communities across the nation follow a uniform pattern of convene → plan → procure → operate, each community, as it performs the drill, produces a unique homespun renewal organization differentially shaped by local social, political, and economic conditions. In this practice, mobilization includes the building and maintaining of an organizational base; planning includes fact gathering, assessment, and strategic and tactical thinking; and negotiation includes persistent pressure and bargaining for sufficient resources to achieve goals.

Resources required may include people, civic values, organizations, jobs, money, space, information, vehicles, skills, expertise, tools, real estate, art, and other things usable in community building. The process best proceeds with an open door, shared assessment of opportunities by those who choose to come through the door, and careful thinking about the future. In two words, it is *rational* and *inclusive*. Community organization is distinct from administration or management in that it is action largely executed in the wider social environment, beyond the boundaries of a single organization, with most of the decision making, advocating, and tactical work done by community people rather than by paid organizers, employees, or board members. Its principal mode is political rather than financial. Its function relevant to a small community is to improve a spatial, multi-organizational sub-world, which is a much more complex entity than any single organization or even any set, system, or network of organizations. A spatial sub-world might be a new suburb beset by racial fears or a tired mill town seeing its school system deteriorating. In an authentic community organization, policymaking and other work related to steering the course is controlled by indigenous people who are residents and volunteers.

THREE KEY INGREDIENTS

The following are the key ingredients that, in combination, set community organizing apart from enterprise and government: (a) influence and power based primarily on volunteer collective action that arises from melding and meshing talents and contributions of people and very much depends on their numbers and level of commitment; (b) decision making that is continually widened to include an increasingly representative body of participants, with its decisions reaching to matters that are public and significant; and (c) initiative, coordination, and facilitation by a special kind of multi-skilled person called a community organizer. Such a person is often experienced in finding recruits and raising money. This multi-skilled organizer is usually a paid professional but can be a volunteer.

As a process of change, community organizing continuously operates on two tracks. Track 1 is the path of pursuit of agreed-on program goals. Such pursuit is done through a variety of strategies and tactics that are considered in this chapter. Track 2 is the path of building, maintaining, and continually renewing an organizational base using methods that are alsodescribed here.

As pointed out in Chapter 3, there are local development organizations that come to focus on a single narrow goal such as affordable housing. Core leadership becomes so absorbed in the technical details of financing, contracting, marketing, and managing that resident involvement is lost, and a potentially powerful community building effort becomes just another single-interest service done by experts without the capacity for transforming the community. This book suggests a comprehensive alternative.

FUNDAMENTALS

As in the world of sports, fundamentals are important in community organizing. Football requires effective blocking and tackling. The qualities a baseball scout looks for in young talent are hitting and throwing a baseball and running. Soccer calls for speed and foot control of the ball. For community organizing, the fundamentals are interaction and extraction.

Interaction is persuasive communication that brings fed up and disgruntled people together for collective assessment of a community's strengths and weaknesses, for understanding the distress and oppression afflicting the community, for determining goals and strategizing on how to accomplish them, and for choosing tactics to achieve goals. It involves periodic reassessments that measure progress and help to guide group decisions for mid-course corrections.

Drawing in an array of participants, interaction energizes and educates them and facilitates their accepting productive roles in the collective effort. It is not comfortable work. Struggle and sacrifice are required, and risk taking is indispensable when building leadership. Progress is measured in the intensity of hope that is generated and in the depth of commitment made by participants.

Interaction, then, is the internal effort, that is, the leadership recruited transferred and melded together with sound working relationships

forming a firm organizational base aimed at community improvement, an effort run by residents and their allies. As with winning in sports, it requires team spirit and confidence for success as well as mutual respect among participants to maintain momentum.

Extraction is finding and obtaining the "fuel" for interaction and the collective change efforts that can flow from interacting. It often speaks in the voice of negotiation rather than persuasion, but always with a hint of the public good at stake. In essence, it is the separation of money, time, and other useful things from people, organizations, and institutions while leaving them satisfied, perhaps even pleased, about providing them. It is a constant procedure accompanying and enabling interaction, with great pools of resources available as targets, a fortuitous reality in the United States. (This is taken up in Chapter 11.)

The medium of extraction is continuous individualized communication with each target (continuous and gentle, yes; continuous and pushy, no). The community group of expanding strength finds many resource targets in its sights but pressures each one only intermittently. Besides the highly visible foundations and government agencies, a vital community group steadily works to obtain regular contributions from its own body of residents. Sharing the burden by residents begets feelings of ownership and loyalty and also fosters a sense of belonging.

Now we examine the dozen key activities that make up the art and science of community organizing.

THE 12 ACTIVITIES
OF COMMUNITY ORGANIZING

For the place community, there are a dozen activities that come into play when community organizing is undertaken by determined local persons able to interact with the neighbors, organizations, and local institutions whose participation is essential to renewal. These are the key activities that constitute the process of community organizing. All are interactional, but at least six can involve extraction as well.

Interactive

1. Creating and spreading a vision

2. Recruiting

3. Developing leadership

4. Forming and maintaining a cadre

5. Launching the organization

6. Researching and planning

Interactive-Extractive

7. Evaluating process and product

8. Staffing

9. Communicating

10. Implementing plans

11. Tapping resources

12. Building and strengthening interorganizational relations

Each of these 12 activities is described here. Examples of these activities as integral parts of the community organizing process can be found throughout the book.

1. Creating and Spreading a Vision

People seeking to change their community come to organizing with goals in mind. To attract helpers and partners, these goals need to be sold in the form of a vision, description, or picture of what the community could be.

The initiator of change might be an individual but is more likely to be a small group. It can be a householder who is tired of petty crime on her block and has persuaded two neighbors to help "do something about it." It might be a retired bus driver living in public housing who wants to create computer learning opportunities for his grandchildren and has enlisted young mothers who share his cause, or a family support agency staff helping single fathers to establish a center for self-employment. Possibly it is a student from a university doing an internship with an urban church that wants to help the people of its neighborhood find energetic would-be homeowners to take possession of several empty

houses for restoration. It could even be a suburban church discovering that a handful of stressed parents are at their wits' end in trying to reach and right their DUI-prone teenagers.

The vision is a mental picture of the transformed community as it might look if a community rebuilding effort succeeds. An example might be an image of future blocks of modest, well-maintained homes and shops populated by welcoming people, replacing today's litter, boarded-up buildings, and discouraged residents. Another example might be an image of a well-tended town, with tricycles on the lawns and energetic people, of all ages and skin colors, painting the home of a sick neighbor. Or, the mental picture could even be that of a street of quality shops, owned and operated by locals, hiring community people at living wages, replacing the current sprawl of "big box" stores operated by low-wage employees working for global owners.

A hopeful vision expresses expectation and confidence. The ability of initiators to create and communicate this vision is the striking activity vital to opening the eyes and winning the interest of contacts. Communicating a captivating vision is an essential skill for bringing people into an improvement effort. Organizers, either volunteer and otherwise, innovate endless ways in which to communicate their enthusiasm. They pull out dramatic drawings or photographs illustrative of their vision. They use relevant news clippings, videos, scale models, magazine articles, books, and case studies to suggest the "new looks" possible. They host articulate visitors to describe the vision they have realized and take contacts to visit a community that is making progress toward realization of a vision.

Initiators and the contacts they are working with invent mental pictures of hope for their families and neighborhood, evoking visual images of cooperating households, productive schools, responding institutions, respectful governments, supporting neighbors, and attractive streetscapes. Gathering together contacts, an organizer challenges them to build a collective vision by dreaming, analyzing, debating, writing on a blackboard, or sketching their own concepts and then gradually merging them. The stimulation of the interaction can produce surprises and fresh new pictures. It can also produce trust of a dynamic variety, a kind viewed as social capital that enlivens small communities and strengthens the bond among residents. (Social capital is examined in greater detail in Chapter 10.)

Perhaps starting with one element on a flip chart, all contacts add elements to a drawing until the group agrees that it is complete. Perhaps "BINGO!" will suddenly arise during a series of sessions of people facing a serious crime condition or the decline of their school system sunk in debt and discouragement. Finding a vision taking hold and raising the sights of others transforms struggle into progress. Denys Candy, an organizer and educator, suggested, "The organizer must orchestrate tangible experiences of the vision in microcosm" (personal communication, August 11, 1999).

A compelling vision inspires and moves contacts to intensify their attention and interest. Spreading a vision is the fruitful process of moving a handful of contacts from being prospects to becoming committed participants. As new people accept participation, their concerns and hopes can be incorporated into the vision, making it a living guiding beacon for the organization being created (or recreated).

2. Recruiting

This is the act of accepting the contact as a committed member who is ready to defend the vision. It means winning a commitment after an organizer's personal interaction over time has generated mutual trust and acceptance. It usually involves a specific invitation to the participant. Serious recruitment takes time, sincerity, respect, good listening, and patience as well as discrete care to ensure diversity of the membership. The organizer looks for a latent receptivity in each person being recruited and seeks to provide an "appropriate incentive" to motivate the person to accept an invitation offered. An appropriate incentive can be any legitimate outcome possible from the change effort that would both serve a need of the person recruited and advance an objective of the collective effort. For example, the person recruited might need a summer job for her teenage son and see this as a possible outcome of the organization's work. It

might be a case of a discouraged householder who believes that "joining up" will provide new hope or of a teen who wants to see a community basketball court built. In sum, recruiting is persistent contact, respectfully and personally done, with a legitimate incentive implied and a clear invitation to join tendered. It is prudent to keep in mind that recruitment is a never-ending process. It is truly relationship building. Productive organizations constantly need fresh blood to keep their efforts vital and to keep their membership representative of all legitimate interests and groups.

3. Developing Leadership

Chaskin, Brown, Venkatish, and Vidal (2001) pointed out that leaders are at the core of a community's capacity to organize. They facilitate and give direction, teach and motivate, initiate activities and opportunities, advocate for community interests, and catalyze the formation of groups to address crises and capitalize on opportunities (p. 27).

Leadership development focuses primarily on individuals. According to Chaskin et al. (2001), "It typically attempts to engage the participation and commitment of current and potential leaders, provide them with opportunities for building skills, connect them to new information and resources, enlarge their perspectives on their community and how it might change, and help them create new relationships" (p. 27).

When a recruit makes the decision to join the pursuit of the vision, it is of utmost importance that this person be embraced and recognized for his or her willingness to sacrifice and work for the cause. Experienced members should pay attention, welcome the new organizational colleague, and provide opportunities for learning about the goals sought and the nature of the organization being formed or renewed. Sometimes a few words may suffice: "Thanks for being here," "This session went well because of what you contributed," or "We'll start forming committees in a couple of weeks, so maybe you'd like to consider which ones interest you." At this level, the maintenance of a mix of colors, ages, incomes, education, and gender is of special importance. Opportunities to take on responsibilities and learn new skills should be freely offered to a newly committed member. The more the new member develops capacity, the stronger the organization becomes.

Risks are involved. Inexperienced members can foul up, but calculated risk taking can lead to a more productive member and perhaps a future leader. (Some new members grow continuously to become heads of organizations, others play specific in-and-out leadership roles as the occasion might demand, while still others remain content and productive in the ranks.) Active members of an organization can learn and grow from failure as well as from success. In general, the risks pay off. A fledgling member may stumble when assigned to give testimony at a public hearing, but by the second or third experience, he or she may prove to be quite impressive. In any case—whether impressive or not—the new member is likely to grow from the effort, and become more productive as a participant, so long as he or she is given support, encouragement, and a bit of gentle guidance. Growth and maturation of members is always a primary goal of organizers.

Early on, initiators and founding members can begin to transfer power and influence to promising recruits. Out of such sharing can come more rapid maturity of members as well as more diverse perspectives and ideas for building the organization. The developing organization will need increasing and varied skills and experience as it reaches different stages of growth. (We see how this need unfolds in the Aliquippa case discussed in Chapter 7.)

4. Forming and Maintaining a Cadre

As new members are welcomed and tested, some harden their commitment and move to the center of the effort, sometimes on their own momentum and sometimes by being pulled there by an organizer. Early on in a viable effort, several such dedicated people will coalesce at the core to become a cadre of adherents. *Cadre* is a classical term that fits well with organizing. It signifies a nucleus or core group, especially of trained personnel or active experienced members of an organization, who are capable of assuming responsible roles and of training and indoctrinating others. Friendship, mutual

support, and a sense of being equal partners will likely come to bind them together.

The cadre will facilitate, shape, and build the new (or renewed) entity as it becomes a permanent neighborhood force with structure and a platform of beliefs and goals. The newborn force will be strong if its cadre members are a diverse lot, representative of a wide spectrum of community interests who involve themselves in the organization's affairs on nearly a daily basis.

Regarding the core group and the organizer serving it, Candy advised, "The organizer's role is to facilitate relationships among the members of the core group" (personal communication, August 11, 1999). He described the core group as creating an "oasis" of mutual support, that is, an inclusive environment where dreams are built on and actions are taken. "Identity and aspirations are celebrated and reflected upon. Space is made for wounds to heal and disappointments to be expressed. Hearts and minds converge to intensify the intention and commitment essential for success." From this generous effort comes the continuity of the organization in both growing and pursuing the projects necessary to realize the central vision.

Like the organization itself, a healthy cadre will experience turnover, with new people flowing in and veterans bowing out from time to time. The enthusiasm, cohesion, and persistence of the cadre will be a principal determinant of the success of the organization. The cadre is the internal engine. Its health is vital to the organization remaining fresh and productive. The case study of the long-lived Hyde Park-Kenwood Community Conference; set out in Appendix 2.B in Chapter 2, confirms the role of the cadre in providing continuity to an organization. By its constant barrage of ideas and issues, the conference always had interesting and significant activities to attract and hold a sufficient number of activists so as to ensure an effective cadre.

Chaskin et al. (2001) suggested that cadre members with shared language and vision are better able to support each other, providing extra encouragement and help with strategy. They maintained that when diverse groups of community people agree on plans and projects, positive outcomes are more likely because of the "multiple points of leverage." On the other hand, they found that cadres typically require more commitment and more training, which can take extra time, energy, and money from those involved. However, Chaskin and his colleagues maintained that the additional gains are worth pursuing (pp. 43–44).

An essential activity for the cadre early on is selecting and holding to firm direction that moves the organization forward to realize its vision. Consensus on direction can avoid false starts, help stay the course, and conserve time—that most precious asset of committed people who bring a new organization to life. A sound direction is always one that reflects the organization's vision.

If the vision is full employment, then the direction is toward employer partnerships and workforce development. If the vision is safety, then it may be light-ups in residents' yards, more beat police, and neighbors learning to protect each other's kids and property. A solid sense of direction gives focus and cohesion, keeping the organization on a logical path. Identification of this course requires thoughtful teasing out to ensure that the direction is compatible with local community conditions, such as the level of employment, and the community's past experience with mobilizing for improvement. Identified and agreed to by the organizing cadre, direction guides a fledging organization until it gains confidence and pushes ahead with certainty.

As the organization reaches certainty, it realizes the need to lock in direction with a formal plan. In time, the persevering organization finds the time and money to create its plan with the expectation that the plan will provide week-to-week guidance and accelerated progress toward the expansion of the program and the achievement of goals. (The process for designing formal plans is set forth in Chapters 8 and 9.)

Direction generally pops into view about the time when two or more persons generate a vision for change in their community and set out to sell it to others while beginning to make it happen. Direction, if paid attention to, keeps on developing and furnishing focus until a formal strategic plan is in place. Then, direction recedes into the background, where it continues to remind the organization of its limits and to goad the organization to remain faithful to its historic purpose.

A great diversity of widely used directions have been developed and identified since community organizing began to flower after World War II. Some of these are described in the next few paragraphs.

Rothman's (1964) three models of intervention, identified during the 1960s, were "locality development," marked by bottom-up planning, resident participation, and neighborhood preservation; "social planning," marked by experts and national data-based problem solving, a top-down model; and "social action," marked by militant advocacy, social justice, and mass organizing. Only relatively recently did Rothman (1995) publish a long overdue reappraisal of his three approaches based on fresh empirical evidence of how community organizations behave in the real world. The result is his recognizing that many community organizations follow a hybrid direction, which combines the qualities of two or more ideal models.

Dreier (1996) called his typology "Community Empowerment Strategies," identifying three single-dimension alternative directions: "community organizing," which mobilizes large numbers of people around dramatic issues to seek change by political pressure; "community-based development," neighborhood-based effort to improve local economic conditions; and "community-based service provision," a social approach built around social services that build human capital.

Fisher (1984) set out what he called "three dominant approaches": "social work," built around consensus and human service centers; "political activism," built on confrontation and heavy power pressure; and "neighborhood maintenance," the conservative approach for homeowners, small business people, and leaders of institutions, with emphasis on consensus typical of a community development corporation (CDC).

Hanna and Robinson (1994) put emphasis on transformation of values and competency within leaders and active volunteers so that they move to a new depth of commitment and desire for change. Their typology consists of the following: "traditional politics," elitist and rational, with a heavy class line; "direct action mobilization," mass based and hard bargaining, with elite people in the leadership; and their own "transformative social change," which seeks to produce a courageous breed of indigenous community people. Its leadership envisions volunteers who become aware and knowledgeable of the societal forces that threaten families and communities. Prescribed are self-directed, nonhierarchical bonding and social action that liberates participants from the mind-set of dependency, freeing them to create small communities imbued with social justice.

The direction with the largest and most dedicated following appears to be that of the Industrial Areas Foundation, derived from organizing practices created by Saul Alinsky beginning back in the 1930s. Warren (2001) described it as engaging "faith traditions in an effort to construct a politics that addresses the concrete needs of families in low-income communities of color and of working Americans more broadly." Building housing, improving schools, and developing job training and other basic needs while strengthening "the frayed social fabric of neighborhood life . . . shrewd and tough political fighters lead the network's organizations with the explicit goal of building political power" (pp. 4–5). There is additional information about these directions in Appendix 5.C.

There are many other brands of direction that have their own training centers, focus their organizing on place communities, and generally follow a power organizing approach. A few of the best known ones are the following:

ACORN: The Association of Community Organizations for Reform Now, with its Institute for Social Justice in Little Rock, has a model of organizing that focuses on solid research and extensive outreach and that is based in place communities.

CCC: The Center for Community Change, in Washington, specializes in broad-based community organizing focused on empowering low-income communities and will provide field training anywhere in the United States where there are serious local sponsors.

CTWO: The Center for Third World Organizing, in Oakland, emphasizes innovative political skills and community and labor organizing for activists of color and also engages in "identity politics."

CTAC: The Community Training and Assistance Center, based in Boston, teaches leadership skills for staff and volunteers of new and established community-based organizations working to renew low-income neighborhoods.

COI: The Consensus Organizing Institute is an organization that turns its back on conflict organizing and the Alinsky tradition. COI brings together, trains, and unites talented indigenous people from distressed communities and links them with concerned regional institutional leaders from business, government, and foundations for joint efforts of neighborhood renewal. COI claims to be different in its positive partnership direction, which promotes cooperation of funders and other regional leaders with neighborhood leaders. In 2002, COI was concentrating its work in the San Diego area, with a focus on workforce development among youth. (See also Appendix 3.)

The Gamaliel Foundation: This organization offers training for neighborhood faith-based groups in a full range of organizing techniques, including co-partnerships between and among organizations. It conducts training at its center in Chicago and as an outreach arrangement anywhere in the United States or beyond.

Midwest Academy: This organization, also based in Chicago, offers activist training that emphasizes basics, including organizing the unorganized, building coalitions, and political context.

NTIC: The National Training and Information Center, sponsored by National People's Action in Chicago, sponsors training on information and research, leadership development, negotiation, strategic planning, and actions.

Highlander Research and Education Center: This organization, in New Market, Tennessee, conducts popular education-focused training and retreats on a tailor-made basis with community groups, especially groups in the Appalachia and the southeastern United States.

OTC: The Organize Training Center, in San Francisco, conducts training for specific projects, including groups from evangelical churches and Bay Area labor unions.

5. Launching the Organization

The cadre gives guidance and support to the members as they participate in choosing structure and strategy and in establishing the organization as a competent and respected entity. For long-term growth and vitality, these decisions are best achieved through an open process with maximum involvement of interested community people. Launching is a process to be done with care, making certain that the emerging organization reflects the varied groups and interests of its community or at least seriously offering them every opportunity to be involved and keeping the opportunity open in perpetuity. This policy and practice of inclusion provides the potential for great staying power, provided the leadership is alert to working out differences among the diverse interests as disagreements arise within the organization. In this sense, a place-based organization is a microcosm of the nation, which overall grows more diverse every year. Wide participation helps an organization to create policies and programs that embody the authentic history, values, and ethnic and economic makeup of the community's population. Inclusion keeps an organization in tune with the community's patterns of association and aware of major strengths and specific distress factors.

No two-community development organizations will be exactly the same because no two local places have exactly the same population mix or environmental conditions. For instance, if the tradition for voluntary organizations in a community is tight decision making and business-like professional implementation, then the structure of the new entity is likely to be designed with a compact board, a paid staff, and a small set of committees carefully selected for their experience and ability to get things done. A community where democratic values have high priority may choose a larger board and numerous committees and be slower to implement but may involve many more people. In either case, it would be important that the structure eventually encompass representation of all population groups in the community (by location, race, income level, gender, religion, occupation, age, etc.). Small details, such as time of board and committee meetings, can be vital as well. Are the meetings set at times of the day when most people are able to attend? During this era of two-job families, Saturday or Sunday afternoons are sometimes best, or perhaps evening meetings that begin at 7:00 and end before 8:30.

A further example involves study of the existing network of organizations in the local community. If there is already a healthy array of nonprofit service and improvement groups, then they might be pulled together into a coalition structure that would undertake to achieve the cadre's mission. Or if the community is barren of existing groups, then a brand new organization with fresh leadership and a body of individual members may be called for.

Coalitions provide instant power but sometimes have difficulty in making decisions and moving quickly because each organization enrolled has its own priorities. Beth Rosenthal and Terry Mizrahi, out of Hunter College's Education Center for Community Organizing, have done extensive studies of coalitions. They defined coalitions as "organizations of independent organizations which engage in collective activity to accomplish specific projects or to influence external institutions while maintaining their own autonomy" (Rosenthal & Mizrahi, 1994, p. 1). They confirmed that coalitions are most useful when there is a proliferation of organizations operating in a field or organizing on the same issue. A new structure of individual members is most useful when there is no effective organization available whose interests match the cadre's interests.

Whether the structure is built from a membership of individuals, a coalition of organizations, or a melding of the two, it will need some kind of web of sub-units (e.g., task forces, action teams, committees)—a few in the beginning and more as it grows. Through these "cells" for investigation, deliberation, recommendation, and action, a role can be provided for every community member willing to contribute time and talent. Such sub-units make possible ongoing inclusion as the effort proceeds. They will vary in size, importance, and longevity, depending on their duties and responsibilities and on the mission of the organization. Some will focus on programs for achieving goals, while others will focus on maintaining and building the organizational base. For instance, a job creation task force may focus on self-employment and capital formation (goals), while a membership committee seeks recruits to make sure that all task forces and committees have full membership bases. Both types of sub-units should be conscious of the two tracks and act in ways to mutually reinforce each other, ensuring strength of both the "goal" track and the "base" track.

6. Researching and Planning

An organization whose leaders and members are in agreement on mission, goals, and vision, and who have constructed a structure and decision system compatible with their community, can keep moving ahead by having an ongoing process of researching and planning.

This means forming a standing committee on planning to gather and assess information related to community conditions and goals, recommend priority projects, lay out plans, and suggest time schedules. Such planning is a reality-based way in which to move the organization ahead. Creative and open research and planning take time and energy, but they produce visible progress and help to maintain community interest, involvement, and support from members and outsiders.

A veteran neighborhood researcher who has won acceptance and trust from grassroots people is Hide Yamatani of the University of Pittsburgh's School of Social Work. For more than 30 years, he has worked for and with people in small communities, often located in predominately African American sections of battered industrial towns as well as within urban neighborhoods. Early on, Yamatani discovered that findings are most revealing, accurate, and useful when a representative community committee is a full partner in commissioning the research and in choosing the specific issues and problems for investigation (personal interview, March 12, 2001). To ensure the representativeness of a community committee, he recommended asking its start-off members to identify missing constituencies and to find authentic representatives willing to make a firm commitment to serve on the committee.

Yamatani has found that a high degree of mutual trust is generated when findings are reviewed and approved jointly by the investigator and the grassroots committee. Such a process, he has found, ensures that the research is done within an adequate and accurate base of contextual knowledge, where researchers truly come to understand the territory. An organization with habits of careful research and reflective planning wins credibility. Credibility is the foundation for organizational longevity and goal achievement.

Two subsequent chapters (Chapters 8 and 9) deal further with the techniques for using research and planning to make an organization productive and influential. It is prudent for a new organization learning how to use research and planning to consult other, more experienced community organizations in its region so as to learn what they have done and how they have done it.

The operating formula for planning is that it be research based; driven by vision, mission, and goals; and open to participation by the whole community.

7. Evaluating Process and Product

The best organized collective of people will make mistakes and miss opportunities, but a habit of evaluation can minimize such missteps and cut the losses. Most evaluation is done internally (i.e., in-house) and is effective so long as it is honest and its purpose is improvement rather than punishment. Every policy, program, and major action, as well as the organizational structure and its functioning, should regularly get an effectiveness exam. Is it being carried out as planned? What works? What does not work? How can it be improved? Who is going to make the improvement? When will the improvement be made?

Evaluation can be a regular item on board and committee agendas. It can be a priority item at annual meetings. It merits the attention of the group's cadre and other top leadership all year long. Candy emphasized that the core group members should hold themselves and the board with which they usually overlap accountable for implementation steps while ensuring that there are processes in place for ongoing learning from each step (personal communication, August 11, 1999). They need to ask themselves, "How can our future actions reflect things we've learned from past and present actions?"

Any serious in-depth evaluation needs a "foreign" ingredient to add objectivity. It might merely be the opinion of a knowledgeable outsider thrown in the evaluation pot with many inside opinions. Or it might be that outsiders are hired to perform the evaluation. However, experienced insiders who have demonstrated their good judgment and fairness, and who are sophisticated enough to know that an honest assessment always helps more than it hurts, increasingly are able to perform trustworthy evaluations.

At times, in the life of a veteran organization, fundamental reassessments have to be made around the following questions. Is the organization's structure still compatible with its vision, mission, goals, and values? Is enough new blood being brought in every year to keep the organization vital and growing? Such assessments are best made as part of a fresh, open planning effort undertaken to update both program and organizational base, as recommended in Chapter 8. Such a reassessment can produce revival of both spirits and aims. The general rule of evaluation is always as follows: *Seek not to embarrass but rather to strengthen.*

8. Staffing

No matter how productive and celebrated an all-volunteer community development organization becomes, it can reach the point where the original cadre of enthusiasts is fading away at the same time that work and opportunities continue to pile up. Then, continuity and growth may be maintained only by hiring paid staff, with the organization making the leap to a larger annual operating budget. It is normal for an active mature organization to have a small staff whose members can ensure the organization's continuity every day, but to the extent possible, an organization will want to keep its important decision making in the hands of volunteer leaders and active members, with periodic inclusive open meetings. In small communities especially, staff members should be facilitators rather than out-front leaders.

There are many qualities to be looked for when choosing a director (or a lead organizer, as a top staff person is sometimes seen). Probably the most important qualities are the following:

Commitment: This person must have firmly held beliefs in the dignity of all people, the necessity of participation, the importance of the small geographic community to human growth and development, the ability to work long hours productively and enthusiastically, and a genuine interest and belief in the mission and goals of the organization.

Compatibility: This should be a warm, likable, and genuine person who is able to get along well with people of all races, income levels, sexes, and the like, yet is a tough internal advocate and supporter for the goals of the organization. (In best practice, external public advocacy and bargaining are done largely by volunteers with staff backup.)

Communication and fund-raising talents: Community organizers must be able to tap the public, the masses, the rich and the poor, and the decision makers of government, business, and media. The lead organizer must know how to train volunteer leaders to mobilize material resources as well as people. This requires skills in communicating and recruiting as well as the ability to find, inspire, and train those residents who already have such skills or the potential for developing them, including bargaining and negotiation skills with institutions.

Cultural competence: The organizer should be willing to become knowledgeable and respectful of the special cultural traits and needs of the different racial and ethnic groups in the community and should demonstrate a patient willingness to help the organization's volunteers share the knowledge and sense of respect.

It is of utmost importance that a staff be diverse—particularly as to race and gender, even when the community it represents is all of one race—if it is to help the organization flourish and have credibility within a diverse society that has massive numbers of active women and people of color, with these numbers growing every year. Every community development group, no matter how geographically insular and set apart, must tap resources in a larger world that will judge it on its respect for people and contributions to the common good of society.

9. Communicating

A key need of every collective body, whether new or old, is to keep members of the body informed and to provide channels for feedback. Two-way shared information flows help people to work intelligently and cooperatively and give them a sense of being recognized. The most common break in information flow is from the volunteer or worker back to a committee chair, officer, or other project leader informing the leader that an assignment has been completed or that a barrier has arisen. Perhaps the message is not sent or is sent and fails to arrive. Such foul-ups weaken the organization.

People are not being left out when they are receiving active signals of response. Information flows breed respect. People who feel respected help to make firm the fabric of an organization. In the 21st-century world of sophisticated Internet communications, the World Wide Web, satellite relays, and cable TV, powerful means are available for keeping in touch with neighbors. There is work to be done to ensure that all community households become wired in.

Organizations use many methods for internal communication, including regular newsletters, periodic mailings, widely distributed meeting minutes, large meetings, e-mail, follow-up phone calls from cadre members, posters on the headquarters bulletin board, 5-minute "update" reports on the doings of the organization at every event, and even in-home kitchen gatherings where appropriate. Of course, the most effective communication is always personal, face-to-face conversation. It is interactive, provides the opportunity for clarifying questions and uncertainties that may be bothering participants, and leads to a sense of comradery. Nothing builds an organization faster or more strongly than do active "partnerships" among members, especially when they are carrying out what they know to be important phases of the organization's work.

If two veteran members are going to the county courthouse to check voting statistics for their community, then they might inform two or three new members of the purpose and work involved and extend an invitation to join in. Even if none can make it, the new members will feel closer to the organization for having been invited.

Every organization needs an open communication loop for passing information related to strategy, planning, implementation, modifications, and evaluation. It also needs to draw on outside information and opinions so that its decisions are not narrow, exclusive, and vulnerable to rejection by community people who do not understand why the decisions were made.

At some point early in the life of a forming or reforming body, outside awareness and public support must be sought. More complicated challenges then come into play. Getting out an accurate message that will be listened to takes planning and careful implementation. Sometimes, media must be used to ensure that the message reaches the broad audience.

For democracy to work, people need information. Most media organizations and their staffs take this responsibility seriously and are open to receiving and considering information and opinions coming from community groups. Accurate significant information, submitted in a timely way, will generally get the message out and over time help to win confidence and influence for an organization. Bobo, Kendall, and Max (1996), in their helpful manual, recommended that there be a plan for using the media, urging, "Approach the job of getting media coverage like any other aspect of organizing" (p. 116). They strongly supported the important practice of organizations putting their active volunteer leaders forward in speaking to the media rather than having staff alone reap this experience. Volunteers learn faster when they face challenging, real-life trials.

A special area of growing importance is cross-cultural communications. Green (1999) warned that cross-cultural communications are difficult to master, with blunders occurring frequently. He suggested an "ethnographic" approach that puts emphasis on indigenous community people as guides and teachers, while the organizer frequently participates as a very active listener and a respectful learner. Green also suggested that "minority professionals have special insights into the communities that they serve. In addition, they are usually sensitive to the way social service organizations affect persons of minority background generally" (p. 184). Green emphasized that using cultural guides is an "example of efficiency" (p. 138) and that, for an organizer to be able to undertake constructive intervention, he or she must be able to recognize and respect the life experience and street wisdom of residents and those they may be able to enlist as supporters.

Green (1999) reported that the organizers who generally work well with community residents ethnically distinct from themselves depend heavily on informed and informative "cultural guides." From his field research, he has learned the following: "Guides can be found anywhere, in any community, and they may or may not be community leaders. More often, they are ordinary people who can articulate well what is going on around them" (p. 93).

Green (1999) sought to make the best of the reality that many white organizers are thrown unprepared into cross-cultural situations and must learn to swim upstream. No matter how competent their training, they seldom can be as effective as the minority organizer working on home ground. Rivera and Erlich (1998) stated bluntly, "There is no stronger identification with a community than truly being a part of it. The most successful organizers are those activists who can identify culturally, racially, and linguistically with their communities" (p. 13).

In summary, there are two levels of communication to consider. The first is keeping back-and-forth flows of information and ideas moving within the organization, ensuring that cadre participants and all members are knowledgeable about what is happening and why. The second is maintaining a stream of significant messages to the community and the wider world beyond. A permanent communication sub-unit can assume responsibility for this. To do its job, such a committee monitors information flows to make sure that they are accurate, adequate, and being received. This requires the committee to have access to everything going on in the neighborhood organization and in fact be part of its policymaking process. The committee will make sure that the organization is responding to questions and suggestions that are coming to it and is not missing promising opportunities.

This includes requests for information from media people who are in position to place the organization's purposes and projects on the public agenda. Funders use media attention as a criterion to judge which organizations have programs that are relevant and effective. If an organization wants 1,000 people at a mass meeting or desires to change the minds of the members of a zoning board, then it will often need media channels. There are a host of useful methods for dealing with media, all of which require skill, technology, and risk taking. For instance, inviting television and press photographers to events can often pay off. Newspapers and television stations are hungry for photo opportunities other than talking heads. Two excellent books on organizing that contain useful material on working with the media are *Organizing for Social Change* (Bobo et al., 1996) and *Organizing: A Guide for Grassroots Leaders* (Kahn, 1991).

10. Implementing Plans

This is the art of getting things done. A confident organization (the only kind to have) pushes ahead to implement a proposal of its planning committee as soon as it makes its way safely through the organization's approval machinery. Strong support within a broad participation process greatly increases the proposal's chances for success. Under such circumstances, the volunteers, money, and other resources needed to carry out a proposal will emerge. (Detailed ideas for an effective participation process can be found in Chapters 6 through 11.)

Beginning a complex project sometimes calls for testing. This means quick action probes to test reactions. For example, a project plan aimed at using citizen patrols to advance the community's sense of safety might need a week of trial runs to test both police relationships and the ability of volunteers to follow a disciplined time schedule.

A broad plan for raising racial awareness might call for pilot interracial gatherings in members' homes. Such meetings could help to discover adjustments necessary to ensure that this tactic has the power to change people's viewpoints and behavior rather than stir their emotions. The organization might want to have a small team of members who act as evaluators for such tests, making the assessment more independent than one carried out by members of the same committee that formulated the plan. Such evaluation would aim at corrections and improvements early on rather than a sweeping judgment on the overall quality of the plan.

11. Tapping Resources

Just as the organization needs steady flows of new recruits, it also requires a steady flow of funds to maintain and grow its base operation as well as separate funds for each of its goal-oriented projects, programs, and actions. This calls for a permanent fund-raising sub-unit or committee that will support those sub-units generating plans that require funding. Producing a steady flow is a test for the organization's capacity to have an impact. What goes on here is the selling of a vision to funders, who might be from governmental, corporate, institutional, or philanthropic segments of the region or beyond, as well as to residents and small businesses from the local community or even to the general public on a broad basis. Local contributions may be modest, but people have a large self-interest in contributing what they can.

Like recruitment of people, recruitment of money requires communication, personal contact, and incentive. Whenever possible, potential outside funders and local contributors alike should be provided with an attractive reason for donating their cash beyond making an investment in the community's future. Such a reason might be the possibility of a sensational breakthrough on a pet issue of the funders, a potential dramatic improvement to the environment where the funders' headquarters is located, an innovative way in which to celebrate a foundation's founder, or showing funders that a modest investment now will likely forestall much larger requests later. There can be various payoffs from keeping the funders' interests in mind.

Ongoing financial support from members of the organization requires special care and communication. Si Kahn, who has spent more than 25 years practicing civil rights, labor and community organizing in the South, strongly urged an organization to send regular reports to all of its members on financial matters (Kahn, 1991). He warned that if the membership does not understand what is happening with the "money," then the result can be a loss of trust in the organization. "If you have a newsletter, provide a monthly report of money coming in and going out. Put together an annual summary that people can understand. Remember that even the most simple financial report can be difficult to comprehend" (pp. 229–230).

The ability of an organization to obtain steady ongoing funding is a concrete demonstration of its vitality and progress. The demonstration is twice as impressive if a respectable portion is raised from the community itself. Grassroots financial support lends credibility and legitimacy. To funders and public alike, it is a sign that the organization has an authentic base and is making headway to achieve its goals. Interested outsiders gain confidence in an organization that shows it can raise grassroots money. It also allows a group to maintain (at least some) control of its agenda because it can dictate where money can be spent or allocated. Outside funds inevitably are tied to specific uses or come with restrictions.

Some of the essential elements of successful fund-raising, beyond maintaining a competent organization with important goals, are friendly face-to-face visits with funders led personally by the organization's top leaders and periodic mobilization of visible support from a widespread and diverse public, with the success confirmed by media attention and impressive turnouts at the organization's events.

A strong organization will seek financial support that is diverse and renewable, with at least a portion of it being nonrestricted as to usage and much of it drawn from the grassroots. (More on tapping resources can be found in Chapter 11.)

12. Building and Strengthening Interorganizational Relations

As a new organization emerges, it may encounter other organizations within its community whose purposes and goals overlap its own. This presents an emerging group with both an opportunity and a barrier. Can cooperation of value to each be worked out so that the wall of separation disappears? Or does the barrier have to be confronted and overpowered? In today's climate of consensus and collaboration, funders smile on cooperation, and partnerships and joint effort can be productive when two or more groups find their interests converge and can cooperate without any group being exploited. But if a local association of old-time residents shoves aside the invitation of a new group, declaring its members to be "upstarts" with "no credibility," then the "upstarts" may have to show their unity, determination, and ability to achieve. Sometimes, calling on a friendly third party to mediate (from either inside or outside the community) can help.

Candy, from his diverse experience with collaboration and coalitions, advised that any cooperation with other organizations should be done with an agreed-on "specific unifying purpose" and "clear set of expectations and tasks" along with spelled out accountability mechanisms. Regarding the exploitation problem, Candy believes that "inequality of power and resources [does] not preclude partnerships as long as the partners are clear about what they are doing" (personal communication, August 11, 1999) and, we would add, so long as the weaker group (in members and/or money) is given respect and treated fairly in joint matters.

Sometimes, the most prudent course is for a cadre that is building a new organization to anticipate competition and conflict and to lay the groundwork for avoiding it or at least reducing the intensity of confrontations to come. This might be done by participation broad enough to give the emerging group authenticity and show that it is open and generous as well as already rooted in the community. Additional insurance can come from a communication campaign early on to educate the local public as to the purposes and significance of the organizing effort and to help curious organizations feel informed and welcome rather than excluded.

An alternative approach to a long-term partnership is the ad hoc, short-term "deal" when two or more groups can cooperate together on a specific matter for a limited time. Collaboration does not always require permanent ties. New organizations may find it best to shy away from entangling alliances until they are strong, knowledgeable, and certain of the benefits to come from a long-term commitment to a partnership or coalition. For example, Marciniak (1981) reported that small Chicago neighborhoods sometimes meld together with the larger "community" of which they are a subsection to gain a stronger voice on some crucial issues

affecting all of them (pp. 51–52). In the future, community forces will require larger and more cohesive alliances at every level up to national and global ones so as to protect and advance people's interests at the level of neighborhood.

THE MONDROS AND WILSON STUDY OF ORGANIZERS

Back in 1984, Mondros and Wilson (1994) began a 10-year study of community organizers employed in 42 organizations in a variety of cities. From their observations, they identified "vision changing," "technical tasks," and "expressive tasks" as the principal activities being engaged in by community organizers. In making their observations, they confirmed the two-track nature of community organizing as organization building and goal seeking.

Mondros and Wilson (1994) saw vision changing as a process in which the organizer helps community people to develop a compelling collective view of what their community could look like in the future, with the view built on positive and honest values.

Technical skills that appear important are the ability to analyze goal-related issues and power relationships and the ability to maintain and strengthen the organizational base while acting on the analysis. Mondros and Wilson's (1994) analysis gave direction to action and provided an estimate of the organizational consequences of dealing with an issue. Such direction derives from understanding of the local political and economic environments. Finally, there is a need for evaluation of the contribution that an issue can make to the organizational base, along with assessment of the impact of the issue on goal achievement.

Expressive skills relate to competencies in group process, including empathy, intervention timing, and the ability to win trust, communicate hope, and help people turn their concerns into public issues that can be acted on, according to Mondros and Wilson (1994).

The successful organizer sheds the image of expert to create personal bonds with members. Mondros and Wilson (1994), after their 10 years of observation, concluded that the able organizer brings facts to analysis and lifts people's sights. The organizer must appreciate members but not be limited by them. The organizer takes the lead in doing the necessary difficult job that nobody else wants to tackle. (Once members and volunteers see that the job can be done and have information on how to do it, the foresighted organizer will leave it to them, even when the risk is high.)

The reader can see that the job is tough even for the dedicated, full-time, paid organizer and perhaps will wonder how a volunteer can serve as organizer for an active organization that faces difficult issues of distress. The answer is that it can be done when there is (a) a large time commitment by the volunteer, (b) a strong cadre that can be leaned on, and (c) the possibility of successful extraction of resources. Whether paid or volunteer, the modern community organizer has to be a shock absorber. Endemic to the job is "suffering" as well as satisfaction and occasional exuberance.

change in a society with a sizable new class of billionaires. This new century could be a stormy era where community building will thrive. Detailed ideas for organizing participation can be found in Chapters 6 through 11.

We have sought in this chapter to describe contemporary community organizing. Once more, it has been defined as mobilization of self-directed community forces aided and facilitated by skilled organizers, both volunteer and professional, to generate the power and plans needed to protect, improve, and vitalize local communities.

For the reader wanting to learn more about the details of community organizing, we have cited works by Bobo et al. (1996), Kahn (1991), Chaskin et al. (2001), and Hanna and Robinson (1994). We would add to these books by Rubin and Rubin (2001) and Staples (1984). All six works are quality overall guides to competent community organizing.

SUMMARY

In general, the early 21st century is being recognized as a time of caution and conservative outlook for new initiatives. But bold voices and tactics are still present, as we learned from the World Trade Organization protests in Seattle in 1999 and from other major street demonstrations that have followed. In small communities, especially those under distress, community organizations with a human services emphasis have been the most numerous. But advocacy remains a basic function of organizing and even disruptive advocacy remains a live and useful alternative and at times is an absolute necessity for getting attention for justice.

In our time, evolution versus revolution takes on great salience as economic bifurcation divides our society, sense of civic duty wavers, all-white outer-suburban communities grow and spread, and the national government responsible for equity continues to be preoccupied with security and hesitant in the face of resurgent budget deficits. The loss of job certainty at all levels of the middle class brings new millions down to the worry level of the working poor and creates growing numbers of Americans with good reason for pursuing drastic community

CONTINUING QUESTIONS

1. What makes a community organization more powerful and efficient—democratic participation or strong administration from the top by experienced experts?

2. Over time, is cooperation or conflict more effective in getting business and government targets to cooperate? Which best achieves a parity of power?

3. Does advocacy and action or compassionate service best serve to reduce distress and to reinvigorate social fabric in suffering communities?

4. What is the best way for an organization to ensure that its cadre remain fresh and vigorous and open to new members?

5. How do distressed small communities achieve diverse effective leadership through the community organizing process?

6. Can the growing numbers of community organizations be fused together in regional and national coalitions to achieve points of influence with state and national public policymaking?

7. What new funding methods and sources can give stability to community organizing and the profession of paid organizers it is generating?

8. Can community people play a larger role in providing and soliciting funding?

9. Can a balance between process and product help to maximize success? What would such a balance be?

Appendix 5.A
Three Organizers at Work

In a sound old suburb, where empty storefronts on the main shopping street and proliferating home burglaries are beginning to worry residents, a concerned homeowner, Carlosa Perez, recently retired, takes the initiative to investigate these signs of decline. After gathering what information she can from shopkeepers, the police, and large property owners, she knocks on doors and discusses her findings with a few neighbors. During a 6-week effort, she identifies three residents who share her concern sufficiently to agree to join her in calling together a church basement meeting. A total of 25 residents gather to hear police reports, and to mull over changing shopping patterns, as described by two local real estate brokers, who project color slides of deserted structures.

A half dozen participants volunteer to join Perez and her three helpers to survey the plans of local businesses and to compare the crime statistics for their community with those from surrounding communities over a 10-year period. The hat is passed for money to pay for mailing to all present a copy of the information to be gathered, and $46 is collected. With the results of their information gathering, Perez and her information cadre seek advice from the State Crime Commission and the County Planning Board as they plot their next move for dealing with the threats to their cherished suburban place. They agree to mail out their information to all who have expressed an interest and hold a report meeting. At the same time, they are asking themselves the question: Is this a one-shot operation, or do we have to form an ongoing organization? How do we involve the whole community in all of this? Where do we get the money to do all of this?

They take these questions to a second, somewhat larger public gathering, where they lay out the results of their survey. Local business people do suffer from an increase in break-ins and shoplifting, with a few considering a move from Main Street to a mall. Homeowner complaints to the police have jumped in regard to both thefts and vandalism. Several in the audience voice fears and propose a variety of actions and approaches that might be taken. Police officers announce that they would willingly cooperate with a campaign of neighbors to help each other protect property. Perez, as chair, encourages all to speak out, while a second volunteer takes notes of what is said.

At the end, several residents volunteer to be part of an expanded leadership group with Perez and her original team, two business owners, and a police officer. The charge to this group is as follows: Survey a wider public, find out what other suburbs are doing, and come back in 60 days with a list of suggested actions. The hat brings in another $76, part of it to be donated to the church where the meetings have been held. An amendment from the floor adds the task of checking where future funds might be found, including an appeal to all residents (how do they take the money of neighbors with flair and good feeling?). Perez makes sure that, before the evening ends, the leadership group's first work session is scheduled with the time and place announced and in a spirit of "this effort is open to all who want to come."

Our experience is that every small community has its Carlosa Perez—sometimes several of them. Such individuals may surface on their own, as in this case, but more often some alerted person, association, or bureau inside or outside the community seeks them out during a time of community crisis and inspires them to get moving.

Carl Redwood is a paid community organizer who assists, teaches, and develops people in an urban neighborhood. Incomes are modest, poverty is a common condition, and many families juggle a love/hate relationship with food pantries, shelters, hospital emergency rooms, and public housing managers.

Redwood tells his resident partners that he is "helping them become community rebuilders" as he assists them in learning tactics for pushing drug sellers off street corner "free trade zones," pressuring advertising agencies to pull down their thicket of tobacco and alcohol billboards, insisting that the mayor consult residents before choosing a new subway route through their community, and ensuring that every resident, no matter how young or old, gets a chance to master the Internet, Web sites, information searches, and other high-technology tools of survival. His top goal is a leadership corps of able people interconnected and spread across the community. (See the accompanying sidebar description of Redwood's model technology network for wiring a small community.)

Model of a Technology Network for a Small Community

Drawing on the skills and experience of Nova Scotia's "Chebuto Freenet," Carl Redwood and community worker colleagues in Pittsburgh's Hill District neighborhood enlisted and facilitated residents and organizations in building the Hill House Community Access Network (HILLCAN) to unify and serve the students, parents, residents, organizations, and businesses.

HILLCAN is a prime social fabric building resource for the Hill. Foremost in the achievements of HILLCAN and its principal sponsor, Hill House Association, has been winning the cooperation of neighborhood groups in establishing three main community access sites and building relationships with other organizations to ensure that all Hill residents are within 10 minutes of a site that provides computer time and access to the Internet and several data networks.

Users are recruited to become members of HILLCAN and are asked to pay a $35 membership fee (if they are able) toward the expenses of the operation. Members have access to electronic mailboxes from which they can send and receive e-mail and also build their own individual Web sites.

Training is provided at each site and at a central lab maintained at Hill House, headed by Chrisholle Thomas-Eugene. As a full time staff member, she recruits and trains volunteers who give time as user assistants at the six sites. All ages of residents, from 6 to 86 years, participate as users, with more than 800 of them being dues-paying members. Neighborhood site locations include the Hill branch library, the Martin Luther King, Jr. Community Reading Center, the New Beginnings Learning Center, the Grace Memorial Presbyterian Church, the Youth Fair Chance Community Center, and Hill House, a one-stop social service shop with several agencies centered in one building.

HILLCAN seeks to accomplish the following:

- Help meet the personal and professional information needs of people
- Foster communication among individuals and the institutions that serve them
- Support community groups in their efforts at professional development, outreach, and community service
- Teach residents to use new software and new online techniques
- Enhance opportunities for sustainable community-based economic development
- Create a favorable environment for business and employment growth through simulating a workplace environment with sites preparing job seekers for high-technology jobs
- Facilitate distribution of the minutes of local organizations and their committees
- Serve as a working model to be replicated in other communities.

Aware of the potency of coalitions, Hill participants have been cooperating with groups in the region to foster and support the creation and linking of community access networks. This multi-organizational effort has been pushing to unlock free cable modems and Internet access for 100 neighborhoods and has been backing an "extendable institutional network (I-Net) to 140 school district, library, and museum buildings, with capability to extend to nearby community sites," according to Redwood. He explained, "We are trying to get the neighborhoods wired before the big AT&T monopoly freezes us out" (personal interview, May 24, 2002). Ed Jackson is a recent addition to HILLCAN as the technology coordinator and speaks proudly that HILLCAN now possesses one of only three wireless Internet sources in the city of Pittsburgh. Because of Hill House's advanced technological systems, it has abilities for interactive videoconferencing, video streaming, and advanced programming. Convinced that the new communications technologies can make community groups more efficient, effective, and influential, Redwood emphasized,

Applications to aid job searches, and the distribution of health services [include] remote medical monitoring and imaging for local clinics and providing the poor [with] less expensive photocopying, postage, overnight services, and long-distance message service. Neighborhoods will be better able to get out the word on their development opportunities. And a well-planned system can include plenty of bandwidth for future expansion needs so Pittsburgh's neighborhoods don't lag behind in the future. (personal interview, May 28, 2002)

Redwood added that there is one big weakness that must be overcome: "We've got to find carrots and sticks to entice legislators and other power holders to pay more attention to e-mail. Too many ignore e-mail as it becomes the low-cost voice of ordinary people, sent out from their homes, workplaces, and neighborhood access sites" (personal interview, May 28, 2002). Evidently, some naive policymakers fail to distinguish between junk e-mail and constituent e-mail.

For several years, Redwood has helped local churches, social service centers, block clubs, schools, a college, a CDC, recreation groups, child welfare and child care agencies, recovery programs, computer learning storefronts, businesses, health care providers, and other collective bodies with a physical presence in the neighborhood to cement together a "Neighborhood Consensus Group." Redwood foresees the consensus group as the heart of an inclusive system through which, in time, residents and their allies will control key community decisions and generate the power to ensure adequate resources from government, businesses, hospitals, universities, and other outside institutions. But he acknowledges that this will be many years into the new century. He understands that progress amid widespread poverty and unemployment comes only after patient, long-term struggle.

One of a few hundred spread across the nation, Redwood is a prototype of today's realistic, competent, committed, place-based community organizer, carrying on an old and honorable occupation: backing up people of a local community toward their learning how to take collective action to pursue objectives that residents themselves identify as essential to the renewal and future well-being of their neighborhood.

The third organizer used historic preservation to help move her small community forward. Shelia Gordon Mendicino is a baby boomer who puts her convictions to work in carefully planned persistent actions that follow the precepts of community organization: Make a plan based on facts, recruit able partners, execute vigorously, and evaluate at every step. After graduation from Indiana University of

Pennsylvania in 1975, she settled in Vandergrift, where she has come to cherish the curving tree-lined streets, the well-built homes, and the distinguished town center planned by the staff of the Boston studio of Frederick Law Olmstead, America's leading planner-landscape architect of the late 19th century, under commission to George McMurtry and his Apollo iron and steel company.

Mendicino recruited among other baby boomers, particularly with fellow parishioners at St. Gertrude Catholic Church, which still occupies the town location designated for it on Olmstead's maps. They talked about the thousands of steel and foundry jobs that were no more, about the closed Apollo mill (long part of the U.S. steel empire), about fading tax revenues, and about empty buildings on the main street. One by one, Mendicino enlisted partners for a study of the town's needs. The carefully done study gathered views from a sample of householders and community leaders.

The results were published and presented at a large community meeting on a snowy night. Out of the meeting came dozens of volunteers who set about organizing a senior taxi service, "meals on wheels," and a renewal of the town's handsome but shabby Casino Theatre, which sat astride of the town's principal business-institutional corner. One of the volunteers was Eugene Iagnemma, a local high school history teacher, who was to form and lead the nonprofit corporation that saw the theater through its restoration and reopening.

By the arrival of the 21st century, the theater was refurbished and being used for locally recognized shows and civic events. Under new owners, the steel mill had been modernized and was producing specialty metals. The Victorian Museum and Historical Society and local town government were carrying on town development. Mendicino was pursuing her career in human services.

On the occasion of the town's centennial in 1995, a town committee published a history of Vandergrift titled *Something Better Than the Best* (Blose et al., 1996). The main author, Kenneth M. Blose, concluded,

> McMurtry's "Better Than the Best" lives on today in a community alive with renewed civic pride.

The celebration of a century of excellence has spurred a concerted move to historic restorations. The majestic Casino Theatre, once neglected and run down, recently reopened its doors to sold-out audiences for live theater presentations. . . . For today, it is enough to note that the idea of "something better than the best" is alive and well in the people of this community. (pp. 227–228)

Blose's words are a rousing tribute to Mendicino and Iagnemma as prescient volunteer organizers.

Appendix 5.B
The Community Organizer

Earlier in this chapter, we identified "a special kind of multi-skilled person," called a community organizer, as one of the three key ingredients of community organizing. From experience, we have found that in small communities, this indispensable facilitator can be either an able and generous volunteer or a trained paid professional. Sometimes in larger organizations, the staff include two or more organizers, as in Boston's Dudley Street Neighborhood Initiative, where each organizer is assigned a different set of activities.

In either case, the community organizer will be engaged in the 12 activities spelled out in this chapter. He or she will be monitoring and coordinating the two-track effort. Having mastered the organization's vision, and perhaps even having helped to create it, the organizer will disseminate it whenever appropriate. The organizer will give quality time to seeking recruits diverse in race, gender, and income who can be given free rein to learn and grow into industrious members and perhaps become part of the continuity crew—"the cadre"—that worries daily about the organization and keeps it productive and moving.

The organizer joins with members and friends of the organization to plan, strategize, and execute—finding resources both inside and outside the community, generating research findings, and mobilizing residents, political allies, and media supporters to bear down on the causes of distress. As such, the organizer is a partner with people seeking the use and revitalization of community assets.

The organizer moves with the pack, eschewing status and credit, confirming the achievements and efforts of members and friends, and working to ensure diversity in board and other leadership. The organizer hangs back to let attention and recognition fall on protégés and encourages them as they step out and take risks.

Candy reminded us that an organizer learns the skills and tools to achieve a balance between group process and outcomes sought, sometimes stated as "group maintenance and program tasks." Balance helps to avoid two common traps: the "all action" or product trap encountered by groups that expend most of their energy on "getting things done," only to be held up at crucial moments because people were inadequately informed or unwittingly excluded, and the "talk forever" or process trap that bogs down groups that "continually process interpersonal issues or have the same meeting several times—a recipe for draining away energy and focus. Success emerges from holding an effective balance between process and outcomes and from recognizing that emotional factors will affect decisions and final outcomes" (personal communication, August 11, 1999).

The organizer steps aside to allow the communication skills of members to be honed, and their ties to the media and funders to be cultivated, through honest and forthcoming relationships. The empowering and sophisticated techniques of gathering relevant facts and using them to plan, convince, evaluate, and educate are continuously worked at, guiding the organization in its planning and implementation decisions. Collaboration is used to boost power when appropriate, with partnerships and coalitions worth investing in when they provide gains to all participants.

The competent organizer keeps one foot firmly in place on each of the two tracks. Always there is recruitment and teaching going on to strengthen the organizational base and the fund-raising to intensify pursuit of program goals with the money sought both inside and outside the walls of the community.

Kahn (1991) called attention to the nobility of the organizer roles, reminding us that as people begin to organize together, they also begin to learn from each other's values. "We are not simply building an organization . . . we are creating a shared sense of history and democratic values, a common set of expectations within which to develop our strategies and tactics" (pp. 283–284).

The productive organizer keeps adding to his or her knowledge, for instance, learning how to assist a weak volunteer board to become a strong one or coming to understand street crime and the ways in which a citizen "blockwatch" program can deflect it. The organizer comes to know where to get help for jobless residents who show talent for self-employment as well as how and when to direct them to go get the help. The organizer learns how to support an alliance of local organizations in their building "big muscle" support for a goal such as controlling the uses of riverfront land in their neighborhood that is being cleared of its railway siding or for building the regionwide influences to open far out suburbs to diverse populations. The organizer can introduce a block club to the recreation facilities of a nearby university from which residents always felt excluded. The organizer knows how to find a translator for participants who have not yet learned English. All this is part of the organizer's work, which can be summarized as finding and training ordinary people to proudly do extraordinary things.

Appendix 5.C
Classic Organizing "Directions"

"Best" practitioners, and the writers who celebrate their work, usually emphasize a typology of three directions mimicking the pioneering analysis of Rothman (1964) while using the three dimensions of small community applied throughout this book: social, political, and economic. Each direction (or approach/model) is generally focused on a single dimension. Practitioners sometimes present only the one direction that they practice and favor, which might be single- or multidimensional. We explore here the work of several key writers and practitioners. An effective organizing effort generally chases an approach early on, giving itself a "disciplinary direction" to ensure that it does not waste resources of money and manpower. The direction helps the cadre and its comrades to hew the line, minimize false starts, stay a course, and conserve time—that most precious asset of volunteers and paid organizers alike.

Alternative Directions

Best known over the years has been the typology of Jack Rothman. His three "models of intervention," originally identified and described back during the 1960s, are locality development, social planning and policy, and social action. At the time of conception, he saw these as three separate and distinct types. Now, he sees them as more fluid and flexible. His original "intervention" descriptions went as follows:

Locality development: This model approach is marked by community preservation and improvement, community competency, and social integration. In general, it is operated by consensus, with community people making decisions and carrying them out. The outcome sought is more capacity for community people to maintain and exercise mastery over their community. An example of direction with a social emphasis is New Bedford's spirits-raising Waterfront Historic Area League (WHALE), a private nonprofit organization, which restored and revitalized the city's historic neighborhood, with lifetime resident John Bullard as organizer.

Social planning and policy: This approach is marked by data-based problem solving and reliance on expertise. This approach uses either consensus or conflict to push for change. The organizer is fact gatherer and analyst, program implementer, and expeditor. The outcome sought is to identify accurately the social service needs of local people and to inform them of their options, leaving people to make their own demands for implementation. Examples of this direction with an economic emphasis are United Way planning councils, which focus on workforce development and housing, and neighborhood planning forums, which initiate planning efforts joined in by interest groups in a small community seeking to implement job creation.

Social action: This approach involves advocacy thrust, commitment to fundamental change, and social justice. In general, it uses conflict. The organizer is activist, agitator, broker, negotiator, and partisan. The outcome sought is to develop power and gain control over decisions affecting the community. Alinsky-inspired organizations, such as BUILD in Baltimore, are examples of this direction with a political emphasis. (Rothman, 1995, pp. 32–33)

Rothman (1995) made a long overdue reappraisal of his models and redefined them as having much more elasticity, calling them "approaches" or "modes" based on his recent empirical evidence of how community organizations behave in the real world. The result is an "interweaving" of the three. For instance, Rothman found that the United Farm Workers union uses advocacy and conflict measures such as picketing, marches, and grape boycotts, as in the Social Action direction, but also uses mutual aid and community building measures that include leadership development, as in the Locality Development direction (pp. 46–58).

Rothman (1995), in his more recent research, found "dilemmas" that belie the purity of his old models. He affirmed that in some locality development organizations there is the usual orientation to self-contained community, but with help coming from external sources such as the Catholic Church's national Campaign for Human Development and the World Health Organization. He also found an increasing number of social planning organizations heavily into participation. His revisions support the rule that local environments shape approach and organizational form and that each small community has its own unique set of local conditions (pp. 46–61).

In Rothman's (1995) search for ways in which to match productive approaches of community intervention with situations of community distress, he cited the relevance of economic context (pp. 59–60). He did so recognizing that a market-dominated society, with its acquisitive ethic, produces social disparity, industrial decay, recurring joblessness, racism, normlessness, and social isolation. Frustration arises because even carefully planned and executed interventions often can accomplish little in redistributing wealth and power or in preventing the victimization of "have-not" households. One has only to consider that during the 1960s the working poor earned 90% of the money they needed to raise a family (two wage earners), whereas today that figure is less than 70%.

Locality development has had its successes in countering social isolation by bringing people together with each other and with local institutions. But it has not always been able to remove the social conditions of normlessness and inequality because of the devastating impact of negative societal forces. Social action has confronted power, Rothman (1995) acknowledged, but it has not shaped a method for rehumanizing the distress makers that it cannot defeat such as drug pushers and those perpetuating racism in outer-ring suburban corporations, schools, and other institutional environments.

Rothman (1995) maintained that his three practice options can be more effective in contemporary society when interwoven creatively into hybrid designs to fit specific community situations. He cited Barbara Ehrenreich for confirmation. Ehrenreich's (1995) statement might serve well young community renewal organizations struggling to find a sense of direction: "This is a time when people looking for change don't have some kind of precise model to inform that struggle for change. Everyone has some responsibility to start imagining, dreaming, inventing, and visualizing the kind of future we would like" (p. 60).

Peter Dreier, another writer, has a typology that confines itself to locality, but in the small community world he finds the same tripartite division by dimensions: social, political, and economic. Dreier (1996) called his typology "Community Empowerment Strategies" and identified the following single-dimension alternative directions:

Community organizing: Mobilizing people to combat common problems and to increase their voice in institutions and decisions that affect their lives and communities. (a direction with political emphasis)

Community-based development: Neighborhood-based efforts to improve an area's physical and financial condition such as new construction or rehabilitation of housing. (a direction with economic emphasis)

Community-based service provision: Involves neighborhood-level efforts to deliver social services (e.g., job training, child care, parenting skills) and is called "building human capital." (a direction with social emphasis)

These are narrow directions that are insufficient by themselves. They depend on other organizations being around to take care of the distress not addressed by the single-dimension approach. For example, if we were dealing here with a community organizing type, then the neighborhood would also need a CDC to work with economic distress and a service provider to handle social distress. From his work as an urban administrator-practitioner and as a political science scholar, Dreier pulled up insights for strengthening community organizations through leadership development and organization building.

Robert Fisher presents a much broader perspective. From his studies of the history of community organizing, Fisher (1984) identified what he called the "three dominant approaches," which he traced back to the 1880s:

Social work approach: This approach is characterized by the social settlement house and, more recently, by human service centers of the kind established in Aliquippa, Pennsylvania. The organizer is often a professional social worker who serves as an enabler, an advocate, a coordinator, and a planner. The problem condition is likely to be social disorganization and conflict. Methods are consensual and gradualist. Goals are group formation, social integration, and quality service delivery. (a direction with social emphasis)

Political activist approach: This approach is characterized by militant confrontation and heavy pressure on the power institutions of society. Power sharing is a major goal. The method is advocacy, involving conflict and negotiation, as used by mass-based organizations such as the Industrial Areas Foundation founded by Saul Alinsky, the National Association of Community Organizations for Reform Now (ACORN), and committees of the unemployed. The organizer is a mobilizer and leadership developer. The problem condition is social and economic oppression sprung out of powerlessness. The ultimate goal is the elimination of social, political, and economic disparities. (a direction with political emphasis)

Neighborhood maintenance approach: This approach is characterized by middle-class residents and their small business and institutional allies who seek to "defend" their communities against change and perceived threats to property values. The "problem" conditions may include racial change, decline in municipal services, deterioration of housing and shopping streets, and increased crime. The organizer might be a volunteer community leader or a paid university trained specialist in urban planning, business administration, community development, or law. The method is hard-line consensus involving peer pressure, lobbying, and legal action. The organizational vehicle might be a neighborhood preservation association or a narrowly focused CDC. (a direction with economic emphasis)

Because small communities, by their nature, have social, political, and economic dimensions, at the same time that they differ widely in the nature of their distress factors, it is expected that there are going to be groups of communities identifying social distress as their principal challenge and concentrating there, while other groups identify either political or economic distress and move to concentrate on one of these. And as Rothman has found, there are mixtures of both distress and revitalization efforts that involve "interweaving." Fisher's historical perspective widens our understanding of the growth and direction of community revitalization approaches. There are also writers who focus on the *participants* in community organizing rather than on their organizations.

Mark G. Hanna and Buddy Robinson, whose transformative model was introduced in Appendix 3.A, added a fresh perspective with their typology sprung out of the soul of the oppressed resident, titled "Strategies for Community Empowerment." Hanna and Robinson (1994) moved to a new depth in the social dimension. They went beyond direct action, with its absorption in taking power, money, service, and infrastructure from external resources, to dig down to transformative changes in the "habits of the heart" of participants in community revitalization. They set out the following typology:

Traditional politics: This involves elite, nonparticipative efforts that bend the status quo just enough to preserve it. It involves rational problem solving, but the income gaps and racism always remain. (a direction with social-economic emphasis)

Direct action community organizing: This involves mass-based organizing. It sometimes uses confrontation. It is power oriented. It aims to bring elites to the bargaining table, where nonelites can negotiate to share their power. (a direction with a social-political emphasis)

Transformative social change: This involves small groups, intensive study and reflection, and people becoming acutely aware and knowledgeable about the oppressive forces that affect their families and communities. Emphasis is on self-directed (nonhierarchical) learning, interpersonal bonds, and a fully collective approach to group awareness, decision making, and social action, which liberates participants from the mind-set of dependency and oppression. (a direction with a social-social emphasis)

Hanna and Robinson (1994) judged the traditional and direct action approaches to social change to be inadequate or even counterproductive: "Such methods do not systematically consider the pervasive character of a culture of domination, nor sufficiently emphasize critical consciousness in the action/goal-oriented methods" (p. 23). They maintained that until the participants themselves are liberated from the mind-set of oppression, the result of any action may merely reproduce the identical negative behavior and unjust institutions that were the targets of reform in the first place, for example, when an elite group of residents and outsiders take over the board of a CDC and suppress participation. They drew on the work of Friere (1972), author of *Pedagogy of the Oppressed,* to recommend "liberating education" as an essential pre-action component of community change, which they preferred to call "overall transformation of a society." They saw such "education"— it might also be called "vision creation" or "leadership development" (p. 22)—as requiring participative research of the kind set forth in Chapter 3.

Hanna and Robinson (1994) called their favored model transformative social change practice: "The development of critical conscious, through problem-posing 'educational-projects,' which should be carried out with the oppressed in the process of organizing them, is the heart of this transformative method" (p. 23), an insight they credited to Friere. They saw this method as leading to liberation from the oppression mind-set.

Some of the characteristics of this method are small group processes of self-directed inquiry, gradual political socialization and awareness, concern with understanding power and community decisions, and formation of support and solidarity groups, self-help economic and social cooperatives, and base ecclesial communities designed for mutual support of members and the sharing of life with neighbors. The person who initiates and guides, supplying spiritual inspiration and a rigorous curriculum, is much more a community educator than a community organizer.

This direction concentrates on change within community people who become aware of restrictions on their dignity and learn collective ways in which to break away from oppression and to build new lives of cooperation, peace, and self-confidence. Only when they reach self-learned enlightenment and liberation are residents ready to employ mainstream community organizing methods, and then on their own enlightened terms. During an age when a seemingly irresistible culture of secular materialism is sweeping the globe, this transformative mode, with its spirituality and empowerment goal, could attract many who are searching for a counterforce movement that is faith based. Without the stability and thrust of ideology, it is difficult to hold an organization together for a long period of education and reflection that has no concurrent production line of concrete outcomes.

The transformative path has the possibility of flowering into a comprehensive model, although its start-up groups begin with a focus on a single-dimension social emphasis. Single-dimension approaches appear to be successful when there is an organization or two in the community taking responsibility for the other two dimensions. For instance, there may be a suburban community with excellent schools and social services, with steadily employed households that have sizable incomes, but also with declining voter registration and turned off attitudes toward politics, reflected by unfilled seats on political party committees and no residents interested in running for municipal office or serving on school boards. Such a place is likely to lack influence and miss obtaining many resources that could strengthen social and economic components. Or a city neighborhood might be stable in money and power but be torn by racial hostilities and need competent diversity organizing with a social emphasis.

Increasingly, however, both experience and studies of efforts, such as those in Dudley Street, Aliquippa, and an array of other neighborhoods and towns across America, confirm that single-dimension approaches do not do the job. The tripartite "social-political-economic" breakdown, when confined to a single dimension direction, is as artificial and outdated as the traditional Rothman models of intervention. Both sets of ideal models advance understanding but fail to provide us with proven "interwoven" guides, as Rothman (1995) suggested in revising his own models. It is now the synthesis demonstrated by the comprehensive prototypes that seems most capable of renewing a community and restoring it to wholeness.

In Chapter 3, we described the Comprehensive Community Initiative, funded by Ford and other foundations, and the family-focused and transformative approaches as models of power relevant to overall renewal. Dudley Street and Aliquippa also represent important examples of comprehensive direction, as do some of the emerging community builders' organizations. (There is a definition of the comprehensive approach in Chapter 1.)

Kingsley, McNeely, and Gibson (1997), in their report developed jointly by the Development Training Institute and the Urban Institute, stated that community building is a direction that downplays resource tapping and its pursuit of money, services, and material benefits for those in distress. Although most of its advocates recognize a continuing need for considerable outside assistance (both public and private), community building's central theme is to obliterate feelings of dependency and to replace them with attitudes of self-reliance, self-confidence, and a passion for social justice. It gives high priority to establishing and reinforcing sound values. In some of this, it is similar to the transformative social change described earlier. Like Dudley Street and Aliquippa, its model organizations set sights on opportunities and distress across-the-board, with all three dimensions getting attention as required. But once a community builds a critical mass of people irresistibly moved by self-reliance, self-confidence, and justice, they are going to move on to seek resources for healing the environment and resisting and modifying external forces oppressing the community.

The community building vision leads toward small communities in which neighbors come to rely on each other, working together on concrete tasks that use newly discovered collective and individual assets and that redistribute human, family, and social capital to provide for a more equitable community. These are not ideas to be imposed from the outside. They are what the leaders of distressed neighborhoods across the nation themselves are saying they want to see accomplished, according to the landmark study conducted by Kingsley et al. (1997).

The Consensus Organizing Institute (COI), based in San Diego, focuses on connecting neighborhood residents to each other through strong social networks and then to resources and opportunities throughout a metropolitan region. Currently in San Diego, COI is organizing networks of parents of preschool-aged children to shape the way in which tobacco tax money is used in their communities and is also working with resident networks and regional leaders to shape a regional growth strategy emphasizing equity and ecological sustainability. In Louisville, COI is organizing resident networks to shape the way in which a new metropolitan government will work with inner-city communities. At the core of COI's approach is the development of productive relationships between neighborhood residents and local government, and COI's strategies include efforts to increase neighborhood participation in elections for local government, according to its president, Richard Barrera (personal correspondence, June 13, 2002).

Traditional Power Organizing

Style and brand name have been central features of community organizing since 1939, when a graduate student named Saul Alinsky and his indigenous sidekick, Joe Meegan, launched the Back of the Yards Neighborhood Council to help oppressed working families on Chicago's South Side push for union recognition, a living wage, and improvements in health care and housing.

Alinsky (1945) took the academic label *community organization* and turned it into *community organizing* with bold moves that tied this revised label to power, pressure, and high-profile public actions. In 1945, he spelled out his approach in *Reveille for Radicals,* thereby drawing coast-to-coast interest in his confrontive approach that rested on displays of people strength through marches, parades of newly registered voters, overflowing public hearings, and sometimes disruptive boycotts, picketing, and sit-downs. Earlier, he had created the Industrial Areas Foundation (IAF), staffed by teams of organizers who carried his irreverent methods to other cities.

When Alinsky began his work, community organization was a social work approach, both professional and bureaucratic, wedded to traditional forms of cooperation and consensus. For example, when social worker Julia Abrahamson became the founding director of the pioneering Hyde Park-Kenwood Community Conference in 1949, she immediately began to shape the new group in an exclusively consensual mode, eschewing the power approach. Throughout the 1950s, Alinsky recruited and trained residents who grabbed headlines with their rent strikes, mass demonstrations, and bold challenges to landlords, employers, and merchants accused of exploiting families in low-income neighborhoods.

Most social work organizations proceeded with their professional and bureaucratic processes even as the neighborhood people they served showed increasing impatience with the chronic impoverishment and joblessness swallowing them. It was the era when Michael Harrington was haunting the offices of the temporary worker employment agencies and roaming the hills of Appalachia searching out the stories and numbers for *The Other America* (Harrington, 1962), his shocking book that would make poverty and 50 million hungry people fully visible in the United States.

Feisty students and faculty in schools of social work, and neighborhood groups in general, began to accept power organizing.

Table 5.1   Typology of Directions for Organizing the Renewal of a Small Place Community

Component	Social	Political	Economic	Comprehensive
Also known as	Social work approach Human service organizing Social fabric Social capital	Advocacy Pressure approach Conflict organizing Direct action Mass-based organizing	Community economic development Enterprise development Affordable housing development Consensus organizing	Community building Holistic community development Comprehensive community initiative Organizing for Community Controlled Development
Major themes	Meeting essential needs of individuals and families Personal development Grassroots delivery of social services	Through a mass base, people bring power structure to table to negotiate sharing of power	Neighborhood-based efforts to improve economic conditions with affordable housing, new and expanded enterprises, and infrastructure	Obliterate feelings of oppression, to replace with sense of self-reliance that is directed to flowering of family and community
Sources of power	Money, ideas, people, alliances with government	People as collective of activists, voters, campaigners	Money and influence Partnerships Property	People and alliances
Orientation	Healing	Influence	Redistribution	Empowerment
Goals of planning	Human needs	Control	Efficiency, stability, living wage Equity, job security	Transform people, build community
Leadership	Grassroots Locally based professionals	Grassroots with elite strains	Elite, top down Neighborhood based	Mixed grassroots and elite Neighborhood based
View held by media	Bureaucratic, rigid, soft-edged, unrealistic	Activist, radical, interesting, disruptive, shrewd-naive	Relevant, hard-edged, often successful, realistic	Struggling, innovative, family centered, overprogrammed
Risk taking	Low tolerance	Unconcerned	High tolerance	Unconcerned but willing to try
Collective form	Social agency, network support group	Mass organization	Housing development corporation Community development corporation	Community-wide initiative
Principal method for seeking change	Collaboration Transformation	Negotiation, intimidation Elections	Deal making	Bag of tools

(Continued)

Table 5.1 Continued

Component	Social	Political	Economic	Comprehensive
Targets of change	Families and agencies	Decision makers	Free market	Society
Five relevant authors	Friere Halpern Hanna & Robinson Horton, Kretzmann, & McKnight	Berry Dionne Rusk Fisher Alinsky	Downs Jacobs Sklar Rothman Wilson	Kingsley, McNeely, & Gibson Stone Marciniak Dreier Rothman

SOURCE: Murphy and Cunningham (2002).

It became a component of various approaches, both new and old, as the spirit of community action swept across the nation during the 1960s and beyond. Some 40 years later, during more conservative times, power tactics are still latent in most organizations, but not so widely used as during the 1960s. There are still brand approaches, with their own training centers, preparing organizers and fostering organizations where power and confrontation are dominant to the approach. Alinsky's IAF, now more than 60 years old, is still ubiquitous and important.

The IAF lays claim to self-sufficient organizing efforts under way in 63 sites in the United States and has relationships with similar projects in the United Kingdom, Germany, and South Africa. One of the most active sites is the Chicago area, where United Power for Action and Justice is what IAF terms an "organization of organizations" with 340 institutional members, including religious congregations, unions, nonprofit health centers, and community organizations from across the region. Wilson (1999) hailed the IAF for its multiracial, grassroots community organizations and pinpointed its Texas Industrial Areas Foundation, "which has created a model statewide network of political influence" (p. 124). Rusk (1999) assessed the IAF through two coalitions of organizations it helped to create. First is San Antonio's Communities Organized for Public Service (COPS), which forged the city's Hispanic population into a successful political force. The second is the church alliances in Northwest Indiana, which reshaped major policies and programs of city and county governments to protect environments of low-income families threatened by business and government projects. Rusk praised the effective power building and deployment by coalitions of Indiana churches and place-based community groups (pp. 263, 279–280). Warren (2001) produced a book-length assessment of the IAF as it works in Texas and the Southwest. He saw the IAF as demonstrating "the possibilities and rewards of value-based politics, of multiracial collaboration, of patient relationship building in local communities" (p. x), and he wound up the book by suggesting that the IAF offers "new models for multiracial understanding and collaboration" and for revitalizing "our democracy by infusing it with an active and empowered citizenry" (p. 264).

Leadership Aid

Included here is a matrix that puts the preceding scramble of directions into a suggested order (Table 5.1). This is supplied as a leadership aid that might be of assistance to a cadre seeking to confirm the policy and program direction of its newly forming neighborhood renewal organization. This matrix is designed to supply, in "quick read" form, a broad range of alternative components that an active cadre could use to overcome barriers confronting its emerging organization as well as to exploit further its assets. Given the reality that every association situation is unique, most cadres have a constant need to find the right combination of components for their particular efforts in their particular environments. In community organizing, it pays to mix, match, and experiment as an organization is built or rebuilt.

REFERENCES

Alinsky, S. D. (1945). *Reveille for radicals.* Chicago: University of Chicago Press.

Blose, K. M., et al. (1996). *Vandergrift, Pennsylvania: The Story of America's first successful, worker-owned planned community.* Vandergrift, PA: Victorian Vandergrift Museum and Historical Society.

Bobo, K., Kendall, J., & Max, S. (1996). *Organizing for social change.* Washington, DC: Seven Locks Press.

Chaskin, R., Brown, P., Venkatish, S., & Vidal, A. (2001). *Building community capacity.* New York: Aldine DeGruyter.

Dreier, P. (1996). Community empowerment strategies: The limits and potential of community organizing in urban neighborhoods. *Cityscape: A Journal of Policy Development and Research, 2*(2), 121–159.

Ehrenreich, B. (1995). From a letter to the membership of the Democratic Socialists of America, dated December 1, 1993, New York. In J. Rothman, J. Erlich, & J. E. Tropman (Eds.), *Strategies of community intervention* (5th ed., pp. 26–63). Itasca, IL: F. E. Peacock.

Fisher, R. (1984). *Let the people decide: Neighborhood organizing in America.* New York: Twayne.

Friere, P. (1972). *Pedagogy of the oppressed.* London: Penguin.

Green, J. (1999). *Cultural awareness in the human services: A multi-ethnic approach* (3rd ed.). Boston: Allyn & Bacon.

Hanna, M. G., & Robinson, B. (1994). *Strategies for community empowerment.* Lewiston, NY: Edwin Mellon.

Harrington, M. (1962). *The other America.* New York: Macmillan.

Kahn, S. (1991). *Organizing: A guide for grassroots leaders* (rev. ed.). Washington, DC: NASW Press.

Kingsley, G. T., McNeely, J. B., & Gibson, J. O. (1997). *Community building: Coming of age.* Baltimore, MD: Development Training Institute.

Marciniak, E. (1981). *Reversing urban decline.* Washington, DC: National Center for Urban Ethnic Affairs.

Mondros, J., & Wilson, S. (1994). *Organizing for power and empowerment.* New York: Columbia University Press.

Rivera, F., & Erlich, J. (1998). *Community organizing in a diverse society* (3rd ed.). Boston: Allyn & Bacon.

Rosenthal, B., & Mizrahi, T. (1994). *Strategic partnerships: How to create and maintain interorganizational collaborations and coalitions.* New York: Hunter College School of Social Work, Education Center for Community Organizing.

Rothman, J. (1964). An analysis of goals and roles in community organization practice. *Social Work, 9*(2), 24–31.

Rothman, J. (1995). Approaches to community intervention. In J. Rothman, J. L. Erlich, & J. E. Tropman (Eds.), *Strategies of community intervention* (5th ed., pp. 26–63). Itasca, IL: F. E. Peacock.

Rubin, H., & Rubin, I. (2001). *Community organizing and development* (3rd ed.). Boston: Allyn & Bacon.

Rusk, D. (1999). *Inside game, outside game.* Washington, DC: Brookings Institution Press.

Scheie, D. (1996, September–October). Promoting job opportunity: Strategies for community-based organizations. *Shelterforce,* pp. 9–11. (Orange, NJ: National Housing Institute)

Staples, L. (1984). *Roots to power: A manual for grassroots organizing.* New York: Praeger.

Warren, M. (2001) *Dry bones rattling: Community building to revitalize American democracy.* Princeton, NJ: Princeton University Press.

Wilson, W. J. (1999). *The bridge over the racial divide: Rising inequality and coalition politics.* Berkeley: University of California Press.

6

PARTICIPATION
Lifeblood of Renewal

The principal asset of any human settlement is its people. Their dreams, skills, and labor make it prosper. Their unity has the power to turn a collection of streets and buildings into a community in the truest sense of the word. Their connectedness, and only their connectedness, can create a desirable place in which to live and work. No genuine renewal happens without the initiative and sustained participation of the community members. No improvement effort fully flowers unless people from every nook, cranny, and interest group invest themselves in the care and "husbanding" of the place and its assets. Residents are primary, but also important are those who work in the community, own property, possess governmental authority, or otherwise have continuing legitimate interest and responsibility but are not residents.

Current research and the experience of the United Nations (1993) in its worldwide quest to understand and promote human development have revealed the greatest progress in nations where ordinary people are pressing to take control of economic and social forces that threaten them. "People today have an urge—an impatient urge—to participate in the events and processes that shape their lives." While recognizing that such a breaking forth of the human spirit can be manifest in anarchy and ethnic violence as well as in the creation of democratic institutions, the United Nations concluded that

people around the globe are demanding a steady advancement toward participation that is centered on greater access to and control over social, political, and economic institutions (pp. 1–2). "The implications of placing people at the center of political and economic change ... call for nothing less than a revolution in our thinking" (p. 8).

In its report 5 years later, the United Nations (1998) focused on the destructive inequities in global consumption. The report saw improvement possible and found the involvement of individuals, grassroots community organizations, and nongovernmental organizations, in addition to business, government, and international institutions, making change happen. It looked to widespread participation to spawn enlightened considerate values, centered on the common good, within the hearts of people in every nation, as we have seen in situations as diverse as the charity of the faith-based women organized by Mother Teresa in India and the unsung labor of volunteers who quietly serve the homeless in every city in America. Private individualized choices may be "legal, affordable, and socially acceptable," yet as the United Nations stated, they can still be "devastating for human development" (p. 87).

The latest UN report (United Nations, 2001), subtitled *Making New Technologies Work for Human Development,* asserted, "Like the printing press of earlier centuries, the telephone, radio, television, and fax machine of the 20th century opened up communications, reducing isolation and enabling people to be better informed and to participate in decisions that affect their lives. . . . The advent of the fax machine enabled much more rapid popular mobilization" (p. 29), aided and abetted by e-mail, the Internet, and cell phones, we would add. According to the United Nations report,

> Basic capabilities for human development are to lead long and healthy lives, to be knowledgeable, to have access to resources needed for a decent standard of living. . . . Without these . . . , many opportunities in life remain inaccessible. . . . Social and political freedom, participation, and access to material resources create conditions that encourage people's creativity. . . . Human development shares a common vision with human rights. The goal is human rights mutually reinforcing, helping to secure the well-being and dignity of all people, building self-respect and the respect of others. (p. 9)

During the past decade, there has been phenomenal growth in citizen organizations inside nations with iron-rule histories, including Indonesia, Slovakia, South Korea, and the Philippines. Citizen groups and church organizations were a major force in the defeat of apartheid in South Africa, the end of the dictatorship in Chile, the overthrow of Communist regimes in Central Europe, the creation of an international treaty prohibiting land mines, and the establishment of the International Criminal Court.

Even the rigid Chinese Communist regime in 1999 was forced to respond to its protesting students and the Falum Gong mediators when these movements mobilized massive nonviolent displays of popular support. The initial response of the government was toleration, which became repression as adherents publicly demonstrated their willingness to risk independent action. The long-term impact appears to be that global forces are putting increased pressure on the Chinese government to allow more freedom. Nongovernmental groups worldwide are now a distinct sector, one that, like government, serves essential social functions involving supplying education, health, and social services and pressuring economic and political institutions for fairness and accountability.

In interviews with 6,100 Americans in 15 mid-sized cities, Berry, Portney, and Thomson (1993) found that participation leads to sense of community, which in turn leads to more active contributions to community improvement. They concluded that participation stimulates understanding among citizens and between citizens and their leaders and that participation begets appreciation of both the limitations and potential of government and the need to move beyond private self-fulfillment. "It can encourage and nurture cooperative efforts to address community concerns, cooperation that is critical in a time of rapid social change and increasingly intense economic pressures" (p. 255).

Participation is a core element in the growth and development of the human spirit. Without it, community cannot exist. The very term *community economic development* denotes a process pervasive with shared decision making, shared work, and shared resources. Participation has as much of an economic dimension as it does an organizing dimension. There is also looseness and confusion about the concept of participation. Examining fruitfully the relation of participation to revitalization of distressed small communities calls for a precise definition. A brief review of the history of participation leads us to the definition.

HISTORY

It was from a diverse and changing Europe that the seeds of new social organization were planted in North America during the 17th century. In Britain, the direct source of the new society, elitism was enthroned at the national level as in most of the rest of the world. Britain, however, was the nation that had created the Magna Carta in 1215, defining a new relationship of shared powers among king and barons and guaranteeing certain liberties for towns and cities.

The spirit of rights of the individual and shared control provided the climate within which the original Virginia and New England colonial settlements were launched. Their ability to follow the spirit was aided by 2,000 miles of ocean that separated their settlements from the absolutist inclinations of British rule.

Virginians met in their first assembly in 1619 to pass local laws. The following year, the Pilgrims established a government of their own when 41 white adult males met aboard the Mayflower before going ashore to begin settlement of the territory they were to call New England.

Colonial towns exercised power through town meetings of their European residents, a participatory form that spread throughout New England and even into Wisconsin. The town meeting, which continues to this day in some of the smaller communities of New England, allows residents to debate and vote directly on town budgets and other policy matters.

During the 19th century, growing volunteer organizations gave millions of American citizens a role in public life through church organizations, charity groups, chambers of commerce, trade unions, and farmer associations such as the National Grange. Early in the century, Tocqueville (1954) commented on American society, "There is no end which the human will despair of attaining through the combined power of individuals united through a society" (p. 199).

During the 1920s, voluntary associations concerned with city planning emerged in New York, Chicago, and elsewhere. Already, there were neighborhood organizations and local institutions challenging downtown elite planners. Rural participation opportunities multiplied during these years with the blossoming of the Federal Cooperative Extension Service, through which committees of local rural people initiated and carried out projects to increase farm production. Out of this model of participation came the farmers' committees that set local production quotas and made other serious decisions for agricultural programs begun under the New Deal during the 1930s.

By the time the nation's single most powerful institution, the national government, came to take the preeminent role in social and economic life during the 1930s, citizen participation was a recognized but not well-developed force in public affairs. After World War II, when the national government turned to domestic programs on a grand scale, it did so with participation as an integral component.

One after another vast new federal program was launched, directly affecting citizens in their home communities. As related in Chapter 2, new programs for renewing cities and reducing poverty stimulated widespread participation, much of it laced with controversy and most of it undermined in time by traditional authoritarian forces of business and government.

Throughout this history, the extension of participation was real but limited. While decisions on public matters moved beyond kings, barons, bishops, and generals, local decision making tended to continue to be dominated by the local elites of small communities. The term *elite* signifies a person who, by education, talents, personality, experience, wealth, position, and/or connections, comes to influence and control people, assets, and events.

When movements of poor people, African Americans, Hispanics, Native Americans, and their allies in distressed communities appeared successful in reallocating power during the 1960s, students, women, consumers, public employees, middle-class environmentalists, urban white ethnics, and prisoners, among others, came to demand recognition for their issues. Since those tumultuous years, participation in public affairs by ordinary people has become more widespread. The number of small communities hatching development organizations has multiplied. However, although participation is more extensive, the reality is that the portion of the population participating in most small communities is still inadequate for serious community power building as to both numbers and representativeness.

The terrorist attacks on the World Trade Center and Pentagon on September 11, 2001, detonated new national and local waves of concern for public matters along with outpourings of generous community activity. This changed climate has led to new attention for civic values within neighborhood and nation, with the meaning and potential of more activist unity a central topic. Stimulation of outpourings of civic involvement have been reported in a few areas as a result of the attacks, but information coming from the nation is too meager to indicate a strong trend. This matter was discussed earlier in the Preface relating to the research of Robert Putnam, whose work gets more attention in

Chapter 10. Basically, Putnam (2002) found a strong renewed urge for civic activity, but not the widespread organizing necessary to release it (p. 1). As of this writing, we must say, the depth and endurance of citizen concern and activity cannot yet be judged. The permanent effect of September 11 on participation, if any, might not be known for years.

The pull of private life had been extra strong since the Reagan presidency, when the public was constantly told that "government is the problem." Active, renewal-committed small communities seemed to be kept going by skeleton cadres of dedicated people, while the majority of residents became infected by the malaise of civic apathy. Even where celebrated rebuilding initiatives have been under way, opportunities have been lost for lack of participation. "Not enough" is the assessment that applies to nearly all of the cases cited in this book. If this shortfall were to remain, then it would bode ill for the future of the nation and its 60,000 small communities.

A decade ago, Berry et al. (1993) did studies in Portland, St. Paul, Birmingham, and Dayton, four cities where participation is promoted by city government. They found that although participation stimulates people to actively work on behalf of their community, the proportion of people continuously involved remains small at less than 17% (p. 292). They concluded that citywide systems of neighborhood associations do affect participation in the city:

> Even though they fall short in getting more people to become active in the political world, particularly low-income people, neighborhood associations do nurture face-to-face participation. This participation, channeled into neighborhood-based activity, changes the balance of power in the city . . . between business and government, on the one hand, and neighborhood organizations, on the other. (pp. 286–288)

The creative and determined organizing breaking forth in more and more communities as reported in this book, together with the "tappable" pools of wealth still held by numerous affluent families, corporations, institutions, and governments, makes accelerated efforts possible, attainable, and (we believe) likely. The stakes are too high, the prospects are too enticing, and community talent is too profuse. America is not going to miss this opportunity. And we believe that the long-term dynamic line of history sketched previously supports this hopeful view, as does the great outpouring of community activity at the Seattle protest during the closing weeks of 1999 and in other places during 2000, 2001, and 2002 (described in Appendix 2.C).

The sweep of history reveals a steady ratcheting up of people pushing and society responding to citizen involvement in public affairs. This movement is associated with rising awareness of the potency of participation and its power to spark individual and collective responsibility for the small place community. With this background established, we now turn our attention to seeking a clear definition of *participation.*

DEFINITION

From history, contemporary events, and a review of the defining literature, we find that participation has three essential elements: inclusiveness, power, and decisions of consequence.

To be legitimate, participation needs to be open and able to attract and include meaningful numbers of ordinary people who are members of the community without important office, wealth, control of information, or other formal power sources beyond their own numbers. These gain influence through the synergism of the participation process itself as they take collective action. Ball and Knight (1999) put it this way: "Pioneers are not always leading lights— that is, powerful people with connections. Just as often, they are moving spirits—local people who have said 'enough is enough, and I am going to do something about it.' These people are at the core of civil society" (p. 22). Ball and Knight further raised the question of why we must listen to citizens and then answered it: "Because citizens know best some things that need to be done and how to do them, and because they can help make societies competitive, caring, cohesive, and corrective, too" (pp. 24–25). We see this illustrated in the Bloomfield-Garfield (Pittsburgh), Dudley Street (Boston), and Lyndale (Minneapolis) neighborhoods, where boards of residents control and deploy large-scale resources. A resident board is also making decisions in Aliquippa, Pennsylvania. This is described in Chapter 7, although participation has been narrowing there during past years, as will be seen.

Inclusiveness means purposefully taking in those interested and willing community members who go about their daily affairs largely unseen and unseeing, not normally active in organizations but surviving, maintaining their households, carrying personal responsibilities for daily quotas of work (whether paid or unpaid), and contributing to the community in quiet ways. Especially important are those persons of limited income for whom survival may be a struggle of tedium and routine, often forced by circumstances into accepting services and money (from transfer payments) they would rather provide for themselves. The quality of participation is ultimately determined by its universality, as reflected in its encompassing of elites and nonelites, haves and have-nots, and participants from all racial, ethnic, and income groups in the community.

The extent of participation must not become fixed at the level of those people who come forward initially. That would mean that the majority of local people would never become involved. It is people of a place able to render decisions based on collective strength that confers a rough parity of influence. And it is also the people of a place becoming aware that their community has barriers to inclusion and taking steps to remove them, whether they be inadequate communications, apathy, the stubbornness of elites, inequality, or plain old intolerance.

Power is control—the ability of a group to get others to act as the group wants them to act. Participation occurs when such control gets into the hands of inclusive groups where ordinary people are present in numbers commensurate with their proportion in the community and where shared power is being exercised over decisions that are significant, as when the Bloomfield-Garfield Corporation builds its public meetings to critical mass sufficient to bring elected political representatives to their meetings, where they are vulnerable to making pledges to support government resource extraction at a scale bold enough to finance community goals once considered unattainable.

In a small community, significant decisions are those in which tangible assets are at stake; for example, a sizable pot of money is to be allocated, a decent-paying job is up for grabs, a site for a new recreation center is to be selected, a candidate is to be endorsed for public office, a bank is to be publicly censured for redlining, a method is to be worked out to ensure diversity on an important neighborhood human service board, a bridge is to be blockaded to pressure government, or a loan is to be made from the neighborhood development fund. These are public matters of substance. Decisions made about such matters are the major action elements of participation.

Participation, then, is defined as a process whereby the people of a community, regardless of income or position, join meaningfully in making social, political, and economic decisions related to the general affairs of the community. This definition helps us to understand when participation is authentic.

In short, *participation* is a categorical term for resident control. It involves a redistribution of power that enables have-nots, previously excluded from political and economic processes, to be deliberately included. People who have not controlled property, money allocations, or hiring contracts begin to do so. Participation is both a process and a product. It is a continuous effort to build leadership and to make planning and development more creative and more relevant. At the same time, it produces outcomes, for example, two new enterprises locating in the community and hiring 115 local workers and the creation of job networks that tie recent high school graduates to future employers. Note the importance of the outcomes suggested to a small community; there is nothing artificial or anonymous about them. Another useful tool for distinguishing between authentic and artificial participation is Arnstein's (1969) ladder.

ARNSTEIN'S LADDER OF PARTICIPATION

Sherry Arnstein, during the late 1960s, was an irreverent researcher and policy planner who

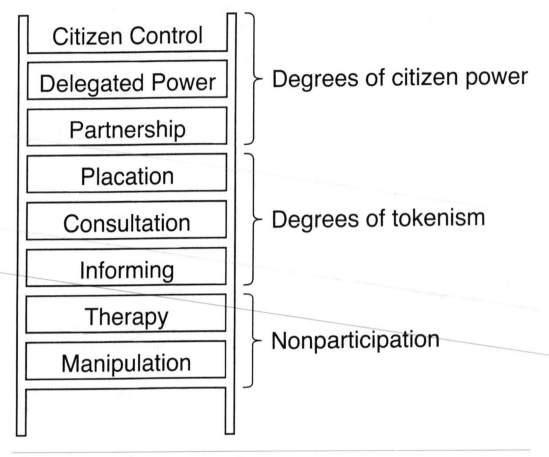

Figure 6.1   Arnstein's Ladder of Citizen Participation

SOURCE: Arnstein (1969).

was retained by the U.S. Department of Housing and Urban Development (HUD) to advise on citizen participation in the then new Model Cities Program. This program was to pour federal money into distressed neighborhoods in 150 cities to underwrite coordinated attacks on poverty and blight. She looked carefully at some of the 1,000 "maximum feasible participation" community action programs funded previously under the Economic Opportunity Act of 1964. She also studied the preliminary struggles of Model Cities Program groups to meet participation requirements. From her observations, she wrote an article that identified gradations of "participation," arranging them as a ladder whose bottom rung was manipulation and whose top rung was citizen control (Arnstein, 1969).

Arnstein's (1969) ladder is a typology supported by considerable case study evidence (see Figure 6.1). It is a genuine and useful portrayal of the complexity and reality of citizen involvement in public affairs. In the 21st century, it may appear a bit simplistic to some, but its bite remains in a world where much activity labeled "participation" is artificial and toothless.

Arnstein's two bottom rungs, manipulation and therapy, are classified as "nonparticipation." Her prime example of manipulation is the rubberstamp advisory board whose members are guided to support a plan for public relations purposes. Therapy arises when "experts" interpret powerlessness as mental illness and subject citizens to clinical group therapy instead of facilitating them to gain influence and economic strength. Simply put, receiving social services is not participation.

The next three rungs upward are informing, consultation, and placation, all degrees of tokenism. Although informing can be a start toward authentic participation, it generally is only a one-way flow of information from elites or officials to ordinary citizens. Consultations involve citizens informing officials through surveys, focus groups, open meetings, and public hearings. Placation encompasses token memberships on policy boards or citizens groups that are left to make plans without adequate technical staff, sufficient time, or enough money to do the job.

The three upper levels represent ascending levels of citizen power. It is here that we begin to find activity that fulfills the requirements of the definition. The three rungs are partnership, delegated power, and citizen control. Partnership is a sharing of power that comes out of negotiation between citizens and power holders. It works only when citizens can demonstrate a mass base and have their own technical staff, lawyers, and adequate financing. In partnerships, there is always the resource problem. Unless each partner organization has roots in an independent power source (e.g., money, a large cohesive body of members, substantial property, several high-status members, continuous sources of useful information, government authority), there is no parity and the partner without a power source is going to be dominated. Delegated refers to negotiated power sharing in which ordinary citizens achieve dominant decision making authority over one or a few significant public matters. It might involve authority to shape a budget, sign off on choice of the staff director, veto the proposed route of a new highway, or make and implement a plan for 200 new houses in the community. An exquisite example is Dudley Street obtaining the power of eminent domain, as described previously. The uppermost rung is citizen control and refers to the situation where "residents can govern a program or an institution, be in full charge of policy, budget, and management, and be able to negotiate the conditions under which outsiders may change them" (Arnstein, 1969, p. 223).

Arnstein (1969) cited the community development corporation "with no intermediaries between it and its source of funds" as a model (p. 223). She also suggested "new community institutions entirely governed by residents with a specified sum of money contracted to them" (p. 224). She estimated that 15 of the first 75 cities with Model Cities Programs "reached some significant degree of power-sharing with residents," adding that "in all but one of those cities, it was angry citizen demands, rather than city initiative, that led to the negotiated sharing of power" (pp. 222–224). (Chapter 7 looks at a community where a board dominated by residents makes all policy decisions, including the making of budgets and the hiring and firing of staff, yet does not enjoy broad-based, community-wide participation.)

After 30 years, the principal barriers alluded to by Arnstein are still around, but some new imaginative mechanisms for dealing with these constraints have developed. She saw large urban governments and service bureaucracies manipulating and placating citizens. Today, as Arnstein foresaw, there are grassroots organizations able to hire their own competent staffs and obtain the assistance of lawyers, accountants, architects, and other experts (sometimes as volunteers). Such community organizations usually can hold their own in negotiating with governments and large institutions. Arnstein's straightforward statement of authentic versus ersatz participation remains an astute analysis of the nature and potential of citizen participation, and it issues a sophisticated warning to citizens of the threats that can subvert their power and influence.

Today, we recognize Arnstein's statement as useful but simplistic. More recent experience has revealed to us that although community decisions may be made through a resident-controlled structure, there may still be a tight small inner group of residents monopolizing decisions. The "iron law of oligarchy," still in effect for humanity, leads to situations where once ordinary folk, rising through grassroots and democratic structure, become members of a policy board and persist in keeping a grip on it in perpetuity. In time, they become an entrenched group that monopolizes all of the power levers to hold office year after year. In other cases, perhaps a dozen residents may set up a community development corporation for their town and begin to operate without ever welcoming in others while preempting the field. Such practices might be said to hang banana peels on the top rungs, with slippage imminent, as outsiders seek to enter. Every organization, no matter how democratic its ideals at its beginning, must vigilantly monitor its inclusiveness or lose it.

BARRIERS TO PARTICIPATION

Significant barriers often face limited-income people who seek to become decision makers in the affairs of their community. Three were identified by Tom Collins, a community educator in Ireland who has worked with community organizations in inner-city neighborhoods and council estates (as public housing is called in Ireland). According to Collins (1992), the first barrier is the natural gravitation of more affluent members to take over organizations in their home community, thus blocking out the less affluent. Second is the general "resource deficiency of the poor," where a group lacks money for staff and expert consultants and attracts too few volunteers experienced in running organizations. Poverty makes it difficult for people to join organizations, sustain membership, and have access to the technical assistance needed for effective decision making. People of little means need to find institutional allies who respect their independence, furnish needed resources, and allow them space to gain experience on their own. Third is the necessity for voluntary organizations to compromise with elites to ensure that the money essential to survival keeps flowing into the organization but at the same time mobilizing numbers large enough to insist that they continue to choose their own board.

An example of this occurred in Pittsburgh when residents of the Central North Side fought against the massive land acquisition of nearby Allegheny General Hospital but had to settle reluctantly for giving up several blocks of residential property in exchange for the hospital agreeing to future limits on expansion and the hospital joining with community groups in a binding control to promote the prosperity of the neighborhood by hiring local residents, underwriting a community organizer, and providing incentives for employees to buy homes in the neighborhood.

Collins (1992) saw the reluctance of the poor to join local organizations as often sound and logical economic thinking. People at all income levels participate only up to the point where the gains from doing so are greater than or equal to the costs. For people of limited income, potential gains have to be perceived as feasible, tangible, and fair (pp. 105–107). Too often, gains offered to them are birds in the bush about to fly south for the winter.

This suggests the need for a multilevel participation strategy in which different people will gain different benefits from participation according to their starting points. Chanan (1999) called this extending vertical participation in which all residents have at least one potential entry point (pp. 37–38). Not everyone will be immediately pulled in at the issue action level; therefore, a multilevel strategy for participation will also speak to building relationships, skills, and knowledge. For those typically excluded, participation in a local residents organization can be an important stepping-stone to making new social connections for mutual support and to building a sense of common interest and purpose in the community. For average residents, Chanan saw taking an active role in a local organization as a way of widening their circle of acquaintances and gaining new skills (p. 37). Young people develop a sense of community responsibility and gain recognition of their talent through participation in sports, clubs, the arts, or youth issue groups. More active community members participate as a way of acquiring and exercising leadership competence and influencing the community's development.

As with any time-consuming and complicated human process, participation has a downside: times where it becomes a burden, a limitation, or even an illogical barrier that must be recognized and somehow dealt with. The most frequent cases involve opportunities. For example, a small community has long sought demolition of a high-visibility row of derelict buildings that shelter cat-sized rats and is a threat to adventuresome children. Suddenly, state money is available but must be applied for within a week together with a careful plan for reuse of the cleared land. Leaders of the community organization want public meetings throughout the neighborhood to decide on terms of a planning proposal. The leadership confers, makes as many phone calls as possible testing resident sentiment, and makes a decision to demand a 6-week delay while enlisting local state legislators to support the delay demand. At the same time, leaders form a planning committee of popular residents to kick off town meetings and start the discussion process without delay. This way of operating is risky; the state may move ahead and auction the land to the highest bidder, likely a real estate speculator from the community, but the community is not going to be caught with a hurried incompetent proposal. It will be respected for sticking to its standards. There will be a sound consensus proposal or none at all.

Then there is the efficiency dilemma. Are costs greater than benefits? The organization in the preceding example obtains its delay, compiles a proposal with considerable participation, submits it, and wins a grant. Some neighbors clamor for a kickoff to launch housing construction, while others want time to work out agreements for residents to get priority on jobs being created. Again, the leadership moves to balance time for a fair agreement versus the desire of most neighbors to see action with new houses popping up. Residents are cajoled to come to meetings (either face-to-face or phone-to-phone), hauled and urged, enticed with food, and rewarded with free babysitting and door prizes of video games, grocery certificates, and power screwdrivers. This results in more discussion, more chances for all to be heard, and more gentle pushing, but with deliberate speed from the leadership cadre. Amid "hurry up" complaints, the agreement is teased out and signed. Shovels are in the ground. Not all are happy, but still the outcome represents a confident beginning and a celebrating community. "Hanging in" prevails. Nobody lost—well, almost nobody. Let us now decide how the houses will be allotted fairly and fully. And so it goes.

Organizations continually confronted with serious and delicate public matters learn to handle them with care and deliberation, balancing participation with opportunity and balancing quick results with the need to hear from all.

An organization's strongest claim to represent its community comes from an inclusive membership and an open decision making process. An organization built on such strengths is in a position to make hard choices and defend them successfully. An organization that decides to pass up a windfall of housing funds because there is not time for adequate community discussion of difficult sensitive issues implicit in the offer is in a strong position to defend itself, and to hold the respect of local people, while responding to critics and objectors. Such an organization will have competent leadership and communication as well as the arguments that make credible explanations to the whole community.

When facing formidable questions with potentially damaging consequences, a community-based organization will try to prepare its members and the public in advance—outlining the nature of the issues and spelling out any possible pitfalls and opportunities that may exist. This paves the way for acceptance of decisions. When decisions are made, the *why* questions are communicated. Going into such tense situations, the organization seeks to invoke all of those who may be affected by decisions that are likely to occur.

PARTICIPATION AND ORGANIZATIONAL STRUCTURE

Three alternative models of organizational structure for a community renewal organization that can contribute to the organization's ability to achieve in-depth participation within its small community are outlined here. These structures can be useful in either building or rebuilding a local renewal body. There are other structures possible, but these three probably are the most useful for ensuring participation. If followed faithfully, any of these models could help residents to achieve broad decision making within their community. The shared contributing of money, the opportunities to vote on policy, and the ensured opportunity to have a vote on at least one important committee or task force are the keys to authentic participation.

1. *Membership Structure:* Residents enroll as individual members, pay dues, and are invited

to volunteer for a project or committee. The dues are essential to promote a sense of ownership. Periodic open meetings are held where members are brought up-to-date on programs, are recruited for committees, and can debate and vote on one or two crucial policy matters in addition to electing board members. This model requires a full-time organizer on staff who is attuned to inclusion and to aggressively reaching out to every interest, race, and ethnic group within the community. A regularly published community newspaper can aid cohesion. (The Bloomfield-Garfield Corporation mentioned earlier uses a version of this model.)

2. *Block Club Structure:* Residents join block clubs that are organized throughout the community's territory. One or two full-time organizers employed by the community-wide renewal organization nurture these clubs. Each block club seeks to deal with its own local distress issues, obtaining help from one of the organizers as needed. Block leaders meet together regularly to coordinate their programs, exchange information with officers of the central renewal organization, and make recommendations on policy. Each block club might select a member for the board, or assembled block presidents can choose all or some of the central board members. Organizers need to be sensitive to the importance of a diversified leadership in each block club. (The Hyde Park-Kenwood Conference (Chicago), during its bold early years, and the Mon Valley Initiative (Pennsylvania), during more recent years, used a modified structure of this type.)

3. *Coalition Structure:* Instead of a body of individual members, the renewal organization is a coalition of groups from the same community. It has its own paid staff, including at least one community organizer. The agreement among the associated groups requires an approved system of participation set up within each member group to ensure that each member of each group has a channel for communicating with the coalition board and shares in its raising of funds. There might also be a process by which any member of a group would be able to run for a seat on the coalition board by filing a petition. For the coalition to sustain its inclusive democratic nature, it will need to hold periodic open meetings where its important issues may be discussed and decided by all present, with the decisions made being either binding or powerful recommendations not to be overridden without serious reasons. Boston's Dudley Street is an example of an organization with a modified coalition structure.

We now look at efforts to deal with barriers and opportunities in two community organizations: the Bloomfield-Garfield Corporation and the Dudley Street Neighborhood Initiative. In later chapters, we revisit such activities more than once.

THE BLOOMFIELD-GARFIELD EXPERIENCE

The authors of this book prepared this brief case study based on 20 years of relationships with the Bloomfield-Garfield Corporation (BGC) and its community. The BGC illustrates the three essential elements of participation: willingness to include all, power, and decisions of consequence.

At the beginning of the new century, BGC (introduced in Chapter 2) had 500 members in 350 households and 45 businesses that paid $5 or more per year to belong to the corporation. Its elected board drew from a membership that held open bi-weekly meetings. In addition, numerous non-dues payers were associated as volunteers, users of services, financial contributors, student interns, nonmember residents seeking information or help, and members of committees, task forces, and institutional partnerships. A monthly newspaper pumped out a steady flow of information about programs of the corporation and the activities of community people. The newspaper was widely circulated, and it informed and educated readers about community matters both great and small. Moreover, BGC has long been partially self-supporting. Like many such organizations, it is making increased use of e-mail, a Web site, and chat rooms to capture the involvement of people not able to attend meetings.

"We never ignore an issue that is brought to us by a community person," said Agnes Brose, one of the staff organizers, who raised her children in Bloomfield-Garfield and who has served as a volunteer, founding board member, board chairman, and office manager during the past 22 years.

BGC's program was evaluated by McDevitt (1992), who quoted a public official as telling her, "BGC is the best community development corporation in the city . . ., firmly community-based" (p. 221). Another respondent told her, "BGC has the ability to go beyond real estate." McDevitt's own assessment emphasized BGC's flexibility, realism, and high energy level (pp. 221–226).

The organization's motto is "pay attention." When a few people on one block call in with a small but real annoyance, an organizer helps them to assemble the block's households. People are urged to speak out and make the issue clear for all. Then, the organizer becomes a teacher. As Brose put it,

> We don't promise to take care of every little complaint. We educate residents on how they can empower themselves, who they have to approach in city government, or what agency they can visit. We depend on their self-interest to get things moving. We don't push people to participate until we have something real to offer them. People should learn at every meeting and go away with something serious to do. They should come out excited, feeling they can control their own lives. Next time, they'll want to bring someone else with them to the meeting. When an issue is solved, we want the original complainers bragging they got it done. (personal interview, November 18, 1999)

The corporation keeps a mailing list of all who are helped. People on the list will be called in the future to assist the organization. Brose observed that volunteers are the glue holding the inner city together in the face of crime, shabby jobs, and shrinking population. At BGC's annual Martin Luther King, Jr. celebration, an all-day open house at a neighborhood church is the focal point, with entertainment by community musicians, dancers, comics, poets, and actors. Original poems are recited, songs are sung, and speeches are made by those in high and low positions. Residents offer their talents, whether they are BGC members or not. Pride abounds, and there is a strong incentive for building participation, with "standing room only" the rule of the day. It is an annual event that BGC describes as "ordinary people paying tribute to an extraordinary man."

BGC and its wise and determined director, Richard Swartz, are strong supporters of the living wage. Low wages are widespread among Garfield's hard-working population. Recently, a household survey sponsored by the Pittsburgh Partnership for Neighborhood Development (2000) reported,

> Garfield residents represent an experienced workforce doing work important to the Pittsburgh economy. Most employed residents started working at 16 [years of age]. But their wages are low. The median annual wage for a head of household was found to be $17,000, an amount well under the poverty line. About 90% of the workforce was employed, with the 10% jobless rate more then double the regional rate. (p. 6)

During recent years, the traditional gulf between the community and its hospitals, nursing homes, and public schools has been reduced through an organizing effort built around the mutual concerns of residents and institutions for safety, a more attractive environment, and living wage work, with the residents needing jobs and the institutions needing reliable, steady competent employees. For this large-scale effort, the corporation united with nearby neighborhoods and formed joint task forces and committees to work on issues that bring institutions and community people together, issues in which both institutional representatives and residents have a self-interest.

Every organization has its difficulties from which all can learn. In spite of their "citizens first" approach, BGC's full-time staff members plead guilty to being quoted too often in the press as organizational spokespersons, a practice they blame on the need for quick responses at times when no volunteer leader is available. This practice can become a barrier to participation where staff members have been around for more than 20 years, as in Bloomfield-Garfield, and yet still have not built a system for resident volunteers to handle sudden requests from the media. Such a practice usually means that the "iron law" is still in force, blocking opportunities to develop indigenous leadership.

The 20-plus years means that the three top staff leaders are experienced veterans with savvy, commitment, and contacts. No other trio in town can match them in dedication and competence. But these are three white people. One African American and one Asian American are now in professional staff slots, and top board officers are often African American (as is more than half of the population). One of the three veteran staff organizers is Richard Flanagan, who leads the youth development program. He defended BGC staff tenure as an unusual case where staff experience and dedication are crucial to a community in severe crisis. He argued that emerging development projects will eventually provide funds to diversify the staff racially, and in 2002 there were signs that this was happening (personal interview, May 26, 1999).

Brose summed up BGC's practices on participation as follows:

We always need members' ideas and energies. Almost year-round, the organization is involved in planning that requires the insight and experience of those who live or work in the community, and we can always find a role for anyone who has the time to help with an after-school program, a door-to-door survey, the publication of our newspaper, or the design of a public art project. (personal interview, November 18, 1999)

The organization's leadership is ever conscious of making the board inclusive, seeking to ensure representation of male and female, old and young, black and white, professional and business, employers and workers, retired and unemployed, public housing residents and homeowners. To run for the board, a person must record at least 6 months of active duty with the organization. "Participation comes first," in the opinion of Brose. "Only then are we able to get into bricks and mortar" (personal interview, November 18, 1999). Brose provided a model for vigorous personal recruiting in handling small, immediate neighborhood irritations with maximum participation. She indicated that she is always ready to welcome in all residents, including the gloomy neighbors who refuse to believe in renewal.

Early in 2000, the BGC, arm in arm with Garfield's Jubilee Housing Association, announced a bashing of both gloom and doom through a $20 million "do it right" rebuilding of Garfield's largely abandoned central hillside. In concert, the adjoining Garfield Heights public housing community unveiled a proposal to tear down its segregated and blighted "project structures and replace them with $30 million worth of attractive mixed-income, mixed-race homes." Construction for the first phase of 50 homes was to begin in the fall of 2002. Brose declared, "We're going to do something bigger than big" (personal interview, November 18, 1999). City planner Christopher Shea, who lives nearby, added, "This is one of those places where African American and white families work together for the community. They are out to dim the lines of race and class." Overall, hundreds of vacant and abandoned houses and apartments will be demolished, freeing tracts of land with a dramatic site and view for rebuilding with resident ideas shaping decisions, but in the long run this will require much more than $50 million in public and private investments.

At the time of this writing, the two sponsoring organizations were pressing government for financial commitments. By the spring of 2002, $1,550,000 was promised as initial contributions to the dramatic housing effort. Throughout the planning, open sessions were held and usually drew 50 or 60 residents. Over 2 years, hundreds of residents took part in these and associated activities aimed at renewing the central hillside. As planning and fund-raising proceeded, BGC kept up a drumfire of new programs to keep interest high. These involved expanded after-school programs for elementary school children, reaching out to diabetics, town meetings for improving the lives of seniors, and campaigns to increase community benefits from the local hospitals and health maintenance organizations (HMOs).

A dramatic campaign, mounted by a multi-community neighborhood organization-trade union alliance under the leadership of Brose, fought to save the jobs of employees at the area's Nabisco plant, which closed in 1999 after 80 years of production, laying off 250 people. Nabisco was pressured to maintain the closed plant and its equipment in working condition until a new owner was found in the Atlantic Baking Group. Residents, government officials, and the Steel Valley Authority were mobilized in the fight. By 2002, Atlantic Baking had the restored plant up and running but was suffering from an uncertain market and a shortage of working capital before its new owners found an investor who helped them to acquire five additional baking plants owned by Keebler, which was expected to stabilize the firm and double employment at the Pittsburgh plant, raising it from 200 to 400. Brose told a *Pittsburgh Post-Gazette* reporter, "I feel very rewarded. It's a great reward for anyone who played a role in this. People have to know if you come together, things can happen. Change can happen" (McKay, 2002, p. A-9).

In 2002, local government was occupied beginning a $10 million facelift for Penn Avenue negotiated by BGC through the city council. Penn is the historic main commercial street that wanders through the neighborhood and connects it with downtown.

THE DUDLEY STREET EXPERIENCE

For a more advanced model of participation and development in a broad strategic planning context, we can look at the work that the Dudley Street Neighborhood Initiative (DSNI) has gone through to create, first, itself as an organization with a mission and direction and, second, its long-range plan for an "urban village" as the center of its revitalization effort, a village now well along in construction.

Medoff and Sklar (1994) described how leaders of Dudley Street agencies, community activists, and interested outside funders began to mobilize against government neglect and business abuse in 1984 and saw themselves building an "organization of organizations" governed by a board that would be "broadly representative of the community" but dominated by traditional leadership from health and human service agencies, community development corporations, local businesses, religious institutions, and city and state governments. This elitist approach ran into a firestorm during an open community meeting called by the leadership in early 1985 to gain public ratification. Residents angrily challenged the legitimacy of the proposed board and launched a process that led to a governance structure with a resident majority, a blend of old and fresh new leadership, including low-income residents and representatives of indigenous community organizations as well as officers of the Riley Foundation, which had made a resource commitment to the new organization.

By 1986, this democratic structure was ready to start defining a plan for use of the neighborhood's large quantities of vacant land. Begun was a bold planning process that was open to widespread participation and was aimed at reflecting community aspirations and building on resilient strengths. Staff members and board leaders made personal contacts to persuade people to join in.

A request for proposals was created and distributed, with several planning firms submitting bids. Resident members of DSNI oversaw the selection process. The firm chosen held an all-day retreat with the staff and board members to clarify roles and expectations. Together, they reviewed the board's vision for the future and identified neighborhood assets, development opportunities, and constraints to action. A resident-directed planning committee became responsible for overall management, meeting every other week with the firm's planners to review progress. Resident committee members made frequent suggestions and modifications. As needed, subcommittees were set up to help assess and rework specific pieces of the plan, allowing additional community people to join in. Residents on the committee and its subcommittees had little or no technical background when they began, but they mastered vocabulary and techniques as the plan took shape, enabling them to challenge the firm's professionals at times.

Throughout the neighborhood, residents were regularly informed of planning progress through knocking on doors, mailings, flyers, newspaper ads and articles, radio announcements, and town meetings. Open, community-wide meetings were held where residents and planners looked at the community with attention to both strengths and needs. Each person attending was invited to join a committee or subcommittee. Focus groups were held, with residents telling their stories, stating their concerns, and suggesting solutions from their own experiences. Surveys sought more information and deeper insights from human service providers. The results were helpful but disappointing in the degree of resident response. Only a small percentage actually became involved.

In time, designers and architects began to sketch out drawings for a renewed neighborhood based on the resident dreams, hopes, and disappointments aired at the open sessions. These often lengthy "charettes" were held at the community center of the local public housing community, with DSNI providing transportation for any who asked for it. In time, an agreed-on plan was approved at public meetings and won support of Boston Mayor Ray Flynn. Today, the community is well along in development of its urban village, centered where Dudley Street and Blue Hill Avenue meet.

For the first time, the neighborhood is achieving a central point of identity—designed for meeting, strolling, watching, and living—with a park, retail shops, and a community activities building. Since its adoption, the plan has sparked and guided building and rebuilding throughout the neighborhood. (A visit by one of the authors [Cunningham] in 1996 found housing construction to be under way on every block—mostly new housing on vacant land but also the upgrading of existing housing—and the creation of small, public open areas for sitting and active play. Significant additional progress had been made by the time of the other author's [Murphy] visit in 1999. The vision of an urban village is now becoming fully realized in bricks and mortar, and the dramatic central point appeared completed when Cunningham made a return visit in June 2002.)

Medoff and Sklar (1994) summed up DSNI's open door planning:

> DSNI had successfully flipped the traditionally top-down development planning process on its head. It had created a new bottom-up, participatory, comprehensive planning process. And it has mobilized sufficient strength to win unprecedented city government support for the residents' vision of a revitalized Dudley. (p. 113)

The Dudley Street case, with its fruitful cooperation between mayor and citizens, has given additional impetus to a restoration of trust between citizens and local government. Peter Dreier, who served 9 years as director of housing at the Boston Redevelopment Authority and was a close adviser to Mayor Flynn, expressed this view:

> Rather than viewing neighborhood residents as passive consumers or clients of government services, it is more appropriate, as well as more efficient and effective, to view them as citizens and partners who can help shape, promote, and even deliver services. In order for America's urban neighborhoods to be healthy, their residents must gain a stronger voice in shaping the physical, economic, and social conditions in their communities. . . . Citizen participation can sometimes be messy and even conflicting, but it often results in better public policy, more cost-effective programs, and a healthier democracy. (Dreier, 1996, p. 123)

Into the new century, DSNI has continued to involve a substantial portion of its population and to realize its urban village in bricks, mortar, and job opportunities. It was awarded the 2001 leadership award by Independent Sector in November 2001. As indicated in Chapter 2, DSNI obtained control over most of the neighborhood's vacant land early on. This was done through DSNI's being legally delegated the power of eminent domain. It is a power that DSNI has exercised on a few occasions when conflicts have arisen with would-be investors as to how certain parcels would be used. DSNI Director John Barros commented, "This power has helped us maintain and enforce our community review process which monitors and protects planning decisions arrived at by open process" (personal interview, May 2002). As a child in Dudley Street, he participated in neighborhood cleanups and was the first youth to serve on the DSNI board. Later, he graduated from Dartmouth worked in the corporate world, and eventually competed successfully for the director position. He believes that indigenous staff members bring extra strength and heads a staff with 9 of 14 members from the Dudley Street community. Before his birth, his family migrated to Boston from Cape Verde. He believes that because of his young age and ethnic background, some people doubted his ability to do the job well, but "over time I believe I have convinced them otherwise" (personal interview, May 2002).

Regardless of which structure a renewal group chooses, there is one overarching quality that requires close attention. It is a quality that helps to ensure that participation will be vigorous and sustained. It is what we have come to call group process.

Group process is consciously making sure that an organization is inclusive and that personal relationships are attended to. It is the mode of operating that emphasizes generous spirit among and between participants and that gives high priority to openness, trust building, respect for diverse views, mutual support, and sharing of decision making. It is continuous information sharing, using e-mail, Web pages, faxes, and other technological means as well as printed newsletters, telephone chains, and face-to-face conversations (with the latter always being the most useful). It is a way that produces cohesion.

Good group process assumes that everyone has a voice worth listening to. There are periodic planned opportunities for people to speak out with the leadership listening. The leadership works to create a "welcoming spirit" with "pay attention" attitudes toward the thoughts of newcomers. There are small social events within the organization (e.g., potluck suppers, backyard parties, cosmic bowling) to firm up the organizational fabric. Experienced members should be designated as hosts to ensure that new members are getting attention and being listened to. Group process in fact needs as much attention as does organizational structure.

If an organization is to build its local community's social fabric, then its internal activities need to be supportive of this goal. Activities such as the sharing of power, maintaining of accessibility, and mutual listening by participants create an environment to which neighbors are freely admitted and by which they are offered the means to transform themselves, learn new skills, and take on civic responsibilities.

Literature and political discourse during the new century put heavy emphasis on people finding a sense of identity amid increasing scale, diversity, conflict, and violence. "Small community" and "participation" are twin elements most cited as the keys to human stability and tranquility. Across America, we find the effort to make sense of a world growing increasingly complex, sterile, and insecure while people desperately seek to counter that sterility and insecurity by seeking a sense of community and family in their own living place amid trusted neighbors. The efforts described in Bloomfield-Garfield and Dudley Street epitomize such seeking. Such community controlled development likely can be launched in any small community, with the community building and achieving in its own way and with its own structure and form.

Delgado (2000), in his principles for community, made as his first principle, "Create community participation stressing inter-ethnic-racial relations." He suggested active group creation such as painting murals, growing beautiful public gardens, building children-designed "playscapes," and erecting large street sculptures (pp. 62–64). Harvard University's William Julius Wilson, whose pioneering Chicago research guides contemporary understanding of black urban poverty in America, urged groups of ordinary citizens of all races to embrace mutual political cooperation as the only path to gaining sufficient influence "to ease their economic and social burdens" (Wilson, 1999, p. 123).

Looking toward a World Summit on Social Development, the United Nations (1993) called for the building of "a new people-centered world order" while finding that "the decentralization of power—from capital cities to regions, towns, and villages—can be one of the best ways of empowering people, promoting public participation, and increasing efficiency." All across the globe, the United Nations finds old models of security, development, market, and international cooperation being challenged by "a profound human revolution that makes people's participation the central objective in all parts of life. Every institution—and every policy action—should be judged by one critical test: How does it meet the genuine aspirations of the people?" (p. 8).

SUMMARY

Participation is necessary for the well-being of the small community, just as it is essential to the health of the human spirit. Its residents and other hands-on stakeholders alone can do the personal, parent-to-child, neighbor-to-neighbor work that is needed to preserve or restore a small community. The more universal the participation, the more likely community change efforts will be authentic and sustained. Close attention to racial and ethnic inclusion is essential if a small community is to attain unity and the power that goes with it. However, inclusion is never easy. Barriers to universal participation exist that can be overcome only by strong incentives and local leaders who recruit personally and persistently. The events of September 11, 2001, and the government's response to them make inclusion more important to society, but only if it is free of partisan bias and derision.

Historically, large governments, business corporations, and institutions are structured to dominate in democracies. Elites of wealth, talent, and position tend to crowd out ordinary people. In most small communities, there are people who are paralyzed by job insecurity, racial fears, lack of education, bad housing, ill health, and/or limited access to networks of contacts and power. Organizing participation requires making a special effort to surmount such barriers and welcoming in all people on an equal footing.

When the vision projected by a change effort is clear, is feasible, and touches real self-interests, numerous people will respond, at least for short periods of time. The comprehensive approach advocated in this book for organizing community controlled development requires a very heavy component of resident involvement, and collaboration with other organizations is needed whenever a partnership must provide the extra leverage to exploit a major opportunity.

Participation can transform people and small communities, but it is a difficult process to keep on track. There is more to be learned about how to do this. For a detailed lesson on local people struggling to rebuild their community, we turn to the Aliquippa story in Chapter 7.

Continuing Questions

1. Would it be more practical to have a few representatives of important interests in a community as the participants and decision makers rather than expend scarce resources seeking widespread open participation? Does a process focus always delay or reduce product outcomes?

2. Is it fruitless to seek to include limited-income residents in participation when they are distracted and consumed by the struggle to survive?

3. What causes paternalism in organizers? How can it be mitigated?

4. Is intensive participation more likely to lead to a cohesive citizenry or to interest group conflict and community paralysis?

5. Can masses of people make good public decisions? Don't large mobilizations just bring instability to a community?

6. How much participation is enough?

7. What new methods need to be devised to ensure that all racial and income groups are included?

8. Can high technology support and enhance participation, or does it merely become another barrier to separate belongers from the masses?

References

Arnstein, R. (1969, July). A ladder of citizen participation. *Journal of the American Institute of Planners,* pp. 216–224.

Ball, C., & Knight, B. (1999). Why we must listen to citizens. In *Civil society at the millennium* (pp. 17–26). West Hartford, CT: Kumarian Press.

Berry, J. M., Portney, E., & Thomson, K. (1993). *The rebirth of urban democracy.* Washington: DC: Brookings Institution Press.

Chanan, G. (1999). *Local community involvement: A handbook for good practice.* Dublin, Ireland: European Foundation for the Development of Living and Working Conditions.

Collins, T. (1992). Participation and marginalized groups. In B. Reynolds & S. Healhy (Eds.), *Power, participation, and exclusion.* Dublin, Ireland: Conference of Major Superiors.

Delgado, M. (2000). *Community social work practice in an urban context.* New York: Oxford University Press.

Dreier, P. (1996, May). Community empowerment strategies: The limits and potential of community organizing in urban neighborhoods. *Cityscape, 2*(2), 121–159. (Washington DC: U.S. Department of Housing and Urban Development)

McDevitt, S. (1992). *Community development corporations: Antecedents, influences, results.* Ph.D. dissertation, University of Pittsburgh.

McKay, J. (2002, April 4). Rescued East Liberty cracker company branches out. *Pittsburgh Post-Gazette,* pp. A1, A9.

Medoff, P., & Sklar, H. (1994). *Streets of hope: The rise and fall of an urban neighborhood*. Boston: South End Press.

Pittsburgh Partnership for Neighborhood Development. (2000). *The Garfield employment study: Profile of a working city neighborhood*. Pittsburgh, PA: Author.

Putnam, R. (2002, February 11). Bowling together. *The American Prospect, 13*(3), 20–22.

Tocqueville, A. (1954). *Democracy in America* (Vol. 1). New York: Vintage Books.

United Nations. (1993). *Human development report*. New York: Oxford University Press.

United Nations. (1998). *Human development report*. New York: Oxford University Press.

United Nations. (2001). *Human development report*. New York: Oxford University Press.

Wilson, W. J. (1999). *The bridge over the racial divide: Rising inequality and coalition politics*. Berkeley: University of California Press.

7

ALIQUIPPA

A Small Community on the Front Line

When much of southwestern Pennsylvania's steel industry collapsed into rust and dust during the early 1980s, the shock to the Aliquippa community inflicted thousands of families with sudden anguish. The timing and scale of the collapse detonated economic and social spasms that reverberate to this day.

Response to the havoc came from residents, their families, and their supporters in local institutions. With dogged locking of arms, they became the Aliquippa Alliance for Unity and Development (AAUD) and dug in for survival and collective recovery. After almost 20 years of triumphs and disappointments, the AAUD has much to teach us about economic development organizing from the sheer hell of trying to resurrect one of America's once-proud industrial towns. Aliquippa's plight matches that of thousands of aging industrial communities racked by technological change and global economics and also ravaged by the plight of "undercrowdedness" that can impair the best laid plans of citizens and their small communities. Aliquippa's history is instructive but is not yet a success story.

Chapter 5 described community organizing as 12 activities for undertaking renewal and rebuilding. Since 1983, residents of Aliquippa and their allies have sought to get their community moving. As the Aliquippa record unfolds in this chapter, the strengths and weaknesses of the AAUD's handling of the 12 activities are assessed, not to render judgment but rather to extract valuable lessons.

The Aliquippa experience is used because it is fresh material, fully available to the authors of this book, and because the issues and events encountered represent an unusually full range of the challenges likely to be met in community economic development organizing. Particularly instructive is Aliquippa's money-raising approach as to both what it has done and what it has not done. Remarkable also is the caution with which the organization has approached forming partnerships with other organizations.

An autonomous and conscientious board of community people has run the AAUD show with both volunteer and paid organizers facilitating. The budget has grown, media have been wrestled with, marches have been joined, videos have been produced, governors have been welcomed, a tottering credit union has been saved (sort of), and an estimated 10,000 struggling people have been aided (some a little, some a lot). In short, we believe that Aliquippa is a valuable story of ordinary people doing extraordinary things and engaged in experiences possible for most citizens to identify with. The community has survived but has not recovered.

The AAUD's basic premise is that a small community can be preserved if both external and internal resources are mobilized through an effort that balances self-help and massive outside investment. Its vision goes beyond the survival of Aliquippa. It has pursued change and development, with special concern for the large poverty population living in and around its Franklin Avenue core. And it has dared to entertain the hope of a stable renewed community where town youth would believe they could stay and prosper.

An abbreviated historical story is presented in this chapter. It begins with the residents pitching in to create a strong organization and a local safety net while moving toward more venturesome goals. The alliance pursues the impossible dream, making deals with other organizations and waking up to the reality of the vast scale of resources needed to approach real recovery. Along the way is a running commentary of what all of this might teach us about Organizing for Community Controlled Development (OCCD). The chapter closes with a summary, a list of hard-to-answer questions, and speculation on the town's future. No matter how bad its situation, every small community has a future to face.

Aliquippa's efforts to fight back, tailor-make its own distinctive renewal organization, and open a path to survival and toward recovery make a sobering case. In addition to attempting to use the 12 activities, the alliance has been a pioneer in combining economic development and human service delivery within a community-organizing framework. We suggest that the reader absorb this useful story while keeping in mind that the 12 activities will inevitably play out differently in each community that organizes itself to pursue unity and development.

BACKGROUND

Aliquippa is a once-prosperous town, only 8 miles from the Pittsburgh International Airport, founded in 1905–1906 by the Jones and Laughlin Steel Corporation for the sole purpose of making steel. It has sought a rebirth through the efforts of 500 community volunteers, 10 paid staff members, and an array of cooperating agencies and institutions. These aligned forces help to launch enterprises, create jobs, provide an abundance of survival social services, rejuvenate real estate, seek to help the school

system be more creative as its student body shrinks, work to beautify the environment, trap outside investments, and attempt to lift the spirits and capacities of a biracial population of 11,734 (U.S. Bureau of the Census, 2000), all that is left in a community that boasted 27,000 people in 1930. As late as the mid-1970s, it was home to 20,000 residents then tied to a vigorous downtown core and a dominant beneficent employer. Today, every move the town makes is affected by its people shrinkage. During the lifetimes of several of its current residents, Aliquippa has lost 55% of its population, while the nation has increased its population by 220% (see Figure 7.1).

The town's sprawling riverfront mill (sold to the LTV conglomerate during the 1970s) employed 10,000 until 1980, when declining national markets forced cutbacks that by 1983 brought mill employment down below 3,000 and by 2000 brought it down to 300. As in industrial communities throughout the nation, the Aliquippa plant closing meant that households and institutions were severely affected, and most local businesses closed or fled to nearby suburban locations. In late 1983, a team of seven graduate social work students from the University of Pittsburgh showed up in Aliquippa to assess the impact of sudden massive joblessness.

LAUNCHING THE ALLIANCE

The student team that came to Aliquippa in 1983 discovered job loss in free fall, 55% of family incomes wiped out, and the downtown Franklin Avenue core disintegrating. They saw central Aliquippa taking on the classic pattern of urban poverty and decay, with impoverished people living in housing that was substandard or subsidized (or both), encircled by town rings of still tidy moderate-income neighborhoods, and relatively affluent outer rings of suburban townships. They found concerned people and anxious organizations but no planning or cohesive organizing. Town government was fractured by infighting and uncertainty and was left rudderless without the strong guiding hand of the steel company. Racial conflicts, rigidly

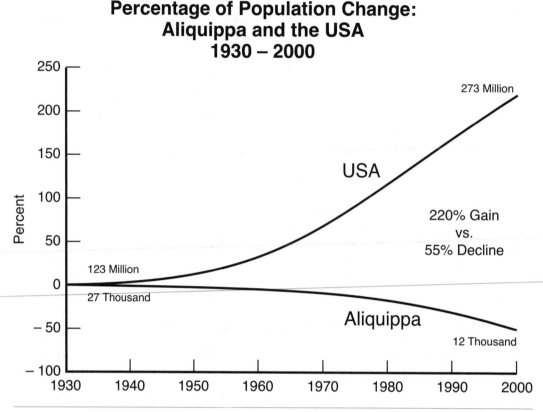

Figure 7.1   Percentage of Population Change: Aliquippa and United States, 1930–2000

segregated neighborhoods, and sometimes-hostile police despoiled social unity. The students' blunt, widely circulated report shook the community and motivated two area residents to bring wise heads together to face the distress.

These resident initiators were Cathy Cairns, one of the graduate students responsible for the shocking report, and Lorenzo Williams. Williams was an officer of the local National Association for the Advancement of Colored People (NAACP), a former welfare caseworker, and a lifelong resident of the town with a degree in community development from Pennsylvania State University who had been looking for a way in which to help get the town moving. Cairns and Williams met when they separately found their way to a regional "comeback conference" of unemployed people. They discovered that they shared hopes for uniting a critical mass of Aliquippa people powerful enough to provoke

change. As an interracial team, they matched the diversity of the Aliquippa community.

Hitting the recruitment trail, they made phone calls, conducted house calls, and cornered people at church gatherings. They went to borough council meetings selling their conviction that there were enough dedicated people in Aliquippa to launch a revival. They listened to people and invited those most interested to gather in the back room of the Brighton Hot Dog Shoppe, which they considered "a neutral location [politically], where the meeting room was free, as long as those attending ordered hot dogs and cokes" (Cairns & Cunningham, 1986, p. 67).

Coming together on July 12, 1984, were 27 chosen hopefuls from in, around, and beyond the town. This group was composed of the mayor and 4 other political activists, 5 attendees from various religious institutions, and 6 business people, half of whom were real estate developers.

There were 3 private citizens, 3 social agency representatives, 2 persons from the University of Pittsburgh, plus 1 each from the hospital, steelworkers union, and a civic group.

Cairns and Williams led a spirited discussion of the crisis, which produced a list of 15 problems, with Problem 1 being "the dependence on and the insensitivity of the steel company." The gathering settled on three aims: town unity, the retraining of displaced workers, and the pursuit of outside aid. All 27 members pledged to stick with the group for at least 1 year.

A handful of them volunteered to convene within a week. Meeting at All Saints Episcopal Church, they chose community pride and job creation as the first targets. Within another week, there was an open meeting at the union hall with a larger group. This group included representatives of the LTV Steel Corporation, who showed no interest in joining a planning effort and left early. Community people agreed to organize a beginning structure with teams to tackle community pride, business and development, health and human services, and police-community relations. These teams quickly moved to plan and produce visible results.

During a lively discussion, this All Saints assembly identified its start-up mission and embedded it in an organization name: the Aliquippa Alliance for Unity and Development. Cairns later explained, "The name was chosen because it stated the group's two purposes—bringing the town together and the creation of jobs while helping the unemployed" (Cairns & Cunningham, 1986, p. 70).

Williams was elected the first chairperson. As an African American growing up in Aliquippa, he knew firsthand the discrimination and tensions associated with employment, housing, and police behavior. There followed 3 months of recruiting, with Cairns, Williams, and a crew of faithful adherents turning out a body of people, some of whom possessed organizational know-how and others of whom began to gain it "on the job" while tracking down needed information, holding town meetings, begging for resources, and sweating out decisions.

To recruit more volunteers, they called on their contacts, followed up on suggestions from clergy and politicians, and signed up people who stopped them on the street to ask questions.

Rather than persuading people, they usually identified people already set to help. The two organizers found that being volunteers themselves made it easier to ask others.

Cairns and Williams and a handful of other regulars provided continuity. From the beginning, this start-up "cadre" was open, with members dropping away periodically and new ones working their way in. In less than a year, a job change pulled Williams out as chair, and Sister Carol Berger filled in. Sister Carol was parish social minister at Our Lady of Fatima Church in adjacent Hopewell Township. Several clergy helped to build the alliance but generally acted as individuals, not bringing along the support of their congregations. Church connections were complicated by the existence of two church ministerial associations separated largely by race, a legacy of Aliquippa's apartheid past. The founding steel corporation in 1906 had set up the town with a separate residential "plan" for each racial and nationality group.

Active cadre members formed a board by consensus (no election). A key member of the leadership core was Mary Ann Ilov, who had previously organized her neighbors to solve a festering road problem and served a spell as treasurer of the borough government. Recently, looking back at the 1980s, she remembered, "It was the political people who quickly moved away from the effort. They were uncomfortable with it. They didn't understand the openness and power sharing. Only Danny Britza, the mayor, stuck it out" (personal interview, August 26, 1997).

Ilov recalled that while several dedicated residents joined the board, she was especially impressed by the new organization's ability to attract volunteers from beyond the town, pointing out that a majority of the 13 citizens serving on the first board of directors lived outside the municipal boundaries of Aliquippa. However, most of the "outsiders" came from nearby townships and represented a church, a hospital, a union, a chamber of commerce, or a school that was located inside the town. Having the town's boundary line separating their homes from Franklin Avenue was of little consequence. Although distress in Aliquippa was most intense and widespread, with its town government and school board both suffering large property tax revenue losses and its public housing sheltering nearly a quarter of the severely impoverished people of the region, there also were numerous households in adjacent communities dragged down by the mill closing that gave the struggle a regional relevance.

Assessment

After 79 years of loyal service from Aliquippa and its workforce, the steel corporation deserted the town's households and institutions with only a handful of jobs left behind. The residents and the institutions assumed the burden of survival and rebirth.

In Aliquippa, two young residents, unfazed by the task and agreeing on a vision for a restored Aliquippa, took the initiative to recruit a diverse team of concerned people from the devastated mill town and adjacent affected communities. They confirmed and filled out the vision and taught recruits how to mobilize others while planning and building an organizational structure. This process involved vision spreading, recruitment, leadership development, cadre formation, the launching of a structured body, and continuous research and planning by this body— the first six activities of community organizing as described in Chapter 5. With persistence, the two volunteer organizers facilitated the launching of a new organization. As with Boston's Dudley Street beginning, institutional professionals were prominent in the AAUD, but unlike the Dudley Street case, there was no struggle for power between institutions and residents in the AAUD. Aliquippa institutions and households alike felt caught in the same cauldron of collapse and cooperated closely with each other. The Aliquippa effort was diminished, however, by its miniscule church involvement, and the opportunity to begin with a widely publicized open board election was passed up. Community elections done with flair and fairness could have boosted credibility and influence as well as attracted a more diverse leadership. Friendly outsiders were appointed to the board so as to enlist able dependable talent quickly. This was a time of crisis. Aliquippa's leadership team believed that the most urgent priority was tangible programs and projects. There were short-term gains from such a direction, but it did not bode well for achieving depth of participation in the future.

BUILDING A SURVIVAL SAFETY NET

A mixture of seasoned board members and promising volunteers moved to lift residents' spirits. Within a few weeks, their Community Pride and Activities Committee had a 2-day Community Days Celebration at Morrell Field with ethnic food booths, professional and amateur talent shows, and a live concert for teenagers. Despite rain showers, the celebration drew hundreds of people. However, many towns' people stayed away, uncertain and suspicious of the new organization. Some were not comfortable with an interracial gathering.

Next came a lively Christmas party for children. Cairns reported,

> No matter what the challenge or personal inconvenience, this committee has moved forward, through buckets of rain on the Santa Claus trucks, scarcity of electrical wiring, banners falling from poles, and hot sausage sandwiches with no buns. Most on this committee had previously worked together to raise funds to benefit the steel union's food bank. The committee members have seen Aliquippa's good days and understand the community spirit needs of the town. (Cairns & Cunningham, 1986, p. 74)

Members of the Business and Development Committee came on board through the Aliquippa Chamber of Commerce and the borough government. The committee consulted economic development specialists to learn about programs that seemed to help in other depressed steel areas and carefully studied their own collapsed area.

Putting its research to work, the Business and Development Committee laboriously compiled inventories of available property in the old downtown business district and sent word of bargain space to organizations, firms, and government agencies that might have an interest in low-cost commercial real estate. The committee sponsored tours of idle sections of the massive LTV mill and took steps to suggest the site to General Motors for location of its Saturn plant. But little came of this, with the town having few assets for attracting investments from outside beyond a riverfront site and an available semi-skilled workforce.

Pastor Charles McClung did work successfully with alliance support to persuade the Episcopal Diocese of Pittsburgh to sponsor the Community of Celebration, a Christian community in Scotland that sought to relocate to a distressed American community where its presence might make a difference. When the community relocated to Aliquippa, it brought leadership, a prayerful membership, and property investments. It purchased and rehabilitated one side of a block of Franklin Avenue for its headquarters and family living quarters. From the time of its arrival, the Community of Celebration became a strength to the town and the alliance, furnishing staff and board members, volunteers for many projects, and a strong spiritual and service presence in the town. The Community of Celebration became the alliance's most steady church-based supporting organization, a genuine element of stability.

A long-nagging source of disunity in Aliquippa had been racial antipathy. Not only had Aliquippa been established with a separate neighborhood for each racial and nationality group (Cairns & Cunningham, 1986), but the town's 657 government-assisted rental housing units isolated people by race. The flash point for racist conflict became the borough police department. Black residents claimed abuse by white officers, while white officers talked about the criminal conduct of black residents.

The Alliance's Police-Community Relations Committee began work in a volatile environment. Its members included top officers of the police force, McClung, the president of the NAACP, an assistant district attorney, the head of the county's women's shelter, Britza, and Cathy Cairns (chair of the committee). It sought to sponsor positive police-citizen dialogue and to assist the police department in upgrading its training procedures and community relations skills, but it found residents reluctant to become involved.

The committee planned a follow-up training program for Aliquippa police that quickly petered out, as the state police were unable to both cover police work assignments during training times and do the teaching. Several Aliquippa officers refused to attend despite direct orders.

Although distrust triumphed in aborting the training, the accompanying publicity did raise public awareness, and outbreaks of overt racism declined. Racism was not an issue that the AAUD would ignore, but the cadre leading the organization began to seek other approaches. In time, the appointment of a black police chief eased the tension. Meanwhile, in its open manner, the Alliance became a visible model of diversity. The informal cadre of active leaders, the board, the committees, the meetings, the forums, the celebrations, and the groups of volunteers working on projects included both black and white residents. However, white residents in outer-edge neighborhoods and the suburban enclaves beyond isolated themselves from central Aliquippa more than ever before.

THE NEED FOR A SOCIAL SERVICE CENTER

The work of the Human Services Committee was more productive. It organized a town meeting at which unemployed residents spoke about their survival struggles to a panel of elected and appointed public officials, with their testimony backed by social service workers who reported being overwhelmed by demands for help. Rising hunger, child and spouse abuse, mental illness, drug use, youth crime, and housing difficulties (e.g., the inability to pay heating bills) were described.

Recommendations from witnesses centered on the need for a multi-service "one-stop shop" service center. The county's social service agencies had become scattered in other towns that were inaccessible to many low-income families. Achieving the center became the focus of the Alliance.

A fund-raising committee headed by board member Richard Dupree was established. By late 1985, the Alliance had purchased an old solid brick building on Franklin Avenue for $9,000 with funds supplied by county government. Mellon Bank, which still had three branches in the borough, contributed $5,000 toward renovation. It was the first of many joint arrangements with county government, which recognized the impotence of Aliquippa's borough government and saw an inexpensive way in which to help out the voters of the largest municipality in Beaver County. Mellon Bank was preparing to partially disinvest in the town and needed a way in which to maintain goodwill with Aliquippa depositors, including some of the business people active on AAUD committees.

Alliance leaders mobilized crews of retired and unemployed workers to gut and remake the spacious interior of the newly acquired building. Their labor began on a February morning in 1986, when Father Jay Geisler of St. Titus Catholic Church on Franklin Avenue celebrated the 7 a.m. mass for volunteers and parishioners and joined them in a march down the avenue to start work.

The transformation proceeded as an all-volunteer operation, with the Mellon Bank funds used for those materials that could not be obtained as donations. Alliance members and merchants supplied pots of chili and pizza, casseroles, cakes, and cash to keep 50 volunteers nourished for several days of plaster demolition, trash removal, and drywall installation. Ilov remembered that "many of the volunteers, black and white, had worked together in the mill and were elated to be together again" (personal interview, August 26, 1997).

Local architect John Tomich donated design expertise. Retired contractor Charles Chilleo and ex-mill foreman George Glomb served as gratis construction chiefs. When Chilleo became seriously ill, Ilov put on a hard hat and filled in. As Mellon Bank money ran out, studs, nails, and other materials were financed by the sale of $10 shares of "stock in Aliquippa" to families, firms, and institutions. More than $4,000 was raised in a week, a promising start to grassroots fund-raising.

As resources were tapped, conversations began with service agencies throughout Beaver County regarding rental of space in the remodeled building, the Franklin Center A total of 19 public and nonprofit agencies, including a service office of the local elected member of the state house of representatives, signed leases. By May 1986, a working center of human development for Aliquippa families was in use with brightly painted offices and light blue carpet. On June 27, Lieutenant Governor William Scranton, III, and three AAUD volunteers simultaneously cut the ribbon officially dedicating the "Franklin Center."

From property acquisition to dedication in 201 days—a volunteer miracle! Aliquippa now had a $150,000 asset created through sweat equity. The town's distressed families had a walk-in location for finding solace and tangible aid, one they could view as their own "people helping people" center. The community had visible evidence that the alliance meant business.

The 250 families per month original projection for center use was soon surpassed, going over 1,000 per month within a year. In 3 years, that figure was doubled, and the center was expanding into the empty Isaly's ice cream building beside it. About 60% of the people using the center were from the town, with the balance being from southern Beaver County. AAUD leaders estimated an even split among black and white residents using the facility. They was a mixture of the new poor who had lost mill jobs and the old poor who were surviving on welfare. By the recession year of 1990–1991, the center would be obtaining and distributing $618,000 in private Dollar Energy funds to match state and federal grant funds for families with shut-off notices from utility companies. The Women, Infants, and Children (WIC) offices in the center would be giving out $550,000 in supplemental nutrition vouchers. These income transfers were an important economic boost to the depressed community.

Assessment

Beyond the six basic interactive activities used in forming the Aliquippa organization, its first action program year was marked by seizing the opportunity to support the move of the faith-based Community of Celebration to Aliquippa and by raising $4,000 through the sale of stock in Aliquippa to community people and their friends. In this program building, there was also use of research and planning, communication, plan implementation, resource tapping, and interorganizational relations. The hustling alliance accumulated recognition and strength, and it did so with volunteer organizers as its key resource. The Alliance learned early to tap both cash and noncash resources. This characteristic conferred extra appeal but extracted a heavy toll from a few generous people. It was useful for winning credibility but rendered the most faithful cadre members vulnerable to burnout. The time for hiring a couple of paid, full-time staff members was fast approaching.

The AAUD gained from the growing experience of its independent indigenous board (although not a board chosen by vote of the community). It benefited from constant recruitment that kept fresh enthusiasm and ideas flowing and shored up the working committees as they pursued AAUD goals. Its leaders recognized the dual effort required for continuity of a healthy renewal organization: first, constantly pushing and pulling to achieve program goals and, second, making certain that the organizational base of workers and money was solid and growing.

Giving top priority to creation of the safety net center was a choice that proved to be achievable. The AAUD learned the wisdom of responding to authentic demand arising from its research and openness. It provided concrete opportunities for participation and produced evidence that the organization was serious. It also marked the AAUD as a welfare service focused on "blacks and poor people." It was another signal to suspicious middle-class residents that the AAUD was intent on serving a limited segment of the population. The AAUD needed to communicate its concern for all people in the community and its conviction that human services strengthened economic and social conditions to the benefit of every citizen. The AAUD had moved well on the development track but needed to catch up fast on the unity track, tightening its bonds not only with the whole population but also with a wider array of organizations.

MOVING ON A
WIDER, RISKIER FRONT

Producing the Franklin Center in 1986 was a milestone. Individuals, organizations, government officials, and the media began to pay attention, and the alliance itself became more confident. With the Franklin Center attending to the emergency needs of families and providing legitimacy to the alliance through its bricks and mortar visibility, the AAUD hardly paused before plunging ahead. Maintaining its efforts to support unity, survival, and human service, the organization moved on to job creation. The new center itself had a job dimension. The AAUD hired Ilov to administer the Franklin Center and hired a receptionist-secretary, Jewel Avery, to assist. In addition, the 19 agencies buying into the center had to supply persons to staff their new Aliquippa offices. But these were token increases. The little city desperately needed substantial job growth. The AAUD saw this as its top priority and as the route to a stronger and wider support base.

The prevailing street wisdom in Aliquippa was that rescue would come via a restarting of the LTV blast furnaces. Had the mill not always come back from shutdowns during its 80 years of life? And if rescue would not come via resurgence by the mill, then it would come via another big corporation, which would arrive to invest in the mill's spectacular, 6-mile wide riverfront site. The town government perfunctorily joined county officials in promoting use of the vast riverfront site, from time to time becoming excited over potential investors expressing interest, but year after year these iffy, media-announced boomlets came to naught. The board decided to find a second building that could become a small-scale business incubator and job producer. Suddenly, and unexpectedly, Mellon Bank stepped forward to offer the AAUD its branch building in an isolated corner of town called West Aliquippa. The bank returned to the Alliance because of its adroit leveraging of the bank's earlier $5,000 contribution and the leadership it demonstrated in mobilizing volunteers to produce the Franklin Center.

Mellon Bank received a tax write-off, and the AAUD began 1987 with an air-conditioned edifice for business start-ups. However, the proud, autonomous, all-white West Aliquippa neighborhood was in an uproar. Upset over losing their bank, the people were confused and afraid as to what the new ownership might mean to them.

Inhabitants saw the AAUD either as a mystery organization or as "that group from Franklin Avenue that includes a lot of blacks." The Alliance invited all of the residents of West Aliquippa to a "reception" in the bank building. Cairns (1991) remembered,

A hundred people showed up in spite of a heavy snow. Black paint had been used to spatter racial graffiti on the outside walls. Black and white board members explained that the building would be the West Aliquippa Business and Technology Center and provide help to anyone who wanted to start a legitimate business.

Tempers cooled, and the Alliance moved ahead on the new incubator with a much-enlarged focus on economic development. The Howard Heinz Endowment gave $60,000 toward renovations and a paid executive director. Cairns was drafted for the position. An interracial team of unemployed steelworkers who had been volunteers in creating the Franklin Center formed the Aliquippa Recovery Krew (ARK), which was promptly awarded the remodeling contract for the new business center.

By early 1988, the West Aliquippa incubator was open with seven tenants, including a fast-growing sitter service that would mind babies, elderly parents, and pets. In time, the Duquesne University Small Business Development Center began offering business plan construction and technical assistance. Business counseling services were provided not only to tenants of the center but also to community people interested in running enterprises from their homes. Teaming up with the chamber of commerce from the town of Ambridge across the river, the AAUD offered a workshop on starting new businesses. About 50 people were expected, and some 200 showed.

With the alliance deep into promoting job creation through self-employment and small business expansion, some of its leadership also became involved in a battle with LTV over retiree pensions and medical benefits that pulled the Alliance back into mass organizing. The LTV corporation had filed for bankruptcy and arbitrarily terminated the health benefits and supplemental pensions that early retirees expected to enjoy until they were old enough for social security.

Militant protesting under the banner of "solidarity" brought lines of angry marchers to Franklin Avenue. In time, the AAUD board became so incensed at the treatment of their retiree neighbors that it issued a public statement in support of solidarity and its cause.

Conflict receded when LTV and the United Steelworkers of America negotiated an agreement to retain partial benefits, although many of the retirees believed that the settlement was unfair.

Continuously, the Alliance sought out potential entrepreneurs to support and existing businesses to help. It offered training and seed money for start-up enterprises. It launched programs to enhance the skills and job readiness of the local labor force. And it began to build a program of youth development and summer employment. During the four years from 1987 to 1990, the alliance raised and spent $700,000 on employment-related projects. Public and private funders alike were putting an emphasis on job creation. The $700,000 was big money to the fledgling AAUD organization, but it was peanuts toward overcoming the massive joblessness that was faced. Overall, job creation programs fell into these categories:

1. *Community enterprise*: These were the small-scale efforts to help new businesses begin or to help old businesses hang on or even expand.

2. *Enhancement of workforce*: There were programs to teach productive work skills, healthy attitudes, and mature human relations.

3. *Youth preparation and development*: There were classes in remedial education, enterprise start-up skills, and achievable career ladders for at-risk youth. Summer youth employment projects offering skills training, work experience, and recreation and fun were begun, as were in-school programs.

A new initiative provided mini-grants to teachers to underwrite progressive learning projects. The alliance created community events for the schools such as a Science Caravan in-school visit arranged with the Buhl Science Center. A specter of doom hung over the school district. Famous for its history of championships in major sports, it faced a loss of enrollment and revenues. The obvious remedy was merger into one of the adjacent stable township school districts.

A project given special attention was the Youth Enterprise Project of 1988–1990, which was supported by a grant from the Appalachian Regional Commission. It sought to test whether young people in their late teens and 20s had the interest and ability to operate enterprises that would contribute to recovery. There were benefits to the participating youth from the training and experience they gained, but no stable youth-owned enterprises resulted. Findings indicated that success would require an established renewal organization to itself form new enterprises, engaging youth as interns with the possibility that they would become owners or partners as they mastered the enterprise process (Martz, 1991).

In general, race relations were improving throughout West Aliquippa, with tighter control by the police chief over the behavior of his officers, but there was at least one incident related to the youth employment project. Youth crews arrived at a work site to find "Niggers Go Home" signs posted. The reaction of neighbors was speedy and positive. They circulated a petition requesting police protection against the "vandals" doing the posting and made clear their public opposition to "hate" behavior.

Moving into the 1990s, there was a central imperative that the Franklin Avenue business district be kept viable or else the AAUD effort would be a lost cause. As a University of Pittsburgh evaluation pointed out, "A ravaged, boarded-up central business district discourages residents from staying or from moving into the area" (Ricci, Singh, Ahlbrandt, Manners, & Trauth, 1994, p. 98). (On a normal business day, 19,000 cars pass through on Franklin, moving from one part of Beaver County to another. But few of these automobiles stop in Aliquippa, according to the Pennsylvania Department of Transportation.)

On November 12, 1991, the *Beaver County Times* ran an editorial titled "Too Far Gone" (1991), attacking the government funds being spent on Franklin Avenue and suggesting that the money be used instead to upgrade the newer outlying Sheffield shopping district. An op-ed page rejoinder endorsed by merchants, city officials, church leaders, and residents stated, "Franklin Avenue *is* downtown Aliquippa." It pointed out that 40% of the town's population lived within walking distance and added,

As people perceive downtown Aliquippa, so they will perceive the entire community; as long as

nothing is done to clean up Franklin Avenue, people will think of all of Aliquippa as that "dark, dirty, deteriorated place" where "the people don't care." … Franklin Avenue is the key to changing Aliquippa's image. (Ritter, 1991, p. A7)

The AAUD pursued a steady program of buying or accepting as gifts a string of key Franklin Avenue buildings, at the same time seeking resources—both money and volunteers—to replace windows, patch roofs, and otherwise preserve the structures. Renewal of the Franklin Avenue core became the central goal of the organization's strategy. The renewal had both a physical (bricks and mortar) dimension and a human development dimension. The physical was real estate and infrastructure. The human development was survival, health, training, education, and employment of core residents. Other sizable projects carried out during the early 1990s were related to this goal. This included projects in the arts and youth development, such as Internet training and printing design, and (to a lesser extent) programs related to the schools and housing. The AAUD was 8 years old now, haunted by the reality that the more it did, the more it saw that more would have to be done.

Even while an occasional new business was opening on Franklin Avenue, an existing business was closing for lack of customers, lack of management skills, or the retirement of an owner unable to find a successor. This happened to the highly publicized Broadcast Café, a new enterprise that for a time seemed to be holding successful teen dances and generating new life in its block. In 1992, the then Pennsylvania Department of Community Affairs (now the Pennsylvania Department of Community and Economic Development) commissioned a study to evaluate the housing conditions and identify the housing needs of Aliquippa, as required because Aliquippa had been designated a distressed community and was subject to certain state regulations. The study found fewer people choosing to live in Aliquippa, with the town's population increasingly made up of the elderly, minorities, and low-income residents. The study reported that 543 (9%) of Aliquippa's housing units were vacant. The positive signs noted were still pleasant residential sections, attractive housing, and improvements under way. More than half (60%) of the town's dwellings were owner occupied (Mullin & Lonergan Associates, 1992). Identified needs were translated by the report into a vision for Aliquippa's residential future. A primary goal suggested was increased homeownership in an effort to keep people from moving out.

Within the pages of the housing study, the importance to Aliqippa of the building of the new Pittsburgh International Airport was noted (Mullin & Lonergan Associates, 1992, p. V-3). When this airport was being built, Aliquippa leaders expected that it would boost the economic fortunes of Aliquippa. However, there has been only marginal gain. If the AAUD had been an established force, joined with other placed-based groups in a sophisticated coalition, then it might have been able to negotiate benefits from the airport, but it lacked the political influence and organized strength to act alone. The weak Aliquippa government also lacked the know-how and passion to advocate and bargain for a deal.

On the organization-building side, the AAUD's newsletter, *Grassroots,* promoted participation, bestowed recognition on volunteers and cooperating organizations, and advertised the Alliance's increasing services. Early on, the publication became an essential communication and organizational tool.

The Howard Heinz Endowment and Vira Heinz Endowment were leading funders for the alliance during this period. In 1987, they contracted with the University of Pittsburgh's Center for Social and Urban Research for an ongoing evaluation of the AAUD and its work. The report of the center for 1987–1990 concluded that "the Alliance has been relatively successful given the constraints within which it is working" and suggested that the Alliance's achievements stimulated positive attitudes among the town's business people. It mentioned commitments made by business people, increased hiring by some employers, and adherence to the principle of people helping themselves while "avoiding the charity model" (Ricci et al., 1991, p. 4).

The AAUD was cautious in joining partnerships, being careful not to make alliances that would limit its independence or give it

responsibilities it could not fulfill. It did achieve stronger ties to several old and new partners, especially local government and the school district. It formed relationships in real estate and youth activities, and it was making a difference in the ability of the poor of Aliquippa's central core to survive. For the overall Aliquippa community, employment opportunities and serious job preparation could be provided for only a few hundred in an area where thousands were idle or underemployed. Move-outs went on, and the sidewalks of Franklin Avenue continued to hunger for pedestrians.

Assessment

A community is a precious human asset. When under distress and assault, the struggle for preservation and resurgence is arduous and painful. And the pain can last a long time. But no other work can be more worthwhile. This is what drives people to stick it out. A persistent and saving quality keeping the AAUD striving forward during its first 8 years (1984–1992) was confidence. Aliquippa's poverty, its fragmentation, its people drain, and its limited clout, which doomed it in the eyes of some, never paralyzed the core cadre of the organization.

The logic driving the AAUD was irrefutable. Social services were a holding action for families. Full recovery would come only with economic renewal, defined as plentiful jobs at decent wages. The leaders knew that it was good jobs that would hold youth, stabilize the population, and restore bustle and shops to Franklin Avenue. But they were to find this a most difficult objective. Investments were moving away from old industrial communities all over America. The steel company had fled. The local government did not see job creation as its responsibility. The Alliance would have to try to do it.

AAUD community organizing during this period gradually shifted away from largely interactive efforts to those that were both extractive and interactive, with a heavy emphasis on extracting cash and noncash resources from outside sources. There was more communication flowing, more implementation of plans, and more entry into interorganizational relationships, although the AAUD was cautious to guard its independence. It found that a partnership could pay off when trust was built, as with the Mellon Bank. As partnerships absorbed more of the Alliance's time and energy, however, it had less to expend on aggressive organizing and mass participation. It found that it paid a price for initiating its important West Aliquippa project without first consulting the local people, thereby starting the relationship surrounded by a suspicious community.

During this growth period, the organization was forced to hire for its human service center first, and then its incubator project ratcheted the organization up another big jump to require the hiring of a full-time director. Staffing during these early years was made easy because the AAUD could turn to tried and true cadre members who were willing to become staff members.

Renewal of the core through real estate development and job creation became a major thrust, but the scale achieved seemed in no way to approach the need. The organization did create some jobs as a by-product of its efforts to preserve and renew buildings. But the AAUD's experience told it that community recovery would require a tremendous expansion of investments from public and private sources. For example, its $60,000 grant was inadequate. It amounted to only about 10% of what would have been much more appropriate and what probably would have been used effectively.

TURNING TO PARTNERSHIPS AND PROFESSIONALIZATION

While the first 8 years were filled with volunteer struggle for survival, largely carried out with informality and the enthusiasm that comes with high-risk community adventure, the next 10 years were to become absorbed in the grinding labor of inching toward recovery. Local cynics dubbed it "chasing the impossible dream," while their hopeful neighbors clung to the founding spirit with predictions of "you ain't seen nothing yet." These latter folks pointed to renewed main street buildings, handsome designer sidewalks and lampposts being installed, youth crowding after-school training classes, a few new riverfront employers hiring workers, and a host of potential funders and

development partners on the horizon. In the rest of this chapter, we look at this changed direction and seek to squeeze out more useful lessons.

Community organizing follows a general rule that "a central notion cuts commotion." In Aliquippa, the renewal of the Franklin Avenue core became the central focus for the AAUD and an opportunity for testing the rule. Projects and programs were brought into line, with their sights converging on the Franklin Avenue target. This focus shaped efforts to increase internal organizational strength as much as it drove services, projects, and events aimed at recovery.

An example of a project that both strengthened and boosted the recovery effort was an AAUD celebration of "womanpower" held in 1993 to recognize active and aspiring businesswomen, their careers, and struggles to mesh career with family life considerations. Ambitious Aliquippa-area women came together to talk about seed money, business start-ups, and being able to juggle a demanding job with a spouse and children. This gathering sought users for the AAUD's West Aliquippa Enterprise Center and for a possible second center to go somewhere on Franklin Avenue. It sought to enlarge the pool of potential job providers as it encouraged would-be entrepreneurs to come out of the closet.

Summer arts activities, including the painting of outdoor murals on empty Franklin Avenue buildings and classes for children, enticed residents to get involved. These activities would eventually blossom into an annual 1-day summer festival, "Aliquippa Embraces Art," with a diverse army of some 100 regional and local artists and their friends participating and many related events emerging. Although these events sometimes are poorly attended, this new engagement with art has drawn attention from press media throughout the region, bringing Aliquippa and the AAUD wider prominence and credibility. The arts bring new people to Franklin Avenue. They enliven lifeless buildings as studio workspaces. AAUD activists dream of art "embracement" creating links among the schools, public art, and Franklin Avenue that might win supporters from the all-white outer sections of the town.

In addition to arts programs, the AAUD launched a "Partners in Opportunity Development" (POD) education program with funds from the Appalachian Regional Commission. In the heavily used Franklin Center, POD offered training in the waiting rooms and halls alongside scheduled classes and meetings. It sought to sharpen and upgrade the skills of youthful residents headed for college or technical training while providing them with guidance for seeking financial aid and counseling on career choices.

AAUD advocacy activity concentrated on Franklin Avenue, putting pressure on banks to maintain their Aliquippa branches. The AAUD joined city and county governments in seeking the release of a $12 million federal transportation department allocation for infrastructure that included improvements for Franklin Avenue. The organization fought against a state proposal to turn the Franklin corridor into an expressway to speed motorists to and from the airport.

The most dramatic change strengthening the core focus was the transfer to the Alliance of Mellon Bank's main branch on Franklin Avenue, an imposing stone structure dating back to the 1920s. The transfer came out of quiet negotiations between the AAUD and the bank and was supported by a jointly filed application for state tax credits. No town meeting for public explanation of the deal took place, in sharp contrast to the unveiling in West Aliquippa. Mellon Bank agreed to pay the acquisition expenses and renovation cost (Cairns, personal communication, October 25, 1993). This deal represented a further exit of banks from Aliquippa, although the bank did sign a lease to maintain a small bank service office in the rehabilitated building, which was renamed "Renaissance Place." A principal purpose of the service office would be cashing welfare checks.

During this period, the AAUD began talks with wholesale grocers, who agreed to study the feasibility of a small supermarket on Franklin Avenue. The study findings were negative, citing Aliquippa's shrinking population. To gain a better grip on its Franklin Avenue strategy, the AAUD and its subsidiary, the low-profile Aliquippa Development Corporation (ADC—inherited from town government), contracted private consultants to study the potential of the avenue. They did this with backing and funds from the Pennsylvania Downtown Center, and the ADC eventually obtained money to assist

merchants in remodeling their storefronts on Franklin Avenue. The study confirmed the weaknesses of Franklin Avenue as a market and the necessity for large subsidies to renovate buildings. It stressed the urgency of the AAUD/ADC taking control of more key properties and pioneering an "incubator without walls" for homegrown enterprises initiated by talented local residents. This meant obtaining government and other outside funds, restoring more buildings, and training and subsidizing talented young people to build a critical mass of new businesses in a completely transformed environment. But the construction and subsidy estimates were enormous.

EDGING TOWARD STAFF LEADERSHIP

In early 1993, the AAUD board and the Aliquippa community were shaken by Cairns's announcement that 10 years was long enough and that she would be stepping down at the end of the year, confident that the organization was solid and ready for a staff transition that would bring fresh ideas, probably new faces, and surely new achievements, including bringing to fruition the establishment of a hospital-related health clinic on Franklin Avenue. She had always believed in the AAUD's appointed resident-based board as the most reliable place for decision making, a belief that sometimes put her in tension between policy-oriented funders who pushed program suggestions at her and residents in the streets who had other ideas, while she and the board were either moving in a third direction or sweating with uncertainty in the middle.

In preparing to leave, Cairns listed the barriers she saw to revitalizing Franklin Avenue and opening more jobs for residents, barriers she judged to be more subtle and complex than those faced in 1983: (a) the absence of a funded technical assistance system able to facilitate would-be investors/industrialists setting up in Aliquippa, (b) the inability to link new entrepreneurs fruitfully to banks and other sources of capital, (c) the lack of a sophisticated workforce able to perform or quickly learn high-performance production techniques, (d) the absence of an energetic system of education and training with links to employers able to ensure training graduates of opportunities to compete for quality jobs, (e) too little power to stop "environmental deals" that trade health and safety for the promise of jobs (e.g., a medical waste disposal plant proposed for Aliquippa's riverfront that the AAUD helped to shoot down), (f) the lack of a feasible land management program to turn downtown Aliquippa into a compact attractive business district able to draw customers and residents to Franklin Avenue, and (g) a dearth of available highway funds and other government aid to plant state-of-the-art public infrastructure in the Franklin Avenue core as a foundation for modern retailing, professional services, and high-performance manufacturing businesses, with contractual arrangements to ensure residents priority access to the new jobs (personal communication, October 25, 1993). Under her list lay buried the central question: Where are the crowds of customers?

During the 1993–1994 period, as Cairns wound down her leadership role, two independent reports saluted the AAUD's achievements under her stewardship while raising searching questions about the obstacles to accelerating progress. These matched and added to Cairns's own list of seven barriers. Both independent reports urged that the alliance seek organizational allies to increase its political influence and to increase its access to major funding sources.

First, a Carnegie Mellon University report (Brown et al., 1993) titled *Building on Unity: A Coalition for Development in Aliquippa,* credited the AAUD with a "giant step" in stabilizing social problems, thus providing a "firm foundation on which development initiatives can be built" (p. 4). Although the graduate student-staff authors assigned an honor grade for the AAUD's development progress, the grade for moving toward unity was close to a "flunk." The CMU team found Aliquippa stuck in the mud of separateness as it concentrated on the Franklin Avenue corridor (pp. 5–8). It suggested more handholding with key local governments and development organizations of the Pittsburgh region. To play hardball in the sprawling Pittsburgh region, the report proposed a new Beaver County growth coalition with Aliquippa as a major player and listed a set of activities for seeking consensus and common goals among the region's major stakeholders (pp. 14, 27–28).

The second outside appraisal was an updated formal evaluation (Ricci et al., 1994) from the University of Pittsburgh praising Cairns for her "flexibility and innovative leadership" and the AAUD for its "variety of business and social service programs" (p. 101). But it raised questions about the focus on Franklin Avenue (pp. 109–110). While conceding that motor traffic on the street remained heavy and that any future industrial development would have to rise from the nearby cleared mill site, the report insisted that "the geography, history, and social conditions of this street and the region it is in may make full-scale economic recovery [of the street] impossible" (p. 110). The university evaluators also recommended a leadership organization uniting Beaver County's 54 municipalities that would move the AAUD to a regional focus within a multi-body alliance (p. 113). The struggling AAUD acted on neither assessment.

Some increased impact came from communications. The organization focused attention on the newspapers and radio stations of Beaver County and the periodic issuance of the newsletter *Grassroots,* with its articles on business start-ups, the latest expansion of human services, and the training offered at the AAUD's Learning and Evaluation Center.

Each planned project and service required meetings and the recruitment of more volunteers to serve on the advisory board, committees, and subcommittees to implement them. Here was a continuously growing process where more residents and outside allies could be plugged in and become part of the structure. The growth put more work on the board and cadre leaders, and it forced the hiring of more staff as funds were available. Staff hiring, when done, was done slowly and carefully.

After an exhaustive national search for a new director, the position was accepted by Pauline Cooper, a community organization graduate of the University of Pittsburgh School of Social Work who since 1988 had been a full-time field organizer for the Mon Valley Initiative (MVI) (described in Appendix 3.C). There, she had won a reputation as a tenacious facilitator and professional of high standards who tirelessly pursued community projects to completion, always involving key resident leaders in the process.

A native of Northern Ireland who was not unfamiliar with community conflict, Cooper took hold of the AAUD in 1994 and moved with confidence not only to maintain momentum but also to accelerate it. Working with the board that had chosen her and a broad array of other advisers, she helped the organization to sort out existing programs and to consider new ones. This review occurred during the summer and fall of 1994, with the result being a newborn strategic plan, largely the work of staff and board members, a style traditionally practiced by the MVI. The plan envisioned numerous partnership ventures with city and county government, the school district, and a variety of other public and private bodies.

New Strategic Plan—But Sticking to the Focus

Projected for the years 1995 to 1998, the new strategic plan was as much a limit-setting document as a goal-setting one (AAUD, 1995). It was tightly confined to six priorities, which were to (a) multiply businesses on Franklin Avenue; (b) upgrade educational opportunities, especially for low-income minority youth seeking to break into the regional job market; (c) enhance relationships with elected officials while working with the City of Aliquippa to set up a community job bank; (d) join existing regional coalitions and attract more resources from outside Aliquippa; (e) build AAUD capacity to plan strategically, raise money, and educate and develop staff; and (f) enhance participation by measuring and responding to "customer" satisfaction levels; by recognizing contributions of staff, board members, and volunteers; and by widening the involvement of the community in AAUD activities. This plan bound the organization to a strong mix of goal-implementing tasks and projects as well as numerous activities to build the muscle of the AAUD itself, a classic two-tract approach. An analysis of the substance and method of Aliquippa's strategic plan can be found in Chapter 8, where it is used as a case example.

The traditional work of organizing-developing-servicing would be maintained with a more conscious effort to publicize these activities.

The plan vowed to "meet regularly with media representatives, expand press exposure," and attract more residents both as users of services and as volunteer workers. Meantime, a group of residents urged on by Ilov and board co-chair Debra Ruckert gathered old photos for a community slide show titled *Aliquippa: the First 50 Years.* The show drew 300 people to the high school auditorium on October 11, 1995, with many traveling from standoffish, uphill white areas. The show reminded the audience of a shared common past, including a "then as now" rigid separation of races.

At the end of 1995, Integra Bank (now National City) announced that it was closing its large Franklin Avenue branch to merge it with a branch in nearby Hopewell Township. In an arrangement mediated by the Pennsylvania Department of Banking, Integra promised to continue to provide basic services 2 days per month from its old building until the alliance could open a new state-chartered credit union. The structure would then be donated to local government to become a large, more dignified town hall, with the bank throwing in $75,000 for renovations. This encouraged Aliquippa public officials to take more interest in the renewal of Franklin Avenue.

On February 14, 1996, a long-time dream was realized with the formal opening of a "downtown" health care clinic next door to the Franklin Center, a move that greatly expanded the health services on Franklin Avenue. It added a much-needed and convenient service. As a new "business," it added an employer and a rent-paying tenant to support one of the newly opened buildings.

At the forefront of such community building was David Blenk, a young architect hired by Cooper in 1994 to be the business district specialist. Blenk helped to guide the planning of the health clinic while he was assisting the AAUD's Business Committee to establish a system for shepherding investors and promoting start-up enterprises. His work began to remove some of the "barriers" to economic progress listed by Cairns before her departure. To carry out the economic goal, he pulled together the AAUD's scattered development components to make them a single program, which added several new enterprises to Franklin Avenue. Other projects he would be helping to launch were the new credit union and a development fund to furnish capital for small businesses.

To advance education, Cooper pushed the AAUD's board and Education Committee to work with the school district as a partner, assisting it to be more accountable for learning, especially for ensuring that students acquire literacy skills. The AAUD had previously forged its operational links to school administration through the school's teachers, parents, and students. In carrying out the new strategic plan, the alliance expanded its school-to-work partnerships to encompass institutional employers, business owners, and postsecondary institutions as comrades in building a school-to-work system that connected directly with school administrators.

In a partial response to the heavy loss of community banking services from Franklin Avenue, the AAUD organized Pennsylvania's first state-chartered community development credit union. The credit union was opened in 1997 by Pennsylvania Governor Tom Ridge (who later became President George W. Bush's director of homeland security) and found itself facing a credit-starved community where small consumer loans were in high demand by a needy and high-risk population, with many not accustomed to borrowing from an institutional lender. In a short time, this new people's institution, run by a local volunteer board, made 100 small loans to local borrowers as well as a few large new car loans that eventually were to become troublesome. It regularly held open meetings to listen to members and provide financial education.

Cooper, Blenk, and cadre volunteers filled the credit union's board and committee positions, hoping to build it through a year of planning. It opened on Franklin Avenue with more than 400 members and $600,000 in deposits, which came from local households, private foundations, corporations, state and county organizations, outside "friends of the alliance," the AAUD's own cash flow, and "conscience" money deposited by some of the financial institutions that had fled Franklin Avenue. AAUD leadership credited the national Community Reinvestment Act and its requirements as being influential in gaining the bank cooperation.

With the assistance of the National Equity Fund of Chicago, a $2 billion nonprofit national "intermediary" set up to assist development organizations in small communities, national funds were brought in to help. Tapping into National Equity's "outside" funds, the alliance carried out a $1.6 million mixed use remodeling of the G. C. Murphy and Oliker buildings on Franklin Avenue to provide affordable rental apartments and space for artists' studios as well as expanded ground floor space for WIC and new enterprises. This was the alliance's first million-dollar project. It was kicked off at a press conference in November 1997, where the then Pennsylvania Lieutenant Governor Mark Schweiker (who later became governor) gave a keynote address and promised that "with a strong public/private partnership firmly in place, we can continue to build a more vibrant Aliquippa for the future" (AAUD, 1997, p. 1).

ASSESSMENT

As an established organization with structure, a veteran leadership core, real estate holdings, a strategic focus, and flows of income (some self-generated), the AAUD was in Aliquippa for the long haul but recognized that all of these assets were not sufficient to move the town to economic recovery. The alternative proposed by the two university assessment teams was to unite with other towns and countywide entities to form a powerful regional development commission that would seek a much grander flow of money from state, federal, foundation, and corporate sources. Realigning strategy and resources to operate through a new multi-organizational countywide coalition, however, was not deemed prudent or potentially productive, as the AAUD would have to give up its autonomy and probably its concentration on central Aliquippa as well.

The AAUD concentrated on the more limited goal of stabilizing the highly visible and symbolic main street while increasing opportunities for the poor and struggling working people who lived on and around it. The AAUD acted as the responsible and compassionate renewal organization doing whatever was feasible. The future of many families and their children hung on the organization's power to attract investments, connect with employers, and engage the Franklin Avenue householders themselves as participants in workforce development and other renewal efforts. These were top priorities; dealing with the more stable residential sections of the community could come later as influence and resources became more plentiful.

More money was being found by the AAUD, and the scale reached seven figures for an individual deal. Time and people constraints were felt in interorganizational relations; there were many partnership opportunities in the arts, public schools, housing, enterprise ideas, and the like, but these partnership opportunities called for planning and selecting, and they called for continually more attention from staff, committee leaders, and board and cadre members, all of whom were already heavily burdened.

The AAUD did see value and potential in temporary ad hoc partnerships so long as they were limited in number, were entered into with trusted allies, and held the probability of a tangible payoff. But in working with allies such as Mellon Bank and the Pennsylvania Department of Banking, the methods followed were those of business and government rather than of the inclusive community organization, providing open opportunities for all residents and other stakeholders to influence program and policy. There also was probably a missed opportunity here for amassing and exercising powers of extraction through strong coalitions formed with other communal groups throughout the county.

When Cairns, the co-creator and organizer who had invested 10 intense years of her life in the AAUD, cut herself loose, a board that was grateful and respectful of her sacrifices and achievements began to take unto itself more power and responsibility with the aid of experienced outside people. It is likely that this shift had been subtly under way for some time and provided one of the tensions that led Cairns to decide that it was the appropriate time to step down. As board members struggled through the separation, they became confident that change at the top of the staff was proper and timely, with most members appreciating how well the retiring director had helped to prepare them to handle the change.

With resolve, the board hastened to step up the AAUD's efforts to find other organizations and institutions to participate in the Franklin Avenue renewal, so that others would share the investment risk and the responsibility for making the effort work. One strong rationale for the Franklin Avenue focus was the AAUD's dedication to the human side of renewal. In Chapter 3, Bratt (1997) was cited as seeing a national lack of public interest in helping poor people as a root cause of the continued decline of low-income neighborhoods. The AAUD moved in a counter-direction, making poverty reduction within its most impoverished sub-area a primary goal.

Waking Up to Reality

Approaching 1998, 500 neighbors, friends, and volunteer supporters were still involved in the AAUD rescue machine, led by savvy board co-chairs Aileen Gilbert and Debra Ruckert and an energetic staff of Pauline Cooper, David Blenk, Jonathan Pettis, and their half dozen dedicated colleagues. Their direction was clear and consistent, as follows. Revitalize the core community by renewing its people and buildings. Use all available resources in so doing, and then reach out to help revitalize and tie in the rings of community and region beyond. At all times, stimulate and draw in those groups, both government and private, that might help to move the mountains.

The AAUD saw a revitalized neighborhood core as eventually casting an attractive new image for all of Aliquippa, an image that could heighten the desirability of the idle steel site and the value of other sections of the town, and maybe even strengthen the rings of suburban townships beyond. And, very important, the strategy they chose could advance justice and reconciliation.

The $1.6 million Murphy-Oliker real estate project meant that the renewal of Franklin Avenue was thrown into higher gear. On the remodeled upper floors of these distinguished old buildings went the first "new" rental housing to open on the avenue in decades, with signed-up tenants waiting to get their keys. Remodeling included a new elevator in the larger Murphy building. The AAUD saw this project as providing a guide for redoing a sound but dilapidated building for joint housing-business use in a low-income community. Support for the venture rested on a creative package of public and private financial aids that drew on state, federal, county, and private foundation money as well as on the heavy use of low-income housing tax credits brokered by the National Equity Fund and its corporate investors. Through a high-risk bank loan, the alliance itself furnished the final $120,000 for the $1.6 million package. The ground floor of the Murphy building was prepared as enlarged space for the WIC program, which had become cramped in the Franklin Center. WIC signed a 7-year lease calling for commercial-level rent.

While the Alliance had progressed to raising about a third of its $600,000 annual operating budget from fees and rents, it had to be continually engaged in finding and extracting the other $400,000. Although from the beginning there has been a flow of miscellaneous small grants and gifts from faith organizations, government, individuals, banks, utility companies, firms, and an occasional raffle or special project, the stable and single largest funding partner since 1986 had been a coalition of foundations formed by the Heinz Endowments, which during the alliance's early years included the Pittsburgh Foundation. The 1995–1998 strategic plan called for "creative solutions to build local capacity," with the executive director taking charge to beef up the fundraising team of board members (AAUD, 1995).

SEARCHING FOR THE RIGHT PARTNERSHIPS

Cooper tried hiring a consultant to help her plan and direct the money-raising effort but soon learned the basic operating rule that no one can replace the director in giving leadership to fundraising. She found that the same rule applied to the other five priorities contained in the 1995–1998 strategic plan. With a million-dollar-plus goal, Cooper and her finance committee wooed foundation and government grantors from throughout the Pittsburgh region, conducted eye-opening site tours for funder program officers and foundation board members, and laid out inventive multiyear proposals. All of the money sources approached were external to Aliquippa and its immediate region. There was no provision for an internal campaign that might tap residents, business people, nearby institutions, and other potential Aliquippa supporters. Time constraints pushed leadership to seek the "biggest buck" per hour invested. This seemed to be the big grant route.

Of particular interest to funders approached were Aliquippa's organizing schemes that linked human services with real estate development,

youth job training with both arts and school improvements, and enterprise start-ups that would assist with innovative capital pools and technical assistance. All of this solidified the choice for partnerships. By 1998, new multiyear foundation commitments totaling more than $2 million were obtained, including a $750,000 Heinz Endowment grant to begin building a $10 million development fund that, if achieved, would bring AAUD programming to the eight-figure level for the first time. Funders with whom new or expanded partnerships were established were the Richard King Mellon Foundation, the McCune Foundation, the Grable Foundation, the Mary Hillman Jennings Foundation, and the Sarah Scaife Foundation. All of these foundations focus on the Pittsburgh region, of which Aliquippa and Beaver County are vital components.

Cooper's professional competence and disarming approach won increased respect for the AAUD with the networks of governments, businesses, and institutions in Beaver County. Inside and outside the organization, she sought specific commitments for volunteer effort from residents and diverse friends and contacts. She encouraged staff to find ways in which volunteers could carry substantial responsibilities and be immersed in decision making. In particular, she sought to involve participants in housing plans, social services, job skills, business education and start-up, youth development, and arts programs.

Cooper saw connections between the empowerment of people and the AAUD program. She described empowerment as happening in a variety of ways: parents becoming active in improving their children's schools, teachers bringing out the talents of their kids through art projects and after-school creative work, high school seniors earning college credits, and students testing their entrepreneurship skills, perhaps by apprenticeships with some of the young businesses located in the alliance's two incubators.

Cooper's vision of empowerment extended to whole organizations. Envisioning the AAUD as a community, she sought to guide it to join other entities as diverse as the County Housing Authority and the Catholic Church to partake in renewal and to share their assets. As mentioned previously, churches generally had not joined in the AAUD effort. Father John Sweeney, pastor of the St. Titus Catholic parish, indicated that his duties in managing a church and school with

180 students (10% black), working with 40 active volunteers who maintained the parish property, and overseeing the annual summer 5-day street festival absorbed all of his time. He said that ministers of Aliquippa's small churches held full-time outside jobs, while those of large churches were as busy as he was (personal interview, June 2, 1998). Sweeney praised the AAUD's work on Franklin Avenue. He described two Franklin Avenues: the quiet one by day and the drug scene by night. His parish has property at two locations on the avenue, and he promised that the one unoccupied property would be "well cared for."

William Farra, long-time leader of the lay Episcopal Community of Celebration whose row of attached houses and church are located on Franklin Avenue, confirmed that Aliquippa congregations were without resources to operate beyond their own institutions. Across the nation, churches are a mainstay of community revival, and in 2002 President Bush was urging the nation's churches to take on the role. Churches often identify their members as neighbors and the church itself as a neighborhood institution, and churches recognize a large self-interest in the condition of their neighborhoods (personal interview, September 18, 1997). This ideal, however, cannot be implemented without resources. Farra is a long-time member of the AAUD board, and many of his Celebration brethren have served as staff and volunteers.

As Cooper facilitated the growth of the AAUD by building relationships with germane organizations, she not only was putting more muscle into the alliance's goal seeking but also was being attentive to her other major responsibility: strengthening the internal organization for the long haul. She did this primarily by fund-raising. She did it also by tightening media connections, tying specific volunteers to specific projects where they fit well, and co-authoring an article for a national publication titled "Youth Revitalizing Main Street" that could help the AAUD access national resources (Twiss & Cooper, 2000). Published in *Social Work in Education,* a widely read social work journal, the article was co-authored by Pamela Twiss, who previously wrote the evaluation of Aliquippa's youth enterprise demonstration (Martz, 1991).

With funding solid for years ahead, in 1998 Cooper revealed that she and her husband were happily expecting their first child and that before mid-year she would step down to become a mother, wife, and community volunteer. Board members were disappointed to lose her but cheered her reason. Being a body of community veterans, they stayed the course and moved forward. They restarted the recruitment process, moved ahead with an extensive search, and ended it quickly by naming Blenk, the staff's business specialist, as executive director.

When Blenk originally joined the AAUD staff in 1994, he found local government still cautious toward planning and development, with the city's professional staff giving no inspiration to elected officials. Seemingly, the activity level had changed little in 10 years. Blenk and Cooper then agreed that a public partnership was vital for new programs and accelerated progress. They began to deal with the council and the city manager, but in 8 months they found that a political coup had wiped out the officials they dealt with and so had to begin anew.

Convinced of the importance of government cooperation and involvement to their goals, they moved to build relations with the new set of officials. They found continued instability among the elected council members but found some consistency and stability appearing among the appointed city hall staff. They discovered that there was staff interest in the renewal of Franklin Avenue, the improvement of housing, the upgrading of the workforce, and the expansion of efforts to bring employers and private investment to the city.

Seeking more active working relationships with the school board, they found the key official to be a solicitor intolerant of citizen groups. At the county level, they encountered policy and operations under the thumb of a traditional elected three-member commission that ran through seven different members in 4 years. County development efforts were largely delegated to a nonprofit county economic development corporation. At the same time, the governor was restructuring the state's departments responsible for development programs toward what he hoped would be a structure allowing a municipality to negotiate a single comprehensive program with the state, thus bypassing departmental complications. For state government, it was a promising era of budget surpluses—an era too good to be true that ended with the economic downturn of 2000 and President Bush's "war on terrorism" launched in 2001. To build and maintain necessary and growing government relationships, the AAUD assigned two staff members: one responsible for programs related to consumer services and one responsible for economic and business programs.

The priority program became amassing the $10 million development fund, completing the renovation of Franklin Avenue structures, and at the same time training, motivating, and placing local people in jobs or self-employment while helping them to become homeowners within Aliquippa. Also high on the list was attracting other diverse investment to the town. Blenk and his board had a vision of upward mobility for the people of the Franklin Avenue core.

The most important breakthrough in all of this was the joining of local government with the AAUD as a partner in the renewal of Franklin Avenue. As a distressed community, the City of Aliquippa had obtained funds to redevelop the lower portion of the avenue toward the river, where commercial structures dominate, while the alliance handles the upper end, where the structures are partly commercial but mostly local government service offices, homes, churches, and nonprofit social agencies. An agreement to this effect came out of the joint work of David Blenk and Rebecca Bradley, the flexible, energetic, young city administrator for Aliquippa. Bradley shared the following view:

> Inside and outside of Aliquippa, people judge the city by the condition of Franklin Avenue. They ignore our attractive and prosperous shopping streets off Brodhead and Kennedy and by habit think of Aliquippa as "decrepit old Franklin Avenue." We have to restore Franklin and we will, with [the] AAUD's help and leadership. (personal interview, August 5, 1998)

She was also upbeat about the $10 million development fund and extra funds the local government had been able to obtain to hire more police. She reported that crime numbers were down, including a sharp reduction in drug crimes, with the latter being due to especially rigorous police enforcement on Franklin Avenue (personal interview, August 5, 1998).

Would a $10 million development fund be sufficient for the Alliance to advance its whole program? No, but it was enough to push ahead dramatically and to link with groups such as the county development corporation and Housing Opportunities of Beaver, private real estate developers, and a few new industrial investors who may see possibilities in the cleared riverfront site. The partnership with the City of Aliquippa was a big boost for this approach. In time, however, the total investment for a recovered Aliquippa would have to be more like $300 million from all sources, both public and private, with other substantial private investments required on an annual basis. Blenk showed a talent for winning the confidence of leading people in the town and in the region around Aliquippa. He and the board members dug in, well aware that no progress toward recovery could be made without large-scale new outside support.

In 1999, Blenk found tough challenges to meet. The credit union, with its low-income clientele, ran into difficulties. The inexperienced staff members were not ready to manage the growing portfolio of small loans made to low-income residents unaccustomed to the ritual of borrowing and repaying. There was also the frustration of restrictions and risk uncertainties when attempting to support would-be entrepreneurs who possessed good ideas but few assets and no track records. Staff and board members moved quickly to a solution that strengthened the capital situation. The credit union was merged with the larger, long-established credit union in the nearby town of Ambridge, which agreed to maintain the Aliquippa office and its low-income customer base (see Appendix 7.C).

To provide capital for high-risk business lending, the launching of the $650,000 Business Loan Fund was sped up using development fund money from the Heinz Endowment, although Heinz announced in early 2000 that it was ending its more than a dozen years of granting operating funds to the AAUD. The Business Loan Fund project began with its loan fund manager hired as a member of the AAUD staff. This project was designed to promote grassroots business education opportunities as well as to lend money. It was to provide both money and technical assistance for individual enterprises. The "individual development account" program that had been launched by the credit union would continue to operate under the AAUD. (This program assisted low-income savers with building capital.) As the organization rode into the year 2000, other critical matters were on its plate.

The city, county, and state were coming to agreement on the comprehensive Franklin Avenue renewal and rebuilding strategy. The school board was yet to join in, a matter that was given high priority by the AAUD. As director, Blenk spent at least 30% of his time on government-related projects, and the AAUD received increasing technical assistance from the state's newly restructured and renamed Department of Community and Economic Development.

Participation was rising in the AAUD school programs staffed by Megan Bursic, a community organizer hired by Blenk and the board.

Even with its continued interest in community organizing, the AAUD board does not have a systematic method by which the larger Aliquippa community can subject the policy-level decisions of staff and board members to scrutiny in public sessions.

As the 21st century arrived, Gilbert and Ruckert moved out of their positions as co-chairs of the board, Gilbert to pursue a long-time dream (see the accompanying sidebar) and Ruckert to become director of a workforce development program in Pittsburgh. Sam Gill succeeded them as the single chair. An African American and a veteran board member experienced in nonprofit finance, Gill was an accountant who worked as the finance officer for the Beaver County Head Start program.

Woman With a Street-Based Dream

Aileen Gilbert is a bright and able African American woman who raised a large family in Aliquippa, including a National Football League lineman. Before her son had become a celebrated athlete, she chaired the AAUD's resident controlled board (1989–1991) and was back as co-chair for 1997–1999. One of her constant concerns was "citizen volunteers" who give up too quickly when the going gets tough. She often told her board, "Most people in the community have no idea to what extent the program has grown or how we have expanded our capacity to work in the community. People come to the Alliance when they need services for their families but rarely get involved in the total program. We need to reestablish and extend our community ties."

Before her term as co-wielder of the AAUD board gavel was completed, Gilbert resigned to go back to college and to "help ignite a civic revival on every street in Aliquippa." After resigning, she revealed her dream: "We'll find a captain in each block to pull people from their homes for talk and plans. What are the worries? What can we residents do about them? This movement has to push up from residents. We've already got Geneva Short listening to neighbors on Wilker Street, where her neighbors are worried about crime. People have to learn what they can do for themselves. There are young people around town with college degrees waiting for direction. A Geneva Short has to be identified and inspired on every block. I will be working on this out of the new community center of the Sound the Alarm Church organization that will be built in Plan 11. That's a neighborhood adjacent to Franklin Avenue, but the center will seek to serve all of Aliquippa, and we'll operate and promote it that way."

Gilbert added: "As this thing grows, with people-concocted changes popping up on all sides of town, blocks will get together in groups to scheme for bigger things like schools and recreation centers, and they'll turn to [the] AAUD for knowledge and resources and to help shape future plans. By then, maybe I'll be ready to try to get back on the AAUD board." (personal interview, January 13, 2000)

There appear to be no established procedures for continuously recruiting and developing volunteers from the community. As needed, staff and board members find people to fill seats on advisory boards and committees, seeking persons with skills and experience appropriate to the requirements of each position. Plans were under way for a Retired Service Volunteer Program that would use knowledgeable volunteers age 55 years or over to assist seniors with applying for tax and rent rebates. The luster of a people's movement was giving way to the spit and polish of a professional organization; however, it was an organization pushing forward plans designed to stimulate an infusion of investments, jobs, construction, and improved incomes for the households of Aliquippa, where median household income has been depressed at half the statewide household median for more than 20 years.

Coming into the year 2000, the AAUD (1999) was following a new 1999–2002 strategic plan completed the previous October, with an emphasis on reducing the heavy unemployment and poverty of the "5,500 low and moderate income residents living in and around the depressed Franklin Avenue core of the city" (p. 1). (This plan is also discussed in Chapter 9.) The six major areas of the plan encompass administrative support; capital and business development; business and economic development; workforce development, including education, training, and strengthening public schools; human and social services; and maintenance of the AAUD's property and equipment.

During the first half of 2001, Blenk accepted a position as executive director of the Oakland Planning and Development Corporation located in the university-rich East End of Pittsburgh. The AAUD board in April 2001 once again began a search and hired Beverly Gillot, a planning and economic development consultant with regional and countywide experience.

During this transition year, three staff members left the AAUD to pursue other opportunities. Among those departing was the energetic development specialist who had been spearheading Aliquippa Embraces Art and a variety of development projects.

Gillot assumed staff leadership, making clear that her focus was on the following:

1. Economic and workforce development

2. More formalized relationships with the government of the municipality, including the possibility that the AAUD would become the city's official redevelopment arm through the ADC

3. Forging strong partnerships with county and regional entities

Board and staff composition and structure were put under review. A new strategic planning process was discussed with the board. Participation and grassroots involvement seemed to be off the agenda. Suggestions were made that "Unity" be dropped from the organization's name.

As the year moved on, Gillot's narrow program view clashed with those of allies both inside and outside Aliquippa, and she had contentious interactions with some government and nonprofit officials. City government took over the ADC and transformed it into the Franklin Avenue Development Corporation with a board appointed by city government (R. Bradley, personal interview, February 26, 2002). Gillot left the organization in January 2002, with the AAUD staff and board quickly bouncing back to the broad program followed prior to Gillot's arrival.

A new hunt for a staff leader was begun. The kind of director to be sought and hired would indicate whether the AAUD was ready to become formal and focused on real estate and redevelopment or would return to its comprehensive roots.

A fact sheet issued during early 2002 (AAUD, 2002) reported that the Alliance's programs during the previous year had "created and retained" 102 jobs and helped start 6 businesses in Aliquippa and the surrounding region, with $1.9 million lent to businesses in the region since 1999. More than 120 senior citizens were assisted with utility bills, tax rebates, and health insurance. Its "Pathway to Work" program helped more than 100 people apply for jobs and promotion and provided 450 households with support for their overdue gas and electric bills. It announced expanded efforts for 2002. Also in 2002, the local Salvation Army was planning to break ground for a new church-community building on Franklin Avenue. Plans were set for a July 27 annual arts festival, and state and federal grants were being applied for, with an annual budget approaching $800,000, 35% of it earned through rents and fees. A Pathway to Work unit was assisting 80 would-be workers to prepare for jobs, and links to growth employees were being sought beyond Aliquippa. In addition, the Community of Celebration began construction of its new $375,000 Chapel of the Holy Spirit on property behind the community's long row of Franklin Avenue homes.

Health services are available daily on Franklin Avenue; a full-time WIC program, family clinic (physician on hand 10 a.m. to 2 p.m.), and a traditional array of services are dispensed to individuals and families by agencies that come to the Franklin Center to meet residents by appointment, or individuals and families can just drop in if in need. After nearly 20 years, the achievements of the AAUD could be summarized in seven words: "community survival, yes; community recovery, not yet." Touching base with the veteran board cadre and the enthusiastic town manager revealed new thoughts, a riverfront steel history museum, masses of senior volunteers and crowds pulled to Aliquippa through the arts, new incentives to be tested to gain more church support, and increases in state money from a new governor (R. Bradley, personal interview, February 26, 2002). Tools of potential are the new Franklin Avenue Development Committee and a new connection with the Beaver County Initiative for Growth headed by local state legislators.

Serious stirrings in grassroots organizing are also being led by the Aliquippa Police Department and the Aliquippa "Communities That Care" (a branch of the national program carried out with state and federal funding). Officer Steve Roberts and organizer Libby Gabauer have already helped residents in the Linmar Terrace and Plan 12 sections to form crime watch groups, with a single group of 25 residents in Linmar Terrace and four block groups in Plan 12 each with a dozen households involved.

On April 27, 2002, these groups with several churches and their youth groups, backed by city government trucks, carried out a "Keep Aliquippa Beautiful" cleanup day. Gabauer described the effort as "families working within their own immediate neighborhood, taking ownership of their surroundings." She talked about plans for three more watch groups (personal interview, April 29, 2002).

A new director for the Alliance was found and in place by early April. Rosanne Stead brought 20 years of experience gained from business, politics, and nonprofit groups, including management of a large bookstore-cultural center, director of a small foundation, and member of a city planning commission. Stead earned a master's degree in urban studies at the University of Chicago. Her community work included serving on the board of a homeless shelter, organizing a campaign to pass a ballot question, and building, strengthening, and making effective the work of several partnerships and coalitions. Organizational skills to which she had been exposed included marketing, recruiting, fund-raising, training, and brainstorming.

Within days of beginning the job, Stead was meeting and building relationships with city and county officials as well as leaders of a host of nonprofits. She spoke with enthusiasm of the hopeful people she was meeting in these work sessions and said that she was "coming on to the job at a time of significant new initiatives in Aliquippa and Beaver County involving new alliances, new resources, and new ideas" (personal interview, April 25, 2002).

Final Assessment

In Chapter 6, we suggested three practical structures for achieving widespread grassroots participation in a small community: individual membership, a block club network, and a coalition with members of each affiliated organization having access to planning decisions. Currently, the AAUD does not employ any of these structures. As the organization matures and seeks to hold, educate, and expand its constituency, one of these three empowering structures might be a useful long-term investment for helping Aliquippa to achieve unity. The alternative would be the formation of a second organization to concentrate on participation and advocacy, including grassroots fund-raising and broad-scale involvement of the community in making of the periodic strategic plans, while the

AAUD focuses on development. This seems to be the dual structure envisioned by Gilbert, the respected former co-chair of the AAUD board quoted in the sidebar earlier. It is a structure commonly and successfully used in many communities and now might be possible through the Communities That Care program.

Gilbert and Ruckert, as co-chairs, at times showed interest in block clubs. There was even mention of using the town's historic company-town residential "plans" as basic units for linking households directly to the AAUD. A dozen of the plans, each originally meant to encompass a single ethnic or class population, are still mapped. They vary in size, with the average number of households per plan being about 300. Such organizing questions would grow in importance if and when the board becomes ready to aggressively expand its focus beyond the Franklin Avenue core.

Some in the organization appear aware of the critical need to gain both breadth and depth of participation, close ties to expanding employers, and increased political clout (including more equal and creative partnerships with various levels of government). There seems to be an awareness of all three needs and concern for dealing with them. But these needs are not yet high enough on the agenda to be funded.

In Chapter 4, there was discussion of the people versus place issue that arises in community renewal. The AAUD has been attacked by the *Beaver County Times* for spending public funds on a place that is not likely to recover. But the Alliance surmounts the issue by also spending heavily on the education, health, and social well-being of the people of this place, which can help provide them with mobility if they choose to exercise it. Such programs also tend to strengthen the place and meld it together. This is strength of the kind pursued by the AAUD during its first 10 years. But it requires organizing as well as development to work. The central resource imperative remains. Without crowded streets, bursting institutions, and fattened inflows of incomes and development funds, the recovery vision is a mirage.

The AAUD has recruited, begged, and hammered its way into being an instrument of change. Each of the 12 basic activities of community organizing has been put to work and found to be useful. The first five—vision, recruitment, leadership development, cadre formation, and launching the chartered organization—were employed adroitly in the start-up, and these same activities have been found useful for reinvigoration along the 20-year route.

Goals were pursued with the aid of research and planning, evaluation, able staff, an implementation process, and partnering with other organizations, although the organization chose to reject the far-reaching recommendations urged on it by assessment teams from the two universities. Base was maintained and occasionally invigorated by tapping new resources and communicating with supporters and target publics. The AAUD has experienced value in preserving a balance between racing the AAUD machine and maintaining it. It has demonstrated the strengths that can show up in dedication of the cadre, commitment to the poor, tenacity in sticking to a core focus, and the relentless tapping of large outside institutions for human and material resources.

For an organization, 20 years is a long time in community renewal. Few stay vigorous and arrive at their 20th year with more strength and resources than they had in their 5th year. But the AAUD clearly has done so. It has skillfully and courageously blended human services, development, and community organizing. But by the year 2002, it appeared to have tilted toward development. Maintaining a comprehensive approach is difficult, but gaining it back after once losing it is a painful and expensive struggle, as many traditional community development corporations found during the 1990s. For at least 10 years, the AAUD kept at its dual mission of unity and development, but the pressure and enticements of development have risen to the top during recent years. In this first decade of the 21st century, the Alliance faces more pressure to shift resources away from the unity thrust and to bet the bulk of its treasury on development. However, if resident interests are to be well served in negotiations with city and county governments, philanthropic foundations, major employers, and other institutions, then the AAUD will need the respect and influence accruing from a large and representative body of active members and programs that bring residents into the action on a large scale. The "experiment" with an economic development specialist as director was not a good fit.

The most significant and useful institutional change probably would be a merger of the public schools of Aliquippa, Hopewell, and Center. The resulting scale and diversity could mean a school system of superior quality for all three communities. State government has the power to create the merger, and so do the federal courts, but fears of public officials prevent it from happening.

We suggest a strategy to explore: the difference that 2,000 or 3,000 young energetic immigrant families could make if they were warmly welcomed wholesale to live in a town with the idle assets of Aliquippa. They could rebuild and live in its now empty houses, launch new enterprises, supply new workforce skills, bring additional political influence, and widen the demand base of the local economy. Perhaps their creativity and enterprise could solve the puzzle of how to exploit the nearby Pittsburgh International Airport and the still vacant stretch of riverfront site hungry for investors.

An appropriate way in which to further evaluate the Aliquippa effort is to measure it against the five principles for saving small communities set forth in Chapter 1:

1. *Inclusion:* From its start, the Aliquippa renewal effort was open and joined in by a significant array of residents and other stakeholders. The name of the organization and its purpose ("Unity and Development") was decided in a public forum. Town meetings and surveys guided programs. Over the years, the effort came to rest on a small professional staff and a working citizen board with legal control backed by a loosely organized volunteer base. More recently, the focus has narrowed further, and there is a tendency for decisions to be made by a few board members and key staff members, with less attention given to interconnectedness and outreach. An ad hoc community-wide committee appointed by the AAUD board might profitably evaluate the question of the state of participation during a time when the little city may be ready for grassroots politics, fund-raising, and mass-based events.

2. *Comprehensiveness:* Social and economic opportunities and pressing needs have been steadily attended to, with the AAUD's first major project being a human services center that serves about 1,000 persons a month. There have been sporadic serious efforts for racial peace; current projects have a heavy emphasis on workforce training, youth career development, enterprise support (including incubators), business loans, and real estate construction and rehabilitation. Political awareness and influence do not yet get attention. There are no civic training sessions to stimulate issue interest; there is no mass power base or active crew of influential supporters continuously advocating with the institutions that control the wealth of the Pittsburgh region and the state of the nation beyond.

3. *Mobilization:* The AAUD has shown that it can assemble impressive crowds for community days, town meetings, protest marches aimed at key causes such as protecting mill pensions, visits by a governor, the premier of a historic town video, parent support groups, arts festivals, Christmas parties, and more, yet there are sections of Aliquippa and environs from which few or no people are drawn and where whole sub-neighborhoods are yet unconnected. The AAUD has had some success in extracting resources from governments, foundations, and banks but has done no sustained grassroots fund-raising involving residents. However, any and all volunteers are still welcome. Planning nearly always remains limited to a staff-board function. The board and staff continue to shy away from becoming part of a countywide power alliance.

4. *Adequate wealth:* Programs to upgrade residents' work skills, establish active connections with growth employers, support family thrift and institutional equity, and seek to obtain more outside investment funds go on. The town remains woefully short of jobs and of human, social, and financial capital, although a relatively small business loan fund is active. Current major programs are summer youth work experience, skills training, and thrift education. No standing task force exists to continually solicit operating and investment funds at a scale that matches opportunities and needs. The community's households continue to be dependent in large part on transfer payments.

The organization seeks every opportunity to apply for grants that might be relevant to its objectives. It has had major government funding for a Pathways to Work program, involving preparedness and training aimed at helping to transition people from public assistance, to career training, to employment; it also assists working clients to plan and achieve career goals. Pathway program services are available free to all Beaver County residents (AAUD, 2002).

5. *Health and spirit:* The intensely used WIC nutrition and education center has been in operation for 16 years. The walk-in health clinic on the main street has had an off-and-on operation but now operates daily with a doctor on hand for a few hours each day. Community spirit has been promoted by residents joining together to create a historic video, the annual Christmas parade, and occasional concerts. Regeneration of the spirit is being held back by lack of church participation. Progress has been made in raising morale of public school parents and students. There is no committee currently focused on strengthening the social fabric. The effort could profit from a periodic reassessment of action plans to ensure their execution with maximum feasible participation.

SUMMARY

Through the AAUD, residents of Aliquippa and their allies from the surrounding region have built a vehicle for planned change that has mobilized a body of residents and supporters and has drawn on an array of individuals, foundations, governments, churches, businesses, and other civic institutions for cash and noncash resources. It is a significant model of what is coming to be called *comprehensive initiative* and *community building.* Such models seek to tackle any serious issue that residents identify and commit to in a spirit of inclusion, civic courage, and fair sharing of the earth's bountiful production. The Alliance has already found the means to survive and gradually grow as an organization over time, and it has the momentum and respect to anticipate a life ahead. But the community body itself, in the face of sparse opportunities and the curse of undercrowdedness,

continues to shrink and stagnate, to cry out for an explosion of population and massive investment, and to intensely use a large, flat riverfront site close to one of the finest international airports on the globe. The Alliance has learned that it can make life a little more bearable for many households, yet it needs many more strong partners and mountains of cash resources that are not yet forthcoming.

People in Aliquippa have built the Alliance through five stages. First, a group of determined local people cast a vision and shaped an organization to achieve the vision. Second, they picked the most immediate need and created a one-stop center where families battered by unemployment and mounting debt could get sensitive support and tangible aid from understanding neighbors. Third, they moved on to find ways in which to create jobs and obtain needed training resources, education, transportation, health care, day care, and motivation. Fourth, they focused on the community's central weakness—undercrowdedness and the failed image of their traditional "main street"— and went to work to turn it around with amenities and connections to employers. Fifth, they have set out to locate financial resources at a scale to jump-start recovery.

With only modest progress to show and too few partners to help finish the task, the AAUD attempts to keep pushing toward its strategic plan objective. It inches forward, tending to favor visible achievement over unity and organization building, and as it struggles to make progress, it faces a challenge to maintain its people involvement. All of this now confronts an enthusiastic new executive director.

CONTINUING QUESTIONS

1. Can small communities with racially diverse populations play a key role in achieving racial healing in America?

2. What is the best way in which to widen participation in a community fragmented by race?

3. What is the responsibility, if any, of successful expanding employers to reach out to assist communities with chronic unemployment?

4. Will private and public funders continue to support Aliquippa-like programs so long as such programs show only limited progress?

5. Will American society's faith in government, seemingly restored somewhat by response to the tragedy of September 11, 2001, lead to societal investments in its depressed communities of sufficient scale to help them achieve true recovery?

6. How can human service programs be used effectively to recruit volunteers for a local community development organization?

7. Do people, including both parents with schoolchildren and voters without school-children, still care enough about their public schools that they will bite the political bullet for them—take on the bias and all the entrenched institutional inertia that undergird school decline and push for radical solutions such as merger and equitable funding?

8. How can state government be brought to live up to its responsibility to ensure quality public education for all of its communities, including distressed communities such as Aliquippa?

9. If religion is tolerant and liberating, then why do many of today's churches display low interest in issues beyond their own internal affairs?

10. Can the catalyst role played by the AAUD be assumed by some larger organization to play a similar role for the whole county of which the alliance is a part?

11. Will America accept the need for nine-figure government transfers to renew severely battered communities?

12. What does an OCCD organization lose when it shifts from a grassroots organizing and volunteer effort to a polished partnership effort?

Appendix 7.A Viewpoint of a Community Critic

Robert L. Reynolds sells mobile phones at the Giant Eagle store on the edge of Aliquippa. He speaks of the sales trade as community building; both are an art rather than a science. Born and raised on Franklin Avenue, he has a love-hate relationship with the town. Good times remembered include streets and sidewalks choked with people—black and white, young and old, blue collar and white collar—all jostling for space. "Look at Franklin Avenue now. It is a pale remnant of its former self," according to Reynolds. He traces the decline of Aliquippa to the assassination of Martin Luther King, Jr., during the 1960s that spawned racial conflicts. When this happened, businesses were frightened away from inner-city streets. The decline of Aliquippa was the product of a plan engineered by "corporate America" that starved the town of resources through redlining. Reynolds attributes the decline to racism, disinvestment, and the lack of leadership by African Americans.

Reynolds believes that Aliquippa faces certain doom. Aliquippa will soon be smothered by the neighboring townships, such as Center and Hopewell, and will become part of a larger entity. "The corpse of the town can then be given a decent funeral. The layers of cynicism and apathy deposited in the town in heaps like slag have smothered the possibility of renewal."

— Brian Conway
Research Assistant

Appendix 7.B Board Members Can Stimulate Participation

Debbie Ruckert, until recently a lifetime resident of Aliquippa and the daughter of a steel-worker, had served several years as an AAUD board member—including 3 years as co-chair—while working full-time and raising a teenage daughter. One of her favorite reminders is the following: "We have two choices in life. We can choose to do nothing and wither away into obscurity, or we can get involved and make a lasting contribution to our world."

She feels strongly that board members of community renewal organizations can raise the quality of resident participation if they do the following:

- Ensure that the services of the organization meet the requests of the community
- Ensure that the organization is meeting its contracted obligations
- Ensure that the staff and other components of the organization are pursuing the policies set by the board

- Accept responsibility for acting as a two-way channel of communication with residents and others being represented
- Advocate the needs of the community at board meetings and in forums and discussions within and beyond the community

Appendix 7.C
Credit to the People:
The Dilemma of
High-Risk Credit Unions

It is our conviction that a community's greatest asset is its people—and that it is working people with adequate credit that keeps a community stable and viable. However, racial and class biases in bank lending procedures force many impoverished small communities to look to themselves to find credit. This situation, as well as National City Bank's decision to close its Aliquippa branch, created the need for something to be done to meet the credit needs of Aliquippa's impoverished core community.

The AAUD has tried hard to create a democratic and prosperous community in Aliquippa. To help achieve this community development goal, it set up a credit union headed by Beverly Sessoms in the former J. C. Murphy building. Informally begun in November 1996 and formally in February 1997, it sought to pool some of Aliquippa's economic risks and assets under one roof. Residents owned the credit union and borrowed its funds. The credit union gave Aliquippa its first stockpile of flexible grassroots money under community control.

It was the AAUD's catalytic role in organizing that lifted the credit union off the ground. It was established with great hope for its potential to breathe life back into the flagging local economy. Technical assistance from across the river (Ambridge New Alliance Federal Credit Union and the Hill District Credit Union in Pittsburgh) seemed to assure it of a promising future. It chalked up major accomplishments in a relatively short period of time. By 1998, it had furnished more than 180 loans and was serving 650 to 700 community residents. However, during this same year, the AAUD credit union ran into trouble. Loans, even of the low-interest kind offered by credit unions, are never easy to pay

back, and in the case of Aliquippa's credit union, some never were paid back. This was the principal factor that led to the credit union's merger with the nearby Ambridge credit union in April 1999. Although it will undoubtedly benefit from the experience, size, and expertise of Ambridge's New Alliance Federal Credit Union, this is at the cost of its identity as a creature of the AAUD's renewal efforts as well as its loss of control over the credit union's board and credit committee.

Credit unions in low-income neighborhoods often run into difficulty. A highly publicized case (similar to that of Aliquippa) is the Central Brooklyn Federal Credit Union in New York City, which opened its teller stations with dreams of people en masse investing savings and taking out loans that would spark neighborhood resurgence. Chartered in 1993, it reached 5,000 members and $5 million in deposits by 1996. But by that year, it was having financial difficulty, weakened by its providing needed but unprofitable services, such as money orders and subway tokens, plus a chronic difficulty with loan repayments. The National Credit Union Administration (NCUA) took control away from the community and placed it under conservatorship. Newspaper reports indicated that regulators faulted the credit union's inadequate bookkeeping, high expenses, and liberal loan and collection practices. (It is good to note that the Central Brooklyn Credit Union was returned to community control in January 2000 and is now a stable ongoing concern.)

Closing troubled credit unions or forcing their merger is a standard action for the NCUA, which maintains that the agency's principal obligation is to protect its insurance fund by promoting large, stable credit unions. With a customer base of 521 low-income designate credit unions, the NCUA (1999) during the period from 1995 to 1999 oversaw 20 mergers and 10 liquidations, a surprisingly high 94% stability rate for this high-risk set of credit unions.

The AAUD's executive director, David Blenk, noted the lessons learned from the merger with Ambridge New Alliance Federal Credit Union. He viewed community participation in credit unions as a strength as well as a source of vulnerability. He stressed the importance to new and small credit unions in poor communities of securing substantial equity (institutional net worth) as a route to stability, of the value of serious and deliberate community participation in credit union decisions, of the need for training for the members of the credit committees, and of the utility of technical assistance from entities such as the National Federation of Community Development Credit Unions, the trade association for credit unions that serve low-income communities (personal interview, March 29, 2001). A constant challenge, however, is how a small community can secure the sustained technical assistance and resources from the outside that is vital to launching and maintaining a small credit union that tends to serve poor people.

— Brian Conway
Research Assistant

Appendix 7.D
Aliquippa Embraces Art

The annual arts festival for 1998 was held on a sunny Saturday in July. Franklin Avenue was festive and bouncy for this day. After a carefree parade of fire engines, senior citizen horn players, and floats spewing wrapped candy pieces to kids sitting along the curbs, black and white art lovers intermingled in vacant lots and unrented storefronts to view traditional and experimental sculptures, murals, photographs, installations, paintings, idols, and icons, many of them interactive. Locals and itinerants grilled and sold chicken pieces, sausages, ribs, and burgers in a smoky central parking lot. Bouquets of gas-filled balloons floated on strings above fireplugs. Children holding soft drinks abounded. Observations and conversations revealed three sources for the crowd: artists and friends, Alliance activists and their contacts, and walk-in people from the humble surrounding homes. Curious residents of neighboring uphill middle-class streets were absent.

The crowd was a happy one. It was an earthy joyful place for a visitor to be. The blackened kielbasa in this setting was delicious. The pro bono bands were professional, and they intensified the magic. A look-alike of Roberto Clemente, the celebrated Pittsburgh Pirates center fielder who died a hero's death taking medical supplies to a remote area of the Caribbean, did a poignant monologue, spellbinding the African American children and captivating adults of both races who massed around him. In numbers, the total crowd at any moment probably was no more than 200—not many for such an event, but they represented a superb gathering in quality. The social fabric was close-knit and gentle, giving off a sense of what the psalms call "the oil of gladness."

— James V. Cunningham

REFERENCES

Aliquippa Alliance for Unity and Development. (1995). *Strategic plan: 1995–1998.* Aliquippa, PA: Author.

Aliquippa Alliance for Unity and Development. (1997, November 11). Lt. governor to keynote Aliquippa ribbon cutting [press release]. Aliquippa, PA: Author.

Aliquippa Alliance for Unity and Development. (1999). *Strategic Plan: 1999–2002.* Aliquippa, PA: Author.

Aliquippa Alliance for Unity and Development. (2002). *Making it happen through leadership and empowerment.* Aliquippa, PA: Author.

Bratt, R. (1997). CDCs: Contributions outweigh contradictions. *Journal of Urban Affairs, 19,* 23–28.

Brown, R., et al. (1993). *Building on unity: A coalition for development in Aliquippa.* Pittsburgh, PA: Carnegie Mellon University, Heinz School of Public Policy and Management Systems, Synthesis Project.

Cairns, C. (1991). [Organizer's typescript diary]. Unpublished manuscript.

Cairns, C., & Cunningham, J. (Eds.). (1986). *Aliquippa update: A Pittsburgh milltown struggles to come back 1984–1986.* Pittsburgh, PA: School of Social Work, University of Pittsburgh, School of Social Work, Three Rivers Community Project.

Martz, P. (1991). *The youth enterprise demonstration: A critical evaluation of three projects carried out in southwestern Pennsylvania.* Pittsburgh, PA: University of Pittsburgh, School of Social Work, Three Rivers Community Project.

Mullin & Lonergan Associates. (1992). *Housing and neighborhood improvement strategy for the City of Aliquippa: An action plan for preservation of the city's residential neighborhoods.* Pittsburgh, PA: Author.

National Credit Union Administration. (1999, September 30). *Report of low income designated credit union: 1995–1999.* Washington: DC: Author.

Ricci, E., Singh, V., Ahlbrandt, R., Manners, S., Keren, D., Musa, D., Trauth, J., & Tucillo, E. (1991). *Evaluation of the Greater Pittsburgh Revitalization Initiative* (progress report, Year 3). Pittsburgh, PA: University of Pittsburgh, Center for Social and Urban Research.

Ricci, E., Singh, V., Ahlbrandt, R., Manners, S., & Trauth, J. (1994). *Greater Pittsburgh revitalization initiative evaluation final report.* Pittsburgh, PA: University of Pittsburgh, Center for Social and Urban Research.

Ritter, D. (1991, November 19). Franklin Avenue is vital to city's future. *Beaver County Times,* p. A7.

Too far gone. (1991, November 12). *Beaver County Times.* [editorial]

Twiss, P., & Cooper, P. (2000). Youth revitalizing main street: A case study. *Social Work in Education, 22*(3), 162–176.

U.S. Bureau of the Census. (2000). [Online]. Available: www.census.gov

8

Forging an Organizational Plan

Both organizations and communities undertake planning to realize their mission and chart a course of action. Organizations do it to make strategic choices for focusing their always limited resources. Communities do it to mobilize all of their assets toward a unified vision of desired community change. This chapter concentrates on ways in which to develop effective organizational plans using participatory decision making, while Chapter 9 focuses on community planning through broad-based participation that is likely to involve several organizations.

Overview of Organizational and Community Planning

The planning processes outlined in this chapter and Chapter 9 are generalized and provide a framework that can be tailored to fit particular conditions. Each organization and community is different; therefore, care should be taken in determining what to do, how to do it, and when to do it while taking into consideration local interest, momentum, urgency, timing, resources, and needs.

Organizational and community planning often overlap and become intertwined. The processes and products are similar, but the focus is different. Both ask and answer the

following questions. What needs doing? How should we do it? Who will do it? When will it be done? What resources are needed? How will success be measured? Organizational planning focuses on planning within an individual organization; community planning focuses on multiple constituencies and organizations planning together at the community level.

Both organizational planning and community planning involve processes that are structured, focused, inclusive, and participatory and that are designed to raise interest, rouse support, and make decisions about the future work of the organization or the joint organizations for the community. Both entail the following:

- Creating a structure to develop, coordinate, manage, and oversee a distinctive planning effort
- Identifying and engaging a wide variety of participants
- Developing a collective vision for the future
- Gathering and analyzing data and information
- Identifying opportunities, assets, problems, and needs and making informed choices as to where to put energy and resources
- Setting agreed-on concrete goals and developing implementation plans to achieve those goals

- Mobilizing and deploying resources to carry out activities
- Monitoring and evaluating progress and revising plans periodically

Both organizational planning and community planning require patience, flexibility, the ability to meld disparate interests and ideas, persistence, hope and a positive outlook, and confidence that the job can be done. Both are grounded in maximum resident participation producing locally grown and rooted plans. The products of such planning processes are widely agreed-on sets of actions (e.g., programs, projects, initiatives, activities, campaigns) that will move an organization or a community from current conditions to a collective (and better) future.

Entire books have been written about organizational and community planning processes. In this chapter, we have distilled our experiences and those in wide-ranging references, but even with this distillation, the processes that follow may seem intimidating and unwieldy. Keep in mind that we seek here to present a wide array of planning elements from which a local community group may tailor-make a successful process for itself. *What is crucial are the spirit and design of the process; what is vital is to produce the plan.* Each of the elements presented here can be modified in scale and detail to match the resources available and the community conditions being encountered. Organizational planning is discussed first because this is where most renewal efforts start.

WHAT IS ORGANIZATIONAL PLANNING?

The focus of an organizational plan is "internal," set on the "micro level". It is a guide for one specific organization to define its roles and activities as it builds sufficient strengths to achieve its goals. It is an organization's path to effectiveness. At times, this work takes place within a community planning process.

As an initial step, organizational planning involves clarifying the collective organizational vision and mission or organizational purpose. The mission might be as narrow as ensuring an adequate supply of quality affordable housing or be as broad as making a commitment to focus on all aspects of community renewal. The plan will detail what activities the organization will carry out and what it will get others in the community and beyond to do with it or for it. The plan will sharpen the organization's internal structure (leadership, management, credibility, communications, and resource base) and solidify the community. Although widespread public input and feedback may be solicited, decision making usually remains within the organization.

In this chapter, we discuss three levels of organizational planning: annual, long range, and strategic. When undertaking their first effort at planning, most groups start by producing an annual or 1-year plan that captures what they want to accomplish in organization building and program activities or initiatives during the next year and what they will need to do to reach their goals. Once a group has developed and implemented an annual plan or two, it begins to see the connections between issues of concern and the fact that many issues require long-term efforts. Eventually, this may lead to developing a long-range plan of 3 to 5 years, again focusing on a series of organization building and program goals and related activities. A shorter term, detailed 1-year plan is then developed to guide implementation.

Both annual planning and long-range planning typically assume that the current situation and trends will continue, with the plan aimed at improving the local community's future. Strategic planning, on the other hand, takes into account the always changing external and internal issues and trends that affect and shape an organization and its agenda. Strategic plans can be short term, 6 months to 1 year, or longer term (up to 5 years). Annual plans are then derived from longer term strategic plans. Many seasoned organizations have moved toward strategic planning because it takes into account the dynamic nature of community organizing, community conditions, and revitalization efforts. Organizations grow into higher levels of planning, with each requiring an increasing amount of skills, expertise, and resources.

WHY DEVELOP AN ORGANIZATIONAL PLAN?

Community organizations operate in an environment of pressing needs and opportunities and demands for action. Why take the time and expend scarce resources to gather information, think, discuss, and reach agreement on a plan? Organizations, which regularly undertake planning, point to the following benefits:

- Organizational agreement, and therefore cohesiveness around what will be done and not done, gives direction and focus and also builds momentum. Priorities and the organization's role(s) are clarified. An organization chooses where it will focus its efforts rather than allowing others to determine and control its agenda.
- Well-designed, participatory planning processes can build an organization. Discussing critical problems and exploring options build teamwork and provide opportunities for new leadership to blossom and develop.
- An organizational plan indicates clear places for people to fit in, thereby using community talent more fully. It is respectful of volunteers' time. People are able to carve out those areas for volunteer effort that will hold their interest and tap their expertise.
- Having a well thought out plan captured in a written document gives an organization a stronger claim to resources. A plan provides a road map to follow allowing for targeting of efforts and more strategic and efficient use of resources. A clear concise plan can be an effective communications tool, marketing the group and its agenda to a wider public.
- A regular cycle of planning allows an organization to develop alertness to and keep pace with changing internal and external community and organizational needs, opportunities, and trends.
- A published and widely disseminated plan document achieves greater accountability both within the organization and to the organization's constituents.

This can increase an organization's credibility and legitimacy, especially among those outside the community giving an organization greater influence. This often translates into more resources and favorable considerations of requests. Plans help to focus efforts and can lead to significant progress toward goals and solid outcomes.

There are, however, some limitations to organizational planning. Barry (1997) found that the costs of planning can at times outweigh benefits; planning consumes time and money that might be spent more productively on other tasks. In addition, planning efforts sometimes get off track; bad decisions are made, brewing troubles surface, and people can become lost in the process or get bogged down in insignificant history and minutia. Therefore, before undertaking a planning process, an organization needs to ask whether the benefits will outweigh the costs. If the answer is no, then it would be wise to postpone planning and to address any urgent issues, design a better process, or seek outside advice. It is also possible to become so wedded to a plan (one that has taken considerable time and resources to design) that flexibility is compromised. The organization must be careful not to see the "plan document" as the final product and the path chosen as unchangeable. It is important to see the plan itself as evolving, taking time to review and update as conditions change or fresh opportunities arise. Kearns (2000) pointed out that an emphasis on data gathering and analysis can "mask the inherent subjectivity of planning efforts and the ease with which they can be manipulated to verify predetermined conclusions, giving a false impression of objectivity" (pp. 38–39).

Some organizations never develop organizational plans as described in this chapter. Barry (1997) pointed to organizations that have gifted leaders with finely developed intuition about what will occur and how their organizations should proceed. Such people know instinctively how to proceed, sometimes without formal planning. Barry stated that if one's organization has such a leader or leaders, then one may want to keep the planning process very simple. Kearns (2000) identified this as a visionary approach to planning. In this type of planning, one "stand[s] with the leader's vision for the organization and work[s] backwards to determine what resources or core competencies must be leveraged to achieve that vision" (p. 32). A cautionary note is in order: Although inspiring leaders are great assets to any organization, it is important that in the majority of cases an organization does not become too dependent on any one leader; even simple plans should reflect the views of those expected to carry out the plans.

Barry (1997) also described what he called "creative muddling" (p. 12), which occurs when a team of skilled people who know each other's talents and abilities work together creatively and opportunistically to achieve a particular purpose. When done well, this can be an effective form of operating. When done poorly, this muddling style can stymie an organization.

When to Develop an Organizational Plan

An organization needs to undertake more formalized systematic planning and decision making when it has done the following:

1. Become a formal structured organization— holding regular meetings, having identified leadership, having a meeting/office space, and having begun the incorporation process

2. Developed a tested sense of direction

3. Made progress on an initiating issue(s) and is getting results

4. Achieved sustained involvement of a dependable cadre of volunteers

5. Tapped resources or assets to bring to the table (e.g., people, money, data)

6. Built history and recognition outside of its own group

It is better for an organization to be proactive rather than reactive when planning. However, in many instances, organizations are "prompted"

into developing their first, and in some cases subsequent, plans. (Such was the case in Aliquippa, Pennsylvania. The accompanying sidebar gives insight into the Aliquippa Alliance for Unity and Development's [AAUD] planning history.) Some more common "detonators" of organizational planning include the following:

- *Funder requests:* Applications for funding often request copies of plans as a condition for receiving a grant. Funders sometimes also suggest and offer to pay for plan development.

- *Organizational crisis:* Loss of funding, loss of key staff and/or leadership, and lack of programmatic results often force people to the planning table. (In most cases, it is better to resolve the immediate crisis with problem solving than to undertake planning while a crisis is beginning to boil over.)

- *Organizational transition:* New board members asking key questions, a new leadership team wanting to make its imprint, shifting from an all-volunteer to a staffed effort surfacing issues of roles and responsibilities, and a new executive director/staff bringing fresh perspectives and skills all can detonate a perceived need for a plan.

- *Community challenge:* Residents asking why the organization is doing what it is doing, especially when resources are scarce, or multiple demands from a variety of constituencies may prompt the need to selectively apply resources for maximum impact.

- *New service area:* A shift in geographical area of focus, especially when an effort starts out in a specific targeted area but perceives expanded need or shifting need, may force the making of a new or enlarged plan.

- *New conditions:* A change in community conditions, often caused by the actions/decisions of others or a change in the economic, social, or political landscape, can force a group to rethink its approach and/or agenda, necessitating the development (or updating) of a plan.

- *Legislative action:* The need to create a plan may occur when programs or funding requirements are significantly altered or when legislation establishes new programs or funding streams (e.g., a shift from "training" to "investment" in the area of workforce development).

ALIQUIPPA ALLIANCE FOR UNITY AND DEVELOPMENT'S PLANNING HISTORY

This brief overview of the three plans that the AAUD has developed illustrates how organizations get more capable and detailed in planning as time progresses. It also indicates the various prompters of plan development and the range of options on which to focus planning. The complexity and breadth of the AAUD's plans mirror its growth as an organization.

AAUD Strategic Self-Sufficiency Plan, 1992–1997

Plan Focus. In 1992, the AAUD was pushed by its funders (in particular one major funder) to develop a strategic organizational plan. The AAUD produced *Strategic Self-Sufficiency Planning, 1992–1997,* which focused solely on the organization's financial status and future funding options. Specifically, the AAUD addressed the ramifications of a reduced core (operational) budget and explored local fund-raising efforts and the pursuit of nonlocal funding streams and project income.

This plan was developed by the executive director and reviewed by the board of directors.

AAUD Strategic Plan, 1995–1998

Plan Focus. This plan broadened its focus to include goals, strategies, and action plans in four issue areas:

1. Building a strong partnership with the community by focusing on the needs of the citizens and businesses in Aliquippa (e.g., business development, recruitment, and retention for Franklin Avenue; upgrading the quality of educational opportunities available to residents to enhance their basic skills and become competitive in the local and regional market; enhancing relationships with elected officials; joining regional coalitions and obtaining resources from outside Aliquippa)

2. Becoming a model for community revitalization by "getting the job done" (e.g., developing creative solutions to build local capacity, facilitating the quality and delivery of each of the AAUD's services)

3. Enhancing staff, board, and volunteer participation in the AAUD and making participation a satisfying process (e.g., developing an awards/recognition system, encouraging participation at board meetings and AAUD events)

4. Creating a renewed spirit within Aliquippa that would ultimately improve Aliquippa's image (e.g., organizing community-wide events, expanding the AAUD's committee structure to involve more residents, developing a community calendar, promoting the good things that happen in Aliquippa)

The board of directors and staff developed this plan. Information reviewed during the planning process included the results of the 1994 Regional Urban Development Action Team (RUDAT) charette and a City of Aliquippa-sponsored comprehensive plan. Progress toward goals was monitored and evaluated, and the plan was reviewed and updated yearly.

AAUD Strategic Plan, 1999–2002

Plan Focus. The third plan that the AAUD produced is the most detailed and comprehensive one. It specifies outcomes that would indicate that goals have been achieved and the actions that must be taken to reach the outcomes. The plan includes a timetable for review and revision and also fixes responsibility for those activities. (An excerpt from this plan can be found later in a subsequent sidebar in this chapter.) The 1999–2002 plan identifies the following seven key areas for concerted effort:

1. Administration (e.g., management, staff supervision, fund-raising, board development, plan updating, increasing community involvement and volunteerism, continuing a reputation as a cutting-edge leader, maintaining strategic community linkages)

2. Capital and business development (e.g., increasing capital available for business expansion and growth; operating a strategic loan fund; establishing local, regional, state, and national partnerships that bring resources, technical assistance, and expertise to the AAUD's development activities)

3. Business and economic development (e.g., operating a small business counseling center, recruiting and retaining businesses on Franklin Avenue and beyond, enhancing Aliquippa's image)

4. Workforce development (e.g., improving the quality of students graduating/exiting the Aliquippa school district; reducing the dropout rate; increasing student attendance; increasing the involvement of parents, the community, and adult role models; increasing the community's knowledge of and preparation for alternative schooling techniques)

5. Human and social services (e.g., placing more individuals in career track jobs, increasing resources for workforce development, retaining skilled people in the region)

6. Existing properties and equipment (e.g., monitoring, compliance, and auditing of all ongoing projects; exploring the reuse or possible sale of currently owned properties; improving the AAUD's technology and equipment resources)

7. Arts programming (e.g., supplementing the arts and music curriculum and addressing the lack of performance space within the school district and in the community, supporting access to art and cultural avenues absent in the community, establishing a national model for economic revitalization through the arts)

The board of directors and staff developed this plan. Among the data used in plan development was information generated from an economic analysis of the area conducted by Carnegie Mellon University. This analysis was funded through a grant from the Heinz Endowments. Following review of the economic data, the AAUD selected out those areas where it could have an impact, set goals and outcomes, and then detailed actions to achieve the outcomes.

The AAUD did not create any specific implementation plans tied to any of its strategic plans. Responsibilities for outcomes were assigned on a staff level, and actions and progress toward goals are monitored through quarterly reporting. (More on implementation plans can be found later in this chapter.)

AAUD Plan Development Assessment

The AAUD altered its course under the pressure of opportunities to get grants and start dramatic programs with youth and real estate development and businesses, and it attempted this through a limited set of board members, staff, and influentials. What might have occurred if the AAUD early on had instituted a regular organizational planning process with widespread participation?

♦ A system of local indigenous fund-raising (mass contributions) and more leverage with funders would have likely resulted in a more diversified and stable funding base (including more sources of grants, more county funding support, etc.)

♦ A formal resident/public participation system and more widespread community connections through a system of block clubs would have likely resulted in more political influence. Although the AAUD has hundreds of volunteers, they are not organized into an on-call base of support. In addition, the AAUD's mobilization for political influence likely would encounter little competition.

♦ Greater loyalty of people to the AAUD and to the community and increased volunteerism and engagement in AAUD activities (the Alliance would have uncovered valuable specialized talents to tap) would have been an additional by-product.

DEVELOPING AN ORGANIZATIONAL PLAN

Internal organizational planning and decision making combines building an organizational base and developing a work program. The focus is on what a *specific* organization will do both short term and long term.

Community organizations are confronted daily with community issues, needs, and opportunities—improved housing, more and better jobs, problem landlords, safety issues, and the like. Organizations in many cases are limited by time and resources as to what to focus on as well as when and how. In addition, opportunities are always present—new resources become available, a problem structure is demolished and a vacant lot is available, a key piece of property has been offered as a donation or is now available for sale, a local employer puts out a call for 100 new workers, and the like.

Effective organizational planning is about an organization knowing its community's needs and assets and balancing these against its capacity to effect change and the opportunity for success. Deciding what to do—which programs, projects,

services, and activities to use—we call *making strategic choices.*

There are many paths to take in making a decision. The path taken depends on an organization's style and the personalities involved. As with any decision, community organizations know that they cannot anticipate everything and cannot know all of the answers upfront. They sometimes do not even know all of the questions to ask. Deciding what to do is not a cut-and-dried scientific process. Even when all of the information is at hand, uncontrollable forces are at work; therefore, planning involves regular monitoring, evaluation, reassessment, and plan revision.

FRAMEWORK FOR ORGANIZATIONAL PLANNING AND DECISION MAKING

As we have seen, serious community controlled development organizations generally spring to life because a few people become concerned about distress or want to seize an opportunity. Their motivating purpose we call *mission,* and the hopeful future images they conjure we call *vision*—two aspirations intermingled and reinforcing. The same reality is to be found in more formal organizational planning, which is the process of building and maintaining an organizational vehicle and developing a specific organizational agenda for renewal.

Our suggested eight-step framework for organizational planning and decision making is outlined in what follows. We begin with getting organized to undertake planning and move through the seven additional steps. Each organization undertaking a planning process needs to tailor the process and its product to its current capacity, resources, and circumstances.

Planning processes (including ours) are laid out in sequential discrete steps that give the impression that if the steps are followed as outlined, then the process will be relatively smooth and the product (plan) will be clear, concise, and correct. But planning is hard work and involves a lot of different people and interests, many unknowns and assumptions, and often a bit of luck. Cautions, pitfalls, and ways in which to minimize problems are included in our description that follows. An outline of our framework for organizational planning is shown in Figure 8.1.

Step 1: Getting Organized

Forming a Core Planning Team

A small group or committee of the leadership team or board of directors (five or six people) is tapped to coordinate, manage, and oversee the planning process. This group meets regularly during the planning process and reports to the leadership team or board of directors. Key staff members should be part of the core planning team.

Many people have concerns about planning and ask whether it will be worth the effort and time. Some have had bad experiences with planning—plans sit on the shelf and are not used, there was unsound decision making, arguments broke out frequently, and the like. It is important to identify any concerns within the organization about planning and barriers that may exist and to determine how these can be addressed. Some suggestions are to discuss the

benefits of planning, acknowledge the previous negative experiences, and involve the whole leadership team or board in designing the planning process.

Designing the Process

It is critical that an organization designs a planning process that fits its needs and resources. Some preliminary questions for the group to discuss are the following:

- What type of plan do we need (e.g., annual, short-term, long range, strategic) and why?
- Why do we want to develop a plan? What are the benefits and costs?
- What are the goals of our planning process (to sharpen organizational focus, to build leadership capacity of core people, to attract new volunteers, to reach agreement and consensus, to maximize results)?
- How much time, and what quantity of resources, can we commit to developing the plan?
- What period of time should the plan cover (e.g., 6 months, 1 year, 2 years)?
- Who will the prime developers of the plan be (e.g., a board committee, the whole board or leadership team, staff/board members/volunteers)?
- How open will the process be? What provisions for input and participation will be made? Who else is critical to include in plan development? When is input appropriate and necessary?
- How much information is needed to make sound decisions? How available and reliable is such information?
- How will decisions be made (e.g., formal vote, majority, consensus)?
- What are the future uses of the plan (both internal and external)?

The development of a plan can take a few weeks or a number of months, depending on the size and structure of the organization, the time frame, resource availability, and the amount of detail wanted in the plan. Some groups meet, gather information, meet again, and then repeat the process. Some groups meet,

FRAMEWORK FOR ORGANIZATIONAL PLANNING

STEP 1: GETTING ORGANIZED Forming a Core Planning Team Designing the Process Deciding on the Scope of Participation

STEP 2: DEVELOPING OR REFINING ORGANIZATIONAL PURPOSE Setting the Context Vision and Mission

STEP 3: TAKING STOCK Progress Assessment Conducting an Environmental Scan

STEP 4: SELECTING PRIORITIES FOR ACTION/ATTENTION Making Strategic Choices

STEP 5: DEVELOPING GOALS AND STRATEGIES Tying Proposed Actions to Outcomes

STEP 6: DEVELOPING IMPLEMENTATION PLANS Long-Term and Short-Term Plans and Objectives Projects, Programs, and Activities

STEP 7: DRAFTING, REFINING, AND ADOPTING THE PLAN

STEP 8: MONITORING AND EVALUATING EFFORTS Checking Progress Toward Goals Reassessing and Revising Plan

Figure 8.1   Framework for Organizational Planning

gather all of the information needed, and then meet and draft a plan.

Deciding on the Scope of Participation

Who to include in the planning, and how to include them, is a critical question. The aim should be to maximize participation—collect more information, ideas, and options; elicit more ownership and buy-in; attract more people to help with implementation; and get greater commitment to the organization's efforts. Maximizing participation is to be done amid pockets of apathy, complex problems, and the challenges and joys of daily life. This involves fully engaging the full board or leadership team, volunteers and staff, residents and others who the organization serves or will affect (e.g., civic club officials, small business owners, rental property owners); and other interested parties (e.g., supportive political leaders, media friends, funders).

A key question to answer is how much internal and external input and feedback is enough to produce a legitimate organizational plan. It is important that there be some open sessions for any persons or other organizations to provide ideas in addition to soliciting data and feedback (described later in Step 3). Critical here is to decide what role the open sessions play– e.g., information only, debate, recommendations, casting votes.

Step 2: Developing or Refining Organizational Purpose and Focus

Setting the Context

This step in the process begins with reviewing the organization's history—why the organization was founded (key organizing issues), the direction being followed, and key accomplishments in both organization building and program activities. This provides everyone with a common organizational view and points of common reference. All of the key players know how and why the organization arrived at the point of formally defining vision and mission.

Creating a Vision and Developing a Mission Statement

We describe vision and mission statement separately. In many organizations, they are combined in one guiding statement.

Vision. It is important that organizational building begin with a shared long-term vision of what people want to happen in their area of interest. If a group of concerned residents is drawn together around the issue of abandoned houses, then their vision could be to have all residential properties occupied and well maintained and to have no abandoned houses in their community. A vision is a shared picture of the future that an organization seeks to create and believes can be accomplished. Vision also includes anticipating what an organization wants to become in the future, discovering what it desires its future reputation to be and what the community and others will be saying, and forecasting what it will have accomplished. If a group has multiple areas of concern, then its long-term vision may be more broad and comprehensive.

Examples of community visions include the following:

- Through a spirit of community cooperation fostered by Bayside Neighbors United, Bayside will be a more diverse and harmonious community where all residents see themselves as neighbors and potential friends and where democratic cohesion will take the place of racial and religious misunderstanding that causes division among residents.
- The Avalon Civic Association envisions its community as a place where every child receives a quality education, resides in a quality affordable home, and is able to secure a living-wage job on coming of age.
- The Roner Springs Community Development Corporation, engaging a wide range of local residents, will work to ensure that Roner Springs will be a people-friendly place where the strengths and talents of all residents are tapped on behalf of the community.

Mission Statement. Based on the future vision, a group develops a mission for its organization— a brief statement specifying the purpose of the organization, that is, why it is in business. If the organization has a mission in place, then the mission should be reviewed and revised if indicated. A mission statement tells what the group will focus on and also, as important, what it will not focus on. The mission serves as a guide and tool for initiating and instructing future members of the organization and outsiders. The mission statement also embodies core values and principles of the organization—the beliefs that people share (e.g., mutual respect, everyone having a voice). In summary, a mission statement clarifies, focuses, commits, and communicates. Examples of mission statements include the following:

- The mission of the Green Street Coalition is to foster family self-sufficiency and build resident capacity to meet long-term life challenges.
- Freedom Hill Inc. was organized to improve its town's economic base through community development and community-building efforts, create a positive town image, and increase homeownership opportunities for residents. In pursuing our mission, we enable neighbors to

make informed decisions about the town's future.

Step 3. Taking Stock

Taking stock involves checking in on the organization's resources, capabilities and progress and, with strategic planning, doing a more in-depth examination—an internal and external assessment. Once assessment and progress information is gathered, it should be captured in a report and discussed by the planning group. (This information becomes the fodder for goal development, a future step.)

Assessing Progress

With annual and long-range planning, an assessment of the organization and progress toward goals is made. An assessment of the organization answers the following questions. What is going well? What, if anything, needs to be changed about how we function and operate? What should we start, stop, or continue? An internal activities progress review is conducted that looks at what has been accomplished and why, what is still in progress, what has not been completed and why, and what has not been started and why. Most often, both types of information are gathered internally through a questionnaire or survey or during planning session discussions. In addition, some organizations develop a questionnaire or survey (phone, mail, or door to door) seeking broad public feedback on their work and operations as well as ideas for future activities, programs, projects, and campaigns.

Green (1994) identified a series of key questions that also can be answered in this "taking stock" phase:

- What need, problem, or value caused the organization to come into being?
- What has changed?
- Are the issues the organization is addressing still relevant?
- Will these changes affect the organization's mission, programs/projects, and/or funding?
- How will the changes affect the planning process?
- Who are the organization's constituents?

- How is the organization meeting its constituents' expectations?
- What will the organization's constituents want tomorrow?
- How will its constituents' needs affect the organization's long-term plan?

Conducting an Environmental Scan

In strategic planning, an environmental scan, often called a "SWOT analysis" (with SWOT an acronym for strengths, weaknesses, opportunities, and threats), involves conducting an internal assessment (organizational strengths and weaknesses) and an external assessment (opportunities and threats outside the organization).

Data are gathered and analyzed concerning the organization's strengths and weaknesses, which include capabilities and resources that the organization can build on or develop and areas that it can improve or change. Examples of areas to examine include board development, administrative practices, financial management policies and procedures, local fund-raising, membership recruitment and retention, and internal communications.

Data are also gathered and analyzed on the opportunities and threats faced by the organization, including constituent needs, competitors and allies, and social, political, economic, and technological forces, changes, and trends. Environmental scans help to determine how external trends and changes might affect the organization and its mission over the next few years. Examples of possible opportunities include the availability of new job training grant funds, a new branch bank scheduled to open in the community during the next year, the creation of a new federal-level housing financing program, Internet access through local schools and libraries, a national funding intermediary selecting a community's region for investment, and the potential formation of a community planning forum. Examples of existing or potential threats include a planned highway expansion and bypass at the edge of the community, a shocking racial incident, a nearby manufacturing plant closing, a stock market downturn that has affected the amount of foundation funds available locally, the election of a community-unfriendly mayor or municipal leader, and continued growth in area unemployment rates.

Strategic planning information-gathering processes for the environmental scan can range between small-scale internal discussions or questionnaires and full-blown organizational and community assessments involving door-to-door surveys. The depth and scope depend on an organization's needs, time, and resources. Organizational assessment information is often gathered through interviews, surveys, questionnaires, and focus groups that include members of the board or leadership team, volunteers, staff, constituents, and others (e.g., funders, business leaders). Community assessment information to identify forces and trends can be gathered by the means already mentioned or through a community scan or assessment (detailed in Chapter 9). An alternative information-gathering method is to have small groups brainstorm during an initial planning session(s) and report back to the full group.

Step 4. Selecting Priorities for Action/Attention

Step 4 involves identifying and selecting critical issues or priorities to narrow the list of possibilities for action/attention to a doable number. Often these are the organizational, programmatic, and community strengths/opportunities or weaknesses/threats that will have the greatest impact (either positive or negative) on the organization, its constituents, and the community. All should fall within the organization's mission. Walsh (1997) suggested that organizations find a sensible entry point on any issue and tackle what they have been positioned to make a difference on and work out from there.

This initiates the "selection" or "focusing" process and involves making choices. At this point, the agreed-on method for making decisions should be tested and (if needed) adjusted. Some groups have had success with a consensus method. Others vote, with each person choosing his or her top three or four choices for further planning and with the top total vote getters being where time is concentrated. (A more in-depth choice process is detailed later in this chapter.)

Step 5. Developing Goals and Strategies

Developing goals and strategies related to the priorities focuses on tying proposed actions to outcomes.

Goals specify how an organization's mission will be carried out. Goals are the intended long-term results (a) of an organization's community development efforts and (b) of the strengthening of the organization. Goals are broad statements that are limited in number. They can be used as tools to assess the success of an organization in fulfilling its mission.

An organization's community development goals and organization-strengthening goals are developed through data collection and analysis as well as issue and opportunity identification and prioritization, as described previously. For community development efforts (e.g., programs, projects, initiatives, campaigns), some examples include creating new housing at a scale and character to appeal to a diverse population, broadening the mix of community businesses to serve both local and regional markets, ensuring adequate and fair community access to mortgage loans and other financial services, and enhancing the image of the community business district. For building the organization, some examples include building an active and diverse membership and volunteer base, maintaining strategic links in the community and beyond, having in operation employee-supportive personnel policies and procedures, creating opportunities for youth to become involved in planning and implementing community projects, developing a more diversified resource base, enhancing volunteer opportunities for senior residents, and strengthening board, staff, and volunteer relationships.

Strategies identify opportunities and a plan for taking advantage of them to meet the goals. Strategies answer the question of *how* an organization intends to accomplish its long-term goals. For example, if the goal is to increase the amount of money circulating (and recirculating) in the community, then one strategy might be to create quality, living-wage new jobs for the unemployed. On the organizational side, if a goal is to stabilize and diversify the organization's funding base, then one strategy could be to develop mission-related, income-producing activities. Because circumstances and conditions change, strategies should be reviewed and revised periodically.

Selecting an Organizational Role in Community Controlled Development

There is a wide range of roles a community group can take in community development and within specific initiatives or projects. The roles are distinct but not mutually exclusive. Roles can change from initiative to initiative and even during initiatives. Also, roles may change or a group may assume multiple roles with any given effort. The role(s) a group assumes depends on several factors, including group capacity (in-house skills vs. skills needed to successfully fulfill a particular role); the mission, goals, and priorities of the group; the opportunity or issue; community needs; access to and availability of resources and technical assistance; and the group's willingness and ability to assume risk. When choosing a role, a group needs to consider the possible organizational impact (e.g., funds, time involved, other pursuits). The following are categories of roles in community development and examples of activities within each role (adapted from Pratt Institute Center for Community and Environmental Development, 2000).

Advocate/Catalyst/Monitor: This organizing role involves creating, securing, and maintaining resources and a supportive climate for community development. It involves advocacy and pressure to get others to act and may involve taking a position or stand. It may involve action to forestall race and class segregation and to reduce tensions. It can also mean being a "watchdog" on government and private sector activities that affect a community. Role examples include the following:

- Monitor bank lending for community reinvestment
- Hosting a community meeting to review a developer's proposal
- Holding a public hearing to gather resident testimony or presenting testimony at local government budget hearings

- Serving as a vehicle for community input and participation in housing policy development
- Conducting a petition campaign for adequate city services
- Promoting the community as an area for investment
- Organizing a community merchants organization
- Publishing opinion pieces in newspapers and a community newsletter
- Holding a festival to celebrate racial/ethnic diversity
- Drawing attention to issues such as slum landlords and street violence
- Participating in or organizing a community planning process

Facilitator/Broker/Supporter: This matchmaker role involves identifying and coordinating community needs, opportunities, and resources and bringing them to the attention of providers and users. Coalitions and clearinghouses often assume this role. Role examples include the following:

- Identifying youth interests and needs and linking them to a local service provider
- Developing a community resource directory
- Linking job sources to potential hires
- Marketing housing and business loan programs to community residents
- Identifying potential homeowners for a new housing development
- Linking community businesses to a local small business development center
- Identifying and screening tenants for a local commercial space
- Issuing requests for proposals for development opportunities in the community
- Researching local real estate practices to ensure equal opportunity, fairness, and inclusion

Developer/Builder/Financier: This role finds a community group as a project initiator and/or planner. It is a production role requiring a group to be entrepreneurial. This role requires specialized technical skills and often has the greatest risks. It is, however, not necessarily the most difficult when compared with mounting an organizing campaign or building community consensus during a planning process. Many groups take on partners (inside and outside the community) so as to successfully execute this role. Role examples include the following:

- Developing rental or ownership housing units
- Buying, rehabilitating, and then selling commercial property
- Assembling a site and putting together a development financial package
- Raising funds for a loan fund for local businesses
- Loaning funds to a developer for a community project
- Creating a community development credit union
- Designing a job training and placement program that ensures diverse gender, racial, and ethnic participation

Owner/Operator/Manager: This "do it your-self" role is closely linked to the developer/builder/financier role. Groups often act solely or in a partnership or joint venture. Role examples include the following:

- Operating and managing a housing loan fund
- Creating and carrying out a job training project
- Owning a commercial building and recruiting tenants
- Developing and operating a child care center
- Operating a youth micro-enterprise program
- Owning and operating a community-based landscaping business
- Developing and managing rental property

Step 6. Developing Implementation Plans

Long-Term and Short-Term Plans and Objectives

Each goal (and accompanying strategy) that is developed will have a series of related objectives. Objectives are short-term, achievable components of the strategy or strategies that go into an action or work plan to explain the steps an organization will take to achieve its goals. They are specific, measurable, and time related. Objectives are typically developed during an organization's annual planning process. (With both long-range and strategic

planning, implementation plans are developed annually.) Examples of goals, strategies, and related objectives include the following:

Goal: Community youth will have long-term economic self-sufficiency.

Strategy: Provide career ladder employment opportunities for community youth.

Objective 1: By June 30, 30 low-income community youth will be trained and placed in part-time summer manufacturing jobs that pay at least a beginner living wage.

Objective 2: Throughout the coming school year, 20% of placed youth will be retained in their positions.

Goal: All residents from the community will have quality affordable housing.

Strategy 1: Provide rehabilitation loans and new housing construction.

Objective 1: Through selective targeted demolition, the number of substandard housing units will be decreased by 10% over the next program year.

Objective 2: By the end of the first program year, financial assistance will be provided for housing rehabilitation to 30 families.

Objective 3: By the end of the second program year, six units of low-income housing and four units of market-rate housing will be constructed and pre-sold.

Objective 4: Housing occupancy will reflect the diversity of the region.

Projects, Programs, and Activities

Building from the goals, strategies, and objectives, long-term and short-term action plans are developed that lay out activities and tasks; fix responsibilities; identify resource needs; identify opportunities for cooperation, collaboration, and partnership; and establish a timetable for implementation, monitoring, and evaluation. (See Appendix 8.A for a sample action plan format.) Action plan activities and tasks are always tested against the following key questions. Will this help the organization to move toward its vision? Is this in keeping with the mission?

To aid in choosing what to do, many organizations develop decision-making criteria that specify what aspects of the goals and strategies should be met through projects, programs, and activities and that act as guidelines by which organizations choose what specifically they will do (e.g., number of jobs to be created, degree of racial mixing achieved in hiring, development of a key site). This is discussed more fully later in this chapter.

Projects, programs, and activities are the day-to-day business of an organization—things that are done to move toward the vision, in line with the mission, derived from goals and strategies, and selected using decision-making criteria. They can include everything from operating a multi-generational family center, to reporting on community lending practices, to planting a community garden, to educating state-level officials on toxic waste dumping.

If an organization already has things under way, then during planning its members need to determine the relevance of the existing work program (e.g., projects, initiatives, campaigns, activities). Some activities under way might no longer address the newly revised mission, goals, or objectives and will not fit the plan. There may be a need to phase out certain activities or get other organizations to take the lead or take them over. It is important to be serious and tough here. Weeding out can help an organization to get much more accomplished in the future.

The accompanying sidebar presents an excerpt from the AAUD's 1999–2002 strategic plan. In this plan, the AAUD (1999) lists organizational and program goals, outcomes sought, actions, responsibilities, and a time frame related to each goal. Annual implementation plans were *not* formally developed to support this strategic plan.

ALIQUIPPA ALLIANCE FOR UNITY AND DEVELOPMENT STRATEGIC PLAN, 1999–2002 (EXCERPT)

Mission

The Aliquippa Alliance for Unity and Development Inc. (AAUD), a nonprofit corporation, exists to improve the quality of life for citizens and businesses of Aliquippa by empowering the citizens and businesses to create and manage economic and social change.

Organization (Administrative) Building Goal #4: Increase community involvement and volunteerism in the programs of the AAUD and the community at large.

Outcomes

1. Increased community morale, understanding, and desire for revitalization

2. More and better programs that benefit the community

3. Broader base of support for all revitalization projects

4. Increased resources to be sought to improve the community

Actions

1. Hold community events, such as the arts festival and breakfast with Santa, that build involvement.

2. Organize community-wide celebrations to honor our accomplishments.

3. Regularly promote the positive happenings in Aliquippa.

4. Develop an awards/recognition system for board, staff, and community.

Responsibility: AAUD executive director, executive committee, board of directors, staff

Time Frame: Continuous

Arts Programming Goal #3: Establish a national model for economic revitalization through the arts.

Outcomes

1. Increased economic flow through the region via tourism opportunity and influx of outside dollars.

2. Aliquippa's activity in the revitalization through the arts, including the Arts/Community Center, receives national coverage and recognition.

3. Support and participation in conferences/symposiums based on economic revitalization.

4. Aliquippa community openly discusses and responds to artistic intervention.

5. Aliquippa youth see the opportunity for culture in their lives.

Actions

1. Establish a system and staff dedicated to the increased viability of the art link in Aliquippa.

2. Initiate programs that are consistent with research of established models.

3. Develop and administer programs which are innovative and attract national attention.

4. Continue the sponsorship of Aliquippa Embraces Art and related economic development activities.

Responsibility: artistic coordinator

Time Line: Continuous with a 5-year time line

Assessing the AAUD plan against our model plan elements detailed earlier reveals several stumbling blocks to implementation. Outcomes sought are equivalent to our element of objectives. Words such as *increased, more, better, support,* and the like are descriptive rather than specific and measurable. This means that it will be very difficult for the AAUD to know whether it has had success, and if so how much, when progress is reviewed. In addition, the actions refer to the broad goal and not to specific objectives. Tying activities/tasks to specific annual objectives would allow closer monitoring of progress and give the AAUD a more complete idea of what was and was not working. Responsibility is fixed to the artistic coordinator in the Arts Programming Goal 3, which permits the coordinator to develop a work plan and to monitor progress. However, by listing responsibilities to a wide range of people and groups in Organizational Building Goal 4, specific responsibility is loose and accountability is slippery. Although continuous as a time frame would seem to cover all bases, what should be emphasized, what is left for further work, and what is the sequential progression and linkage of steps are not apparent.

On the plus side, the AAUD delineated both organization-strengthening goals and community development goals. This demonstrates an understanding that any work program needs to be supported by an ever-stronger organization.

Step 7: Drafting, Refining, and Adopting the Plan

The following series of activities can be described as "wrapping up" the planning process.

A draft plan document is prepared for review. All goals, objectives, and activities must link and must not compete or cancel each other out. Resource needs must be reasonable, or the plan must include goals, objectives, and/or tasks to address shortfalls later. There must be full agreement if an outside person or organization is named as a responsible party.

The plan is refined. It is best if one or two (but no more) people make the needed changes to the draft plan. This second draft is then reviewed for agreement, and a final plan document is produced.

The draft plan process can be conducted at a face-to-face session or by written comment. However, an open meeting where people can discuss, debate, and reach agreement is always superior to written comments sent by mail, fax, or e-mail. Notification of the review meetings must be clear, timely, and communicated without missing any appropriate stakeholders.

It is important for the organization to formally adopt the plan. This may include holding a vote at a board or membership meeting. This reinforces people's agreement, ensures that organizational resources are committed, and seals ownership.

The next step is to disseminate copies of the plan to members, other organizations, the community, funders, and other stakeholders as appropriate. Many groups produce a plan summary document to distribute and keep the full plan as an internal document. Community briefings also strengthen community knowledge and ownership of the plan.

The final step is to assess the planning process. Determining what went well and what needs to be changed to improve the plan development process should take place while the experience is still fresh in people's minds. This is often the time when organizations consider seeking professional assistance to co-design and facilitate the following year's planning process.

Step 8: Monitoring and Evaluating Efforts

Checking Progress Toward Goals

Monitoring and evaluation are the processes and methods that an organization sets up periodically to check on progress toward community development and organization-building goals and objectives. These can be informal or formal and can represent time set aside to assess and make corrections or adjustments. Monitoring of progress should be done on a monthly basis at the committee or board of directors level. Evaluation often occurs on an annual basis (or at more frequent intervals if an effort is new or if activities were based on many assumptions).

"Go/no go" points are part of the regular monitoring process. These are points in time when an organization assesses whether or not to proceed with particular activities in its plan or to put on hold what is under way until circumstances change. For example, assume that with current financing, a planned housing project is not feasible. Does the organization put the housing project on hold and wait for additional resources to become available sometime in the future, or does it proceed along with the project and actively push funders/financiers for needed resources? The answer will differ for each organization, depending on urgency, priorities, need to succeed, competing interests, and the like. From an organizational standpoint, go/no go points might be reached when pivotal questions are faced such as adding additional staff, dropping an old program that is obsolete, increasing membership dues, expanding the board, and moving the organization's office.

Evaluation should be seen as a genuine tool for learning and building understanding and support because the process allows an organization to measure impact or progress and determine what has been effective and ineffective. It is key to study, judge, understand, and learn. Many see evaluation as something to be thought about and "done" at some future date, yet designing a monitoring and evaluation process and procedures needs to be addressed at the same time a plan is developed.

Evaluation involves comparing results with outcomes sought, that is, progress toward goals. Outcomes sought should be evident in goals and objectives. Also as part of the plan development process, markers of progress need to be developed. Internal markers of progress determine how well the organization is doing what it is doing; external markers determine whether what the organization is doing is what it should be doing. Once markers are agreed on, the next step is to decide what data can be used to measure progress and success. This allows a group to gather information and document results along the way. It is crucial to gather information in a way that it can be used. Information should include hard data (e.g., number of housing units produced, number of jobs created) as well as descriptive data (e.g., well-told stories from consumers, interview results).

There are several key questions that need to be addressed in designing an evaluation process, including the following. What is the purpose of the evaluation? Who will be the audience(s)? What questions will guide the process? Who will conduct the evaluation? Who will interpret the results? Who will prepare the evaluation report? How and when will results and lessons learned be communicated? To whom will they be communicated?

Monitoring and evaluation can be complicated. It is also difficult, in many cases, to draw causal relationships between what an organization has done and the outcomes. For this reason, it is important to get guidance and ongoing technical assistance from people experienced in setting up a system and in conducting monitoring and evaluation processes.

Reassessing and Revising the Plan

With an annual plan, it is now time to begin the planning process once again. Every year, an organization with a developed long-range or strategic plan should set aside time to review the remaining years of the plan in light of the current situation of the organization and the community. A full annual plan for the year ahead should be developed, and the remainder of the plan should be updated and revised (if indicated). Changes should be communicated to appropriate stakeholders and allies.

CHOOSING A STRATEGIC NICHE

Choosing specifically what to do among competing ideas/interests and when to act to achieve needed outcomes and maximize resources is often the most important decision an organization faces in community renewal. We now offer some thoughts and guidance drawn from the Pratt Institute Center for Community and Environmental Development (2000).

Many opportunities and choices exist regarding what an organization can or should do. A group hears of an effort by another community organization, a piece of property becomes available, or new program funding is announced. It is tempting to seize one of those ideas and begin implementing it given the levels of community need and the expectation for results—to take an opportunistic approach. An opportunistic approach can be used to help an organization get started, but it is not advisable in the long run. A planned strategic approach based on immediate local conditions and circumstances is called for to enhance chances for success.

To be strategic, a decision will involve balancing knowledge of the community and the opportunities therein against the strengths of the organization and its members and the availability of resources. The choice of "what to do" is made following such an analysis taking into account the mission and goals of an organization. Effective decision making includes gathering and processing information (e.g., testing assumptions, analyzing data); reviewing, assessing, and evaluating possibilities; and selecting specifically what initiatives to undertake or which projects to pursue.

The strategic niche diagram (Figure 8.2) presents a framework of the elements that need to be considered in determining an organization's strategic niche. *Strategic niche* can be defined as the area of work chosen by an organization suited to its unique resources and its assessment of community needs and opportunities. Descriptions of the four elements to be considered (organizational interest and capacity, community conditions, market opportunity, and resources) follow.

Organizational Interest and Capacity. The mission, goals, interests of the people within the organization, role required or desired, and capacity within the organization as may be determined by an organizational assessment are key to discerning a strategic niche. The capacity includes quality of organizational

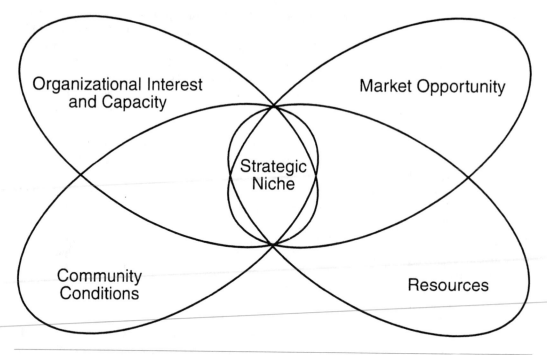

Figure 8.2   Elements for an Organization to Consider in Determining Its Strategic Niche.
© Patricia W. Murphy

leadership, degree of constituent involvement and accountability, ability to form and hold a collective vision, clarity of goals and objectives, organizational time availability, organizational technical expertise with similar endeavors, availability of internal resources, sufficient staff and volunteers, effective communication and reporting mechanisms, well-developed management and administrative capabilities, effective decision-making structure, organizational credibility, track record, and political clout.

Community Conditions. Priorities, needs, problems, issues, opportunities, strengths (both people and place), and assets make up community conditions. These are determined by a community assessment best carried out with constituent and community support, participation, and decision making. Examples of community conditions might include the state of the community economy, sizable new private or public construction of buildings or infrastructure, the community's current media image, the lack (or presence) of cooperation among local elected officials, the impact of proposed zoning changes, and the state of race relations.

Market Opportunity. When determining strategic niche, the "market" must be assessed. The demand for a project, product, or service and the prospect of success are taken into account. Need is not enough; actual demand must be determined. This includes taking into account projects and programs of other organizations so as to avoid duplication.

Resources. The availability and access to capital (both financing and funding), technical assistance, skills and expertise, and staffing as well as access to and willingness of other actors (e.g., government officials, realtors, property owners, businesses, other community organizations) to participate, prospects for future funding, and prospects for future partnerships are considered in the resource portion of the strategic niche.

Making a Strategic Choice: Selecting Ideas and Allocating Resources

Whether ideas come out of a proactive mode (e.g., community assessment, brainstorming session) or whether an organization finds itself reacting to opportunities that literally drop into its lap, it is a good idea to have many ideas percolating at once.

Sometimes ideas will not be readily visible or accepted as real possibilities, and a lot of faith and legwork may have to go into them before others can recognize and buy into their possibilities. It often takes a long time for an idea to come to fruition—to take hold and blossom. And at any stage during the project or program development process, any number of things can go wrong or be delayed such as the loss of a major employer with whom an organization has a job training contract, a 3-month delay in getting a zoning change needed for a real estate project, and an unsuccessful application for money for a community revolving loan fund. Therefore, it is important to have multiple efforts and multiple possibilities. Some will be in the beginning stages; others will be in full swing. Some may be more modest but more visible (e.g., turning a vacant lot into a community parklet), while efforts that will have more impact take longer to plan and execute (e.g., starting a community development credit union, mounting a lawsuit for the state and school board's failure to provide adequate education for community children).

This, however, requires some kind of process for deciding how to allocate resources in the pursuit of possible projects, programs, and/or activities. The opportunistic approach might work for a while, but a strategic approach is recommended. To make a strategic choice, however, the ideas need to be screened so as to get to the few that suggest and deserve further exploration and testing. The few that make the most sense are those in which an organization will put the most time, effort, and resources for assessing and testing.

Making a strategic choice is a repetitive process of assessing an organization and its environment, identifying needs and opportunities, and generating ideas and options for addressing them. This is done to determine whether an opportunity is "real" or "feasible"— whether there is need and demand, whether it is doable under the conditions that prevail, whether the capacity and resources exist and are accessible, and whether it is right for the organization given its goals and interests.

To decide what to look into further and to whittle down the number of ideas, opportunities, and options, criteria are needed to assist in decision making. Goals and priorities determine these.

An organizational assessment (both strengths and weaknesses) will suggest capacity, readiness, and a possible role in an activity or project. The opportunity assessment criteria (community conditions, market opportunity, resources available, and organizational interest/capacity) are used to decide when to move ahead or when to pass. Just because an opportunity presents itself does not mean that it has to be pursued now or ever. From time to time, an organization will need to reassess, reanalyze, and retest assumptions and facts. Also, factors and the opportunity environment may change. What looks like a good opportunity today might not be a good opportunity tomorrow (e.g., property could be pulled off the market, development/rehabilitation funds might not be available). Conversely, what does not appear to work today may reemerge as a real opportunity as the environment changes (e.g., new actors become engaged, the organization gains new skills, more resources become available). For these reasons, it is important to build in go/no go decision points and to schedule stops at each of these points for deliberation and decision.

An organization needs to have a variety of activity options from those in the development stage to those nearing completion. If an organization puts "all of its eggs in one basket," then when a problem occurs or an effort stalls, there is a tendency to try to push ahead; often, there is frustration and perhaps loss of credibility. By working on several things at once, bumps in the road will not completely halt the organization for lack of alternatives.

Decision Criteria/Assessment Factors

The part that an organization expects community development programs and projects to play in its strategy will help to define its venture selection criteria. These criteria are especially important in helping an organization to narrow down its first wide list of project or program possibilities to those most in keeping with its mission.

The criteria should be explicitly linked to an organization's community development goals.

If a primary goal is to increase employment opportunities or increase jobs for low-income community members, then one criterion should be that the project creates job opportunities for community residents. A very good idea that some organizations have adopted is to set priorities on each criterion. Then, if an organization cannot find a project that fits all of them, it will be able to select and implement first the venture that promises to meet the organization's most important goal. These criteria will also be one measure against which an organization can gauge project performance.

While setting out clear goals and criteria, an organization should also be careful not to overload ventures by expecting them to achieve too many goals. Setting too many goals for a project or program can be one of the biggest obstacles to making it work. This is one reason why it is important for an organization to develop an overall community development strategy so that the project or program will be expected to achieve only the goals most appropriate to it, not all of the organization's community development goals. For example, too many goals related to one project might look like the following. An organization decides to assist in the development of a locally owned business, thereby meeting a business development goal. It might also want the particular business to guarantee good-paying jobs for long-term unemployed local residents and offer youth needed after-school jobs as part of a workforce development goal. A blight removal goal would lead the group to want the business to be housed in a now-vacant building in need of major repair to boost the image of a key block. In addition, the group might want the business to become a major depositor in the community credit union to help boost the credit union's asset base. Some of the goals might be in conflict such as expecting employment of long-term unskilled unemployed when skilled workers are needed by the particular business. Also, the business might do better in a different location or in a new building. Being a major depositor in the credit union might prevent the business from developing a relationship with a non-community-based financial institution that in the future could provide it with much-needed capital for expansion.

An organization's community development strategy/long-term approach is also crucial to evaluating whether or not an opportunity meets certain criteria. Sometimes, a project or program will not fit into a 1-year time line or even into a 2- or 3-year time line. For example, although a project might not be able to create many jobs during the first few years it is in operation, it might have significant job creation potential over a 4- or 5-year period. If an organization expects too much from a project or program in the short run, then it might not only fail to achieve its short-term goals but also might lose its long-term potential.

Decision criteria can help an organization to select projects and programs by identifying those that fit in most closely with a variety of community development goals and overall mission and strategy. The criteria should spell out business and social expectations so that these can be balanced with each other. An organization may have established "large profit potential" as an objective for launching a new retail business. As a single criterion, that might lead the organization to choose a liquor store. However, social goals, such as the impact of the venture having a positive effect on the image of the community and the organization, might eliminate this venture possibility.

Another example of balancing social and business criteria is demonstrated by looking at how an organization would choose to develop a parcel of vacant land. Even if it narrowed down the use of the land to housing, the organization would still need to choose among a variety of options: single family, multifamily, senior highrise, townhouse, rental versus homeownership, and the like. Spelling out the primary target population, what kind of jobs and how many jobs the project should provide, and what level of risk the organization should assume could give the organization a sound and consistent means of making this choice. Developing and using such decision making criteria can help an organization to minimize conflicts, build consensus, make more fruitful strategic choices, and maximize impact.

The following guidelines for considering a project, program, or activity from organizational, community, and business/economic perspectives have been adapted from those created by Linda Gardner of the National Economic Development and Law Center (Gardner, 1983, pp. 101–102). Each organization should develop its own criteria, based on these guidelines. These guidelines have a primarily "economic" focus. Similar criteria could also be developed with a "political" and/or "social" focus.

Guidelines for Considering a Project, Program, or Activity From an Organizational Perspective

Does the proposed opportunity:

- Have a great likelihood for success?
- Provide for maximum organizational involvement (and/or control) in decision making?
- Develop organizational and staff capacity to undertake an enhanced role and increasing community economic development responsibility?
- Match or fit the organization's mission, strategy, and goals?
- Provide enhanced training and experience for staff and board members?
- Provide for significant or increased participation of the community in the organization?
- Address a key site, critical issue, and/or major community need?
- Provide for positive public relations for the organization?
- Require more time than is available? Will it require diversion of time, money, and energy from other pursuits?
- Maximize financial benefits to the organization from rents, royalties, fees, interest, securities, shared profits, and/or assets?
- Maximize the ratio of organizational investment to financial return?
- Have a manageable level of risk?

Guidelines for Considering a Project, Program, or Activity From a Community Perspective

Does the proposed opportunity:

- Have community support? Is it needed and wanted?
- Address the unique needs and circumstances and also build on the strengths of the community and its members?
- Generate community pride and community spirit?

- Help or harm the community's image?
- Provide the opportunity to increase community cohesiveness and cooperation?
- Provide for a significant or increased level of community participation and involvement? Of community control? Of community decision making?
- Develop the leadership assets of community residents?
- Increase community political strength?
- Provide community education opportunities?
- Provide community residents with more locally produced goods and services?
- Provide existing community businesses with expanded or new opportunities?
- Strengthen community members' employment and work skills?
- Expand the number of, and access by community residents to, quality living-wage jobs?
- Present a positive image to outside business, financial and political interests, and institutions so that outside participation and investment in community revitalization is encouraged?
- Create significant opportunities for community members to assume key decision making, management, and/or directorship responsibilities?
- Increase community ownership of resources to provide increased control over their use of any income derived?
- Preserve or enhance the community's natural resources or create environmental pollution, causing problems with noise, air, odor, and health quality?

Guidelines for Considering a Project, Program, or Activity From a Business/Economic Perspective

Does the proposed opportunity:

- Have a demonstrated market?
- Have a growing or expanding community or external market?
- Capture a sufficient share of the market to ensure success?
- Create undue risk in case of failure (e.g., large debt, unused or unusable buildings and equipment, unemployment)?
- Have special labor, licensing, or environmental requirements?

- Have the potential to break even or generate a profit within a reasonable period of time?
- Require substantial future reinvestment to maintain or expand its stability and profitability?
- Present the opportunity for venture self-sufficiency?
- Present the opportunity for community ownership?

Summary

Organizational planning is not a "one-shot deal" but rather a continual process of identifying and assessing what needs to be done, selecting where to focus based on an agreed-on mission, developing and implementing activities, assessing progress, and evaluating results. Organizational plans should serve as a guide to where an organization's efforts and resources will be targeted. Plans (and planners) should remain flexible—open to opportunities and aware that setbacks can occur. Periodic monitoring and plan revision greatly supports being flexible.

Chapter 9 focuses on creating a comprehensive community plan. We define community planning, review why and when to develop a community plan, and lay out a planning model. Important to the process, as with organizational planning, are widespread participation, flexibility, and a results orientation.

Continuing Questions

1. What responsibility does an organization have in facilitating leadership development in a planning process? Should training be provided for willing but inexperienced participants?

2. How much internal and external input and feedback are enough in making an organizational plan?

3. How much of the planning and implementing should residents and their community group do, and how much should "outside experts" do?

4. Are public hearings useful in organizational planning (either formal or informal)? Under what conditions?

5. What practical role can focus groups play in helping an organization to shape or assess its agenda?

6. What kinds of noneconomic rewards can be provided for dedicated volunteers who make extraordinary contributions to plan development?

Appendix 8.A
A Sample Action Plan Format (for use with Step 6 of the framework for organizational planning)

Building from goals, strategies, and objectives, action plans specify what will be done, by whom, by when, and with what resources. They serve as annual work plans for board members, staff, volunteers, and members.

Goal development: From critical issues, areas of concern, areas for attention, opportunities, and new areas to explore, develop both short-term and long-term broad goal statements. Prioritize the goals.

Objectives: For each goal, determine specific, measurable, time-limited objectives.

For each objective:

Activities and tasks: List out activities and tasks for the short-term. Think practical and doable.

By whom: Assign responsibility. Who is responsible for carrying out the activity or task? Who will be the primary point person or group? Think internal (within the group) and external (outside the group).

By when: Establish a time line. Fix a date for when each activity/task should be carried out or completed. Use the dates as a guide for monitoring.

Coordinated with: Determine whom you need to coordinate with, work with, check with, and/or report to within and outside the group. (This can be a person, a committee, an organization, etc.)

Resources needed: Determine your resource needs—funding, in-kind services, people, places, things, materials, technical assistance, information, projects or programs already in place, and the like.

Assumptions/Information needed: What assumptions are you making? What has to happen before starting or completing any particular objective, activity, or task? What information do you need—data, knowledge, answers, and the like? Should information gathering also be a task?

Obstacles: What are the obstacles you face—roadblocks, pitfalls, and absolute must-haves to succeed?

Contingency plan: What is your contingency plan? What alternative courses of action can you take?

Reporting: To whom must or should you report (both internal and external)? When and how often? What format (either oral or written)? Who will report/prepare?

Monitoring and updating: What is your early warning system to alert you that something has changed? What are the benchmarks for success or failure? How will you keep your finger on the pulse? What process and methods will you use to check whether or not deadlines are met? How and where will you get feedback?

Evaluation: How do you define success? What indicators will be used to measure success? What data will you need to collect? When will you evaluate, and who will do the evaluating? What process will you use? How will you use the evaluation information (both internal and external)?

REFERENCES

Aliquippa Alliance for Unity and Development. (1999*). Strategic plan 1999–2002.* Aliquippa, PA: Author.

Barry, B. W. (1997). *Strategic planning workbook for nonprofit organizations* (rev. ed.). St. Paul, MN: Amherst H. Wilder Foundation.

Gardner, L. (1983). *Community economic development strategies: Creating successful business Volume 1.* San Francisco: National Economic Development and Law Center.

Green, F. L. (1994, February 1). Strategic planning: A blueprint for success. *CAN Alert,* pp. 1–3, 9. (Santa Cruz: California Association of Nonprofits)

Kearns, K. P. (2000). *Private sector strategies for social sector success: The guide to strategy and planning for public and nonprofit organizations.* San Francisco: Jossey-Bass.

Pratt Institute Center for Community and Environmental Development. (2000). *Nuts and bolts of community development training program* (rev. ed. developed by R. Bryant, P. Murphy, & W. White). Brooklyn, NY: Author.

Walsh, J. (1997, January). *Stories of renewal: Community building and the future of urban America* [report]. New York: Rockefeller Foundation.

9

Unity in Creating a Comprehensive Community Plan

Strong effective plans for community revitalization generally arise from an array of hopes and ideas, articulated by a broad range of community interests in an open and structured process. Participating interests can span nonprofit/community sector organizations, encompassing block clubs, social service agencies, neighborhood watch groups, informal support groups, community development corporations (CDCs), neighborhood cleanup groups, civic associations, and faith-based initiatives, as well as reach out to public sector organizations, including libraries, schools and colleges, municipal and county governments, and private sector groups such as for-profit businesses, chambers of commerce, real estate developers, banks, and institutional employers (e.g., hospitals). A plan thoughtfully produced from such a mélange of interacting participants becomes an authentic road map for community change.

Some fundamental differences exist between organizational planning and community planning. As we saw in Chapter 8, the focus of an organizational plan is "internal," or on the "micro level," in that it is a guide for one specific organization's roles and activities in renewal and in increasing its power and ability to implement plans. Although widespread input and feedback may be solicited, decision making usually remains within the one specific organization. For

example, a nonprofit civic association may enlist the help and ideas of a church, several businesses, a bank, and homeowners in drawing up their association plan, but the final decisions on what to do, and on how and when to do it, rests with the initiating organization, the civic association. (Often, however, the development of the individual organization plan takes place within a community planning process; several of the participating groups may be making their own individual organizational plans at the same time as they are participating in the community planning process.)

In contrast, the focus of a community plan is "external," or at the "macro level," in that it is about developing a road map among many groups and institutions in a community where organizations plan and implement together. The community plan serves as an umbrella under which numerous interests (residents, organizations, and groups) create and coordinate complementary efforts to achieve a collective community vision. It often resembles a coalition model where the decision making is collective. Coordination and monitoring often reside with a representative community planning committee or forum. Boston's Dudley Street is an example of this type of planning effort.

The Dudley Street Neighborhood Initiative (DSNI) community planning process involved a

178

broad spectrum of neighborhood-based and neighborhood-serving interests. Community planning forums were held, with residents and organizations developing a collective vision, analyzing information and community data, and developing broad short- and long-range goals and related projects and activities for a targeted area. Implementation of the planned activities was spread among many organizations depending on their missions, existing plans, and resources. For many years, the DSNI itself did not implement any projects or programs; initiative partners carried out the plan. In contrast, the Aliquippa Alliance for Unity and Development has not produced a community plan by our definition. The Alliance produced organizational plans that cover many social, political, and economic aspects of the community, but it has produced these plans internally with minimum input.

DEVELOPING A RESIDENT-DRIVEN COMMUNITY PLAN

What Is Community Planning?

Community planning is both a process and a product. It is a process of taking stock, building consensus, and developing a future-oriented community vision. Ideally, the products of this process will be realistic and implementable plans and will involve a broad range of "committed" community actors—residents, organizations, agencies, institutions, businesses, governments, funders, investors, and others with a legitimate interest. In a best-case scenario, a community planning process is initiated by one or more local community organizations or a cadre of residents determined to produce a feasible agenda for revitalization. Such planning offers an opportunity for people to better understand their community's distresses and opportunities and become united in a renewal effort. Although the process can stretch over a long period of time, it is well to keep in mind that plan making is but one part of an overall community-organizing and revitalization effort and not the end product.

Many communities operate under "community plans" that are developed by local governments or planning departments with community (public) participation limited to input or comment—without fundamental community controlled analysis and decision making. Schorr (1997) noted, "Despite evidence that supports maximizing discretion at the point where the problem is the most immediate, it is the rare public official who dares to rely on discretion to improve the effectiveness of local programs" (p. 79). Furthermore, Schorr found that standardized solutions, developed outside the community, have been found to be "notoriously unreliable because they reduce the reliance on local knowledge and skill and limit the flexibility of people at the front lines to solve the problems they encounter" (p. 79).

A community developed plan is essentially a set of data-based recommendations embodying the ideas of a widespread array of interests about how to improve a residential place—translating strategic thinking into tangible, fundable, measurable goals, objectives, and activities and providing a shared vision for the future (Mourad, 1996, p. 1). The plan identifies mechanisms for implementation, assigns roles and responsibilities, establishes time lines, identifies resource needs, and sets out success measures. A competent plan is more than a wish list. Its recommendations are based on systematic analysis of data collected in and about the community and represent a consensus of the participants in the process as to what is feasible within the time frame established.

A community plan can be *targeted,* focusing on a few agreed-on issues or a specific geographic area, or *comprehensive,* focusing on many or all aspects of the quality of life in the whole community. The scope of the plan may vary according to need or urgency as well as fiscal and time constraints. In any case, the plan in time should reflect broad community consensus on the specific priorities and outcomes sought.

The plan should be viewed as an evolving document that constantly needs to respond to changing social, political, and economic conditions. Successful implementation requires ongoing assessment, periodic corrections, and attention to maintaining a consensus of community participants.

Why Develop a Community Plan?

A plan can help a community and all of its parts move from passivity and decline to vision and purpose. This happened in Dudley Street, as the neighborhood became proactive, with its people taking control, moving from "Why don't they?" and Why did they?" to "Here's what we're going to do" and "Here's what we need others to do." In this way, planning draws out community momentum and gives each participating interest an appropriate role toward advancing implementation, efficiency, and unity.

An open process can expand resident participation, providing opportunity for locked-out people to have a stake. The dialogue, exploration, and debate generated can strengthen social fabric by building community connections and trust through stepped-up resident interaction. The act of planning also builds problem-solving and decision-making capabilities. An inclusive process can unify diverse sections of the community.

By engaging local organizations and institutions as well as other key interests, the process can create an infrastructure to sustain efforts, build an institution(s) where none exists, and strengthen existing relationships and linkages to maximize resources and impact. An example of a new institution would be the creation of a community newspaper where none exists to inform residents about each other and thereby tie people together. In many communities, organizations with compatible missions and goals exist, but there is little connection between them. An open planning process can help point to areas for collaboration and partnership, stimulating a more coordinated effort and enhancing outcomes for the whole community. Being open to all parties of interest, both within and beyond the community, gives force to implementation. Planning builds capacity and credibility. This process can help a community to gain visibility and stimulate action. A plan that taps substantial resources (social, political, and economic) can be used to attract outside investments and leverage new resources.

By fixing responsibility, individual, organizational, and sector (public, private, and community) accountability can be enhanced. Knowing who is to do what by when, with an agreed-on leadership monitoring progress, ensures and expedites implementation.

Lastly, developing and implementing a community plan produces noticeable and sometimes dramatic changes. The bright new and remodeled housing and parklets that continue to rise throughout the Dudley Street community, helping to create a feeling of renewal and hope, are an example of this.

When to Develop a Community Plan

Sennett (1994), in an article titled "At the Drawing Board," identified five signs that indicate the need to develop a community plan:

1. When a portion of a community is besieged by outside development forces or a market condition of gentrification, a self-made plan is one way in which to establish the resident's claim on the future.

2. When a community is cut off from surrounding communities and outside support systems, planning can mobilize and energize agents for revitalization within the community and can raise the area's profile enough to garner significant outside assistance.

3. When community organizations in the area cannot agree on a revitalization agenda, a consensus-building process can produce common goals and coordination of efforts.

4. When participation in community organizations is dwindling, planning can be part of an overall organizing effort and can engage or reengage community interests with attractive ideas that will offer incentives and opportunities to many new participants.

5. In a case where top-down outside planning has marginalized community residents, ignoring their needs and viewpoints, community-initiated intervention through planning can block a top-down move, keeping control with those who will have to live with the results. (p. 11)

It is important to note that it is in a community's best interest to organize a planning process, even a modest one, early on before being pushed by major threat or crisis. An early process will enable the careful working out of how to be proactive rather than reactive.

COMMUNITY PLANNING
PROCESS MODEL

Developing a Process and Structure for Community Planning

Many models of planning exist. The one suggested here is resident initiated and controlled and taps into a community's own problem-solving abilities. In this model, organizing and planning go hand in hand. This model can be adapted to any community, with individual community circumstances guiding the specific planning path to be followed.

Key advantages of this model are that it has the following characteristics:

Inclusive: Community residents are widely recruited to become primary actors in the planning and decision-making processes, including helping to determine how the plan is conceptualized, designed, implemented, and evaluated. Providing education on issues and engaging other residents in data gathering and analysis make issues and information more easily understood and facilitate decision making as well as a sense of ownership of the plan. The broad array of key interests is engaged in the process from the start.

Flexible: Planning is tailored to specific local conditions, an essential requirement when renewing a small place community.

Comprehensive: The plan is community focused but takes into account relevant forces and opportunities outside the community.

Process and product focused: The process builds the capacity within the community to implement and sustain efforts, build institutions, enhance and expand participation, achieve consensus, and build collective power. The process also builds social fabric and trust by increasing neighborhood connections, communications, and interactions. The products are a series of actions and tactics to be carried out. They can be as varied as a movement to get banks to offer low-interest loans for property rehabilitation to the holding of a special event to celebrate the rising test scores of community children. The ultimate outcomes sought are measurable progress toward agreed-on goals.

Results oriented: The effort requires a "planning while doing" approach, not a "plan then do" one. Developing a community vision and long-term plan while simultaneously winning short-term visible results keeps people engaged in planning and implementing. The cleanup of a vacant public lot illegally strewn with garbage (short term) can provide the spark for a citywide cleanup of vacant lots and for the enforcement of city code violations on a systematic year-round schedule (long term).

Community specific: Decisions are based on a realistic understanding of a community's conditions, assets, and resources grounded in data gathering and analysis.

Resource maximizing: Building partnerships and linkages both internal and external to the community is critical for planning and for amassing and leveraging resources for implementation in this model.

Self-assessing: Developing a system of monitoring and evaluation to assess progress and outcomes and to plan revisions keeps the effort on track and keeps the participants focused and accountable. This model of planning is continuous, with plans responding to conditions as they emerge.

The diagram in Figure 9.1 shows our suggested community planning process.

The Community Planning Process

1. Form a coordinating committee to guide and manage plan development and implementation.

2. Decide on a planning process model and plan focus.

3. Reach out to maximize participation.

4. Develop a collective future vision.

5. Identify community assets, strengths, issues, concerns, and needs.

6. Gather and analyze data and information.

7. Develop broad goals and specific measures of success.

8. Develop alternative strategies and project ideas, test out, and select.

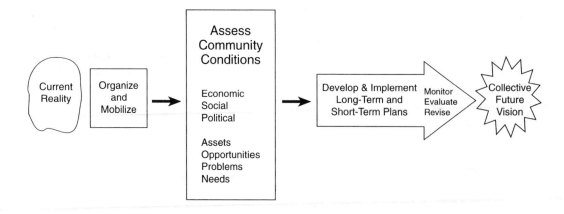

Figure 9.1   Community Planning Process.
© Patricia W. Murphy and James V. Cunningham 1999

9. Build a long-range plan and a short-term action plan.

10. Mobilize resources (both internal and external).

11. Implement the short-term action plan.

12. Monitor and evaluate process, products, and outcomes.

13. Update and revise the plan.

14. Celebrate successes.

Step 1: Form a Coordinating Committee to Guide and Manage Plan Development and Implementation

The catalyst for a community planning process may be a small cadre of interested residents, a single organization, or a group of organizations. No matter the initiator, essential to plan development and implementation is a long-lived structure that includes a diverse group broadly representative of all sectors of the community. This coordinating committee must be strong and stable enough to provide guidance and coordination during planning and keep in place a data-gathering and analysis system, a community communications process, and systems for monitoring and evaluation as the plan is being implemented.

Kinsley (1997) identified three groups of people needed to move plan development and implementation from beginning to end: a core group (planning process initiation), a coordinating committee (planning process oversight and facilitation), and a project team (planning process operations) (pp. 56–57).

The *core group*—3 to 10 people or organizations that initiate the planning effort—is often initially a loose-knit group whose members talk of improving their community, are clear that something must be done, and are committed to making it happen. In many cases, it is an individual or a single organization that quickly finds interested others and brings the group together. This core group may first meet in someone's living room, at a community group's office, or at a local restaurant. The group might include a wide range of people such as a block club president, a church pastor, a business owner, a community council member, the executive director of the local community development corporation, and a number of interested residents. The core group's decisions will focus on forming a coordinating committee. If leaders who represent only a fraction of the community initiate the planning effort, then they should not move ahead until a representative structure is in place and is accorded wide community support. Why? As the planning begins, those left out can move to halt the process through public statements and actions. This can delay progress and cut off needed resources. Often, public and private sector allies or potential allies will pull out support in the face of community controversy.

The *coordinating committee* (called planning forums or planning collaboratives in some communities) is composed of 10 to 15 people, each of whom is connected to more than one group or represents more than one sector of the community. The coordinating committee is more formal and is charged with building community trust in the planning effort, overseeing the process, monitoring progress, and selecting a project team.

The *project team* of 4 to 7 people is responsible for the day-to-day operation of the planning process—recruiting volunteers, working with the media, handling meeting logistics, and facilitating (or assisting in facilitating) meetings. Project team members may be staff or volunteers drawn from the coordinating committee members.

Step 2: Decide on a Planning Process Model and Plan Focus

With a diverse and recognized planning group in place, the effort moves forward. Sometimes, it is best to launch short cycles of planning followed by periods of implementation, with resident priorities setting the course, as we saw in Dudley Street. Quick victories and visible results, especially when widely publicized, can boost morale, unite participants, and gain credibility inside and outside the community.

Strengthening a community through an inclusive process means finding people and financial resources. Availability and access to technical assistance, information resources,

and funding will help to keep the planning productive. It can take time to build up to having all of these resources.

At the beginning, then, the coordinating committee *preliminarily* agrees on the scope of the plan—whether the plan should be targeted (focusing on a handful of pressing concerns) or be more comprehensive (focusing on many or all aspects of the quality of life in the community). In a community that is just embarking on organizing residents and building one or more community organizations, most early attention is on recruitment, leadership development, finding resources, and small concrete achievements such as Aliquippa's Community Days and town meetings early on in the Pennsylvania community. Visible activity and results are essential to win public acceptance. During this early phase, a community must be careful not to lock itself into long-term decisions and unrealistic commitments. Early direction also depends on past relationships of the groups and institutions involved and on the degree of trust among them.

The answer as to whether a short-term or long-term plan should be developed depends on the purpose of the plan, the level of people and informational resources available, and local community conditions at the time. Difficult and complex issues (e.g., job development after a major employer shuts down) call for long-term planning, while more simple objectives (e.g., getting a traffic light installed at a dangerous intersection) can be handled in the short term. A long-term view requires confidence in future flows of human and financial support. Such supportive community conditions make it safer to take risks for the future.

Several additional issues will need to be addressed as the process gets started. These include (a) how decisions will be made and (b) whether outside assistance will be required to help design and facilitate the planning process. The coordinating committee can discuss and prepare recommendations for decision making by all of the parties (e.g., groups, organizations, residents, other stakeholders) participating in the community planning process.

Decision-making considerations include the method or methods for deciding (e.g., majority vote, consensus) who makes decisions (e.g., organizational representatives, individual residents, interested people who work in the community, anyone who attends) and when decisions are to be made (e.g., on the spot, after formal review by participating organizations, following a community public hearing).

Many community planning efforts have benefited greatly from assistance in process design and facilitation. Dudley Street contracted with an out-of-state firm that provided expertise and technical assistance to the planning process. Other organizations have sought assistance from planning consultants, university planning or urban studies faculty members or interns, community planning and design centers, and/or municipal planning officials. Outside assistance can provide neutrality (when situations become contentious or to prevent one person or organization from dominating), knowledge of efforts beyond the specific community generating broader thinking, and connections to resources. Outside assistance must work for and with the community, however, or else a "top-down" plan will result.

Step 3: Reach Out
to Maximize Participation

A community planning process should be grounded in organizing and work for broad-based participation from all sectors, including residents (long term and new, homeowners and renters), human service agencies, community organizations, faith-based and religious institutions, business groups, civic clubs, youth groups, community-serving institutions, senior citizen groups/retirees, public safety officers, school personnel, realtors, and commercial property owners. Special outreach efforts are needed to ensure that all income levels and ethnic/racial backgrounds, as well as all geographic corners of the community, are represented. In most cases, one or more persons should be specifically assigned the outreach task. It is important to ensure that those who are directly affected by the issues are personally invited to be involved. All relevant community resources are to be identified and tapped, new relationships and partnerships are to be forged, and key issues and concerns are to be heard. Broad-based participation builds a constituency whose members can then argue for plan implementation

and resource allocation. With such support, the plan cannot be dismissed as the work and wishes of one narrow interest group. It then becomes a plan that is easier and safer for funders to support.

Planning process leaders need to be alert to identifying incentives for gaining initial and continued involvement beyond weak motivators such as "having a voice" and "seeing community progress." Incentives can range from participant photographs and name recognition in the newsletters of participating groups to discount coupons from local establishments, child care and full meals at planning sessions, door prizes awarded at meetings, and the chance to meet with "big name" celebrities. Buttons, T-shirts, and/or colorful posters with a catchy community slogan can also serve as incentives.

Early in the process, the coordinating committee needs to establish relationships beyond the community to better access essential information and help secure resource commitments prior to implementation. Such relationships might be established with planners, architects, community design centers, colleges and universities, foundations and governmental funders, financial institutions, investors, developers, and (when indicated) the news media. In addition, it is important to include in the planning process those who can directly influence issues or opportunities such as elected political office holders, concerned business leaders, and other decision makers.

An authentic inclusive process has a majority of residents among its body of founding decision makers. Residents gain ownership of planning efforts by polling, organizing, and having open meetings to decide on issues, priorities, goals, policy questions, implementation strategies, resource allocation, and outcomes as well as by contributing funds to finance the planning. A well-developed outreach strategy is needed to guarantee widespread participation. Outreach can include the use of flyers, announcements, newsletters, press releases, mail and phone surveys, focus groups, open community forums, workshops, town meetings, and other personal face-to-face tactics. But the heart of outreach is door knocking and striking up conversations at fast-food restaurant counters, bars, grocery stores, Little League games, firehouses, ethnic clubs, pizza parlors, and other gathering places.

Special intensive techniques are often necessary to reach groups of people long isolated from the daily ebb and flow of community interaction. This might involve a start-up blitz of daily face-to-face encounters for 2 or 3 weeks.

During the planning process, the joint planning group can build confidence in the effort by distributing a planning newsletter, giving progress reports, and providing open briefings where all questions can be addressed with frankness and respect (see accompanying sidebar). Some communities use an organization or community Web site to post information and solicit feedback. Intensive outreach needs to continue throughout the process. It is crucial to be open and sensitive to feedback.

Planning Makes a Difference: The Lyndale Neighborhood Planning Process

The Lyndale Neighborhood Association (LNA), founded during the early 1970s, is the primary "plan and act" vehicle for the racially diverse residents, numbering more than 7,700, in this Minneapolis neighborhood. Planning and doing helped to move the community from "the fear, crime, and suburban flight of the 1980s to confidence, safety, and revitalization" by the late 1990s (Gosiewski, 1999, p. 1). The LNA maintains that planning made a difference because, through its planning processes during the 1990s, the community created and renewed a unifying vision for Lyndale, identified issues on which people wanted to work, pinpointed the assets and talents of residents and stakeholders, leveraged resources from funders to implement the community's plans, created new structures in the community to put implementation on the fast track, and formed new partnerships. Population in Lyndale is also on the rise, with a growth of more than 400 residents between 1999 and 2001 (Lyndale Neighborhood, 2002).

Throughout the 1980s, a small group of dedicated volunteers served the LNA. In 1990, more than 400 survey forms were distributed to neighbors by two hired residents, with the help of LNA steering committee members, seeking to identify talents, interests, and willingness to get involved in the association. A neighborhood after-school mentoring project was started with the help of more than a dozen residents who expressed interest in mentoring youth on their returned surveys.

In 1991, the Exodus Community Development Company approached the Northwest Area Foundation to fund redevelopment of the hardest-hit block in Lyndale. Impressed by the plan, the foundation funded a 16-month planning process for the whole community.

Some 400 Lyndale stakeholders (residents, organizations, and institutions) created a unified vision and plan for the community after gathering data through surveys, focus groups, and the census and reaching consensus on objectives and strategies during a marathon series of 90 large and small community meetings. The meetings provided for plan feedback, which the LNA steering committee used to organize and guide plan implementation. The Lyndale plan was ratified at a November 1992 general membership meeting of the association. As the plan was ratified, LNA staff and volunteers formed neighborhood committees to coordinate efforts in youth and families—human development, safety and crime, housing, economic development, environment, and art-culture. The Northwest Area Foundation provided $282,000, and the City of Minneapolis Neighborhood Revitalization Program (NRP) provided $700,000, toward implementation. In 1993, 150 residents and LNA staff developed more detailed work plans for their volunteer efforts in crime prevention, youth and families, and housing/economic development. These three plans were merged and became Lyndale's First Step NRP plan. Implementation soon began. By then, the Housing and Economic Development Committee had evolved into the Lyndale Neighborhood Development Corporation (LNDC) to play a leading role in plan implementation.

In 1995, Lyndale neighbors produced a comprehensive NRP plan that envisioned spending $3,750,000 to improve Lyndale over 3 years. Past planning efforts had increased the vision and capacity of the committees and volunteers. From 1996 to 1998, residents developed specific plans to invest the NRP funds in their neighborhood. By 1999, Lyndale estimated that the $2,500,000 in NRP funds invested had leveraged the investment of more than $65,000,000 in revitalizing properties and $2,000,000 in revitalizing people.

In 1999, Lyndale embarked on a new round of planning, the Lyndale Planning Odyssey, developing Lyndale's vision for 2000–2003. Spearheaded by the LNA, numerous community partners joined in plan development, including neighborhood churches, the Lyndale school, Painter Park, the Blaisdell YMCA, the Harriet Tubman Women's Center, and Horn Towers Senior Housing. Throughout this 6-month process, the LNA, grounded in resident input and initiative, solicited planning input through community meetings, its Web site, and resident-hosted "home planning events." For these events, the LNA provided a detailed checklist of meeting invitation preparation, list of discussion topics, note takers, an experienced facilitator, and stipends for meeting refreshments. More than 400 residents participated in planning events.

To maximize resident participation, a series of community meetings were organized by regions, stakeholder groups, and issues. The LNA and local community institutions hosted the meetings. The stakeholder group meetings included Latino families, Somali elders, and youth, all of whom had powerful reactions to being heard and experiencing Lyndale as a community that would support their efforts (LNA, 2000). In all of the meetings, participants envisioned solutions to issues they were facing, how the neighborhood as a whole could enhance or coordinate those solutions, and what parts of the solutions individual residents were committed to implementing.

Three themes emerged in the planning process as neighborhood priorities: (a) economic development that focused on developing innovative ways for neighborhood investment to stay in the neighborhood, (b) affordable housing to respond to a market shift with home values rising 70% in a 1-year period and rents rising at a similar rate, and (c) engaging harder to reach community members in community-building efforts. Throughout the 1990s, the face of Lyndale had changed dramatically through continued immigration of Latinos, Somalians, and a smaller number of East Asians. The engagement of youth was seen as critical; the planning kickoff event was held at the Lyndale school with more than 200 residents, including 50 teenagers, in attendance. The neighborhood continues to commit itself to diversity and participation, seeing these as its greatest strengths.

In their comprehensive community planning process, Lyndale residents reaffirmed the community vision "to create a stronger sense of community pride, which encompasses and celebrates the diverse people mix and creativity of all. We seek to use these positive talents to develop a visibly safe, clean, stable and nurturing, and economically viable neighborhood that promotes feelings of eagerness to learn and grow" (LNA, 2002). The community mission and values statements embrace social fabric building as key to community development: "We believe building community is connecting people with one another. Neighbors that know each other and look out for each other are safer. A neighborhood where people know their neighbors, share experiences with their neighbors, and are connected to the community's resources will be more stable. A community that has a high level of trust, enthusiasm, and confidence encourages economic investment, growth, and jobs. We seek to achieve our goals in a manner that: fairly recognizes all people and institutions of the neighborhood, strengthens reciprocal relationships with one another and the larger community, and addresses problems at their roots in an attainable, sustainable, and empowering manner" (LNA, 2002).

The LNA embraces "planning while doing." During the 1999 process, approximately 90 resident-led projects were implemented (LNA, 2000). Progress through planning is evident. State grant funds for crime prevention through environmental design that were secured in 2000 have supported alley and block improvement projects, new neighborhood welcome signs, building and parking lot lighting, and a peace park; residents, businesses, and organizations partnered to stage a 3-day community festival in September 2002; a neighborhood task force has been meeting to provide input into the planning process for a $104 million housing and commercial development, Nicollet Lake Commons, at a key intersection; a project advisory committee participates in infrastructure design and construction review for a major ramp access project; cleanups, block parties, and paint-a-thons, in addition to a small business revolving loan program, spur business district revitalization; and the LNDC participates in a working group developing a community land trust for south Minneapolis.

In the spirit of access and openness, the LNA Web site (www.lyndale.org) provides a community calendar, a local business directory, organization information, project and program updates, contacts, resources and membership meeting minutes. Most important, the Web site details opportunities for all residents to get involved. The "Building a Better Neighborhood" section offers a range of ways for people to connect to each other and work for a better neighborhood—knowing their neighbors; knowing the parents of young people on their blocks; welcoming new people to their blocks; calling 911 whenever something wrong happens; being block club contact persons; supporting neighborhood businesses; cleaning up their yards, streets, and alleys; voting; telling others about the good aspects of the neighborhood; and turning their ideas into projects (LNA, 2002).

Step 4: Develop a Collective Future Vision

A vision statement answers the questions "What do we want our community to be?" and "When what we want to change does change, what will our community be like?" It incorporates participants' dreams and hopes for themselves, their families, and the community as a whole. It describes how the renewed community will look and feel, and it includes what participants want to preserve and create. Kinsley (1997) suggested that it is helpful to have people come together to form a vision by generating ideas around specific categories: "arts and culture, built environment, business and jobs, social fabric, education, skills and talents, the government, health, history and tradition, the natural environment, and recreation" (p. 113). This aids in stimulating thinking and ensures that a broad view will develop. By developing a collective future vision at the start of a planning process, those involved begin to understand the outcome sought and become enthusiastic about it. A stronger plan results if groups and

organizations that participate share their organizational vision—what they hope to achieve for their "community," their constituents, and consumers. By melding these diverse visions, participating groups can move beyond an inward focus to a broader community-wide vision and a sense of unity.

Graphically capturing the vision can provide a permanent (and portable) record. Communities have had planning participants create future vision collages, murals, community vision quilts, maps, and displays that are on view during and after the planning. Such graphic visuals serve as rallying points and motivators, and they can be used to spell out community hopes and dreams to potential resource and assistance providers.

Community and organization cohesion can be strengthened during a community planning process. By sharing their backgrounds as a prelude to setting priorities, participants begin to build personal relationships and a shared history from which they can shape a unified future vision. Mulling over zoning codes and population and housing data together builds common knowledge. Willingness to compromise can create trust. Celebrating accomplishments generates community spirit. When residents reveal their assets, opportunities for mutual help emerge. For example, in a discussion on the environment, long-time residents may reminisce about all of the trees that had to be cut down to make way for widening roads and sidewalks, new residents with young children may discuss the lack of park and playground facilities, while businesses may discuss a lack of parking. Perhaps by pooling resources, the group can suggest that a local organization buy two large side-by-side houses that are slated for demolition near the town center, tear them down, and create a metered parking lot with a green space on the side for benches, trees, flowers, and playground equipment and with the money from the meters being used to fund future community projects.

Some community organizations and institutions will join in a community planning process with their own organizational plan already in place. Participating in the process presents such organizations with additional options and resources and can also open up their internal planning processes to many new voices. For example, the chamber of commerce uses the diverse participants to assess chamber members' marketing strategies to better hear what customers want. The CDC begins to include public housing residents in its discussions of a new homeownership project. The men's homeless shelter invites close-by residents to join in planting a shelter vegetable garden, thereby creating neighbors rather than dissenters.

Participating organizations, through sharing their own plans and agendas, can find opportunities to coordinate, partner, or collaborate, thereby maximizing resources, increasing the effectiveness of their services and efforts, and avoiding duplication or working at cross-purposes. For example, a family center links its families to an existing child care service rather than creating its own, a community food bank enlists participating church youth groups as volunteers, or a nonprofit housing corporation connects with the local hardware store that donates "fix-it kits" (including a tote bag with a hammer, different-sized nails, a wrench, a yardstick, various screws and a screwdriver, and several paintbrushes) to the organization's next 10 new homeowners.

Step 5: Identify Community Assets, Strengths, Issues, Concerns, and Needs

A solid plan recognizes connections among community problems and issues, builds on strengths, and integrates strategies and activities to maximize outcomes. It examines program, service, and policy levels from a local to a national perspective, including the impacts of external institutions, public policies, and private sector market dynamics (Kubisch et al., 2002, p. 80). A solid plan moves beyond "local" to identify, analyze, and challenge the institutional, structural, and systemic forces that affect families and communities.

Although the outcomes sought are community specific, planning typically examines the following: the formal and informal community economy; asset and income generation; availability and access to capital and credit; workforce development and employment; business creation, development, and expansion; education and training; community/public safety; community parks and recreation areas; health and human services; housing and shelter; capital and infrastructure improvements (including transportation); natural resources, environment, and beautification; arts and culture; social fabric (including community cohesion and pride); and governance structures, political organization, and all power-oriented activity related to public matters.

Many communities have adopted an *asset-based approach* to planning—melding community planning, organizing, and development into a single process for revitalization. As described by Kretzmann and McKnight (1993), this approach identifies what is already present in the community, not what is problematic or absent. An asset-based approach implies an "internal" focus—concentrating on building on the existing capacity of residents, organizations, and institutions. This focus on existing assets in distressed communities does not imply that such communities no longer need additional resources; it suggests that the likelihood of attracting outside resources increases dramatically when local communities are mobilized and act to use internal resources showing visible improvements that tell funders and financiers that the community is a sound investment. This approach requires "mapping"—taking inventories and plotting assessments—of three levels of building blocks.

In conducting a community assets inventory, all communities will find that they have a variety of formal and informal resource systems (individual, institutional, and community) available to help residents and assist in community organizing and revitalization efforts.

Communities have found that the actual process of mapping community assets strengthens the links among participants and motivates participation, collaboration, and commitment to action. Following are Kretzmann and McKnight's (1993) community building blocks.

An Asset-Based Planning Approach

Level 1: Primary building blocks are assets and capabilities located inside the community and largely under community control. These include assets of all individuals (e.g., skills, talents, experiences) and businesses (including home-based ones). Organizational assets include citizen and business associations and spiritual, religious, social, and cultural organizations.

Level 2: Secondary building blocks are assets within the community but largely controlled by outsiders. These include public institutions and services (e.g., schools, libraries, police and fire departments, parks), private and nonprofit organizations (e.g., hospitals, social and human service agencies, colleges and universities), and physical resources (e.g., vacant land, housing, environmental resources, commercial and industrial buildings).

Level 3: Potential building blocks are resources originating outside the community and controlled by others. These include public capital improvement expenditures, public information, and transfer payments.

By examining primary, secondary, and potential building blocks, a community can identify its assets and strengths, issues, concerns, and needs and have a balanced perspective on its situation.

Step 6: Gather and Analyze Data and Information

A sound plan is based on hard data and the systematic analysis of information collected in and about a community, often produced by community residents and organizations. In addition to gathering data about the community, information about opportunities, events, and forces impinging from the outside is obtained. Categories can range from physical (land use), to social (sense of community), to economic (income flows) as well as from quantifiable (demographic) to highly narrative (history of the area). In his text *Planning Local Economic Development Theory and Practice,* Blakely (1994) pointed out that good information equals good decisions.

An assessment is also done of the external environment beyond the community, starting with the adjacent areas that most greatly affect the community. These might contain a cluster of other communities, and perhaps a downtown or county seat, having potential impact on the community being planned for. This external assessment is less detailed, focusing on major potential impacts and limited to the principal institutions, employers, forces, taxing bodies, issues, power groups, and plans of others likely to have a significant influence. Planning and development efforts of other communities that might compete with or complement the community's plan, such as a major new housing development and a special business loan program, should be considered. This is often called a close-in environmental scan.

A less detailed scan is conducted for ascending wider environments, including the region, state, nation, and globe, with only the most relevant issues, trends, and institutional forces being considered such as value shifts, changing political alliances, technological advances, collapsing economies, large-scale welfare experiments, and privatization. For example, a Wal-Mart is moving in, most households now have e-mail, the schools all are being transformed into district-wide magnet schools, or a riverfront redevelopment will make available riverfront sites for private housing but close off the community's informal boat launching sites and a couple of prized fishing spots.

A community planning process can develop the leadership talents of participants. Quality information gathering, discussion, deliberation, and decision making as well as the need to problem solve during the process provide a strong opportunity for residents to gain skills and use their capacities for community improvement. As the process proceeds, new people can come forward or be tapped to lead discussion groups, organize and facilitate planning sessions, present research data and facts, serve as communication links with churches and block clubs, and negotiate with resource providers in the public and private sectors.

Data to Collect

A thorough analysis of the economic, social, and political conditions (strengths and opportunities as well as weaknesses, problems, and issues) of the community and its residents is needed to build a descriptive neighborhood profile. In addition, historic information should be gathered and analyzed to interpret and predict trends. Much of the data needed may already have been collected. It is important to check local newsletters and newspapers and locally generated reports, assessments, and maps as well as the research files, libraries, and Web sites of government agencies and departments, planning commissions, public utilities, real estate offices, financial institutions, local businesses and industries, and colleges and universities, among others, for recent reports that may contain relevant information. Local libraries and health departments are often useful sources for census and vital statistics.

The following *categories of data/information* may be collected and analyzed. *What* is collected, *how* it is collected, and *how much* is collected depend on the specific community and issues affecting it as well as the resources available for planning. (See Appendix 9.A for a detailed listing of data to examine in each of the following categories.)

- Demographics
- Land use and zoning
- Economic activity
- Housing
- Business/Commercial

- Manufacturing/Industry
- Employment
- Environmental
- Public health
- Education
- Public safety
- Transportation and access
- Social and human services
- Arts and culture
- Social fabric and cohesion
- Government structure and political organization

Information should be collected systematically with the best available analytical techniques employed to avoid faulty findings. Besides Internet and library searches, a variety of ways in which to collect useful information exist. These include the following:

A "windshield" survey: Volunteers and/or staff drive or walk down every street and alleyway to record information about conditions. Surveyors might use a checklist or tailor-made form.

A door-to-door survey: Volunteers and/or staff go to all households, businesses, and organizations to conduct face-to-face interviews. For those who are not in or who cannot be interviewed at the time, follow-up visits should be scheduled or a questionnaire may be left and picked up at a later date.

A structured set of key interviews: Such interviews are held with knowledgeable people who are authentic representations of each and every population group in the community.

A mail-out survey: Volunteers and/or staff mail or deliver a simple clear questionnaire asking recipients to complete and mail back. Follow-up reminder phone calls may be needed.

Meetings: "Town hall" or community meetings can generate firsthand information. Such gatherings usually form the core of any community planning process. Heavy personal recruitment and the use of publicity techniques are usually required. Community gatherings are best held at well-known, accessible places—a community center, a local school, or a community organization's office. It is important that the place or places chosen be "neutral"—viewed by the majority of the community as a place where all will be welcome. At town hall or community meetings, information is gathered through questionnaires or recorded discussion groups. Public hearings of the type organized in Aliquippa, Pennsylvania, are another method; they are done with an open microphone and a tape recorder while allowing speakers to turn in written statements. Reports on meeting proceedings should be made widely available.

Base maps: Maps and charts that show community conditions are secured or produced. Typical base maps include land use and density (e.g., residential, business, industrial, public), zoning, traffic circulation, housing type and conditions, community facilities, urban design features, amenities, and any special topographical elements such as hillsides, railroad lines, streams, and hills.

Sometimes, there is need to gather additional data as planning proceeds to assist with difficult and complex decisions. The data-gathering and assessment process established during planning can become a permanent monitoring tool for a community organization, helping it to discover distress at an incipient stage.

Mourad (1996) suggested that the following questions be asked in analyzing data (both facts and opinions) collected:

- How do the community's conditions compare with those of other communities?
- Are conditions stable or changing?
- What conditions affect the largest number of people?
- Are conditions a serious problem or a minor inconvenience?
- Do a lot of people in the area recognize a common need?
- What facilities or services are inadequate to meet needs?
- Are there large groups with special needs?
- What conditions are dangerous to health and/or safety?
- What conditions have a negative effect on community attitudes or pride? (p. 2)

During plan development, a community should also identify any factors that might limit success currently or in the near future. These could include external market forces, capital availability, political climate, national and regional issues, special characteristics of the community, discrimination and biases (e.g., racism, gender bias), and community politics.

Step 7: Develop Broad Goals and Specific Measures of Success

The data analysis should give a picture of where a community has been, where it is currently, and where trends suggest it may be going. Issues and opportunities will be revealed. It is time to set priorities by voting on the most pressing issues or those opportunities that could bring maximum impact. It is also helpful to determine where "the energy is"—those issues and opportunities that capture the most interest and attention.

Once priorities are established, goals are developed. Goals are the intended results of community development efforts. There are usually short-term (1 year or less) and long-term (more than 1 year) goals. It is important that goals be reasonably attainable. Examples of (in most cases) impossible community goals include living-wage jobs for every resident within 1 year and the rehabilitation of every storefront on main street within 18 months.

At this point, it is also important to agree on measures of success, even though evaluation is a future activity. Measures will differ for each community. Many communities start by asking, "How will we know when we have succeeded?" Criteria for success (both quantitative and qualitative) may be developed that answer questions related to impact (What effect have we had? Has what we have done made a difference?), product (What has been done?), and process (How fairly and efficiently has it been done?). Many groups also work to identify best practices looking to successful efforts of others and set benchmarks against which progress is later measured.

A community may look for primary direct outputs—numbers, costs, distribution of benefits, and/or changes in economic indicators. Often, such information can be compared with results in a similar community; however, differences in community conditions may make one community incomparable with another. The community also looks for indirect outputs such as an increase in home maintenance, an increase in community or organizational capacity to make decisions, and an increase in community self-help. Ultimately, success means that momentum has built within the community and that people are able to build on the changes occurring and may even increase grassroots control.

As a field of practice, community development has not yet developed a widely accepted code of standards or criteria for evaluating performance and outcomes. However, in 1998, the Development Leadership Network, a national network of community development practitioners, mounted the "Success Measures Project," 2 years of structured grassroots dialogues across the United States leading to definitions of benefits and indicators to measure the success of community development programs and activities. Examples of housing indicators include monthly housing cost and affordability, wealth/equity creation, housing quality, and environmentally sustainable design and construction (Development Leadership Network, 1999).

In addition, many communities are developing sustainability indicators. Examples from the Urban Ecology Coalition in Minneapolis include indicators such as the percentage of residents who feel safe in their neighborhood, the number of residents who share skills or barter services with each other, the percentage of neighborhood children who attend schools in the neighborhood, the percentage of residents who regularly celebrate their ethnic or cultural heritage, and the percentage of residents who earn a living wage (Crossroads Resource Center, 1999). (More on criteria for success and evaluation can be found in Step 12.)

Step 8: Develop Alternative Strategies and Project Ideas, Test Out, and Select

A variety of means to achieve goals are available. As pointed out in Chapter 8, strategies answer the question of *how* a community intends to accomplish its long-term goals. For example, will it seek to stop money from leaking out of the community by establishing more local shops or by creating quality new jobs for the underemployed or unemployed? Or, will it try both strategies or perhaps an entirely

different strategy? Because each community's circumstances are different, what worked elsewhere might need to be reshaped or not pursued.

Selecting and prioritizing is best accomplished using agreed-on criteria for decision making. It is important to ask, "If we do the following, then what can we expect to be the direct and indirect impact or outcomes?" Rubin and Rubin (1992) suggested the following three questions that can help community planning groups to choose from among alternative solutions. Is the solution worth the effort? Do alternative solutions produce more benefits at less cost? Who gets the benefits, and who pays the costs? Kinsley (1997) suggested asking the following questions. What are the benefits? What are the problems? Why do it? What problem will it address, or what need would it fulfill? What barriers to success could it address? Decision-making criteria suggested in Chapter 8 could also be used in selecting and prioritizing alternative strategies and project ideas. Testing out and selecting means that some ideas will move forward and some will not; the answer can be "not this" or "not now."

Step 9: Build a Long-Range Plan and a Short-Term Action Plan

As with the organizational plan detailed in Chapter 8, a long-range community plan looks a few years into the future and lays out a general direction, broad goals, and a sequence of steps. A short-term community action plan, like an organizational action plan, provides detail, using precise language to list the specific actions that will occur (with priorities and sequences), and lists out rejected alternatives (and explains why). For each goal, it includes a series of objectives that are short term, achievable, measurable, necessary, and feasible. Each objective has a set of related activities and tasks.

The short-term action plan also identifies responsible parties (implementers) and potential collaborators, and it suggests resource needs (including cost estimates, personnel, technical assistance) and indicates where these resources could or will be found. It is important to be sensitive to existing successful efforts in the community when developing the action plan. Finally, a timetable of target completion dates is established. Included in this short-term action plan are monitoring, reporting, and evaluation activities. It is wise to have contingency plans, if possible, for times when funds disappear, partners back out, or leadership changes. Laying out an organized plan of action helps to highlight conflicts or linkage opportunities between different planned activities and tasks.

Schorr (1997) found that the most promising community rebuilding initiatives

> all use a comprehensive lens as they survey both problems and opportunities. They all understand the necessity and effectiveness of working simultaneously on economic and physical development, service and education reform, and community building. But they are strategic in choosing where to begin, in sequencing their activities, and in how much they take on at once. (p. 27)

Kinsley (1997) suggested seeking small solutions that are usually more flexible, less expensive, and more manageable than larger solutions: "When a community embarks on a diverse effort that includes many small projects, each of which can produce results, then the potential for success is high" (pp. 28–29). Some might not work out, but others will succeed, and the overall effort will be a success.

Once a draft of a multi-year plan is completed, a community-wide meeting should be held for community review and adjustment. Such a meeting provides a good opportunity to recruit the additional volunteers and supporters needed for implementation. Strong community support for a plan is essential for securing resources and the support of officials and other key actors. Organizing this community-wide

draft plan assessment should be a high priority, complete with an adequate budget.

Step 10: Mobilize Resources (both internal and external)

As decisions are being made as to what to do (what to include in the plan), a decision has to be made as to whether it is desirable to include items for which there are no foreseeable resources. A community can plan conservatively in anticipating resources, it can plan boldly and then do whatever is necessary to amass the resources, or it can do something in between. A community is well advised to take a risk and include an item or two with high risk but great potential. A little faith in the future can keep a community energized if the prospects are exciting enough. Sometimes, daring objectives can help to raise new funds. Perhaps a funder can be lined up in advance if there are any high-risk funders around. The funder might even be invited to help shape the project.

A solid planning process will include early on those persons within and outside the community who can assist with mobilizing resources or who have actual decision making authority over resource allocation in the private, public, and community sectors. Successful initiatives draw extensively on resources outside the community, including public and private funds, professional expertise and technical assistance, and partnerships that bring clout and influence that can reduce or remove obstacles to success (Schorr, 1997, p. 28). It is important to keep everyone informed as planning proceeds through newsletters, briefings, and/or face-to-face meetings. (See the accompanying sidebar on the Greenpoint community.)

Community Consensus: The Greenpoint 197-a Plan, 1998

The Greenpoint community, earning its name from the expansive lush greenery before early 19th-century development, is located in the northernmost portion of Brooklyn in New York City. Greenpoint neighborhoods, tied together by a sense of community identity and a common future, share a vibrant and active commercial strip that reflects their diverse ethnic populations, a thriving historic district, and fine examples of urban architecture. The "197-a plan," 1998 (with the "197-a" coming from a section of New York City's charter regarding plan development for communities), emerged during the late 1990s from more than a decade of community activism and builds on Greenpoint's assets—its architecture and urban fabric, its people, and its spirit and spirituality (Greenpoint 197-a Committee, 1998, p. 1). The plan was prepared by the Greenpoint 197-a Committee for Brooklyn Community Board One, with significant technical assistance and outreach support from the Pratt Institute Center for Community and Environmental Development.

Beginning in the late 1950s, public policies "allowed" Greenpoint's eastern sector to become a magnet for noxious uses and, by the late 1980s, a dumping ground for swarms of garbage trucks off-loading at waste transfer stations. After petitions, letter-writing campaigns, testimony at hearings, and the formation of action committees to fight detrimental facilities, Greenpoint residents, community organizations, business leaders, and Brooklyn Community Board One members began working together as the Greenpoint 197-a Plan Committee to devise a plan to guide the community's future. Greenpoint residents see their plan as a "blueprint to inform, monitor, and guide" New York City agencies and private or nonprofit developers about how "Greenpoint can best be developed and how its problems can be redressed" (Greenpoint 197-a Committee, 1998). The 197-a plan offers recommendations for the entire community—residential areas, industrial zones, and commercial strips—and addresses all major aspects of Greenpoint life.

The plan's primary focus was to propose appropriate rezoning and development of the East River waterfront to allow for increased public access and open space. Major objectives were aimed at strengthening and diversifying Greenpoint's economic, social, historic, and cultural base and at integrating Greenpoint into the broader New York community. Among these were the following objectives (Greenpoint 1997-a Committee, 1998):

1. Revitalize and make publicly accessible Greenpoint's historic waterfront.

2. Clean and renew Greenpoint's environment through monitoring industries, eliminating the negative effects of their by-products, and regreening the neighborhood.

3. Build on Greenpoint's historic mixed-use character by reusing vacant buildings and land to create a mixture of residential, commercial, workshops, high-performance businesses, studios and parks, and open spaces.

4. Foster a renaissance in Greenpoint through historic preservation and the creation of additional cultural and educational facilities.

5. Retain jobs in active, compatible, clean, and nonpolluting industries, and encourage clean industries to remain in the community so as to promote employment and business opportunities for local residents.

6. Provide for needed senior citizen, youth, and community services such as day care centers, schools, and an up-to-date computer technology library.

7. Maintain and improve mass transit in the area.

8. Ensure that the Department of City Planning immediately begins the process of rezoning the six proposed rezoning study areas in Greenpoint to achieve the objectives proposed in the 197-a plan.

For more than a decade, members of the community sought public input on Greenpoint waterfront planning. Through public forums, workshops, discussions, and local newspapers, collaboration among residents, community groups, merchants, manufacturers, and others resulted in the creation of a community revitalization plan that reflects a consensus of different neighborhood interests. The participatory and inclusive process included three major public forums in 1997 and 1998. Each forum was advertised in local newspapers and via flyers (in English, Polish, and Spanish). Forums included slide shows and question-answer sessions. Recommendations from the forums were also distributed in several languages. In addition, more than 9,000 copies of the proposed plan in newspaper format were distributed door-to-door throughout the community. Special meetings were also held with the Greenpoint business community, and a waterfront tour was conducted for city and county officials.

Once finalized, Community Board One submitted the 197-a plan to the Department of City Planning for extensive review in 1998. Meetings with all relevant government agencies were held throughout the spring of 1999, including planning, parks and recreation, transit, housing, environmental protection, and transportation. After several years of negotiations with the Department of City Planning over plan contents, the Greenpoint 197-a plan was approved with modifications by the City Planning Commission in December 2001 and was adopted by the New York City Council in January 2002 (J. Lawrence, Community Board One, personal communication, August 2, 2002). Grounded in hard facts from extensive data collection and analysis, the Greenpoint 197-a plan is a blueprint for the community's future as an ethnically vibrant, mixed-use, mixed-income community with maximum access to public open space and its waterfront.

The Greenpoint 197-a Plan Committee, an independent committee, was organized in 1998 to write and complete the plan. It worked with many organizations in preparing the 197-a plan for Community Board One, among them the concerned Citizens of Greenpoint Inc., the Friends of India Street Pier, the Greenpoint Civic Council, the Greenpoint Monitor Museum, Greenpoint Property Owners Inc., Hispanos Unidos de Greenpoint, Neighborhood Roots, the North Brooklyn Community Development Corporation, and many community activist residents. Numerous other stakeholders participated in some of the discussions.

The Greenpoint Waterfront Association for Parks and Planning (GWAPP) came into existence in May 2000 as an umbrella organization that encompasses many of the organizations that worked on the 197-a plan. The GWAPP is also actively involved as a community organization implementing recommendations of the plan along with the New York City Department of City Planning, other city agencies, Community Board One, and other local organizations (J. Lawrence, Community Board One, personal communication, August 2, 2002). The Greenpoint 197-a plan, 1998, is posted on the Web site owned and maintained by the GWAPP (http://gwapp.org/gwapp/01-introduction.pdf).

(Greenpoint's adjacent waterfront neighborhood, Williamsburg, concurrently developed a complementary 197-a plan. Both communities began waterfront planning in 1989. In 1996, residents of Greenpoint concluded that its issues and geography required a separate 197-a plan.)

Step 11: Implement the Short-Term Action Plan

Implementation will be occurring as plans are being developed aimed at "short-term victories." It is important to maintain a mix of short- and longer term activities to help keep momentum going. The strength and structure of community organizations and institutions can be tested during implementation when both expectations and energy are high. It is important to plan projects, programs, and activities as well as to plan for continual development of the community's organizations and institutions.

Key for successful implementation is building people support during the planning process by including people of all kinds, whether they have worked on the plan making or not. People will help to provide momentum by their numbers, by their influence as individuals, and by their collective cohesion.

Step 12: Monitor and Evaluate Progress, Products, and Outcomes

Being able to measure, evaluate, and report results is key to keeping local residents and organizations hopeful and committed and to engaging further local, state, and national groups and resources. These activities are also critical in keeping the effort consistent with community needs. They make the next step, updating and revising the plan (as well as expanding), possible.

Monitoring and evaluation involve keeping up with implementation and deciding whether the plan is still feasible or whether it is off base. It is important to see a plan as a dynamic evolving document that continuously responds to changing economic, social, and political conditions. A permanent implementation committee or community planning forum can be set up to periodically and systematically monitor and measure directions, accomplishments, and impacts and then determine areas for improvement. The implementation committee/planning forum should also stay informed of proposed new developments and be ready to react proactively. Communication of progress to constituents and the public demonstrates the willingness to be held accountable for actions taken.

When designing a planning process, upfront agreement on the form of monitoring and evaluation is needed. What specific measures or milestones will be used to evaluate progress toward goals? Who will conduct the evaluation? How will the information gathered be used, and who will use it? The data gathering itself should be continuous and may involve a year-end review session, a town meeting, or a series of focus groups. In addition, the planning and monitoring structure and process should be reviewed to see whether there are any changes that are needed to ensure future success.

Kubisch et al. (2002) noted some lessons learned from the Aspen Institute's Roundtable on Comprehensive Community Initiatives for Children and Families. They acknowledged that "the process of community change is exceedingly difficult to map and track" (p. 70). Also, long-term outcomes—significant changes in community-wide indicators of family and community well-being—are unlikely to show up within most funders' time frames. Therefore, "pathways to achieve change" as well as markers of progress—the link between activities and outcomes—must be identified to demonstrate whether an initiative is on track (p. 70). Kubisch et al. also spoke to the need for ongoing learning by developing a continuous process of feeding back information that can guide management and decision making within and external to the community (pp. 73–75). Community change participants are also called on to test new strategies, learn from them, and disseminate the results so as to add to the community revitalization knowledge base (pp. 76–77).

Step 13: Update and Revise the Plan

Once an assessment or evaluation of the progress on the short-term plan is completed and community circumstances are reassessed, the long-range plan should be reviewed using an open feedback process and, if indicated, should be modified, with a new or revised short-term action plan put into motion. The process of updating and revising the plan should be an open process so that, once again, agreement can be reached on who will do what, when, and how.

Step 14: Celebrate Successes

Achieving long-term outcomes can take years of effort. At times, people's energy may lag, hopes may be dashed, and public support may wane. Because momentum is critical to keep moving forward, attention should be paid to acknowledging small successes. A stop sign is finally installed, a new park is dedicated, one new business opens on the commercial strip, a volunteer makes his or her first public presentation—all of these offer opportunities to celebrate and spark new commitment and energy.

SUMMARY

Both organizational planning and community planning provide blueprints for sustained strategic action. Maximum outcomes are achieved through processes that are highly inclusive and participatory, systematic and structured, and based on facts and data, with progress and results that are monitored and evaluated. Plans are meant to be dynamic—subject to modifications and revisions. Both community planning and internal organizational planning are integral parts of community controlled development; they build social, political, and economic strength. These processes can commence at any time and be designed to meet time and resource constraints. There is never a "too late." The small community that successfully struggles through the rigorous and sometimes painful activities described in this chapter, and that ends with a long-term guide for change accepted and cheered by all parties, need have no fears. Its brilliant future is assured.

Continuing Questions

1. Under what conditions (and with what prerequisites) should a community engage in a comprehensive community planning process?

2. How can a variety of community organizations and interests balance individual opportunities and challenges with a commitment to a long-range plan?

3. Should achieving consensus during a planning process always predominate? Under what circumstances, if any, should the majority rule?

4. Once a community plan is completed and adopted, how should opportunities that arise but are not part of the original plan be addressed?

5. Under what circumstances, if any, can plans produced without significant constituent or community participation be valid?

6. Is it prudent and useful to ask elected officials to endorse a community plan? What are the advantages and disadvantages?

7. What level of resources (people, time, and funds) should be spent ensuring media cooperation with communication of plan contents to the public?

Appendix 9.A
Suggested Data to Collect in Planning Efforts

Data should be collected internal and external to the community. Categories of data should be analyzed overall and in terms of race/ethnicity, gender, age, class, and other specific attributes to see whether there are patterns of inequity:

Demographic data: Number, size, gender, and age; racial and ethnic composition; marital status; proportion of households with children, proportion of male- and female-headed households

Land use and zoning data: Residential, business/commercial, industrial/manufacturing, institutions; green space, parks, and recreational space; vacant land and buildings

Economic data: Per capita and family income levels and sources; median household and family income; distribution of personal income; poverty rates; range of occupations with salary data; flows of pensions and entitlement payments; bank and thrift institution lending; performance and compliance with the Community Reinvestment Act

Housing data: Type/Construction, conditions, density; supply and demand; sales and prices; rent levels; proportions of household income spent on housing; waiting time for subsidized housing; distribution of affordable housing throughout the community; migration patterns into or out of the community; average length of residency; home-ownership levels and patterns; demographics of homeowners and renters; tenure versus turnover; vacancies (number and length); mortgage market trends; real estate sales market activity; rental market activity; housing assistance and loan program availability and use; home maintenance and repair activity; building permits; zoning codes

Business/Commercial data (retail trade area): Age, construction, and condition of commercial buildings; average store size; current merchant mix including number and kind of retail stores; sales volume; prices charged; business hours of operation; consumption by residents at local stores; outside and inside appearance of stores; ownership and management data; transportation to and from the area; parking availability;

pedestrian amenities; commercial crime; business/retail trends; vacancies and turnover; commercial real estate activity and trends; business lending practices and trends

Manufacturing and industry data: Range, size, and nature of local manufacturers and industries; ownership and management data; employee workforce profile; wage, salary, and benefit scales; future trends; openings, closings, and relocations

Employment data: Workforce participation; unemployment and underemployment rates; skills of unemployed and underemployed persons; income and educational levels of residents by employment/job type and category; wages and benefits; job tenure; business and industries where residents work; commuting patterns to places of employment; training and placement services

Environmental data: Environmental quality data and statistics (land, vegetation, air, and water); amount of toxins released by local firms; quality of public services (waste removal, street cleaning, and rodent control); quantity, location, and toxicity of brown fields; number and location of environmentally remediated sites; lead content in homes and soil; location and amount of green ways, green spaces, parks, parklets, and community and yard gardens; utility consumption; number and nature of green building initiatives and practices; population of fragile species; number of bikeways, rails-to-trails projects, and outdoor recreational venues

Public health data and vital statistics: Birth and death statistics and trends; health status of residents; primary health hazards to the population; locations of hospitals and medical facilities; number of residents with and without health insurance coverage; number of babies born at adequate birth rate; age of birth mothers; number and location of community-based or alternative health care facilities; number, location, and use of community food banks; percentage of children participating in free breakfast or lunch programs

Education data: Educational achievement; high school graduates who go on to college; graduation rate of public and private high schools; school dropout statistics; per capita and per student expenditures; adult literacy rate; number of public, private, parochial, vocational, and technical schools as well as colleges and universities; number of residents involved in lifelong learning; use of educational facilities for after-school programs and activities; number of residents (parents/guardians) involved in school community councils or parent-teacher associations; number, nature, and functioning of school governance and advisory bodies

Public safety data: Crime and incidence statistics including the nature and frequency of crime; "trouble" spots; juvenile justice data; amount and nature of public safety resources; police accountability; fire prevention and firefighting; code enforcement; number of residents participating in community crime prevention programs; number and effectiveness of police/community councils

Transportation and access data: Availability and accessibility of private and public modes of transportation; distance to and from major employers; number, nature, schedule, and cost of public and private road construction projects

Social and human services data (e.g., child welfare, child care, health/mental health, substance abuse, senior care): Availability and accessibility of services and providers; service needs (type and amount) that are and are not being met by existing services or facilities; service eligibility requirements or restrictions; location of services and facilities; transportation access to services or facilities; relationships among providers and with the community; formal and informal helping/support networks

Arts and culture data: Number and community activity level of artists living or working in the community; number and location of community murals or community artwork; number and schedule of cultural productions staged in the community; percentage of residents who regularly celebrate their cultural heritage; number and nature of, as well as participation levels at, multicultural activities and events; availability of arts programs and instruction at local schools

Social fabric and cohesion: Number of residents active as volunteers or in the governance of binding institutions and activities, including organizations of faith or spirituality, schools, ethnic clubs, athletic teams, coffeehouses, bowling leagues, community libraries, book clubs, historic societies, block clubs, and community organizations; number and circulation of community newspapers and local organization newsletters; an inventory or calendar of community events and celebrations along with participation levels; number of residents who volunteer for community service work or for work at local organizations; number of residents who share or trade skills; number and nature of hate crimes and racial incidents; levels of cohesion, with special attention paid to the dynamics of and attitudes toward race, ethnicity, and class

Government structure and political organization: Percentage of eligible voters registered and turnout; number, nature, and activity of local political committees, clubs, and representatives; number and tenure of resident-elected officials; number, nature, activity, and power of community advocacy organizations; number of local boards, authorities, commissions, and planning councils; community governance and representation; demographic and other characteristics of elected officials and community leadership; condition of local party organizations, number of active workers, and level of year-round meetings and special events; information on independent political groups; political agenda of any alliances or coalitions in the area; power of school boards, zoning commission, and the like to make public decisions; lobby groups in the nonprofit sector

REFERENCES

Blakely, E. J. (1994). *Planning local economic development theory and practice* (2nd ed.). Thousand Oaks, CA: Sage.

Crossroads Resource Center. (1999). *Neighborhood sustainability indicators guidebook.* (working draft produced for the Urban Ecology Coalition). Minneapolis, MN: Author.

Development Leadership Network. (1999). *Success measures guidebook* (Version 1.0). Boston: Author.

Gosiewski, S. (1999). *Planning makes a difference! A history of Lyndale's recent planning efforts.* Minneapolis, MN: Lyndale Neighborhood Association. Available: http://lyndale.org/lna/odyssey/recent.htm

Greenpoint 197-a Committee. (1998). *Greenpoint 197-a plan* (prepared for Brooklyn Community Board One, with technical assistance from the Pratt Institute Center for Community and Environmental Development). Brooklyn, NY: Author.

Kinsley, M. (1997). *Economic renewal guide: A collaborative process for sustainable community development* (3rd ed.). Snowmass, CO: Rocky Mountain Institute.

Kretzmann, J. P., & McKnight, J. L. (1993). *Building community from the inside out: A path toward finding and mobilizing a community's assets.* Evanston, IL: Northwestern University, Center for Urban Affairs and Policy Research.

Kubisch, A., Auspos, P., Brown, P., Chaskin, R., Fulbright-Anderson, K., & Hamilton, R. (2002). *Voices from the field II: Reflections on comprehensive community change.* Washington, DC: Aspen Institute.

Lyndale Neighborhood. (2002). [Online]. Available: www.lyndale.org/welcome

Lyndale Neighborhood Association. (2000). *The Lyndale neighborhood's comprehensive community planning process* (report to the McKnight Foundation). Minneapolis, MN: Author.

Lyndale Neighborhood Association. (2002). [Online]. Retrieved April 20, 2002, from the World Wide Web: www.lyndale.org/lna.html

Mourad, M. (1996, June). Community collaboration: The power of a neighborhood planning process. *Cost Cuts,* pp. 1–3.

Rubin, H. J., & Rubin, I. S. (1992). *Community organizing and development* (2nd ed.). Boston: Allyn & Bacon.

Schorr, L. (1997, Fall). Community rebuilding: Something important is happening. *Family Resource Coalition of America Report,* pp. 27–29.

Sennett, F. (1994, April–May). At the drawing board. *The Neighborhood Works,* pp. 10–17.

10

MAXIMIZING SOCIAL STRENGTH

We have been seeking to understand small community through the study of each of its three dimensions. In the beginning, we assessed power and its uses in shaping the political dimension. We have opened up questions about resource flows, connections, and conflicts that are embedded in the economic dimension. In the Aliquippa case, we saw how power and resources are intertwined in real life. In Chapters 8 and 9, we looked at ways of linking people, power, and resources through planning. In this chapter, we explore how the social dimension can help community people to achieve their collective goals. What is sought is a sustainable harmony of the three dimensions where equity, equality, and well-being are maximized. To perform this guiding role, the social dimension obviously must be strong enough to draw together the political and economic dimensions in ways that serve the mission of community people and their allies.

Social strength is an indicator of a community's grit and resilience. It encompasses social fabric, social capital, and social services, which in combination make up the communal infrastructure of a residential place, give it unity, and make it a force. It is a force that can protect and build the community's togetherness, as people in Aliquippa (Pennsylvania), Bloomfield-Garfield (Pittsburgh), Dudley Street (Boston), Hyde Park-Kenwood (Chicago), Lyndale (Minneapolis), Rollingwood (Austin), Valmeyer (Illinois), and Vandergrift (Pennsylvania) have defended and built their togetherness, fragile as it may appear at times.

Strength-based social infrastructure can allow for internal conflicting beliefs without the outbreak of hate crimes and family feuds. Alive at opposite poles, it is what allows a community to embrace equal opportunity and, at the same time, to "tolerate" a public meeting by the Aryan Nation in the neighborhood park.

Infrastructure is also strengthened on a microcosmic level when members of a new generation opt to stay in the old neighborhood to raise their children, when mothers and fathers share child-rearing duties and teenagers mow the yards of senior citizens, when churches operate food banks or raise money to help individual families overwhelmed by catastrophic medical bills, when families work together to acknowledge and preserve historic landmarks, when garden clubs adopt neighborhood vacant lots or highway miles and commit to beautifying the landscape, and when families—even a whole block of them—adopt homeless people, see to their shelter needs, and set them on a path to stability.

Knowledge about social strength relative to community renewal has been accumulating for a long time, but there continues to be fragmentation and confusion. We provide the following set of brief definitions and distinctions, followed by case examples and commentary, with the hope of advancing the search for clarity and communal depth.

THE THREE COMPONENTS

The term *social strength* denotes an overall condition of well-being in the personal and public lives of people in a small community, marked by proactive and fruitful interrelationships among them, a comfort with collective planning, and action as they encounter serious needs and opportunities. Social strength appears to rest on three components.

1. Social Fabric

We looked at social fabric in Chapter 4, where we described it as a tough underlying web of human relationships. It consists of people of a small community interacting as neighbors, friends, blood relatives, customers patronizing the same shops, residents using the same services and institutions, people sharing the same local history, and (in time) people trading information in helping each other to grasp opportunities and navigate daily life. It is this web of connections that leads the residents of a Hyde Park-Kenwood to continue to plan together for 50 years and that leads the people of Dudley Street to feel confident in taking on the power of eminent domain. Individual relationships grow and multiply, beget attachment, and contribute to maintaining the underlying web of cohesion.

And more happens. At some point in the web, clusters of mutually supportive behavior appear. Such points are marked by continuous relationships formed around specific interests. Such interests can range from seeking job openings, to finding affordable shelter, to raising children, to pursuing robust health, to improving the schools, to expanding green space and girls' sports. As these thickened points in the web become intense and stable, they give birth to new directions, convictions, suspicions, attitudes, alliances, and ideas—all of them potential assets.

2. Social Capital

The authors of this book first encountered the term *social capital* in Jane Jacobs's *The Death and Life of Great American Cities,* where she wrote about the uses of city neighborhoods, making the following declaration:

> A good city neighborhood can absorb newcomers into itself . . . , and it can protect a reasonable amount of transient population, too. But these increments or displacements have to be gradual. If self-government in the place is to work, the underlying float of population must be a continuity of people who have forged neighborhood networks. These networks are a city's irreplaceable social capital. Whenever the capital is lost, from whatever the cost, the income flow from it disappears, never to return until and unless new capital is slowly and chancily accumulated. (Jacobs, 1961, p. 138)

James S. Coleman has brought this concept to visibility during recent years. Residents driven by their desires to explore opportunities and reduce personal and community distress push themselves beyond the individual relationships of social fabric to form stable intense networks built on mutual interests within the context of wider social systems (Coleman, 1988).

To Coleman (1988), social capital is the nonmonetary wealth produced by the benign energized interaction that occurs continuously within networks, much of it spontaneous and serendipitous, "making possible the achievement of certain ends" (p. S98) such as trust, norms of behavior, mutual supports, sense of direction, and valuable information flows. All of these "ends" are also products that can create further assets, which is the essence of capital. From the elbow rubbing, cell phoning, and joint experimenting within networks of interconnected people, participants gain energy, ideas, and skills enabling them to plan and act in more productive ways. Social capital becomes richer as transformation occurs within network members, freeing them from the limitations of oppression. An increase in trust, for example, allows the group "to accomplish more than is possible without it" (pp. S100–S101).

The information flows that become available to members of an active network can bring useful facts such as sources of low-interest loans, advance warning on plant closings, scholarship sources, tax breaks for the elderly, and guidance on where to find a reliable plumber. Finally, Coleman (1988) imparted this knowledge: "A prescriptive norm within a collectivity that constitutes an especially important form of social capital is the rule that one should forgo self-interest and act in the interests of the collectivity" (p. S104). As the bonding of members within a collectivity becomes more secure, members may modify personal priorities and shift their loyalty to the newly emerging common purpose. In such a situation, we can say that the newly forged purpose is a product of social capital.

Robert Putnam, the Harvard University professor worried over Americans losing their connectedness, celebrates social capital building as the way in which to restore cooperation and the habit of generous civic activity. In "Bowling Alone: America's Declining Social Capital," Putnam (1995) emphasized two components of social capital: civic engagement and trust. He defined civic engagement as the degree to which citizens participate in activities that affect all levels of the political decision-making process—activities such as voting and membership in special interest lobbying groups. High levels of social capital are found where individuals trust or feel a mutual sense of obligation toward each other, with trust creating a sociable environment where people expect others to behave in accordance with social norms that encourage reciprocity.

Putnam researched the development of 20 regional governments organized in Italy in 1970. Some since then have built vigorous, abundant local societies, while others have withered. Putnam (1993b) and his colleagues did not find politics, ideology, traditional wealth, or social stability associated with the difference; rather, they found "civic engagement, voter turnout, newspaper readership, membership in music societies and literary circles, Lions clubs, and soccer clubs." Successful are the regional places where citizens tussle with public issues, where people trust one another to act fairly and obey the law, where there are honest leaders committed to equality, social and political networks organized horizontally rather than hierarchically, and "civic communities [that] value solidarity, civic participation, and integrity" (pp. 35–37).

Putnam (1993b) maintained, "Racial and class inequalities in access to social capital, if properly measured, may be as great as disparities in financial and human capital, and no less portentous." In other words,

It's not just social capital, period. It's social capital that cuts across the cleavages in American society. That is, it's not enough that we all start bowling again. There have to be bowling leagues in which people of different races are connecting with one another. If we can solve this one, if we can get more active people working in contexts that respect American pluralism, many of our other problems, to begin with our politics, will be different. (p. 39)

Many others now hail the importance of the concept. Lang and Hornburg (1998) noted that social scientists emphasize two main dimensions of social capital (p. 4). Social glue is the degree to which people participate in group life and includes the amount of trust or level of comfort that they feel when they participate in these groups. Social bridges, the links between groups, are vital because they connect groups to each other and give members access to the broader society through a chain of affiliations. In their article, "What Is Social Capital and Why Is It Important to Public Policy?," Lang and Hornburg noted that "the amount and nature of social capital varies tremendously by location." with some places (e.g., many affluent suburbs) having a lot of financial capital and low social capital, while many low-income communities are low in financial capital but abundant in social capital (p. 4). They cited the economic importance of social capital to immigrants and racial minority groups—linking people to diverse groups and the wider society, thereby gaining access to greater opportunities. In spite of all the positives attributed to social capital, they went on to say that "social capital, in and of itself, does not always correlate with healthy, democratic, and economically vital communities" (p. 6). Their examples of the negative aspects of social capital included political machines, old-boy civic networks, the efficiency of cronyism in resource distribution, and the tight-knit white neighborhoods in American cities that "make such places unfriendly, and at times deadly, for some outsiders, especially minorities" (p. 7).

Midgley and Livermore (1998), for instance, stressed social capital's potential for improving the quality of societal institutions, especially by bringing trust into economic relationships. Midgley and Livermore were also careful to set out the limitations of the social capital direction. They pointed out that a narrow approach can fail to include the whole community in its planning, leaving out the poorly educated and least organized, who may have the most to gain from this direction.

Midgley and Livermore (1998) also raised a warning regarding the possibility of local elite leaders taking over development programs for their own uses if they are more interested in profits than in reducing poverty. Also, they suggested that the emphasis on a local approach might leave out adequate seeking of external resources that are needed by deprived groups in the community. In fact, they insisted that local economic development based on social capital has to double its efforts to seek outside investments if a small community's social, political, and economic needs are to be met and its assets are to be developed. Purely self-contained efforts may leave the small community itself "bowling alone" if it does not seek to tap the available resources of the wider world— whether it is job-seeking help for low-skilled residents or reconciliation processes taught by experienced makers of racial peace who can offer knowledge and support to a group of inexperienced residents seeking a new spirit of reconciliation for their gated suburb.

Ideological opponents of government involvement in the economy might claim that purported benefits of social capital eliminate the need for government aid in which public support is desperately required. Coleman and Putnam have argued strenuously that social capital is a supplement—not an alternative—to an effort to renew and strengthen a distressed community. No effort for small community renewal should ever arbitrarily close itself off from legitimate outside resources. Now, we move onto the third component of social strength.

3. Social Services

Beyond the individual relationships that make up the web of social fabric, and beyond the focused networks, groups, and informal social institutions and their products that constitute social capital, are the collective bodies— formal in their makeup—that produce and provide healing, helping, and developmental services to community people. Their services might relate to physical or mental health, child care, geriatric supports, coming-of-age youth, recreation, job readiness, spiritual growth, computer competence, adoption, problem pregnancies, assertiveness, hobbies, household finances, race and reconciliation, or one of dozens of other significant matters related to personal and family wellness and development.

Over time, residents or organizations serving the community distribute these services in accordance with demand. Residents of a small community may identify a serious service gap and take action to provide it themselves or to stimulate others to do so. For instance, the health committee of a renewal organization might find a demand and market for abstinence education for youth. After a wide and unsuccessful search to find a competent existing group to offer the service, the health committee links the education department of the local hospital with a faith-based coalition of youth leaders to research and establish the program, promising to find the money to support it.

Community renewal groups, desperately seeking a gap-filling job service to employ parents being moved off public assistance, might canvas all available private, public, nonprofit, indigenous, and professional organizations and find that none is able or willing to risk time and money, leading the renewal group to organize its own experimental job service. If the new entity persists, and it is able to train, place, and tap into abundant flows of resources, then it takes a respected place in the galaxy of organized services in the community.

In creating or rejuvenating a social service, a community group has the opportunity to broaden and strengthen the focus. Most social service providers focus on their own specialty— what they do. We suggest that they also give serious attention to *how* they are doing it. It is reasonable and helpful for a community group to raise questions with the leaders of a prospective social service partner. Are providers linking the people they serve to each other for peer support? Are they linking people to competent but obscure outside resources that have expertise that is not available in the community? Are they facilitating links among sets of resources? Are they tapping into talented people for involvement as volunteers? Are they finding and using informed natural helper networks? Is advocacy part of their agenda? Do they cultivate and hire talented local people? Do they open themselves up to listening to their volunteers and others from the area they serve? Do they solicit outside views relative to planning, policymaking, and evaluation systems? Do they have local people on their governing board and committees? Each community group will approach this sensitive relationship in its own way and with its own questions based on local conditions.

We see now how the fabric of human relationships (the networks, alliances, and institutions arising from these relationships), teamed with the organized suppliers of social services, emerges as a special kind of infrastructure forming the social dimension of a small community—a combination we term the "social strength" of a place. It is a dynamic bundle of assets to be celebrated, nurtured, and built on. It also is an infrastructure that requires human labor to operate it and thereby becomes what is coming to be called a "social economy," which can be a source of career opportunities for a community's workforce.

Fabricant and Fisher (2002) cautioned,

> Communities are not isolated islands. Poor neighborhoods are affected by economic and political decisions made elsewhere. The capacity of poor neighborhoods to mount a political response to damaging trends and/or policies is in direct portion to its stock of social capital. More to the point, the effectiveness of social change initiatives depends as much on residents having better resources and information as on strong networks of social solidarity. Only by struggling to integrate social services, community building, and social change initiatives can social service agencies contribute to arresting and reversing the decline of very poor communities. (p. 4)

Hard Rock Cases

With the components of social strength defined, we now seek to clarify further the role of these components in real-life communities by drawing on case studies. We start with Sara Rimer of the *New York Times* describing a patch of Philadelphia's social fabric, which grows into social capital building and easily can be projected as spilling over into social services, as we will show:

> Dorsha Mason, 80, crippled and bent by phlebitis and arthritis, rises from bed in the row house of the old North Philadelphia neighborhood where she has lived for more than half a century, inches her way across her living room with her walker, and opens the front door. Her neighbors do not have to worry. The open door says she has made it through another night. Up and down the block, neighbors echo the signal. Across from Mrs. Mason, Rachel Lockhart, 83, opens her door, and so does Mary Little, 80, next to her, and Amanda Riley, 89, two doors down. On the corner, Katherine Jones, 66, opens hers.
>
> They have lived side by side on this short block of red and white row houses, most of them for 40 years and 50 years. They raised their children together, and paid off their mortgages by scrubbing other people's floors or working in the factories that brought tens of thousands of black families here from the South.
>
> They went to church together singing in the choir and cooking for the needy. Through it all, they always made time for the neighborhood; organizing meetings and voter registration drives, sweeping the streets, planting prize-winning gardens. (Rimer, 1999, p. 1)

This brief sketch readily can lend itself to hypothetical extension into a full portrait of social strength—in fact, one illustrative of the whole three-stage system of social strength. Social fabric was forming on Mrs. Mason's West Hagert Street some 50 years ago when the women met as young mothers and began to connect as neighbors facing similar responsibilities for parenthood while enjoying the pride of homeownership. Acquaintanceships blossomed into a friendship network that gained stability and utility for the women as well as spillover benefits for the community.

The network became a major asset in their lives, a place where limits on the outdoor conduct of their children and other norms for their block could be assessed, agreed to, and later enforced. An additional valuable piece of social capital added to the thrust that held together their lives as neighbors was the system of mutual supports that evolved. Their needs and talents took them beyond their West Hagert Street to satisfy spiritual, emotional, and artistic desires through a neighborhood church. They cooked for the poor and helped to organize voter registration campaigns to benefit their wider community. Their stability and generosity made them both receivers and providers in the local world of social services centered in their case around a church. It is easy to imagine them sharing homegrown greens with neighbors who did not own land for backyard gardens and helping their children's schools to raise money for field trips to the zoo and science center. Imagine the power and support that a dozen such networks can bring to a single school. The three stages of social strength become quite visible in such a case, "neighbors specializing in assisted living—the informal, unpaid kind" as Rimer (1999, p. 32) reported it.

Let us look at a less sanguine case to understand how lack of social strength hurts. The following is a paraphrased account of a case compiled by Steven Ginsberg of the *Washington Post* that was reprinted in the *Pittsburgh Post-Gazette:*

> Franklin, Virginia, is a 19th-century industrial town of 8,000 set along the Blackwater River, with a paper mill that employs 2,200. Slightly more than half the population is black, and the races have long lived apart, separated by the railroad and by feelings of suspicion and disrespect toward one another.
>
> When Hurricane Floyd sent river waters crashing through the town in September 1999, great damage was done and the two racial groups were suddenly working together for survival of themselves and the town. With calamity upon them, blacks and whites consoled one another. They labored side by side at relief centers helping those whose homes were destroyed. They cleared debris from the dripping streets and found common ground in their shock. Black and white women united for a solid month to cook and serve meals to relief workers who came from other communities.

> As the clean-up, restoration, and resettlement made progress, the tenuous unity dried up along with the soaked houses warmed by the southern sun. Complaints of unequal treatment began to be muttered by residents of both colors: there were whispers of a relief board dominated by white members, while some whites who led the clean-up effort said blacks could have done more to help their own section. Trust plummeted. Black physician Alvin Harris declared, "We live in a world of fiction here, where emotion between black and white is more important than fact. It goes back to the Civil War; we still ain't finished." (Ginsburg, 2000, p. A22)

Why was Franklin restoring its walls of separation? One possible answer appears simple enough: no social strength. From the facts presented, it seems that connections had never been established between the races. The town had sprung up as two isolated sections, separate and unequal. It is hard to believe, but in such a small community during a period of more than 135 years, there never grew up enough healthy black-white relationships to create social fabric reaching across the town. There was never the close human contact and common use of facilities needed to sweep out Civil War bitterness.

No doubt, there is a separate pool of social strength in each half of Franklin. But no single small community can truly prosper without a seamless fabric and the shared assets of social capital with which to build trust and mutually accepted norms. These might have solidified the recovery. Separate social services in a historically divided community slowed the rebuilding and prolonged the suffering of the dispossessed. From this drag-down into an antipathetic past, let us fast-forward to a spectacular future plan for a leviathan grid of small linked neighborhoods in California.

Proposed for the Santa Clarita Valley in Los Angeles County is Newhall Ranch, planned as a residential sub-region of 22,000 homes for 75,000 people in a state that adds 12,000 people to its population every week—enough for one new suburb. As the state's major metropolis, Los Angeles has a demand for 25,000 new housing units a year. The Newhall Land Company owns vast tracts of land in the valley. Over many years, it will use 19 square miles for the project, with half of the project area kept as open space. Roughly half of the homes are to be single-family freestanding homes, with the other half being a mixture of townhouses and rental apartments. A small percentage of the homes will be set aside for lower-income households. Some environmental organizations have opposed the project on the grounds of sprawl, overcrowding of land, inadequate community facilities, and a host of other growth issues. Los Angeles County has approved the project, and Newhall Ranch construction will move ahead.

Over the life of the project's construction, 3,000 or 4,000 people can be expected to move in each year. Now, the reader should think hypothetically about the first year of construction, with 3,500 homes coming to market within a few months of each other; while buyers from the valley itself, from nearby places, and from far away places all are moving in at the same time— most of them strangers to each other. What can be done to help such a set of new small communities build social strength early on?

Celebrations and low-key social events can be held to facilitate relationships and accelerate the growth of social fabric among the newcomers, starting even before they haul in their furniture. Social capital can be gained by promoting the forming of stable networks for trust building and the establishment of norms as well as for collective planning and action. Social services can be developed by encouraging and facilitating new residents' assessing existing social services in the valley, with a view toward identifying gaps and planning to preempt any crisis. A college or university in the region might supply student interns to do the organizing, or the organizing might come from a family support center of proven competence.

Contracting out the organizing of a social strength start-up project to a neutral professional source, such as an institution of higher learning or a creative family support center, would give the project a modicum of independence, which is important in gaining cooperation from new residents. It would provide both the collegiate staff and the residents with freedom to innovate, at arm's length from the company, in what would be a pioneering undertaking. Such an experimental project could have significance for the marketing of housing,

community building, and the training and education of community workers. The undertaking might be further enriched by linking it with existing public schools, health centers, and human service agencies, as partners in the "First Year" events, for Newhall Ranch.

These three cases—Philadelphia, Franklin, and Los Angeles—illustrate in different ways the meanings and applications of the three stages of social strength. The social component of community is open-ended, and its strengthening can be approached from every point on the compass. The literature on social strength is vast and rich, but most of it has been out of the reach of residents of distressed neighborhoods as well as of most community organizers. There is much more knowledge to be passed on to would-be organizers and to anyone with a serious interest in saving America's small communities. Just as with the literature on community organizing, we select prudent and useful publications on social strength and provide the reader with a few samples of the respective authors' wisdom, hoping that the reader may further explore the books that seem most useful.

EXPLORING SOCIAL STRENGTH: PRIZED READING

We start with Roger Ahlbrandt, whom we already introduced in Chapter 4 (Ahlbrandt, 1984; Ahlbrandt & Cunningham, 1979). Ahlbrandt was well known to the authors of this book and was a scholar blessed with wisdom, practicality, and wide-ranging interests, from the resurgence of the world steel industry to the efficiencies that derive from resident choices being sought out and listened to by governments. For a half dozen years during the late 1970s and early 1980s, he poured his energies into the relation between people and their neighborhoods. His rigorous surveys and analyses of resident choices convincingly linked resident relationships, values, institutions, and information flows with attachment and loyalty to their neighborhoods. From his survey research, he and his colleagues formulated classic recommendations for strengthening social fabric. His ideas are found in two books: *A New Public Policy for Neighborhood Preservation*

(Ahlbrandt & Cunningham, 1979) and *Neighborhoods, People, and Community* (Ahlbrandt, 1984). Most of the ideas remain alive in, and relevant for, this 21st century:

- Leaders of a neighborhood organization should study their community's social fabric to understand it and become conscious of its importance.
- Maintenance and strengthening of social fabric should be a continuing goal of a small community renewal organization, with the organization's structure designed to maximize human socialization and joint effort.
- Programs should be formulated to promote networks of kin, friends, and neighbors, with this objective kept in mind when planning social events, festivals, fund-raising walks and races, ethnic fairs, recreation and sports activities, cultural events, and new social services.
- Because homeownership promotes longevity of residence, which in turn can strengthen social fabric, it should always be considered as a goal. In general, vital small communities require a broad mixture of housing types and prices to diversify and enrich the fabric.
- A local renewal organization should ensure that there are adequate communication flows to keep residents informed about their neighbors and about issues affecting the community. A vigorous public flow of information is vital to maintaining healthy social fabric. Community newspapers are especially effective. In addition, e-mail networks are increasingly useful as computers become more available and accessible in small communities.
- Quality neighborhood institutions should be celebrated and supported, especially those that provide a focal point for bringing people together. This includes shopping streets, recreation and performing arts centers, and small local places for eating and/or drinking.
- A neighborhood renewal organization and its leaders should be known for fairness and wholesome values, including a continuing willingness to offer technical assistance to worthwhile new block clubs, associations, and businesses.
- Neighborhood preservation and vitality require a comprehensive program, tailored to local conditions and carried out with enthusiasm.

(Ahlbrandt, 1984, pp. 196–197; Ahlbrandt & Cunningham, 1979, pp. 208–209, 215)

The work of Ahlbrandt and his collaborators has stood the test of time, and several more recent books add to and embellish this classic foundation. Kretzmann and McKnight have operationalized some of the social capital and asset theory propounded by Coleman and Putnam. Kretzmann and McKnight's (1993) manual, *Building Communities From the Inside Out: A Path Toward Finding and Mobilizing a Community's Assets,* is particularly useful.

The basic Kretzmann and McKnight (1993) theme is that small communities cannot be renewed by concentrating on their distress; rather, they must be renewed by locating and using the assets, skills, and capacities of residents, citizen associations, and local institutions (p. iii). Research tools were suggested, including a "capacity inventory" of residents and citizen associations, with church and cultural groups being given priority. Methods were described for residents entering into partnerships with branch libraries, schools, community colleges, police, hospitals, staffed parks, and other more formal local institutions, many of which are directed from outside the community.

Kretzmann and McKnight (1993) gave an example of building social strength through "rediscovering" a park as a community asset, rich in skilled adult personnel and in attractive well-equipped outdoor and indoor spaces. Residents identify the park in a community inventory, cultivate its staff, find their need for more users, and promote use of the park for an annual "Back to School" parade, as a location for weekly nature-oriented art classes taught by public school faculty members, and as a place for senior citizen summer picnics, with the park staff arranging for city-owned vehicles to transport the seniors and police officers serving as volunteer coaches for park sports leagues. All of these joint activities promote resident relationships, induce the formation of friendship groups and active committees, and stimulate richer service programs that advance physical and mental health. Such initiatives are at the heart of the assets approach.

The Kretzmann and McKnight (1993) manual also proposed ways in which small communities can "capture" local economic assets that are already in place, starting with a compilation of the budgets of neighborhood institutions, an estimate of potential savings being accumulated by neighborhood households, and an inventory of "hidden" assets such as abandoned land, unused indoor space, and waste materials. It reported a partnership among a community development corporation (CDC), technical assistance organizations, and a high school that enables students to create school-based enterprises, including a catering business to serve staff and people working nearby. Students also operate a resale shop that is open to the student body and the community.

Kretzmann and McKnight (1993) closed with a five-step model for an asset-based community development initiative and suggested ways in which people and institutions from outside the community can support a resident-oriented community-building activity. As a wrap-up, they crowned their model with a prescription for a "neighborhood development trust" that would mobilize resources inside a single modernizing small community, with the realistic assumption that "in the long run, the primary neighborhood development resource must be the investment of time, money, and problem-solving capacity by the people in the neighborhood" (p. 361).

Describing the suggested trust as "a local structure specifically designed to identify, support, and invest in small local community enterprises," the Kretzmann and McKnight (1993) manual listed these ingredients for the trust:

- A start-up endowment of about $930,000 (presumably from an outside foundation or government source) to give the new entity 5 years to become established and financially independent
- Gifts and investments from the capital held by individuals, associations, enterprises, and public bodies living or rooted inside the community
- Directors of the trust to be neighborhood people with diverse constituencies who personally make an investment or represent a local entity making one
- An experienced professional manager paid for out of the start-up endowment

- The intention to convene groups and interests around development issues, stimulate investment in small local community enterprise, and "create a focus or a long-term vision for the neighborhood" (p. 364)
- Consideration of possible projects for investment such as a neighborhood radio station, a marketplace for artisans, and incentive grants for local businesses to create intern opportunities for enterprise-minded local high school students
- Grants to convert vacant land to vegetable gardens, loans to redesign local vacant facilities for new productive uses, and awards to local block clubs that create initiatives for child care, gardening, energy conservation, or youth employment

Organization strengthening is seen as a benefit that can flow from such a trust. "The citizen problem-solving purposes of the [trust] can be achieved by limited investments in local planning processes that convene a broad range of community investors to create a vision for the neighborhood's future and plans for mobilizing a wide range of constituencies in implementation" (Kretzmann & McKnight, 1993, pp. 361–366).

The Kretzmann and McKnight (1993) manual is a potent document for stimulating fresh ideas within the movement to rejuvenate America's small communities. For instance, one of its appendixes is a list of 223 neighborhood associations found in Logan Square, one of Chicago's multi-neighborhood communities of the type defined by Marciniak in Chapter 4. Many of these little associations go unheralded, yet they serve real needs. Kretzmann and McKnight maintained that every neighborhood has hidden groups that are assets. Some of the 223 associations discovered in Logan Square were called "Anin Art Puppet Theater," "Danish Rosary Group," "Fullerton Avenue Merchants Association," Painters Local #147," "SELSA Block Club," and "VFW Chicago Blackhawk Post #7975" (pp. 120–125). If only a quarter of the 223 could be activated in a single local coalition, it would indeed be a mighty force for its community.

In a more recent book, McKnight (1995) gave us a song for this chapter:

We all know that community must be the center of our lives because it is only in community that we can be citizens. It is only in community that we can find care. It is only in community that we can hear people singing. And if you listen carefully, you can hear the words: I care for you, because you are mine, and I am yours. (p. 172)

The third book we recommend is Robert Halpern's scholarly history of neighborhood-based poverty initiatives, *Rebuilding the Inner City* (Halpern, 1995). Halpern, mentioned briefly in Chapter 2, teaches and researches at Chicago's Erikson Institute for Advanced Study in Child Development, an affiliate of Loyola University. Making a sweeping review of neighborhood-based reform initiatives across the 20th century, Halpern (1995) mapped cycles of glory and despair, pointing to dedicated and often creative crusades of hope and brilliant strokes that too often turn to ashes, disappointment, and frustration—unless propped up by a financial angel.

Starting with the settlement houses and Charity Organization Society and its volunteers during the 1890s, Halpern (1995) analyzed the continual rises and falls of efforts by neighborhood people and their allies to achieve social strength and a decent life in their small communities, particularly those beaten down by poverty and isolation.

Throughout most of the hundred-plus years from the 1890s onward, the reform attempts met hostility and disrespect from officials and professionals who resented uncredentialed amateurs taking leadership roles in community health, housing, education, welfare, planning, and other "professional preserves." As reported in Chapter 2 of this book, neighborhood-based movements assumed influential places during the populist and progressive eras prior to World War I and later during the Great Depression, when community activists and their neighbors sought to improve health and housing conditions for families and boisterously demanded jobs for idle breadwinners.

Resources remained scarce for neighborhood programs until the passage of the landmark Housing Act of 1949, which brought large amounts of money as well as destructive programs on which to spend it, including the juggernauts of urban renewal and high-rise public housing. Both of these disrupted neighborhoods at the very time that the southern outmigration of poor people was applying massive pressures on old housing stocks in the North.

Halpern (1995) showed that as housing grew scarce, the government financed urban renewal that cleared tens of thousands of units of "substandard but affordable housing," while federal mortgage subsidy funds slipped away from cities, to be used instead to promote suburban residential development, and city factory jobs followed the white workers who were relocating into the new suburban houses. "These programs also permitted suburban governments and developers to exclude African-Americans, cutting them off from the most powerful wealth generation machine the middle class has ever known, i.e., the appreciation of those homes over the decades" (p. 3). The location and design of large public housing projects intensified segregation, and the federal highway program further isolated neighborhoods, often leaving them without ready access to social services.

Federal activism and cash did pour into neighborhoods in the face of the militant civil rights pressures of the 1960s. The money funded human services, including Head Start, community health centers, the Neighborhood Youth Corps, and mental health centers, with community action programs providing resources for planning coherent anti-poverty efforts that included resident involvement. However, government flows of resources into neighborhoods declined during the 1970s and 1980s, along with the state of the economy, as "stagflation" struck. Then came the election of President Ronald Reagan, who gave priority to defense spending while turning off government aid to urban neighborhoods and social services.

Business and government decisions during recent times have further oppressed older neighborhoods and towns, as many of the remaining manufacturing jobs have been shifted to the outer-suburban rings and as public and private decision makers have refused to invest in, insure, support, or interact with old neighborhoods and their residents. Halpern (1995) observed, "Rather than reshaping the larger social context, each new initiative is progressively shaped by that context" (p. 5). Halpern found a tendency to use timid interventions for addressing deeply rooted problems such as persistent inequality and social exclusion. However, he did have modest praise for the Dudley Street Neighborhood Initiative (DSNI), crediting it with "progress in meeting its objectives" (p. 204).

The lack of opportunity, the sense of exclusion, and the closed isolation of today's inner-city neighborhoods concerned Halpern (1995). He indicated that they lack networks that can provide entry to the world of jobs. Children can grow up 20 minutes from downtown business and cultural districts and never see them (p. 199). Halpern concluded that Americans have been far more likely historically to use the idea of community to exclude and divide than to include, and he repeatedly illustrated this by pointing out societal efforts to segregate and isolate the poor.

For the future, Halpern (1995) noted his worries about impoverished communities that continue to possess relatively few resources beyond their own residents and internal institutions. He viewed this poverty condition as preventing such neighborhoods from gaining the influence they need to break out for a new run at the middle-class way of life. He recognized social fabric and social capital as assets that poor communities do have, but he pointed out that even these are fragile in the current political environment.

Like Grogan and Proscio (2000), Halpern (1995) forced our face toward the fire of reality, but without the same flamboyant hope and "signs of new vitality" that the former saw "everywhere" in cities (Grogan & Proscio, 2000, p. 28). There have been benefits to small communities from building internal social strengths, and these have tempered the hardships of the poor. Participation once aroused has tapped into the energies and imaginations of residents in building a sense of community and inspiring civic activism and leadership, but it has created few jobs. Planning and self-governance efforts have made local government more sensitive and shown society the logic of the neighborhood as an organizing center. Neighborhood mobilization has challenged the conventional excuses for the necessity of inequality. There have been modest institutional

and legal reforms projecting influence beyond the poverty neighborhoods as well as the shaking loose of some token public and private resources to be invested in these neighborhoods, but there has not been the outside connections with influence and clout that can produce the enormous scale of resources required for reaching parity with the larger society at the scale of nine figures as required, for instance, for Aliquippa.

Halpern's (1995) sobering major finding is that, to date, the historic experience with neighborhood initiatives is at best an ameliorative, rather than a transforming, problem-solving strategy. In spite of evidence to the contrary, such as the persistence of low wages and means-tested supports too low to meet basic family needs, we are still fooled into believing that people single-handedly create and perpetuate their own hardship (p. 221).

Halpern (1995) put the finger on social weakness as a central reality:

> The most basic reasons for the prevalence and concentration of social problems are found in the primacy of the marketplace in defining people's worth and entitlement, and in shaping social relations in a limited sense of social obligation, in the continued social and political sanctioning of exclusionary housing practices, and in the resulting feelings of exclusion, of being trapped, of anger, despair, depression, futility. (p. 228)

Halpern (1995) insisted that reform programs must go beyond the inner city to penetrate both the close-in and far-out suburbs (no matter how exclusive); to find common ground for working to ensure that living places everywhere rise above the distress of racism, civic disengagement, and economic insecurity; and to find new kinds of mutual concerns that can connect the separate worlds of center city and outer suburbs. "Both local government and private institutions like churches and youth serving organizations must address the task of recreating a measure of human contact between inner-city neighborhoods and surrounding parts of the city" (pp. 231–233). In effect, what seems to be called for are socially concerned people and institutions in small communities creating local reform organizations that not only renew their own neighborhoods but also link to each other to build regional and national understanding, cohesion, and the political resolve to shape universal respect and equity. Halpern expressed a dim sobering view of the future of small central-city communities, close-in older suburbs, and aged industrial towns.

In *Dry Bones Rattling: Community Building to Revitalize American Democracy*, Mark Warren examined how the Industrial Areas Foundation (IAF) networks in Texas and the Southwest, led by committed people of faith, rebuild social capital while promoting racially inclusive democratic participation (Warren, 2001). As Warren, an assistant professor in Fordham University's Department of Sociology and Anthropology, began his research on the IAF networks, Putnam's (1993a) study on governance in Italy, *Making Democracy Work: Civic Traditions in Modern Italy,* was published. This pushed Warren (2001) to "consider the IAF strategy as an effort to make democracy work" (p. x).

While Putnam focused on the decline in social capital in most forms of associational and group life, Warren (2001) was particularly concerned with the decline of stable institutions of community life that in the past played an important role in sustaining an active democracy through connections to the political system such as the linkage of local branch political organizations and unions to community institutions and organizations (e.g., fraternal organizations, parishes, local business associations) (pp. 15–16). Warren also noted the decline of locally rooted but nationally federated organizations, such as the Parent Teacher Association (PTA) and the American Legion, that connected people to government and structured the engagement of people in political action.

Although there has been growth in small (often self-help) groups below local community organizations and institutions, and there has been growth in national movements and advocacy groups above these organizations and institutions, Warren (2001) maintained that building such social capital might not be sufficient if community organizations and institutions remain detached from the political system. *Dry Bones Rattling* laid out Warren's four-part framework for building social capital to revitalize democracy. His framework is as follows:

1. Building social capital needs to start with the institutional life that exists in local communities.

2. Given that these institutions and the social fabric of communities are weak, there is a need to develop cooperative ties and enhance the leadership capacity of community members.

3. Local communities can be isolated and inward looking, requiring the development of broader identities and a commitment to the common good; social capital needs to be bridged across communities, especially those divided by race.

4. Effective power requires identifying or developing mediating institutions capable of intervening successfully in politics and government; "building strong communities with diverse connections may not matter if they lack the power to shape their own development." (pp. 19–20)

For Warren (2001), religious congregations stand out as institutional bases for democratic action because, even though church attendance has been declining, congregations represent the largest form of social connectedness in the United States, have staying power, and embody strong traditions through which participants learn and express the value of community and reciprocity. In addition, faith-based efforts can infuse political action with commitment to social justice and racial equality.

In examining the Texas IAF network, Warren (2001) found organizations in which "people themselves actively participate in democracy" (p. 4). He challenged "conventional assumptions that religious intervention in politics can only mean the effort to impose a group's moral teachings on society" (p. 4). Warren viewed the IAF organizations as political rather than religious, engaging faith traditions in building political power to address the needs of families in low-income communities of color—power that results in new housing, improved schools, jobs training and jobs, and strengthened social fabric. Warren cited the IAF network organizations as a core example of community building—revitalizing democracy at the ground level by focusing on "patient relationship building at the local level, with efforts directed towards concrete improvements to communities where families live and work . . . rooted in community institutions that engage the participation of Americans often left out of elite-centered politics, especially women and people of color" (p. 9).

Warren's (2001) in-depth study of the Texas IAF provides sound lessons on democratic action, the development of statewide issue campaigns and regional networks, the building of multiracial coalitions (Warren's "bridging social capital"), and leadership development and decision-making processes in participatory democratic organizations.

Lisbeth Schorr is a researcher, teacher, writer, and activist who has long been concerned with the quality of social service interventions that are aimed at strengthening families and neighborhoods. Schorr's work is based out of Harvard University and the Aspen Institute, where she helps to lead the Comprehensive Community Initiatives for Children and Families. For many years, she has done close personal observation of interventions known for their innovation and impact, a search that has taken her into small and large communities scattered throughout the nation. Her book is *Common Purpose* (Schorr, 1997), a 500-page distillation of what does and does not work in reforming and renewing social services. Her ideas are relevant to us because her most universal solution calls for change to be initiated in and through the nation's small place communities.

What does not work, according to Schorr (1997), is dependence on the large bureaucratic systems such as the police, job training, economic development, health and mental health, public education, and child welfare. In her view, these systems are constrained by laws, rules, and regulations and are being run by officials unable to reframe their missions and restructure their operations so that their agencies can be responsive to specific individuals, families, and communities. Her research has found only a few rare cases of reform from within. In Schorr's view, what works are programs that are neighborhood based, have plentiful support from outside forces and institutions, and do not hold back from both challenging and partnering with the rigid bureaucracies. After a lot of time in the field doing hands-on study of neighborhood change efforts, Schorr is enthusiastic and

hopeful for the new comprehensive initiatives in community building and rebuilding.

Schorr (1997) named four elements that she believes give promise to these programs. First, they get beyond individual problems to comprehensive efforts that take in the social, the political, and the economic. Second, the community's own resources and strengths are used as the foundation for designing changes. Third, successful initiatives draw extensively on outside resources, including public and private money, expertise, and new partnerships that bring clout. Fourth, effective initiatives run on one or more possible theories of change that connect programs with desired outcomes. When a community organization makes an overall long-range plan, it seeks to link its mission to specific goals and programs to be carried out in the future. This is the "change theory" process that we have dealt with extensively in this book, particularly in the two planning chapters (Chapters 8 and 9).

Schorr (1997) also laid out conditions that can help to make community building work. These involve access to information about what works, new forms of "nontechnical" technical assistance; connections to far-flung influential people who are able to affect external decisions that influence the neighborhood, and more appropriate and higher levels of funding. She suggested an interesting system of locally based and nationally linked intermediaries to perform the national functions essential to success in the neighborhoods. In her view, all of this is best put in place by a powerful new national public-private partnership. And she warned that this will take a long time to construct before it will begin producing a new brand of flexible, user-friendly services and resource flows.

One extra quality to which Schorr (1997) paid attention is the spiritual. Finding it important to practitioners and volunteers in community undertakings, she reported that religious faith, prayer, trust in a higher power, and healing relationships with faith-based professionals are increasing. Schorr stated, "My own conclusion, after reviewing available evidence, is that it may be easier to establish strong relationships in settings with a spiritual or religious foundation than in secular settings, but faith-based auspices are not the only ones that can cultivate transformative relationships" (p. 17). The sense of being part of a movement that transcends the individual's material needs contributes to success. She cited a foundation officer who believes that "'we should not underestimate the importance of faith as a core value' providing the extra element that makes it possible to persevere in the face of stress and uncertainty" (p. 17).

The distinguished MacArthur fellow William Julius Wilson, in his plea for "a national multiracial political coalition with a broad-based agenda" (Wilson, 1999, p. 4), denoted religious organizations as an important and necessary component in any serious campaign to end social inequality (p. 6). Citing the late Saul Alinsky's still very potent IAF, Wilson suggested that its church-based organizing approach be taken as a model for grassroots coalition building. Wilson argued that the "worldview common to the Catholic clergy, Protestant ministers, and other active practitioners of Judeo-Christian creeds provides a foundation that allows for trust as its starting point" (p. 88).

Wilson (1999) maintained that the religiously oriented leaders of social and ethnic groups can perceive the commonality of their economic and political interests because they share the fundamental belief that all people are "children of God," a common identity starting point for a coalition. He pointed out that the IAF builds a consensual political strategy on the intersection of faith and action, framing issues in a wide context of religious and family issues and being "careful to define issues in race-neutral terms" but in fact addressing issues of race by confronting the problems of the poor and overlooked (pp. 85–91).

Newark's New Community Corporation (NCC) has combined religion and opportunism and is grounded on religious teachings of social justice, according to Schorr (1997). "[The] NCC can adopt and shift as opportunities present themselves without fear of losing its way. Its social justice goals keep it focused" (p. 352). Sister Stanislaus Kennedy, a fabled Irish organizer well known for building her nation's imaginative street-based services for homeless children and youth, touted the link of services to justice:

> If our relationship with our own self is right, then we are at peace with ourselves and in ourselves; and if our relationships with other people and with the world are right, then we have justice. But we can't have right relationships with others unless our relationship with our self is right so we can't have justice without peace. And if our relationship with God is right also, then we have true peace with justice. (Kennedy, 1998, p. 117)

Kennedy also contended, "There is no human person who does not pray, one way or another, whether formally and consciously or simply in experiencing fleeting or more sustained moments of connection with God" (pp. 117–118).

One trap that social service reform at the neighborhood level has to avoid is the pitfall of dependence on what are at best short-term, emergency handout programs. Janet Poppendieck, in her study of emergency food, warned of the allure of quick results. Poppendieck's (1998) book, *Sweet Charity,* made the case that charitable assistance often raises a barrier between "providers and clients" that robs users of their dignity and motivation. She called for advocacy organizing that gives hungry people the training and vision to be capable themselves of pressing for policy changes.

Poppendieck (1998) found inequality to be more pronounced now than at any point since World War II:

> Poor people have lost—have been deprived of—rights to food shelter and income that were theirs twenty years ago. The Personal Responsibility and Work Opportunity Act of 1996 (Welfare to Work) and the end of welfare as we know it are only the culmination of a long, dreary process that has undermined the nation's fragile safety net. The erosion of the value of the minimum wage, a reduction in the purchasing power of public assistance, the decline in job security, and wave after wave of cutbacks in food assistance, housing subsidies, and welfare benefits have reduced the share of income going to the bottom layers of our society, and curtailed the legally enforceable claims that people in need may make upon the collectivity. (pp. 4–5)

We have laid out a few choice useful books. An additional way in which to extract knowledge about the social dimension is to look at the seven principal community case studies in this book to assess their organizational strengths, weaknesses, and missed opportunities on the social front. Such an assessment can be found in Appendix 10.A.

Concerned about the communal aspects of the living place, we have employed the metaphor *fabric* and found that it does advance our understanding, but not so far as we might like. We know that no matter how tight the warp and the woof are locked in, the fabric still can be rent apart by hostility and bias. A responsible renewal organization stays alert to the condition of its fabric. The fabric can be dampened by apartheid, with its handsome texture losing its tension and snap. It can be attacked by downsizing and lose its ability to support the lives of children and their families who depend on it.

But the bright side is that we are not helpless. Through commitment, organizing, and planning, we can together repair and create new tools of progress, take new actions, find new solutions, and extract more resources. Just as the determined people of a community can mobilize to reform their schools, build affordable housing, or preserve wooded open space, they can also enlarge and toughen their social fabric, employ it as a base from which groups can meet, build trust, invest, and fill the holes of vital but missing social services needed to maintain and enliven the minds, bodies, and hearts of themselves and their neighbors. Social strength can be consciously nurtured.

The people of a small community draw their collective strength from the social dimension. They overcome civic apathy to pile up influence and power to help residents find living-wage jobs. They stand together against bias. That is the model for Organizing for Community Controlled Development (OCCD) set forth in this book, and it is one course the American people can follow to freshen and recast their society, starting at home in their own blocks and neighborhoods and working upward on the steps of alliances and coalitions to achieve a national interconnectedness that eventually may let them relax and enjoy the fruits of universal unity and fair play economics.

In Chapter 11, we examine the methods and resources to finance and support community controlled renewal efforts.

SUMMARY

The small place community derives its strength in large part from the willingness of its residents and other stakeholders to relate to each other and do collective work on behalf of the common opportunities and common needs of the place. Much of the thrust of collective effort comes out of the social dimension of the community. This chapter has identified and defined three elements of the social dimension—social fabric, social capital, and social services—that together make up social strength. Each of these three feeds on the others. Sources are suggested for learning more about the three elements and how they can be used for community growth. Maximizing social strength *must* be a core activity of all community efforts and be done from a stance that is proactive and purposeful.

CONTINUING QUESTIONS

1. Can social fabric be consciously created, or is it best left to the serendipitous choices of individuals?

2. Is there enough strength within the social dimension to help reduce the latent racism that seems to lurk in small communities during our time?

3. Are there forms of community activity with visible results through which we can observe the community being strengthened?

4. How far can we go in using dedicated, life-experienced, nonprofessional residents as full-time providers of social services in their own small community?

5. What are the principal qualities needed by a professional organizer seeking to win the trust of oppressed community people and facilitate their building social strength in their small community?

Appendix 10.A
Comments on Building Social Strength in Seven Case Communities: Aliquippa, Bloomfield-Garfield, Dudley Street, Hyde Park-Kenwood, Lyndale, Rollingwood, Valmeyer, and Vandergrift

Aliquippa

Social services were a major concern of the Aliquippa Alliance for Unity and Development (AAUD) from its beginning because family survival was the immediate priority of most of the Pennsylvania town's households after the collapse of the local steel company during the early 1980s. As reported in Chapter 7, human service needs were the subject of town meetings and hearings early on, and the alliance moved swiftly to respond to a rising tide of demands for a one-stop service center. The center was created with donated money and volunteer labor, and demand was found to be several times what had been expected. An indigenous staff was recruited. After 17 years, the Franklin Center continues to serve 1,000 or more families per month.

During the same early period, social fabric was promoted by the AAUD itself with its numerous committees and events, including community festivals, a Santa Claus parade, and eventually an annual arts festival. A great variety of committees and task forces have kept networks of volunteers totaling more than 500 occupied in rebuilding and rejuvenating the community. Gains in social strength have been substantial but always limited by racial walls of separation that have existed in and around the town since its founding. Also, an opportunity never developed has been involvement of users of the Franklin Center in the ongoing volunteer work of the alliance. As members of the organization's cadre often remark, "The Aliquippa Alliance for Unity and Development has paid much more attention to development than to unity."

Bloomfield-Garfield

Traditional social services were left to other organizations in and around Dudley Street. The Bloomfield-Garfield Corporation (BGC) follows a similar program pattern in Pittsburgh. It concentrates on advocacy, community maintenance, housing and other real estate, police protection, participation, special events communications (in the form of its own newspaper), and youth development. But its involvement with social services is through partnerships with hospitals, schools, a branch YMCA, and other existing organizations. There are a few annual celebrations, an arts festival, a summer day for busloads of families at famed Idlewild Park, and other events that help to maintain and enrich social fabric. The one service offered is an extensive, year-round, staffed youth development schedule tied to a rehabilitated church building for indoor programs. The BGC is flexible and opportunistic. If there is an overwhelming crisis demanding attention, as happened with youth when shootings began to occur in the streets during the early 1990s, then the BGC will probably move fast with a large-scale response, as it did with youth development.

Dudley Street

Boston's Dudley Street is an outstanding case of diverse people uniting on a common ground and using advocacy to capture city hall support. It won foundation commitments that were parlayed into a spectacular beginning for renewal of a battered and dumped-on central-city neighborhood. It has been a disciplined effort to stick to the possible and make visible progress in renewing the community. As Schorr (1997) described, social services were left out of the early planning because Dudley Street leaders were "skeptical of becoming involved with human service agencies, which they see as responding only to symptoms" (p. 356). Schorr could not help wondering "whether, despite its impressive victories," the neighborhood had paid "a price in adopting an ideology that limited its ability," during its early years at least, "to engage with the police, the social service system, the education system, the job training system, or economic development to impact more profoundly the lives of neighborhood residents" (p. 356). The DSNI did involve youth directly through the organization's own programs. A Youth Committee designed and painted a large outside wall mural that contained many familiar faces of neighborhood teenagers and younger residents. The committee helped to organize summer recreation on a few of the plentiful vacant lots. There were also Dudley's Young Architects and Planners, a more mature group that participated in early planning activities by community residents and their professional partners. This group contributed drawings and models as participants in the neighborhood's open planning sessions. (A further contribution was a group member who grew up to gain the knowledge and experience to become the DSNI executive director. See page 120.)

Hyde Park-Kenwood

Hyde Park-Kenwood's social strength comes from the historic move made a half century ago when white residents stood up during a crisis time of racial move-ins to say that they would not flee to the Chicago suburbs but rather would stay and try to join arriving black neighbors in building an interracial community of high standards through a community conference. Some 54 years later, the neighborhood, with its University of Chicago base, remains at least biracial but very much gentrified classwise.

Programs during recent years have been directed toward maintenance and renewal aimed at keeping the neighborhood attractive and safe. This means supporting police protection and housing code enforcement as well as monitoring public infrastructure and green spaces to ensure a quality environment. Keeping community residents informed, in part through cooperation with the feisty weekly newspaper (the *Hyde Park Herald*), has always been a major activity. Today, the Hyde Park-Kenwood Community Conference publishes a newsletter, cooperates with a wide array of other organizations, advocates on key public issues, but provides no social service programs. These are left to numerous other experienced agencies in and around the neighborhood. The conference does help them to toot their horns.

Lyndale

In its journey from fear and crime to confidence and revitalization, the Lyndale

Neighborhood Association in Minneapolis combined planning and doing as a unique tactic for moving ahead in a productive and exciting manner. Youth were trained in useful and highly efficient survey work. The method used involved delivery of surveys, call backs, and analysis of the returned surveys under experienced mentors, with immediate follow-up on small actions to demonstrate to residents that their ideas were being heard. The resident responders listed their assets and talents and were quickly called and assigned plan elements. Some formed partnerships to do team projects as tutors, recruiters, or money extractors.

A total of 90 large and small meetings were held throughout the community to create a unified vision, with meeting participants later becoming members of implementation teams to act in human development, safety and crime, housing, economic development, environment, or arts/culture. Start-up funds raised for implementation amounted to $982,000, with the amount eventually rising to approximately $2,500,000, which leveraged additional private and public investments of $67 million, the kind of scale needed by Aliquippa and Bloomfield-Garfield.

Rollingwood

Rollingwood, as described in Chapter 2, is a high-income, overwhelmingly white residential suburb on the outskirts of fast-growing Austin, the Texas state capital. With a total population of 1,403 (according to the 2000 census: 1,282 whites, 69 Hispanics, 32 Asians, 0 African Americans, and 20 others), Rollingwood has its own municipal government. It began as a village in 1955 and officially became a city in 1960. Homes that once brought five-figure prices now sell for $500,000. Its local government informally shares community leadership with the Rollingwood Neighborhood Association (RNA). Neither entity pays its leaders, with volunteering being a way of life in this 1-square-mile suburb. Day-to-day city business is affected at all levels by the flows of direct democracy and citizen participation, with government focusing on the political and the RNA focusing on the social.

Government decides the power issues related to land use, tax rates, and sewer hookups linked to Austin. The RNA provides the city's social fabric through network building, summer barbecues, neighborhood watches, and beautification projects. An RNA veteran observed, "A lot of neighbors are concerned about keeping taxes low while still getting good services. So, we don't say, 'Oh, let's let the city do it and we'll just pay a higher rate.' We go to the nursery and buy plants for the city park and plant them ourselves."

Ryan Kelley, the city manager, described the Rollingwood service system as "personalized." He added, "People come in needing a permit. I sit down with them and explain the procedures, answer their questions, and get them understanding what to do before sending them away to the proper official in Austin or the county. Sometimes it's hands-on, like the time a panicked lady called to say she couldn't turn off her big new sprinkler. We sent the police chief and a park worker to help her" (phone interview, May 8, 2002).

"On bigger issues, city council meetings sometimes draw a crowd. [The] council will sit there until 1 a.m. if necessary to listen to everybody. We can't furnish a big array of services like Austin [can], but we can and do concentrate on a few basics" (R. Kelley, phone interview, May 8, 2002). Kelley pointed out that Rollingwood invests its tax revenues in twice-weekly garbage collection and a seven-person police force. "An Austin neighborhood with our size population would be lucky to have the services of two officers," he emphasized.

Susan Welker, a resident who was president of the RNA in 2001, praised the willingness of residents to give their time and talent to civic issues and community events. "Events draw plenty of volunteer helpers, and city council elections achieve close to a 100% turn-out of registered voters" (phone interview, May 8, 2002).

Welker admitted that among all of the openness, elbow rubbing, and events organizing, she has encountered some friction, but she insisted that in her working with fellow residents she has found them to be mostly civil and generous. Paid membership for 2001 was 117 of the 400-plus households, with some families volunteering for activities without ever bothering to join. Because there are no paid staff members, $10 dues income is adequate.

Welker helped the neighborhood association to expand its resident relationship-building program so as to include multi-house garage sales, a Valentine Day ice cream social, and "Halloween Safe Stops," with the latter being card tables set up on street corners on Halloween night with lit candles and a friendly adult handing out glow-in-the-dark necklaces, ready to assist any child who is lost, frightened, or otherwise needing assistance. Welker started an RNA newsletter, which came out "about every other month or so" during her year as leader. She found it to be a boon for keeping residents connected.

Welker spoke with pride of other leadership thrusts she has been involved in, including the evening of September 11, 2001, when there was an RNA meeting scheduled. She and her leadership decided to go ahead with the meeting despite the terrorist attacks on the United States earlier in the day. Moving it to city hall, they made it an outlet for feelings about the morning's attacks. "It gave us a sense of bonding and set a direction for the community, which has given strong support to the nation and its leaders" (phone interview, May 8, 2002).

At another time, in a rare move, the RNA endorsed Welker in testifying at a council meeting on a volatile political issue involving the hours that a newly arriving Albertson's grocery could stay open. Albertson's wanted to stay open 24 hours a day, while the community wanted an early evening closing. Welker joined forthrightly in speaking out at the contentious proceedings, which eventually led to a 10 p.m. compromise. "We could get into this one," said Welker, "because we were opposing outsiders with a united community behind us. For most issues, the community is split and we have to stay out" (phone interview, May 8, 2002).

On the political front, this small community has widespread civil and civic activity. With its unemployment rate of less than 1%, it suffers minimal job insecurity. But on the social front, with diversity rising, there appear to be chores yet to be planned and implemented. For instance, Welker commented that the local police seemed especially diligent in watching black drivers when they are using Rollingwood streets. Rollingwood is not a gated community, although a council member has introduced an ordinance to control the length of cut grass, which is reminiscent of a privately controlled community. People with money and credit are free to buy and move in. Constant change is a certainty here, as in most communities. This community's high level of participation will likely serve it well as change challenges it in the future.

Valmeyer

In the Valmeyer case, where a whole Illinois town relocates itself to high ground away from the flood plain, the relocating residents are interested more in bread, butter, and bricks-and-mortar matters than in social services. Residents do provide locations for replacement churches and a public school, but they otherwise appear to depend on outside sources to take care of their social needs. It would appear that households sheltering a total of only 500 people were not a critical mass that had to think about their own services beyond what the churches could furnish in emergency situations. They did plan a few hangouts that could generate interacting, and they recognized the gap left by their inability to attract a replacement general store, which had been the old town's center for "rubbing elbows." Perhaps the gap could provide the opportunity for launching a self-developed co-op store run by residents.

Vandergrift

Steelmaker George G. McMurtry "dreamed of a town where his steel workers could govern themselves, own their own homes, teach their own children, and worship in their own churches. In a time when most steel towns were nothing more than a cluster of ramshackle homes along muddy streets, McMurtry was planning a monument to Victorian architecture and modern landscaping ideals. [The] dream became a reality in 1895 when the town of Vandergrift was born" (Laero, 1996, pp. xxiii–xxv). So wrote Pastor James E. Laero of Bethal Family Church for the 1995 Vandergrift Centennial. Vandergrift, Pennsylvania, prospered until the collapse of the steel industry during the early 1980s, when the town's mill closed. Through the leadership of two town

volunteers, a modest resurgence has occurred over the past 20 years.

First came Sheila Mendicino—a housewife, mother, and counselor—during the 1980s to recruit a cadre out of St. Gertrude's Church and undertake a full-blown study that included a sample survey of households and town leaders.

Results were presented at a town meeting, which led to volunteer committees organizing a senior transportation system, meals on wheels, stepped-up public safety directed at drugs and vandalism, and a nascent history project. The results brought in agencies to provide job training and to help secure tenants for closed storefronts. Supports for a growing senior population and restless teens brought stability to the town.

During the 1990s, volunteer Eugene Iaghemma, high school teacher, led development of the Victorian Vandergrift Museum and Historical Society and eventually the Casino Theatre Restoration and Management Inc., which exploited the town's history as a pioneering planned industrial community with a significant design embracing curvilinear streets and a central village green fitted into the contours of a hilly site.

Hundreds became involved in the history effort, capped by the restoration of the shabby old Casino Theatre, once the jewel of the central village green in downtown Vandergrift. It now has year-round programs of stage shows, town meetings, and a variety of other public events. Historic marches, celebrations, publications, exhibits in the theater's museum, and community dinners have increasingly made the town's history visible. Shared history has been used to protect and grow the town's fabric.

References

Ahlbrandt, R. S. (1984). *Neighborhoods, people, and community.* New York: Plenum.

Ahlbrandt, R. S., & Cunningham, J. (1979). *A new public policy for neighborhood preservation.* New York: Praeger.

Coleman, J. S. (1988). Social capital in the creation of human capital. *American Journal of Sociology, 94*(Suppl.), S95–S120.

Fabricant, M. B., & Fisher, R. (2002). *Settlement houses under siege: The struggle to sustain community organizations in New York City.* New York: Columbia University Press.

Ginsberg, S. (2000, January 2). Town rebuilds its racial walls. *Pittsburgh Post-Gazette,* p. A22. (Reprinted from *The Washington Post*)

Grogan, P., & Proscio, T. (2000) *Comeback cities: A blueprint for urban neighborhood revival.* Boulder, CO: Westview.

Halpern, R. (1995). *Rebuilding the inner city: A history of neighborhood initiatives to address poverty in the United States.* New York: Columbia University Press.

Jacobs, J. (1961). *The death and life of great American cities.* New York: Vintage Books.

Kennedy, S. (1998). *Now is the time: Spiritual reflections.* Dublin, Ireland: Town House.

Kretzmann, J., & McKnight, J. (1993). *Building communities from the inside out: A pathway toward finding and mobilizing a community's assets.* Evanston, IL: Northwestern University, Center for Urban Affairs and Policy Research.

Laero, J. (1996). Introduction. In K. Blose (main author) et al., *Something better than the best.* Vandergrift, PA: Victorian Vandergrift Museum and Historical Society.

Lang, R. E., & Hornburg, S. P. (1998). What is social capital and why is it important to public policy? *Housing Policy Debate, 9*(1), 1–16.

McKnight, J. (1995). *The careless society: Community and its counterfeits.* New York: Basic Books.

Midgley, J., & Livermore, M. (1998). Social capital and local economic development: Implications for community social work practice. In M. S. Sherraden & W. A. Ninacs (Eds.), *Community economic development and social work* (pp. 29–40). New York: Haworth.

Poppendieck, J. (1998). *Sweet charity.* New York: Penguin Books.

Putnam, R. D. (1993a). *Making democracy work: Civic traditions in modern Italy.* Princeton, NJ: Princeton University Press.

Putnam, R. D. (1993b, Spring). The prosperous community: Social capital and public life. *The American Prospect,* pp. 35–42.

Putnam, R. D. (1995, January). Bowling alone: America's declining social capital. *Journal of Democracy, 6*(1), 65–78.

Rimer, S. (1999, November 7). Joined at the stoop: Neighbors till the end. *The New York Times* (national ed.), pp. 1, 32.

Schorr, L. (1997). *Common purpose: Strengthening families and neighborhoods to rebuild America.* New York: Anchor Books.

Warren, M. (2001). *Dry bones rattling: Community building to revitalize American democracy.* Princeton, NJ: Princeton University Press.

Wilson, W. J. (1999). *The bridge over the racial divide: Rising inequality and coalition politics.* Berkeley: University of California Press.

11

TAPPING ESSENTIAL RESOURCES

This chapter concentrates on the all-important flows of money and other resources that a community effort must obtain to make renewal happen, including funds donated both from inside and outside the neighborhood. Suggested here particularly are methods for securing discretionary, unrestricted, and renewable revenues—the kind that bear the givers' personal stamp of "we care." This chapter builds on the brief description of resource tapping found in Chapter 5, where such work was viewed as 1 of the 12 essential activities of community organizing. It also builds on the real-life experiences found in case studies set out in the previous chapters.

America is a generous society. Individuals and private institutions now give more than $200 billion annually to every type of cause (AAFRC Trust for Philanthropy, 2002). Three quarters of the money comes from individuals, who historically are the most stable givers, little affected by recessions. Another 12% of giving comes from foundations, and 5% comes from corporations. This array of givers, plus potential givers not yet effectively tapped, is open to all small communities willing to compete. There are whole books written on the seeking of resources. In this chapter, we mention and recommend a few of the most useful ones.

We affirm the following as key ways and means in which to secure resources. Face-to-face asking is the most productive way in which to tap into support. The serious committee volunteer or board member prepares for a first contact by making sure that he or she can articulate the group's goals after learning about the priorities and relevant connection of the prospective donor (whether an individual or an organization). Respected volunteers, who have been trained to be attentive listeners, often make the best solicitors. Such volunteers always take the time to learn how their organization's need for money might be linked to an interest of the funder (e.g., both might have a concern for children or for job creation through home-based enterprises). Moreover, often when a volunteer solicitor discusses expected benefits of a proposed program, the spotlight should be on the community's people or even on the donor, not on the organization seeking the funds. When approaching outsiders, the cause of community building is what counts, not the enhancement of the organization promoting its cause. Continued strengthening of the organization and securing operating funds is crucial, but the most effective way in which to gain donor support is through highlighting programs, initiatives, and outcomes. Effective volunteers are prepared to cite specific programs and opportunities and build a case for potential results such as the safe attractive streets and brighter children that can result from donor investment. The first people to be asked should be the officers and other cadre members of the asking organization. Resource tapping has more credibility when the leaders of the asking organizations are known to be contributing, no matter how little they are able to give. A foundation is always impressed by donations coming from program beneficiaries such as community residents, local shopkeepers, and any neighborhood organizational partners who put money on the table.

Opening up and maintaining resource flows is rewarding organizational work that can begin as soon as the first volunteer recruits are pulled together to consider starting an organization, whether it is to be an association of individuals or a coalition of existing groups. Immediately, the hat can be passed to pay for sending out future meeting notices and for coffee and bagels. Then, the giving can build upward from the initial members. Names of all givers should be recorded from the beginning on a donor list, which can be continuously added to and periodically used for solicitation. Klein (2002) reported that "mailings to current donors are getting returns of 10% or better" (p. 5). Fund-raising is work that grows as the organization grows. It is related to both building the organization base and achieving the organization's goals. In fact, the vigor of the resource flows in large measure determines the vigor of the organization. Tapping resources is creative work that instills dedication and builds competency in the leaders, staff, and volunteers who do it.

Resources are money, people, goods, and services. *Tapping* means obtaining these for free. Money is the most flexible and useful resource and is the most common type of outside contribution. Its universal acceptance as a medium of exchange makes it the most desirable one. But one must keep in mind the usefulness of many noncash resources such as shares of stock, vans, office furniture, and professional guidance (e.g., an expert's help with mailing list construction, public relations, financial accounting, or legal matters).

In creating (or renewing) an organization, we can tap volunteers from the beginning to have fresh energy and test the drawing power of the vision. The organization seeks enough volunteers so that there are a few special ones who plunge in extra deeply, take hold with tenacity, and make a commitment of daily participation. As explained in Chapter 5, these special volunteers become the cadre members who assume responsibility for making sure that meetings are held, planning is done, and plans are implemented, including the tapping of resources. They exemplify the *people* resource. But all who give or lend their talents in any way,

whether short term or long term, also constitute this resource. A lawyer who donates 6 hours of time to aid the organization in obtaining its nonprofit charter and Internal Revenue Service (IRS) tax exemption letter and a musician who plays the accordion gratis at fund-raising events are people resources, as are an array of others who contribute time and talent, no matter how humble the talent.

Useful goods are always a resource. If a friendly institution or firm supplies six functioning "pre-owned" computers for the organization's start-up office, if volunteers make organizational calls endlessly from their home telephones without reimbursement, and if a local hospital or church furnishes meeting space complete with coffee regularly and without charge, then the organization is tapping into *goods* resources. And if a local copy shop prints the two-page newsletter free of charge each month, then that is a *service* resource.

People, goods, and services can be valuable but sometimes are clumsy to match with specific organizational needs. Whenever accepted, they can be given a monetary value and sometimes are counted as matching funds for a grant. However, money, particularly discretionary money, is always the most valuable and appreciated resource. Its flexibility moves the organization's machinery with superior ease.

A small community renewal group with a respected growth record early on usually creates a finance committee with a connected resource development team as part of the organization's permanent structure. This committee-team combination would be responsible for the activities already mentioned in this chapter. The finance committee assists the staff and board members in making and holding to a budget while keeping the development team guided and encouraged in finding the funds required to implement the organization's plans. Together, the committee and team ensure that the organization has sufficient resources to carry forward its plans and achieve its objectives. In some organizations, separate but equal committees that work closely together undertake the finance and fund-raising functions. In some small organizations, especially new ones, the two functions may originate as a single entity.

Required for the finance committee are two or three committed leader types from the central cadre, at least one of whom is a board member. This is important because financial planning and fund-raising often involve policy matters. There is much to be gained from having an understanding banker, accountant, or lawyer on the finance committee if that is possible. But not all three are needed; one is enough. Both committee and team can benefit from well-connected and deeply loyal outsiders to broaden the universe of contacts.

The finance committee should be a wise and dedicated crew that helps to bring stability and influence to the organization. The allied resource development team requires people of energy who know what they are talking about and exude hope. The team's membership likely rotates in accord with the scale and objectives of each campaign undertaken. As the size and complexity of the finance, budgeting, and fund-raising grow, finance and resource development leaders (and often members) should have significant experience, knowledge, and hard-learned understanding of what is involved and what needs to be done.

Wise words on the kind of persons needed for finance and fund-raising work came down to us from Harold J. Seymour, a high-stepping resource wizard out of a rebellious and creative decade. With Seymour (1966), pride of association came first for both volunteers and any staff involved. He defined pride as strong motivation for supporting both cause and organization:

> Pride is nurtured by communication and ceremonial. But the one thing that triggers it into action better then anything else is actual participation in program. . . . This involves consistant attendence at meaningful meetings and stated sevices. . . . It involves acceptence of real responsibility for committee work. (pp. 6–7)

In other words, there is no place here for those with a tentative or nervous commitment.

Seymour's (1966) central thesis was that a cause for which big money is sought requires relevance, importance, and urgency:

- A cause is *relevant* when it is a major public need or problem of the day, affecting the personal interests, loyalties, and concerns of a large body of people.

- A cause is *important* when it is recognized as such in its own field and within its own sphere of influence.
- A cause is *urgent* when it establishes and maintains a public image of crisis within a mood that tolerates no talk of compromise or costly delay.

An example might be the following. A sudden epidemic of teenage suicide strikes neighborhoods across a metropolitan region, affecting urban and suburban communities and school districts (i.e., relevance). Fear and sorrow provoke pleas by parents, churches, mayors, and teenagers themselves for gatherings where teenagers and community leaders talk it out and launch actions of reconciliation and healing (i.e., importance). Media attention multiplies as local gatherings draw together youth, school leadership, and nationally recognized professionals for frank and open expressions of feelings, experiences, and insights (i.e., urgency).

The proposals, communications, and negotiations that go into obtaining resources are high-order operations. The volunteer officers and members leading these operations need to be especially reliable people who are certain of what they are doing. And they should always have the personal support and involvement of the heads of the board and staff. The work of the finance committee and development team (whether separate or merged) should provide a steady rising stream of resources for the base operation and for the specific projects and programs the organization decides to undertake. All of those concerned with resources should be given recognition for their work in the meetings and publications of the organization.

This team will need to be conscious of flows of incoming resources from both internal and external sources. Although the reality is that resources for reviving a distressed community must come heavily from the outside, every community has internal resources, will grow stronger as it draws on its own supporters, and will gain more attention and help from the outside when it maximizes the use of inside resources. Funders do respect self-help.

Consider firms, institutions, foundations, governments, and individuals of all income levels (both internal and external) as targets that have a stake in the campaign. Keep the results out-front to inspire and keep pressure on potential givers. Large givers are impressed with well-kept finance records that can be shown to help control expenses. They expect applicant organizations to submit neatly prepared reports and other required documents on time.

Besides keeping the top leaders of the organization visible and active in negotiating with the gatekeepers to money, goods, and services that might be extracted from inside and outside the distressed community, there are other healthy practices for the committee and team to follow:

- The organization should continually seek to broaden the sources of funding. A variety of sources helps to avoid dependence and reduces the threat of sudden gaps of funding that can paralyze and slow down an organization. Pauline Cooper, an executive director of the Aliquippa Alliance for Unity and Development (AAUD) in Pennsylvania during the 1990s, moved quickly to diversify sources soon after she became director. Her sources included philanthropic foundations; local, county, state, and national governments; staged events; earned real estate rents and fees; and annual mail appeals to an ever-growing mailing list (personal interview, February 2002). A diverse resource base that includes unrestricted funds also enables an organization to take on tough issues that funders will not or cannot support.
- The organization's vision of a restored and renewed community should be linked to a donor's mission in clear and hopeful terms. The vision pursued should be pictured as able to speak a refreshed regional environment. The potency of the community organizing-economic development combination in use should be emphasized. Donors should be told how their money is to be spent. They should be driven through the community and shown concrete achievements, stopping at the homes, shops, and offices of cadre members and other volunteers so that donors can hear the dreams spelled out directly by community people who are beneficiaries of programs.
- Personal contacts should be established with all funders so that they can be asked directly

face to face. Asking face to face is better than asking by telephone, asking by telephone is better than using a handwritten note, using a handwritten note is better than mass mailing, and so on. Personal fund-raising always does best.

- The organization should realize that the resources are out there. Fully 85% of Americans give to one or more charitable organizations. Religion receives the largest share. Every small community and region in America has generous contributors (both large and small) and many potential givers who have not yet been reached with an inspiring vision. They have to be shown a transformation that interests and excites them, and they have to be directly asked to support it. Many donors give simply because they are asked; this is the most basic rule to learn first—to ask well.
- A financial team that is serious operates with a plan and a time schedule, both of which are formulated openly within the community.
- The organization should spend time learning about the interests, history, and relationships with other organizations of potential donors and finding ways in which the donors' concerns can dovetail with those of the organization so that both the organization and the donors gain from their investments.
- An event that loses money can be turned into an asset through an assessment that reveals how mistakes can be avoided in the future.
- Even if an organization is able to hire a staff person for fund-raising, the responsibility remains with the board. Staff members are only for facilitation.
- Transforming donors into grassroots fund-raisers is a solid path to expanding income, according to Melissa Bangs of the Share Foundation: Building a New El Salvador, whose organization has showed how to do it. Her organization's donors have proved to be seekers whose own commitment makes them especially credible when they ask (Bangs, 2002).
- A small organization that lacks monetary power can still have people power, and people power can often persuade funders to change. Confident seekers can count for as much as concrete goals laid out.
- Successful fund-raising locks in enthusiastic volunteers and empowers them as well. The

AAUD persuaded the National Equity Fund (NEF) to send a representative to Aliquippa and changed the NEF's "no" to a "yes." The NEF (2002) now boasts that it is the nation's largest nonprofit syndication of low-income credits, with $3 billion to help finance 50,000 affordable homes.

- Resource tapping often is more connections than cause—but not always.
- The organization should find a way in which to get potential donors involved—asking for their advice, getting them to take slots on the committee, putting them in the next parade, and so on.
- Funders' refusal to pay for community organizing efforts can be challenged. If funders want the organization to be strong and self-reliant, then the organization should show them how such power can come only from organizing.

There is a historic difficulty in obtaining foundation money for community organizing and a comparative ease in obtaining foundation money for community economic development. Many potential givers have to be sold on the extra potency of the comprehensive approach that integrates power organizing with development. Articulate residents can best make successful pitches. The ability to sustain a rising budget over time breeds self-confidence in members and respect from outsiders.

A special resource of value to organizations is a well-invested reserve fund of reasonable size that provides a quick source of funds when high-potency opportunities arise. A prudent organization limits use of the fund to projects that will advance the organization's plan. Outside funders seldom give for this purpose, but as the organization builds streams of income from its own grassroots campaigns, it can build its own reserve fund and thereby increase its autonomy and independence.

As mentioned earlier in this chapter, there is a massive literature on resource gathering. We mention and recommend next four of the most useful publications that, along with the other material in the chapter, can give the reader a beginning operating knowledge of resource tapping.

FOUR USEFUL PUBLICATIONS

These are four publications widely used and acclaimed. Two come out of practitioner experience and emphasize grassroots fund-raising. One comes from a major corporate funder, supplying handy guidance for tapping into all kinds of cash and noncash "stuff." And one arises out of the national academic-government-large foundation grant triangle. These publications are helpful for making resource-raising teams more effective. They are also recommended for use in training new volunteers.

It was noted in Chapter 5 that a good organizer has a foot on each of the twin pedals of building the organization and achieving the community's goals. Grassroots fund-raising is a means of advancing toward these two ends simultaneously. Local small community-generated funding is as much recruitment, participation, and leadership development as it is program implementation. It is ordinary people building their own strength. By its very nature, it is people-to-people work. It is money that is internally extracted and internally controlled. This brings to the organization an extra dimension of independence, an additional modicum of self-sufficiency, and a slightly more reliable financial base. This way of raising money is rooted in Arnstein's participation tradition, as laid out in Chapter 6. It provides a more secure and independent base from which the small place community may push ahead freely with organizing community controlled development.

Joan Flanagan's classic, *The Grass Roots Fundraising Book,* is biased toward money generated from inside an organization and its community. Flanagan (1995) outlines an argument against exclusive reliance on external grants to keep an organization afloat, cheering for dues and pledges from members and believers. Her thesis is simple but not simplistic, persuasive but not pushy. Her book, written in an earthy style, is a manual of what, why, and how of bottom-up fund-raising.

Flanagan (1995) shows how grassroots giving leads to more committed members, better leaders, a successful organization, and greater self-sufficiency. To Flanagan, money raised from members, friends, and community residents is the best kind—discretionary. She emphasizes,

"Never underestimate the moral advantage of raising your own money" (pp. 2–3).

Grassroots fund-raising is a little like dating. It demands that one person ask another for something desired. It involves appealing to another's self-interest, and the outcome is likely to be successful when the appeal is made personal. It takes courage to ask. Success makes people feel good about themselves. Often, the fear of rejection turns people away from taking the step of asking, but failure to ask can waste an opportunity. And, like dating, fund-raising can be fun. The comparison stops there.

Fund-raising, of whatever kind, does not just happen. It flows from an organization's direction and planning, calling for courage, no small amount of persistence, and lots of sheer elbow grease. The time and effort to prepare pays off handsomely. Flanagan shows how smart plan making gives the organization credibility and status while opening opportunities for new people to enter the fold and exercise skills of leadership and organizing.

Most community organizations rely on sources of funding outside themselves, with governments and foundations (both family and corporate) being the principal sources. In addition, a growing number of intermediary organizations accumulate money from business and public sources and distribute it (along with technical assistance) to local community groups. (Profiles of two intermediaries in Portland, Oregon, can be found later in this chapter.) The money obtained through these sources is then added to money raised by the grassroots members. With the contraction of government and the increase in nonprofit groups trying to extract foundation money, community organizations will increasingly have to turn inward to find the money that ensures viability.

Grassroots fund-raising does not confine an organization to its own members. It can also include raising money from the general public. This form of fund-raising helps an organization to increase the amount of money and members available to it, but more significantly, it provides public attention. It is a useful recruitment tool because it involves tangible commitment. The accompanying sidebar on Kiltimaugh illustrates grassroots fund-raising at its best.

The Kiltimaugh Renewal:
A Case Study of Residents Opening Their Wallets

Kiltimaugh is a miniature community in western Ireland that fell into a swamp of economic depression during the 1980s and pulled itself out, largely with its own money, during the 1990s. John Higgins, the organizer who facilitated this residents' triumph, described the pitch of the door-knocking volunteers challenging their neighbors as follows: "Would you not think that to save Kiltimaugh is worth giving the price of two pints of Guinness per week?" (Higgins, 1996, p. 159).

The Kiltimaugh community of 2,500 awoke to its misfortune, much as Aliquippa did, when a major manufacturing plant closed, and student researchers reported that youth were emigrating in droves. By 1990, 40% of the structures of its once proud main street lay derelict, much as had Aliquippa's 10 years earlier. Both towns found their misfortunes widely publicized in the national press. A further similarity is that Kiltimaugh was located a 20-minute drive from a major airport but lacked the power ties with government to make an economic connection. In the language of west Ireland, Kiltimaugh was a "tombstone village."

As in Aliquippa, concerned Kiltimaugh people realized that government was not going to rescue them from their misery, leading them also to a self-help direction. Among the assets that built Kiltimaugh confidence was a history of intense community spirit linked to enthusiasm for sports and the arts as well as generosity toward the poor. Kiltimaugh people took pride in their place and quickly began work on a prospectus for overcoming their ill fortune—a wish list of resources and actions to fill up their idle shops and put their jobless to work.

Then, a major difference showed up between the two communities in their method for tapping resources. Without waiting for good deeds and visible achievements to point to, Kiltimaugh mobilized 20 energetic "collectors" to take the new prospectus into homes to ask wage earners to sign pledges of 2½ punts (the former currency of Ireland, the equivalent of about U.S. $3.25) per week for operating and investment funds. Letters were sent to émigrés all over the world offering them the opportunity to assist in the rebirth of their native community.

Within 4 years, the campaign was to bring in 111,000 punts (the equivalent of about U.S. $150,000), which became the resource base for leveraging millions more. Kiltimaugh people spoke with their wallets, provoking respect and support from government, business, and institutions. Response was widespread and diverse, although the people keeping the campaign fresh and moving were the usual small, dedicated core cadre that one finds engaged in every successful community renewal effort.

Higgins (1996) seemed to differ with the broad involvement theme of this book, stating, "Nothing will happen . . . if we go overboard on democracy and wait for maximum participation. Experience shows that a handful of people will eventually be the workers to undertake the projects and see the plan to completion" (pp. 153–154), later adding, "You can go to your community selling nothing more than hope, provided that you have a credible group of people with a credible and cohesive argument" (p. 160). In fact, Higgins and his crew of residents did get maximum participation of a sort through the diverse and extensive mass of people, most with limited means, who put out their 2½ punts every week. But his words do give us an excellent working definition of the essential cadre component of community organizing.

"IRD Kiltimaugh Ltd.," the CDC formed early in the effort, set its mission as "to develop the economic potential of Kiltimaugh and environs to its fullest". It proceeded through committees to set priorities, broker with lenders, hunt out investors, guide new ventures, lobby government for infrastructure, and initiate partnerships with other groups to carry out hosts of development activities. Its ownership of the nonprofit company whose assets jumped from zero to more than a half million punts in 4 years buoyed people of the community. One priority was to maximize flows of money into the community. Toward that end, the CDC organized the remaining merchants, and new ones who opened shops, to give tokens to customers (one token for every 5 punts spent), with each token being a ticket for a weekly lottery offering substantial prizes, leading to an annual culmination drawing for a new automobile. Through quality cultural and artistic programs rooted in Kiltimaugh tradition, the CDC began to bring in flows of art lovers and tourists to enjoy the feel of what became an "artisan village." Human service needs were met with a variety of supports.

During the first 5 years, bank activity shot up by 50%, a hotel was constructed, new shops opened, the town's beautiful old streetscape was restored, and the investments of the residents were multiplied. Media exposure spread the Kiltimaugh story throughout Ireland and onto the continent.

For the future, the organization and its citizen owners aim to continue raising 32,000 Euro per year as their own share of an investment that must be at least 250,000 Euro annually to keep pace with the promise of the prospectus. (As of January 1, 2002, Ireland's currency changed to the Euro.)

The conclusion of the Higgins (1996) report was that achievement and new hope come from marrying community endeavor and goodwill with professional expertise. The Kiltimaugh experience also confirmed the confidence and force that come to a community that is firm and systematic in drawing resources from itself. More people involved in the process means more in results.

> Grassroots fund-raising is an inward-looking funding tactic. The political benefits of this are less obvious than the financial ones. In any given organization, the fund-raisers are power holders. Thus, if ordinary people in the community are to control their destiny, then they must play a role in raising money. By so doing, this can simultaneously raise their sights, heads, and goals. There is no denying that money empowers.

The second of the recommended publications has been developed over 15 years by Pittsburgh's Mellon Financial Corporation (2000), whose community affairs division has been supporting small community survival and renewal efforts for many decades, as the case study on Aliquippa in Chapter 7 documented in detail. The latest edition of the Mellon guide for nonprofits is titled *Discover Total Resources*. The bank describes its 54-page booklet as "neither a textbook nor a directory." It is rather a descriptive checklist to be used as a guide, or self-audit, by staff, board members, and volunteers to assess the degree to which they are tapping a full range of community resources—people, money, goods, and services (p. 1). More than 400,000 copies of the booklet have been distributed. It is now available on the Web (www.mellon.com/communityaffairs/guide.html).

This Mellon guide follows a rational corporate approach, with a Seymour-like reminder to "determine who you are, where you want to be, and what you need to get there" before approaching any potential donors (Mellon Financial Corporation, 2000, p. 2). Mellon suggests a long-range resource plan that is reassessed regularly. "A healthy organization continually reviews program goals in light of available resources and other external factors. It is this ability to *adapt resources* to needs that distinguishes the *successful*" (p. 3, italics in original).

This publication is particularly helpful in four areas. First is its emphasis on nonprofit groups drawing on their own organizational families, making sure that they offer every opportunity to members, supporters, and residents of the community to participate in funding local programs, events, and services while at the same time explaining how these local dollars help to strengthen the community (Mellon Financial Corporation, 2000). An aid to doing this that is suggested is the "contributor choice" program of United Way, which can be used by employed persons of the community to make regular contributions to any recognized nonprofit of their choice through payroll deductions. Second, this booklet goes beyond money to people resources, providing ideas for obtaining loaned experts from corporations and institutions, college interns with appropriate skills, and diverse types of volunteers with useful and varied experiences and talents, with the added advice, "Have fun! People will volunteer more if they enjoy the experience" (p. 8). There are do's and don'ts on the art of obtaining pro bono services of loaned executives, and Mellon recommends making a strong written case on the need for them. "List all the ways your organization helps a corporation. Also, list all the ways their executives can help your organization" (p. 9). The guide also advises on getting the best from interns: "Assign them specific work projects, rather than general duties. Projects are easier to manage and evaluate and [are] more meaningful to the interns" (p. 10).

Third, there is considerable insider information for getting at more difficult and less known resources, including bequests, endowments, bank trusts, and low-cost loans known as "program-related investments" from national foundations and from some "hidden" sources of goods and services.

The Mellon guide reveals that phone calls and visits to bank trust officers can result in listings of little-noticed trust funds and the eligibility requirements for tapping them (Mellon Financial Corporation, 2000, p. 28). It also suggests that if an organization produces a grant proposal that it believes is unique or of possible national significance, the proposal should be sent without hesitation to a major national funding source.

The guide gives tips for follow-up after a proposal has been submitted, including acknowledging a rejection with a "thanks for the consideration" note (there may be a "next time") (p. 31).

Mellon places a heavy emphasis on people as the prime resource and supplies several ideas for obtaining noncash goods and services. Listed for looking into are the used and surplus goods of corporations, discounted new products, cooperative purchases involving joint use of equipment, and systems for bartering services among organizations.

Fourth is an array of techniques. The Mellon guide reports that funders have a growing respect for partnerships and tend to favor organizations that demonstrate talent for finding partners and using them to make themselves more efficient.

The Mellon guide advises giving each event and project of an organization its own budget to ensure that attention is given to finding the money and to make it easier to conduct a cost-benefit assessment of each program piece to make sure it is worth keeping. Nonprofits are advised to get rid of events that constantly lose money or that bring too little return for the effort. (Of course, there is always the event with special impact or significance that is worth keeping in spite of its losing money.) A final Mellon admonition offered is a reminder not to forget to include "people enjoyment" in the planning.

The third published source that has stood the test of time is a guide to preparing major grant proposals, *Getting Funded,* by Mary Hall. This is for the growing organization that has made its mark locally and needs a large amount of additional money to take advantage of a promising and significant opportunity or to expand the testing of an innovation that has already proved to be productive (Hall, 1988). Hall is a distinguished educator and foundation executive with experience in both the public and private sectors, largely in the northwestern United States.

While the Flanagan (1995) book is helpful in building a resource-seeking effort that is diverse, lively, and participative, and while the Mellon Financial Corporation (2000) guide aids us in being diverse, pragmatic, and definitive, Hall (1988) shows us the rigorous path to the larger, focused, multi-year grants of foundations

and the U.S. government. While the first two publications lean to tactics, Hall's is more strategic with a longer range perspective.

Hall provides useful checklists, with the sobering thought that the preparation time required for a major grant might be a full year of research and decision making. She stresses the importance of questions such as the following. What comparative advantage can the organization bring to the proposed project? Does the organization have the resources of time and money to create a competent proposal and then to pursue its funding to the end? Each of Hall's 14 sections has a set of questions to challenge the proposal writer, and she provides thoughts on how to create proposal ideas, define purpose, integrate evaluation, lay out a budget, and make the submission. Hall's technical details on budget preparation are especially useful.

Hall's theme is that a winning proposal is the product of a process that takes advantage of all potentially helpful collaborators after a careful and deliberate decision has been made that obtaining a grant is desirable and feasible. She is persistent in pressing the importance of quality data gathering and in taking time to build a force of partners who will become actively involved in advocating for the proposal. Along the way, she cautions that great care must be taken to make sure that the proposal makes a strong case for the worth and high priority of its central idea.

An organization giving adequate attention to demonstrating its ability to perform is another message conveyed by Hall. She suggests careful documenting of past successes. And she adds that an experienced professional, other than one of the proposal's authors, should edit a completed proposal. Hall believes that a proposal should largely stand on its own merits and should be submitted only with the support letters that are required. She discourages large numbers of marginal support letters from friends who are not involved in the proposed project.

Another clearly written guide arising out of local experience comes from Kim Klein, whose *Fundraising for Social Change* is known for its excellent chapters on direct mail, planned giving (including endowments), telephone solicitation, major gift campaigns, dealing with anxiety, and raising money in rural areas. Klein's (2001a) fundamental themes that come through are that if organizations want money, then they have to ask for it, and if organizations systematically ask enough people, then they will get it. The latter can relieve much anxiety, she has found.

Klein is a long-time continuous student of fund-raising. In addition to her books and frequent articles, she publishes the national *Grassroots Fundraising Journal,* a six-times-a-year update on the field, now in its 20th year.

The fourth edition of Klein's (2001a) book, *Fundraising for Social Change,* cleared up the misconception that most nonprofit funding comes from corporations and foundations in the private sector. Klein reported,

> Most charitable dollars come from government programs. The fact holds true despite the extensive cutbacks in government funding of nonprofits that characterized the 1980s and early 1990s. . . . Following government dollars, more money is given to nonprofit organizations by individuals than by any other source, including corporations and foundations combined. (p. 6)

Klein's book focused almost entirely on how to raise money from the enormous market of individual donors.

As stated before, private individuals and organizations now give more than $200 billion to nonprofits annually, with most of it coming from individuals, 10% from foundations, and the remaining 6% coming from corporations. (We note that religious organizations receive the bulk of individual donations, with most making "asks" each and every week.) Many foundations receive perhaps 100 proposals for every 2 grants they hand out, and in general, most of their grants are given only for short-term projects or programs. More that 1.1 million organizations have IRS letters of designation making them eligible to apply for grants. Klein (2001a) pointed out, "Several million more small, grassroots organizations doing important charitable works are not registered—new start-ups, organizations that use little money such as neighborhood block clubs, organizations that come together for a one-time purpose such as cleaning up a vacant lot or protesting something" (p. 5).

Klein (2001a) noted that 82% of the money donated by individuals is given away by people living in families with incomes of less than $60,000. Poor and working-class people tend to give away more money as a percentage of their incomes than do upper middle-class and wealthy people, probably because the need is so much clearer to them (pp. 5–9). She concluded,

> A broad base of individual donors provides the only reliable source of funding for a nonprofit year in and year out. The growth of individual donations to an organization is critical to its growth and self-sufficiency. Further, relying on a broad base of individuals for support increases an organization's ability to be self-determining. (p. 9)

Klein (1999) has also done some thinking about the especially important question of how to keep funding operations fresh and productive. She compares fund-raising to a car in that both need care. "The trick is to anticipate wear and tear and deal with it before damage is done" (p. 9). She finds that too many fund-raisers get tired of the routine and start taking shortcuts that ruin their effort. Her recommendations are to periodically recruit new volunteers for the fund-raising team leadership and to change the tactics; instead of an event, "send a mail appeal inviting people to stay home . . . , a phantom event" (p. 9).

All fund-raisers find that strategies do wear thin. A fund-raising event, Klein (1999) reports, takes a year to plan and bring into being but becomes a bore "after seven or eight years" (p. 9). It is the same with a quarterly mail appeal; it has to be redesigned and written differently every few years. Klein advises that an organization's fund-raising team evaluate its campaign, approaches, and tactics every year to make sure that they are producing as needed and expected. Adding this to the aforementioned frequent rotation of people on the team makes possible a continual stream of fresh perspectives.

Klein (2001a), in her book *Fundraising for Social Change,* has a whole chapter on "the thank-you note" and the Internet as a tool of growing usefulness when used properly. She warns that it can steal away a lot of valuable time and "has exponentially added to the isolation of many people who confuse chat rooms with community" (p. 286). Of much interest, too, are her words on nonprofits starting small businesses. She believes that although there are success stories, most such enterprises have failed. Klein has important advice about hiring a paid fund-raiser, the distinction between the role of the staff and the role of the board in fund-raising, how to approach financial trouble, and the question of clean and dirty money. Klein (2001b) likes to remind organizations that "people are more important than profit" and that "good staff develops out of an understanding of process" that is people sensitive (p. 3). More insights and pointers from Klein, including the *Grassroots Fundraising Journal,* can be found on her Web site (www.chardonpress.com).

Both Hall and Klein urge organizations to be systematic about building and maintaining resource-tapping capability by keeping the process in tune with the mission and employing the tools of planning, public relations, and political persuasion. They agree that resource gathering needs to be a permanent organizational component that is reassessed and rejuvenated regularly.

(The reader should be reminded that all sizable public libraries, and even some branches, maintain lists of potential funders, valuable collections of publications, books, electronic materials, and other sources on fund-raising that are helpful to nonprofit organizations.)

A CASE FOR STABLE FUNDING

During the 1990s, which was a difficult and conservative decade for small community organizing and development efforts, community voices from across the nation raised a cry for more certain and more abundant funding. A case was made that there is now an opportunity for the nation to preserve a priceless asset by using the energies and talents of untold millions of community people motivated to make small communities stable and livable.

Peirce and Steinbach (1990) helped to set off the opportunity alarm with their concrete reports on widespread achievements and possibilities. Providing considerable evidence, they declared that "the failure of the community development movement is unthinkable" (p. 73). They argued that during an age of social distress

and fragmentation, the movement promises a "personalized, neighborhood-based" renewal that is essential for a strong national economy and a united tranquil nation—needs echoed by voices high and low since the terrorist attacks of September 11, 2001. "Community development organizations are not just a minor local phenomenon. They are an absolute national necessity" (p. 73). Long-term, persevering supporters are needed to help the movement stay alive and grow.

Eisen (1992), in her study of foundation support for comprehensive community initiatives, reported that funders increasingly are recognizing the need for patience as they find the comprehensive process requires more time than anticipated and that the traditional annual funding cycle does not apply to such initiatives. She concluded that comprehensive community revitalization requires long-term, deep-funding support, an appeal strongly supported by the long histories of the Aliquippa (Pennsylvania) and Dudley Street (Boston) cases and to a lesser extent by the Hyde Park-Kenwood (Chicago) case.

The Center for Community Change (CCC), with its extensive experience in assisting organizers and their organizations, maintains that the opportunity must be met by ensuring core support for all local development organizations that have proven their worth (Mott, 1996). The CCC has called for each region of the country to find coalition leadership able to produce a long-range plan for maximizing the amount of general operating support available for its grassroots community groups. Citing the 200 alternative community funds in the country, the growing community foundations, and the numerous pots of money still available in governments, corporations, traditional foundations, and intermediaries, the CCC insists that such guaranteed support is feasible.

Andrew Mott, long time CCC staff member who now heads the Independent Community Learning Project to improve training of community leadership, concluded, "No part of the country offers community groups the full range of support which would maximize their growth and accomplishment [and enable] the nation to take full advantage of the remarkable potential of grassroots community organizations" (Mott,

1996, p. 105). The authors of this book agree that such systematic funding could be a strength for society, provided that the community groups match the outside funding with a broad-based stream of contributions from within their own communities, accompanied by procedures for accountability to their constituents. The match need not be dollar for dollar, but it should be substantial, with each group raising local funds up to its potential.

Andrew Mott Speaks Out for Scale

Increasingly, the rising mismatch between resources available and resources required frustrates efforts toward renewal and justice in poverty-affected small communities and in many communities that are only partially poverty stricken. The yawning abyss grows ever wider and deeper. The CCC is an organization that has helped hundreds of low-income communities' push for survival and equity since the 1960s. While heading the CCC, Mott (2000) laid out the reality of where low-income neighborhoods stand. His words, summarized here, have relevance for all distressed small communities that lack an adequate scale of resource flows for achieving renewal:

> At first (in the 1960s), American society and the federal government responded positively (to calls for supporting neighborhood rebuilding). Public opinion polls then showed massive support for new measures to create greater equality and opportunity . . . , but by 1975 the movements had run their course. . . . Since then, the nation has shifted back and forth from eras of conservative government to periods of moderate reform. At no time, however, has there been another wave of strong, positive federal support for poor people, minorities, or the organizations representing them. The prevailing policy direction has been conservative, with continuing devolution and cuts in federal programs for the poor. It is remarkable that this 25 years has also witnessed a burgeoning number of low-income and moderate-income community groups throughout the country. . . . They have developed creative programs, built housing, created jobs, delivered services, turned neighborhoods around, influenced the policies of banks and government agencies, and transformed

the lives of their leaders and many people they serve. They have much to be proud of.

> But despite these heroic efforts and remarkable achievements, poor people are being left farther and farther behind, and their communities are too often continuing to decline. The gains low-income people make in their neighborhoods are severely limited without massive investment from government and the private sector.

> Recently, perhaps in their frustration at the intractability of so many social problems, many foundations have initiated their own anti-poverty and community improvement programs. Collaborative by design . . . and often bringing "movers and shakers" into decision-making from the beginning, most foundation initiatives are loathe to challenge the policies and practices of major public and private institutions.

> Moreover, such initiatives have a difficult time attracting large numbers of community people into leadership positions or creating a sense of ownership among neighborhood residents, as most of the initiatives do not emanate from self-organizing or the community's own initiative. These factors limit their potential for promoting public policy change. This could change if funders fundamentally changed their approach—shifting the balance of power and initiative to community residents who are highly motivated to press for policy changes. (pp. 28–29)

Through the Industrial Areas Foundation (IAF), led by organizers developed in the tradition of Saul Alinsky, oppressed groups have been gaining power by mobilizing mass-based faith coalitions that demand just shares of public resources for distressed neighborhoods (Halpern, 1995; Rusk, 1999; Wilson, 1999). In Chapter 2, the extent of this IAF resurgence was reported in some detail. Options for the expanded movement has been financed through a new strategy created under the leadership of Ernesto Cortes, Jr., founder of Communities Organized for Public Service (COPS) in San Antonio, which became the model for the IAF spread through Texas and beyond. As described by Warren (2001), the IAF's base operating revenue comes from a 1% to 2% assessment on the budgets of institutions (mostly faith-based) that are affiliated with the IAF. These funds pay for hiring organizers, an activity that many foundations and other funders have been reluctant to underwrite. According to Warren, these dues take care of about one third of the IAF organizations, and the IAF "struggles to maintain the percentage as a way to guarantee its independence and to demonstrate continued support from its base" (p. 38).

The balance of the budget comes from a mix of local businesses (of various sizes) and from foundations (mostly large national ones). Warren (2001) viewed the Catholic Campaign for Human Development as the largest single funder of Texas IAF organizations and "in fact probably the single largest funder of poor empowerment groups of all kinds across the country" (p. 38). During recent years, secular foundations, including Ford, Rockefeller, and Schumann, have provided large grants to support the IAF network of training institutes.

Rubin and Rubin (2001) made a case for funds to be tapped by community organizations through ownership of mortgageable assets, fees for assisting with real estate and business deals, owning and renting property, revolving loan funds, credit unions, federal tax credits, and other innovative sources, most of which we find on stage in the Aliquippa case study (pp. 207–210). Rubin and Rubin also were confident that every small community can produce a steady stream of funding internally through carefully organized campaigns led by volunteers, as colleges have done with their annual giving funds (p. 379).

The Development Training Institute and the Urban Institute, in their joint study of the community-building approach (Kingsley, McNeely, & Gibson, 1997), also advocated a plan for mounting a national campaign to help boost and stabilize funding for local community groups and their programs. They suggested that leadership for such a national campaign come from relevant national foundations, national interest groups such as the National Congress for Community Economic Development (NCCED), and appropriate federal agencies. Their vision is for a new, diversified national fund to provide resources for local community-building strategies and national support networks, with the money coming from governments (federal, state, and local) and the private sector including national and local foundations as well as other private groups (pp. 50–51).

Bridge to Resources:
A Case Study of "Intermediaries"

A small community development organization, especially a young one, may be far away from the money and knowledge it needs to flourish. The distance for a rural or small town organization may be spatial, while for an urban organization it may be political, with there being no connections to downtown decision makers. To bring the small community and its development organization closer to essential funds and technical assistance, the "intermediary" has been invented, with major examples than can now be seen in at least 30 places in the United States, most of them urban places. Kingsley et al. (1997) called attention to the increasing role that community foundations have played in stimulating and financing intermediaries or in assuming the role themselves in some of these places (pp. 56–57). They viewed this as significant because community foundations where assets spring from numerous diverse individuals, families, and businesses, rather than from a single wealthy family or corporation, already have more than $12 billion in assets and are growing rapidly. Pablo Eisenberg, long-time national advocate for disadvantaged people and their communities, believes that community foundations can build bridges to small risk-prone local associations that traditional foundations shun. (See Chapter 12 for more on community foundations.)

Intermediaries have long existed in the form of United Ways and the social concern offices of religious judicatories, which provide information, training, and technology transfers as well as allocations of funds to human service agencies. In addition, a variety of federations and councils inspired and shaped by nonprofit groups in cities, counties, and multi-county regions advance joint interests through research, advocacy, and lobbying and collaborative projects. Often, intermediaries link grassroots community-based organizations to governments, universities, and other institutional storehouses of wealth and talent. To provide support for small community development organizations, intermediaries began to appear during the 1960s in the form of citywide neighborhood coalitions and community action organizations sprung from the "War on Poverty." A city where the distress-fighting organizations of small communities have had especially effective help from intermediaries is Portland.

Portland, a growth city of a 550,000 people in the state of Oregon, anchors a region where people cherish their environment. Neighborhoods are treated with respect and supplied with quality public services. A civic spirit of fairness reigns, but sharp differences also exist among the citizens as to how much aid government should give to voluntary organizations. Some believe in the efficacy of government and favor extensive support, while others hold that government is a shortcut to waste and dependency and that neighborhood groups are best operated by volunteers who look for funds and technical aid to their business and residential neighbors and other private sources.

Portland's Office of Neighborhood Involvement (ONI) came into being during the early 1970s at the initiative of a handful of volunteer groups that formed a loose coalition in the northwest section of Portland (ONI, 2001). By 1975, they had persuaded city government to establish the ONI with a small paid staff hired from among leaders of the associations. The ONI was set up as an autonomous bureau of the city, with its staff given civil service protection. From the beginning, this staff served as an organizing force, helping residents who asked for assistance in forming or strengthening an association. (During the early years, this bureau was called the Office of Neighborhood Association.) Increasingly, the residents who lead the associations have been economically secure homeowners.

In time, six sections of Portland, encompassing most of the city, had coalitions of neighborhood associations working to preserve and improve their sections. The ONI furnished a budget to each coalition to underwrite a small office and coordination staff. Through this structure, the city met its state and federal participation obligations, operated an anti-crime campaign, and offered training to the leadership of the associations.

Today, there are 95 associations, grouped into seven incorporated coalitions. Each coalition negotiates an annual contract with the ONI spelling out the obligations of the coalition and

the specific assistance to be furnished by the ONI. It is an arms-length process, with the coalitions and their affiliated associations maintaining their autonomy. The ONI's role, besides funding and technical assistance, is coordination, liaison, and some quiet advocacy on behalf of neighborhoods.

Annually, each coalition and its affiliated associations determine priority public works requests for their section of the city and submit them to the ONI, which seeks to move the most feasible and urgent requests through the appropriate city bureaus. Each coalition receives about $130,000 in hard city funds for operations annually (except that one coalition with an oversized territory receives double funds). These operating funds are over and above any public works allocations.

The ONI's success is testified to by its longevity; a quarter century of service was celebrated in the year 2000. Leadership dubious of the competency of government now dominates most associations, so contraction rather than expansion is likely to be the direction of this innovative and pioneering intermediary during the immediate years ahead.

Portland's other intermediary is younger, is a much bigger spender, and supports much more drastic programs of change. It is the Neighborhood Partnership Fund (NPF), a division of the Oregon Community Foundation managed by its own neighborhood-oriented staff. It directs its attention to supporting the community-building efforts of residents and business people in the city's severely distressed neighborhoods.

Founded in 1990, the NPF is a partner of the city government's Bureau of Housing and Community Development (BHCD) in funding and mentoring 11 community development corporations (CDCs) that are struggling to revitalize 23 neighborhoods, largely in the north and northeast sections of the city (NPF, 1997, 1998). The 11 development corporations pursue housing construction, business district rebuilding, workforce education, and upgrading of health and day care. The 23 neighborhoods involved have diverse populations of African Americans, Native Americans, people of Hispanic and Asian origins, and white Americans.

The NPF has a professional staff of five, and it gathers, manages, and distributes more than

$2 million per year. In addition, with assistance of the national Enterprise Foundation, it provides $2 million in short-term construction loans for bricks-and-mortar projects in the 23 neighborhoods. Since 1990, NPF organizations have produced more than 3,500 affordable housing units and thousands of square feet of revitalized commercial space, leveraging more than $50 million in investments in the process.

To qualify for inclusion in the programs, local organizations must undergo an organizational assessment and submit a work plan. The NPF and city staffs believe that these requirements have stepped up the competence and productivity of participating organizations as well as improved communications and accountability within the program. Each neighborhood organization works with a contract representative who acts for both the NPF and the BHCD.

Training in financial management, board responsibility, staff cohesion, and strategic planning is part of the relationship. Know-how is provided for linking residents to workforce development and sometimes directly to jobs. The partnership believes that job training and placement will increasingly be a neighborhood-level activity assigned to CDCs and other community-based organizations. Other technical assistance concerns resource connections, services for the homeless, youth involvement, public safety, and innovative problem solving.

There are separate programs to recruit and educate future staff members for local organizations, with the priority being on women and people of color. This "Human Capital Initiative" helps promising individuals to formulate career plans and gives special attention to recruiting candidates indigenous to participating neighborhoods. A related concern of this initiative is the raising of salary levels for neighborhood staff.

The NPF is an independent nonprofit organization and has its own 21-member "advisory board" along with an independent board of directors. Among the board members are bankers, corporate executives, educators, designees of the Oregon Foundation and of city government, and 3 neighborhood representatives.

The NPF board is most proud of its ability to attract local and national funds, its fruitful collaboration with city government, and the community building it has facilitated through assisting neighborhood organizations to expand their programs beyond housing.

The NPF sees a need for its work to continue well into the 21st century. It continually pushes neighborhood organizations to increase their capacity and makes future funding dependent on their doing so. The NPF also is considering expansion of its program into small communities beyond the city of Portland.

Key parts of its program seek to increase the involvement of employers and educators in neighborhood workforce improvement, to step up the redevelopment of real estate, and to renew the public's sense of hope and pride in Portland's now distressed residential communities.

Intermediaries, like all funders, experience tensions at times with the organizations they support, especially when they differ over goals, priorities, and/or means. This is the reality in Portland as in other cities. Tensions are endemic to interorganizational relationships, especially where there is a pecuniary nexus.

There are major issues to be worked out in the future among intermediaries and local community renewal groups regarding power, control, and policymaking. Meantime, the intermediary continues to provide one source of sustainable resource flows for small communities. It is also in a position where it can nudge community renewal groups to broaden their indigenous fund-raising. But leaders of community renewal groups must always be on guard to protect their autonomy. As Rubin (2000) warned community leaders, "Obtaining funds from intermediaries and foundations entangles community-based development organizations within a complicated, evolving, and controlling political world" (p. 99).

Go For the Money

In this chapter, we have preached an orthodox path: Accrue a permanent resource-tapping team that does its homework, researches prospective givers, services their history and giving records, and sends out trained volunteers in pairs (sometimes with staff or board members) for straight-up face-to-face asking, all the time getting full support and participation from the group's top leadership and at times involving this leadership in the face-to-face asking.

Such a team confronts a daunting task during the 21st century. The money is there, but the suppliants are legion. Although the stock market decline has reduced foundation assets, there are still considered resources out there for which to be completed. We are now approaching the largest transfer of wealth in the nation's history as baby boomers inherit their parents' material and liquid assets.

There the money is, and so is the competition. Worldly wise, dogged nonprofit marketers parade a limitless number of compelling causes, reaching from heart transplant equity, to stopping genetically modified food, and on to quality opera for the outer suburbs and cyber-centers for children in low-income neighborhoods. Assertive imagination and energy is required to compete in such an extraction market. How does renewal of a withered 1920s bungalow suburb or a historic and distressed 1890s mill town match the expectation and significance of launching the careers of 50 promising young entrepreneurs in their own hometowns in west Africa? It is not a snap, but this book has been written to make the case that saving America's small communities can match the significance of any other cause if brought to high profile by a united participatory community overcoming despair with solid achievements. We acknowledge that in the short term, cause may sometimes have little to do with obtaining a large grant (while connections are everything), but in the long run, it is cause and substance that prevail.

In these remaining paragraphs, we search the realities of the enigmatic economic environment that carried over from the 1990s into the 21st century, and is our hunting ground for resources, whether we fathom the economic environment or not.

Shaping this environment is disparity, the yawning widening chasm between the affluent and the abject, between those with stock accounts and those who cannot catch up with their debts no matter how many jobs their households carry and how deft they are at juggling their payment books and credit cards. It is a near equal split. Some 48% of American households own stocks, and the other half own none. Among the roughly 35 million affluent households, one in five already has assets of $1 million or more, in large part a result of the rocketing stock and home prices of the past dozen or so years. During the 1990s boom, poverty declined from 15.0% of the population to 12.7% and has remained stuck there since. In 2000, President Bill Clinton climbed onto podiums across the nation to implore people and their leaders to dedicate the growing abundance to banishing disparity. The response was not overwhelming. Then came a recession, tax cuts, and the "War on Terror" to end the surpluses and bring back an annual national deficit. The near term is likely to see increased stability but no return to the buoyancy of the 1990s. The great wealth will remain with the upper 20% of householders. Any resources for widespread indebt renewal of distressed communities probably will have to come through more aggressive and progressive tax and spending policies and from the sacrifices and sweat of community people themselves.

Fully 80% of the rapid growth in the net worth of affluent families since 1995 came from capital gains on stock shares and homes. The overall savings rate among people in the bottom 52% of incomes was negative given that any savings by this group was overcome by consumer debt. During the past decade, the median family indebtedness for all families rose from $23,000 to $33,000. The Federal Reserve indicated that between 1993 and 1998, households with a head under 35 years of age saw their assets decline by 30%, while one in eight families spent more than 40% of their income on debt payments.

Poverty, job insecurity, and other economic distress remain very much alive and virulent in a third of the nation's small communities, with weak spots in another third. Giving has generally increased, but not for human services, which include causes such as traditional charity and small community renewal. Kilborn (1999) that human services received only 9.2% of all giving in 1998, compared with 13.9% in 1970. Religion and culture receive more than 90% of current giving. Households gave 2.5% of their incomes to charity in 1988 but only 2.1% in

1998. Consumer debt flourished and spread during the 1990s, while the proportion of givers shrunk from 75% to 70% of the population. After inflation, a household's average annual gift to human services fell from $270 in 1998 to $250 in 2001. Philanthropic contributions by corporations, typically about 1% of their profits and about 5% of all giving nationally, have been declining more than have those by individuals.

Kilborn (1999) speculated that in moving to the outer-suburban ring, with its gated and other exclusionary communities, affluent people who rally to help hurricane victims seen on television "do not see the need around the corner" (p. 48). Kilborn quoted the Memphis Urban League president as charging that prosperity during the 1990s undermined sharing and the bonds of neighbors and communities while turning people into protectors of wealth. "The result of prosperity is isolation, arrogance, and in-your-face. This among people who were once interdependent in terms of basic survival needs" (p. 48). Kilborn's report ended with a suggestion by Elizabeth Boris of the Urban Institute that this "wealth protection" may rise because the newly rich have not yet "learned to give" (p. 48). This is a notion to be tested by resource-seeking teams in small communities everywhere. Perhaps many have never been asked before to give to a serious civic cause.

Eisenberg, the lifetime fighter for distressed communities who advised in the creation of this book, has been going about the nation imploring funders to reach down deeper to assist and empower small communities, particularly those beaten down by poverty and low wages. He especially sees regional foundations, such as the Chicago Community Trust and the Oregon Community Foundation, as able and appropriate to help because of their broad giver bases. He believes that government should require foundations to give away more than the current 5% of assets per year, which he finds to be much too low to meet the needs of a society struggling with poverty and class divisions (Dyer, 1999).

Aiming hardballs at the rich and near rich is Claude Rosenberg of San Francisco, himself a rich giver who has set up his own $32 million foundation. His studies reveal that wealthy Americans could double or triple their giving without reducing the quality of their lives, but he believes that too few do it because they base giving on their incomes rather than on their accumulated wealth.

Rosenberg calculates that a couple with $50,000 to $75,000 of income and $118,000 of assets could afford to increase donations by about 21%. Families with earnings of $100,000 and $1 million of investments could give away $16,000 without changing their way of life, which would be six times current giving. For the roughly 111,000 families with annual incomes of more than $1 million, the increase could be 10-fold. The average income for this group is $2.8 million, with assets of $21.2 million. Rosenberg figures their painless annual gift at an average of $1.2 million a year, compared with their actual annual gift of $120,000 (Johnston, 1999).

Rosenberg's pitch is, "It is very much in the interest of the wealthy to give away more and create a society where they can live safer, happier, better lives." Peter Lynch, the famed money manager, and former President Jimmy Carter are among those who endorse Rosenberg's direction. "A lot of people have been waiting for some validation that it is all right to give a lot more," Rosenberg tells people. "I am giving it to you based on research." All resource-tapping teams should take note. (See Rosenberg's Web site [www.newtithing.org] for more information.)

We know that a small place community, with or without an intermediary connection in its own regional environment, faces an array of public, nonprofit, and for-profit institutions affecting it from the outside as it struggles to preserve and improve itself. These include foundations, banks, county governments, police departments, media, unions, universities, the U.S. Department of Housing and Urban Development (HUD), faith-based associations, and profit-seeking corporations. Some of these institutions are pillars of the region that are laden with influence and resources, while others are from beyond the region but also possess vast political and economic powers and control wealth at the state and national levels. Local fund-raising teams out of small communities over time are well advised to become familiar with these sources of information, power, and cash, starting with those from the immediate region who are most likely to be interested and generous.

Pauline Cooper, who as the director of the AAUD helped its board and staff to raise millions of dollars in grants and gifts, suggested that fund-seeking teams carefully build staunch relationships of understanding and trust with foundations, governments, and wealthy donors. "Involve them, seek their advice and opinions, invite them to join an advisory board or a task force, get them to give testimony—help them to experience the struggle" (personal interview, February 2002).

And now emerging is a largely ungoverned global economy for which nations are seeking to build new institutions of order. Who will benefit from these is not yet certain, as we discussed in Chapter 2 probing the Seattle protests of 1999 and the series of demonstrations that followed into the new century. Controversy rages around this establishment of a new global order. Fears and disagreements abound as to what would constitute a productive and equitable world system. It will be useful over time for cadre leaders and other key activists in small community renewal organizations to stay abreast of this controversy and seek to shape it when opportunity arises, most likely through regional and national coalitions.

As we know, resources originate from the productive work of a nation's people using tools, equipment, processes, and smart thinking to continually make themselves and their workplaces more creative and prolific. People in the United States produce more than $10 trillion worth of goods and services a year. It is an astounding mountain of resources that usually rises each year. It is from this yearly creation of wealth that comes both the savings and current income that become the target of fund-raising and other resource tapping by small communities and their renewal organizations. During the decade of the 1990s, this annual gross domestic product (GDP) grew vigorously without interruption for 10 years, the longest continual period of steady growth recorded. The boom ended in 2000. Unemployment has risen steadily since, now nearing a 9% real rate, made up of the official rate of 6% for idle workers actively looking for work plus 3% for discouraged workers who want a job but have quit looking. Economic indicators are mixed for long-term, but near-term looks like a mean money season for small communities. In

any case, there remains a well-stocked hunting ground for communal resource tappers, but a difficult one. Careful planning and persistence are demanded more than ever to secure the scale of resources required, to enable people to create just and healthy small communities.

SUMMARY

Obtaining adequate money and other resources to fuel serious and successful revitalization of a distressed small community is always possible in America's prosperous society, but it requires systematic, continuous, and imaginative work by an aggressive finance group positioned as a key sub-unit of the renewal organization. This team works from a plan and is most likely to thrive when it gets respect and cooperation from throughout the organization for the essential work it does. We have seen that the staff-board team in Aliquippa has concentrated on foundation and government grants with considerable success. But the AAUD has yet to further strengthen itself with a broad-based annual campaign among local residents, businesses, institutions, and other place stakeholders, as occurred in the Kiltimaugh community.

Organizational strength increases when money and other necessary resources are raised both from within the community and from outside it. Substantial flows from the people inside make outsiders more willing to give. One of the most overlooked organizational opportunities for most small community development organizations is the possibility to transform residents into financial stakeholders.

Donors respond best when asked face to face by someone they trust or admire. An organization's leaders confirm the importance of tapping when they actively join in the asking. The potency of combining community organizing and economic development can be a compelling selling point to funders (both individual and institutional) especially when they see the participants opening their own wallets, no matter how humble the contents.

Resource tapping is an important participation activity for training volunteer leadership. There is a storehouse of knowledge about resource-raising. Four publications that have proved their worth as training aids have been suggested. Regional intermediaries have been proposed as an aid to stabilizing neighborhood organization budgets in urban areas, with a case study of Portland's two intermediaries presented to illustrate the strengths and weaknesses of this special type of support institution.

The scale of resource needed for small community revitalization should never be underestimated.

CONTINUING QUESTIONS

1. How does an organization maintain its independence when it is accepting large amounts of grant money from outside funders?

2. To maintain a sound representative organization exercising local control, what portion of an organization's budget needs to be raised locally within the community?

3. When time and volunteers are in short supply, under what conditions is it still worthwhile to spend effort pursuing noncash contributions? In general, should small organizations hold off on seeking such contributions, or are the possibilities too good to pass up?

4. How much grassroots fund-raising is enough? Is grassroots fund-raising an exercise in gaining credibility, a means of enhancing community participation, or both?

5. How can better, more productive partnerships be built? Religious organizations receive most of the charity dollars. How can community economic development organizations build partnerships with religious organizations (and other faith-based groups) to share in these funds?

6. Can small community renewal groups deal as equals with intermediaries? If so, then under what conditions or stipulations?

7. What are the best ways in which to train volunteers to be effective askers?

8. How do we best present the case for funding community organizations to a broad array of potential donors including foundations?

REFERENCES

AAFRC Trust for Philanthropy. (2002). *Giving USA.* [Online]. Retrieved May 30, 2002, from the World Wide Web: www.aafrc.org/images/graphics/chart1.jpg

Bangs, M. (2002, March–April). Streets of Hope Campaign: A case study in transforming donors into grassroots fundraisers. *Grassroots Fundraising Journal, 21*(2), 4–7.

Dyer, E. (1999, October 20). Wealthy charities must do more at grassroots, advocate says. *Pittsburgh Post-Gazette,* p. B8.

Eisen, A. (1992). *A report on foundations' support for comprehensive neighborhood-based community-empowerment initiatives.* Unpublished report initiated and funded by East Bay Funders, the Ford Foundation, the New York Community Trust, the Piton Foundation, and the Riley Foundation.

Flanagan, J. (1995). *The grass roots fundraising book.* Chicago: Contemporary Books.

Hall, M. (1988). *Getting funded: A complete guide to proposal writing* (3rd ed.). Portland, OR: Continuing Education Publications.

Halpern, R. (1995). *Rebuilding the inner city: A history of neighborhood initiatives to address poverty in the U.S.* New York: Columbia University Press.

Higgins, J. (1996). *The Kiltimaugh renewal: Best practice in community enterprise.* Dublin, Ireland: Oak Tree Press.

Johnston, D. C. (1999). *Donors' assets—Where the money is: The chronicle of philanthropy.* [Online]. Retrieved July 15, 1999, from the World Wide Web: www.newtithing.org/content/donors.html

Kilborn, P. (1999, December 12). Charity for poor lags behind need. *The New York Times* (national ed.), pp. 1, 48.

Kingsley, G., McNeely, J., & Gibson, J. (1997). *Community building coming of age.* Baltimore, MD: Development Training Institute.

Klein, K. (1999, January–February). When fundraising strategies wear out. *Shelterforce,* pp. 9–29. (Orange, NJ: National Housing Institute)

Klein, K. (2001a). *Fundraising for social change* (4th ed.). Oakland, CA: Chardon Press.

Klein, K. (2001b). Letter from the publisher. *Grassroots Fundraising Journal, 20*(4).

Klein, K. (2002, January–February). Raising money in uncertain times. *Shelterforce,* pp. 4–6. (Orange, NJ: National Housing Institute)

Mellon Financial Corporation. (2000). *Discover total resources: A guide for nonprofits* [booklet]. Pittsburgh, PA: Author. (Community Affairs Publications, One Mellon Center, Suite 1830, Pittsburgh, PA 15258)

Mott, A. (1996). *Building systems of support for neighborhood change.* Washington, DC: Center for Community Change.

Mott, A. (2000, March–April). Building power. *Shelterforce,* pp. 28–29. (Orange, NJ: National Housing Institute)

National Equity Fund. (2002, March). [advertisement]. *Affordable Housing,* p. 9.

Neighborhood Partnership Fund. (1997). *Synergy: 1996–1997 progress report.* Portland, OR: Author.

Neighborhood Partnership Fund. (1998). *Neighborhood Partnership Fund* [program brochure]. Portland, OR: Author.

Office of Neighborhood Involvement. (2001). *Update: Neighborhood involvement directory.* Portland, OR: City of Portland, Office of Neighborhood Involvement.

Peirce, N., & Steinbach, C. (1990). *Enterprising communities: Community-based development in America, 1990.* Washington, DC: Council for Community-Based Development.

Rubin, H. (2000). *Renewing hope within neighborhoods of despair.* Albany: State University of New York Press.

Rubin, H., & Rubin, I. (2001). *Community organizing and community development* (3rd ed.). Boston: Allyn & Bacon.

Rusk, D. (1999). *Inside game, outside game.* Washington, DC: Brookings Institution Press.

Seymour, H. (1966). *Designs for fund-raising: Principles, patterns, and techniques.* New York: McGraw-Hill.

Warren, M. (2001). *Dry bones rattling: Community building to revitalize American democracy.* Princeton, NJ: Princeton University Press.

Wilson, W. J. (1999). *Bridge over the racial divide: Rising inequality and coalition politics.* Berkeley: University of California Press.

12

CAPITAL FORMATION

Building Community Financial Assets

Access to credit and capital is a basic civil right.

—motto of National Community
Reinvestment Coalition

In all communities, residents and businesses have a range of financial service needs. These include consumer loans for appliances, cars, education, and home improvements and purchases as well as business loans for start-ups, working capital, cash flow, inventory, and equipment. Residents and businesses also have a need for checking accounts, savings accounts, check cashing, and money order purchases. A basic problem in distressed communities is the availability of and access to financial capital—cash and cash equivalents—through a system of financial transactions and services. Many communities were and still are redlined by major financial institutions; that is, the communities are seen as too risky or not profitable for lending, investment, or the provision of consumer services. Also many financial institutions have closed branch offices in distressed communities when overhead costs became too great to make it worthwhile to provide for the needs of small savers. Bank acquisitions and mergers have consumed, and in some cases have eliminated, "neighborhood" banking. This has meant that

for some communities where lending had once been available for home purchases, rehabilitation, and improvements as well as for consumer loans and small business start-ups and working capital, credit is no longer available. Without the investment power that access to credit provides, a community's infrastructure fails; housing deteriorates, businesses collapse, commercial properties are no longer maintained or are vacated, and ultimately its public services such as schools and streets decline due to a falling tax base and disinvestment.

A lack of access to capital and credit has a debilitating effect on every effort to rebuild and revitalize small communities. Poor communities have cash and income, but most is spent on necessities (e.g., housing, food, clothing), with little left to put into savings or investments that create wealth and permit the accumulation of assets. What little is deposited as savings or otherwise invested is usually deposited into institutions controlled by nonresidents and not reinvested into the community of origin.

A variety of factors inhibit access to cash or credit by individuals and families in distressed communities. Traditional financial institutions look for a borrower's ability to repay so as to minimize the risk associated with lending. Many people in distressed communities have limited income and little or no savings. Many do not have bank accounts because their cash comes in and goes out immediately, and they cannot maintain minimum balances. In many distressed communities, no traditional financial institutions exist; access is determined by a person's mobility—the ability to travel to another community. Residents of distressed communities may have no jobs, lack a stable environment, and have poor or no credit histories. Traditional financial institutions see all of this adding up to the inability to repay and poor credit risk. Lender bias is also evident in distressed communities. Because the transaction costs for loans are relatively the same whether the loans are large or small, small loans are not seen as profitable. Many lenders are hesitant to loan to minorities, women, and the elderly; as mentioned before, redlining can cut off a whole community from banking services. Lack of credit can result in families being prevented from obtaining the car transportation essential to finding and holding jobs.

Lack of access to certain kinds of capital is widely regarded as the greatest impediment to the growth of entrepreneurship (American Assembly, 1997, p. 6). Businesses require financing when they want to start up or expand so as to support planning and research, buy or rent equipment in a building, hire employees, stock inventory, pay utilities, and/or cover other operating expenses. Businesses use two types of money: equity and debt capital funds. Equity financing is capital given to a business in exchange for a share of ownership and a claim on the income it is expected to earn in the future. Such funds typically come from the personal savings of the entrepreneur, from other investors recruited, and from selling shares of stock to the public. A public sale usually will not be successful until a firm has an established record for sales, management capacity, and at least positive prospects for profits. Equity financing is not a debt that has to be repaid at a certain time. Debt capital is received through a loan. Regular repayment of the funds borrowed plus interest is required. Access to capital for new, small, and minority- and community-owned businesses is limited, inconsistent, and unpredictable. There are significant barriers to securing debt capital. Equity capital and early pre-development funding are generally not available. Early-stage capital is often the most important, yet it is the most difficult to secure. Low-income individuals interested in self-employment and business creation have difficulties in accumulating sufficient funds to start businesses. They have limited personal savings, face prejudice from lenders, and have little collateral to offer in exchange for loans. Such entrepreneurs also face redlining when financial institutions and insurance companies refuse to support investment in businesses located in what are perceived as high-risk communities. Financial institutions tend to favor larger firms because the costs associated with making a lending decision—information gathering, transactions, administrative activities—tend to be the same whether the investment requested is small or large.

Community development corporations (CDCs) and other community-based development groups have found several advantages to pursuing capital formation activities on a local community level. Social goals can be addressed while meeting the financial needs of the community. People of color and women can gain increased access to needed capital and credit, and there can be increased support for community-based initiatives that have job creation potential. For example, an unemployed woman could secure a small loan from a community microenterprise program and open a family day care home, providing her with an income and enabling others to reenter the workforce with minimal child care concerns. Only one major disadvantage exists to pursuing local capital formation in terms of economic development: It only indirectly creates jobs, and these are usually few in number. Increasing the access to capital and credit also provides only one ingredient for successful business development: funds. For small businesses to succeed and grow, they also need technical and management assistance. The greater the extent that these are provided in tandem with funds, the greater the likelihood that jobs will be created and sustained.

This chapter looks at four approaches to capital formation: (a) advocacy and organizing to persuade financial institutions to make specific investments or types of investments in distressed communities, (b) building institutions by creating community development investment institutions that are based in and serve distressed communities, (c) building individual financial assets through the creation of individual development accounts, and (d) creating local money systems.

ADVOCACY AND ORGANIZING FOR COMMUNITY REINVESTMENT

The history of the Community Reinvestment Act (CRA) began long before its enactment by Congress in 1977. Traditionally, financial institutions in the United States have had an obligation to serve the public because of privileges they receive from the federal government that other businesses do not receive. For example, financial institutions have charters to do business, obtain federal deposit insurance, and borrow money under special arrangements from the Federal Reserve and the Federal Home Loan Banks. These privileges gave rise to the principle, found in U.S. banking laws starting in the 1930s, that financial institutions should serve the convenience and needs of their local communities.

During the years leading to the passage of the CRA, there was considerable concern about ensuring fair access to credit and equal lending practices and patterns, especially in inner cities. Community groups spoke out against redlining—the perceived practice of drawing red lines around disfavored neighborhoods where money would not be lent, regardless of the creditworthiness of the individual loan applicants. Many believed that financial institutions, which accepted deposits from within the communities but invested them elsewhere, aggravated the visible economic decline of urban areas. Local activists determined that their communities were experiencing systematic disinvestment, not individual negative lending decisions by loan officers. From dispersed local efforts, a

national movement grew during the 1970s. With this as a backdrop, the attention of Congress was turned to the problem of revitalizing neighborhoods and the role that financial institutions could play in that effort. Prior to the passage of the CRA, Congress enacted the Home Mortgage Disclosure Act of 1975 (HMDA), requiring financial institutions to make public their data on home mortgage activity, including the race, income, and gender of home mortgage borrowers as well as the census tracts in which the loans were made. HMDA data, along with CRA performance ratings, give community members a clear picture of where they stand.

The CRA, which became effective in 1978, outlaws redlining by affirming that financial institutions have an obligation to provide equal treatment to all communities for which they are chartered. They are required to help meet the credit needs of their entire service areas, including low- and moderate-income sections and residents. The CRA requires that regulatory agencies (a) use their authority to encourage institutions to reinvest in their home areas, (b) regularly assess CRA performance of the institutions they supervise, and (c) take CRA performance into account in determining whether to allow financial institutions to expand their business in certain ways. For example, if an institution were found to have a poor record of providing credit or fulfilling other local financial service needs, then it could be denied approval to offer new services or to pursue profitable mergers, acquisitions, or branching opportunities. The CRA does not require financial institutions to make loans that could jeopardize their safety, nor does it dictate the types, amounts, or terms of the loans they make. The act provides guidance as to how a bank's record of satisfying its obligation of helping to meet the credit in its local community will be assessed by federal regulatory agencies.

Information looked at by bank examiners (which can and should be monitored by community groups) includes that which can answer the following questions. How actively does a bank lend in its community? How does the bank deliver its products? How extensive are a bank's community investments? Such information includes detail on the following six principal matters that could be measured against objective data on the area's credit needs:

- The extent of the institution's marketing efforts to communicate with members of the community regarding the credit services being provided
- The institution's participation in governmentally insured, guaranteed, or subsidized loan programs for housing, small businesses, or small farms
- The geographic distribution and volume of the institution's credit extensions, applications, and denials
- A record of opening and closing offices
- The practices intended to discourage applications for credit such as prescreening
- The institution's participation, such as investments, in local community development and redevelopment projects or programs

This information is to be compiled and analyzed regularly by the financial institutions themselves.

This information is available to community groups and the public. By gathering and analyzing it, community groups can proactively respond to such data and approach financial institutions prior to any regulatory examination to advocate for service improvements.

Since the enactment of CRA legislation, there have been scores of agreements between communities and financial institutions providing for ending discriminatory practices, improved services, and sometimes specific financial settlements to compensate for past practices. To maintain or improve their community reinvestment performance, lending institutions have an incentive to make formal agreements with community organizations that commit to specified levels of lending, investments, and services in underserved communities. Often, lending institutions will enter into agreements with community groups when federal regulators are considering their applications for charters, mergers, acquisitions, relocations, consolidations, or establishment of branch offices. In such cases, lending institutions want to convince regulators that they will work with community groups to increase the access to capital and credit for underserved populations.

At first, banks feared regulatory rejection and only reluctantly complied. Now, in some cases, there has emerged a culture of willing compliance, as evidenced by the proliferation of bank community development departments and programs oriented toward helping low-income areas. Some financial institutions also have come to recognize that there is business—good profitable business—in distressed communities. At the same time, however, private financial institutions have an underlying aversion to government regulation, and their trade associations constantly lobby to weaken provisions of the current law—sometimes successfully, as with the Gramm-Leach-Bliley Financial Services Act of 1999 (the Financial Modernization Bill), allowing banks to merge with finance, insurance, and securities firms but without requiring these merged entities to be covered by the CRA. In response, community groups under the umbrella of the National Community Reinvestment Coalition co-sponsored the Community Reinvestment Modernization Act of 2001 (H.R. 865), which will update the CRA to ensure that it keeps pace with the many changes in the financial industry. (H.R. 865 was slated to be reintroduced in the 108th Congress in 2003.)

Even with substantial and long-term local- and national-level activity around, many communities remain unaware of the potency of the CRA.

A community group (or a coalition of community organizations) can challenge a financial institution's application for a charter, merger, and the like by participating in the application process in two ways. It can file negative comments on an application—a challenge—and/or file a formal request for a public meeting or hearing on the issues raised in the challenge. Use of the amplifying voice of the media is critical in making information on policies and practices widely known. The National Training and Information Center (NTIC) noted that whether a group wins or loses a CRA challenge, the action makes other lenders take notice (NTIC, 1990, p. 167). Other lenders who want to develop reinvestment programs prior to being challenged often approach groups that have used the CRA process to negotiate reinvestment programs (p. 172).

To unite and harness community reinvestment efforts across the United States, the National Community Reinvestment Coalition (NCRC) was founded in 1990 by 16 national, regional, and local organizations (NCRC, 2002). The NCRC, a national nonprofit organization with more than 640 dues-paying nonprofit organizations as members located in every state, works to make community reinvestment activism a common local occurrence and to promote increased community-lender partnerships. The NCRC provides accurate and up-to-date information on national policy opportunities and potential setbacks to community reinvestment, and it also offers research services, technical assistance, and education programs. In addition, National People's Action (NPA), a part of the NTIC, that has been active on the CRA since the 1970s, is running a year-round campaign to strengthen CRA regulations by organizing hearings throughout the United States for regulators to hear how the CRA needs to be improved (NPA, 2002).

From 1977 to late 2001, banks and community organizations entered into more than 400 CRA agreements worth in excess of $1 trillion in reinvestment for traditionally underserved communities (NCRC, 2002). The NCRC (1996a, 2002) and the NTIC (1990) provide examples of financial institution commitments that have been made to meet community credit needs. These include the following:

- Loans to specific low- and moderate-income areas
- Specific dollar allocations for targeted lending
- Commitments to loan to minorities in proportion to their percentage of the general population
- Below-market interest rates
- Programs to reduce or eliminate mortgage loan-closing costs
- The elimination of minimum loan amounts or higher fees or costs for small loans
- Reduced downpayment requirements
- Longer maturity (longer payback period) for home improvement loans
- Grants to build the capacity of community-based organizations
- The creation of community review boards

Several examples illustrate the magnitude (and potential impact) of some CRA agreements. In the winter of 1995, The Pittsburgh Community Reinvestment Group (PCRG), a coalition of 32 community organizations, successfully protected a CRA lending agreement with Integra Bank that was endangered by the bank's pending merger with National City of Cleveland. Integra had previously committed $1.4 billion for community development and affordable housing in Pittsburgh's low-income communities. This agreement was threatened because National City had a tradition of not signing CRA agreements with community groups. The PCRG mobilized its membership and spearheaded a successful letter-writing campaign to the Federal Reserve Board. PCRG efforts resulted in an increase of the total loan amount to $1.67 billion. Through the year 2000, the loan pool included $275 million for residential first mortgages in low- and moderate-income communities, $94 million for second mortgages, $780 million for nonprofit developers and minority- and women-owned businesses, and $41 million for home improvement loans (NCRC, 1999).

In a second example, the Community Reinvestment Association of North Carolina (CRA-NC) in 1996 negotiated a $465 million, 3-year agreement with First Union Bank, one of the largest banks in the United States. The agreement covers a range of lending and marketing activities, including new affordable homeownership mortgages, special outreach to North Carolina's Hispanic residents, and expansion of First Union's network of school savings banks (NCRC, 1996b, p. 8).

Also in 1996, the California Reinvestment Committee (CRC) and the Greenlining Institute secured a $45 billion CRA agreement with Wells Fargo Bank that responds to priority lending needs in low-income communities. Wells Fargo has committed 60% of its $7 billion affordable housing component of the CRA agreement for low-income rental housing construction. The bank has agreed to direct the bulk of its $25 billion in small business lending toward loans of less than $50,000 that are needed by very small businesses in distressed and low-income communities (NCRC, 1996a, p. 6).

In a fourth example, the Chicago CRA Coalition, with 100 member organizations, negotiated a $4.1 billion, 6-year agreement with First Chicago Bank in 1999. The agreement will result in 5,200 more small business loans and 36,000 home loans over the six years. First Chicago's market shares of home and small business loans will be higher in lower-income communities than in upper-income communities. Important victories in this agreement include an $800,000 increase in the bank's downpayment assistance to low-income first-time homebuyers and the bank's agreement to open four full-service branches in low-income neighborhoods. In addition, an advisory council that includes community organizations was to be created to monitor the bank's progress in meeting agreement goals (NCRC, 1999).

As a final example, in the fall of 1999, the Detroit Alliance for Fair Banking (DAFB) signed a $918 million, 3-year community action plan with Michigan National Bank (NCRC, 1999). The action plan, designed to enhance the economic recovery of the city of Detroit, includes 3-year targets of $34.6 million in residential lending, $39 million in home equity/home improvement lending, $670 million in commercial/small business lending, and $105 million in commercial real estate lending. The plan also contains a strengthened commitment to diversity in recruiting, hiring, and advancing; to increasing minority procurement; and to maintaining existing banking services in Detroit.

Groups are also pushing the insurance industry on reinvestment issues. A coalition of Massachusetts community groups secured passage of precedent-setting state legislation requiring insurance companies to disclose the geographic distribution of their policies and providing financial incentives for offering policies in traditionally underserved communities (NCRC, 1996a, p. 1).

The late 1990s saw a focus on subprime and "predatory" lending" by community groups, regional and national groups (e.g., the NCRC, the Neighborhood Reinvestment Corporation, the NPA, the NTIC), and the U.S. Department of Housing and Urban Development (HUD) in attempting to expose and reduce unethical, exploitive, and destructive practices.

Subprime lending, most often on home refinancing, involves providing credit to borrowers with past credit problems, often at a higher cost or on less favorable terms than the conventional market. A HUD (2000) study of subprime lending found that the number of subprime refinance loans increased 10-fold between 1993 and 1998. Subprime loans were also three times more likely in low-income neighborhoods than in high-income ones and were five times more likely in black neighborhoods than in white

ones. In addition, homeowners in high-income black neighborhoods were twice as likely as homeowners in low-income white neighborhoods to have subprime loans.

Predatory lending is any unfair credit practice that harms a borrower or supports a credit system that promotes inequality and poverty. Goldstein (1999) defined predatory lending as occurring when "a set of loan terms and practices target a particular population and take advantage of the borrower's inexperience and lack of information, to manipulate a borrower into a loan [he or she] cannot afford to pay or defraud the borrower." Predatory lending hits homebuyers with excessive mortgage fees, interest rates, penalties, and insurance charges that raise the cost of buying a home by thousands of dollars. Targets for home equity loans are often low-income elderly homeowners. When an elderly homeowner defaults on the usually large loan with the home as collateral, foreclosure occurs. The rise of predatory lending targeting limited-income residents and communities increases the likelihood of foreclosures, displaced residents, abandonment of properties, and community destabilization (Seidman, 1999, p. 15).

To fight and stop subprime and predatory lending, groups have organized to take legal action to enforce fair lending practices and to increase (fair and just) competition for their services. For example, during the late 1990s, the NCRC at the national level and member organizations at the state level launched an anti-predatory lending campaign. In October 2002, a $484 million consumer protection agreement was reached with Household to halt predatory lending practices. This came about through years of advocacy and action by NCRC, Acorn and state attorneys general (NCRC, 2002). The NCRC has also published an "Anti-Predatory Lending Tool Kit" (available on its Web site [www.ncrc.org/svcs.toolkit_w_covers.pdf]). In 2002, the NCRC members were advocating for new predatory lending consumer protection in more than 30 states (King, 2002). In September 2002, Citigroup agreed to pay $215 million to the federal government and hundreds of victims of the company's subprime affiliate, the Associates. This agreement was a direct result of organizing by National People's Action and local affiliate groups (NPA, 2002). Groups were also educating community consumers and providing close follow-up to first-time homebuyers. As Seidman (1999) stated, "Credit delivered irresponsibly—particularly to those who can least afford to lose—is worse than no credit at all" (p. 16).

Community-based advocacy and organizing taken to the national level can have a substantial impact. In early 2001, the Predatory Lending Consumer Protection Act was introduced into Congress as part of the LaFalce Financial Services Consumer "Bill of Rights." In May 2002, it was introduced in the Senate and was scheduled to be reintroduced in the 108th Congress in 2003.

COMMUNITY DEVELOPMENT FINANCIAL INSTITUTIONS

A community development financial institution (CDFI) is a financial intermediary that has community development as its primary mission, developing a range of programs and methods to meet the needs of low-income communities (National Community Capital Association, 1999). CDFIs are specialized financial institutions that operate in market niches that have not been adequately served by traditional financial institutions. The first CDFIs were organized during the mid-1970s. By early 2002, more than 500 CDFIs were serving urban, rural, and reservation-based communities in all of the U.S. states, the District of Columbia, Puerto Rico, and the U.S. Virgin Islands (U.S. Department of the Treasury, 2002).

CDFIs capture and recycle the financial resources in a community (plug leaks), attract and circulate additional financial resources, and target resources to traditionally under-served markets and community-based development activities. Investments in CDFIs, which generally pay a below-market rate of return to investors, come from financial institutions, foundations, individuals, religious institutions, and others. CDFIs also demonstrate that losses are not inevitable when lending to and investing in limited-income people and distressed communities. They also can raise the level of competition in financial markets. Community Development Financial Institutions generally have the ability to make smaller loans, schedule longer repayment terms, and offer more flexible interest rates. CDFIs are locally accountable lending structures that come in a range of forms and sizes.

In 1994, the Community Development Financial Institutions Act was signed into law creating the CFDI Fund, under the U.S. Department of the Treasury. From 1996 through early 2002, through competitive grants, the CFDI Fund invested over $500 million promoting community and economic development in underserved markets through grants and loans for investment purposes, technical assistance, and operating support (U.S. Department of the Treasury, 2002).

We examine several community development financial institutions: community development credit unions, loan funds, community development banks, and community foundations.

Community Development Credit Unions

As we discussed in Chapter 7, in connection with the Aliquippa Credit Union, a community development credit union (CDCU) is a credit union that serves a community of predominantly low-income people, with the goal of developing that community. CDCUs may be the best replicable model for providing affordable capital and financial services in low-income and very low-income communities (Tansey, 2001, p. 2). The common bond uniting members of a CDCU is association (as with faith-based credit unions) or residence (geography). CDCUs serve the credit and financial service needs of their members. In essence, CDCUs are nonprofit financial cooperatives—financial institutions that are owned and managed by depositors— and they are federally or state chartered. Every CDCU is unique and tailored to its community. There are some CDCUs with more than 50,000 members and more than $100 million in assets. There are also some CDCUs with a few hundred members and less than $100,000 in assets (National Federation of Community Development Credit Unions [NFCDCU], 2002). Community groups and community-based organizations such as churches are frequently the organizers of CDCUs.

A CDCU gives residents the opportunity to bank at a local institution while at the same time investing in local businesses and property. CDCU members buy one share and in return have one vote. This vote enables them to select the CDCU board and loan committee and to determine which CDCU goals, priorities, and economic development projects will receive support. CDCUs lend money to members, local entrepreneurs, cooperatives, community-owned businesses, and community-based real estate ventures. (Very small CDCUs tend to make only personal loans to members.) The flow of funds from local residents to financial institutions outside of local control is slowed, and investment in community enterprises and projects is encouraged.

In addition to lending services and loan products, many CDCUs offer checking and savings accounts, payroll deductions, automated teller machine (ATM) access, individual retirement accounts (IRAs), and certificates of deposit (CDs or share certificates). CDCUs also cash transfer payment checks (e.g., public assistance, supplemental social security). Some CDCUs, in response to the needs of their members, serve as informal educational institutions, providing financial, tax, and housing counseling. A number of CDCUs have established youth credit unions with a primary emphasis on savings.

CDCUs have lower overhead (e.g., modest offices, lower staff salaries, extensive volunteer participation) and cooperative ownership (which does not expect a market rate return on investment) and therefore are less costly to operate than traditional financial institutions. As a result, they can charge less for their services and can extend credit to creditworthy people who are regularly turned down by banks—single women, the elderly, those with limited incomes, and first-time borrowers.

Deposits from nonmembers are accepted by CDCUs. Many also seek below-market rate deposits and grants from socially oriented investors such as concerned individuals, churches, foundations, banks, and corporations.

Community groups and faith-based organizations wanting to form CDCUs do not have to go it alone. Assistance is available from the NFCDCU (www.natfed.org). The accompanying sidebar profiles the development of a community development credit union in New York's Lower East Side.

Stimulating Community and Economic Development With a CDCU

In 1984, the Manufacturers Hanover Trust Company closed its Lower East Side branch in New York City, leaving a 100-square-block area and more than 50,000 residents without a bank. Two years later, after months of negotiations and a challenge to Manufacturers Hanover under the provisions of the CRA, area residents succeeded in forming the Lower East Side People's Federal Credit Union (LESPFCU), a member-owned, federally chartered and regulated nonprofit organization. As part of its agreement with the community, Manufacturers Hanover gave the credit union the vacant building for 3 years rent free. The company also agreed to make $150,000 worth of renovations and to deposit $100,000 interest free in the credit union. The LESPFCU bought the building from Manufacturers Hanover in 1989 for $90,000.

The goal of the LESPFCU is to stimulate the economic and community development of the Lower East Side by providing a safe, sound, and democratic alternative to traditional banks. Anyone who lives or works on the Lower East Side is eligible to become a member of the credit union for a $30 deposit. The credit union offers personal checking and savings accounts, ATM access, and personal and home mortgage loans. It also offers small business loans of up to $25,000 and microenterprise loans of $10,000 or less to small-scale home-based businesses. Since 1996, the LESPFCU has been certified as a CDFI by the U.S. Department of the Treasury's CDFI Fund. With nearly 4,000 area residents and employees as members and assets of $4.8 million, the LESPFCU's two branches serve nearly 10,000 Lower East Side residents. Since its founding, the credit union has reinvested more than $5.7 million in loans to its community.

SOURCE: Lower East Side People's Federal Credit Union (2002).

Loan Funds

Loan funds are pools of capital established specifically to make loans in situations where conventional sources of financing are lacking.

Community Development Loan Funds

Community development loan funds (CDLFs) are financial intermediaries that accept loans from socially motivated investors and then reinvest the proceeds in community-based organizations and development projects. CDLFs combine the short-term goal of meeting the immediate capital needs of their communities with the long-term goal of effecting social change at the community level. CDLFs are privately owned, nonprofit charitable organizations that stimulate new and expanded investments by individuals and organizations in housing, business, and economic development projects in low- and moderate-income communities. CDLFs are frequently lenders of last resort, providing capital that is not available—or not available on affordable terms—from conventional sources. CDLFs are more flexible on collateral requirements and more liberal on loan structure and terms than are conventional sources. Loans usually range from $5,000 to $50,000 for terms of 1 to 5 years.

CDLFs are usually established by coalitions of community-based organizations and/or institutions. There is no minimum amount of equity or loan capital required to form a CDLF, although in general start-up costs should cover 2 years of operations plus an additional amount for loan loss reserves—a range of $50,000 to $150,000. Sources of grants and loans to capitalize and operate a CDLF come from individuals, religious organizations, foundations, and corporations. An example of a CDLF with a wide range of lending services is described in the accompanying sidebar.

Coalition-Sponsored Community Loan Fund

Founded in 1985 by a coalition of religious institutions and community leaders, the Boston Community Loan Fund (the Loan Fund) is a nonprofit, nonsectarian membership organization. The Loan Fund is part of Boston Community Capital, a community development financial intermediary that invests in projects that provide affordable housing, good jobs, needed goods and services, and new opportunities. The Loan Fund provides below-market financing to nonprofit community organizations that develop and preserve housing for low-income people in the Boston area and also provides construction and working capital loans to nonprofits that serve the community. In addition, the Loan Fund provides new and emerging housing groups with technical assistance so that they can become qualified developers and borrowers. Technical assistance also is provided to all borrowers before, during, and after loans are made to ensure the success of projects. The Loan Fund supplied more than $22 million in loan capital during the 1998–2001 period to qualified organizations, created or preserved hundreds of units of affordable housing, and approved non-housing loans supporting commercial development, child care facilities, youth service organizations, environmental preservation, a school for troubled boys, and a teen pregnancy prevention program. The Loan Fund maintains an excellent record, with total losses of less than one third of 1%.

SOURCE: Boston Community Capital (2002).

Microenterprise Loan Funds

The primary goal of microenterprise loan funds (MLFs) is to help people attain economic self-sufficiency through small (micro) business development. An MLF is a nonprofit revolving loan fund that makes very small, short-term loans for working capital to individuals who want to start or expand very small businesses. Microenterprises are businesses that can be established for less than $10,000 and that employ no more than five people. In the United States, many MLFs are modeled after successful efforts in Bangladesh (e.g., the Grameen Bank) and Indonesia (Louis, 1997; Yunus, 1997). These loan funds are vehicles for reaching low-income entrepreneurs and aspiring entrepreneurs such as street vendors, home manufacturers, farmers, and fishers. Because of their small size, microenterprises have few resources and little expertise. Conventional financial institutions generally avoid these small enterprises because the service costs on the loans needed are often larger than the loan amounts sought. In addition, microenterprises also often lack the collateral necessary to secure conventional loans.

In addition to providing loans, MLFs offer business assistance in planning, marketing, management, and operations. If the small enterprises become large enough to approach mainstream financial institutions, then MLFs can help them with the loan application process. Some MLFs are organized around peer groups that allow creditworthy borrowers to receive loans based on character references and acceptance by their peers in the peer borrowing group. The peer group (usually five to eight members) becomes responsible for loan repayments by its members. Micro loans typically range from $250 to $5,000, with a brief payback period of typically less than 1 year. Loan repayment rates are high, and default rates are nearly nonexistent—a better record than that for conventional financial institutions.

Community groups and other nonprofit agencies, as well as local and state governments, have started MLFs. Capitalization of MLFs comes from public, private, and community sector contributions and grants and from social investors.

The Association for Enterprise Opportunity (AEO), founded in 1991, is a member-based national trade association of more than 400 organizations committed to microenterprise development. These microenterprise programs serve thousands of low-income and disadvantaged entrepreneurs across the United States. The AEO provides public advocacy, increases the awareness of the microenterprise strategy, and works to remove the barriers that impede low-income individuals. The AEO also provides training and peer exchange to its members, organizes an annual conference, develops resource materials for the microenterprise field, and works to expand the funding base for programs (AEO, 2002). The Chicago-based Women's Self-Employment Project, detailed in the accompanying sidebar, is a prime example of microenterprise lending.

Microenterprise Success for Women

The Women's Self-Employment Project (WSEP) was established in 1986 to raise the income and degree of economic self-sufficiency of low- and moderate-income women in the Chicago area through self-employment and asset development. WSEP, a U.S. Department of the Treasury-certified CDFI since 1999, provides business loans that range from $100 to $75,000 (start-up micro loans range from $100 to $5,000, business development loans range from $10,000 to $35,000, and business expansion loans range from $35,000 to $75,000). WSEP also provides peer lending support networks, an entrepreneurial training program, marketing assistance, and business growth guidance. Since 1986, WSEP has provided business training, tools, and information to more than 7,000 women and provided training and technical assistance to more than 2,500 low-income women. More than $1.6 million in micro loans have been disbursed to low- to moderate-income women to start and grow their micro businesses, with a cumulative repayment rate of 82%. As a result of WSEP's efforts, more than 800 businesses have been started, more than 500 businesses have expanded, and more than 2,000 jobs have been created or retained.

WSEP participants, all of whom are women, have ranged in age from 19 to 75 years. Fully 83% are African American, 10% are Caucasian, and 4% are Latino. Of the total participants, 34% receive some form of public assistance, 46% work at full- or part-time jobs, and 78% are the primary sources of income for their families. More than 82% of WSEP businesses are home based, and 10% are located in storefronts. Nearly one third (32%) of WSEP businesses employ additional employees. Businesses created have included apparel, business services, arts and crafts, cosmetology, and food.

Working across the United States and internationally, WSEP provides consultation, research, services, and technical assistance in microenterprise program design, development, and operations. More information on WSEP can be found at www.wsep.net.

SOURCE: Women's Self-Employment Project (2001, 2002).

Revolving Loan Funds

Revolving loan funds (RLFs) are pools of capital established specifically to make loans where conventional sources of finance are lacking. RLFs assist in the financing of housing and business development, often tailoring their loans to the needs of borrowers in ways that conventional lenders cannot. As the loans are repaid, the money returns to the fund to be loaned again for similar purposes. RLFs do not necessarily focus on helping low-income people. RLFs are generally funded by government programs (e.g., Community Development Block Grants). The primary goal of RLFs is to preserve and create employment opportunities in their target areas. RLF loans are usually made to individually owned small and medium-sized businesses and tend to be larger than CDLF or microenterprise loans. Many RLFs also are structured to invest in housing development. RLF loans typically have longer terms and lower interest rates than do conventional sources of financing. Community groups can encourage local government agencies to create revolving loan funds, or they can create their own.

Community Development Banks

Community development banks (CDBs) are typically full-service commercial banks that direct the flow of assets and services back into a geographically specific low-income area. CDBs are established expressly to apply the corporate strategy and resources of banking to stimulate the redevelopment of its surrounding community. They have been referred to as "banks with a heart." CDBs mount active reinvestment programs and provide consumer, commercial, and neighborhood development loans, as well as training and technical assistance, to local ventures in spite of their higher than normal risk. CDBs also attract new outside capital into a community. The accompanying sidebar on ShoreBank illustrates the range of impact of community development banks.

The First "Bank With a Heart"

The first and most notable development bank is South Shore Bank in Chicago (now Shore Bank). The ShoreBank Corporation acquired the South Shore Bank in 1973 when the predecessor bank tried to leave the South Shore community. South Shore is 2 miles square, has a predominantly African American population, has a poverty rate of 27.3%, and is located 9 miles south of Chicago's Loop. To capitalize the bank, numerous organizations and churches provided funds, and South Shore Bank pioneered the linked deposit strategy (where resultant financing made available from deposits is targeted to specific venture types and geographic areas) to attract other socially motivated investors.

Shore Bank serves individual consumers, businesses, faith-based and religious groups, and community organizations, providing personal financial services, consumer loans, home equity loans and lines of credit, business loans, business cash management services, and commercial deposit accounts. Shore Bank is also a major real estate lender in Chicago's South, Mid-South, and Westside neighborhoods. Shore Bank has loaned more than $525 million during the past decade to more than 13,000 businesses and individuals in its priority communities—and made 847 loans, totaling $107.7 million, in 2000 alone (ShoreBank, 2001).

The ShoreBank model has expanded to Cleveland, Detroit, and Washington State, and its consulting company affiliate, ShoreBank Advisory Services, is assisting in establishing small business lending programs in places as diverse as the Caucasus, the Middle East, Mexico and Central America, and the United Kingdom.

SOURCES: Blakely (1994, pp. 195–197); ShoreBank (1999, 2001).

Community Foundations

A community foundation is a tax-exempt, nonprofit, autonomous, publicly supported, nonsectarian philanthropic institution with a long-term goal of building permanent funds for the broad-based charitable benefit of the residents of a defined geographic area (Council on Foundations, 2000). There are more than 600 community foundations across the United States, organized on an individual city, town, county, or state level. Such foundations serve urban, suburban, and rural areas. We have already mentioned the activities of community foundations in Chicago and Portland in previous chapters.

A community foundation functions like a permanent community savings account, where the community—personified in the foundation's board and decision-making body—has a say over how to distribute the earned interest. Donors contribute money, stock, life insurance, real estate, or other assets as planned gifts or bequests payable on the donors' deaths. Contributions to a community foundation are pooled and "endowed"; they are never spent. Instead, they are permanently invested to produce income. This income is then used to make grants to fund-determined eligible groups and activities. Community foundation endowments range in size from less than $100,000 to more than $1 billion.

A community foundation's assets come from numerous, widely diverse sources with locally based interests—individual donors, public and private organizations, governments, and private foundations. Many community foundations solicit contributions from people of means. Some, however, target a wide range of donors, permitting even communities with "modest means" to create and operate community foundations.

In addition to making grants, community foundations can convene community stakeholders, foster partnerships, broker technical assistance, leverage other resources, and build bridges among people, places, and organizations—a true capacity-building aide for communities striving to help themselves (Aspen Institute, 2000).

Community foundations help to maximize the current and long-term impact of charitable activities in a community while providing donors with financial advantages such as tax savings and recognition. Donors are assured that their gifts will benefit their community in perpetuity. Such foundations also ensure that community donations stay in the community, benefiting community-based organizations and efforts. The importance of community foundations in renewal is captured in the accompanying sidebar on the Community Foundation of Lower Flatbush Valley.

Preserving and Conserving Community Assets

Founded in January 1998, the Community Foundation of the Lower Flathead Valley in Pablo, Montana, brings together tribal and nontribal members to work on projects preserving and conserving the cultural, natural, and human resources of the valley with a special emphasis on meeting the needs of children. In 1999, the foundation distributed $14,750 to 11 valley organizations. Grants, ranging from $500 to $3,000, supported a summer reading program, repairs to two community centers, a summer activities and photography program, youth recreation programs, local reading programs, and several local history programs (Community Foundation of the Lower Flathead Valley, 2000). In 2000, the foundation upped its grant making, awarding 21 grants totaling $72,062, ranging from $271 to $19,000, to a similarly wide variety of community group and institution projects (Community Foundation of the Lower Flathead Valley, 2001). In the recession year of 2002, 17 grants totaling $28,182 were awarded (personal communication, Community Foundation of the Lower Flathead Valley, June 15, 2002).

BUILDING INDIVIDUAL FINANCIAL ASSETS

To build personal financial assets and economic standing through education, business creation, and homeownership, most people need some savings or credit histories. Assets provide families with a financial base to weather unexpected events and allow them to think and plan for the longer term. The accumulation of assets, rather than just income, plays a major role in allowing people to escape poverty and achieve wealth (Sherraden, 1991; Schreiner et al., 2001). Sherraden (1991) found that the accumulation of assets also improves family stability and provides a foundation for risk taking (pp. 180–181). Assets also increase political participation because people have greater incentives and greater resources to participate in the political process (p. 165). The concept of individual development accounts (IDAs) emerged to make asset accumulation possible for low-income people previously blocked from so doing. IDAs are leveraged, restricted investment accounts that help low- and moderate-income individuals to build savings; they are essentially subsidized savings accounts. When IDA holders make deposits, those funds are matched primarily by external sources (e.g., foundations, corporations,

religious institutions, government). Savings can be used for education and training, homeownership, and the development of home-based and microenterprise businesses. IDA programs have built budgeting, finance and investment training, and technical assistance into their efforts and are structured to provide long-term and sustained support for participants. An idea under exploration is to have individuals make monthly contributions to the IDAs of families, friends, or community residents.

IDA programs help to achieve a number of important community development goals. They increase an individual's or a family's savings for investment-related activities, encourage long-term thinking and planning, and increase a participant's economic literacy. Support for IDAs has been growing since the Corporation for Enterprise Development (CFED) launched its $11 million, 4-year (1997–2001) IDA American Dream Demonstration (ADD) project in 1996 in 13 host organizations and since Congress passed legislation allowing states to create IDAs (Zdenek, 1996). The CFED (2002) noted the following as of December 2001:

- IDA programs existed in more than 350 communities (more than 10,000 participants), with numerous community programs in development.

- A total of 28 states had included IDAs in their Temporary Assistance for Needy Families (TANF) plans, 27 states had passed some form of IDA legislation, and a few states had IDA legislation pending.
- Several national foundations were supporting the downpayments on the ADD project, a 2,000-account IDA demonstration in 13 sites across the United States.
- Through the federal Assets for Independence Act of 1998, a $125 million, 5-year demonstration project, IDAs were expected to reach an additional 30,000 to 40,000 working poor Americans by the year 2003.
- A May 1999 ruling made IDAs count toward CRA credit under a wide range of tests.

IDAs have spawned a movement, with the CFED sponsoring the *Assets* newsletter, an IDA network (www.idanetwork.org), and an annual IDA learning conference. The CFED, in partnership with the Fannie Mae Foundation and the Capital Area Asset Building Corporation, has developed a Children and Youth Savings Accounts/IDA Project (CFED, 2002). The CFED is also working with Congress and leaders in asset building and children and family development to build support for a national Children's Savings Account policy aimed at reducing intergenerational poverty and asset inequality (R. Bryce-LaPorte, CFED, personal communication, September 23, 2002).

The accompanying sidebar describes a collaborative approach to IDA program development and operation.

San Francisco Bay Area IDA Success

A community-based organization collaborative in the San Francisco Bay area, led by the East Bay Asian Local Development Corporation (EBALDC), moved from an extensive 2-year design and development phase to program implementation in April 1998, becoming California's first functioning IDA program. The collaborative and the EBALDC sponsor the New Employee Asset Building Program as well as the original ADD.

The Bay Area IDA Collaborative partners offer its participants a comprehensive network of resources and services to increase self-sufficiency and wealth accumulation, including credit counseling, first-time homebuyers training, microenterprise training, and personal finance education. As part of the collaborative's support, each month IDA participants attend one of six Savers' Clubs, where they learn about a range of financial topics and share their financial concerns. Volunteers, who also lead workshops, facilitate Savers' Club meetings.

Local contributions to support the IDA program come from 15 groups, including foundations, banks, the United Way, and community-serving agencies. National demonstration sponsors include the Corporation for Enterprise Development and the U.S. Department of Health and Human Services.

Since beginning operations, the collaborative and its participants have managed 16 organizational partners and 4 banking partners, enrolled more than 250 IDA program participants, and accumulated more than $235,000 in participant savings and matches. Among the participants, more than 10% of savers have purchased homes, and more than 30 savers have drawn down, investing more than $50,000 in savings plus matches toward their asset goals. In addition, more than 150 participants had been referred to credit counseling, homeownership workshops, and microenterprise training. The Bay Area Collaborative has created a Spanish-language IDA program and laid the groundwork for a Youth IDA Program.

SOURCE: East Bay Asian Local Development Corporation (1999, 2002).

GRASSROOTS ECONOMICS: CREATING LOCAL MONEY SYSTEMS

Hundreds of U.S. communities issued their own money during the Great Depression of the 1930s because banks had closed and the deposits they held had disappeared. Local money systems enabled local labor and resources to keep producing and recirculating. Since the 1980s, local money systems have been created in the United States by individuals, small groups, and nonprofit organizations in low- and middle-income communities to sustain local economic resources, support local connectivity, and strengthen community networks. In addition, such local systems give residents, especially those with limited cash income, a new way in which to obtain needed goods and services. Community currency is seen as a catalyst for building local economic interdependence and as fundamental to greater community economic self-reliance.

There are a few thousand community money systems in operation across the globe—some having less than 100 participants, others serving a few thousand people (Brandt, 1999, p. 30; Douthewaite, 1996). Systems operate in a variety of ways; some print paper money, others use time dollars where each person's hours of service have the same value, and still others use mutual credit systems where people accrue credits for work valued at market rates (often called local exchange trading systems [LETS]). With these systems, transactions are independent of the external money flow. In the United States, about 10 LETS systems were operating during the mid-1990s; however, there were more than 150 time dollar systems in operation (Douthwaite, 1996, p. 90). Additional systems were online by 2002 (Local Exchange Trading Systems, 2002). Two variations on local money systems are illustrated in the accompanying two sidebars.

Ithaca Hours

Since 1991, Ithaca, a city of 30,000 in New York, has issued more than $85,000 of its own paper currency called Ithaca *hours* to more than 1,000 participants. Building on their own strengths and resources, participants list the goods and services they have to offer in a catalog and then use the hours they earn to purchase goods and services from others. About $500,000 of local trade has been added to the "grassroots national product" (Glover, 1999). The hour notes, in $10 denominations (the average level of hourly wages and salaries in the area), buy a wide range of local goods and services, including child care, car repair, roofing, electrical work, gifts, and nursing care. Hour notes are accepted by restaurants, movie theaters, the bowling alley, and grocery stores, and they can be used for downpayments and home mortgage payments. More than $10,000 of local currency has been donated to 60 nonprofit community organizations by the Ithaca hours governing body (Glover, 2002). In an effort to spread the concept, Ithaca hours has made available a "Home Town Money Starter" kit.

Member Organized Resource Exchange

Ten low-income neighborhoods in and around St. Louis participate in Member Organized Resource Exchange (MORE) time dollar (Brandt, 1999). Created during the early 1980s by the Grace Hill Settlement House, the non-currency-based "hour for hour" system has involved approximately 6,000 people, who provide each other with a wide range of services such as child care, housecleaning, rides to medical appointments, snow shoveling, and tutoring. Some participants receive credit for helping their neighbors; others receive "payment" for volunteering in Grace Hill's programs. A computerized tracking system records all of the services given and received by members. Grace Hill has also started a "Time Store" stocked with donated goods and supplies, many of which are solicited by the members.

SUMMARY

In all communities, residents and businesses have capital and credit needs. Capital plays a critical role in providing growth for the future. Lack of access to capital and credit is a basic problem in distressed communities. Community controlled development organizations—individually, in coalitions, or in partnership with other nonprofits and the public and private sectors—have shown that they can help willing people of limited means to obtain capital for any worthwhile project. They can also serve as advocates and catalysts in CRA challenges, stop bank branches from closing, push for the creation of revolving loan funds, and negotiate investments/deposits to CDFIs. Likewise, they can monitor CRA agreements; organize groups to develop, invest in, or join CDFIs; market traditional bank products; capitalize loan pools; and co-insure loans. Community groups can also identify and refer applicants to financial institutions, provide credit counseling services and budgeting classes, manage and operate credit unions, loan funds and IDA programs, and create community foundations. Furthermore, communities can create their own currency to bolster the multiplier effect—increasing the recirculation of local dollars.

All of the preceding examples require community groups to build linkages to other organizations within and outside their communities. Groups also need to gather and analyze data to gain a detailed understanding of their communities' (e.g., individuals, families, entrepreneurs, businesses) credit needs, capital flows, local banking practices, and barriers to asset accumulation.

CONTINUING QUESTIONS

1. How can a community organization successfully educate its residents on the value of saving and building assets for family stability and growth?

2. Can such savings be accumulated in ways that build the local community?

3. How can a neighborhood organization best support strong vigilance by government to prevent redlining of small communities?

4. Is ours a society that encourages saving as much as it does spending and consumption? What can be done to promote savings?

5. How can local financial institutions help to maximize participation? What training opportunities does local capital building create that can enhance community leadership?

REFERENCES

American Assembly. (1997). *Community capitalism: Rediscovering the markets of America's urban neighborhoods* (Proceedings from the 91st American Assembly). New York: Author.

Aspen Institute. (2000). *The Rural Development and Community Foundations Initiative.* Washington, DC: Author. Retrieved July 12, 2000, from the World Wide Web: http://aspeninst.org/rural

Association for Enterprise Opportunity. (2002). Retrieved September 20, 2002, from the World Wide Web: www.microenterprise.org/whoweare/profile

Blakely, E. J. (1994). *Planning local economic development: Theory and practice* (2nd ed.). Thousand Oaks, CA: Sage.

Boston Community Capital. (2002). Retrieved March 12, 2002, from the World Wide Web: www.bostoncommunitycapital.org/loan/fund/index.html

Brandt, B. (1999, June–July). Low-income groups try out community money systems. *Dollars and Sense,* pp. 30–33.

Community Foundation of the Lower Flathead Valley. (2000). Retrieved July 12, 2000, from the World Wide Web: www.lfvcf.org/enter.html

Community Foundation of the Lower Flathead Valley. (2001). Retrieved February 15, 2001, from the World Wide Web: www.lfvcf.org/enter.html

Corporation for Enterprise Development. (2002). Retrieved February 16, 2002, from the World Wide Web: www.idanetwork.org/assets/winter2002/winter2002.html

Council on Foundations. (2000). *What is a community foundation?* [Online]. Retrieved July 12, 2002, from the World Wide Web:www.cof. org/whatis/cofservices/4community/community.htm

Douthwaite, R. (1996) *Short circuit: Strengthening local economies for security in an unstable world.* Dublin, Ireland: Lilliput Press.

East Bay Asian Local Development Corporation. (1999). *Join the Bay Area IDA program and start saving for life: Bay Area Collaborative IDA program brochure.* Oakland, CA: Author.

East Bay Asian Local Development Corporation. (2002). *Bay Area Collaborative IDA project description.* [Online]. Retrieved September 21, 2002, from the World Wide Web: www.ebaldc.com/contents/ned.htm

Glover, P. (1999). *Grassroots economics.* Retrieved November 11, 1999, from the World Wide Web: www.context.org/iclib/ic41/glover.html

Glover, P. (2002). *Creating community economies with local currency.* [Online]. Retrieved February

22, 2002, from the World Wide Web: www.lightlink.com/hours/ithaca_hours/intro.html

Goldstein, D. (1999). *Understanding predatory lending: Moving toward a common definition and working solutions.* Washington, DC: Joint Center for Housing Studies and Neighborhood Reinvestment Corporation. Available on the World Wide Web: www.nw.org/network-strategies/campaign/publications/pdf/predatory_lending1199.pdf

King, L. (2002, Spring). NCRC members advocate for new predatory lending consumer protection in over 30 states. *NCRC Reinvestment Works,* pp. 1, 4.

Local Exchange Trading Systems. (2002). Retrieved February 16, 2002, from the World Wide Web: www.transaction.net/money/lets

Louis, E. T. (1997, July–August). Grameen's lessons. *Dollars and Sense,* pp. 30–31.

Lower East Side People's Federal Credit Union. (2002). Retrieved March 28, 2002, from the World Wide Web: www.lespfcu.org/pfcu.html

National Community Capital Association. (1999). *Frequently asked questions about National Community Capital Association.* [Online]. Retrieved November 11, 1999, from the World Wide Web: www.communitycapital. org/cdfis.html

National Community Reinvestment Coalition. (1996a, June–July). *NCRC Reinvestment Compendium.* (Washington, DC: Author)

National Community Reinvestment Coalition. (1996b, November–December). *NCRC Reinvestment Compendium.* (Washington, DC: Author)

National Community Reinvestment Coalition. (1999, Winter). Detroit Alliance for Fair Banking and Michigan National Bank establish $1 billion development plan for Detroit. *Reinvestment Works,* p. 12. (Washington DC: Author)

National Community Reinvestment Coalition. (2002). Retrieved March 12, 2002, from the World Wide Web: www.ncrc.org/cra/index.html

National Community Reinvestment Coalition. (Fall 2002). NCRC victorious in effort to change Household's practices. *Reinvestment Works,* pp. 1–2. (Washington DC: Author)

National Federation of Community Development Credit Unions. (2002). Retrieved March 3, 2002, from the World Wide Web: www.natfed.org/home.html

National People's Action. (2002). Retrieved May 1, 2002, from the World Wide Web: www.npaus.org/issues/cra/npa-recommendations.htm

National People's Action. (September-October, 2002). NPA celebrates Citigroup $215 million settlement for predatory lending practices. *Disclosure,* p. 1. (Chicago, IL: Author)

National Training and Information Center. (1990). *CRA handbook.* Chicago: Author.

Schreiner, M., Sherraden, M., Clancy, M., Johnson, L., Curley, J., Grinstein-Weiss, M., Zhan, M., & Beverly, S. (2001). *Savings and asset accumulation in individual development accounts, downpayments on the American Dream Policy Demonstration, a national demonstration of IDAs, accumulation in low-resource households: Evidence from individual development accounts.* St. Louis, MO: George Warren Brown School of Social Work, Center for Social Development.

Seidman, E. (1999, Winter). Targeting vulnerability: The crux and cure to predatory lending. *Neighborworks Journal,* pp. 14–17.

Sherraden, M. (1991). *Assets and the poor: A new welfare policy.* Armonk, NY: M. E. Sharpe.

ShoreBank. (1999). Retrieved November 30, 1999, from the World Wide Web: http://sbk.com/history.html

ShoreBank. (2001). Retrieved April 13, 2001, from the World Wide Web: www.shorebankcorp.com

Tansey, C. D. (2001, September). Community development credit unions: An emerging player in low-income communities. *Capital Xchange,* p. 2. (Washington, DC: Brookings Institution Center on Urban and Metropolitan Policy and Harvard University Joint Center for Housing Studies)

U.S. Department of Housing and Urban Development. (2000, August). Subprime lending more likely in minority and low-income areas. *Recent Research Results,* pp. 1–2. (Washington DC: Author)

U.S. Department of the Treasury. (2002). *Inside the CDFI Fund.* Retrieved March 3, 2002, from the World Wide Web: www.cdfifund.gov/overview/index.html

Women's Self-Employment Project. (2001). *WSEP organizational brochure.* Chicago: Author.

Women's Self-Employment Project. (2002). *Primary mission and organization performance.* [Online]. Retrieved September 23, 2002, from the the World Wide Web: www.wsep.net

Yunus, M. (1997, July–August). The Grameen Bank story: Microlending for economic development. *Dollars and Sense,* pp. 27–29.

Zdenek, R.O. (1996, September–October). Creating stakeholders with individual development accounts. *Shelterforce,* pp. 18–20. (Orange, NJ: National Housing Institute)

13

NEIGHBORHOOD PRESERVATION THROUGH AFFORDABLE HOUSING

Don't move, improve.

—slogan of Banana Kelly Neighborhood Improvement Association,

South Bronx, New York City

The general welfare and security of the nation and the health and living standards of its people require a decent home and suitable living environment for every American family.

—National Housing Act of 1949

Housing is a basic building block of communities and the land use that most directly affects residents. The availability of and access to safe, affordable quality housing directly affects community welfare, social fabric, and community cohesion. Quality housing therefore is a major contributor to the well-being of community residents. As a major component of the built environment, a community's housing stock is the embodiment of the perception (and reality) of the decline or prosperity of a community and its residents.

The housing challenges facing a distressed community can include substandard housing; the lack of income to pay mortgages, rent, or utility bills; rising and excessive rents; overcrowding; unfair housing practices and barriers to homeownership; an abundance of absentee landlords who leave property in disrepair; and steeply escalating real estate values that squeeze out lower-income and eventually moderate-income residents. The long-term trend of the reductions in the numbers of rental units affordable to extremely low-income and very low-income households accelerated during the late 1990s—a critical shortage problem, according to the U.S. Department of Housing and Urban Development (HUD, 2001, p. 1).

Community-based housing and neighborhood preservation activities and programs include efforts in which community members, home-owners, tenants, and locally based organizations with partners and collaborators join together to intervene in conditions and factors that adversely affect the stability of the community, the housing stock and housing market, and the quality of life of residents. Such initiatives include organizing and advocacy to increase the availability and access to decent housing, community and consumer education, and the provision of services or resources needed for housing. In addition, community-based housing initiatives include the production, rehabilitation, management, and/or ownership of housing.

Four measures (each linked to all of the others) can be used to assess housing in a community and the housing options presented to current and former residents:

1. *Accessibility:* Is there fair and equal access to a resident's or potential resident's choice of housing type and location?

2. *Adequacy:* Is the quality of the housing high? Is the housing safe and habitable? Does it meet fire, health, safety, and building codes? Does it meet family size and needs?

3. *Affordability:* Is there a range of opportunities to rent or own for all members of the community? Are there adequate resources to preserve and maintain both the interior and exterior of the housing? (According to the federal government, housing is considered affordable if it consumes no more than 30% of a household's income.)

4. *Availability:* Is there a range or diversity of types to serve the needs of all members of the community?

FORCES AFFECTING HOUSING MARKET STABILITY AND HOUSING OPTIONS

There are a variety of economic, social, and political forces that affect the stability of a community's housing market and housing options. All affect housing accessibility, adequacy, affordability, and availability to some degree. Some forces are locally based and can be locally influenced or countered. Many are beyond a single community's ability to change—but they must be identified and dealt with nonetheless.

Burgess's filtering-down theory explains how different socioeconomic groups come to occupy particular neighborhoods (Blair, 1995, pp. 244–245; Burgess, 1925). Filtering is a process in which higher-income groups move farther from a city and lower-income groups move into the vacated housing. As incomes among high-income groups rise, demand for housing increases. Some buy newly constructed houses that will likely be located farther from the heart of the city where vacant land is available. It is often less expensive to build on vacant land, and inner-city lots are generally too small to accommodate the preferences of upper-income households. Blair (1995) identified three likely possibilities of who occupies and what happens to the vacated houses:

1. *No filtering:* Families from similar economic backgrounds purchase the vacated housing. There is no change in the economic status of the neighborhood. This does not increase the amount of housing available to lower-income people.

2. *Complete filtering:* A comparable income group is not willing to pay prices of housing, even though the quality of units has not deteriorated. Housing prices fall and homes become available to lower-income households.

3. *Filtering and adaptation:* Houses often undergo some adaptive change when they filter to a lower-income group. Lower-income families may not be able to afford the same level of maintenance. Some may wish to divide the houses to accommodate more people, and single family units will become multi-family units, thereby increasing density. Higher-income people will begin to move out at an accelerated pace due to congestion, noise, fear, real or perceived increases in crime, and increasing limited-income families moving into the area. After a certain concentration of a group has moved, a community may "tip" and filtering may accelerate. (pp. 244–245)

When landlords reside in the buildings they rent, they tend to maintain property better than if they live elsewhere. Research findings also suggest that when landlords live in the community, they tend to maintain their rental units better (Porell, 1985, p. 116). When landlords move from the community, the quality of the housing stock may fall, accelerating the filtering process.

Blockbusting refers to real estate activity whereby brokers encourage whites to sell at low prices, preying on fears that non-whites are taking over the neighborhood or community. Real estate dealers hope to either purchase the properties cheaply and then resell them at a substantial profit or simply turn over properties to earn commissions. Redlining, as described in Chapter 12, occurs when lending institutions withhold mortgage financing from potential buyers in neighborhoods or communities that are undergoing economic transition to lower-income groups. If mortgage funds are not available, then the price of housing will tend to fall, speeding the process of change. A community with a high degree of homeownership can tip toward a high concentration of renters that tend to be more transient and less invested in the community. Although outlawed since 1968, unscrupulous real estate practices continue to be used in ways that have the effect of replacing segregated white communities with segregated non-white communities. These practices include blockbusting, racial steering, and redlining. Active community-based fair housing organizations work to prevent them, but such practices still occur in ways that isolate and segregate poor and non-white families.

Housing segregation results in limited housing choices and speeds up the cycle of community decline (Blair, 1995, p. 255). People find themselves housed in areas that might not suit their housing preferences and in areas that might not offer attractive appreciation potential. They have less access to jobs in the outer-metropolitan rings where much job growth is occurring. Housing segregation occurs from lender discrimination, blockbusting, steering by real estate agents, and the relatively limited incomes of persons of color forcing them to locate in areas of low-quality (less-costly) housing. Many persons of color are hesitant to locate in white communities because they anticipate hostility or at least not a welcoming environment.

Lending discrimination means that properties will tend to be rental rather than owner-occupied ones. Difficulties in obtaining mortgage loans reduce property values because few can afford to purchase a home without a mortgage. When property values soften, fewer potential buyers will be interested in an area.

Gentrification is a pattern of change in the profile of a neighborhood's population accompanied by an increase in housing values resulting from an influx of high-income owners into previously lower-income urban neighborhoods (Holcomb & Beauregard, 1981; Keating & Smith, 1996). Gentrification is something that happens *to* a community (especially a poor community) when the location is convenient and the housing is basically attractive, even if dilapidated (Rubin & Rubin, 1992, p. 117). It may also occur if the larger environment has some spectacular quality such as a major university, a waterfront, a government capital, or a truly historic link. Also termed neighborhood upgrading and reverse filtering, gentrification typically involves higher-income newcomers (often single white professionals) replacing lower-income, long-term residents (often persons of color). Often called "urban pioneers," such newcomers have moved into older neighborhoods, acquired homes cheaply, restored dilapidated housing, and created market demand for housing and services by upgrading the community. In the process, they have often eliminated below-market housing, especially for renters, and converted rental housing into condominiums, thus causing the displacement of many residents (limited-income and working class persons) who are unable to afford higher housing costs. It has been argued that once there have been substantial shifts in the incomes and lifestyles of residents of such neighborhoods, it is inevitable that middle- and upper-class newcomers will drive out lower-class residents because of incompatibility. Holcomb and Beauregard (1981) found that gentrification is often erroneously perceived as a migration back to the city by middle- and upper-income people and is interpreted as a vote of confidence that carries the hope for urban revival (p. 41). Research suggests that gentrification actually may be only retaining those who were already in the city and lived in other locations or providing housing for the educated sons and daughters of city dwellers (Chicago Rehab Network, 1993).

The government assists and encourages gentrification by providing grants and loans for housing rehabilitation to eligible households, declaring historic districts and landmarks, improving public services, and making capital investments such as sewage system and park improvements. Government further stimulates renovation through strict code enforcement and by allocating tax dollars to these areas. Homeownership is encouraged through tax concessions and subsidized low-interest loans. Moreover, the resultant increases in property tax assessments speed the flight of original residents and free more housing for gentrifiers.

The costs of displacement not only are financial (e.g., moving expenses, security deposits, increased rent, new utilities) but also are social (e.g., loss of community ties, reduced proximity to friends and relatives and to medical and other social services) and emotional (e.g., the trauma of displacement from familiar locations).

Sarkissian (1976), in her historical review of "social mix in town planning," argued optimistically that greater socioeconomic diversity in neighborhoods would help to promote a stable social mix of community leaders, provide alternative role models, encourage artistic diversity, encourage cultural cross-fertilization, increase equality of opportunities for low-income persons, avoid residential instability, reduce social tensions, and prepare residents for life in a diverse world. Time has shown that the many forces and trends Sarkissian envisioned could come into conflict and provoke consequences opposite to her prediction; for example, affluent newcomers can drive out people with low or modest resources, stamp on blue-collar values, and increase real estate speculation. This poses a dilemma for many distressed communities—how to attract and retain middle- and upper-income residents (a process that will likely push up housing prices), but doing so without displacing people of modest incomes. There is no easy solution to this.

During the 1950s and 1960s, many inner-city neighborhoods were destroyed by "slum" clearance to make way for redevelopment. Large-scale transportation system developments (highways, mass transit links, and nodes) still threaten and negatively affect many communities. Urban renewal and transportation system development typically occur in limited-income communities and communities of color, which are picked both for their locations and for the lack of influence of residents to stop redevelopment. These practices have also resulted in resident and business displacement.

HOUSING MARKET ANALYSIS

It is important that strategies, short- and long-term plans, and programs and activities emanate from sound current data and information. Housing market data can be collected as part of a community planning process or as part of an organization's planning process. Once collected and analyzed, the data should be used to inform where to intervene (both condition/issue and location), how to intervene, and when to intervene. They should also serve to guide each organization in finding its niche and particularly its role in housing revitalization activities.

Information typically gathered in a housing market analysis is listed in the accompanying sidebar. Much information may be on hand from studies and surveys and can be found in a library or a local planning department. However, property information usually needs to be gathered by going door to door and observing or assessing. All information should be updated on a regular basis so that changes (both positive and negative) can be assessed and any changes in strategies and plans can be made. It is helpful to map any relevant information and to take photographs of each property, developing a "montage" or streetscape so that areas of particular strength or weakness (including clusters of property) can be easily identified. A thorough housing market analysis can also be used to build a case for additional resources, the development of special targeted programs, and changes in housing policy. The gathering and analysis of housing data offers an important opportunity for community participation and community education.

Information to Gather for a Housing Market Analysis

It is important, when analyzing housing data, to look for patterns and trends in all of the following categories, based on population characteristics such as gender, age, race, and ethnicity, to determine what positive or negative forces are at work:

- Population demographics of the community and settlement patterns of the residents (past, current, trends)
- Housing stock
    - Supply: amounts, characteristics (type of structure, year built, plumbing, condition)
    - Residential building activity: (current, planned) construction, rehabilitation, demolition, conversion
- Market conditions
    - Occupancy (rent, own, lease)
    - Tenure of occupancy
    - Vacancy
- Mortgage market
    - Sources and availability of funds and access to funds
    - Interest rates and terms of mortgages
    - Mortgage and deed recordings
- Sales market
    - General market conditions
    - Speculative versus contract building
    - Marketing experience (new and existing)
    - Price trends (new and existing)
    - Unsold inventory of new houses (price, months unsold)
    - Houses under construction
    - Foreclosures
- Rental market
    - General market conditions
    - New rental housing (year, type, rents, marketing experience, competitive status with existing rental housing)
    - Rental housing under construction (volume, type, quality, probable marketing schedule) and rental housing committed but not started (volume, type, quality)
    - Foreclosures
- Housing demand
    - Quantitative demand: projected increase in households, by tenure, by geographic submarkets
    - Qualitative demand: single- and multi-family, potential for subsidized housing
- Zoning
    - Location of and restrictions on residential and mixed use

The Chicago Rehab Network (1993) suggested the following as major "housing misery" indicators that signal a housing crisis in a community. A community will be on its way to crisis if only a few of these indicators are present. Many of these indicators require comparisons with other communities. A crisis is indicated when the following conditions exist:

- The median household income is at or below the government poverty level
- At least 40% of renters spend more than 35% of their incomes on rent
- Single-family homes drop in value
- Loans made by conventional lenders decrease
- A high number of housing units are lost (over the preceding decade)
- A high number (or an increase in the number) of demolitions or demolition court filings occurs
- At least 4% of residential buildings are abandoned
- More than 25% of lots are vacant
- A significant number of children suffer from lead poisoning (pp. 12–13)

Housing and Neighborhood Preservation Tool Kit

A useful and informative tool for housing and neighborhood preservation is the "Equitable Development Toolkit: Beyond Gentrification" (available through PolicyLink [2002] at www.policylink.org). The tools, based on the most successful strategies developed in culturally diverse communities, include model policies, case studies, ordinances, and resources in the areas of affordable housing, controlling development, financing strategies, and income and asset creation. Among the numerous equitable development "principles in action" are understanding the economic, political, and social forces at work in the community; assessing, mapping, and analyzing the potential for displacement; supporting resident participation in land use planning; stabilizing current residents; building public awareness of the issues; promoting diverse homeownership opportunities; and planning for newcomers to promote a diverse community mix and to ensure affordability.

HOUSING-RELATED ORGANIZING AND ADVOCACY

The first federal fair housing law was passed in 1968 after the murder of Martin Luther King, Jr., who with others in the civil rights movement brought national attention to the widespread problem of housing segregation. The Fair Housing Law made numerous practices illegal—from steering, to segregated neighborhoods, to discrimination in the sale and rental of housing. Although fair housing enforcement has become sophisticated, community-based organizations continue to be actively involved in organizing and advocating for fair housing because once overt bias practices are now subtle or covert. Organizing and advocacy may take the form of participating in a community-wide or region-wide effort frequently coordinated by a fair housing group. Activities usually focus on tenant, homeowner, and real estate agent education regarding fair housing legislation, monitoring (and testing) of real estate, lending and insurance practices, and (when necessary) assisting with legal actions. The accompanying sidebar highlights a far-reaching fair housing education and outreach effort.

Comprehensive Fair Housing Education and Outreach

The Fair Housing Council of Suburban Philadelphia aggressively identifies new forums through which to spread the fair housing message to the public, public officials, building owners, and the real estate industry. The council has created a referral network that will assist fair housing advocacy groups and others involved in fair housing to better inform their clients of their rights and resources to assist with cases of discrimination. Employees of social service agencies serving women, low-income residents, minorities, and persons with disabilities receive fair housing training. The council also provides continuing education opportunities to realtors, housing managers, and landlords as well as training and technical assistance to zoning boards. In 2001, the council trained more than 100 housing counselors. A newsletter, the *Delaware County Fair Housing News,* informs more than 1,100 readers on fair housing issues.

SOURCE: U.S. Department of Housing and Urban Development (2002a).

Community-based organizations are also involved in the preservation of low-income housing through local- and regional-level low-income housing coalitions and as members of the National Low-Income Housing Coalition (NLIHC). Housing affordability, especially among lower-income renters, has been at a crisis stage for many years. One third (36 million) of American households are renters (NLIHC, 2002b). On average, across the United States, a person or family must earn $14.66 per hour—nearly three times the federal minimum wage—to afford to rent a two-bedroom apartment at fair market rent (NLIHC, 2002b). On the local, regional, and national levels, low-income housing preservation activities include education, research, technical assistance, monitoring the impacts of legislation, policy creation, and education of government officials (lobbying). The NLIHC's (2002a) *Advocate's Guide to Housing and Community Development Policy,* available on the Web at www.nlihc.org, is an excellent resource for community groups wanting to influence housing programs and legislation.

The accompanying sidebar describes housing trust funds and highlights the National Housing Trust Fund Campaign, a nationwide affordable housing organizing effort endorsed by more than 3,000 organizations, municipalities, and elected officials.

Preserving Affordability: Housing Trust Funds

Housing trust funds are distinct funds established by legislation, ordinance, or resolution by cities, counties, and states to receive public revenues that can be spent only to support the production and preservation of affordable housing. A key characteristic of a housing trust fund is that it receives ongoing revenues from dedicated sources of pubic funding such as taxes, loan repayments, and fees. More than 250 state and local housing trust funds have supported hundreds of thousands of affordable housing units (NHTF, 2002). According to the National Housing Trust Fund Campaign, these housing trust funds spend more than $500 million for affordable housing every year, and the amount is increasing (NHTF, 2002). On average, another $5 to $10 is leveraged in other public and private resources for every $1 committed to a housing project by a housing trust fund. Housing trust funds support a wide range of low- and very low-income housing activities, including preservation of existing housing, new construction, emergency repairs, homeless shelters, and housing-related services. Housing trust funds "enable jurisdictions to elevate their funding of critical housing needs by committing resources to a process that treats affordable housing as an essential component of maintaining healthy communities" (NHTF, 2002). Proponents of housing trust funds point to jurisdictional documentation of increased jobs, growing sales taxes, higher property tax revenues, and many other economic benefits. The Center for Community Change's Housing Trust Fund Project (www.communitychange.org) is an excellent source for information and technical assistance.

The National Housing Trust Fund Campaign, coordinated by the NLIHC, is seeking to create a national trust fund program through legislative action. The campaign is working to ensure an adequate amount of affordable housing and to demonstrate that investment in housing is an economic stimulus. More information about the national campaign can be found at www.nhtf.org.

Organizing, advocacy, and action related to the Community Reinvestment Act have decreased redlining and made home repair and mortgage loans more available in limited-income and distressed communities.

Many groups are active in historic preservation, identifying individual properties or whole areas that have historic (as well as social and cultural) value to the community. Historic preservation organizing and advocacy activities can include lobbying for historic designation on the local, state, and/or national levels; "stopping the bulldozers" in an effort to preserve valued and valuable property; assisting historic property owners with securing financing; and organizing a community effort to buy and rehabilitate a community landmark property.

On a more local level, community groups advocate and organize for and against zoning, for and against development and redevelopment projects, and for funding to support community-based housing initiatives.

HOUSING STABILIZATION AND PRESERVATION

Housing stabilization and preservation initiatives, also called incumbent upgrading, include a range of activities and programs that help to preserve the quality of housing by stemming the deterioration of the existing housing stock or retaining vacant housing stock for future use. Such efforts encourage the preservation of a community, maintain attractive older housing, attract additional investment, often increase assessed value, and do not displace residents. Housing stabilization and preservation activities also reduce the potential financial windfall of many traditional gentrification projects (Rubin & Rubin, 1992, p. 118).

There are a variety of reasons why a community's housing stock may begin to decline. In many communities, the housing stock is aging, requiring costly repair and replacement action. Life factors (e.g., divorce, illness, job loss, more children) challenge residents' ability to maintain or sustain continual ownership. Often, residents have little or no income for maintenance and upkeep, or they lack the knowledge and skills needed to do regular maintenance. Landlords, especially those who live outside the community, frequently delay or neglect common maintenance. People planning to move or who fear property value decline tend not to invest in maintenance and improvements to their homes (Galster, 1987).

A leaky roof today, if neglected, can become a major costly roof replacement in the future. A hanging gutter, if not repaired, can lead to major water damage and costly future repairs.

The delay or neglect of routine home maintenance and improvement, no matter the cause, can lead to further deterioration and in some cases abandonment (not always the occupant's choice). Abandoned properties can become a significant safety problem and are eyesores that visually and spiritually chip away at a community's core. If unaddressed, many abandoned properties are demolished, leaving vacant lots. Such lots often become overgrown and littered with trash. Vacant lots also break up the visual integrity of a street and place large gaps between neighbors. A vacant lot means the loss of an opportunity for a family to stay in or join a community.

Community organizations coordinate, carry out, and participate in a variety of activities and programs aimed at the stabilization and preservation of a community's housing stock. The most effective efforts include a combination of activities, full use of community volunteers, and the participation of others with a stake in the community. Many of these efforts also present a good opportunity to employ residents, provide skill and preemployment training, and offer entrepreneurial opportunities to residents and the community sponsor. Community groups take on a range of roles—advocating for the creation, continuation, or expansion of programs; monitoring program operations; coordinating and facilitating the efforts of others; and developing, operating, and managing efforts as nonprofit or for-profit enterprises.

Resources to fund stabilization and preservation activities can come from grassroots fund-raising efforts, donations, corporate and foundation grants, the public sector, and the private sector.

Following are some examples of housing stabilization and preservation activities engaged in by community-focused housing efforts.

Code Enforcement. There are three basic steps involved in code enforcement: research, education, and action. Community groups must become familiar with the fire, health, building, and safety codes and regulations in their area as well as the agencies responsible for oversight and enforcement. An inventory of the housing stock and a basic conditions report will provide direction as to which properties are in most violation or pose the greatest hazard. Care must be taken to advise and educate all property owners on the codes and regulations so as to alert them to make necessary repairs and improvements. If repairs or improvements are not made voluntarily, then action is taken to persuade the property owner to act, with citing for code violations as the final recourse. Code enforcement can pose a dilemma for community groups because there are usually limited-income property owners (including senior citizens) who cannot afford the needed repairs. Efforts must be taken to ensure that such property owners are not forced out or financially penalized. In cases where violations are not severe enough to have property owners fined, community groups often provide volunteers to help with the repairs or even post property owner identification signs on buildings that are soon to be in violation in the hope that public pressure and embarrassment will push the owners to improve the properties. Valuable to many community groups are computerized property records by street address for every property in their neighborhoods, which keep track of conditions of and changes to local property and record significant events at and in properties such as change of use, interior remodeling, fires, arrests, crimes, zoning violations, and visible exterior decline or improvement.

Paint-Ups, Fix-Ups, Spruce-Ups. Such efforts are aimed at using volunteers and donated materials and supplies to do moderate exterior and interior repairs to homes owned or occupied by limited-income or fixed-income residents. Volunteers may come from the community group, community residents, faith-based organizations, employees of community institutions and businesses, and the United Way or other corporate volunteer efforts. Materials and supplies are donated from local and regional/chain businesses, with tools often being left with the homeowners. An example of this type of effort is "Christmas in April," which operates nationwide.

Christmas in April recruits groups of volunteers, often corporate volunteer teams, with a wide range of skills to fix up the homes of limited-income homeowners, often identified by local community organizations. Interior and exterior painting, porch repair and construction, window repair, carpet replacement, and the like

are done by teams of volunteers with donated (or low-cost) supplies.

Weatherization Programs. Such programs are often coordinated, marketed, and operated by community groups, utility companies, and local governments or redevelopment authorities. The focus is on energy efficiency and cost savings on utility bills in addition to low-cost or no-cost improvements to the exterior of homes provided by new windows and doors, caulking, and weather stripping. Such repairs also improve exterior property appearance.

Home Repair Programs. These programs offer low-cost or no-cost inspections, low-cost on-site repairs, design assistance, and/or education for homeowners and renters so that they are able to make their own repairs. Home repair programs present the opportunity for employment of community residents and youth as a training ground or the first step to entrepreneurship. Home repair programs often incorporate a tool lending library—a source of home improvement tools on loan to community residents. In addition to lending tools either free or for a small fee, the tool lending libraries often provide advice on tool use and on home improvement and maintenance techniques. Tool lending libraries are usually initiated and run by community groups. Local businesses donate materials or make available expert employees to instruct residents on home maintenance. Home improvement workshops provided on-site or at a community site offer residents the opportunity to learn essential home maintenance and repair skills such as proper use of power tools and how to fix simple plumbing problems. Such skills can provide cost savings in both the short and long term.

Housing Resource Bank/Donated Materials Warehouse. Such banks and warehouses are operated by nonprofit organizations that solicit and receive noncash resources (e.g., building materials and supplies, the use of trucks or tools) from private businesses and use recycled or bulk-purchased materials for distribution to community-based organizations or individual residents so as to implement housing improvement projects. Housing resource bank staff members are available to give technical assistance either on-site or at the resource bank. Such programs are often coupled with home repair programs.

Community Skills Bank. This is a registry of people signed up to volunteer their time and talents, specifying in advance the skills they are offering, the times they are available, and any other conditions they have set for volunteering or bartering their work. An organization can list kinds of assistance available in a systematic way and then match volunteers to residents' needs and to community projects. A skills bank offers a way in which to draw on expertise located outside the community in professional firms, social service agencies, businesses, and corporations and to put these people to work for a distressed community. The result can be sizable money savings for residents. By serving as a "capacity inventory," a skills bank matches needs with the capabilities of residents. The skills bank or barter exchange can be operated by an existing organization but can also be the impetus for establishing a new organization. Such efforts can also serve as a referral file to match area residents with neighborhood jobs.

Low-Interest/No-Interest Home Repair Programs. Many organizations offer loans at low or no interest to pay for materials and labor to do basic maintenance, make modest repairs and improvements, and bring properties into code compliance. Home repair loan pools may be funded and operated by a community-based organization, offered through a local bank, or funded by and housed in the local government. Community-level programs often reduce or eliminate loan interest for volunteer time with community improvement projects.

Sealing Buildings to Preserve Them for Future Use. Typically, it is the responsibility of building inspection departments (or property owners) to seal (close up) vacant property. However, after such properties are sealed, they often become unsealed due to weather, vandals, squatters, drug dealers, and the like. Once they are unsealed, vacant buildings can become health and safety hazards, and additional deterioration may take place, necessitating demolition in the future. Community groups have organized to monitor and report unsealed vacant property. They have also formed building sealing crews that receive a contract fee from the local government to keep buildings sealed. In addition, groups have used resident and other volunteers to seal such buildings. Local artists then paint and decorate the bare plywood (often painting curtains and window panes) to camouflage vacancy and boost curb appeal.

Demolition and Recapturing of Materials for Reuse. If a property deteriorates to the point where it must be demolished, then the recapturing and reuse of building materials (e.g., bricks, flooring, some mechanicals, plumbing) can help to offset the costs of other repair, rehabilitation, and construction projects in the community. These activities often can be opportunities for youth training and employment as well as for small business development. Salvaged materials businesses that market wares beyond the community can be solid local economic generators, especially if they are community owned and operated.

HOUSING DEVELOPMENT: REHABILITATION AND CONSTRUCTION

Housing development goals and activities are shaped by community conditions, local trends, opportunities, and organizational/community capacity. In distressed communities, housing development goals are often focused on community stabilization and on providing long-term, affordable quality housing for existing community residents who could not otherwise afford the decent, safe, and accessible housing that is currently available on the private market—especially if housing values are increasing. It is important for affordable family housing to be part of the larger community vision and plan (Jones, Pettus, & Pyatok, 1995). In many cases, the development of affordable housing stands out as a symbol of hope and a better family and community future. In other instances, it fits in with the existing housing as a complement to the present and a bridge to the past.

Housing development activities include housing rehabilitation and construction for rental housing or homeownership aimed at the whole range of community residents—individuals and families, seniors, the homeless, substance abusers, persons with special needs. Such housing may be permanent, transitional (temporary), or supportive (offering a range of social and physical services).

Community groups play a variety of roles in housing development—from influence to control. They rally and sustain community support for or against a proposed project. They negotiate to ensure maximum benefits to their community. They pull together and shape the various elements of a project so that it meets regulatory and funding source requirements, and they coordinate/integrate the diverse resources of the project development team (community, public, and private). They directly provide project funding or stimulate funding from other sources. Community groups are also marketers that convince others that their community is a good place in which to live, do business, and invest. Community groups are also directly involved in the development and management of the housing produced. They do so as sole developers (e.g., arranging all of the financing, managing construction) or in partnerships with other nonprofit or for-profit developers. Community groups have also sought to influence (and sometimes control) the real estate practices in their community through cooperation with, and pressure on, their local real estate brokers, even extending this to outside brokers operating in their community.

During the early 1980s, as the federal government began sharply cutting assistance for low-income housing, only a few community organizations had the capacity to fix up more than a few buildings or had the capacity to undertake complex housing projects that required multiple sources of funding. Even fewer had the capacity to manage rental housing occupied by populations weighed down by social and economic distress. Now, community development corporations and other types of community-based organizations have moved to the forefront of the nation's housing revitalization efforts to become the major producers of affordable housing in distressed communities (Dreier & Atlas, 1992; Vidal, 1992). More community-based organizations focus on rehabilitation—improving the quality and appearance of existing buildings—than on new construction due to greater average cost per unit of new

construction and because many urban neighborhoods offer limited amounts of vacant land suitable for new construction (Vidal, 1992).

There are numerous reasons why community groups get involved in housing production. These include the following:

- To compensate for the lack of market activity or for-profit housing development activity in their community ("Unless we get into real estate development, no one else will do it")
- To ensure that housing activities meet the community's needs (e.g., affordability, accessibility, adequacy) and are of maximum benefit to community residents
- To build indigenous know-how and offer opportunities for entrepreneurial development
- To create individual, family, and community assets (generational equity)
- To increase locally owned housing, leading to greater community stability
- To eliminate blight and halt deterioration
- To make a visible impact on the community, thereby attracting additional resources, interest, and market activity

Community groups also get involved in housing development for less than strategic reasons, including the following:

- *Opportunity:* When a site becomes available or a property is available free of charge
- *Pressure from funders, the community, or peer groups:* Especially given that housing is a visible tangible product
- *Housing program availability:* When funding and technical assistance for housing development are readily available
- *Revenue generation:* The belief that housing development presents an opportunity to generate significant revenues for their organization's operation leading to financial independence

Apart from the direct impacts on a community resulting from housing rehabilitation or construction, indirect impacts appear when other developers, investors, or residents respond to community groups' accomplishments by making new investments themselves. Upgrading the value of one parcel encourages more productive use for adjacent properties. This requires that other local players become aware of the groups' accomplishments, decide that they represent or signal a substantial change, and develop confidence that the change is likely to last (Vidal, 1992). Community group housing activity also has the potential to influence the level of interest and activity among networks of bankers, private developers, and local government officials that is crucial to attracting new resources. Such activity can also influence the attitudes and behavior of community residents—increasing community pride and hope for the future.

However, in housing policy circles and in the field, several criticisms and shortcomings of many community-based housing strategies are voiced: (a) the lack of impact (the relatively small number of units produced in proportion to the need and costs of production), (b) the lack of expertise (resulting in the uncertain ability of nonprofit community groups to increase production, scale, and management capacity), (c) the long lead times needed for groups to gain or secure the technical expertise needed to successfully develop housing, and (d) the difficulty of trying to attack problems at a local level whose roots are regional, national, or even international. In addition, housing strategies often consume all of the time and energy of an organization, leaving no time for other important community issues.

Sullivan (1993) reported that as many community groups, especially community development corporations (CDCs), have put more and more housing in place, they have gone beyond traditional development and landlord roles to deal in innovative ways with the multiple needs of residents. In some cases that grew out of service provision or community organizing, groups have moved into housing. In other cases, CDCs that began with a housing emphasis have begun to link services and organizing to their housing. Many groups have developed a multifaceted, place-based renewal strategy. Through their own or outside property management, the CDCs have used resident selection and eviction to control the composition of residents of their buildings. Through property management's enforcement of rules, and through provision of or referral to social services, some CDCs have worked with individuals and families to overcome problems and foster personal development. In addition, some CDCs have focused their workforce development efforts on increasing the income potential of tenants. Through tenant and community organizing, CDCs have changed the ways in which residents relate to one another. Through advocacy, some CDCs have strived to change the way in which their neighborhoods and residents are treated by powerful forces from outside the neighborhoods.

Making Housing Affordable

In cities, most homeowners below the poverty line are paying more than 30% of their incomes for housing (Jones et al., 1995, p. 14). In the majority of communities, new affordable housing for limited-income families is rental housing because it is the type of housing most affordable to households in need. However, given the opportunity, many of these families would prefer owning their own homes. Although rental housing is typically less expensive to develop on a per unit basis, many communities prefer homeownership to rental housing because they perceive it as being more stable and less politically controversial. It is important to note that the financial responsibilities associated with homeownership (e.g., regular payments, maintenance, replacement costs) can be difficult for limited-income families (and increasingly also for middle-income families). Community groups can, however, provide training grants and moral support to help families develop.

Following are a variety of strategies and programs that community groups use to make housing affordable to community residents.

Mortgage assistance programs make homeownership available to limited-income individuals and families. Such programs can do this in distressed and higher-income communities, particularly during times of inflated interest rates. Mortgage assistance programs are used to subsidize a portion of the front-end costs of constructing or renting properties, effectively lowering mortgages. They are used to subsidize monthly payments to cover the cost of what a family can afford in the face of high-cost financing. Funds are lent as a low-interest or no-interest deferred second mortgage so that the homeowner can obtain a smaller conventional first mortgage from a financial institution. The homeowner pays little or no interest on the second loan, as payments are deferred for a number of years or put off until the house is sold.

Lease-to-purchase programs can make homeownership possible for first-time buyers who do not have the funds for downpayments. With such a program, a portion of the rent (lease) payment for a specified period of time goes toward the future downpayment costs on the residence.

Sweat equity housing provides a family that works on the renovation or construction of its future home with an opportunity to build up equity in the property through its own labor. The value of the sweat equity is often counted toward the downpayment price of the property. Sweat equity housing projects usually involve limited-income people who have never owned homes and cannot qualify for conventional mortgages. Such projects also greatly reduce labor expenses, site acquisition costs, and contractor fees, and they often use recycled or bulk-purchased material. Habitat for Humanity, described in the accompanying sidebar, is internationally known for its use of sweat equity to make housing affordable.

Habitat for Humanity International

Millard and Linda Fuller founded Habitat for Humanity International in 1976. A nonprofit, ecumenical, Christian housing ministry that aims to eliminate poverty housing from the world, Habitat for Humanity has a wide range of people working together in equal partnership, fostering new relationships and a sense of community as well as building and rehabilitating housing. Affiliated groups are independent and locally operated nonprofits responsible for their own fund-raising, staffing, volunteer recruitment, and publicity. There are more than 1,900 active affiliates in 83 countries, including all 50 U.S. states, the District of Columbia, Puerto Rico, and Guam. By 1998, Habitat for Humanity (affiliates) was the largest nonprofit builder of affordable housing in the United States. Habitat has built more than 100,000 houses worldwide (30,000 in the United States), providing more than 500,000 people in some 2,000 communities with safe affordable shelter.

Habitat for Humanity operates under a unique set of guiding principles. It accepts no government subsidy and relies totally on contributions to fund construction and administration. It focuses on homeownership only and uses contributed funds, rather than bank mortgage loans, to provide no-interest mortgages. It also depends heavily on sweat equity and volunteer labor. Habitat for Humanity estimates that its approach reduces construction costs by at least 60%.

SOURCE: Habitat for Humanity International (2002).

Limited equity cooperatives (co-ops) are a form of affordable, resident-controlled homeownership in which a nonprofit corporation, made up of the people who live in the housing, owns the housing. The housing can be apartments, townhouses, or individual houses. Co-ops are often developed by a community-based nonprofit corporation that may or may not have a continuing relationship with the project. Residents are shareholders, with each purchasing a share in the co-op, and are entitled to long-term leases on their units and votes in corporate governance. As co-owners, the residents manage the property and engage services to ensure effective management. Mutual housing associations are similar to co-ops in that residents are encouraged to think and act more like homeowners than renters, but they do not have any legal ownership of the housing development. The accompanying sidebar provides an example of a mutual housing project.

Excellence in Mutual Housing Development

The Rocky Mountain Mutual Housing Association (RMMHA) transformed Denver's decaying Heritage Estates into a largely resident controlled, 326-unit, affordable mutual housing development. Key to the success of the development was resident organizing and leadership, a major effort to eradicate criminal activity, and extensive renovation guided by a resident renovation committee. The RMMHA also put in place an extensive property management monitoring system to identify negative trends before they become major problems. Heritage Estates was one of three housing projects to receive the 1998 Metropolitan Life Foundation Awards for Excellence in Affordable Housing in the property and asset management category.

SOURCE: Fromm (1999).

"*Co-housing*" is an intentional community that a group of homeowners may choose so as to share resources and other aspects of their lives (Jones et al., 1995, p. 16). This type of housing usually includes shared facilities for meals, work, and social interaction, and it often also includes shared child care. Some co-housing communities stress racial/ethnic, income, and/or age diversity.

Land and building donations and bargain price sales support the development of affordable housing, while the donor or seller is compensated through tax benefits. This greatly reduces the cost of housing, offers a way for a community to gain control of a site, and protects the property from being used for purposes that might harm the community or displace residents. To proceed, two things are needed: a qualified tax-exempt (nonprofit) organization to receive the property and a seller who is ready, willing, and able to donate or sell at a reduced price and is responsive to working with the tax-exempt organization to reach mutually agreeable terms.

Community groups employ a variety of strategies and programs to help ensure affordable housing for residents. Mortgage assistance, lease-to-purchase, sweat equity, limited equity cooperatives, and land donations and bargain sales, used individually or in combination, can expand housing opportunities in any community.

A FOCUS ON HOMEOWNERSHIP

Many believe that the higher the number of homeowners, the higher the degree of neighborhood stability, connection, and pride. Community groups that pursue homeownership over rental housing cite the following as their rationale:

- Homeowners are more likely to maintain their property due to their pride in ownership (fewer deteriorated properties).
- Homeownership (owning rather than paying rent) can be a good financial investment (a financial incentive to invest in the community).
- Owning a home provides for a scheduled savings accumulation of equity (an asset-building opportunity).
- The same mortgage payment monthly offers stable housing costs (predictable budgeting).
- Increasing value/appreciation accrues (a return on investment).
- Owning a home garners tax benefits to owners (with tax deductions reducing taxable income).

However, there are some disadvantages to homeownership, including the high cost, the possibility of foreclosure, the decreased mobility that could affect job access and flexibility, and the need for and cost of ongoing repairs and maintenance. Community groups have developed homeownership counseling programs to maximize the advantages and minimize the disadvantages of homeownership.

Homeownership counseling programs offer information, advice, and assistance to families on locating, purchasing, and maintaining their homes. They help people to improve their housing conditions and meet the responsibilities of homeownership and tenancy. They also advise on ways in which to avoid mortgage payment delinquencies and foreclosures. Nonprofit community organizations operate the majority of such programs. These programs reduce a neighborhood's mortgage default and foreclosure rate. As residents follow better maintenance practices, the community's appearance improves, and as they follow energy conservation practices, they save on their utility bills. Such programs offer pre-purchase and mortgage default counseling, energy conservation counseling, and education on purchase procedures, property care, and maintenance. Many community groups have enlisted financial institutions to pay for such housing counseling programs.

National intermediaries, such as the Neighborhood Reinvestment Corporation and the Enterprise Foundation, afford member groups and their communities program packages, technical assistance, and financial support to promote and increase homeownership, including rehabilitation and construction assistance, organization and project financing, and program guidelines for homeownership counseling and homebuyer assistance. Successful homeownership projects are desctibed in the two accompanying sidebars.

Best Practices in Homeownership No. 1

Cobb Housing Inc. (CHI) has made homeownership a reality for hundreds of families in Cobb County, Georgia. Homebuyer educational seminars and homeownership counseling through CHI's HOMEstart program have reached more than 750 people, a home/rescue default counseling program has served more than 250 participants, and a FirstHome Downpayment Assistance program has assisted more than 125 families in becoming homeowners. CHI also assisted the residents of the Marietta Roosevelt Circle Project to work closely with the police department on crime and drug problems and to secure funding from a local builder to build additional affordable homes nearby (U.S. Department of Housing and Urban Development, 1999). In 2002, CHI was developing affordable new and rehabbed single-family homes and, as a United Way community partner, was working with the Individual Development Accounts Program as a savings tool for homeownership.

Best Practices in Homeownership No. 2

Working in five of the poorest colonias (housing subdivisions originally established by for-profit developers along the Texas-Mexican border, with many lacking running water, sewers, and electricity) in two counties of the Rio Grande Valley, the Community Development Corporation of Brownsville (CDCB) in Texas has created a cost-effective way in which to replace substandard housing and dilapidated shacks with well-designed houses for homeownership. The CDCB's efforts target single female heads of households, the elderly, and large families. In collaboration with the Mennonite Partnership Building Initiative and YouthBuild Brownsville, the CDCB demolishes poorly built homes and, with cost-saving techniques, reconstructs new homes on the lots. Cost-saving measures include salvaging windows and other usable parts and using church volunteers and YouthBuild trainees. The CDCB, working with seven different funding sources, provides no-interest mortgages that can be fully repaid in 10 years. Low-income families become owners of small (680- to 700-square-foot) quality homes for just $83.33 a month. The CDCB's goal is to reconstruct at least 15 houses each year. Its effort won a Maxwell Award of Excellence for the production of low-income housing for its work in the colonias.

SOURCE: Fannie Mae Foundation (1999, pp. 3, 16–19).

Other Strategies and Mechanisms for Community Stabilization

A *land bank* is a community-owned and -managed nonprofit corporation that acquires properties through purchase, loan, or donation and sells them to suitable buyers who will occupy them. Land banks also often acquire contiguous parcels of land (vacant or with structures) so as to assemble sites suitable for multi-unit housing developments. "Land banking" is the term used for the acquisition and holding of properties by land banks and other community-based organizations. A *land trust,* also a community-owned and -managed nonprofit corporation, acquires and holds property in stewardship for the common good of the community, making it permanently affordable through long-term leases. Land trusts develop housing through new construction or renovation and most often sell the units to low-income families. With a land trust, a community gets permanently affordable land and homeowners receive the advantages of owning their own homes, including security, appreciated value, and tax benefits (Pitcoff, 2002). Both land banks and land trusts help to save properties that are key to an area's stabilization. These include properties owned by private absentee landlords or public agencies. Land banks and land trusts can work to counter real estate speculation, reduce displacement of residents, eliminate blight, increase homeownership, and control property for the community's common good. Prime organizers for such initiatives can be community-based organizations, coalitions active in community revitalization, community institutions, or local government agencies. (Information on the Institute for Community Economics, one of the proponents of land trusts early on, can be found on its Web site [www.iceclt.org].) The accompanying sidebar illustrates a community-based land bank.

Land Banking in Fells Point

Baltimore residents faced with the prospect of a superhighway dividing their Fells Point neighborhood organized as the South East Community Organization (SECO) to block the highway's construction. They won the fight and went on to tackle another one: deterioration in absentee-owned buildings. Speculators who boarded them up and waited for increases in property values were buying these buildings. The group formed a land bank (financed by a foundation), purchased houses on the open market, and identified suitable new homeowners. Some houses were offered as is, while others were rehabilitated first; some were sold outright, while others were sold through lease-to-purchase arrangements. The city provided low-cost renovation loans. In all, more than 110 properties were land-banked throughout Fells Point and adjacent neighborhoods. When the land bank had completed its job in promoting resident homeownership, it was able to close its doors, and SECO moved on to the next phase of its neighborhood revitalization.

Receivership occurs when a court names a person or group to carry out an order requiring the repair or management of a neglected private property. The court intervenes after legal action has been taken against the property owner for problems such as health code or building code violations and the owner has not responded satisfactorily (if at all). To preserve the property, someone is appointed the receiver. In communities where vacant, abandoned, or neglected housing is a problem, community-based receivership can save buildings from continued disuse or eventual demolition. Receivership can also lead to obtaining the title to a property without having to pay a purchase price. During a receivership process, the court appoints a person or an organization to act as its agent to carry out a court order to manage or repair a property. Receivership comes to an end in one of two ways. If the order is fulfilled, then the owner reimburses the receiver for any expenses/costs, the court dismisses the receiver, and the control of the property goes back to the owner. In the other way, if the receiver acquires the property through liens or a tax sale, then the receiver becomes owner and fully responsible for repair and future good management of the property. Local and/or state legislation must be in place establishing a receivership program.

Low-Income Housing Communities

A particular area of challenge for many communities is the condition and nature of government-sponsored and -assisted housing. This section examines "Section 8" project-based properties and public housing communities. Low-income housing advocates and resident groups have long lobbied for changes in public and assisted housing. Quality public and assisted housing is a key to a stable life, and for some it is a stepping-stone to homeownership.

Section 8 Project-Based Properties

Section 8 properties are owned and managed by private individuals or companies that receive subsidies from HUD for each unit. HUD Multifamily Assisted Housing housing was developed between 1966 and 1983 for families, the elderly, and people with disabilities. Properties range from high-rises to scattered site individual homes, with the subsidies attached to the units. If individuals or families move from the units, they do not take the subsidies with them.

Project-based Section 8 contracts were for only a 20-year period, with the first contracts set to expire in 1998 (and a total of 1 million contracts on assisted housing units expiring over the subsequent 10 years). Congress, realizing that properties were being subsidized at a rate higher than the market rents for units in a given area, created the "Mark-to-Market" Program in 1998. Under this program, for owners to renew their project-based Section 8 contracts, new mortgage restructuring plans have to be put in place, and the physical conditions of their

buildings must be assessed and repairs made. (The Mark-to-Market Program was set to expire in 2001 but will continue until 2006.)

HUD Multifamily Assisted Housing and the Mark-to-Market Program affect a community's development in several ways. Project-based Section 8 properties are usually found in lower-income distressed communities. Some communities in the midst of revitalization processes look for the demolition of their existing project-based Section 8 high-rises and for the opportunity to move the subsidies into more community-friendly housing (e.g., single-family homes, townhouses). In strong rental markets, owners have opted out of the Mark-to-Market Program, deciding that there is enough demand for their housing in the rental market that they no longer need to subsidize their units. As a result, thousands of low-income families, the elderly, and the disabled in these strong rental markets are losing their housing. Housing advocacy groups in such areas are working to get state and city preservation ordinances passed stating that owners who opt out of their properties need to first notify the cities and give them the opportunity to buy the buildings.

Another tactic in preserving HUD Multifamily Assisted Housing is promoting nonprofit or tenant ownership of these properties. In early 2000, legislation was introduced in the U.S. Senate that would preserve such affordable housing with an emphasis on local nonprofit management. The Local Initiatives Support Corporation (LISC) is providing technical support to groups working on this important issue. (For more information, see LISC's Web page [www.liscnet.org].)

Public Housing Communities

Public housing was created by the Housing Act of 1937 as part of the Roosevelt administration's New Deal, with the belief that such housing would be transitory. Local housing authorities were established to build and administer public housing. (HUD was not created until 1965.) The Truman administration in 1949 was more ambitious, aiming to build 800,000 units across the country. Initially, public housing was targeted toward households that were negatively affected by the Depression but that, after a few years of "housing support," would be able to move to afford housing in the private market in middle-class communities. That underlying conception was the rationale for building far fewer housing units than the number of needy families; over time, units would be circulated to others in need (Jones et al., 1995). After World War II and the postwar economic recovery, many residents of the original public housing moved to suburban communities, aided in part by federal programs such as Federal Housing Administration (FHA) mortgage insurance, which encouraged loans to whites in the suburbs but not to people of color. Few such loans were available to anyone in central cities. Federally aided highway construction did help families to relocate to other housing. Again, white homeowners were helped the most. In the place of middle-class residents who moved out, a less economically mobile population began moving in. Over time (possibly by design) across the country, public housing communities became as racially segregated as private housing and, where they once were economically integrated, became home to mostly limited-income residents. Dreier and Atlas (1992) painted a somewhat different picture but cited similar results. They stated that public housing advocates initially envisioned housing for the poor, as well as for the middle class, but the real estate industry, fearing "socialism" (government competition and control of middle-income housing), successfully lobbied to limit public housing to the poor.

While more than 65% of low-rise public housing communities and the majority of other public housing, especially in smaller cities, are well managed and provide decent housing for residents, many such communities, particularly in big cities, are plagued with problems—high vacancies, deteriorating physical structures, high crime rates, and other social ills (Pollack, 1999). Atlas and Dreier (1994) noted that one major problem with public housing stems from decades of federal underfunding, leading to deferred maintenance and subsequent deterioration.

In 1989, Congress appointed the National Commission on Severely Distressed Public Housing to examine the depth of the challenges facing the nation's public housing stock. The commission found that 86,000 of the 1.2 million public housing units were severely distressed due to physical deterioration, increasing levels of poverty, and inadequate and fragmented services, among other factors. The government's response was the Urban Revitalization Demonstration Program, which became the HOPE VI Program in 1992. HOPE VI was created to "forever change the nature of public housing communities." The HUD flagship HOPE VI Program is aimed at breaking down the economic isolation and segregation by creating economic diversity and vitality in public housing through creating a safe, attractive, mixed-income, and mixed-race environment. HOPE VI focuses on four goals: resident self-sufficiency, community-enhancing physical design, mixed-income neighborhoods, and fiscal sustainability through public-private partnerships. This deconcentration or economic integration involves admitting families headed by working adults with somewhat higher incomes into public housing communities that were once populated nearly exclusively by very poor families. Efforts are also focused on resident management and ownership and the linkage of residents to support services such as child care, health care, education, job training and placement, and substance abuse treatment. Between 1993 and the end of 2001, HUD's HOPE VI Revitalization Grant program had awarded 165 grants to 98 cities to demolish severely distressed public housing (HUD, 2002b).

In some cases, initiatives are under way to reduce the density of public housing (through demolition and new construction with no one-to-one replacement of rental units) and to offer homeownership opportunities in the surrounding communities. These "public housing revitalization" initiatives are concurrent with welfare reform and encompass a new thrust toward "self-sufficiency" for the very poor.

Not all residents in public housing support HOPE VI revitalization of their communities; they fear displacement, loss of community, and even homelessness. In some cases, resident involvement in planning and decision making has been sparse, making lawsuits possible. Concern is also voiced that residents, relocated during demolition and construction or during rehabilitation, will not be able to return to their new mixed-income communities because federal housing law no longer requires one-for-one low-income unit replacement. In effect, long-established community supports, including social fabric, will be severed. As incomes become mixed, it is hoped that residents will become more diverse racially while establishing new long-term communities.

Pollock (1999) offered Baltimore's "The Towns at the Terraces" as a HOPE VI success. The former Lexington Terrace Project was demolished to make way for new mixed-income homes, senior housing, parks, and community centers. All low-income families will receive computers, and their homes will be wired for the Internet. Two major reasons cited for Baltimore's success are significant public housing resident input throughout the redevelopment process and cooperation from the private and public sectors.

With public housing so squarely on the national agenda, many communities are recognizing that the so-called long-isolated (often hidden) pockets of the very poor are in many cases neighborhoods with economic, social, and political strengths as well as challenges like so many other communities. Many families reside in public housing communities by choice. In some areas, public housing communities are becoming an integral part of the larger communities in which they are found.

In addition to the NLIHC, the Center for Community Change's Public Housing Initiative is one of the leaders in helping to protect and improve public housing and in helping resident organizations to increase their power and capacity so as to improve their communities. The center's initiative also focuses on educating and influencing federal and local policymakers. More information on the initiative can be found on the center's Web site (www.communitychange.org).

SUMMARY

A built environment can last more than a century and has a great impact on people's lives. An analysis of the community housing market and its characteristics suggests a wide range of opportunities for community controlled development organizations to ensure the accessibility, adequacy, affordability, and availability of quality housing to community residents and others who may be attracted by such opportunity.

Housing preservation and stabilization activities and initiatives can preserve housing quality and retain vacant housing for future use. The availability of housing development programs and financing support the entry of many community groups into the housing arena. A focus on building affordable homeownership opportunities for households at all income levels can help to stabilize a community and engender community pride. A strategic point of entry into housing and neighborhood preservation for many organizations is organizing and advocacy. Widespread and deep participation by all of a community's interests should be part of any community's housing and neighborhood preservation plan.

CONTINUING QUESTIONS

1. Can a community achieve substantive impact only by supporting or initiating large-scale construction/rehabilitation efforts? What does it take for small-scale efforts to make a discernible impact?

2. Under what housing conditions and with what actions can resident propinquity lead to greater interaction and tolerance among people with social and cultural differences?

3. What housing policies and practices can promote fairness and diversity while making a community both livable and affordable?

4. Is there inherent conflict in working to provide quality low-income housing and working toward the economic diversification of a community by also producing middle-income and upper-income housing?

5. What role can and should community controlled development organizations (not just low-income housing groups) play in addressing the barriers to fair and affordable housing? What responsibility do they have in making sure that the voice of all community interests is heard in policy formulation and implementation?

6. How can a community group engaged in housing production (e.g., construction, management, ownership) not have its entire agenda consumed by that activity? What options does the group have to build a comprehensive agenda?

7. Should government monitor neighborhoods and communities and take initiative when housing indicators signal a pending crisis? How would such government activity link/integrate with a neighborhood's community renewal efforts? Would such monitoring work for or against the interests of low-income households?

8. When undercrowding is a factor, how can a community best shape its housing strategies and plans to overcome this housing defect?

REFERENCES

Atlas, J., & Dreier, P. (1994, September–October). Public housing: What went wrong? *Shelterforce,* pp. 4–5, 27. (Orange, NJ: National Housing Institute)

Blair, J. (1995). *Local economic development analysis and practice.* Thousand Oaks, CA: Sage.

Burgess, E. W. (1925). The growth of the city. In R. Parks, E. Burgess, & R. McKenzie (Eds.), *The city* (pp. 47–62). Chicago: University of Chicago Press.

Chicago Rehab Network. (1993). *The Chicago affordable housing fact book: Visions for change* (3rd ed.). Chicago: Author.

Dreier, P., & Atlas, J. (1992, November–December). A housing policy for the 90's. *Shelterforce,* pp. 2–19. (Orange, NJ: National Housing Institute)

Fannie Mae Foundation. (1999). *Maxwell Awards of Excellence Program for the production of low-income housing: Case studies of the awardees and finalists, round eleven.* Washington, DC: Author.

Fromm, D. (1999, Spring). Best practices at their very best. *Building Blocks,* pp. 8–10. (Columbia, MD: Enterprise Foundation)

Galster, G. C. (1987). *Homeowners and neighborhood reinvestment.* Durham, NC: Duke University Press.

Habitat for Humanity International. (2002). Retrieved February 22, 2002, from the World Wide Web: http://habitat.org/how/factsheet.html

Holcomb, H. B., & Beauregard, R. A. (1981). *Revitalizing cities.* Washington, DC: Association of American Geographers.

Jones, T., Pettus, W., & Pyatok, M. (1995). *Good neighbors: Affordable family housing.* New York: McGraw-Hill.

Keating, W., & Smith, S. (1996). Past federal policy for urban neighborhoods. In N. Krumholz & P. Star (Eds.), *Revitalizing urban neighborhoods.* Lawrence: University Press of Kansas.

National Housing Trust Fund. (2002). *Background information on housing trust funds in the United States.* Prepared by the Housing Trust Fund Project of the Center for Community Change for the National Housing Trust Fund Campaign, Washington, DC. Available on the World Wide Web: www.nhtf.org/about/background.pdf

National Low-Income Housing Coalition. (2002a). *Advocate's guide to housing and community development policy.* Washington, DC: Author.

National Low-Income Housing Coalition. (2002b). *Rental housing for America's poor families: Farther out of reach than ever.* Washington, DC: Author. Available on the World Wide Web: www.nlihc.org/oor2002/introduction.htm

Pitcoff, W. (2002, January–February). Affordable forever: Land trusts keep housing within reach. *Shelterforce,* pp. 13–15. (Orange, NJ: National Housing Institute)

PolicyLink. (2002). *Equitable Development Toolkit: Beyond gentrification.* [Online]. Retrieved April, 2002, from the World Wide Web: www.policylink.org

Pollack, N. (1999, Autumn). Knocking down the past to build the future. *Enterprise Quarterly,* pp. 10–14.

Porell, F. W. (1985). One man's ceiling is another man's floor: Landlord manager residency and housing conditions. *Land Economics, 61*(2), 106–118.

Rubin, H. J., & Rubin, I. S. (1992). *Community organizing and development* (2nd ed.). Boston: Allyn & Bacon.

Sarkissian, W. (1976). The idea of social mix in planning: A historical review. *Urban Studies, 13,* 231–246.

Sullivan, M. L. (1993). *More than housing: How community development corporations go about changing lives and neighborhoods.* New York: New School for Social Research, Community Development Research Center.

U.S. Department of Housing and Urban Development. (1999). *Best practices in housing and community development.* [Online]. Retrieved December 9, 1999, from the World Wide Web: www.hud.gov/fha/best/hsg_best.html

U.S. Department of Housing and Urban Development. (2001). *A report on worst case housing needs in 1999: New opportunity amid continuing challenges* (executive summary). Washington, DC: Author.

U.S. Department of Housing and Urban Development. (2002a). *Best Practices 2000 Program and geographical winners: Pennsylvania.* [Online]. Retrieved February 22, 2002, from the World Wide Web: www.hud.gov/bestpractices/2000/prog_pa.html

U.S. Department of Housing and Urban Development. (2002b). *National fact sheet: FY2001 HOPE VI revitalization grant awards.* Washington, DC: Author.

Vidal, A. (1992). *Rebuilding communities: A national study of urban community development corporations.* New York: New School for Social Research, Community Development Research Center.

14

BUSINESS DISTRICT RENEWAL

Transforming a Shopping Area

"Can all commercial districts thrive? Should all survive?"

—Questions from the field

A small community's face to the world historically has been its shopping district, conveying the community's state of health to society while fulfilling essential and important economic and noneconomic purposes. In distressed communities, signs of decline are likely to appear first in the shopping district. Abandoned vacant storefronts, a dwindling body of shoppers, a poor mix of goods and services, vacant littered lots, and an increase in real and perceived crime are sure signs of a business district and community in distress. Yet in some troubled neighborhoods, businesses manage to thrive amid closures. Maintaining a healthy shopping district during a time of mega-malls, downtown revitalizations, smaller households, out-migration of people and industry, and expanding outer suburbs is at best difficult, but it is necessary for true community revitalization.

Neighborhood commercial corridors have long suffered from poor image and disinvestment. Politicians, city agencies, and corporations in many cities have turned their attention and their capital to the revitalization of their traditional downtown commercial business districts. Neighborhood-oriented and small town business districts are left to revitalize themselves, building on internal assets and resources. Revitalization is the culmination of years of commitment, trust building, organizing, motivating, and planning. The road to success is a long one, but the payoffs and benefits to the community can be significant. Still, not all districts will or can survive or thrive.

In spite of negative societal forces, a broad array of local-level business district revitalization programs are under way in a wide variety of settings reflecting diverse economic levels, locational characteristics, markets, and scales of operation. Support for such revitalization exists from the local level to the national level, and some success is to be noted.

Local business district decline can result from a variety of deep-seated economic, physical, political, social, and human (exerted by individuals) pressures. A local community's ability to influence, change, or even control such forces is a great challenge. Some districts bounce back easily; most will remain static or continue to decline without intervention.

Moreover, improvement in one business district is sometimes at the expense of an adjacent district, especially in no-growth areas. The competitive relationship of one community or neighborhood to another area or areas determines the extent and type of revitalization that may occur.

In this chapter, we examine the economic and noneconomic contributions of business districts to communities, review distress factors, and outline two approaches to renewal—adjusting to a smaller market and adjusting to a changed market—and related activities. The chapter concludes by raising several critical continuing questions regarding business district renewal.

Economic and Noneconomic Contributions of Community and Neighborhood Business Districts

From a purely economic standpoint, questions abound on the contribution of community and neighborhood businesses to the overall economy of a city or county. Yet such commercial districts represent a large investment in real estate and public infrastructure, and combined they are a large part of a city's or county's overall economy. In addition, as part of a larger, long-term strategy of community controlled development that includes housing rehabilitation and construction, job creation and business/commercial/industrial development, and retention and recruitment, business district renewal efforts can make a significant contribution to building or maintaining a well-rounded, functioning community. Although the economic contributions may be limited or in question, the noneconomic value of community and neighborhood business districts is evident.

From an *economic* perspective, small community and neighborhood commercial districts affect communities in the following eight major ways:

1. They provide options for needed goods and services at the local level, close to home. (Many districts can cover the basics; however, they might never challenge shopping malls or downtowns for convenience or on a wide-ranging array of goods and services, big-ticket merchandise, and number of sales transactions.)

2. They offer convenience as a source of supply for local consumers. This is particularly true when local stores are within walking distance and near transit stops.

3. They provide employment opportunities. (However, most jobs are entry level, near minimum wage, with limited upward mobility.)

4. They can serve as an entry point for entrepreneurial learning because many small businesses require less start-up capital and experience and need the small buildings, which can serve as "incubator" space for start-ups because of the low rent. (However, many of these businesses are one-person shops with little hope for expansion.)

5. They preserve some older buildings. Smaller businesses can use older buildings more effectively due to small square footage needs. Older buildings usually command less rent than do newer buildings. (However, rehabilitation costs can be very high, thus requiring substantial public investment.)

6. They make a contribution to the local tax base through property tax and sales tax revenues, although they often lack the scale and intensity of larger developments.

7. They can provide locally based cyclical income flows, with minimal economic leakage when employers and employees patronize other local stores alongside residents shopping in the community. Resident support of local stores, rather than "big box" retailers, means that profits remain in the community instead of being sent to corporate offices in other towns or states. (See the diagram of Al's paycheck [Figure 4.6 in Chapter 4] circulating through his neighborhood as it multiplies its local economic impact within the neighborhood.)

8. They can stimulate housing investment and vice versa.

The *noneconomic* contributions of small business districts center on the small community or neighborhood as a social and political entity. Among the contributions are the following four benefits:

1. Business districts can serve as "community centers," becoming a focal point for activity and social interaction and providing a setting for diverse interpersonal contacts.

2. Business districts can be a source of identity, image, and place identification—important factors in determining residents' hopes and expectations for their communities' futures.

3. Business district vitality is often cited as an attribute deemed desirable, and as such, it is a necessary component of a complete community. (Although in decline during past years, one-of-a-kind homegrown shops are becoming "chic" and numerous on some vintage shopping streets in mature suburbs. Clustered in affluent inner-ring suburbs, such shops diversify suburbia as they are patronized by former urban dwellers who prefer to go to smaller, more focused niche stores built to imitate Jacobs's [1961] walking-scale urban neighborhood of the early 1960s.)

4. Small community business areas create opportunities for residents and merchants to connect to local-level political development. Revitalization efforts require organizing to determine and carry out plans, to tap outside funding, and to exercise clout.

DISTRESS FACTORS IN LOCAL COMMUNITY BUSINESS DISTRICTS

Small community business districts are those that primarily draw customers from a very localized residential market and are generally retail oriented.

A commercial district is a product of market area demand and is dependent on the support, stability, and needs of the households and business/institutional consumers from the market area. Goldstein and Davis (1980) described a cycle of disinvestment or no investment that has taken place in many small, localized commercial districts: Either the community economic system is losing its ability to generate needed goods and services (quantity, quality, or access to) or the market for what it has to offer is dissipating (declining or going elsewhere) (pp. 5–7). Therefore, the district has less capacity to attract and hold elements necessary to keep viable and has a weakened ability to compete for the market or markets available. These factors lead to an image of decline (e.g., vacancies, physical disrepair, litter), real and perceived safety/security issues, a poor business mix, and marginal businesses (e.g., poor quality of goods, less variety of merchandise, poor service), resulting in further deterioration of the market.

Multiple factors, often interrelated and interdependent, are involved in business district decline. These factors include market, image, infrastructure, district characteristics, economics, local government regulations, revitalization strategies, and level of community organization. Each district will have its own set of factors—some of which can be changed, others of which cannot be changed. Plans for business district renewal are based on assessments of these factors.

Market

A declining or inadequate market challenges many districts. The result is less sales volume, resulting in less profit and therefore less money to reinvest in the business for needed improvements. Others face a stagnant market—one with no growth potential. Some districts, however, have a hidden opportunity—an underserved market with untapped expenditure potential. Residents may have the will (the need and the money) but not the way (no local providers of wanted goods and services).

The following four major issues and factors influence local central city and old town markets:

1. *Increased competition from malls, big box stores such as Wal-Mart, specialty stores, shopping areas, and downtowns:* Many local districts have too many single-purpose stores and little destination shopping. Shoppers have to make too many trips or too many stops at the local level to get their shopping lists filled. The mall competition and big box stores make it easy to make one stop and satisfy all shopping needs.

2. *Change in the retail environment at the local level:* There are fewer "mom and pop" stores. Many local restaurants are now fast-food chains. Many corner grocery stores are now

quick-stop convenience stores with gas pumps. Traditional anchor stores such as grocery stores, "five-and-ten" stores, department stores, and other large retail tenants have closed, moved, or become mega-stores in outlying areas.

3. *Suburbanization:* The shift of population to the newer low-density outer suburbs has decreased the population and market base in most inner cities, industrial towns, mature suburbs, and other older small communities.

4. *Decreased income levels of residential areas surrounding older community business districts:* Less money for households to spend leads to decreased sales and decreased profits for local businesses. Many just hang on offering marginal goods and services, or they go out of business.

Research finds that despite lower household incomes, some industrious inner-city areas (where there has not been great population loss) can concentrate more buying power into a square mile than do many affluent suburbs. Porter and Blaxill (1997) found that many inner-city neighborhoods are badly underserved—"untapped market potential"—and estimated that in 1997 approximately 30% (or more than $25 billion) of inner-city retail demand was unmet (p. A22). Porter's (1995) research suggests that retailers' failure to respond to this market is a matter of an absence of strategy. Porter found that there are numerous challenges that can deter entry into an inner-city market—theft, crime, regulatory complications, neglected business infrastructure, and community resistance. The U.S. Department of Housing and Urban Development (HUD) in 1999 reported that the economic potential of America's low-income urban and rural communities is enormous (HUD, 1999). Focusing on retail buying power and sales patterns in 539 U.S. central cities, HUD found many inner-city neighborhoods suffering from significant "out-shopping"; they have too little retail to meet demand and tap the buying power of their own residents. The retail markets in inner-city neighborhoods (those with higher poverty and lower incomes than those that surround them) are huge. For example, HUD reported that the inner-city neighborhoods in New Haven,

Connecticut, possess $1 billion per year in retail purchasing power (30.4% higher than 1998 estimated retail sales); other figures included those for Allentown, Pennsylvania ($307.9 million, 7.4% higher); East St. Louis, Illinois ($226.7 million, 21.9% higher); and Baytown, Texas ($249.7 million, 17.0% higher) (pp. 25–26). The barriers to business development in these "new markets" include the lack of capital and the lack of technical expertise.

HUD (1999) also found major untapped markets in rural areas. For example, the Pine Ridge reservation, with approximately 11,000 residents, had $60 million to spend on retail needs; however, most spent off the reservation due to little commercial activity on it (p. ix). The counties that make up the Mississippi Delta had $95.7 billion in retail purchasing power, yet poverty in the delta was nearly 21% in 1995 (p. ix). HUD suggested that high-tech communication can fuel business mobility to rural areas that have competitive advantages of inexpensive land and lower average labor costs. In partnership with governments and community groups, such businesses can grow a rural job base.

Some businesses, particularly chain retailers such as Pathmark supermarkets, Rite-Aid drug stores, and Payless ShoeSource footwear stores, are returning to inner-city neighborhoods. Grogan and Proscio (2000) cited two major reasons for this return: (a) the increase in housing investments and homeownership along with the accompanying decrease in crime and decay and (b) the amount of untapped disposable income. "The density of inner-city neighborhoods makes up in volume what those neighborhoods lack in individual earnings or wealth" (p. 128). When there are local stores, more of this family money is spent on necessities. In addition, suburban markets are becoming more and more saturated, and many customers are looking for non-mall shopping experiences (p. 133).

Poor or Negative Image

Real or perceived crime, vandalism, and lack of security plague many business districts. People do not shop, park, or spend social time where they feel unsafe. Many businesses do not remain open in unsafe areas after 5 p.m. Some close permanently. Vacant lots and abandoned buildings, often strewn with litter, garbage, and trash, convey the image of a community under assault. Such areas may attract drug traffickers, further reinforcing the image that a particular part or the entire business area is not a place to frequent.

Infrastructure/Physical Deterioration

Demolition of buildings without replacement leaves vacant space. This reduces the amount of retail/commercial space available and causes a "sawtooth effect"—one or two buildings surrounded by vacant lots and a few more buildings several parcels away. When businesses are not clustered, shoppers are inconvenienced and unable to do multiple-destination shopping in one stop.

Aging buildings are a particular challenge due to the high cost of improvements and lack of investment by owners. Some existing older spaces are too small for contemporary retail uses. Often, small spaces will not support sufficient inventory for the sales volume required. In many districts, some second and third floors are unusable due to a lack of easy access or a failure to meet code requirements.

Inadequate municipal services leaves streets and sidewalks in disrepair. This makes driving through and walking in the district a hazard. Often, people will go elsewhere just to avoid potential accidents or traffic problems caused by crumbling streets.

Scarce, mismanaged, and/or overpriced parking prompt many shoppers to head for the malls, strip centers, or even city center shopping districts. If their time is limited, many drivers would rather not spend it circling the block looking for parking spots. In addition, double-parked cars often block smooth travel on shopping streets. Metered parking works well only if there is turnover in parkers. Often, shoppers and nonshoppers park in short-term spots for hours on end; shop owners and employees often do the same.

Business District Characteristics

Poor relationships between property owners and tenants can lead to a lack of timely repairs and maintenance, creating shabby buildings that are unwelcoming in appearance. In addition, strained landlord-tenant interaction can cause leasing problems—a new tenant is delayed or a current tenant leaves sooner than expected. Many proprietors do not own the space they operate in, so the landlord-tenant relationship is crucial, as is the commitment of the landlord to keeping the space up to code.

Low resident ownership of retail and commercial space also negatively affects business retention. Because the bottom line is business profits, even resident business owners will consider relocation if a district declines.

Small business districts are also strained by inadequate facilities or services to attract and keep employees and even people who may work in or near the districts. Most residents need access to day care, transportation, health, community facilities, and/or some kind of service while going to or from their places of employment. Many will shop near home or on the way home rather than patronize close-to-work shops when services and amenities are lacking.

Economic Factors

Several economic factors lead to a high merchant or business turnover rate or poor quality of stores. Commercial redlining creates barriers to credit or capital to start, operate, or expand businesses, thus slowing or prohibiting financing for renovations, inventory expansion, and capital improvements.

Poor business management often leads to marginal businesses with out-of-date merchandise, inadequate inventories, lack of services, poor management practices, low quality/high prices, and/or inconvenient or inconsistent store hours of operation. Only a "captive" market will remain as customers. The longevity of a business is no guarantee that management is sound.

With increasing frequency, small businesses are being displaced in districts where the market has potential or is untapped. Large businesses or chains, and others that do not fit the traditional nature of the district, take space. Often, multiple small businesses are forced out, with their buildings being sold and subsequently demolished to make way for the new.

Lack of skilled or experienced workers, or skilled workers who are employed outside of the area, may make new businesses hesitant to open or relocate and at times cause existing businesses to scale back or close.

The final economic factor relates to normal attrition of small businesses. Some owners retire; others make life or career changes, shutting down their businesses. Frequently, however, a lack of entrepreneurs to replace retirees or others leaving their businesses (buy-outs) mandates permanent shutdowns.

Local Government Regulations

Lack of or inadequate zoning regulations can cause a lack of cohesion or clustering of stores in business districts. Some regulations are overly restrictive such as those prohibiting food establishments or shopping from being mixed with offices. Many districts face ordinances and regulations that impede business operations. For example, loading restrictions may limit the types of merchandise that can be delivered and offered. Lack of codes, obsolete codes, or unenforced codes (e.g., building, fire, health, safety) can lead to unsafe and unsightly conditions and can be a cost barrier to new tenants.

Past or Current
Commercial Revitalization Strategies

A focus on downtown/central-city business district revitalization can draw needed resources, potential tenants, and current shoppers away from community and neighborhood business districts.

Extensive demolition to amass land for future development (in some cases by the use of eminent domain) has devastated many commercial areas—displacing or forcing the closure of businesses, relocating residents (shoppers), and disrupting traffic patterns and access. People have to shop elsewhere and may establish new "shopping loyalties" or preferences that might not be recaptured at a later date.

Changes in traffic patterns have proved to be debilitating to some small business districts. These changes, often done in the name of progress or benefit, have included closing entire districts to vehicles to encourage a pedestrian atmosphere and rerouting traffic via bypasses and expressways—cutting communities in half

and severing business districts from former markets.

Level of Community Organization

This final factor in business district decline is one that most, if not all, districts can successfully address with local resources: the lack of business community cohesion. Local enterprises not being organized for advocacy, planning, management, and marketing means that there is no group to dream, steer, or marshal renewal efforts. Lack of community-based organization-business community partnerships with the public and private sectors means that valuable financial, regulatory, and technical assistance resources are going untapped. Collective efforts are critical in business district renewal.

TWO APPROACHES TO
BUSINESS DISTRICT RENEWAL

Presented here are two basic approaches to business district renewal: adjusting to a smaller market and retapping a changed market. The basic strategies involve both economic and physical solutions. Comprehensive business district renewal programs also address social, political, and human issues, and they involve advocacy and action.

Central is the need to generate or catalyze private investment and a range of economic end products in the neighborhood by creating certain preconditions (e.g., dealing with safety, physical conditions, and market) and also dealing with a range of elements in the development of a favorable economic and physical environment (e.g., upgrading the area and the quality of merchants, focusing on making them more competitive). Emphasizing specific economic end products—improved store mix, new retail development, more interesting and exciting goods, technical assistance to retailers, and development of financial mechanisms and incentives—does this (Goldstein & Davis, 1980, p. 5).

With both approaches, the process is aimed at making a local business district more competitive through the following:

- Upgrading the district so that it becomes safe, convenient, and attractive to customers, with loyalty of nearby residents restimulated
- Engaging in retail development, which enlarges the variety of stores to offer customers more choice at attractive prices with more personal service (e.g., upgrading the merchants, developing the businesses, doing more aggressive recruitment of firms offering an assortment of goods and services not now available in the district)
- Creating a climate in which ongoing reinvestment rises sufficiently to demonstrate that revitalization is under way and thereby attract new public and private funds to the area
- Developing visible programs that encourage improvements of the surrounding community
- Integrating business district renewal into overall community economic development plans and initiatives

The *Business Opportunities Casebook* (Rocky Mountain Institute, 1990) presented several principles of economic revitalization related to business district renewal that confirm the preceding ideas and offer new ones:

1. *Plug economic leaks.* This is accomplished by identifying supportable market gaps, improving access to capital and credit (both businesses and residents), and connecting local businesses to local suppliers. Plugging leaks also includes activities that increase the amount of spendable income of residents through their capture of more transfer payments and energy rebates.

2. *Support existing businesses.* This is accomplished by reducing imports (buy local) or finding additional exports (increase trade area beyond neighborhood), establishing business assistance programs, increasing capital and credit through loans and banks, and identifying market niches and expanding current business operations. Activities that support existing businesses also include marketing and promoting the businesses and community as well as publicizing business district design and image improvements.

3. *Encourage new local businesses.* This is accomplished by finding and putting to work underused local assets (talent, experience, and knowledge of residents) and by promoting and assisting the start-up and operation of local businesses through entrepreneurial development, education, and assistance.

4. *Recruit compatible businesses.* This is accomplished by developing targeted business recruitment and incentive programs that strengthen the existing business mix, thereby increasing the availability and variety of goods and services.

Business District Renewal Approach 1: Facing the Shrunken Market

Where a market has dissipated, declined, or shifted, renewal efforts may initially or permanently involve the following:

- Consolidation of the business strip (downsizing) and/or selection of target or core areas for improvement
- Seeking of alternatives to traditional anchor stores
- Relocation of remaining merchants in deteriorated areas to fill vacancies in stronger core areas
- Identification of new uses for vacant retail storefronts (e.g., office, service, housing)
- Selection of new uses for vacant lots (e.g., parks, green space, walkways)
- Land assemblage for new development, sometimes through selective demolition or use of eminent domain
- Identification and attraction of new markets outside or within the community (e.g., the discount store trend)
- Targeted business expansion, development, recruitment, and clustering of related stores serving a similar income group

Business District Renewal Approach 2: Facing the Changed Market

In cases where an adequate or underserved market exists, business district renewal involves increasing the ability of merchants to compete for and service the market. The primary focus is on the following:

- Increasing the business mix and products (both quantity and quality) through business expansion, development, recruitment, and horizontal clustering of stores offering a similar range of goods and services to a broader range of income groups
- Developing a core of specialty or niche shops (with local owner-operators where possible)
- Innovative marketing and promotion of the district and its merchants, with enough freshness to be featured in the business pages of the region's newspapers

CREATING A BUSINESS DISTRICT RENEWAL PROGRAM FOR ACTION

Business district renewal programs should be tailored to each district and be comprehensive, addressing the economic, market, physical, social, political, and organizational causes of decline and instability. Efforts should have sequential activities that create the preconditions for private investment, with the sequencing determined by district needs and opportunities, funds available, and the local implementing organization's capacity for planning and action. The creation of public-private-community partnerships (both resources and interests) and commitment with community-/neighborhood-level planning, coordination, and implementation is essential. Key is the commitment and direct action of local merchants and business owners. Successful renewal programs are grounded in a realistic market analysis and are captured in a long-term vision and plans.

A basic goal of community economic development is the stimulation of private investment. In declining areas, lack of investment or disinvestment is the norm. In such cases, the public and community sectors need to serve as catalysts or generators for revitalization. The public sector must take a catalyst's role in providing support for revitalization activities and in developing preconditions that will attract and hold private investment. Public sector support can create a sense of confidence and commitment for revitalization among residents, business owners, and potential investors and developers. Support can include many functions—from

funding and financing to code enforcement and public space improvements.

In many cases, merchants and shoppers need to be given confidence by actions on the part of government in dealing with fundamental issues before reinvestment will occur. Confidence at the local level is also built through the existence of local leadership and community pride. The need for community-/neighborhood-level clout and organizing is clear. Community organizations need to integrate the local businesses into the development of local political capacity. Therefore, a primary focus needs to be organizing and building politically capable merchant associations that help to determine and participate in both planning and implementation.

The private sector, made up of bankers, merchants, investors, realtors, developers, public utility representatives, and the like, also has a role in initiating the reinvestment process on which further new development or investment in the community depends.

Successful efforts require taking risks, making hard decisions on where resources should be targeted, and managing community expectations and needs versus market realities and basic economics.

DEVELOPING A BUSINESS DISTRICT RENEWAL PROGRAM

We focus on two critical steps in developing a business district renewal program: organizing and planning. These form the foundation for a strong, community-led organization that is prepared to choose and implement a revitalization strategy tailored to the needs, resources, and conditions of the neighborhood.

1. Organize a Business District Revitalization Group or Committee

Business district revitalization efforts often start as a response to community concerns—littered sidewalks, graffiti, few customers, and/or high building vacancy or crime rates. Neighborhood residents, business or property owners, local government, or other stakeholders may voice these concerns. However, the concerns must be matched by a genuine desire to address and correct them. It is this desire that will drive the revitalization effort. It takes persistent organizing and trust building to begin, sustain, and initially lead the process. A lengthy organizing process should be planned on and expected.

The key to a successful revitalization effort is to follow a process that is inclusive, builds ownership, makes room for input and participation, builds a shared vision and consensus, and is ongoing. It is important to build a base of support and to include those who have resources to assist in the effort—economic, political, technical, and financial—as well as ideas, enthusiasm, and willingness to work over the long term. Essential stakeholders (e.g., public officials, business leaders, merchants, residents, property owners) should be engaged in the process, and care should be taken not to leave out any groups. Also included should be supporters, neutral parties that might need to be engaged, and nonsupporters or competing interests that might need to be monitored, countered, or converted. Once all possible stakeholders have been identified, decisions must be made as to why, how, where, and when to involve them. Some stakeholders might not recognize their vested interest; they will need to be educated, and their commitment will need to be built, through a shared vision and impacts on their bottom lines.

Many community business district renewal efforts are housed with a community development corporation (CDC) or another community-based organization (CBO), with the CDC or CBO organizing a merchants group. In other cases, the business group may be willing to spearhead efforts with the CDC/CBO participating. The sponsoring organization can provide an existing and established support base, leadership experience, a network of contacts and resources, staffing, and funding to the initial revitalization effort. Its sponsorship is a pledge to lead and sustain the initial efforts and to support future business and property owner-led endeavors.

The board or coordinating committee that is built should be diverse and inclusive, with broad-based stakeholder representation. The identification of potential merchant-leaders is key for the sponsoring organization. Is there a business person who currently holds a community leadership position? Is there a resident who has earned the respect of the local business community? Is there someone who is vocal either in identifying community problems or in pushing for revitalization? Is there someone who recognizes his or her stake in the community and the need to protect that stake?

Beyond the board or coordinating committee, specific committees such as fund-raising, communications, marketing and promotion, and business recruitment should be used as a way of building more people into the program. Nonboard members should be used on committees or task forces, with board members as chairs.

It is important to gain support. It is best to start small and focus on immediate problems that can be solved easily; these can build early credibility. Many stakeholders will require proof that revitalization is possible and that the sponsoring organization is dedicated to success. Small improvement projects, such as vacant lot cleanups and tree or flower plantings, can serve a number of functions for revitalization leaders. First, these projects bring stakeholders together to work as a community. Participants have the opportunity to meet and develop relationships and to build trust with fellow community stakeholders. Second, it shows both those who participate and those who choose not to participate what a team can accomplish. Third, the project is an improvement that benefits everyone. All of these build neighborhood energy, enthusiasm, and commitment to the revitalization cause and even larger efforts.

Establishing and maintaining contact with stakeholders, the community at large, and potential supporters and resource providers is important. A variety of contact mechanisms may be used—face-to-face meetings, on-the-street chats, membership and outreach, a newsletter, reporting systems, planning process involvement, and public relations. The "sales" efforts of revitalization leaders—their enthusiasm and word-of-mouth marketing—are essential to gaining increased participation and support and to sustaining energy.

It is important to have a mix of access points to the organization such as regular publicized meetings at a convenient time (especially for business owners), periodic open meetings, and a mix of meeting types (e.g., business education, information gathering, socials, annual meetings, community meetings, public hearings). There should also be a mix of ways in which to participate such as membership, discussion groups, the board, committees, task forces, advisory groups, and short-term projects.

2. Develop a Long-Term Strategy and Plan

The development of a business district renewal strategy and plan should be part of an overall comprehensive community planning effort. Strategies and plans should accomplish the following:

- Identify business district strengths and opportunities, constraints and weaknesses, and trends.
- Have renewal plans based on an analysis of hard data. A market analysis and an analysis of existing conditions should be conducted. Building and land use maps should be assembled or created, and a "photoscape" of the district should be produced.
- Build on assets. New projects or programs should build on past successes where feasible and thereby increase overall impact.
- Define a target area. Targeting reduces the level of effort and finances required, increases impact, and heightens visibility.
- Set priorities. These should make a noticeable improvement in the area and lay the groundwork for future projects.
- Build a track record. Specific, manageable doable tasks and activities should be identified. It is important to stay focused and within the organizational capacity.
- Develop long-term, multi-year plans with short-term, 1-year action plans.
- Examine and evaluate opportunities and efforts every year. Data should be reviewed and, where indicated, updated regularly. Data should be checked against outcomes and incorporated into plan revision. It is important to communicate results, successes, and remaining barriers.

Strategies and plans are developed by taking a hard look at a business district. A realistic market analysis points out both the positive and negative features of the district. Typically, a market analysis will look at the trade area (geographic limits within which a business district can reasonably be expected to provide goods and services), the character and composition of the people who live and work in the trade area, the major competition, the character and composition of existing business in the district, and the attitudes of those who shop, work, use, and do business in the district (through surveys and interviews). A market analysis should calculate realistic sales potential based on a researched market potential and should suggest the nature and type of businesses that may be expected to operate successfully as well as those currently in the district that can be strengthened or expanded. (See Hyett & Palma [1989] and Wiewel and Mier [1981] for detailed descriptions of a business district market analysis.)

Baseline business district economic data should also be gathered and used to track and assess progress. Such data include number and nature of businesses, number of employees/jobs, dollar value of public improvements, business tax base, building ownership, building conditions, number and value of property transactions, and dollar value of property improvements.

BUSINESS DISTRICT RENEWAL PROGRAM COMPONENTS

A useful framework in which to examine business district renewal activities is the Main Street Program (*www.mainst.org*) of the National Trust for Historic Preservation that "enables merchants to preserve the vital, eclectic, central business district and once again make it the heart of the community" (Necciai, 2000, p. 8). Main Street puts forth a four-component comprehensive revitalization program: organization, design/image/environment, promotion and marketing, and economic revitalization/restructuring. Most successful programs are a combination of those components. Different components may be emphasized at different times and are often phased or staged, depending on the district's nature, needs, and opportunities; the resources available; the degree of public and private support; and the local implementing organization's capacity. For example, business development activities will be stressed in areas with a weak market, while business recruitment can be focused on more successfully in areas with a stronger market because the untapped market will attract potential merchants. Occasionally, historic preservation provides the spark and focus, as we saw in the Vandergrift case discussed in Appendix 5.A.

In declining or declined districts, emphasis has to be placed on building an organization (for planning and coordination), improving design and image (especially public safety efforts and cleanup), combating a negative image, and assisting existing businesses. Efforts will also include community group control of real estate to "jump-start" private investment or make a case that the risk of private investment is manageable. In a district with fewer problems or one with a market that is "untapped," more time will be spent on appearance, events, marketing, enhancement of existing businesses, and business recruitment because the district's "take-off point" is higher up the scale of things to do for stabilization and renewal. Many groups have tried to jump-start a very depressed district through buying and rehabilitating properties and attempting to fill them with businesses. Many of these efforts falter or fail even with substantial public investment because public funds cannot take the place of a weak market or get those who comprise the existing market to shop where they are afraid to go.

There is a caveat with standardized programs on the national and local levels: They do not fit all problems and may fail at solutions because neighborhoods often vary even within a single city. Therefore, programs need a great degree of flexibility.

The four Main Street components, working best when approached sequentially, are outlined next.

1. Organization. This means that there must be an organized strategy and an active organization at its center to plan, coordinate, manage, and monitor efforts and to serve as a funding conduit and develop public relations and outreach strategies and plans. The organization also serves as a communications link among all

players, especially small businesses and property owners, and other interested parties. Efforts are often housed with a CBO/CDC, or a merchants organization with ties to the CBO/CDC, and can be a committee or task force of an existing or start-up group. One organization need not be the sole implementer; however, there should be a central point for plan development, management, monitoring, and revision. The Main Street Program model includes having a Main Street manager as staff and organized active committees. The most successful organizations have a broad base of support and participation from many stakeholders, including local businesses, civic groups and associations, district and neighborhood residents, shoppers/consumers, realtors, property owners, local industries, schools, financial institutions, architects and contractors, developers, faith institutions, and local government. The goal is to have the views, ideas, skills, and resources at the table necessary to spearhead and sustain a renewal effort.

2. Design/Image/Environment. This area encompasses improvements to the exterior and interior property appearance and condition (e.g., buildings, lots), including historic preservation, public space improvements, landscaping, parking, transportation, traffic, public safety (e.g., policing, security, crime reduction), infrastructure improvements, public services, and public area maintenance. The design/image/environment area is not an end in itself; a focus on this component alone cannot overcome basic business problems. Efforts need to be tailored to the district and should build on strengths. This component needs to include incentives for property improvements (e.g., loans, grants) and technical assistance. Efforts should also include zoning and land use controls, creation of regulations and ordinances (e.g., signage, parking, historic preservation, architecture), flexible code enforcement (e.g., building, fire, safety, health), and actions against owners of vacant and deteriorated property.

3. Promotion and Marketing. Efforts here work to establish a new or improved unified business district image, refocus the community in a more positive way, and increase sales through increased foot traffic. This component includes group promotions and advertisements, special sales and sale days, and special events and activities. In addition, many efforts include publication of a business district newsletter and the development of a district logo. The creation of positive public relations comes about by aggressively facing a negative image or negative news and systematically establishing and maintaining good media relations. It is important to market the community, not just the business area. Promotion and marketing efforts are more successful if they target selected customer groups (e.g., workers, residents, seniors, employees).

4. Economic Revitalization/Restructuring. This means positioning a business district for success in the current economy. The work in this area should be a later-phase activity because it requires numerous resources—people, funds, expertise, programs, and public and private support. Strategies and plans need to be based on an analysis of factors that can lead to a new market position for individual businesses and for the district. Economic revitalization and restructuring activities include business development (e.g., financial and business technical assistance, counseling and education for retention, expansion, start-ups), business recruitment (e.g., outreach campaigns, marketing, location or relocation incentives), and real estate development (e.g., marketing property, site acquisition and development, incentives for acquisition, rehabilitation and new construction). The main goal here is the highest and best use of real estate (both buildings and space). Business recruitment is one area where one can work to improve the business mix by targeting businesses for selective recruitment (know which businesses one wants and does not want). The use or development of entrepreneurial programs and/or incubators is an alternative to business recruitment in that they represent "homegrown" business development. Another alternative is business expansion, which may involve expanding the square footage and/or product lines of existing businesses. It is prudent to focus business assistance and attention on the stronger and/or willing rather than on businesses that are more marginal. It is important to remember that some businesses will and should fail if they are not adequately serving the community with quality products, competitive prices, and good service.

Economic revitalization and restructuring also involves exploring opportunities to "control" real estate through the acquisition and development of key sites and properties. In addition, efforts should include creating and promoting a climate to engage private developers by offering incentives, providing assistance, and/or creating joint ventures. Many efforts also need to include the creation of tax abatements and incentives, incentive grant programs, and reduced interest rates and revolving loan pools; the use of the Community Reinvestment Act to meet small business credit and capital needs; and (sometimes) the offering of interest rate subsidies.

BUSINESS IMPROVEMENT DISTRICTS

Business improvement districts (BIDs) are created through local legislation and are most often established when a majority of business district property owners agree to assess themselves an additional fee to provide supplemental services to their business districts (Jackson, 2000). In some areas, BIDs are known as special service districts. Most BID legislation requires a petitioning process that must meet two tests: the agreement of the majority of the property owners within the district and the majority of the value of the property in the district. The most common use of BID funds is to improve basic services to the public by supplementing city/municipal services—removal of trash and litter, upgrading of sidewalks and streets, beautification and landscaping, and security. Many BIDs are working to build alliances with human service providers so as to find long-term solutions to panhandling and vagrancy problems. Others have provided respite centers for the homeless within their districts, and some are helping to establish one-stop service centers. BIDs have no extra-governmental powers; the nature of the services that BIDs perform is negotiated with local government. A locally-based sponsoring group, usually composed of property owners, business owners, and (in many cases) community organizations, provides oversight and coordination of BID activities.

The accompanying sidebar illustrates the challenges, successes, and range of activities and influence of a Main Street Initiative in a Philadelphia neighborhood.

Main Street on the Rise

The CDC of Frankford Group Ministries (CDC-FGM) serves Frankford, a racially diverse urban neighborhood of more than 43,000 in northeast Philadelphia. Focusing on increasing Frankford's self-reliance through housing and economic development initiatives, CDC-FGM has spearheaded the transformation of the Frankford business corridor since 1993. Experiencing a vacancy rate of 40% among 300 commercial properties, CDC-FGM in 1994 was instrumental in organizing property owners and two local business associations to create the Frankford Special Services District along a 13-block corridor. The district is a privately directed municipal authority created under the Municipal Authorities Act of 1945 and Philadelphia City Council legislation. CDC-FGM manages the day-to-day operations of the district. Through assessments charged directly to property owners, the district provides graffiti removal, supplementary sidewalk cleaning services, and a Safety Ambassadors patrol. The district has been able to leverage additional private and public investments to expand its efforts. In 1996, as part of a pilot program, CDC-FGM was awarded National Main Street designation from the Local Initiatives Support Corporation's (LISC) Neighborhood Main Street Initiative.

Organization building has been important to the initiative's success. CDC-FGM, as the Frankford Main Street Initiative, has secured the active involvement of community-based organizations and civic associations, business associations, merchants, bankers, attorneys, hospital representatives, and design professionals. Volunteers representing this wide variety of stakeholders participate in committees on design, promotions, business loans, land use, image, and public relations.

Through the program, the Frankford Main Street Initiative has leveraged more than $500,000 from the City of Philadelphia for new business district sidewalks and additional public and private investments for new facade improvements to district storefronts. Marketing and promotion activities have included development of an annual calendar of events as well as organization of art festivals and holiday events. CDC-FGM has also been successful in leveraging more than $4 million in local, state, and national public and private grant funds for the purchase and renovation of existing commercial properties along Frankford Avenue. CDC-FGM organizing, planning, and implementation efforts have paid off, with a drop in commercial vacancy rates by one half and more than 26 net new business openings.

Staff members of the Frankford Main Street Initiative serve on local community and business boards. Staff members also serve as advisers to the Southeastern Pennsylvania Transportation Authority's $150 million Frankford Transportation Center Project scheduled for a 2005 completion. The transportation center will be the new end-of-the-line destination for the Frankford Elevated Train Service and bus depot. This transit node project is expected to greatly increase the 60,000 riders who currently pass through the station on their way to Philadelphia's central city and to create significant retail opportunities along the Frankford business corridor.

SOURCE: Local Initiatives Support Coalition (2002).

SUMMARY

Integrating business district renewal with overall community economic development efforts—housing, social welfare, quality of life, industrial development, job creation, and the like—can help to create a climate that attracts new residents and new business and industry (e.g., employers, employees, private investment), expands the disposable income of current residents, and expands the market by increasing access and appeal.

However, business district renewal is becoming increasingly complex. Many regional, state, national, and global factors are beyond local control and not predictable. Social, financial, and political forces have been added to the basic economic and physical issues facing business districts. Managing community expectations and needs in light of market realities and economic trends becomes a primary challenge, but without a strong commercial center, a community cannot be strong.

Business district renewal is not as simple as the cookie-cutter approach that is used to explain it in most "how to" manuals. This view misses the dynamic nature of the forces that affect business districts, many of which are outside of community control. A simplistic cookie-cutter view also may unfairly raise expectations in depressed areas. Business district renewal is not just a series of steps to take; in some cases, it requires actual artificial manipulation of market and economic forces such as subsidizing for-profit businesses, operating 100% facade improvement grant programs, and finding ways in which to boost population.

Many business and commercial district programs and manuals assume that local shopping has a bright future—that a small community need only tap "untapped" expenditures or pools of government or foundation funds, focus on underserved markets, create a "catchy" theme to attract shoppers, and make appearance improvements. DiBart, Lebowitz, and Cohen (1980), in *The Role of Neighborhood Business in Neighborhood Stability,* spoke to the lack of consensus during the early 1980s regarding the economic future of small community- and neighborhood-based commerce. Opinions ranged from optimistic ("The latest potentials of urban neighborhoods are merely waiting for the right mixtures of stimuli to reach their take-off points") to pessimistic forecasts citing the overdevelopment of commercial space (vacant stores are commonplace even in strip malls), mobility, urban crime, and shifts in shopping patterns. This lack of consensus still prevails; however, many experts accept Porter's (1995) message and HUD's findings that America's inner cities are the next retailing frontier. But great care in doing sound research, planning, and investing is needed to achieve profitable renewal districts.

CONTINUING QUESTIONS

1. Is there a potential negative impact from dramatically upgrading a community business district? Consider the possible effects of displacement of community- or neighborhood-serving businesses, real estate speculation, increased taxes and property assessments, escalating rents, and alterations in local shopping habits. (See DiBart et al. [1980] for a discussion on this issue.)

2. What is the impact of business district renewal efforts on low- and moderate-income people? What are the costs to households with limited mobility if neighborhood-serving businesses are gone? If the strategy is to target low- and moderate-income people as the primary customer market (e.g., recruiting low-price discount stores and outlet stores), does this limit the future of the community for upgrading the economic base?

3. Can or should all small business districts survive? Have some outlived their usefulness or ability to compete? Should some marginal districts be consolidated with stronger neighboring districts to serve more than one residential area? Given limited public resources, should criteria be developed for selecting only the most promising areas for revitalization and for targeting investment? What would those criteria include?

4. What are the measures of success for business district renewal? How can the diversity of communities and situations be addressed?

5. What is the impact of business district renewal efforts on housing improvement and vice versa?

6. What is the interrelationship between downtown (central business district) renewal and outlying local business district renewal?

REFERENCES

DiBart, R., Lebowitz, B., & Cohen, R. (1980). *The role of neighborhood business in neighborhood stability: An information bulletin of the Community and Economic Development Task Force of the Urban Consortium.* Washington, DC: U.S. Department of Commerce, Economic Development Administration, Division of Economic Research.

Goldstein, B., & Davis, R. (1980). *Neighborhoods in the urban economy.* Lexington, MA: Lexington Books.

Grogan, P., & Proscio, T. (2000). *Comeback cities: A blueprint for urban neighborhood revival.* Boulder, CO: Westview.

Hyett, D. G., & Palma, D. P. (1989). *Strategic retail market analysis.* Washington, DC: Hyett-Palma Publications.

Jackson, E. (2000). *Why Mark Rosenman's wrong about business improvement districts.* Washington, DC: International Downtown Association. Available on the World Wide Web: www.ida-downtown.org/legislat/index.html

Jacobs, J. (1961). The death and life of great American cities. New York: Vintage Books.

Local Initiatives Support Coalition. (2002). *LISC Neighborhood Main Street Initiative Network site summaries: Frankford Main Street.* Retrieved September 24, 2002, from the World Wide Web: www.liscnet.org/whatwedo/programs/mainstreet/net_info/phila.shtml

Necciai, T. A. (2000, April). The four stanzas of our battle hymn: The Main Street approach. *PHLF News* (special issue). (Pittsburgh, PA: Pittsburgh History and Landmarks Foundation)

Porter, M. E. (1995, May–June). The competitive advantage of the inner city. *Harvard Business Review,* pp. 55–71.

Porter, M. E., & Blaxill, M. (1997, November 24). Inner cities are the next retailing frontier. *The Wall Street Journal,* p. A22.

Rocky Mountain Institute. (1990). *Business opportunities casebook.* Washington, DC: U.S. Small Business Administration, Office of Business Development.

U.S. Department of Housing and Urban Development. (1999). *New markets: The untapped retail buying power in America's inner cities.* Washington, DC: Author.

Wiewel, W., & Mier, R. (1981). *Analyzing neighborhood retail opportunities: A guide for carrying out a preliminary market study.* Chicago: American Planning Association.

15

WORKFORCE DEVELOPMENT

Strengthening the Economic Base of the Small Community

Back in Chapter 4, we suggested that a neighborhood economy is two sets of reciprocal flows of money and resources passing back and forth from and to households that buy products and sell labor as well as to and from firms and institutions that sell products and buy labor. The householders are all of those living within the geographic confines of the neighborhood. Some workers in these households may be employed within the neighborhood, but generally most work outside it. These householders demand and buy goods and services from a wide array of firms and institutions. A few of these may be inside the neighborhood, but most are outside it. (See Figure 4.1 in Chapter 4.)

To make goods and provide services, the producing/service firms and institutions need land and its products, capital, and labor, including a few people with the talents of entrepreneurship. They purchase these inputs from the households paying them salaries, wages, rents, interest, and dividends.

Because the neighborhood is a residential community, the principal product exported is labor, while most goods and services purchased come from outside the neighborhood. We could say that the principal activities of a neighborhood economy nearly always are exporting and importing.

LABOR IS KEY

The reality is that for most small residential communities, the quantity and quality of labor being exported determines the economic condition of the place. High per household salaries and wages make for affluence, moderate salaries and wages make for modest comfort, and small paychecks make for hardship and even patches of impoverishment. Of our seven key case communities, Rollingwood (Texas) is affluent, Hyde Park-Kenwood (Chicago) is mixed affluent and modest comfort, and the other five are struggling places of modest comfort and substantial hardship. Leaders of these five small communities understand that prosperity is tied to the numbers of householders employed and to the levels of their talents and skills. To seek economic improvement, the key is workforce development. This chapter concentrates on the following question: How can a neighborhood development organization help to raise the quantity and quality of jobs held by its residents?

Distress is deep and paralyzing to a small community when job loss, employment insecurity, unemployment, and low wages pervade its households. And all small communities feel the hurt and hope of the business cycle with its periodic rises and dips. Since the fading of the

World War II boom during the 1970s and the upsizing of technology and downsizing of workforces, job "nerves" have become a continuous source of distress for families and their local labor markets, even when the overall economy radiates prosperity as it did for most of the 1990s. The slowing of the economy since the start of the 21st century has been particularly debilitating to those communities already hobbled by abandoned factories, social isolation, poverty, discrimination, and educational deficiency. We saw this especially in Aliquippa (Pennsylvania), which has been caught in the travail of joblessness for more than 20 years. Too often, small communities and their renewal organizations choke up when facing unemployment (either chronic or occasional). This chapter contains tested working models for facing job insecurity and doing serious workforce development.

The civilian labor force in the United States is 140 million persons. Most of these are members of one of the nation's 71 million families, with a family being defined as "a group of two or more persons residing together who are related by birth, marriage, or adoption" (U.S. Department of Labor, 1996, p. 3). More than 6 million of these families have at least one household member who is unemployed. Joblessness is a distress that is not easy to deal with at the level of the small community, linked as it is to regional, national, and global economic forces. We find this difficulty present in Dudley Street (Boston), Bloomfield-Garfield (Pittsburgh), Aliquippa (Pennsylvania), and other cases cited in this book. All of America's 60,000 small communities suffer from unemployment, or the threat of unemployment, to some extent.

Large regional organizations, as well as state and national development bodies, are set up to give attention to job needs and are increasingly available to assist groups in small communities. Some small community renewal groups have attempted job programs. Most of them, like the Aliquippa Alliance for Unity and Development (AAUD), have had limited results so far. There is growing experience with such efforts, and more effective technical assistance is becoming available, although there are not yet general models of

absolutely proven dependability. We do know that innovation and local custom tailoring are called for, and probably always will be, as illustrated in the neighborhood models presented later in this chapter. But having rushed into the age of information technology in a relatively short time period, we are still struggling to learn how to fit all types of people into the changed economy so that they can enjoy a reasonable share of the nation's growing wealth. Reaching people through local community organizations appears to be an important way in which to do it—but a way that requires care and cooperation from beyond the neighborhood as well as a lot of alert local community planning that shapes and drives vigorous initiatives. Such special effort is necessary because of the erratic and often destructive nature of the free market economy with its churning employment practices.

The U.S. Department of Labor (2000) reported that even during the 3 years from January 1997 to December 1999, a period of overall job expansion and declining unemployment, a total of 7.6 million workers were displaced from jobs (p. 1). The fact that this mass displacement came during one of the most spectacular economic booms in U.S. history makes the scale of the "downsizing" significant and ominous.

This paradox springs from the amorality of the global market economy and of those who run many of its firms and institutions. It is ruthless in its drive for short-term efficiency, even pushing profitable firms to downsize their workforces as a means of building more capital, gaining more market share, further enhancing stockholder values, and ballooning compensation for executives rather than taking the far-sighted route of developing and retaining loyal quality workforces. It is a drive that now intensifies every year. In an overlapping study covering the 3 years from January 1999 to January 2002, the displacement count jumped to 9.9 million, with 4.0 million of these having worked for their employers for 3 years or more (U.S. Department of Labor, 2002, p. 1).

Mass layoffs have become so common that the Department of Labor now distributes a special monthly news release to report them. The global economic forces that affect the demand for workers, down to the level of the small community, are volatile and unpredictable, often oppressing a quarter or a third of the world while the rest of the world is enjoying boom times. These shortsighted drives are likely to be with us for a long time, bringing misery to families and small communities and wasting billions of days of potentially productive work due to forced idleness of able people. The sooner a small community creates a workforce plan and energetically pursues its implementation, the sooner the community can begin to break free of economic oppression.

The 8 million American families out of 71 million that now experience unemployment on any one day add up to considerable human distress, and the number could easily jump to 10 million at any time. Even in a tiny middle-income community of 800 households, there are likely to be 70 or 80 families living with job distress. In a typical low- to moderate-income neighborhood of 2,500 households, there could easily be at least 300 or 400 families troubled by joblessness, or the threat of joblessness, on a given day, while in an upper-income suburb such as Rollingwood, we found only 3 households suffering from unemployment in 2002.

For an organization at the small community level to help its jobless residents secure decent permanent jobs, astute organizing that forges close links to growth employers is called for. These usually are located outside the community. A neighborhood system of direct involvement with job seekers is required, especially one that also can help to meet the needs of employers for reliable employees. Components of the system are assessment of the strengths of resident job seekers, placement in intensive skills training or internships, help to seekers in locating and linking to information and employer networks, guidance to navigate employment interviews, and practical supports to retain jobs (when required) such as health restoration, child care during odd hours, transportation, expensive required tools, and work clothing.

An outstanding case of a productive workforce development process that has been used in dozens of neighborhoods is the San Jose Center for Employment Training (CET) with its real work environment method. It goes all the way back to the 1960s.

The CET was organized by Father Anthony Soto, then a Catholic pastor in a low-income Hispanic neighborhood, and Aussell Tershy, a community organizer, with $75,000 they obtained from the Catholic archdiocese of San Francisco. Starting as a west coast branch of the Opportunity Industrialization Center (OIC), the program became independent as the CET during the early 1970s and eventually spread its branches and affiliates through several western states.

In time, the *Wall Street Journal* gave recognition to CET. Bleakley (1994), a staff writer, reported that the CET community-based programs had graduated 60,000 trainees, 70% of whom were high school dropouts, "most of [them] hard-core unemployed welfare mothers, those with little or no work history, and people with past substance-abuse or law-enforcement problems" (p. B1).

Harrison and Weiss (1998) identified the CET as a hub-spoke type of network in which a small community development organization is usually in the center, initiating role. It represents a powerful method for nonprofit community-based organizations taking the lead to ensure that their residents have good jobs. Harrison and Weiss found that it is "one of the few training programs in the nation, subject to rigorous research, showing long-term positive impact on participants' earnings" (p. 50). Its trainees are placed into jobs at higher rates than are those from other programs in the same cities, stay in those jobs longer than do other trainees, and enjoy substantial gains in earnings over time. These results are achieved with very disadvantaged populations.

The CET has three basic strengths:

1. It has established strong, close trusting links with quality employers, which hire many of its graduates.

2. It has strong sustaining and motivating values derived from its history and the community forces that nurture it, including the Hispanic community, the Catholic Church, and the United Farm Workers Union.

3. Its training is carried out in a "real-life" production environment where there is a time clock, demanding corporate instructors, and hands-on machines from the very first day.

This is an expensive system in staff time. A large community organization would need to budget and raise substantial extra funds. A small organization with limited funding would need to recruit generous and knowledgeable volunteers. This means finding able people with experience, perhaps young retirees (in their 50s or 60s) who have worked in middle-management jobs and have both experience and contacts. Such volunteers would be useful in approaching growth employers for cooperation with the effort. Many firms are not experienced in working with community groups and are likely to be more receptive to requests for cooperation if contacted by volunteers with business experience who speak the corporate language.

Establishing links with growth employers is a challenging extraction exercise. It usually involves long-term, substantial personal communication by community organization leaders with firm officials and the offering of incentives that reward the cooperating firm. Rewards can include job applicants who are custom recruited and prepared to meet the employers' precise requirements, public recognition of the firms' cooperation that will strengthen their pubic images, and an opportunity to work with other employers on common needs while gaining useful business information in the process.

Because the U.S. labor market has become a volatile arena, many displaced workers, as well as persons new to paid work, are hired every day as others are furloughed. In a year's time, a large segment of the nation's families may suffer directly from job insecurity, either actually experiencing layoffs or seriously worrying about them. In its August 1998 update on worker displacement, the Department of Labor reported that only 6 million of the 8 million workers furloughed from full-time wage and salary jobs during the 1995–1997 period had been reemployed, with nearly 1 million still unemployed and 1 million gone from the labor force. In our culture, joblessness and concern about its imminence damage people's equanimity and self-confidence. These conditions disrupt and discourage community effort, and they depress consumer markets unless they are made issues for rallying people, collectively building hope, and showing results in restoring people to decent jobs.

Important lessons have been learned since employment insecurity began to be tackled by a few community organizations during the 1960s.

Many additional organizations engaged the issue during the 1970s. As outlined in Chapter 2, these early efforts produced a few large and productive initiatives, such as Newark's New Community Corporation, Brooklyn's Bedford-Stuyvesant Restoration Corporation, and San Jose's CET, but most of the smaller organizations arising out of local communities were not able to mount any long-lasting employment programs. Since then, new efforts have been made across the country that give more attention to employer links, especially regional alliances, workforce networks, and job initiatives that include banks, business firms, universities and community colleges, school districts, nonprofit social support neighborhood associations, Workforce Investment Act (WIA) groups, local governments, economic development agencies, and other regional bodies now wired into workforce development. There have been both successes and failures, and there has been much knowledge accumulated. We present here what seem to be the eight most important lessons.

1. Mobilizing Local Communities to Help Do the Job

Edward J. Blakely, the veteran practitioner and researcher in economic development who has directed the design and implementation of projects at regional and local levels and headed the planning department at the University of California, Berkeley, is the author of the classic manual, *Planning Local Economic Development,* an important guide to understanding the issues and technology relevant to small-scale economic development (Blakely, 1994). He is a firm believer that "locally based economic development and employment generation is more likely to succeed if initiated at the community/local level rather than elsewhere" (p. 27). In the manual, he encouraged neighborhood groups to compete for jobs for their residents while warning that "solutions to community problems will not succeed if they are not targeted to specific groups and linked to the total regional economic system" (p. 27).

From his work, Blakely has come to strongly support the notion that communities, irrespective of their size or location, must consider their economic destiny a major component of their agenda given that the possession of a job and economic security are the hallmarks of citizenship in the United States and that no small community can prosper without healthy internal economic flows and fruitful links to vigorous external labor markets and financial resources.

Mass layoffs are a disaster for a locality, making it essential that leaders mobilize their resources to create alternative economic and employment opportunities. "Local neighborhoods are not powerless to act. They do have resources that can be mobilized to stimulate both improved economic performance and increased employment" (Blakely, 1994, p. 7). Blakely (1994) cited many examples from his experience and noted that the federal government strongly supports policies to create jobs where people live rather than requiring people to move or make long inefficient commutes. Blakely emphasized that government furnishes funds to improve people's skills so that they are able to compete with foreign labor by being more productive.

There has long been support for small communities selling themselves as attractive locations for firms wanting to tap local resources, especially skilled and productive labor. Today, the quality of the workforce and the availability of a system that can help to provide upgraded skills are the top priorities for companies looking for new locations. In addition to productive workers, firms are interested in locations near their markets and suppliers and also near "intellectual assets" such as colleges and universities as well as clusters of facilities and amenities that provide a pleasant way of life and other especially well-suited resources and infrastructure that might be available.

Blakely (1994) cautioned against using cash subsidies as bait, reminding us that there is considerable evidence that the cost of subsidies ultimately is borne by workers and taxpayers of the community (p. 58). Too often, firms spend down a subsidy and leave. There is also the danger that a big new company from the outside, attracted by subsidies, will push small local firms out of the market, as we have seen in cases of "big box" retailers and highly advertised national chain stores selling designer clothing or family meals. In the manual, Blakely supported incentives over subsidies, suggesting that local

areas can provide attractive business parks, small manufacturing workshops, information and finance systems, research facilities, and "an aggressive local government with a flexible approach to incentives" (pp. 72, 202, 272).

2. The Welfare-to-Work Program Opportunity

With the passage and signing of the 1996 Personal Responsibility and Work Opportunity Reconciliation Act (PRWORA), responsibility for moving welfare recipients into paid jobs was mandated to state governments, with block grants furnished to states to implement the process. Within federal guidelines, each state has the discretion to design its own program, usually contracting with a variety of public and private provider agencies to assist recipients who must begin to support themselves through paid work within tight time limits. In fact, recipients are limited to 5 years of public assistance in their lifetimes, although some loosening of this requirement seems to be under way. Public and private provider organizations generally welcome cooperation from neighborhood groups that want to aid local residents in moving from welfare to work.

Teaming up with state- or county-financed providers that supply basic education, skills training, and job referrals may greatly strengthen the ability of a community group to help its low-income residents become employed. At the same time, the community group might assume an advocacy role and become aggressive and demanding to ensure that residents receive fair treatment as to job openings, wages, and working conditions.

The community group might identify and refer its eligible recipients to quality training and then follow up to ensure that the trainees gain direct access to employers in their own area. Community groups are likely to be the best recruiters for these programs provided that they have built trust with the community through widespread participation of residents and friendly relations with other local organizations. Sometimes, on-the-job internships can be arranged, as can tangible aid, support, and coaching on the job to ensure retention. Morale can be boosted by arranging for child care and transportation and by celebrating milestones such as "6 months in the workforce and still employed."

A new type of especially helpful provider in some states is the family support center. Located in small local communities, public housing communities, and urban and old suburban neighborhoods, such centers focus on health for parents and children, education and support in parenting, and economic independence. Their staff members are trained professionals and paraprofessionals, often indigenous to the community. These centers are found in highly visible, easily accessible locations and often are in buildings that provide other human services. Parents most often play a large role in planning programs and operating the centers. Such centers can make efforts to build connections to employers in the community, seeking to open jobs to community residents. They can make useful partners for community development groups. With their well-organized constituency, such centers may be able to take a strong leadership role in persuading the local community to initiate a new workforce development effort with wide support and participation.

3. Creating New Jobs Within the Community

When available jobs are too few to meet the demands of a community, as is often the case, the development organization can try to create jobs in its own community through several means.

David Scheie reported how the Fifth Avenue Committee in Brooklyn's Park Slope area created jobs through "an environmentally sound" Eco-mot dry cleaning franchise, an auto repair training business, a painting service, a beverage vending firm, and a technical assistance service for small housing contractors. Other new jobs came from training schools that drew on government funds as well as from an organizing campaign to form a union for temporary workers to resist unsafe working conditions and pressure employers for permanent jobs. The committee also campaigns for wages sufficient to raise a family and seeks opportunities to promote capital formation and innovation that can lead to increased self-employment. It seeks to place apprentices with existing local businesses

and does not hesitate to seek job and business start-up opportunities outside its neighborhood (Scheie, 1996, p. 9).

For both inner-city neighborhoods and rural-small town communities, there is often the reality that available jobs are now far away, requiring an automobile to reach them. Many growth employers have moved out to landscaped industrial parks adjacent to "safe, attractive all-white" suburbs. This situation may call for creating jobs closer to home while at the same time finding ways in which to link far-away jobs to the community. Sometimes, this means providing innovative transportation. In Chicago, the nonprofit suburban Job-Link Corporation combines carpooling with community organizing and job placement to help residents of inner-city neighborhoods find work in the growing firms in the suburbs (Bardoe, 1996, p. 19).

A housecleaning cooperative in Healsburg, California, has been cited as a reproducible effort at local job creation by the Center for Community Change (1997). Eight Hispanic women with organizing assistance from the faith-based Sonoma County Community Organizing Project formed the cooperative. Church announcements and some media publicity helped to gain sufficient customers to afford a Yellow Pages listing. It is now a going operation, with participants earning an average of $10.50 per hour (p. 20). The center suggests that some PRWORA money be used to establish community and public service jobs, particularly in quality day care centers serving people making the switch to work.

4. Workforce Improvement: Training and Education

J. Mac Holladay, who has directed state development programs for many years in South Carolina, Mississippi, and Georgia, confirmed that quality of the workforce is the single most important factor in economic competitiveness (Holladay, 1992, p. 34). When a firm considers a location for investment, before it considers climate, transportation costs, government subsidies, local taxes, major league sports, and other amenities, it assesses the skills, health, work ethic, and availability of the local workforce. Profits come from productivity, and the skills and energy of firm employees largely determine the level of productivity. Thomas (1994), in a study of job creation, found that tax dollars are better spent on training than on direct subsidies when a local or state government is seeking to attract business investment (p. 18).

Efficient training and education are key. *Efficient* means that classroom and internship learning is tightly focused on an expanding occupational field where it is known that jobs are growing and available. It also means that the teaching is done seriously by knowledgeable people who care about the goals of the program and that "fluff" is eliminated so that job-seeking residents can be ready for work in minimum time. Fluff could include extensive testing and imparting background technical information that might wait to be better communicated by a future employer.

In Aliquippa, we have seen a broad program of job skill improvement offered to residents through individualized computer skills training provided at the AAUD's own training sites. Referrals are also made to specialized courses operated by the county's publicly funded training agency. In Pittsburgh's Oakland neighborhood, the local community development corporation (CDC) provides job readiness training for residents, particularly those aiming to work at the large University of Pittsburgh Medical Center nearby. Through its "Job Links" services, the Oakland Planning and Development Corporation has an ongoing relationship with the medical center, can help to arrange appointments for interviews, advocate for neighborhood applicants, and give other aid to aspiring job seekers. This program has operated with positive results for more than a dozen years (Harrison & Weiss, 1998, pp. 115–118).

Every small community has some comparative advantage in training. It may have an institution in its area that is a potential source for including residents in its training such as a hospital, a college, or a sports arena. The training could take the form of an internship or volunteer learning, and colleges can sometimes include job skills training within their public service or continuing education programs as well as in their own employee operations. The University of Pittsburgh School of Social Work has a program, created during 1989–1991, under the leadership of Mary Page, that assists low-income single mothers. The University Community Career Development Program offers job readiness training, mentorships, supportive services, and job placement within the university and its medical center, including ongoing supports after employment. It has placed more than 100 women in full-time permanent jobs, with many moving up the career ladder and some attaining homeownership. Nearly all of these women are African American single mothers.

A useful starting point for community development organizations desiring to expand training programs for their residents is to build ties with nonprofit regional organizations that are focused on jobs and workforce development. In any area, these might include the following:

- The federal job training system, including city and county workforce development boards and nonprofit skills training organizations that are funded by the WIA (using both state and federal money)
- The state jobs service that lists job openings and makes referrals as well as manages the unemployment compensation system
- The adult education and career training institutions that include community colleges, vocational-technical schools, and extension-continuing education units of colleges and universities
- Social service systems that provide child care and help with substance abuse, mental health, and family supports

To build a profitable relationship with such resources is a standard exercise in community organizing. Contact is made with resources deemed most useful, leading to conversations between leaders of the local renewal organizations and staff of the resources. Assessments are made as to how residents in need of help might be matched with available social services. All of this is followed by implementation. To be successful, such arrangements require regular communication, with recognizable benefits accruing to both parties. These benefits could be jobs for the community and enhanced reputations for the providers. Successful outcomes would strengthen the fund-raising capability of both the community group and the social service organization. A community plan, as suggested in Chapter 9, would probably include a workforce development component.

5. Linking to Jobs in the Region

Scheie (1996) recommended that local community groups study business and economic trends in their whole region to identify types of jobs for which there is growing demand and to learn more about how their residents might be connected to, and prepared for, such positions. He cited four common principles:

a. *Have focus:* It is important to be clear about which body of job seekers and which set of employers to concentrate on at any one time and to be realistic about the capabilities of each. It is also important to know the selected job seekers and employers and their requirements well, and time should be budgeted for this. Scheie suggested possibly focusing on one regionally strong growth industry about which the local community group can become expert.

b. *Be flexible:* Tactics should be adjusted as resources and opportunities change while keeping within the chosen focus. For instance, because on-the-job technology is changing rapidly, training must be continually updated even for lower-level jobs.

c. *Cross boundaries:* Community organizers must understand for-profit firms, what moves them, and how they operate. An organization's cadre and staff circulate continuously in diverse networks—"staying informed, seeking openings to be useful, following up to avoid losing earlier gains" (p. 11). The key boundary to be crossed is the one that has long separated employers from community activists: the traditional business leaders' suspicion of non-business promoters and fear of falling into a swamp of community controversy if they become involved in community activities. Congenial personal relations need to be established between neighborhood leaders and business leaders.

d. *Cement relationships:* It is crucial for organizers and their cadre colleagues to work with relevant leaders of firms and other organizations whose strengths complement theirs. Scheie made a strong case for the gains that can flow from combining community organizing with economic development: "Ultimately it's the information flow and ingenuity that results from mutual respect and an ongoing appreciation for what each party brings to the table that will make the difference between real gains and frustrated hopes" (p. 11). He viewed the two approaches as making a potent combination.

Bill Freed, who heads the national FREEdLANCE Group for Career and Workforce Innovation, strongly recommends that local community organizations seeking knowledge and contacts related to building workforce enhancement for their residents join the Workforce Professional Network in their region and become active: "If there isn't one yet, organize it." Freed and his group have assisted in the formation and growth of such networks in many parts of the country. Freed is an enthusiastic and imaginative creator and facilitator of such networks, out of which come spirited career development programs and services as well as cooperation, coordination, mutual trust, and joint undertakings by workforce-oriented organizations of a region. Freed's product is social capital, and he might be labeled a "social capitalist" (personal interview, May 31, 2002).

In their positive assessment of San Jose's CET, Harrison and Weiss (1998) saw its success as coming in large part from the center and its staff gaining the confidence and trust of several large employers in the area (p. 70). The CET's success also came from being one of a handful of community-based programs that opened doors to high school dropouts while combining academics with job training skills.

Where a distressed community with a high level of joblessness is located in a growing regional economy, the community's development organization might work with a cluster of expanding businesses in a particular industry. The key here is an in-depth understanding of the forces affecting the targeted industry and identification of joint needs by the firms. A community group might help the firms to obtain quality, low-cost market research and/or to secure hard-to-find information on technological modernization, specialized financing programs, or real estate development, but it will eventually get around to a joint plan for workforce skills training. This cooperation is most successful where an industry requires occupations for which there is widespread demand and for which the community's residents have aptitude and interest. The development organization then can join in arranging for appropriate training for the residents and for their placement in jobs. The Center for Community Change (1997) pointed to the Portland Development Commission in Oregon, which provides such links for firms producing semiconductors, metal products, and health care services. An intermediary called Job Net links employers to community-based organizations in northeast Portland, and these organizations are able to supply residents to fill the jobs, with relevant training done by nearby community colleges (p. 7).

6. Changing and Improving Job Policy

The Center for Community Change, which helps more than 200 grassroots organizations build their strength, keeps pushing for a national response to meet the surprisingly high unemployment in many small communities. Writing for the center, Okagaki (1997) recommended that the nation invest in economic development activities that

> foster creation of a large number of living wage jobs. This has not happened. First, the general direction of federal policy is toward contraction and retrenchment rather than greater investment. Second, federal policy has seldom explicitly linked economic development with poverty alleviation. (p. 11)

Stable community organizations are free to press local and state governments for such a job policy. Nearly every section of the nation now has one or more advocacy coalitions concerned about job creation, the living wage, workforce advancement, and related issues. Acting with and through such coalitions can be an efficient use for the time of two or three of a renewal group's talented and energetic volunteers who are out to cause significant change. There seems to be a broad-based body of national strength building around this thrust of ambitious volunteers. Making contact with the Center for Community Change in Washington, D.C.,

would be a practical first step in getting ideas on how to move forward at the local level.

One creative local-level policy that some groups have pushed forward is the "first source" agreement, where a firm receiving substantial assistance from a local government agrees to interview local residents as the first group of potential employees looked to for filling available jobs. Molina (1998) described a first source program in Berkeley that uses zoning, contracting powers, and occasionally low-cost financing to leverage employer participation. Negotiations with employers often lead to the signing of first source agreements. Under the agreements, both contractors that build new buildings and businesses that occupy new buildings can be subject to first source mandates (p. 21). More than 2,300 Berkeley residents have been placed in jobs since 1986 at a median wage of $8.57 per hour (p. 24).

A distressed section of a city may have vacant blighted sections in potentially prime locations adjacent to downtown or a waterfront that would be attractive to real estate entrepreneurs. Nearby neighborhood organizations can sometimes join together to campaign for a "deal" between investors and local government to develop the site, with inclusion of a first source contract. When several small communities share interest in a site, they are most likely to find success if they do their advocacy as a coalition effort, a tactic that can help to avoid conflict among their local peer groups.

7. Cultural Competence

The relevance and importance of community organizers, employment recruiters, and other outreach staff being knowledgeable about and sensitive to diverse races and cultures is of double importance when they are deployed in the context of workforce development. Jobs and careers are essential, life-sustaining elements providing opportunity and satisfaction to human existence. In the Dudley Street neighborhood, José Barros, a community organizer up from the streets, talked about his long years of living in the Dudley Street area as he emphasized the warm response he gets from youth of color because he shares their roots and speaks their Spanish and Cape Verdean languages as well as English:

I have always been able to win the trust that brings cooperation and involvement from people of all the cultures, ages, and occupations. The young come to the job program because I ask them, and I explain the usefulness and the opportunity [the program] offers. They respond when I tell them how the program is going to create an urban village with a chance for education and training that will open the way to permanent jobs which pay enough to enable residents to afford some of the new housing they see being built in Dudley Street. (personal interview, June 14, 2002)

Barros regularly helps staff from other cultural backgrounds come to understand his Cape Verdean culture.

8. Other Workforce Issues

Blakely (1994) expressed concern that American manufacturing workers are not getting sufficient on-the-job training to remain competitive in the global marketplace. He cited data to show that Japanese auto workers regularly receive four times as much training as do American auto workers, thus making the latter more vulnerable to layoffs. He also strongly endorsed community-organized, customized skills training that would provide training either at an employer's site or at a local college, with the training specifically designed to meet employer specifications. Such customized training can be used to attract business because it reduces an employer's costs. Blakely pointed out that although such cooperation with employers usually involves new firms moving into an area, it may also be possible with existing firms that are expanding. He cited the Ohio High Unemployment Population Program (HUPP) as an innovative example of a program that provides such training and employment services to chronically unemployed minority males. Employers are used as a home base for a combination of on-the-job training and education that earns a credential or degree for each participant (pp. 206–208).

Increased government subsidy for support positions such as teacher aides, recreation workers, playground assistants, library pages, and outreach workers in human service agencies is another means of job creation. Such an arrangement can often be linked with the welfare-to-work program.

A skills inventory covering people available for work in a community, as an aide to filling job openings that have become known to a community development group, can make a community service faster and more efficient. An aggressive organization might gather unemployed people into a local cooperative service business or an advocacy organization to push government to initiate a first source agreement.

Discrimination can be a barrier to employment, with race, gender, and disability all possible roadblocks that must be thought about and handled firmly but sensitively. The Berkeley program cited previously and the Neighborhood Employment Network (NET) in Minneapolis have been especially successful in benefiting minorities, according to Molina (1998) in her report for the Center for Community Change (pp. 26–27).

In 1995, the Annie E. Casey Foundation funded a $30 million "Jobs Initiative" in six cities that tests community groups, employers, foundations, and community colleges working together to find effective ways in which to help disadvantaged workers secure living-wage jobs. In a progress report, the foundation set out lessons learned about race and regional labor markets. Employment discrimination was found to be a pervasive reality, with cultural awareness a current step in the workforce process. A growing network of individuals and organizations with experience in facing barriers to race, ethnicity, and gender has developed whose thinking should be tapped, as many new approaches and tools are needed. But great care and caution is advised every step of the way. The dangers, pitfalls, and unknowns remain numerous (Annie E. Casey Foundation, 2001, p. 19).

A community organization in a small community that wants to follow a consensus approach to jobs can find many ways in which to cooperate with employers and even provide them incentives. However, when friendly overtures are not accepted, advocacy and even confrontation can be considered to bring an employer to the table for negotiation. There are many ways in which to do this—firm talk, pointed press releases, marches, picketing, boycotts, and the like. Bardoe (1996) reported how advocacy has been used to obtain job commitments for neighborhood residents from United Parcel Service in Chicago and from Trailblazer Arena Construction in Oregon (pp. 9–14).

There are also regionwide advocacy efforts related to job rights and equity issues. In many cities, living wage campaigns are under way to raise local wages to a level to keep workers out of poverty. (A living wage is based on actual local living costs, determined by local surveys, and in most communities in 2002 came to about $10.00 per hour plus health benefits for a family of four with two wage earners.) Some community groups insist that they will help to fill only jobs that are full-time and pay a living wage.

As the government welfare-to-work program continues to face the limitations of sub-poverty wages and shortages of support services, many neighborhoods will face crises involving ex-welfare recipients unable to survive in low-wage jobs. This is going to set up a need for local community renewal organizations and their allies to join coalitions of socially concerned groups lobbying for humane changes to the PRWORA that would include government-financed jobs, more diverse and substantial training programs, and intensive support services. Renewal organizations in small communities can sometimes find powerful allies among social welfare groups for such reforms. Lens and Gibelman (2000) argued, "Advocacy is an essential and ongoing component of professional practice that is both consistent with ethical mandates and the 'person-in-environment' orientation that is the special province of social work practice" (p. 619). They also reminded us that advocacy is a much more potent tool when it is used productively to influence the shape and course of events rather than to just respond to them.

The following is one emerging model for carrying out effective workforce development programs in a small community.

A Small Community Model for Workforce Development

Liberation theology was summed up in the memorable phrase "option for the poor." The model developed by Robin K. Rogers while with the Allegheny County Commission on Workforce Excellence is such an option for the small community facing job distress and wanting to give priority to its poor (series of personal interviews, 1999–2000). It is a model rooted in the Kretzmann and McKnight (1993) assets approach to community organizing that puts emphasis on the skills and talents of community people. The need for such a model arises from the growing numbers of people who are either working poor, inexperienced welfare recipients soon to be pushed into the job market, or even worried middle-class people sensing that their skills will soon be obsolete. These three groups constitute the principal target population of the model, although it could serve any person or small community that is helping residents to find jobs.

The model calls for the creation of a partnership arrangement among employers, would-be employees, and both regional and local community organizations. It is directed not only at job creation but also at employee retention.

Two societal pressures help to call this model into being. One is welfare reform, with its "work first" approach pushing unprepared people into the job market, and the other is the global market, pressing nations to lift the productivity of their peoples. Demands for expansion of sophisticated training are likely, at some future time, to be backed by government-guaranteed jobs. Employers will probably be brought in more often as on-the-job trainers and be given attractive government contracts. Community groups can be part of this process by gathering systematic information about their resident workforces, by using the information to lobby for humane and effective changes to the law, and by preparing would-be job hunters to apply successfully for entrance into quality training and placement when they are provided.

The model also makes the case that there are two things the small community can do to increase job retention rates among low-skilled people who are already employed. First, the community can identify through research the supports (e.g., health, child care, transportation, housing) and working conditions (e.g., flextime, on-the-job skills upgrade training, mentoring, conflict resolution procedures, transportation pools) that promote worker job retention. Second, it can use this knowledge as a bargaining chip for joining partnerships with employers.

The wise, deal-making farmer selling livestock at a market knows his products and the market for them just as he knows the contours of his land. The Rogers model sees a future where small community renewal organizations will be as sharp as the farmer because they will know the employment market as well as the hopes, fears, and expectations of community people through regular skill and interest inventories. When armed with this information, their bargaining power will be strengthened. By wearing a path between themselves and employers, organizations can play an advocate role on behalf of job seekers eager to enter or rise up in the labor market. The advantages of the model are as varied as the small communities in which it potentially could be used. It puts to work the social work principle of "starting where the client is," it helps to build agency collaboration within and between communities, and it enhances the capacity of small communities to tackle job insecurity and inadequate wages. The outcome could be a win-win situation for all involved; employers get skilled employees willing to stay for the long haul, employees get living wages with the potential for upward mobility, and the small community gets a workforce for a more vibrant economy and has its homes filled with secure and spending households. Few small communities have reached such a sophisticated level. Most do not yet have any workforce-building program, and those that do are still at the gate doing "job placement" and assistance with résumé writing and interviewing skills. Only strong, high-quality programs will begin to improve stability and reduce employment insecurity. There are a lot of lost and bewildered communities out there on this issue. But as coalitions of experienced and responsible organizations, agencies, institutions, and firms are formed, community organizations can affiliate to gain access to sound and fair ideas as well as useful technical knowledge.

To wrap up, the model sees the small community as the stable out of which solutions to job insecurity and unsustainable wages can come in a way that empowers the community and strengthens participating firms and the local community economy. It asks something of employees, employers, training providers, and community organizations. More specifically, it puts demands on community organizers to have skills, knowledge, and experience in agency collaboration (sharing resources, risks, and rewards) and in building human capital. It demands that employers think locally about employment and the role they can play in revitalizing their environment. And finally, it puts demands on community people to develop their own capacities, talents, and gifts through education and training to enable them to be productive and stable. The elements of the model are summarized in the accompanying sidebar.

General Community-Based Employment Model for Development Organizations in Small Communities

1. Make an inventory of job-distressed residents to learn their goals, skills, needs, and work potential.

2. Approach nearby employers regarding their workforces, training requirements, and any expansion needs such as additional land, zoning modifications, and capital infusion.

3. Join or form a workforce alliance with development organizations in nearby job-distressed communities, growth employers of the immediate region, training institutions, the local official (WIA) workforce system, and other relevant and interested groups.

4. Choose an institutional training resource and other essential institutional supports.

5. Complete a workforce training agreement with all interested parties and implement training and job placement from a central location such as the facilities of a participating employer or community college or a regional technical high school.

6. Make sure that community groups supply follow-up supports for graduates of the training, including (as needed) mentoring, guidance counseling, home purchase assistance, substitute job placement, day care, health care, transportation, legal aid, and additional training and education.

SPECIAL
MANUFACTURING APPROACH

When a strong community renewal organization aims to include manufacturing employers and job seekers in its workforce effort, additional planning is required to help its residents capture some of the more lucrative jobs in goods-producing firms. This section focuses on this special opportunity and describes tested new tactics and techniques available for community organizations that aim to pave the way to manufacturing jobs for their residents.

Back in 1970, there were some 21 million manufacturing jobs, which represented 28% of total U.S. employment. Since then, the number has been slowly falling. The prospect is for manufacturing jobs to continue to shrink in numbers but to continue to offer opportunity to workers with strong basic talents, particularly proficiency in math. In 2001, there were fewer than 19 million manufacturing jobs, which represented only 15% of all jobs. Technology continually makes it possible for fewer people to manufacture more goods. Meanwhile, service jobs have grown to nearly 100 million and represent 80% of national employment. Although service jobs are far more numerous, the goods-producing manufacturing positions are more likely to be well paid with benefits and with the possibility of collective bargaining to enhance the status and security of workers. Moreover, since 1970, most manufacturing work has moved from being routinized and strength based to being complex and knowledge based, requiring skills in reading, writing, computer operation, and problem solving in addition to math. More and more, it has become an occupation of critical thinking backed by continuous learning. This has resulted in a sustained demand for creative workers with high technical competence, while there is an oversupply of low-skilled would-be workers. The latter often are left out of the labor market but need to be looked at as potential material for innovative training and education.

Although a useful rule of thumb is that goods making, rather than service providing, pays off in better jobs, the amount of capital involved in manufacturing, and therefore the risks, can be much greater.

There are local development groups that have pushed ahead as active partners and been successful helping to launch, retain, or even expand goods-making operations. The Small Business Administration has reported that a group of citizens in Chippewa Falls, Wisconsin, a community of 12,000 people, created Spectrum Corporation, a general partnership that has found local capital to support business development at lower-than-usual interest rates. The group's first project was to purchase an Illinois firm employing 55 people and move it to Chippewa Falls, where it soon expanded to employ 140 persons (Rocky Mountain Institute, 1990, p. 50).

Pittsburgh's Northside Civic Development Council assisted low-income single mothers to plan and begin a sewing cooperative, Northside's Own, that produced elegant specialty clothing for the local market and looks to exporting. Such manufacturing efforts are bold undertakings and are very difficult and time-consuming to organize, but they (sometimes) are a way in which to bring back decent-paying manufacturing jobs to distressed communities that long ago lost their stable employers.

Such dramatic undertakings are a temptation, but launching one or more can be diverting and overwhelming to a comprehensive renewal and local development organization engaged on many fronts. There can be favorable situations where the large risks can be undertaken prudently, but often small community organizations lack the time, capital, expertise, and networks of close partners to be able to be out-front in a manufacturing enterprise. Most professionals involved in helping manufacturing enterprises to start up or grow advise local nonprofit development organizations to play a peripheral support role rather than attempting to initiate or help run manufacturing enterprises.

In an extensive study of successful local projects, Mayer (1998) found that industrial retention and expansion programs can assist manufacturing firms already in a given location to stay and grow. The kind of smaller, locally owned manufacturing businesses most likely to welcome help from a community renewal organization have many incentives to stay where they are, which makes the task doable. A manufacturer generally seeks to avoid the costs (both financial and operational) of moving to another location. There is usually a strong reason why the firm selected its current location, and it likely still has ties that keep it in place. The community renewal group seeking to find good jobs for its unemployed residents will logically begin by seeking a relationship with nearby manufacturing firms, starting with any that might exist within the boundaries of its own small community but extending out to others within a feasible commute distance. Supporting and facilitating the survival and growth of such firms can be a profitable role for an organizing for community development (OCCD) group.

Mayer (1998) confirmed that caution is warranted for most small communities. As indicated, equity and operations involvement in just one small manufacturing plant can so absorb the time of an inexperienced development organization and its leadership that there is no time left for building the organization and operating a strong comprehensive program. But there are several constructive support roles that a community group can play in promoting manufacturing employment without being forced to neglect its other programs.

To survive and expand manufacturing, firms often need to remain competitive in the local marketplace. Particularly for smaller companies, an effective industrial retention and expansion program operated by a savvy community group can provide assistance in areas such as marketing, technology, and finding qualified workers.

Mayer (1998) warned that the central players in such an effort must include a "strong and consistent" voice for serving the disadvantaged or else this essential goal, crucial to reducing economic distress within small communities, will be lost (p. 2). And there always must be care that the firms involved have an effective mechanism to communicate their business needs to the leadership cadre operating the renewal group such as a central phone contact who is easy to reach. Such communication usually will run smoother if a couple of employer representatives become active members of the community organization's cadre.

Mayer (1998) reported that manufacturing support programs he has looked at always make communications between leaders of the community program and managers of the firms a key activity, with the community people receiving continuous reports about the firms' ongoing needs and maintaining working relationships to better serve them, if possible gaining their direct participation in the selection of trainees. He strongly supported firm representatives being part of a joint leadership running the support program.

Business services that can be furnished through a cooperative community group are many. These can include finding sites for expansion and developing the space, intervening with local governments to ease permit and other regulatory processes, providing technical assistance with general management, and assisting with marketing and technology, often concentrating on modernization. At times, there can also be help with strengthening firms that are at risk of shutdown or departure; aid in obtaining financing or direct loans from a community group's own development fund (as in Aliquippa); help with networking such as joint purchasing, peer learning, and production collaborations; help with transferring the business to successors; and aid in workforce activities to serve existing workers as well as facilitating the recruitment of new employees. Community job linkage programs can improve poor people's access to manufacturing employment while assisting employers to gain information and help in identifying new markets for firms, new product development to add to traditional lines of products, and even assistance in opening overseas foreign export markets (Mayer, 1998, chap. 2).

Although such manufacturer assistance programs can operate with modest staff size and limited budgets, they do often rely on partnerships to deliver their services. Community program leaders recognize the advantage of drawing on other players with the expertise, resources, and control that they lack. Partners for such programs can include the firms themselves; successfully employed residents who found jobs through the programs, government agencies, outside funders, investors and lenders, experienced consultants, utility companies, veteran workers, and trade unions as well as community organizations.

An important reality is the length of time it takes to make such a program effective and productive. It does not happen fast. It takes considerable study and relationship building in the beginning as well as careful planning and experimental testing of techniques. Programs must be shaped to local conditions for trust building among the partners. The minimum time required for a program to show consistently positive results and to develop steady momentum is probably 5 years. It took 10 years for Aliquippa to get into such a program, and the AAUD is still struggling to produce jobs with it.

Earlier in this chapter, we set forth an eight-point community-based model built from research, experience, and current work that involves a pilot project to take advantage of the government's WIA program, which requires a large role to be taken by business.

Now, we turn to Barry Maciak, who for 15 years has specialized in the care and growth of small and not-so-small manufacturing firms. As a roving business consultant, he has assisted many companies in the 20- to 300-employee range to stabilize and strengthen themselves, sometimes by expansion. Maciak began his professional life as a community organizer fighting poverty during the 1970s and has learned over time that organizing activities such as aggressive recruitment, collective decision making, reality-based planning, open communications, and outside resource tapping can be used to help networks of manufacturers collaborate to remove the barriers they face to growth and stability.

During recent years, Maciak has found shortages of able technical production workers to be the major barrier for small manufacturing companies.

I have seen community-based firms turn down sizable orders offered to them because they couldn't find enough skilled employees. The big regional economic development organizations have not utilized their resources to create a practical rapid response system to deal with this need. During a period of relatively low unemployment, the community has a rare opportunity to not just place unemployed residents in jobs but to move underemployed residents into value-added jobs with growth opportunities. (series of personal interviews, 1999–2002)

During the mid-1990s, Maciak became involved with several machine shops desperate to find a way in which to obtain more qualified workers. With Duquesne University's School of Business as the overall sponsor of the effort, Maciak facilitated a process of planning by a team of firm owners and managers. They quickly realized that they would have to initiate their own recruitment of potential workers and find resources themselves to do the necessary customized training.

Arrangements were made for machine shop executives to tell their story to a room full of foundation executives, who responded to the opportunity to stimulate the local economy through machine shop expansions and living-wage manufacturing jobs. A group of the funders pooled $125,000 to underwrite research and the design and implementation of a small machine shop training plan.

With participation of the owners and managers, Maciak and university staff were able to recruit local high school graduates who had tried higher education but had dropped out after 2 or 3 years for nonacademic reasons. Recruitment was by direct mail and interviews, and those selected were sent to a quality technical-adult education center jointly operated by 11 school districts in the region's main industrial valley. Here, each trainee received 17 intensive weeks of machinist training tailored to the specifications of the machine shop planning team. A total of 15 recruits graduated; with each getting three or four job offers. Maciak expected those who would stick to be earning more than $40,000 after 4 years. In January 1999, 35 more graduated, with recruitment leveling off at 120 per year, the then anticipated equilibrium number. State government and Duquesne, along with the machine shop firms involved and the supporting foundations, shared the cost of $5,500 per graduate. Eventually, Maciak wants to see the trainees also contributing to the costs when feasible.

Maciak is now putting this machine shop model to work in a larger scheme that will include local development organizations from urban neighborhoods, industrial towns such as Aliquippa, and other small communities. He believes that strongly rooted community groups, with established lines to their residents, can be efficient in finding eligible recruits for the training classes.

Maciak was concerned because the first class of machine shop trainees was nearly all white males. The program has since tied in well-established local organizations that have begun to find competent women and minority candidates for machinist occupations and a host of other manufacturing occupations. Also, he has added a remedial education component to help bring promising candidates up to speed. His 2001 classes were 22% African American and 8% female. He continues to work to attract a more diverse flow of applicants.

There is also the function of post-training supports for graduates as they become employed. In some cases, they will need a mentor or sponsor only to listen and give encouragement. But in other cases, there is a need for concrete aid with child care, transportation arrangements, health care, and frequent "talking it over." Maciak will look to community groups for such backup and monitoring in future programs.

When community groups are new to workforce development and job support, Maciak sees them as often needing advice and guidance in understanding business culture and how to establish a successful working relationship with this sector, at the same time helping business people to understand the purposes and potential for the community sector. His model calls for recruitment and training centered in a "manufacturing workforce clearing house" located at a university, a large multi-service community center, the cooperative ministry of a network of churches, or a similar stable nonprofit institution. It would have a small staff of business recruiters who would locate and engage promising small firms in business networks. These networks would follow the machine shop pattern of identifying barriers to growth and planning how to overcome them while engaging community groups in the process.

Community organizations would join such efforts at any appropriate point to negotiate a role both useful to the network and productive for meeting its own community employment needs. In particular, community organizations likely would bring selected job-seeking recruits to the operation. Each small community organization later would be looked to for post-training supports for their residents newly employed in manufacturing. Maciak believes that community groups will need additional resources and very able volunteers to do this follow-up support well. He sees it as a difficult undertaking for most neighborhood organizations. Alert community renewal organizations would move to join such a potent joint effort on their own initiative, long before being invited.

Maciak emphasizes that the machinists project succeeded because the people who participated from the firms, foundations, and educational institutions were decision makers—owners, managers, board members, executives, lead supervisors, and others with real power and influence in their home organizations. He

believes that this is essential, just as bringing in women, minority, and low-income trainees is essential, to make the program work and serve its long-range goals.

VISIONARY LEADERSHIP

Like any initiative, performance excellence in workforce development depends in part on the quality of the leadership. In one sense, leadership lies in the hands of the Workforce Investment Boards (WIBs) created by the WIA. These systemwide partnerships of employers, community-based organizations, one-stop services, and training providers must set strategic direction, create a strong customer orientation, and communicate clear and visible values throughout the system. An effective leadership structure and the ability to accomplish these objectives from the top down are certainly important components in the ultimate success of any performance excellence initiative.

But as anyone who has participated in a major change initiative knows, grassroots leadership is equally critical to the success of a change effort. If the people "in the trenches" do not exercise their leadership skills—innovating, influencing, creating, problem solving, decision making, and collaborating—then new programs and initiatives will die on the vine. A high-performing workforce development system requires leadership at all levels if it is to succeed.

The FREEdLANCE Group for Career and Workforce Innovation

Beyond machine shops, Freed is looking next for manufacturing job opportunities in other industries such as robotics. Besides recruitment and post-training supports, he would look to local development organizations to add grassroots fund-raising, as well as more clout with government, to the network effort (personal interview, May 31, 2002).

The general community-based workforce development model described earlier must be modified to accommodate manufacturing employment. This requires a more intensive relationship with employers and more careful and selective recruitment of trainees. If a community-based development organization is already involved in a workforce alliance with other community groups, then the focused manufacturing effort might be a special project of the alliance or a pilot effort to be linked to the alliance if and when it succeeds. If an organization has no employment program, then it might enter the field by starting with manufacturing. In any case, the steps for getting under way are summarized here.

A team of committed volunteers and staff from the community group (or alliance of community groups) proceeds patiently to open communications with small manufacturing firms within commuting distance of the target workforce. If possible, the team should have, as a member or an adviser, a person who is an experienced and savvy professional—at home with business attitudes and interests. Acting in pairs, members of the community team would approach selected employers to determine their willingness to cooperate with a community program. The test is to have employers reveal their needs and interests and to accept community groups as partners able to make a contribution to the partnership effort.

Sometimes, community representatives first seek to identify small concrete matters of mutual interest to both residents and firms such as traffic flows, parking, public safety, clean streets, and green space. Then, one or more such improvements can be sought immediately to establish a pattern of cooperation that "warms up" the two sides working together before they come to the more complex payoff issues of workforce and training.

Specific employer needs would be hammered out, and community representatives and their organizations would recruit resident prospects, inclusive of race, gender, and ethnicity. Potential training institutions and funders would be brought into the mix. Employers would play a lead role in designing the training curriculum and would participate in the teaching. A component of the training might be internships at employer firms.

Participating employers would have the first opportunity to interview the training graduates. Those not hired immediately would have additional interviews set up for them by community representatives. The community group or groups involved would take responsibility for seeking to ensure that each newly hired person had adequate child care, transportation, health care, and other essential supports. Like all community-based efforts, it is probable that each partnership would develop its own specific characteristics reflecting the special conditions of its region and cluster of small communities. Maciak believes that the time has come when employers are ready to solidify such partnership efforts so long as their product costs are not driven up. The revised model focused on manufacturing is summarized in the accompanying sidebar.

Community-Business Manufacturing Employment Model

1. A local community organization, or a set of organizations such as a coalition, establishes relationships with growth manufacturing firms located within commuting distance of the targeted workforce.

2. Community representatives and business representatives agree on priority needs and opportunities in a joint planning process.

3. Firms and community organizations jointly carry out small concrete projects of mutual interest and work their way to workforce development.

4. Community groups identify residents ready for training who might meet the workforce requirements of firms.

5. Agreement is reached on a training plan with firms, and the involvement of an appropriate institutional training resource, such as a community college, is secured.

6. Training is implemented, and graduating trainees are guided into jobs with cooperating firms and other employers.

7. Community groups furnish follow-up support for newly hired graduates of training.

8. Firms and community organizations jointly evaluate results and move to an improved second stage.

Remember that the well-being of the small community's people is dependent on stable, decent-paying jobs. After a model is chosen, it should be adapted to the local conditions, and work should begin right away if the goal is to strengthen the neighborhood economy.

SUMMARY

Community-based organizations seeking to reduce job distress of their residents can launch their own workforce development initiative, join with other organizations in creating one, or work to strengthen an existing one. Community groups should arm themselves with detailed knowledge of the skills and training needs of local job-distressed residents and see the strengths and weaknesses of their community and region.

Building a workforce development program requires relationships with growth employers that include joint planning and implementation of the relevant, agreed-on customized training and placement. Firm needs and community needs guide creation of a realistic plan that includes placement and follow-up to ensure that newly hired residents have supports essential to becoming stable members of the workforce.

Key factors in the program are employer cooperation, competent selection of trainees, trainee enthusiasm, quality skills training, timely placement of graduates in living-wage jobs, and post-hire supports.

For a small community group to newly enter the workforce field, an essential step is to join any existing, legitimate, local and regional workforce networks, including the one or more linked to the government-mandated WIB.

CONTINUING QUESTIONS

1. What fair and effective incentives can be used to win involvement of employers in small community workforce development?

2. How can community involvement be maximized in a highly organized, information technology training system?

3. Who pays for training?

4. How can a community renewal organization get business participants to understand how the living wage can help to build a vigorous local economy of benefit to all local businesses?

5. As global forces make job security less certain, what role should government assume to remove the uncertainty? Has the time come for government to be the employer of last resort? How can such government activities mesh with the plans and programs of small communities?

6. Is the organizing of community workforce initiatives an important and complex specialty calling for a new kind of organizer with special training and experience?

REFERENCES

Annie E. Casey Foundation. (2001). *Taking the initiative on jobs and race.* Baltimore, MD: Author.

Bardoe, C. (1996). *Employment strategies for urban communities.* Chicago: Center for Neighborhood Technology.

Blakely, E. J. (1994). *Planning local economic development* (2nd ed.). Thousand Oaks, CA: Sage.

Bleakley, F. (1994, October 4). Center's mix of study and skills is a hot job-training model. *The Wall Street Journal,* p. B1.

Center for Community Change. (1997). *Jobs: Some organizing strategies.* Washington, DC: Author.

Harrison, B., & Weiss, M. (1998). *Workforce development and networks.* Thousand Oaks, CA: Sage.

Holladay, J. M. (1992). *Economic and community development: A southern exposure.* Dayton, OH: Kettering Foundation.

Kretzmann, J. P., & McKnight, J. L. (1993). *Building communities from the inside out.* Evanston, IL: Northwestern University, Center for Urban Affairs and Policy Research.

Lens, V., & Gibelman, M. (2000). Advocacy be not forsaken! Retrospective lessons from welfare reform. *Families in Society, 81,* 611–618.

Mayer, N. S. (1998). *Saving and creating good jobs: A study of industrial retention and expansion programs.* Washington, DC: Center for Community Change.

Molina, F. (1998). *Making connections: A study of employment linkage programs.* Washington, DC: Center for Community Change.

Okagaki, A. (1997). *Developing a public policy agenda on jobs.* Washington, DC: Center for Community Change.

Rocky Mountain Institute. (1990). *Business opportunities casebook.* Washington, DC: U.S. Small Business Administration, Office of Business Development.

Scheie, D. (1996, September–October). Promoting job opportunity: Strategies for community-based organizations. *Shelterforce,* pp. 9–11. (Orange, NJ: National Housing Institute)

Thomas, C.M. (1994). *Getting the "jobs" done.* Pittsburgh, PA: University of Pittsburgh, Institute of Politics.

U.S. Department of Labor. (1996, June 16). Employment characteristics of families: 1996. *News.* (Washington, DC: Bureau of Labor Statistics [USDL 97-195])

U.S. Department of Labor. (2000, August 9). Worker displacement during the late 1990's. *News.* (Washington, DC: Bureau of Labor Statistics [USDL 00-223])

U.S. Department of Labor. (2002, August 21). Worker displacement, 1999–2001. *News.* (Washington, DC: Bureau of Labor Statistics [USDL 02-483])

16

Organizing for Community Controlled Development and the Promise of Coalition Politics

This book has suggested ways in which residents of small place communities might unite to plan, find resources, and regenerate their local places while reconnecting themselves to public responsibilities. In this final chapter, we restate the definition and importance of our Organizing for Community Controlled Development (OCCD) model of renewal, reiterating its major characteristics. We also look beyond today's fragmentation of communal power centers to a cohesive national alliance through which community interests would seek to establish parity with the powers of government and business so as to claim and bargain for a scale of resources adequate to recovery and resurgence of the nation's small place communities, permanently establishing communal influence in the process.

Organizing for Community Controlled Development: Reviewing the Nuances

OCCD offers a comprehensive approach and direction for preserving and improving the places where we live. *It is people coming together within their shared living place to plan and deploy resources in ways that enhance the local community, enrich society, and advance social justice.* OCCD encompasses all aspects of community life—the social, political, and economic dimensions. In review, the definitional components of OCCD are as follows:

Organizing: This represents the mobilization and constructive deployment of community residents and allied stakeholders. Organizing embraces a planned approach that draws resources from within and without the community and allows for local control of the community's future.

Community: This recognizes and values place (community as a common geography), common interests that unite, and participants with capacities and needs they share.

Controlled: This asserts that people who are organized and mobilized have earned the right to decide the future of their place by creating a common vision and comprehensive plan through widespread participation.

Development: This affirms that a community's future can be transformed. Social change can be social justice when there are adequate flows of social, political, and economic resources drawn from appropriate institutions and individuals outside the community as well as from the diverse interests within the community.

This *tri-dimensional, place-based renewal approach* is put forward in response to the following three specific conditions of distress:

- *Racial antipathy:* Residential and economic segregation supported by infrastructure (e.g., policies, laws, practices, beliefs, norms, media, language) remain in place supporting personal and institutionalized prejudice, oppression, and racism. OCCD recognizes this antipathy and offers strategies that uncover, confront, and address.
- *Erosion of civic involvement:* Low participation pervades in the political process where policies are shaped and institutionalized, resources are targeted and apportioned, and far-reaching decisions are made that affect the fiber of our small communities. In many communities, there is disillusionment and alienation. OCCD offers mechanisms for residents and community stakeholders to reengage in meaningful dialogue, decision making, and collective action.
- *Economic disparity and joblessness:* The community economy is part of an unregulated global marketplace in a system that creates and supports disparity in employment and compensation as well as wealth. OCCD employs strategies that seek to capture and bolster local economic flows and to challenge and change systematic disinvestments and poverty wages.

The following five *principles* undergird OCCD:

- *Inclusion:* The people of a community can best supply the ideas, decisions, and collective strength to revitalize and preserve it.
- *Comprehensiveness:* The social, political, and economic dimensions all require attention, with priorities tailored to the unique traditions, strengths, and challenges of each particular community.
- *Mobilization:* This is organizing inside the community and reaching outside it to build productive linkages (partnerships and collaborations) that tap new power to help maximize legitimacy and credibility as well as material resources.
- *Adequate wealth:* This represents sufficient resources to lead to self-sufficiency and dignity

for households and continuing independence and vitality for the overall community. A new handbook that is particularly useful for activating this principle is Mihailo Temali's *The Community Economic Development Handbook: Strategies and Tools to Revitalize Your Neighborhood* (2002). It is a lucid and compact guide for organizing, funding, and producing new growth enterprises, partnerships with expanding employers, and solid upgrading of the work skills of residents. It appears a powerful tool for the determined and daring renewal group.

- *Health and spirit:* This refers to the quality of relationships and availability of services to provide physical and spiritual well-being of people and place.

Community renewal is a long-term undertaking; successful efforts require sustainability. If a community is to provide what is needed and expected, then it requires sustained attention from those who live and work there and share responsibility for the community's health. OCCD therefore focuses on both process and product—building an organization capable of leading and sustaining renewal efforts and developing and successfully implementing community-tailored strategies and initiatives. Characteristics of such an effort include the following:

- *Place based:* While people may have ties and concerns beyond their place community (e.g., identity, issues, friends, networks), OCCD is always centered on the renewal of a particular place, a territory of defined boundaries (whether formal, traditional, or informal). Place grounds efforts and defines participants and beneficiaries.
- *Resident led:* Leadership and decision making rest with those who will be affected by decisions and actions. The group includes a trusted "cadre" to guide and facilitate both the renewal process and the product as well as to ensure steady growth to the body of interested residents and their allies who join in.
- *Continual "people" development:* Resident talents and skills (both apparent and latent) are noticed and marshaled on progressively more detailed and complex initiatives, while new leaders are actively identified and groomed to produce and apply knowledge, courage, concern, and cooperation.
- *Deep authentic participation:* A conscious, proactive concerted effort is made to reach out

to and welcome *all* community members. Entry points to the organization and its efforts are varied to accommodate people's availability and interests. Gaps in representation and participation are monitored and filled aggressively. Cultural competency is an articulated value—in the organization and the community. This moves beyond "tolerance" and "multiculturalism" to knowledge of and an abiding respect for others and their cultures as well as a willingness to adjust or change what and how things are done to ensure full participation. "Participation" also means that the process is open to those involved being fully engaged—from idea generation, to decision making, to implementation, to evaluation. Organizational "power" does not remain in the hands of a few.

- *Grounded in community organizing:* Renewal efforts require broad-based mobilization and the exertion of influence and power both to get things done to benefit the community and to stop things that negatively affect the community. All legitimate tools and tactics, no matter how disruptive, are used on behalf of the community agenda.
- *Justice based:* Residents and their organizations understand that not having decent shelter or a family-sustaining wage moves distress beyond individuals and community. Housing development must be coupled with fair housing activities, job creation must be coupled with living-wage campaigns, and community-based residential and small business loan programs must be coupled with Community Reinvestment Act vigilance. Fairness, equity, and redress are as much a part of community renewal as is building new rental housing, operating a business district facade improvement program, or establishing a day care cooperative at a family support center.
- *Open continual organizational and community planning:* Decisions are based on serious assessment and research, not assumptions. Plans have well-defined strategies and goals grounded in mission, and they build on community assets/strengths and address community challenges in all dimensions of the community—social, political, and economic. Input, decision making, and feedback are distributed widely among many participants. Planning systems keep alert to relevant opportunities. Information flows are continuous and open.

- *Strategic resource development:* This refers to the tapping of internal community resources and the extraction of external community resources at a "scale" that meets the test of "whatever it takes." There is a focus on "grassroots" fund-raising—amassing unrestricted and renewable funds—helping to ensure that the community, and not an outsider, is the decision maker.

There are many place-based change efforts under way in the United States, and new groups are organizing every day. Their potential can be great if most of them take in-depth risks and become realistic about scale in a society very rich at the top and growing richer. OCCD is an aide in broadening and strengthening the community renewal movement. We hope that it guides new efforts and challenges existing ones.

BEYOND THE SMALL COMMUNITY: POWER AND INFLUENCE AT THE NATIONAL LEVEL

The authors of this book have confidence in the OCCD model. We believe that if the model is faithfully pursued, it can bring serious change and improvement to a small community. We recognize, however, that during this 21st century, every small residential place, no matter how rigorously mobilized as a determined and generous neighborhood, is subject to societal entropy—negative social, political, and economic outside hits that wear away at its unity, undercut its confidence, and raise barriers to its obtaining a fair share of the nation's flows of resources.

Our OCCD model of change spelled out in this book offers a process and pattern for the organizing of civil society from the ground up through reinventing and revitalizing the nation's network of small residential places. We offer this out of our lifetimes of experience that have concentrated on such places. We are not equipped to suggest a design for a broad new national movement of communal interests, but we do affirm the urgent need for such a political construction that would be inclusive of small communities and their interests and whose strength and reach would go beyond anything that currently exists. It should combine the communal forces that champion fairness and human development in our national life and draw in the compatible third-sector (national) power centers in the nation.

Envisioned are tons of neighborhood organizations connecting upward from their small place communities, ascending through regional and state networks to a national apex interconnected with other national third-sector alliances toward equity and sharing. Separate and distinct, this third sector of national power would enroll a vast array of organizations and groupings that are built around notions of reciprocity, community, and distributive justice. The essential values in such bodies are respect for the dignity and worth of every single person on earth and the right of every person to be included in the decision making that affects his or her well-being.

Even in the rich and free United States, a growing majority feel the sting of bias, the frustration of political hopelessness, and the anxiety of financial insecurity. The spread of "Enron ethics," wiping out the pension investments and savings security of millions of middle-class working people, opens the door to fields of disillusioned wealth holders, rendering them susceptible to enrolling in a movement for fairness.

Add the Seattle protesters of 1999 to those who have joined in to demonstrate for clean water and trade union advancement, along with the vast millions of hidden poor being affected by the shift of federal priorities from human needs to defense, home security, and tax cuts for the affluent, and the numbers look like a political majority that reminds us that it is only a short time since the 2000 presidential election, when less than half of the electorate voted for the winning side.

In our time, it would appear that a vast public is ready to consider supporting a national coalition of communal interests that would seek diligently to redirect national policy toward a new goal of fairness, with neighborhood alliances among the active participants.

During recent years, there have been many wise voices calling for such national bodies of communal interests. At stake are issues vital to small place communities, including the three emphasized in this book: racial hostility, civic apathy, and economic insecurity. Neighborhood-based change-seeking groups can be key potential partners in this mainstream movement where they would coalesce with numerous sectors of society suffering from distress, unfairness, and oppression since the unusual presidential election results of 2000.

Activist writers have proposed a new fairness movement for a long time. Fisher (1984), for instance, was groping in that direction during the mid-1980s when he wrote,

> What neighborhood organizing movements need . . . are ongoing, national political organizations which can provide direction and motivation for local efforts, which, in turn, can be guided and reinvigorated by struggles in communities and workplaces at the local level. Without the continuity provided by a federated national organization, neighborhood organizing projects usually start their work anew, in a vacuum, without the benefit of historical experience or perspective, and generally must survive on their own, against powerful forces and odds, and without supports. (p. 161)

The voices have become more numerous during recent years. Poppendieck (1998), author of the remarkable report on hunger, *Sweet Charity,* stated straightforwardly,

> I believe that many are potential recruits for a movement to challenge unfairness and address the growth of inequality . . . , a movement for fundamental reforms . . . , not a movement built around hunger which would be aiming too low. We need to aim for the creation of a just and inclusive society that taps everyone's potential and makes us all better off in the long run. (p. 314)

Another significant voice has been the Aspen Roundtable on Comprehensive Community Initiatives for Children and Families. The roundtable's *Voices From the Field II* "Call to Action" spoke to undoing racism and beyond local connections and political mobilization to achieve social and economic justice (Kubisch et al., 2002). "Community change efforts have promoted collaborations across racial and cultural lines but have not taken the lead in advocating for responses to the fact that all levels of the political economy sort Americans by race —institutionally, geographically, and psychologically" (p. 97). Individual and community gains are undermined by deeply entrenched white privilege and stereotyping of minorities, "as revealed in the policies and practices of public education, housing, employment, transportation, law enforcement, and other social institutions" (p. 97).

The roundtable stated that by focusing on race-related disparities, an organization or a community would be pulled toward strategies that address institutional and systemic issues. However, "without sophisticated strategies for using structural, institutional, policy, and social levers for change, the work of CCIs [comprehensive community initiatives] will be merely palliative rather than transformative" (Kubisch et al., 2002, p. 103). Community-level political engagement at increasingly wide levels is required. Residents' power needs to be mobilized and exerted to influence political forces and policy decisions beyond the community (p. 85). Coalitions across neighborhoods should be built to maximize the base and influence of constituents (p. 84).

The roundtable also called for community alliances with local, state, and national groups that advocate for disadvantaged groups, noting that "much of the national reform work that has important salience to distressed communities—from civil rights to trade policy—has operated without strong community-level engagement in recent years" (Kubisch et al., 2002, p. 103). The roundtable had a firm position that creating and sustaining connections between communities and the policy, research, and social action arenas "should be on everyone's agenda. . . . This work must be central to future action on the part of all the participants in the ecology of change" (p. 103).

Rusk (1999) observed that existing and emerging regional alliances are the basic building blocks for new national communal power. Rusk sees powerful components coming from groupings of central-city and suburban churches and from the civil rights and environmental movements. Rusk sees the ranks already forming:

A new reform movement is beginning to move across the face of the land. . . . I believe that the chorus of voices will rise, region by region, across the nation until a new set of rules has been created, state by state, for communities. These rules

will emphasize our mutual responsibilities and the reality of our interdependence. (p. 335)

Rusk cited the Northwest Indiana Federation of Interfaith Organizations as an effective local growing alliance exercising great strength. He maintained, "The moral dimension is necessary to push the calculus of common political self-interest to the point of critical mass" (p. 334).

Bobo, Kendall, and Max (1996) advised,

Strong individual membership organizations must be built that mobilize large numbers of citizens on progressive issues. Nonetheless, there are major social issues, particularly at the state and national levels, that require broad-based coalitions, built upon those membership organizations, in order to win. Building coalitions that are strong enough to challenge societal structures, and making them work effectively, requires tough analytical strategic thinking, clear understandings about how coalitions work, savvy staff, hard work, and tender loving care. With such attention, coalitions can change the political landscape for the next century. (p. 77)

The pleas get ever more pressing and insistent. Mott (2000) advised,

To generate the constituency, power, and movement to bring about large-scale gains in life prospects for poor people, community groups must dramatically increase their ability to influence the policies of major public and private institutions. This will require either the rekindling of a mass movement or a series of changes in the priorities and behavior of all the actors in the field of community change. (p. 29)

Perhaps the vision has been best put forward for Americans by Wilson (1999), whose call is so fully designed and argued that it filled a book. He carefully laid out a reasoned and bold scheme for a multiracial political coalition to combat and counter the dividing of American society into haves and have-nots. Wilson argued, "A large, strong, and organized political constituency is essential for the development and implementation of policies that will reverse the trends of the rising inequality and ease the burdens of ordinary families" (p. 1). Throughout his book, *The*

Bridge Over the Racial Divide, runs his insistence that networks of neighborhood institutions and organizations are necessary components of any irresistible force.

In his book, Wilson (1999) envisioned a constituency that includes African American, white, Latino, Asian, and Native American populations, fighting for justice and fairness for all Americans affected by the decreased demand for low-skilled labor and by the widening disparities in incomes and wealth, marked by the stagnation of real wages during the past two decades. He proposed a coalition that moves beyond the racial divide long blocking political unity among the masses of ordinary citizens, a mainstream coalition that would cast a broad positive vision of American race relations.

Wilson (1999) proposed a political message asserting that racial and ethnic groups long seen as social adversaries are in fact potential allies for a reform coalition "because they are all negatively affected by impersonal global economic changes" (p. 77).

The nature of Wilson's national multiracial coalition would be officially bipartisan and would exert pressure on the leaders of both major political parties to create and support policies to help ordinary families who seldom own stocks but constantly struggle with debt. Groups would be interconnected through local, regional, national, and global networks using the mobilization and communication techniques pioneered in Seattle in 1999. Religious organizations, community organizations, and labor unions are looked to for mobilizing very large numbers.

Wilson (1999) maintained that the most powerful motivation for unity and group action resides in economic insecurity that results from the decline or stagnation of real incomes linked to changes in the economy, including the global economy (p. 4). He indicated that a majority of the population now suffers from such insecurity and could unite around common grievances that make reasonable and modest demands. Following are a few of Wilson's facts:

- Male high school graduates with 5 years of work experience have lost 30% of their real incomes.
- If economic trends in place before 1973 had continued rather than being dragged down, a young high school male graduate would be making an average of $33,000, rather than $13,000, in 2003.
- Since the early 1970s, household real incomes for the lower 80% of the workforce have stagnated or declined.
- Between 1984 and 1994, real income of employed college graduates increased by 1%. For high school graduates, it fell 3%. For dropouts, it fell 10%.
- Massive job shifts from cities to suburbs are taking jobs away from lower-income groups.
- Manufacturing jobs are now 70% suburban, and the percentages are nearly as high for wholesale trade and retail trade. City residents increasingly live isolated from job opportunities.
- Today, the divide between the growing suburbs and the stagnant cities is a racial divide.
- If current trends continue, then one half of children from all races will experience at least part of their childhoods in single-parent families.
- Many middle-class families are among those suffering a decline in their living standards.
- More than 14 million Americans have suffered some unemployment since 1998.

The direction advocated by Wilson (1999) was organizing bridges among groups now divided to lay the foundation for multiracial political cooperation. He viewed this goal as being sought through a new public dialogue on how our problems should be defined and how they should be addressed that would draw together Americans left out of the wealth-building explosion of the past decade.

For a successful alliance, Wilson (1999) maintained that those enrolled must include not only neighborhood and other grassroots groups but also the poor and working poor; the in-debt middle class; all others concerned with job security, health, education, and the environment who come from many classes and backgrounds; and all those alarmed by inequality and the ethnic and cultural splitting apart of society. Wilson observed that the key to a successful movement is to mount an effort that benefits all responsible and well-meaning groups in the society. "In the final analysis, unless groups of ordinary citizens embrace the need for mutual political cooperation, they stand little chance of generating the political muscle needed to ease their economic and social burdens" (p. 123).

Wilson (1999) cited the Living Wage Campaign in 33 cities as a coalition already under way, along with the grassroots efforts of the Industrial Areas Foundation in 40 communities from California to Massachusetts. His book closed with an appeal to "the American people, and especially the leaders of the poor, the working classes, the displaced and the marginalized, the downsized and the de-skilled, to set aside differences and work together to discuss, in vocabularies that reject the particularisms of race, the true task before us" (p. 128).

The coalition notion is resonating in many places with many people. Dissatisfaction runs high in the society, and at some point during the first decade of the 21st century, one or more severe economic downturns are likely. Sometime in the near term, the flashpoint may dip very low, with an economic crisis exploding on us. At that time, the forces mentioned here may be able to come together to realize this vision shared by so many prophets.

Fisher and Shragge (2000) maintained that an effective counterforce built around opposition to the new global corporate order would ensure justice and equity. They viewed it as arising from renewed youth activism in a unifying social movement against corporate abuses and global oppression, an effort that will put conflict and protest back in the community agenda (p. 11).

Meantime, for the small place communities, the time and opportunity for change is right now. Whether a wealthy outer suburb haunted by racial fears or a city neighborhood desperate for jobs, the change in climate can be achieved by collective work that starts today with phone calls to a few concerned neighbors.

We wish the reader success at organizing and community building.

REFERENCES

Bobo, K., Kendall, J., & Max, S. (1996). *Organizing for social change: A manual for activists.* Santa Ana, CA: Seven Locks Press.

Fisher, R. (1984). *Let the people decide: Neighborhood organizing in America.* Boston: Twayne.

Fisher, R., & Shragge, E. (2000). Challenging community organizing: Facing the 21st century. *Journal of Community Practice, 8*(3), 1–19.

Kubisch, A., Auspos, P., Brown, P., Chaskin, R., Fulbright-Anderson, K., & Hamilton, R. (2002). *Voices from the field II: Reflections on comprehensive community change.* Washington, DC: Aspen Institute.

Mott, A. (2000, March–April). Twenty-five years of building power and capacity. *Shelterforce,* pp. 28–29. (Orange NJ: National Housing Institute)

Poppendieck, J. (1998). *Sweet charity? Emergency food and the end of entitlement.* New Caledonia: Penguin Books.

Rusk, D. (1999). *Inside game, outside game.* Washington DC: Brookings Institution Press.

Temali, M. (2002). *The community economic development handbook: Strategies and tools to revitalize your neighborhood.* Saint Paul, MN: Amherst Wilder Foundation.

Wilson, W. J. (1999). *The bridge over the racial divide: Rising inequality and coalition politics.* Berkeley: University of California Press.

INDEX

Action plans
    community, 192-193, 195-196
    format, 176-177
    organizational, 167-168
Adequate wealth
    as a principle for saving small communities, 7
Advocacy
    part of the organizing process, 78-79
    See also Disruptive advocacy
Affordable housing
    co-housing, 270
    cost of housing, 268
    housing trust funds, 263
    land donations, 270
    land trusts and land banks, 272
    lease-to-purchase, 269
    limited equity cooperatives, 269
    Low-Income Housing Tax Credits, 39, 41
    mortgage assistance programs, 268-269
    mutual housing associations, 269-270
    National Housing Trust Fund Campaign, 263
    programs, 268-270
    sweat equity, 269
    See also Homeownership; Low-income housing
Agricultural extension
    county agents as organizers, 15
    participants and leadership required, 15
    Smith Lever Act, 15
Ahlbrandt, R.
    generators of relationships, 54-56
    neighborhood surveys, 53
    recommendations for strengthening social
        fabric, 206-207
    small community tied to relationships, 54-55
    social fabric, 54-55
Alinsky, S.
    approach to organizing, 16
    biographer, 17
    direct action model, 18
    spread of Alinsky model, 18
    start of organizing work, 16
    traditional power organizing, 103, 105
    See also Industrial Areas Foundation
Aliquippa, PA
    Beaver County Growth Coalition, 137
    church involvement/role, 127, 129, 142
    community description, 125
    distress, 125, 127-128
    disunity of racial antipathy, 129, 133
    Franklin Avenue business district assessment, 133, 136
    housing market assessment, 133-134
    impact of steel collapse, 124, 125
    loss of banking services, 129-130, 138, 139
    population change 1930-2000, 126
    undercrowdedness, 124
    See also Aliquippa Alliance for Unity and
        Development
Aliquippa Alliance for Unity and Development (AAUD),
    Aliquippa, PA
    advocacy efforts, 136
    Aliquippa Community Development Credit Union,
        124, 138, 139, 143, 151-152, 246
    Aliquippa Development Fund, 143
    Aliquippa Embraces Art, 135, 152
    Blenk, D., 138-145
    board of directors, 127, 129, 140, 144, 150-151
    business district renewal program,
        128, 133, 138, 140, 143
    business development initiatives, 132, 135, 143
    Cairns, C., 126-137
    case study, 124-153
    commercial real estate development projects, 136, 140
    community planning process, 179, 191
    Cooper, P., 137-142
    education programs, 135-136
    evaluation of efforts, 134, 137, 146-149
    founding and early organizing, 125-128
    funding sources, 129, 131, 132, 134, 139
    fund-raising techniques and results, 141, 237
    housing study, 133-134
    human services center development, 129-131, 146, 215
    introduction, 12
    job creation activities, 131-132
    partnerships, 139, 140-142
    Police Community Relations Committee, 129
    public safety initiatives, 146
    racial antipathy responses, 129
    social strength building, 215
    staff transitions, 136, 137, 142, 145, 146
    start-up cadre, 127
    strategic organizational plans,
        138, 145, 158-160, 168-169
    youth-focused programs, 132, 139
    workforce development program,
        132-133, 145-146, 293, 298
    See also Aliquippa, PA
American Dream Demonstration project, 252-253
    See also Individual Development Accounts

American Indians
    activist campaigns and movements, 20
    followed civil rights model, 20
Annie E. Casey Foundation Jobs Initiative, 301
Annual planning
    definition, 155
    organizational, 155
Arnstein's ladder of participation
    origin of, 111-112
    rungs of the ladder, 112-114
    See also Participation
Asset-based community development model,
        188-189, 207-209
    See also Kretzmann, J. and McKnight, J.
Asset-based planning
    community assets and strengths, 188-189
    community building blocks, 189
    community capacity inventory, 207
    See also Community planning; Kretzmann, J. and
        McKnight, J.
Assets for Independence Act of 1998, 253
Association for Enterprise Opportunity
    and microenterprise loan funds, 248-250
    description, 249
Assumptions underlying this book
    collectivity, 5
    entropy, 5
    essentiality, 5
    feasibility, 6
    flexibility, 6
    human dignity, 6
    local uniqueness, 6
    resource reality, 5
    survival imperative, 5

Barelas Neighborhood Association, 12, 54
Baroni, G.
    influence on President Carter, 22-23
    number of resident-led renewal organizations, 11
    on social fabric, 53-54
    role in HUD, 22-23
Barros, J.
    DSNI homegrown director, 120
    eminent domain, 120
    See also Dudley Street Neighborhood Initiative
Bay Area IDA collaborative
    description of IDA program, 253
    See also Individual Development Accounts
Bedford-Stuyvesant Restoration Corporation
    as earliest CDC, 20, 38
    fathered by Senator Kennedy, 20
    Rusk cites increasing poverty, 41
    workforce development program, 295
Berry, J.
    citizen groups as primary political force, 4
    definition of citizen groups, 4
    growing power of citizens, 24
Berry, J. M., Portney, E., and Thompson, K.
    devaluation of participation, 3
    on participation and community distress, 108-110
    volunteer achievements, 3-4

BIDs. *See* Business Improvement Districts
Blakely, E.
    business attractors, 296, 297-298
    dearth of on-the-job training, 301
    economic distress as major component of community
        agenda, 295-296
    locally based economic development and employment
        generation, 295
Blakely, E. and Snyder, M.
    on gated communities, 2-3
    Whitley Heights, CA case study, 64
Blenk, D.
    Aliquippa Alliance business district specialist, 138
    tenure as executive director, 142-145
    See also Aliquippa Alliance for Unity and
        Development
Blockbusting, 259
Bloomfield-Garfield Corporation (BGC)
    annual Martin Luther King celebration, 117
    Bloomfield as example of stage 4 and 5 decline, 63
    board of directors, 118
    Brose, Agnes, 116-119
    business district renewal efforts, 119
    case study of, 12, 116-119
    evaluation of, 117
    Flanagan, Richard, 118
    introduction, 12
    low wage issue, 117
    media relations, 117
    participation philosophy, 118
    rebuilding central Garfield, 118
    relations with local institutions, 117
    response policy, 117
    saving the cookie plant, 118-119
    social strength building, 215
    staff, 116-119
    stage of decline, 63
    Swartz, Richard, 117
Bobo, K., Kendall, J., and Max, S.
    need for national coalitions built on local membership
        organizations, 315
    recommended reading for community organizing, 93
Boston Community Loan Fund, 248
    See also Community Development Loan Funds
Brose, Agnes, 214–218
    leader of Save Cookie Plant campaign, 118-119
    staff organizer, 116-117
    participation philosophy, 118
    response to community members, 117
    See also Bloomfield-Garfield Corporation
Building communities
    diversity and responsibility, 1
    links to government and business, 1
    year-round participation, 1
Bush, President G. W.
    free trade, 34
    support for faith-based organizations, 3, 142
    role of non-profit sector in problem solving, 3
Business creation, 283
    See also Principles of economic renewal
Business district distress factors

business district characteristics, 281
disinvestments, 281
economic, 281-282
infrastructure/physical deterioration, 281
level of community organization, 282
local government regulations, 281
market, 279-280
poor or negative image, 280-281
revitalization strategies, 282
See also Business district renewal
Business development
in manufacturing, 304-308
See also Principles of economic renewal
Business district planning
characteristics of, 284
steps in, 284-286
See also Business district renewal
Business district renewal
Aliquippa, PA, 128, 133, 136, 138, 140, 143
approaches to, 283-284
Bloomfield-Garfield, Pittsburgh, PA, 119
business district distress factors, 279-281
Business Improvement Districts, 288-289
CDC of Frankford Group Ministries, 289
chain retailers return to inner city, 280
design, image and environment, 287
economic revitalization and restructuring, 288
Frankford Main Street program, Philadelphia, PA, 289
Main Street Program components, 286-288
market analysis and assessment, 280
organizing, 284-286, 287
participation in, 285, 287
planning, 284-286
private sector role in, 284
program for action, 284-286
promotion and marketing, 287-288
public sector role in, 284
See also Business district renewal organizing; Business
districts; Principles of economic renewal
Business district renewal organizing
board/coordinating committee, 285
CDC role, 284-285, 287
Main Street program component, 287
participation/inclusion, 285-286
revitalization group/committee, 284-285
Business district revitalization. *See* Business district
renewal
Business districts, small community and neighborhood
causes of decline, 279-282
disinvestments cycle in, 277, 279
displacement, 281
distress factors, 279-281
economic contributions of, 278
non-economic contributions of, 278-279
See also Business district renewal
Business dominance, 1915-1930
over government and community sectors, 15
role of Andrew Mellon, 15
Business Improvement Districts (BIDs)
description of, 288
Frankford Main Street Program, 289

Business recruitment, 283
business attractors, 296, 297-298, 304-305
See also Principles of economic renewal
Business retention, 305

Cadre
cadre accountability, 87
cadre facilitation, 83
definition, 83
formation and maintenance, 83-85
role in community planning, 182
Cairns, C.
co-founder of the Aliquippa Alliance for Unity and
Development, 126-127
first executive director, 132
tenure as executive director, 132-137
See also Aliquippa Alliance for Unity and
Development
Candy, D. M.
balance between group process and goals, 98
cadre accountability, 87
cadre facilitation, 83
coalitions require clear agreed-to purpose, 92
organizer and tangible vision, 82
Capital formation
advantages of capital formation activities, 241-242
advocacy and organizing, 242-246
Aliquippa Community Development Credit Union,
124, 138, 139, 143, 151-152, 246
American Dream Demonstration project, 252-253
Bay Area IDA Collaborative, 253
Boston Community Loan Fund, 248
community development banks, 250-251
community development credit unions, 246-247
community development financial institutions, 246-252
community development loan funds, 248
community financial service needs, 241
Community Foundation of Lower Flathead Valley, 252
community foundations, 251-252
definition of financial capital, 240
factors inhibiting access to capital and credit, 241
Home Mortgage Disclosure Act of 1975, 242
individual asset accumulation, 252-253
individual development accounts, 252-253
local money systems, 254
Lower East Side Peoples Federal Credit Union, 247
microenterprise loan funds, 248-250
National Community Reinvestment Coalition (NCRC),
243-245
National People's Action, 244-245
predatory lending, 245-246
revolving loan funds, 250
role of capital in community economy, 240-241
ShoreBank, 250-251
subprime lending, 245
U.S. Department of Housing and Urban Development,
245
Women's Self-Employment Project, 249-250
See also Community Reinvestment Act of 1977
Carter, President J.
Baroni appointment to HUD, 22

jobs shift away from cities, 23
support for small communities, 22
Case studies
Aliquippa Alliance for Unity and Development,
Aliquippa, PA, 12, 59, 124-153, 158-160,
168-169, 179, 191, 215, 237, 246, 293, 298
Barelas, Albuquerque, NM, 12, 54
Bloomfield-Garfield Corporation, Pittsburgh, PA, 12,
63, 117-119, 214-218, 215
Dudley Street Neighborhood Initiative, Boston, MA,
12, 13, 55, 120, 178-179, 215-216, 300-301
Franklin, VA, 205
Hyde Park-Kenwood Community Conference,
Chicago, IL, 12, 18, 20, 26-31, 72-73, 216
Kiltimaugh, Ireland, 225-227
Lyndale, Minneapolis, MN, 12-13, 185-187, 216
Newhall Ranch, CA, 205-206
Portland, OR, 232-234
Rollingwood, TX, 59, 216-218
Vandergrift, PA, 96-97, 218
Valmeyer, IL, 56, 218
Whitley Heights, Los Angeles, CA, 64
CDCs. *See* Community Development Corporations
CDCUs. *See* Community Development Credit Unions
CDFIs. *See* Community Development Financial
Institutions
CDLFs. *See* Community Development Loan Funds
Center for Community Change (CCC)
case for stabilizing operating support for
CDCs, 230-231
jobs policy organizing, 300
public housing initiative, 275
Center for Employment Training (CET)
assessment of workforce development model, 299
workforce development model, 294-295
Chaskin, R., Brown, P., Venkatish, S. and Vidal, A.
competency of leaders, 82
shared language and vision, 83
Chicago Rehab Network
gentrification research, 259-260
housing misery indicators, 261-262
Cisneros, H.
compromise on people vs. place policies, 62
Citizen groups
as primary political force, 4
definition of citizen groups, 4
growing power of citizens, 24
role in defeat of apartheid, 108
Citizen participation
definition, 110-111
relation to urban renewal, 18
role in rebuilding, viii
self-created networks and indigenous organizations, 18
See also Participation
Civic apathy
2000 election as symbol of, 3-4
as major source of community distress, viii
distress and apathy, 4
erosion of civic involvement, 3-4
roots of civic paralysis, 3
See also Community distress

Claim to represent a community
defending hard choices, 115
inclusive and open, 115
paving way to acceptance, 115
Class inequality
in access to social capital, 202
Coalition politics
as national movement of communal
interests, 313-317
broad-based coalitions built on local membership
organizations, 315
community alliances with state and
national groups, 315
national coalition for economic and social
justice, 314-315
regional coalitions as building blocks for national
communal power, 315
Coalition renewal approach
connections to growth areas, 50
veteran CDCs contract with small organizations, 50
maintenance of community identity, 49
Mon Valley Initiative example, 50
Pittsburgh Partnership for Neighborhood
Development example, 50
shared objectives essential, 49
Coalitions
across racial and cultural lines, 313-317
advice for operating coalitions effectively, 86
against injustice and inequity, 313-317
definition of coalition, 86
effective operation of, 86-87
Living Wage Campaign, 317
low-income housing, 263
Massachusetts Association of Community
Development Corporations, 42
national coalition for economic and social
justice, 314-315
regional coalitions as building blocks for national
communal power, 315
national movement of communal interests, 313-317
See also Industrial Areas Foundation
Code enforcement
as government stimulator of renovation, 260
housing stabilization and preservation, 264-265
housing inventory, 264-265
COI. *See* Consensus Organizing Institute
Coleman, J.
definition of social capital, 201-202
Communal interests
communitarian organizer, 14
examples of gains, 14-15
resurgence of, 24
See also Coalition politics, Communal power,
Communal sector
Communal power
and community organizing, 78
definition of, 78
historic dominance of business, 13-14
relation to global organizing, 31-36
risks involved, 78
systematic process, 78

resources required, 79
  See also Coalition politics, Community power
Communal sector
  citizen roles in, vii-viii
  consensus with business and government, 21
  definition, vii
  historic dominance by business, 13-14
  preservation and strengthening of, vii-viii
  relation to global organizing, 31-32
  urban pioneers, 19
  See also Communal power, Societal struggle
Communication, 88-90
Community assessment
  community capacity inventory, 207
  data gathering and analysis, 188-189, 197-199
  factors underlying decline and revitalization, 76
  stages of neighborhood conditions, 62-63
  See also Community data gathering and analysis;
    Market analysis and assessment
Community data gathering and analysis
  categories of data, 190, 197-199
  community meetings, 190-191
  community surveys, 190
  importance of involving local people in research, 87
  in community planning, 189-191
  See also Community assessment; Market analysis and
    assessment
Community development
  need for neighborhood-based renewal, 230
  neighborhood-based reform initiatives, 209-211
  See also Community Development Corporations
Community development banks
  definition of, 250
  characteristics of, 250
  ShoreBank, 250-251
  See also Capital formation
Community development corporations (CDCs)
  activities of, 38
  aided by new Tax Credit program, 39
  Anner and Vogel on need for mass support from
    grassroots, 42
  benefit from Community Reinvestment Act, 33
  Bratt answer to CDC criticism, 41
  Brophy and Shabecoff affirm brick and mortar not
    enough, 42
  case for stabilizing operating support, 230-231
  criticism of the CDC movement, 39-43
  definition, 20
  Eisenberg on taking responsibility for CDC failures, 43
  evaluation of CDC funding and technical assistance, 41
  Fisher questions direction of CDCs, 39
  Grogan and Proscio defend city CDCs, 43
  history of the movement, 20, 38
  Lemann attack on CDC programs, 40
  move toward comprehensive planning, 43-45
  Peirce and Steinbach assessment, 39-40
  organizing and development in combination, 42
  programs and funding sources, 39
  role in business district renewal, 284-285, 287
  Rusk on Bedford-Stuyvesant, 41
  Shiffman and Motley critique, 40

shift to comprehensive approach, 43-44
  Stoecker makes case for CDC weakness, 40
  Traynor charge that CDC is a dependency model, 40
Community development credit unions (CDCUs)
  Aliquippa Community Development Credit Union,
    124, 138, 139, 143, 151-152, 246
  definition and purpose, 246-247
  capitalization of, 247
  characteristics and services of, 247
  Lower East Side Peoples Federal Credit Union, 247
  National Federation of, 247
  number of, 246
  See also Capital formation
Community development financial institutions (CDFIs)
  community development banks, 250-251
  community development credit unions, 246-247
  community development loan funds, 248-250
  community foundations, 251-252
  definition, 246
  history, 246
  legislation, 246
  types of, 248-250
  See also Capital formation
Community development loan funds (CDLFs)
  definition and purpose, 248
  Boston Community Loan Fund, 248
  capitalization of, 248
  characteristics of, 248
  See also Loan funds
Community distress
  and participation, 108
  as disintegration of political structure, 70
  as unraveling social fabric, 69
  as weakening of the local economy, 70
  business district, 279-282
  breakdown between social structures
    and individuals, 69
  causes of, 65
  definition, 65
  external forces, 65
  factors underlying decline and revitalization, 76
  growth of disparities between whites and
    people of color, 2
  impact of sprawl, 66-67
  micro forces of, 69
  negative individual behavior, 69
  three major sources of, viii
  undercrowdedness, 65-66
Community economy
  cash flow diagram, 71
  distress factors, 70-71
  economic contributions of business districts, 278
  economic factors in business district decline, 281-282
  key economic terms, 73-75
  plugging economic leaks, 283
  role of capital in community economy, 240-241
  See also Local economy
Community foundations
  as alternative funders, 230
  capitalization of, 251
  characteristics of, 251

Community Foundation of the Lower
     Flathead Valley, 252
   definition and purpose, 251
   stimulator and financier of intermediaries, 232
   See also Capital formation; Foundations
Community meetings
   use in community planning, 184, 190-191
Community organizer
   description of three organizers work, 94-97
   Mendicino, S. as example of, 96-97
   Mondros-Wilson study of organizers, 92-93
   principal skills of organizers, 92
   Redwood, C. as example of, 94-95
   three requirements for a volunteer
         organizer to be effective, 93
Community organizing
   additional recommended reading, 93
   Alinsky approach to 16-18
   as uniting process for change, 78
   business district renewal, 284-286
   capital formation, 242-246
   definition, 79-80
   direct action model, 18
   growth at neighborhood level during 1970s, 21
   housing, 262-264
   improvement associations and civic clubs, 17
   Industrial Areas Foundation (IAF), 16-17, 211-213
   interaction and extraction, 80
   local organizations differentially founded, 79
   modern era beginning post World War II, 17
   nobility of organizer roles, 98
   potent method for influencing government, 56
   three key ingredients, 79-80
   three dominant approaches, 100
   traditional power organizing, 103, 105
   twelve activities of community organizing, 80-92
   typology of directions, 104-105
   workforce development, 295-296
Community planning
   Aliquippa Alliance for Unity and
         Development, 179, 191
   asset-based approach, 188-189
   benefits of, 179-180
   business district planning, 284-289
   CDCs move toward comprehensive planning, 43-45
   collaboratives, 183
   community assessment, 188-191, 197-199
   comprehensive, 179
   coordination of, 182-183
   community capacity inventory, 207
   decision-making considerations, 183-184
   definition and scope, 178-179
   difference from organizational planning, 154-155, 179
   Dudley Street Neighborhood Initiative,
         Boston, MA, 119-120, 178-179
   forums, 179, 183
   goal development, 191-192
   Greenpoint 197-a Plan, 193-195
   housing market analysis, 260-262
   impetus for plan development, 180
   implementation, 195-196

importance of involving local people in research, 87
   Lyndale, Minneapolis, MN, 185-187
   measures of success, 192
   model, 181-182
   monitoring and evaluation, 191-192
   outreach, 184-185
   participation, 179-180, 184-185
   role of public sector, 178-179
   resource mobilization, 193
   strategy development and selection, 192
   targeted, 179
   types of community plans, 192
   updating and revision of plans, 196
Community power
   community power structure, 56
   Dudley Street as example of power usage, 13
   Fisher and Shragge on social moderation, 25
   identity politics, 24
   Putnam on time for aggressive organizing, viii
   sources of communal power, 13
   See also Coalition politics, Communal power
Community Reinvestment Act of 1977 (CRA)
   agreements, 244-245
   as a response to redlining, 242
   and housing, 263
   campaigns, 243-244
   challenges by community groups, 243
   community lending commitment examples, 244-245
   history and background, 22, 242
   National Community Reinvestment
         Coalition (NCRC), 22, 243-244
   National People's Action (NPA), 244-245
   National Training and Information
         Center (NTIC), 243-244
   regulatory agency requirements, 242-243
Community renewal approaches
   community building, 102
   comprehensive renewal approach, 43-48
   coalition renewal approach, 49-50
   matrix of directions, 104-105
   neighborhood-based reform initiatives, 209-211
   transformative social change approach, 101-102
   See also Coalition renewal approach; Comprehensive
         renewal approach; Transformative social change
         renewal approach
Community surveys, 190
   See also Community planning
Comprehensive renewal approach
   combination of organizing and development, 43-44
   assessment of community building, 47-48
   Comprehensive Community Initiatives (CCIs), 46-47
   definition and description, 43-44
   emerging consensus around approach, 43-48
   New School for Social Research evidence,
   foundation support for, 230
   Pitcoff assessment of CCIs, 46-47
   team assessment of community building, 47-48
   CDCs moving toward comprehensive planning, 43-45
   transformative tradition, 43-44
   values of, 45
Comprehensive Community Initiatives (CCIs)

assessment of CCIs, 46-47
foundation support for, 230
See also Comprehensive renewal approach
Comprehensive community planning.
   See Community planning
Comprehensive community plans.
   See Community planning
Comprehensiveness
   as a principle for saving small communities, 7
Congress of Industrial Organizations (CIO), 16
Consensus Organizing Institute (COI)
   connecting residents to resources
      and opportunities, 103
   parents reshape spending of tobacco money, 103
Cooper, P.
   partnership building, 141-142
   tenure as Aliquippa Alliance executive
      director, 138-142
   See also Aliquippa Alliance for Unity and
      Development
Core operating support for community development
   case for, 230-231
   national funding campaign for community
      development, 232
Corporation for Enterprise Development
   American Dream Demonstration project, 252-253
CRA. *See* Community Reinvestment Act of 1977
Cultural competency
   inter-ethnic racial relations, 121
   cross cultural communication, 89
   Dudley Street workforce development
      program, 300-301
   use of indigenous community people as
      guides and teachers, 89
   white organizers unprepared, 90
Cunningham, J. V.
   biography, x

Darity, W. and Myers, S.
   widening of racial gap, 4-5
Delaware Community Reinvestment Fund
   linking neighborhoods to regional growth, 50
   Ogontz Avenue example, 50
   poverty alleviation, 50
Delgado, G.
   identity politics, 24
   half of population suffering from decline, 24
Delgado, M.
   inter-ethnic racial relations, 121
   use of murals, public gardens, play-scapes, and street
      sculptures, 121
Destructive forces
   discrimination, 68
   impoverishment, 67
   political imbalance, 68
   redlining, 68
   social service fragmentation, 68
   suburbanization, 66
   unfair and illegal housing practices, 68
   weak labor market, 67
Dionne, E. J., Jr.

as a prophet, viii
citizen roles in rebuilding, viii
era of the swaggering capitalist, vii
definition of communal sector, vii
predicted era of reform and rebuilding, viii
Discover Total Resources fundraising guide, 227-228
Discrimination
   affect on housing market stability and options, 259
   negative economic impact of, 68
   in employment, 293, 301
   in housing lending, 259
   racial steering, 259
   redlining, 68, 259
   restrictive covenants, 17
Disinvestment
   impact on housing, 258
   impact on business districts, 277, 279
Displacement
   as a result of urban renewal, 260
   by transportation systems, 260
   by urban pioneers, 259
   housing, 259-260
   social costs of, 68
   financial and social costs of, 260
Disruptive advocacy
   adapted to neighborhood organizing, 16
   Alinsky use of, 103
   as a change tactic, 16
   industrial strikes, 16
   mass disruptive protests in factories and
      neighborhoods, 16
   useful alternative, 93
   See also Advocacy
Distress. *See* Community distress
Donors
   approaching, 229-230
   giving levels, 220, 236
   involvement in organization, 223-224
   solicitation of, 220, 229
Downs, A.
   Bloomfield-Garfield as stage 4 and 5
      decline example, 63
   factors underlying decline and
      revitalization (adaptation), 76
   stages of neighborhood condition, 62-63
   quality life for poor requires end to poverty, 63
Dreier, P.
   politically savvy Boston housing director, 120
   Dudley Street effort assessment, 120
   three empowerment strategies, 100
DSNI. *See* Dudley Street Neighborhood Initiative
Dudley Street Neighborhood Initiative (DSNI)
   asset concept use, 55
   astute power game: Mayor Flynn joins in, 120
   community planning process, 119-120, 178-179
   Drier assessment: neighborhood clients
      grew into partners, 120
   DSNI excels via indigenous staff, 120
   early history, 119
   eminent domain, 120
   example of use of community power, 13

fruitful joint efforts breeds citizen-city trust, 120
introduced, 12
Riley Foundation as model partner, 12
social strength building, 215-216
vision of "urban village", 120
workforce development program, 300-301

Economic disparity and inequality
    and resurgence of communal interests, 24
    disparity in net worth, 235
    growth of in America, 24, 213
    national movement to address growing inequality, 314
    shaping the fund-raising environment, 235
    See also Economic insecurity
Economic insecurity
    as major source of community distress, vii
    as motivation for unity and group action, 316
    half of population suffering from decline, 24
    includes disparity and joblessness, 4
    sophisticated skills required for decent jobs, 4
    legions of people of all races and classes face
        future insecurity, 4
    unemployment and low wages wreak havoc, 4
Economic renewal
    principles of, 283
Economists' doubt. See People vs. place:
        the economists' doubt
Ehrenreich, B.
    dehumanizing impact of low-wage work, 43
    importance of envisioning the future, 101
Eisen, A.
    study of foundation support for Comprehensive
        Community Initiatives, 230
Eisenberg, P.
    myth of good news, 43
    on Community Development Corporations, 43
    on text books, xi
    taking responsibility for failures, 43
Election 2000
    cities held their own, 4
    vast mobilizations only able to bring out
        half the vote, 3
Environmental scan. See Organizational planning
Equitable development
    principles in housing, 262
    tool kit, 262
Evaluation
    of community plans, 191-192
    of organizational plans, 170-171
    of process and product, 87-88
    Success Measures Project, 192
    See also Monitoring and evaluation

Fabricant, M. and Fisher, R.
    on social change and social capital, 204
    threat represented by drive to privatize, viii
Factors affecting housing market stability and options
    blockbusting, 259
    displacement, 260
    filtering, 258-259
    gentrification, 259-260

lending discrimination
    racial steering, 259
    redlining, 259
    segregation, 259
    transportation system development, 260
    urban renewal, 260
Fair housing
    Law of 1968, 262
    legislation, 262
    education and outreach, 262
    Fair Housing Council of Suburban Philadelphia, 262
    See also Housing organizing and advocacy
Faith-based organizations
    and housing development, 269
    and social strength building, 211-213
    Habitat for Humanity, 269
    Hyde Park-Kenwood Community
        Conference origin, 27
    role in political coalitions, 213
    role in workforce development, 297
    See also Industrial Areas Foundation;
        New Community Corporation
Falum Gong
    massive non-violent displays of alternative belief, 108
Family support centers
    role in workforce development, 297
Fifth Avenue Committee, Brooklyn, NY
    workforce development program, 297
Filtering down, housing
    and adaptation, 258
    description of, 258
    gentrification as reverse filtering, 259
    impact on market stability and options, 258
    theory, 258
Fisher, R.
    direction of CDCs questioned, 39
    mass disruptive protests in factories and
        neighborhoods, 16
    neighborhood base for early activities, 14
    need for neighborhood connected national political
        organizations, 314
    three dominant approaches to community
        organizing, 100
Fisher, R. and Shragge, E.
    global corporate order counterforce, 317
    on social moderation, 25
    radical positions on redistribution, 25
Flanagan, J.
    grassroots fund-raising tips and
        techniques, 224-225
    importance of grassroots fund-raising, 224
Flanagan, R.
    youth organizers, 118
    views on staff tenure, 118
    See also Bloomfield-Garfield Corporation
For profit corporations
    as source of resources, 227-230
    giving levels, 220
Foundations
    community, 230, 232, 251-252
    giving level of, 220, 229

issue of long-term foundation grants, 46
solicitation of, 228
See also Community foundations
Frankford Main Street program, Philadelphia, PA
Business Improvement District, 289
CDC of Frankford Group Ministries, 289
description, 289
See also Business district renewal
Franklin, VA
social strength building, 205
Freed, W.
community manufacturing employment
model, 307-308
workforce network concept, 299
Funding
core stable operating support for community
development, 230-232
issue of long-term foundation grants, 46
need for resource diversification, 232
new sources of, 21-22
requirements for cause funding, 222
See also Intermediaries; Resource development
Fund-raising. *See* Resource development

Gans, H.
renewal destruction blamed on business lobbies, 19
Garvin, C. and Cox, F.
growth of community organizations in the 1970s, 21
new sources of funds for community groups, 21-22
Gated communities
Blakely, E. J. and Snyder, M. on, 2-3
number of, 3
See also Whitley Heights, CA
GDP. *See* Gross Domestic Product
Gentrification
as reverse filtering, 259
Chicago Rehab Network research on, 259-260
definition and description, 259
Equitable Development Toolkit, 262
housing, 259-260
government role in, 260
Global organizing and its relation to communal power
Barcelona, 35
Davos, 33-34
Detroit-Windsor, 34
Genoa, 35
Montreal, 33
New York City, 35
Quebec City, 34
Seattle, 31-33
US domestic protests, 635-36
Washington, DC, 35-36
Goals and strategies
community, 190-191
community strategy development , 192
decision criteria/assessment factors, 173-176
definition, 165, 191-192
developing, 165-166, 191-192
evaluation of success, 170-171, 191-192
monitoring and evaluation, 170-171, 196
organizational, 165-172

strategic choice, 172-173
strategic niche, 171-172
Goldsmith, S.
faith in neighborhoods, viii
Grant proposals
Hall, M. tips and techniques, 228
reliance on, 228
preparation of, 228
See also Resource development
Grassroots fund-raising
description, 224, 225
events, 229
importance of discretionary funds, 221, 224
Kiltimaugh, Ireland case study, 225-227
tips and techniques, 224-225, 228-230
See also Resource development
Great Depression, the
Civilian Conservation Corps, 16
national government assumes public
welfare role, 16-17
participation model of agricultural effort, 16
Roosevelt, Franklin as the pragmatist President, 16-17
Green, J.
cross cultural communication, 89
white organizers unprepared, 90
Greenpoint 197-a Plan
community goals, 194
development of, 193-194
participants in, 194-195
planning process, 193-195
Grogan, P. and Proscio, T.
argument for place-based investments, 62
central city revival involves CDC network, 43
chain retailers return to inner city, 280
defense of CDCs, 43
government has helped empty cities, 62
neighborhood mobilization, 210
social strength building, 210
Gross Domestic Product (GDP)
growth in 1990s, 237
Group process
creating a welcoming spirit, 121
definition, 121
new members getting attention, 121
seeking sense of community and family, 121
sharing of power, 121
small social events, 121
See also Participation

Habitat for Humanity,
sweat equity housing development model, 269
Hall, M.
grant proposal preparation, 228
grantwriting, 228
Halpern, R.
history of neighborhood-based reform
initiatives, 209-211
use of community to exclude and divide, 210
weaknesses in social fabric, 210-214
Hanna, M. and Robinson, B.
definition of transformative tradition, 49

description of techniques, 49, 101-102
Friere, P. as source of theory, 101
transformative social change, 101-102
Health and spirit
as a principle for saving small communities, 7
Historic preservation, housing, 263-264
See also Housing
HMDA. *See* Home Mortgage Disclosure Act of 1975
Home Mortgage Disclosure Act of 1975, 242
Homeownership
Cobb County Housing, GA, 271
Community Development Corporation
of Brownsville, TX, 271
co-housing, 270
disadvantages of, 270
government role in, 260
Habitat for Humanity, 269
impact of redlining, 259
importance of, 270
land banks, 272
land trusts, 272
lease-to-purchase, 269
limited equity cooperatives, 269
mortgage assistance, 268-269
mutual housing associations, 269-270
rationale for, 270
receivership, 272
Rocky Mountain Mutual Housing
Association, CO, 270
South East Community Organization,
Baltimore, MD, 272
sweat equity, 269
versus rental housing, 268
See also Housing
Hoover, E. M.
affluent residents benefit most, 61
doubts about efficiency of renewal spending, 61
migration as appropriate alternative to
place prosperity, 61
See also People vs. place: the economists' doubt
Horwitt, S.
Alinsky as advancer of radical idea, 17
Housing
accessibility, 258
adequacy, 258
affordability, 258, 263
assessment measures, 258
availability, 258
case for socioeconomic diversity in, 260
Community Reinvestment Act of 1977, 263
development, 266-268
discriminatory practices, 258-260
displacement, 259-260
equitable development, 262
factors affecting housing market stability
and options, 258-260
filtering, 258
gentrification, 259-260
historic preservation, 263-264
homeownership programs, 260, 268-271
Home Mortgage Disclosure Act of 1975, 242

Housing Act of 1937, 257
Housing Act of 1949, 18, 19, 257
importance of, 257
Low-Income Housing Tax Credits, 39, 41
market analysis, 260-262
negative impact of unfair/illegal practices, 68
organizing and advocacy, 262-264
rental housing, 258-259, 268
stabilization and preservation, 264-266
segregation, 68, 259
U.S. Department of Housing and
Urban Development, 273-275
See also Affordable housing;
Fair housing; Low-income housing;
Public and assisted housing
Housing development
and construction, 266
community-based organization
involvement in, 267
community organization roles in, 267
criticism of strategy, 268
goals, 266
impact of, 267-268
rehabilitation, 266
Housing organizing and advocacy
Community Reinvestment Act of 1977, 263
fair housing, 262
Housing Trust Fund campaign, 263
low-income housing coalitions, 263
Housing stabilization and preservation
and housing decline, 264
benefits of, 264
code enforcement, 264-265
community-based activities and programs, 264-266
community skills bank, 265
demolition/recapture of materials, 266
donated materials warehouse, 265
home repair programs, 265
housing resource banks, 265-266
incumbent upgrading, 264
low/no interest home repair, 266
paint-ups, 265
sealing buildings for future use, 266
weatherization, 265
Housing trust funds, 263
See also Affordable housing
HUD. *See* U.S. Department of Housing and Urban
Development
Human service organizations. *See* Social services
Human services. *See* Social services
Hyde Park-Kenwood Community Conference
case study, 26-31
faith-based origin, 27
goal: interracial community of high standards, 27
introduction, 12
pioneer in supporting preservation
and rehabilitation, 20
relation to urban renewal, 27-28
residential development, 18
social strength building, 216
use of block clubs, 27

IAF. *See* Industrial Areas Foundation
IDAs. *See* Individual Development Accounts
Impoverishment
    negative economic impact of, 67
Inclusion
    as a principle for saving a small community, 7
    lessons of, viii-ix
    See also Participation
Individual Development Accounts (IDAs)
    American Dream Demonstration project, 252-253
    Assets for Independence Act of 1998, 253
    Bay Area IDA Collaborative, 253
    characteristics, 252
    Corporation for Enterprise Development, 252-253
    definition, 252
    importance of individual asset accumulation, 252
Industrial Areas Foundation (IAF)
    and social strength building, 211-213
    as model of traditional power organizing, 103, 105
    as multiracial coalition, 213
    community organizing campaigns, 211, 213
    fund-raising, 231-232
    focus: communal power, racial equality and social
        justice, 211
    largest effort, 85, 105
    regional network building, 211-213
    sources of financial support, 231-232
    spread to 63 sites in US and foreign countries, 16-17
    See also Alinsky, S.
Interaction and extraction
    definitions, 80
    the fundamentals of community organizing, 80
    See also Community organizing
Intermediaries, funding
    definition, 232
    issues related to, 234
    Local Initiatives Support Corporation (LISC), 50
    Pittsburgh Partnership for Neighborhood
        Development, 50
    Portland, OR, 233-234
    regional, 39
    role of, 232
    types, 232
    United Way, 232
International Institute
    organizing of immigrant communities, 14
Inter-organizational relations
    building and strengthening, 91-92

Jacobs, J.
    attack on urban renewal, 18-19
    definition of social capital, 201
    description of destructive process called sprawl, 66-67
    small community formed by "continuity of people", 53
    small diverse mass of people necessary for
        community vitality, 66
Job creation and development
    as locally-based employment generation, 297
    collaborations and partnerships, 294-295
    components of neighborhood system for, 294-295
    first source agreements, 300

industrial job retention and expansion, 304
Job Link Corporation, Chicago, IL, 297
Jobs Net, Portland, OR, 300
linkage to growth employers, 295
Living Wage Campaign, 302
linkage to regional jobs, 299
manufacturing, 306-308
on-the-job training, 301-302
use of family coaches to support trainees, 42
See also Workforce development
Job retention
    community model for employee retention, 302
    industrial job retention and expansion, 304-305
    See also Workforce development
Jobs
    living wage jobs, 302
    manufacturing, 316
    national jobs policy campaign , 300
    social capital as a source of, 210
    suburbanization of, 316
Judd, D. and Swanstrom, T.
    declining power for distressed urban communities, 4
    Los Angeles street rebellion, 2

Kahn, S.
    members being within their life experience, 56
    nobility of organizer roles, 98
    politics as a useful strategy for involvement, 56
    potent method for influencing government, 56
    regular financial reports to board, 91
Keller, S.
    definition of friendship, 54
Kennedy, President J. F. and Johnson, President L. B.
    oversight of far reaching changes affecting small
        communities, 21
Kiltimaugh, Ireland
    grassroots fund-raising initiatives, 225-227
    importance of professional expertise, 226
    maximization of dollar flows in a
        community, 225-227
    role of volunteers in fund-raising, 225-227
Kingsley, G., McNeeley, J., and Gibson, J.
    assessment of community building as a comprehensive
        approach, 47-48
    community building approach, 162
    dependency replaced with self-reliance, 102
    National Funding Campaign for Community
        Development, 232
    place investment necessary, 61-62
    role of funding intermediaries, 232
Klein, K.
    giving levels, 229
    grassroots fund-raising tips and techniques, 228-230
Kretzmann, J. and McKnight, J.
    asset-based community development model,
        188-189, 207-209
    asset-based planning, 188-189
    community building blocks, 189
    community capacity inventory, 207
    community planning, 188-189
    strengthening social fabric, 207-208

Labor force
   characteristics,293
   nature of labor market, 293-295
Labor market
   nature of, 293
   negative economic impact of weak market, 67
   suburbanization of jobs, 316
Launching an organization, 85-87
Leadership, 82
Lemann, N.
   attack on CDC programs, 40
   hopeful views for promoting public education, safety,
      health and social services, 40
   old neighborhoods unstable for place-based
      investment, 40
   suggests CDCs shift to program for improving schools
      and police protection, 40
LISC. See Local Initiatives Support Corporation
Living Wage Campaign
   as example of a coalition effort, 317
   living wage jobs, 302
Loan funds
   Community Development Loan Funds (CDLFs), 248
   definition, 248
   description, 248
   Microenterprise Loan Funds (MLFs), 250
   Revolving Loan Funds (RLFs), 250
   See also Capital formation
Local economy
   cash flow diagram, 71
   definition of a neighborhood economy, 57
   economic base built on labor exports, 51
   examples of activities for increasing the flows, 57
   four circular flows of spending and receiving, 57
   key economic terms, 73-75
   local multiplier effect, 73-74
   See also Community economy
Local Initiatives Support Corporation (LISC)
   low-income housing preservation program, 273
   Main Street program, 289
   Mon Valley Initiative funder, 50
   funder of small regional neighborhood coalitions, 50
   See also Intermediaries, funding
Local money systems
   characteristics, 254
   community currency, 254
   history, 254
   Ithaca Hours, 254
   Local Exchange Trading Systems (LETS), 254
   Member Organized Resource Exchange
      (MORE), 254
   See also Capital formation
Low-income housing. See Affordable housing; Public and
   assisted housing
Low-income housing preservation
   Housing Trust Fund Project, 263
   HUD Multifamily Assisted Housing Preservation
      Program, 273
   low-income housing coalitions, 263
   National Housing Trust Fund Campaign, 273
   National Low-Income Housing Coalition, 263

   See also Affordable housing; Public and assisted
      housing
Low-wage work
   as a major force disruptive of small communities, 42
   Ehrenreich exposes the dehumanizing impact, 43
Lower East Side Peoples Federal Credit Union, 247
   See also Community Development Credit Unions
Lyndale Neighborhood Association, Minneapolis, MN
   comprehensive community plan, 185-187
   Hero card, 13
   introduction, 12-13
   priorities of, 13
   social strength building, 216

Maciak, B.
   manufacturing workforce development
      model, 304-308
   manufacturing business
      development, 304-308
   manufacturing employee recruitment and
      training, 306-307
   role of community organizing in workforce
      development, 304-308
Main Street program
   components, 286-288
   National Trust for Historic Preservation, 286
   See also Business district renewal
Manufacturing employment
   business services, 305
   community business manufacturing employment
      model, 307-308
   community job linkage programs, 297-300
   industrial retention and expansion
      programs, 304-305
   manufacturing assistance/support
      programs, 305
   manufacturing employee recruitment and
      training, 306-307
   manufacturing employment model, 306-307
   networks, 295, 297, 306, 307
   special manufacturing approach, 304-307
   See also Workforce development
Marciniak, E.
   defining the small community in Chicago, 73
   differential functions of the small community, 73-74
   need for alliances with other community
      organizations, 92
   understanding 2 levels of urban neighborhoods, 73-74
Market analysis. See Market assessment and analysis
Market assessment and analysis
   business district, 280
   buying power in inner city neighborhoods, 280
   housing, 260-262
   housing misery indicators, 261-262
   factors affecting housing market stability
      and options, 258-260
   untapped markets in inner cities, 280
   See also Community assessment, Community data
      gathering and analysis
Massachusetts Association of Community
   Development Corporations

eighteen member groups expand to do development
and organizing, 42
McKnight, J.
vision and definition of small community, 53
See also Kretzmann, J., and McKnight, J.
Medoff, P. and Sklar, H.
asset concept used in Dudley Street, 55
Mellon, A., Treasury Secretary
conservative policies listed, 15
dominated economic policy during 1920s, 15
financial collapse result of Mellon tight-fistedness, 15
Mendicino, S.
community organizer example, 96-97
Microenterprise loan funds
Association for Enterprise Opportunity, 249
characteristics, 249
capitalization, 249
definition, 248
purpose and goals, 248
Women's Self-Employment Project, 249-250
See also Capital formation; Loan funds
Mobilization
as a principle for saving small communities, 7
neighborhood, 210
See also Community organizing
Mollenkopf, J.
Alinsky inspired resistance, 19-20
author of critical studies of urban renewal, 18-20
business/government partnerships, 19
destruction and displacement of black communities, 19
Mondros, J., and Wilson, S.
longitudinal study of organizers, 92-93
principal skills of organizers, 92
three requirements for a volunteer organizer to be
effective, 93
See also Community organizer
Monitoring and evaluation
of community plans, 191-192
of organizational plans, 170-171
Success Measures Project, 192
See also Evaluation
Mother Theresa
example of charity of a faith-based woman, 107
Mott, A.
case for core operating support for CDCs, 230-231
on national coalitions, 315
on national movement of communal interests, 315
on systematic funding for community
development, 230-231
Mourad, M.
community data collection and analysis, 191
Multiracial political cooperation
Living Wage Campaign, 317
national level, 317
Wilson, W. J. on, 317
Mumford, L.
neighbors can establish a sense of belonging, 53
Murphy, P.
biography, ix
Mutual housing associations, 269-270
See also Affordable housing

National Community Reinvestment Coalition (NCRC)
anti-predatory lending activities, 245
Anti-Predatory Lending Tool Kit, 245
Community Reinvestment Act campaign, 22, 244
description, 243-244
See also Community Reinvestment Act of 1977
National Congress for Community Economic
Development (NCCED)
emerging consensus on comprehensive
programming, 43-44
National Federation of Community Development Credit
Unions, 246-247
See also Community Development Credit Unions
National Low-Income Housing Coalition
Advocates Guide to Housing and Community
Development Policy, 263
National Housing Trust Fund Campaign, 263
on housing affordability, 263
National People's Action (NPA)
Community Reinvestment Act campaign, 243-244
predatory lending education and action, 245
See also Community Reinvestment Act of 1977;
National Training and Information Center
National Training and Information Center (NTIC)
Community Reinvestment Act campaign, 243-244
See also Community Reinvestment Act of 1977;
National People's Action
Natural allies
definition, 11
listing of, 11
See also Natural enemies
Natural enemies
definition, 11
listing of, 11
See also Natural allies
NCCED. *See* National Congress for Community
Economic Development
NCRC. *See* National Community
Reinvestment Coalition
Neighborhood
importance and function of, 1
Neighborhood-based reform initiatives, 209-211
Neighborhood conditions
assessment of, 62-63
five stages of, 62-63
Neighborhood economy. *See* Community economy; Local
economy
Neighborhood preservation. *See* Housing
Neighborhood Reinvestment Corporation (NRC)
anti-predatory lending campaign, 245-246
New Community Corporation, Newark, NJ
an earliest CDC, 38
business representatives excluded, 20-21
focus on social justice, 213
history, 20-21
role of faith in, 213
self-directed planning, 20
social service reformation, 213
social strength building, 213
Pratt Institute Center for Community and
Environmental Development study, 20-21

Newhall Ranch, CA
    social strength building, 205-206
Nixon, President R. M.
    community development through citizen action and
        private business effort, 21
Non-Governmental Organizations (NGOs)
    distinct sector serving essential societal functions, 108
    pressing economic and political institutions for
        accountability, 108
NPA. *See* National People's Action
NRC. *See* Neighborhood Reinvestment Corporation
NTIC. *See* National Training and Information Center

Oakland Planning and Development Corporation,
    Pittsburgh, PA
    workforce development program, 298
OCCD. *See* Organizing for Community
    Controlled Development
Organizational claim to represent a community
    making and defending hard choices, 115
    paving the way for acceptance, 115
    validation by open decision-making, 115
Organizational planning
    action plan format, 167-168, 176-177
    Aliquippa Alliance for Unity and
        Development, 158-160
    benefits of, 156
    decision criteria, 173-176
    definition, 155
    developing goals and strategies, 165-172
    difference from community planning, 154-155, 178
    environmental scan (SWOT analysis), 164-165
    framework for, 160-162
    impetus for, 157
    implementation plans, 167-169
    levels of, 155-157
    limitations of, 156
    mission development, 163-164
    monitoring and evaluation, 170-171
    participation in, 156-157, 162-163
    plan adoption, 169-170
    process design, 161-162
    project selection criteria, 175-176
    research and planning, 87
    reassessment and updating, 171
    role selection, 166-167
    selecting priorities, 164
    strategic choice, 172-173
    strategic niche, 171-172
    vision development, 163
Organizational roles in Organizing for Community
    Controlled Development
    advocate/catalyst/monitor, 166
    developer/builder/financier, 167
    facilitator/broker/supporter, 167-168
    owner/operator/manager, 168
Organizing
    See also Business district renewal; Community
        organizing; Housing
Organizing for Community Controlled
    Development (OCCD)
        as response to economic disparity and
            joblessness, 312
        as response to erosion of civic involvement, 312
        as response to racial antipathy, 312
        characteristics, 312-313
        definition and components, 6, 78, 311
        organizational roles in, 166-168
        principles, 7, 312

Participation
    addressing barriers to inclusion, 111
    Arnstein's ladder of participation, 111-114
    and community distress, 108
    as promoter of accountability, 78
    barriers that remain,114-115
    block club structure for, 116
    coalition structure for, 116
    core element in the growth of the human spirit, 108
    definition, 110-111
    devaluation of participation, 3
    downside of involvement, 114-115
    economic dimension as well as organizing
        dimension, 108
    essential elements of, 110
    group process, 121
    historic background of, 109
    in business district renewal, 285, 287
    in community planning, 179-180, 184-185
    in fund-raising, 221, 224, 226
    in organizational planning, 156-157, 162-163
    membership structure for, 115-116
    ordinary community members make participation
        genuine, 110
    participation prone structures, 115-116
    power measured by control achieved, 111
    proposal for multi-level participation, 114
    quality of inclusiveness determined by
        universality, 111
    significance of decisions measured by tangible
        assets involved, 111
    the efficiency -dilemma, 113
    unequal resources within collaborations, 114
    See also Inclusion
Partnerships
    Aliquippa Alliance for Unity and Development, 139,
        140-142
    Dudley Street community-city government, 120
Peirce, N., and Steinbach, C.
    assessment of CDCs, 39-40
    need for neighborhood-based renewal, 230
People vs. place: the economists' doubt
    Cisneros compromise proposal, 62
    ignore social costs of displacement, 62
    migration as an alternative, 62
    old neighborhoods unstable for place-based
        investment, 40
    place investment necessary, 61-62
    people prosperity definition, 61
    question spending on distressed areas, 61-62
    the place prosperity fallacy, 62
    See also Hoover, E. M.; Lemann, N.; Winnick, L.

Personal Responsibility and Work Opportunity
Reconciliation Act of 1996
advocacy to improve, 302
description of, 213, 296-297
impact on workforce development, 302
welfare to work, 213, 296-297
PICCED. *See* Pratt Institute Center for Community and
Environmental Development
Pingree, H., of Detroit, reform mayor (1890–1897), 25-26
Pitcoff, W.
assessment of Comprehensive Community
Initiatives, 46-47
Place prosperity. *See* People vs. place prosperity: the
economists' doubt
Planning. *See* Community planning; Organizational
planning
Political imbalance
negative economic impact of, 68
Poppendeick, J.
increase in inequality, 213
national movement to address growing inequality, 314
Populist and progressive movements
decline of community-based power during
World War I, 15
failure to alter power alignment, 15
source of power in local rural communities, 14
values of the movement, 15
William Jennings Bryan, 14
Portland, OR
funding intermediaries in, 232-234
Neighborhood Partnership Fund, 232-234
Office of Neighborhood Involvement, 233
Oregon Community Fund, 233
public support for community development, 232-234
Porter, M. E. and Blaxill, M.
buying power in inner city neighborhoods, 280
Pratt Institute Center for Community and Environmental
Development (PICCED)
approach to organizational planning, 171-173
cash flow diagram, 71
role in Greenpoint 197-a Plan development, 194
study of New Community Corporation, 20-21
Predatory lending
anti-predatory lending actions, 245
Anti-Predatory Lending Tool Kit, 245
counter campaigns, 242-246
definition, 245
impacts of, 245
Predatory Lending Consumer Protection Act, 246
subprime lending, 245
Principles of economic renewal
business creation, 283
business development, 283
business recruitment, 283
Principles of Organizing for Community Controlled
Development
adequate wealth, 7
comprehensiveness, 7
health and spirit, 7
inclusion, 7
mobilization, 7

Project selection criteria
business/economic perspective guidelines, 175-176
community perspective guidelines, 175
organizational perspective guidelines, 175
use of in organizational planning, 174
Public and assisted housing
as part of larger community, 273-274
assessment of, 274
Center for Community Change Public Housing
Initiative, 275
creation and growth of, 273-274
Housing Act of 1937, 273
impact of FHA mortgage insurance, 274
Mark to Market program, 273
multifamily assisted housing, 273
Multifamily Assisted Housing
Preservation Program, 273
Section 8/project-based housing program, 273
U.S. Department of Housing and Urban
Development (HUD), 272, 274
See also Affordable housing
Public sector
involvement in community planning, 179
role in business district renewal, 284
role in housing, 257, 273-275, 262
Purpose of this book, 9
Putnam, R.
concept of "bowling alone", 202
decline of social capital, 103, 207, 211
findings on political consciousness and engagement
reawakening, viii
inequality in access to social capital, 202
social capital as civic engagement and trust, 202
on time for aggressive organizing, viii

Racial antipathy
as a source of distress in small communities, 2-3
effects of intolerance, 3
Racial equality
Industrial Areas Foundation focus, 10
Racial inequality
growth of disparities between whites and
people of color, 2
in access to social capital, 202
race disparity in employment and compensation, 4
poor people of color isolated, 2
widening of racial gap, 4-5
Racial steering and segregation
in housing, 259
versus socioeconomic diversity, 260
Rae, D.
undercrowded cities, 63-64
undercrowded neighborhoods must
mobilize, 63-64
Reagan, President R.
goals to help business, cut federal aid, promote
privatization, 23
drastic tax cuts, 23
increase defense spending, 23
rich benefited from policies, 23
cut social programs, 23

a politics of moderation, 23
proliferation of community groups, 23
Redlining
    as impetus for Community Reinvestment
        Act of 1977, 242
    as factor affecting housing market stability
        and options, 259
    definition, 259
    negative economic impact of, 68
Redwood, C.
    example of community organizer, 94-95
    technology use in community renewal, 95-96
Regional growth
    neighborhoods linked to growth, 50
Rental housing
    decrease in, 268
    importance of, 268
    maintenance of, 258-259
    versus homeownership, 268
    See also Housing
Residential settlements
    economic roots of, 2
Resource development
    Aliquippa Alliance for Unity and Development, 141, 237
    core operating support, 230-232
    Discover Total Resources, 227-228
    donors/donations, 220, 223-224, 229, 230,
    foundations, 220, 228, 229, 230, 232
    for profit corporations, 227, 228, 229, 230
    funding intermediaries, 233-234
    giving levels, 220, 229, 235-236
    grants, 228
    grassroots fund-raising, 221-230
    Industrial Areas Foundation, 231-232
    key ways and means to secure resources, 220
    Kiltimaugh, Ireland, 225-227
    maximization of dollar flows in a community, 225-227
    need for resource diversification, 232
    organization of activities, 221-222
    participation in, 221, 224, 226
    range of resources, 221
    role of Development Team, 221-222
    role of Finance Committee, 221-222
    volunteer use and roles, 11, 225-227
    See also Funding; Fund-raising
Resource mobilization
    in community planning, 193
Revitalize, definition of, 78
Revolving loan funds (RLFs)
    definition, 250
    description, 250
    See also Loan funds
Rogers, R. K.
    small community model for workforce
        development, 302-303
Rollingwood Neighborhood Association, TX
    introduction, 59
    social strength building, 216-218
Roosevelt, President F. D. R.
    disruptive protests, 16
    Federal Emergency Relief Act of 1935, 16

job infrastructure programs, 17
liberal program set up, 16
response to desperate public, 16
Rosenthal, B. and Mizrahi, T.
    advice for operating coalitions effectively, 86
    definition of coalition, 86
Rothman, J.
    models of intervention, 182-184
Rubin, H., and Rubin, I.
    on need for resource diversification, 232
Rusk, D.
    assessment of Bedford-Stuyvesant, 41
    growth of disparities between whites and
        people of color, 2
    regional coalitions as building blocks for national
        communal power, 315
    race makes the difference, 67
    on national movement of communal interests, 315

Schorr, L.
    community versus public sector planning, 179
    community participation in planning, 179
    social service reformation and renewal, 212-213
    strategic choice in comprehensive planning, 193
Sectors of society
    business, 13
    communal, vii-viii
    government, 13
    pressures on business and government in cities, 14
    sources of power, 13
    struggles among sectors, 13
Segregation
    as factor affecting housing market stability and
        options, 257
    housing, 68, 259
    historical perspective, 2
Seymour, J.
    fund-raising, 222
    requirements for cause funding, 222
Sherraden, M.
    importance of individual asset accumulation, 252
    role of asset accumulation, 252
ShoreBank. *See* Community development banks
Sklar, H.
    growing economic inequality in America, 24
    widespread misery making opportunity for
        communal forces, 24
ShoreBank: *See* Community development banks
    See also Community development banks
Small community
    clues to survival, 75-76
    continuity of people as essential element, 53
    definition and essence, 1, 53
    defining the small community in Chicago, 73
    differential functions of the small community, 73-74
    differential renewal strategy for each, 54
    destructive forces, 66-68
    dimensions of, 5
    estimated number of in America, 1, 9
    functions and importance of, 1
    McKnight, J. vision of, 53

scale of, 54
scale related to location, 54
three sources of vitality, 54
tied to relationships, 54-55
Small community renewal
    CDCs as preferred instrument for, 38
    Comprehensive Community Initiatives as
        model of choice, 44
    definition, vii
    diversity and civic responsibility, 1
    examples of small renewal actions, 5
    fruitful links to governments and businesses, 1
    key renewal issues, 7-8
    year-round participation, 1
Small community renewal organizations
    goal and attitude of, 12
    no known careful estimate of numbers, 11
    seven examples of, 12-13
    types of, 11-12
Social capital
    and social change, 204
    as source for jobs, 210
    Brophy and Shabecoff affirm brick and mortar not
        enough, 42
    decline, 202-203
    definitions, 201-203
    framework for rebuilding, 211-212
    impact of loss of, 201
    importance of, 202
    negative aspects of, 202
    See also Social fabric; Social strength
Social fabric
    common history, 54
    components of, 201
    definition, 201
    definition of friendship, 54
    friendship networks, 54
    generators of relationships, 54-56
    internal communication mechanisms, 55
    kinship networks, 54
    local institutions, 55
    neighborhood surveys, 53
    neighbors, 55
    recommendations for strengthening social
        fabric, 206-207
    shared values, 55
    small community tied to relationships, 54-55
    social fabric holds Valmeyer, IL together, 56
    strengthening of, 206-208
    weakness in, 210-211
    See also Social capital; Social services; Social strength
Social justice
    Industrial Areas Foundation focus, 211-212
    linkage to social services, 213
Social Security Act of 1936, 16
Social services
    as component of social strength, 203-204
    creation of, 203
    elements of promise, 212
    linkage to social justice, 213
    negative economic impact of fragmentation, 68

New Community Corporation, 213
reformation and renewal, 212-213
role in social change, 203
role of faith, 212-213
See also Social capital; Social fabric;
    Social strength
Social strength
    as social infrastructure, 200
    building, 206-208
    components of, 201-204
    definitions of, 200-201
    social strength building case examples,
        204-206, 215-218
    See also Social capital; Social fabric;
        Social services
Societal struggle
    business sector, 13
    government sector, 13-14
    sources of power, 13-14
    tripartite paradigm of, 13-14
    See also Communal sector
Sprawl
    a discussion of definition, 66-67
    how to transform into smart growth or
        sustainability, 66-67
    Jane Jacobs's classic description, 66-67
    See also Community distress
Stoecker, R.
    case on CDC weakness, 40
    volunteer grassroots control with experienced large-
        scale execution, 49
Strategic choice
    decision criteria and assessment factors,173-175
    definition, 172-173
    project selection criteria, 175-176
    See also Organizational planning
    Strategic niche
    choosing an organizational niche, 171-172
    definition, 171-172
    diagram, 172
    four elements of, 171-172
    See also Organizational planning
Strategic planning
    definition, 155
    See also Organizational planning
Strategies. *See* Goals and strategies
Strengthening
    definition, 78
Suburbanization
    impact on housing, 209
    of jobs, 316
    negative economic impact of, 2, 66
Subprime lending. *See* Predatory lending
Swartz, R. *See* Bloomfield-Garfield Corporation

Tapping resources. *See* Resource development;
    Funding; Fund-raising
Transformative social change
    renewal approach
    definition of transformative tradition, 49
    description of techniques, 49

Technology
    participation and access to resources encourage people
        creativity, 108
    enables citizen organizing in authoritarian
        states, 108
Traditional power organizing
    description, 103, 105
    Industrial Areas Foundation model, 104
    world-wide spread of, 104

Undercrowdedness
    definition, 63
    in Aliquippa, PA, 124
    in cities, 63-64
United Nations
    human development proceeds best where
        people press for power, 107
    meeting the aspirations of the people test, 121
    more equality in global consumption when
        grassroots and NGOs mobilized, 107
United Way
    as a funding intermediary, 232
    as an IDA funder, 253
    contributor choice, 227
Urban renewal
    and housing displacement, 260
    as force affecting housing market stability
        and options, 258
    attacked by Jane Jacobs, 18-19
    charged with being under control of private
        corporate developers, 19
    citizens and neighborhoods revolt to limit
        destruction, 19
    conflict among communitarian, business, and
        government interests, 19
    critical studies of urban renewal, 18-20
    destruction of poor communities, 18, 209
    generates conflict, 18
    Halpern alleges used to stem tide of African
        American migration, 19
    helped to detonate the communal revolt
        of the 1960s, 20
    Housing Act of 1949, 17-18
    Hyde Park-Kenwood Community Conference case
        study, 18, 26-31
    political entrepreneurs, 18
    role of urban pioneers in counter
        movement, 19-20
    supported by building trade unions, 18
U.S. Department of Housing and Urban
    Development (HUD)
    and capital formation, 245
    and housing, 273-275
    and anti-predatory lending, 245
    HOPE VI housing program, 274-275
    influenced by Geno Baroni, 22-23
    public and assisted housing, 273
    Mark to Market housing program, 273
    Multifamily Assisted Housing program, 272
    Section 8 housing, project-based housing
        program, 273

untapped markets in inner cities, 280
    See also Low-income housing communities;
        Public and assisted housing

Valmeyer, IL
    example of social fabric holding a
        community together, 56
    social strength building, 218
Vandergrift, PA
    social strength building, 218
Vietnam War
    opposition to, 20
Vision/visioning
    creating and spreading, 81-82
    importance of, 101
    in community planning, 187-188
    in organizational planning, 163
    shared language and vision, 83
    vision changing as principal
        skill of organizer, 92
Volunteers
    lack of skills and experience, 3
    outstanding achievements, 3
    shortage of, 3

Warren, M.
    faith-based organizations and social
        strength building, 211-213
    framework for rebuilding social capital, 211
    mediating institutions and political intervention, 211
    Industrial Areas Foundation organizing, 211-212
Washington, Mayor Harold, 25-26
Welfare to Work. See Personal Responsibility and Work
        Opportunity Reconciliation Act of 1996
Whitley Heights, CA
    case ends in bitterness, 64
    case study, 64
    gates a contradiction to community, 64
    resistant homeowners overreach, 64
WIBs. See Workforce Investment Boards
Wilson, W. J.
    importance of coalitions, 315-316
    Industrial Areas Foundation as
        multiracial coalition, 213
    mutual political cooperation as path to
        parity of power, 6/222
    national multiracial political alliance of communal
        forces, 315-317
    economic insecurity as motivation for unity and group
        action, 315-317
    role of faith-based organizations in
        political coalitions, 213
    Winnick, L.
    abandonment of place a greater evil, 61
    federal spending shifts, 61
    logic of economists' doubt, 61
    migration not an ideal alternative, 61
Wolfe, A.
    roots of civic paralysis, 3
    Women's Self-Employment Project, 249-250
    See also Microenterprise loan funds

Workforce development
Aliquippa, PA, 132-133, 145-146, 293, 298
Annie E. Casey Foundation Jobs Initiative, 301
Bedford-Stuyvesant Restoration Corporation,
Brooklyn, NY, 295
business services for, 305
campaign for jobs policy, 300
Center for Employment Training, San Jose,
CA, 294-295, 299
community-based employment model, 307-308
community business manufacturing employment
model, 307-308
community job linkage programs, 297-300
community mobilization for, 295-296
cultural competency in, 300-301
Dudley Street Neighborhood Initiative,
Boston, MA, 300-301
employment discrimination, 293, 301
faith-based organizations support for, 297
Fifth Avenue Committee, Brooklyn, NY, 297
first source agreements, 300
industrial retention and expansion programs, 304-305
Job Link Corporation, Chicago, IL, 297
Job Net, Portland, OR, 300
job creation and development, 42, 294-295, 297, 299,
300-304, 306-308
job retention, 302, 304-305
labor force characteristics, 293
linkage to growth employers, 295
linkage to regional jobs, 299
Living Wage Campaign, 302
living wage jobs, 302
manufacturing assistance programs, 305
manufacturing employment model, 306-307
models for, 302-308
nature of labor market, 293-295
neighborhood system components, 294-295
Oakland Planning and Development Corporation,
Pittsburgh, PA, 298
on-the-job training, 301
partnerships for, 302
Personal Responsibility and Work Opportunity
Reconciliation Act of 1996,
213, 296-297, 302
role of community organizing in workforce
development, 304-308
role of family support centers in, 297
small community model, 302-303
special manufacturing approach, 304-307
networks, 295, 299, 306, 307
suburbanization of jobs, 316
University Community Career Development Program,
Pittsburgh, PA, 298
Workforce Investment Act, 307
Workforce Investment Boards, 307

Yamatani, H.
importance of involving local people in research, 87

ABOUT THE AUTHORS

Patricia Watkins Murphy is President of Cornerstones for Development, a for-profit firm that works on the local, regional, and national levels with the community, human service, public, and philanthropic sectors by providing consultation, training, and technical assistance to build resilient and inclusive organizations and communities. She has more than 20 years of experience in working for and with community-based and community-serving organizations and human service providers as a staff member, a volunteer, a board member, a consultant, and an educator in community organizing and development. Prior to establishing Cornerstones for Development in 1992, she worked alongside residents of Pittsburgh neighborhoods as executive director of the Stanton Heights Civic Association, associate director of the Hill Community Development Corporation, and economic development planner at the Community Technical Assistance Center. As an adjunct professor at the University of Pittsburgh's School of Social Work, she teaches graduate courses in governance, grant proposal writing, community organizing and development, and working with diverse populations. As an organizer committed to community-led social change, she has served as a board member and an active volunteer with many Pittsburgh-based nonprofits and nationally with the Development Leadership Network. She is currently on the board and is the grant-making committee co-chair of the Three Rivers Community Foundation, which funds community-led economic and social justice initiatives, and serves on the steering committee of the Regional Coalition of Community Builders, of which she is a founding organizer.

James V. Cunningham was born in Chicago, where he did political and neighborhood development organizing during the 1950s before moving to Pittsburgh, whose neighborhood people in 1959 were beginning to participate in the city's renewal effort. As an organizer for the Allegheny Council to Improve Our Neighborhoods (better known as ACTION-Housing), he helped neighborhood people to build organizations that gave them a voice in decisions that affected their lives. Pittsburgh issues, then as now, were race, jobs, and who makes the public decisions that affect families and small communities. After working for 7 years with residents and their allies, he began to teach community organizing at the University of Pittsburgh's School of Social Work. He helped to create a master's program, built on 50% time in field experience and 50% time in academic studies, which drew a steady stream of students from the United States and abroad. Along the route, he published four books: *The Resurgent Neighborhood* (1965), *Urban Leadership During the Sixties* (1970), *A New Public Policy for Neighborhood Preservation* (1979, co-authored with Roger Ahlbrandt), and *Building Neighborhood Organizations* (1983, co-authored with Milton Kotler). He retired from full-time teaching in 1997 and continues to teach part-time and write while serving as a volunteer with the Race and Reconciliation Dialogue Group of St. Paul Cathedral Parish and with the "Living Wage" campaign for the Pittsburgh region.